THE OXFORD ENCYCLOPEDIA OF
BIBLICAL INTERPRETATION

Editorial Board

THE OXFORD ENCYCLOPEDIA OF
BIBLICAL INTERPRETATION

Steven L. McKenzie
EDITOR IN CHIEF

VOLUME 2

Metaphor Theory and Biblical Texts–Womanist Interpretation
Topical Outline of Contents
Directory of Contributors
Index

OXFORD
UNIVERSITY PRESS

OXFORD
UNIVERSITY PRESS

Oxford University Press is a department of the University of Oxford.
It furthers the University's objective of excellence in research,
scholarship, and education by publishing worldwide.

Oxford New York

Auckland Cape Town Dar es Salaam Hong Kong Karachi
Kuala Lumpur Madrid Melbourne Mexico City Nairobi
New Delhi Shanghai Taipei Toronto

With offices in

Argentina Austria Brazil Chile Czech Republic France Greece
Guatemala Hungary Italy Japan Poland Portugal Singapore
South Korea Switzerland Thailand Turkey Ukraine Vietnam

Oxford is a registered trademark of Oxford University Press
in the UK and certain other countries.
Published in the United States of America by

Oxford University Press
198 Madison Avenue, New York, NY 10016

Library of Congress Cataloging-in-Publication Data

The Oxford encyclopedia of biblical interpretation / Steven McKenzie, editor in chief.
pages cm
Includes index.

ISBN 978-0-19-983226-2 (set : alk. paper) — ISBN 978-0-19-999335-2 (v.1 : alk. paper) —
ISBN 978-0-19-999336-9 (v.2 : alk. paper)

1. Bible–Criticism, interpretation, etc.–Encyclopedias. 2. Bible–Hermeneutics–Encyclopedias.
I. McKenzie, Steven L., 1953–
BS511.3.O88 2013
220.603—dc23
2012041156

3 5 7 9 8 6 4 2

Printed in the United States of America on acid-fre

Abbreviations Used in This Work

// or ||	parallel passages
§	Section
Acts	Acts of the Apostles
Add Dan	Additions to Daniel
Add Esth	Additions to Esther
Ag. Ap.	Josephus, *Against Apion*
Amos	Amos
Ant.	Josephus, *Jewish Antiquities*
B. Bat.	*Baba Batra*
Bar	Baruch
B.C.E.	Before the Common Era (= B.C.)
Bel	Bel and the Dragon
C.E.	Common Era (= A.D.)
cf.	*confer,* compare
ch./chs.	chapter/chapters
1–2 Chr	1–2 Chronicles
Col	Colossians
col./cols.	column/columns
1–2 Cor	1–2 Corinthians
d.	died
Dan	Daniel
Deut	Deuteronomy
DH	Deuteronomistic History
DSS	Dead Sea Scrolls
Dtr	Deuteronomist
E	Elohist source in the Pentateuch

Eccl	Ecclesiastes
ed.	editor (pl., eds.), edition
1 En.	*1 Enoch*
Eph	Ephesians
Ep Jer	Letter of Jeremiah
1–2 Esd	1–2 Esdras
Esth	Esther
Exod	Exodus
Ezek	Ezekiel
Ezra	Ezra
4 Ezra	*4 Ezra*
Gal	Galatians
Gen	Genesis
Gen. Rab.	*Genesis Rabbah*
Hab	Habakkuk
Hag	Haggai
HB	Hebrew Bible
Heb	Hebrews
Hos	Hosea
Isa	Isaiah
J	Yahwist source in the Pentateuch
Jas	James
Jdt	Judith
Jer	Jeremiah
Job	Job
Joel	Joel
John	John
Jonah	Jonah
Josh	Joshua
Jub.	*Jubilees*
Jude	Jude
1–2 Kgs	1–2 Kings
KJV	King James Version
Lam	Lamentations
Lev	Leviticus

Lev. Rab.	*Leviticus Rabbah*
lit.	literally
Luke	Luke
LXX	Septuagint
1–2 Macc	1–2 Maccabees
3–4 Macc	3–4 Maccabees
Mal	Malachi
Mark	Mark
Matt	Matthew
Mic	Micah
ms/mss	manuscript/manuscripts
MT	Masoretic Text
NAB	New American Bible
Nah	Nahum
n.d.	no date
NEB	New English Bible
Neh	Nehemiah
Nid.	*Niddah*
n.p.	no place
NRSV	New Revised Standard Version
NT	New Testament
Num	Numbers
Num. Rab.	*Numbers Rabbah*
Obad	Obadiah
OG	Old Greek
OL	Old Latin
OT	Old Testament
P	Priestly source in the Pentateuch
p.	page (pl., pp.)
1–2 Pet	1–2 Peter
Phil	Philippians
Phlm	Philemon
Pr Azar	Prayer of Azariah
Pr Man	Prayer of Manasseh
Prov	Proverbs

Ps(s)	Psalm(s)
Q	*Quelle*, a hypothetical source used by Matthew and Luke
Q	Qumran
Qoh	Qoheleth
r.	Reigned
Rab.	*Rabbah*
Rev	Revelation
rev.	Revised
Rom	Romans
RSV	Revised Standard Version
Ruth	Ruth
1–2 Sam	1–2 Samuel
Sanh.	*Sanhedrin*
Sir	Sirach
Song	Song of Solomon
SP	Samaritan Pentateuch
supp.	Supplement
Sus	Susanna
1–2 Thess	1–2 Thessalonians
1–2 Tim	1–2 Timothy
Titus	Titus
Tob	Tobit
v./vv.	verse/verses
vol.	volume (pl., vols.)
Vulg.	Vulgate
Zech	Zechariah
Zeph	Zephaniah

THE OXFORD ENCYCLOPEDIA OF

BIBLICAL INTERPRETATION

M

CONTINUED

Metaphor Theory and Biblical Texts

Metaphor (Gk. "transference") is a mode of expression, whereby one thing is understood and described in terms of another. For example, in God's promise of covenantal renewal to Israel: "I will *take* you *for my wife* forever" (Hos 2:19), the relationship between God and Israel is conceived and described in terms of espousal, or in God's condemnation to Israel: "I *planted* you as a *choice vine*, from *the purest stock*—How then did you turn degenerate and become a *wild vine*?!" (Jer 2:21), the same relationship is understood and described in terms of horticulture.

Metaphor is frequently discussed along with metonymy, synecdoche, simile, or allegory. Metonymy is a mode of expression whereby a whole being, concept, or event is understood and described in terms of its part, or vice versa (e.g., "throne" for "dominion as a whole": "to set up the *throne* of David over Israel and over Judah, from Dan to Beer-sheba" [2 Sam 3:10]). Synecdoche is a mode of expression whereby a genus is understood and described in terms of its species, or vice versa (e.g., "bread" for "food in general": "one does not live by *bread* alone" [Deut 8:3]). The oft-confused distinction between metaphor, metonymy, and synecdoche can be put in terms of their respective, operating principle: metaphor is based on analogy, metonymy on partonomy, and synecdoche on taxonomy. Hence, as the linguist Ken-ichi Seto often puts it, "Snow White" is a metaphor, "Red Riding Hood" is a metonymy, and "Little Mermaid" is a synecdoche.

Simile, on the other hand, is a nonliteral comparison introduced by *like* or *as*. It is a kind of metaphor (Stern 2000, pp. 229–232). The difference between simile and metaphor is rhetorical in that a simile (e.g., "God is *like* my shepherd") is less direct and less emphatic than the corresponding metaphor (e.g., "God *is* my shepherd"). Allegory is a symbolic representation of an idea or principle by means of figuration, such as drama, narrative, or painting. It is frequently referred to as an extended metaphor (e.g., Quintilian, *Institutio oratoria*, 8.6.44). Like metaphor, allegory operates according to the principle of analogy. However, unlike metaphor, allegory generally prioritizes the idea it communicates over the specific figuration it employs. It follows that in allegory, insofar as the clarity and communicative force of the idea is maintained, different images and motifs can be employed. In metaphor, this is not always the case.

Previously, general scholarship, with some important exceptions (e.g., G. Vico, F. Nietzsche, E. Cassirer, I. A. Richards, S. Pepper, M. Black, N. Goodman), usually treated metaphor as a (mere) stylistic device—a linguistic phenomenon limited mainly or solely to a specific aesthetic discourse such as poetry or oratory. Today, metaphor is regarded primarily as a conceptual phenomenon—a fundamental principle of human cognition that operates in all forms of symbolic activity. This is due, largely, to an interdisciplinary study known today as cognitive linguistics and science, which gradually emerged in the 1970s and 1980s through an integration of research undertaken in a variety of fields, including anthropology, biology, computer science, linguistics, neuroscience, philosophy, physics, and psychology (see Ungerer and Schmid 2006; Kövecses 2010). The emergence of this interdisciplinary study introduced a "cognitive turn," in that it shifted the logical priority of scholarship from the study of language to the study of mind. The same kind of cognitive turn is also taking place in biblical studies. There is a growing amount of scholarly works that explore the hermeneutic force of the cognitive approach to the analysis of biblical religion and literature in general, and of biblical metaphors in particular (see van Wolde 2009 and Jindo 2010 and works cited there). As the amount of literature in metaphor scholarship has grown unceasingly, what follows will consider mainly issues and recent studies on metaphor that may facilitate the researcher in developing effective tools for biblical interpretation.

Below, the term "metaphor," when used as an abstract noun, designates the phenomenon of metaphor; and when used as a concrete noun, designates a specific verbal utterance understood metaphorically.

General Scholarship on Metaphor. Prior to the cognitive turn, the dominant conception in the general scholarship on metaphor was the rhetorical one, which can be traced back to the writings of Aristotle (*Poetics* 21, 1457b9–16 and 20–22; *Rhetoric* III). Although what Aristotle really meant is much debated, he is usually regarded as a major proponent of the rhetorical notion of metaphor, according to which metaphor functions as an ornament superadded to the content of the utterance; it follows, therefore, that the content can be extracted from the metaphor and re-expressed in a literal way. Underlying this view of metaphor as paraphrasable or dispensable is a dualism of form (metaphor) and content (proposition). For instance, if we consider a metaphorical utterance, "Man is a wolf," the proposition of this utterance will be something like "Man is fierce and alarming," and the word "wolf" is understood as a stylistic component operating to evoke feelings and attitudes associated with the notion of "wolf." This dualistic conception also underlies what came to be two dominant traditional theories of metaphor, i.e., the substitution theory (i.e., metaphor as a substitution of a corresponding literal expression; e.g., "Man is a wolf" = "Man is fierce and alarming") and the comparison theory (i.e., metaphor as a condensed or implied comparison; e.g., "Man is a wolf" = "Man is *like* a wolf"). During the Renaissance, the rhetorical notion of metaphor was reinterpreted not as a stylistic ornament but rather as an effective tool for persuasion. It is perhaps in this context that negative views on metaphor as deceptive and undesirable, such as Hobbes's and Locke's, are best understood (Stern 2000, p. 263). Be that as it may, it is not an exaggeration to describe the twenty-two hundred years of metaphor theory as variations of, or responses to, the "Aristotelian" (if not Aristotle's) notion of metaphor (Johnson 1981, especially pp. 3–47).

What generally has been neglected in this history of scholarship is the poetic or mimetic function of metaphor, the notion that a metaphor in poetry operates as a construct of a poetic reality. In his *Poetics*, Aristotle's discussion of *mimesis*—the essential representation of human experiences—does seem to indicate an awareness of this poetic function of metaphor without explicitly addressing it. But in the succeeding millennia, this poetic conception of metaphor was overshadowed by the rhetorical conception and, consequently, was rarely discussed with any degree of sophistication and thoroughness (e.g., Richards 1936; Ricoeur 1977; Harshav 1984; White 1996; Stern 2000).

Studies of Metaphor in Modern Biblical Scholarship. Until the mid-twentieth century, the main concern of modern biblical scholarship was historical (e.g., the authorship and prehistory of biblical texts, the actual history of ancient Israel and its religion, etc.). From the pre-modern works, we have a vast amount of philosophical and exegetical inquiry—inquiry that pertains to the interpretive issues of figurative and, especially, anthropomorphic expressions in the Hebrew Bible, such as Moses Ibn Ezra's *The Treatise of the Garden on Figurative and Literal Language* and *The Book of Discussion and Conversation* (12th c.) or the first part of Maimonides' *The Guide for the Perplexed* (12th c.; see Cohen 2003 for medieval Jewish approaches to biblical metaphor)—as well as Robert Lowth's classic work *Lectures on the Sacred Poetry of the Hebrews* (1753), which presents an extensive disquisition of images and figures in biblical poetry (especially lectures 6–9). In modern biblical studies, however, only since the 1970s has particular focus been directed toward metaphors as literary components. This new approach should be viewed in the context of a broader development—the increasing recognition of the literary analysis of biblical texts as a scholarly discipline within biblical studies. It is mainly in the work of scholars well-versed in literary criticism and the method of close reading, such as Robert Alter (1985), Francis Landy (1983), and Meir Weiss (1984), that this new literary approach to the Bible in general, and the analysis of biblical metaphors in particular, has been developed.

Concomitant with this rise of the literary approach to biblical literature, there arose a trend of analysis known as rhetorical criticism, of which James Muilenburg was the major proponent. The basic concern of this approach is the relation between "linguistic patterns" and the "predications" (i.e., propositions) that those patterns convey. Metaphor is grouped among the "many and various devices by which the predications are formulated" (Muilenburg, "Form Criticism and Beyond," *JBL* 88 [1969], p. 8). This approach supposes the dualistic assumption that metaphors and other tropes are superadded to (hence, separable from) the core content of an utterance.

The rise of this literary approach had an appreciable impact upon mainstream biblical scholarship: a number of scholarly works have offered meaningful interpretations of metaphor in specific biblical passages, and several collections of essays that focus on biblical metaphors have been published (e.g., Camp and Fontaine 1993; van Hecke 2005; van Hecke and Labahn 2010). So far, however, metaphor has not been regarded as one of the primary topics of research in modern biblical scholarship. This is a striking omission in view of the fact that the extensive use of images and figures is one of the most distinctive characteristics of biblical poetry.

Basic Patterns of Research in Modern Biblical Scholarship. There are four main patterns of research on biblical metaphors. They are not mutually exclusive, but rather are compatible with each other; a certain degree of overlapping is found in many of the works reviewed below.

Theory-Oriented Pattern. This research pattern applies theoretical models to the analysis of biblical metaphor. Works that belong to this category include G. B. Caird's *The Language and Imagery of the Bible* (London, 1980), Peter Macky, *The Centrality of Metaphors to Biblical Thought* (Lewiston, 1990), and David Aaron's *Biblical Ambiguities* (Leiden, 2001). These works examine the phenomenon of biblical metaphor with a careful consideration of major existing theories of metaphor. Their scope of interest includes the relationship between the thought and language of biblical religion in general and the role metaphor plays within biblical thinking in particular. On the practical side, these works seek to elucidate the mechanism of metaphors and develop a means of identifying and classifying them according to their type and function. These works are useful when read at the very early stage of analysis to attain an overall understanding of metaphor and other tropes.

Metaphor-Oriented Pattern. Under this heading are the works that explore a specific metaphor throughout the Bible. These works seek to identify the frame of reference to which a given image refers, as well as the associations and connotations it may evoke, thereby delineating its significance within the belief system of ancient biblical religion. The works of this group include Elaine Adler's "The Background for the Metaphor of Covenant as Marriage in the Hebrew Bible" (PhD diss., U.C. Berkeley, 1990), Marc Brettler's *God Is King* (Sheffield, 1989), and Gary Anderson's *Sin: A History* (New Haven, 2009). Exegetes will find this research pattern useful, inter alia, for two kinds of investigation: (a) for determining the semantic range of a given metaphor, in light of which they can evaluate their own interpretation, and (b) for exploring the conceptual world of biblical religion and its history.

Text-Oriented Pattern. The works that follow this research pattern examine a variety of metaphors in a specific biblical text. Examples of this group include Daniel Bourguet's *Des Métaphores de Jérémie* (Paris, 1987), Katheryn Darr's *Isaiah's Vision and the Family of God* (Louisville, 1994), and Emmanuel Nwaoru's *Imagery in the Prophecy of Hosea* (Wiesbaden, 1999). Studies under this category generally present an insightful analysis of metaphors as they appear in their immediate context, but they do not always succeed in integrating those insights into a broader framework.

Method-Oriented Pattern. Studies within this research pattern seek to develop an exegetical method that enhances our understanding of metaphors in their literary context. An inquiry of this kind requires not only a penetrating exegetical sensitivity and sound command of literary criticism, but also an ability to formulate a working method in a way readily comprehensible and applicable. For this, and other reasons, the literature of this pattern is deficient and, therefore, more is sorely needed.

Among the biblical scholars who have made significant contributions in this field is Meir Weiss, who has applied the method of Total Interpretation to the analysis of poetic images (1984). He stresses the importance of the total context of images, analyzing them not in isolation but in relation to, and interaction with, all the structural elements of a given composition. Weiss also warns against the tendency of philological leveling, which regards the parallel uses of the same image as equivalent, thus overlooking the distinctive use of the image in respective contexts; see, e.g., his analysis of the recurring divine metaphor of roaring in the prophetic writings, such as Jeremiah 25:30, Amos 1:2, and Joel 4:16 (Weiss 1984, pp. 239–240).

Another significant contribution was made by Edward Greenstein (2009), who suggested three exegetical directives for unpacking poetic metaphors in the book of Job, namely, to consider their "ramifications," "specific concept," and "intertextual function." By the term "ramifications," Greenstein differentiates the secondary meanings of a given image and the connotations it evokes from its primary contextual meaning. For instance, "fire," depending on the context, may evoke in biblical readers a sense of divine presence (Exod 24:17), divine word (Jer 20:8–9), destruction (Jer 21:10), anger (Jer 21:12), purification (Mal 3:2–3), or love (Song 8:6). By assessing the range of its ramifications insofar as they are pertinent to its given context, the reader may unexpectedly attain a more meaningful and richer interpretation of that metaphor. By "specific concept," Greenstein refers to the extraordinary specificity of the poet's imagery. The poet may use metaphors in a precise, deliberate, concentrated fashion. To examine the author's precision is to discover that the imagery, which at first sight may seem to embody a very vague notion, contains a rhetorical or poetic concept exactly fitted to the narrative's development in its particular context. By "intertextual function," Greenstein means an allusion to a concept or a passage in other biblical texts. For instance, the biblical expression "outstretched arm" (Exod 6:6; Deut 4:34; 5:15; 7:19; 26:8) may evoke in readers the concept or story of the exodus from Egypt. To read a passage while considering this function is to see how the author plays with the traditional knowledge associated with that image and adds new meaning to it. These three directives are very promising in advancing our understanding of metaphors not only in the poetry of Job but also in other biblical texts as well.

With all the contributions of these different research patterns, there are still hermeneutic considerations through which they can be substantially advanced. Of particular import is the following aspect of poetic metaphor that has not been adequately considered (this oversight is especially manifest in studies that adopt the third research pattern): that the meaning of poetic metaphor is not always fixed in its immediate syntactic or literary context but can extend beyond it. In other words, metaphors that appear in different sections of a given literary composition may be part of the same conceptual framework, giving structure to the same poetic reality. The reader, therefore, must actively sort and integrate dispersed elements within the text—elements whose connections are not always immediately apparent—in order to reconstruct that poetic reality and, ultimately, the drama of the work itself (Harshav 1984; Jindo 2010).

The Cognitive Turn in Metaphor Scholarship. As noted earlier, the cognitive turn in general scholarship has introduced a notion of metaphor primarily as a cognitive process, a conceptual (rather than a linguistic) phenomenon. Scholars who initiated this turn have developed a firm theoretical framework and effective methodological tools for conducting a systematic and empirical analysis of the relationship between language and mind. Consider, for example, the following expressions that English speakers use to describe their life experience in terms of journey:

> I am *at a crossroads*. I've *lost my way*. He is *headed in the right direction*. You are *on the right track*. It's *a dead end*. This will *lead you to where you want to go*. *Where* am I?

At first glance, these expressions may not seem metaphorical at all, but a closer examination reveals that beneath them are systematic correspondences between two conceptual domains, whereby speakers understand and experience life in terms of a journey. The basic correspondences of the two conceptual domains can be presented as follows:

JOURNEY		LIFE
the traveler	→	the individual
the journey	→	life
the distance covered	→	the progress in maturity
the obstacles encountered	→	hardships in life
decisions about the direction	→	decisions about what to do in life
the destinations	→	wishes and plans to achieve in life

As the chart shows, metaphorical communication involves the juxtaposition not merely of two individual concepts (e.g., the traveler and the person) but of two conceptual domains (e.g., journey and life). In other words, metaphor involves a *mapping of structure* from one domain onto another.

Cognitive scholars have observed many other instances of this sort in the everyday use of language. Below are but a few examples:

> AN ARGUMENT IS WAR
> Your claims are *indefensible*. He *attacked every weak point* in my argument. His criticisms were *right on target*. I *demolished* his argument. I've never *won* an argument with him.
>
> IDEAS ARE FOOD
> My idea is still *half-baked*. Your classmates won't get your theory—you need to *spoon-feed* them. Let me *digest* it. Her theory is *warmed-over*. His presentation gave us *food* for thought.
>
> THEORIES ARE BUILDINGS
> Is that the *foundation* for your theory? The argument is *shaky*. We need *to construct a strong* argument for that. We need to *buttress* the theory with *solid* arguments. The theory will *stand or fall on the strength of* that argument.

In each case, language users understand and experience one domain in terms of another.

The same holds true for biblical metaphors. Take, for example, the following metaphorical expressions, all of which are related to horticultural imagery:

זרע אברהם "the *seed* of Abraham" (Isa 41:8); פרי בטן "*fruit* of the womb" (Gen 30:2); פרי מעלליו "*fruit* of his deeds" (Jer 17:10); עקרה "the barren (lit. *uprooted*)" (Gen 11:30); נכרת מעמיו "*cut off* from his kin" (Exod 30:33).

A close examination of these expressions reveals that behind them are the conceptual mappings between the domain of human life and that of horticulture. The correspondences of some of the basic elements can be laid out as follows:

The chart clearly illustrates that the language user experiences and understands human life in terms of horticulture (though, perhaps, unconsciously in most cases). This underlying concept was widely shared in the ancient Near East, as the same metaphorical mappings can be found also in other Semitic languages; for example, in Akkadian, the word *zēru* "seed" (cf. זרע in

HORTICULTURE		HUMAN LIFE
tree	→	person
fruit	→	child, or the result of one's deed
seed	→	descendants
uprooted tree	→	the one who lacks productive potency
soil	→	world (cf. Ps 52:7), Land of Promise (cf. Exod 15:17), or temple (cf. Ps 92:14)
being cut off	→	death, annihilation
water	→	divine word or instruction (cf. Ps 1:2–3)
source of living water	→	God (cf. Jer 2:13)

Heb.) is also used for "descendants," and *inbu* "fruit" (cf. ענב in Heb.) for "children, offspring."

The basic features of metaphor that cognitive scholars have identified through these and many other empirical data can be summarized as follows: (1) conceptuality—metaphorical linguistic utterances are manifestations of metaphorical concepts and the conceptual world of language users; (2) systematicity—elements of one conceptual domain are systematically mapped onto the elements of another domain; (3) ubiquity—metaphor is ubiquitous in everyday discourse, not limited to a specific aesthetic discourse such as poetry or oratory; (4) fundamentality—metaphor, in many cases, operates subconsciously and remains unnoticed by language users, and yet it is fundamental to the cognitive activity of human beings and ultimately to the conceptualization of reality.

Considering these features of metaphor, the following points emerge as basic heuristic principles in dealing with metaphors:

(1) Because the phenomenon of metaphor is first and foremost conceptual, the exegete should clarify the interrelations of metaphorical verbal expressions on the conceptual level and the cognitive orientation as reflected in the use of these expressions. The exegete may, thereby, realize that metaphorical expressions that seem unrelated on the textual surface level are, in fact, conceptually interrelated on the deeper level.

(2) Because the phenomenon of metaphor involves systematic correspondences between two conceptual domains, the exegete should approach metaphor holistically and not atomistically. Thus, even if the exegete happens to explore only one correspondence in a given metaphorical concept (e.g., between "tree" and "person" in the earlier example), the exegete should explore it in light of the whole of the given metaphorical concept. Indeed, both the semantic and conceptual significance of each correspondence is determined in relation to other correspondences, as well as to the whole.

(3) Because the conceptual information upon which metaphorical communication is established is already known to language users and therefore, usually not spelled out in a given discourse, the exegete must clarify this information. Put differently, language users usually do not transmit new conceptual information in metaphorical communication but manipulate the conceptual system known beforehand to their audiences. Therefore, the exegete must clarify the conceptual information in case it is not fully articulated in the given discourse.

The explanatory power of the cognitive approach to metaphor has been demonstrated through its application to a variety of cultural and literary studies, ranging from general analysis of the metaphor in culture, to specific analyses, for example, of political and social discourse in the United States, to the analysis of literary works by Dante, Shakespeare, Dickinson, Yeats, Wordsworth, and Haiku poems (see, e.g., Kövecses 2010, especially, chs. 4, 5, 13, 14, 18). In biblical scholarship, too, this cognitive turn is gradually taking place (see works cited earlier).

Metaphor and the Study of Biblical Religion. Metaphor analysis can substantially enhance our understanding of biblical religion. Take, for example, the biblical metaphor of God as king. Biblical authors portray God with such terms and images as "glory" (Ps 24:8), "honor and majesty" (Ps 96:6), "judg[ing]" (Ps 96:13), "majestic" (Ps 93:4), "mighty" (Ps 24:8), "rod [or scepter]" (Isa 10:5), "strength and beauty" (Ps 96:6), and "throne" (Ps 93:2), all of which convey royal overtones. Whoever considers such terms merely as a stylistic or emotive device designed to evoke an overwhelming sense of divine majesty, however, overlooks the terms' cognitive value because beneath them lies a fundamental metaphorical concept of biblical cosmology. That is, biblical writers conceptualized the complex operation of the cosmos in terms of a human polity and their deity as the supreme authority. In cognitive linguistic terms, a conceptual domain of human polity was systematically mapped onto the domain of the cosmos. The basic correspondences of the two domains can be presented as follows:

HUMAN POLITY		THE COSMOS
king	→	God
king's dominion	→	cosmos
royal palace	→	temple, celestial or terrestrial
royal capital	→	Jerusalem
royal manor	→	Jerusalem, the land of Israel
royal garden	→	the garden of Eden
royal council	→	heavenly council
council members	→	celestial beings, prophets
king's confidants	→	Abraham, Moses, prophets
palace attendants	→	priests
palace workers	→	Levites
royal messengers	→	prophets
constituents	→	Israelites, humans, or all the creatures
taxes	→	tithes
tributes	→	cultic offerings
loyalty	→	devotion
disloyalty	→	idolatry
lese majesty	→	sacrilege/blasphemy

As the chart shows, this metaphorical mode of conceptualization involves the juxtaposition not merely of two individual concepts (e.g., king and God) but of two conceptual domains (e.g., human polity and the cosmos). The monotheistic system thereby transferred not only the constituent elements of the source domain but also the relations and tensions inherent within that domain. These are the tensions and interactions—the very elements which give vitality to the biblical drama—that the atomistic kind of conventional approach overlooks in its analysis of metaphors in biblical literature, thus inevitably producing a static interpretation of them and, also, undermining the significance of each element within the broader context.

Metaphor analysis also enables us to recognize the hitherto overlooked nuances and meanings of biblical ideas and motifs. As the preceding chart shows, for example, the biblical motif of prophetic intercession—e.g., Abraham's intercession on behalf of Sodom (Gen 18), Moses on behalf of the people of Israel (Exod 32—33), and Jeremiah on behalf of Judah and Jerusalem (Jer 12, 14—15)—which is hitherto treated discretely, is best understood in light of this royal metaphor. This intercessory role is typologically equivalent to the royal functionary called the king's *ibru* in Mesopotamia (cf. חבר in Heb.) or רע(ה) המלך "king's friend" in Israel (e.g., 1 Kgs 4:5; 1 Chr 27:33). This official served at the royal court as an advisor to, or "confidant" of, the king in his palace or ruling territories. Consider, for example, the following lines from a so-called boundary stone, *kudurru*, of Nebuchadnezzar I that describe the king's *ibru* as a valued advisor to the king:

> PN son of PN the *ibru* of his lord (the king)
> Who stands before the king,
> The servant whose counsel was always chosen.

In this respect, the prophet is God's *ibru* (cf. "The LORD used to speak to Moses face to face, as one speaks to רעהו—his *friend* [or confidant]" [Exod 33:11]). Just as the words of the *ibru* are highly esteemed in the royal court, so, too, the prophet's intercession is greatly valued in the council of God. Hence, we read: "Surely the Lord God does nothing, without revealing his secret to his servants the prophets" (Amos 3:7). Metaphor study, in short, is a key to identifying the overtones, connotations, and implications of biblical ideas and motifs.

The previously mentioned kind of sociomorphic conceptualization is not unique to biblical religion. Indeed, both Mesopotamian polytheism and biblical monotheism shared the same mode of, and model for, conceptualization: they both perceived the cosmos as a state. The difference between the two religious systems lies in the specific political model through which they perceived the operation of the world, namely, an oligarchic versus an autocratic model. The polytheistic mind perceives a plurality of divine wills behind the operation of the world, whereas the monotheistic mind intuits the supreme and ultimate will of a single deity behind it (see Jindo 2010, pp. 75–100, and works cited there). Clearly, metaphor played a crucial role in the formation of the worldview and self-understanding of ancient people in both Mesopotamia and Israel.

As the previous example illustrates, delving into the meaning of metaphor reveals the inner world of biblical authors—how they conceived of God, humans, and the world.

Metaphor and the Study of Biblical Literature. Critics have commonly understood poetic metaphor in biblical literature solely as an artistic flourish intended to create certain rhetorical effects. Seen this way, metaphor appears expendable and unrelated to the core content of the composition—however engaging it may be, aesthetically or otherwise. The case can be made otherwise—namely, that metaphor is the very essence of biblical literature. Literary images and expressions that appear as metaphors in a literary work can function as conceptual constructs of a poetic reality to orient, or reorient, the perception of the reader. As Shelley puts it: "Poetry lifts the veil from the hidden beauty of the world, and makes familiar objects be as if they were not familiar."

Metaphor communicates two kinds of knowledge—*propositional* and *perspectival*. Propositional knowledge, on the one hand, here refers to a descriptive knowledge about beings, conditions, or events, be they observable or imaginary, factual or hypothetical. Perspectival knowledge, on the other hand, refers to ways of seeing and thinking, or particular modes of cognition, whereby people perceive and experience such beings, conditions, or events. Put differently, we communicate through metaphor not only *what* we think, feel, or believe but also *how* we think, feel, or believe. Accordingly, the interpretation of a metaphor substantially changes depending on the interpretive assumption of each reader as to which knowledge the metaphor is primarily conveying, and what function that metaphor is meant to serve.

Take, for example, the utterance, "You [God] brought them [the people of Israel] in and *planted* them on the mountain of your own possession" (Exod 15:17). The utterance involves a metaphor of planting, by which the transporting of the people is conceived and described. A question then arises: How much substantive value should we assume in the cognitive function of this metaphor? If we assume the minimum, we would understand the function of the verb "plant" as stylistic—as a (mere) restatement of the verb "bring," adding some aesthetic or emotive quality. In this reading, the utterance is stating, essentially, the same proposition twice; namely once literally and once metaphorically that God brought the people to the Land of Promise. Hence, the metaphor is not part of the core content of the utterance. If, however, we assume the maximum, we would understand its function as cognitive—as a mode of orientation that is meant to direct or redirect the perception of the reader. In this reading, the utterance is meant to present not only a proposition, but also a specific viewpoint through which to perceive that proposition; namely, the Exodus event as God's plantation project. Just as ancient rulers planted pleasure gardens in or around their palace, God here appears as a divine king who finds an exquisite plant (Israel) on his military campaign (Exodus) and plants it upon his manorial mountain (the Promised Land) to create his treasure garden (cf. Isa 5:1–7; Jer 2:21; Ezek 15:6; Hos 9:10; see Jindo 2010, pp. 151–179). Hence, in this reading, once we paraphrase the metaphor, we lose the very perspective the utterance is designed to communicate.

The reader, thus, can de facto approach the same metaphor as a stylistic or as a cognitive device, and the preference for one or the other depends on the reader's assumption as to the primary goal of the authors, namely, to convey a proposition or a perception, to assert a dogma or represent a drama.

It is not hard to imagine why the latter conception of metaphor—as a mode of communicating perception and insight—has been generally overlooked in scholarship. This negligence stems from a perceived familiarity with the use of metaphorical language that is taken for granted. Readers accustomed to the use of metaphor only or mainly as rhetorical embellishment have presumed that this is the *only way* to use metaphor and that metaphor is being used this way in biblical literature. In this reading, as soon as the propositional meaning of the metaphor is fathomed—be it with or without rhetorical considerations of that metaphor—the goal of interpretation is assumed to be accomplished.

There are many other playful, yet fundamental, uses of poetic metaphor—such as "Janus metaphor," "mixed metaphor," and "revivification of dead/conventional metaphors"—the recognition of which can substantially enhance our reading experience and appreciation of biblical literature. These and many other poetic uses of biblical metaphors have not received the attention they merit and await a thorough monograph-length analysis.

In a word, poetic metaphor as a mode of orientation is *double-directed*. Internally, it operates as a conceptual construct to reproduce a drama of the composition in the mind of readers. Externally, it directs readers to perceive their reality in light of that drama, thereby enabling them to recognize the relations and distinctions they may not have previously noticed. In this way, readers can approach metaphor in biblical literature—and in fact in all mytho-poetic literature—as an indispensable mode to reveal the "metaphysical truth" (Henri Frankfort) underlying the events unfolding in the human world. Readers thereby receive what one may call the very essence of biblical literature—to wit, biblical insight into reality.

[*See also* Allegory and Allegorical Interpretation; Cognitive Linguistics and Biblical Interpretation; Exegesis; Inner-biblical Interpretation; Intertextuality; Literary Criticism, Literary Theory, and the Bible; Rhetorical Criticism; *and* Semiotics.]

BIBLIOGRAPHY

Alter, Robert. *The Art of Biblical Poetry*. New York: Basic Books, 1985. A collection of essays that include sensitive and imaginative analyses of biblical poems and metaphors.

Black, Max. *Models and Metaphors: Studies in Language and Philosophy*. Ithaca, N.Y.: Cornell University Press, 1962. A collection of seminal essays on metaphor and its distinctive cognitive value, as well as on other related issues in analytical philosophy, including Black's seminal "interaction" theory of metaphor—metaphorical meaning as emerging through the selective interaction between systems of implications or "associated common places."

Camp, Claudia V., and Carole R. Fontaine, eds. *Woman, War and Metaphor: Language and Society in the Study of the Hebrew Bible. Semeia* 61. Atlanta: Scholars Press, 1993. A series of essays by various biblicists with an attempt to introduce exemplary discussions related to biblical metaphors.

Cohen, Mordechai Z. *Three Approaches to Biblical Metaphor: From Abraham Ibn Ezra and Maimonides to David Kimhi*. Leiden, Netherlands: Brill, 2003. A lucid and informative study of medieval Jewish approaches to biblical metaphor and related literary issues in the Spanish exegetical tradition.

Greenstein, Edward L. "Remarks on Some Metaphors in the Book of Job" (in Hebrew). In *Bible and Exegesis IX*, edited by Shmuel Vargon et al., 231–241. Ramat-Gan, Israel: Bar-Ilan University Press, 2009. An earlier, English version of this article is "Some Remarks on Metaphors in the Poetry of Job." SBL annual meeting, Atlanta, Ga. 22 November 2003; The University of Wisconsin, Madison, 22 March 2004. Presents three interpretive principles for attaining richer meanings of poetic metaphors in Job.

Harshav [Hrushovski], Benjamin. "Poetic Metaphor and Frames of Reference: With Examples from Eliot, Rilke, Mayakovsky, Mandelshtam, Pound, Creely, Amichai, and the New York Times." *Poetics Today* 5 (1984): 5–43. Reprint in *Explorations in Poetics*, 32–75. Stanford, Calif.: Stanford University Press, 2007. Presents a sophisticated and pragmatic theory of poetic metaphor, which can substantially enhance our understanding of complex literary phenomena of metaphor.

Hecke, Pierre van, ed. *Metaphor in the Hebrew Bible*. Dudley, Mass.: Peeters, 2005. Papers discussing various aspect of metaphor research in the Hebrew Bible.

Hecke, Pierre van and Antje Labahn, eds. *Metaphors in the Psalms*. Leuven, Belgium: Uitgeverij Peeters, 2010. Articles addressing interpretive, conceptual, and/or functional issues of metaphors in the book of Psalms.

Jindo, Job Y. *Biblical Metaphor Reconsidered: A Cognitive Approach to Poetic Prophecy in Jeremiah 1–24*. Winona Lake, Ind.: Eisenbrauns, 2010. Presents an interpretive approach that enables the reader to consider the hitherto generally overlooked cognitive and creative function of poetic metaphor in biblical prophecy.

Johnson, Mark, ed. *Philosophical Perspectives on Metaphor*. Minneapolis: University of Minnesota Press, 1981. An anthology of metaphor theories with a critical survey of the history of metaphor scholarship and a very helpful annotated bibliography of major works in metaphor studies.

Kövecses, Zoltán. *Metaphor: A Practical Introduction*. 2d ed. Oxford: Oxford University Press, 2010. A very accessible introduction to the cognitive linguistic account of metaphor.

Landy, Francis. *Paradoxes of Paradise: Identity and Difference in the Song of Songs*. BLS 7. Sheffield, UK: Almond, 1983. An eloquent study of the poetry and imagery in the Song of Songs.

Ortony, Andrew ed., *Metaphor and Thought*. 2d ed. Cambridge, UK: Cambridge University Press, 1993. One of the best available anthologies of contemporary theories of metaphor.

Richards, I. A. *The Philosophy of Rhetoric*. London: Oxford University Press, 1936. Includes the so-called "interaction" theory of metaphor that is meant to do justice to the creative power and complexity of metaphor.

Ricoeur, Paul. *The Rule of Metaphor: Multi-Disciplinary Studies of the Creation of Meaning in Language*. Translated by Robert Czerny et al. University of Toronto Romance Series 37. Toronto: University of Toronto Press, 1977. English translation of *Métaphore vive*. Paris: Seuil, 1975. An exhaustive, interdisciplinary examination of metaphor theory from Aristotle to the present by one of the most distinguished philosophers of the twentieth century.

Stern, Josef. *Metaphor in Context*. Cambridge, Mass.: MIT Press, 2000. A penetrating full-scale research that seeks to develop a formal theory for metaphorical interpretation.

Ungerer, Friedrich, and Hans-Jörg Schmid. *An Introduction to Cognitive Linguistics*. 2d ed. Harlow, England: Pearson, 2006. A lucid, comprehensive overview of cognitive linguistics.

Weiss, Meir. *The Bible from Within: The Method of Total Interpretation*. Translated by Baruch J. Schwartz. Jerusalem: Magnes, 1984. An English, revised translation of *Ha-Mikra Ki-demuto*. 2d ed. Jerusalem: Bialik Institute, 1967. An excellent introduction to holistic reading of the Bible, which presents, inter alia, meticulous analyses of poetic imagery in biblical literature.

White, Roger M. *The Structure of Metaphor: The Way the Language of Metaphor Works*. Oxford: Blackwell, 1996. Full of insightful discussions and has a fine and concise bibliography of theoretical studies on poetic metaphor.

Wolde, Ellen van. *Reframing Biblical Studies: When Language and Text Meet Culture, Cognition, and Context*. Winona Lake, Ind.: Eisenbrauns, 2009. A programmatic work which introduces cognitive linguistics to biblical studies.

Job Y. Jindo

MIDRASH

The term *midrash* (Hebrew root *drš*, "to investigate, seek, search out, examine") is often used generically to refer to any act of interpretation, but in its strictest and most precise sense it refers to rabbinic biblical interpretation, to both the process of interpretation as well as the fruits of exegetical inquiry. The act of interpreting the Bible was an engagement not only with the written word but also with the practices and beliefs of the Jewish people. Through the midrashic process, the rabbis made the Bible relevant to their contemporaries, taught moral lessons, told fanciful stories, and developed as well as maintained theological beliefs and ethical codes of behavior.

When literary theory emerged as a burgeoning field of inquiry, intersecting with other areas of studies within the humanities in the 1970s, scholarship in midrash and aggadah (narrative) began to reflect a focus on the literary features of rabbinic literature. Current research demonstrates an interest in the literary earmarks of legal texts, and should thus be examined in light of literary motifs, themes, and structure. While rabbinic biblical interpretation and narratives are analyzed in terms of their literary quality, at the same time they are regarded as artifacts that function as conveyors and mediators of rabbinic culture. The historical import of these literary sources is therefore undiminished to the extent that they yield insight into the milieu of those who recorded, transmitted, and lived by them.

Rabbinic literature is commonly divided along chronological lines as well as according to genre.

Collections of works of rabbinic sages of the first two centuries C.E., all in Palestine, known as *tanna'im* (oral teachers), are referred to as tannaitic (70–200 C.E.). Those of rabbinic sages (*amora'im*, "expositors") of the third through fourth centuries, also of Palestinian provenance, or fifth century in Babylonia, are called amoraic (200–500 C.E.). The tannaitic midrashic corpora comment on biblical verses successively. They provide explications on verses in Exodus, Leviticus, Numbers, and Deuteronomy. Compilations include: Mekhilta de Rabbi Ishmael on parts of the Book of Exodus, the Sifra, Sifre Numbers, and Sifre Deuteronomy. They also cover nonlegal passages, but because they primarily deal with legal verses more thoroughly, they are designated as *midreshei halakhah* (legal rabbinic interpretation). Tannaitic collections are further divided according to two rabbinic "schools," those of Rabbi Akiva and of Rabbi Ishmael, both of whom lived in Palestine in the first half of the second century C.E. Scholars assign collections to either rabbi based on a set of criteria: exegetical terminology and hermeneutical methods employed, teachings attributed to named rabbis, and fundamental exegetical approaches to scripture.

Unlike the tannaitic corpora, which are mostly halakhic, amoraic midrashim are almost entirely aggadic, and also almost entirely of Palestinian provenance. Rabbinic compilations of the amoraic period are either ordered according to a verse-by-verse exegesis (like tannaitic midrashim) or are a series of sermons based on the verse at hand. The latter type are known as homiletic compilations, whereas the former type are aggadic exegetical compilations. Premier examples of aggadic midrashim are Genesis Rabbah and Lamentations Rabbah, two of the Midrash Rabbah collections of the books of Torah and the five *megillot* (scrolls) of Lamentations, Esther, Ruth, Song of Songs, and Ecclesiastes. In addition to Leviticus Rabbah, Deuteronomy Rabbah, and Numbers Rabbah, other compilations such as Pesikta de Rab Kahana on selected passages or sections read on special Sabbaths or festal days are arranged homiletically. In these works, chapters comprise homilies that by and large cohere around a particular topic. The collections of homilies moreover share a structural arrangement: a series of proems (*petiḥtot*), the body (*gufa*) of the homily, and in many instances an eschatological ending or peroration. The *petiḥta*, a verse usually from the Writings, is also an earmark of the aggadic compilations, whether exegetical or homiletical. Through a chain of interpretations, the seemingly extraneous verse is connected to the verse under discussion. This structure exemplifies a fundamental aspect of midrash, namely the desire to unite the diverse parts of the tripartite canon—Torah, Prophets, and Writings (TaNaKh)—into a harmonious, seamless whole that reflects the oneness of God's Word.

As we move into the medieval period, from approximately 640–1000 C.E., in addition to compilations similar to those of the classical period, we notice the emergence of an innovative form of interpretation in which biblical narratives are used didactically to impart religious lessons on such themes as the chosenness of Israel, the Sabbath, the centrality of Torah study, and the observance of mitzvot (commandments). *Pirke de Rabbi Eliezer* (*PRE*), of the eighth or early ninth century, also discusses the calendar and astronomy, and is replete with stories and legends found in earlier texts such as Jubilees. The work therefore integrates the structure of classical midrash within the framework of recounting biblical history. Even later midrashic works such as the Yalkut Shimoni and the Midrash Ha-Gadol of the fourteenth and fifteenth centuries not only anthologize earlier midrashim, but also supplement traditional material. Thus, while the period approximately between the sixth and fifteenth centuries reflects inter alia an attempt to compile scriptural interpretation of earlier generations, the later compilations supplement the classical texts of the fifth and sixth centuries. The nature of rabbinic interpretation and the very process of textual transmission, accommodate emendation even as they attempt to preserve both text and tradition.

The starting point of midrashic inquiry is the biblical text and can be characterized by a versocentric quality. Through philological associations and intertextual wordplay, the rabbis unpack the meaning of biblical verses. Moreover, by drawing on verses from the Prophets (Nevi'im) and Writings (Ketuvim) to explicate a verse in Torah, the rabbis demonstrate the underlying notion that TaNaKh is a seamless whole whose parts shed light throughout from beginning to end. For example, on Genesis 1:1, we read in Genesis Rabbah: R. Oshaya opened his explication of the verse: "I was with Him as a nursling (*amon*), a source of delight every day; rejoicing before him at all times" (Prov 8:30). By drawing on a variety of verses (Num 11:12, Lam 4:5, Esth 2:7), the midrash offers different explanations for the meaning of *amon*—"tutor," "covered," "hidden," and "great." The connection is philological, based on assonance between *amon* in Proverbs 8:30 and a word in each prooftext. In this manner, the midrash unpacks Proverbs 8:30, which in turn explicates Genesis 1:1, "In the beginning God created." In the final interpretation, "*Amon* is a workman (*uman*)." Torah (Wisdom) speaks: "I was the working tool of the Holy One, blessed be He." The midrash continues:

> In human practice, when a mortal king builds a palace, he builds it not with his own skill but with the skill of an architect. The architect moreover does not build it out of his head, but employs plans and diagrams to know how to arrange the chambers and the wickets. Thus God consulted the Torah and created the world, while the Torah declares, "In the beginning God created," beginning referring to the Torah, as in the verse, "The Lord made me as the beginning of His way" (Prov 8:22).

Tannaitic/Halakhic Midrashim. As previously mentioned, the earliest midrashic collections are referred to as either tannaitic or halakhic because they essentially, although not exclusively, deal with Jewish law (halakhah). The Mekhilta de Rabbi Ishmael is one of the most frequently cited collections as well as one of the earliest compilations of midrash. The rabbis whose statements are recorded lived in Palestine during the first two centuries C.E. A verse-by-verse exposition of Exodus 12:1—23:19, the Mekhilta often expounds every word of the verse. It also includes interpretations of Exodus 31:12–17 and 35:1–3. Although the Mekhilta de Rabbi Ishmael concentrates on the halakhic portions of Exodus, it also contains extensive aggadic sections. It is divided into nine tractates: Pisḥa (Exod 12:1—13:16) discusses laws regarding the particulars of the first Passover sacrifice; Beshallaḥ (Exod 13:17—14:71) deals with the exodus from Egypt; Shirta (Exod 15:1–21) is an elaborate commentary on the Song at the Sea; Vayassa' (Exod 15:22—17:7) takes up the Israelites' wanderings in the desert; Amalek (Exod 17:8—18:27) focuses on the war with Amalek and ensuing events; Baḥodesh (Exod 19:1—20:23) is an extended explication of the many laws contained in this section, and is the longest treatise of the corpus. Kaspa (Exod 22:24—23:19) continues the discussion of specific laws, and Shabbata (Exod 31:12–17; 35:1–3) ends the compilation with a detailed discussion of two passages pertaining to the laws of Shabbat.

The Sifra ("book") is an early running exegetical commentary on Leviticus in its entirety. This collection of midrashim overwhelmingly, perhaps almost exclusively, discusses halakhic matters. Like the Mekhilta its language is mishnaic Hebrew, but also contains several Greek words. To date, Neusner (1988) is the only English translation of the collection.

Other noteworthy tannaitic midrashic compilations are Mekhilta de Rabbi Simon bar Yoḥai, Sifre ("books") Numbers and Deuteronomy. The Sifre Numbers commences with the first legal material in Numbers.

Like Sifre Numbers, Sifre Deuteronomy covers legal as well as narrative sections of the book. It explicates Deuteronomy 1:1–30; 3:23–29; 6:4–9; 11:10–26; 31:14–32, 34. Narrative portions include the prayer of Moses, the Shema, the song and blessing of Moses, as well as his death. Both R. Hammer (1986) and Jacob Neusner (1987) produced translations. Hammer's translation includes important parallel passages and useful information to help the reader situate the work vis-à-vis other rabbinic texts.

References to compilations as either halakhic or aggadic can be somewhat misleading, although this is less the case with respect to aggadic midrashim in which little if any halakhic discussions are found. The Mekhilta and Sifre Deuteronomy, for example, share features of aggadic texts even though they are halakhic expositions.

For example, Sifre Deuteronomy 343 on Deuteronomy 33:2 offers the following comment on the words, "The LORD came from Sinai":

> When the Holy One, Blessed be He, is about to exact punishment from Seir, he will shake the entire world with its inhabitants just as he shook it with the giving of the Torah. . . . The matter may be compared to a king who wanted to give a gift to one of his children but the king was afraid on account of his brothers, his friends and his relatives. What did the son do? He stood and dolled himself up and cut his hair. The king said to him, "To you, I am giving you a gift." Thus, when Abraham our father came into the world something unfit came from him–Ishmael and the sons of Keturah. They became more evil than the previous ones. And when Isaac came, something unfit came from him, Esau and all the chieftains of Edom. They became more evil than the previous ones. When Jacob came, nothing unfit came from him, but rather all the children born to him were perfect, as it is said, "And Jacob was a perfect man dwelling in tents" (Gen 25:26). The Holy One, Blessed be He, said to him, "I am giving the Torah to you," as it is said, "The LORD came from Sinai; he rose upon them from Seir."

In this halakhic compilation, we read a midrash that is aggadic in terms of its form and content. We are introduced to a parable, in Hebrew *mashal* (*meshalim*, pl.), that explains why Israel is given the Torah. Israel is set apart from all the unfit, unworthy issue of Abraham and Isaac because *it* chose to set itself apart. The king wanted to give something special to one son, but did not do so until the son set himself apart. So, too, God gave the Torah to Israel when it set itself apart through righteous behavior.

While there are fundamental differences between the halakhic and aggadic compilations, we should keep in mind that these are broad terms that ought not limit our perception of the works as first and foremost compilations of interpretation that employ scripture as a springboard for theological, social, and cultural musings.

Aggadic Midrashim. The Midrash Rabbah ("The Large Midrash"), a major compilation of rabbinic interpretations of the books of Torah and the five *megillot* (scrolls)—Lamentations, Esther, Ruth, Song of Songs, and Ecclesiastes—is a collection of aggadic (folkloric or non-halakhic) literature, for the most part composed in Palestine over a period of several hundred years. Based on internal evidence, Genesis Rabbah dates from the fifth century, and the latest, Numbers Rabbah, is from the twelfth century.

Genesis Rabbah is a good example of an aggadic exegetical compilation. Here we find both simple and elaborate explanations of words and phrases of the verse at hand. Most *parashiyot* (chapters; *parasha*, sing.), except for 13, 15, 17, 18, 25, 35 and 37, contain one or more *petiḥtot* (*petiḥta*, sing.), a verse usually from the Writings, especially from Psalms or the Wisdom Literature, sometimes from the Prophets, but rarely from the Torah, that is seemingly extraneous but through a chain of interpretations is connected to the verse at the beginning of the section. So, for example, Genesis Rabbah 33:2 on the second half of Genesis 7:1 ("And the LORD said to Noah: 'Come, you and your entire household unto the ark; for you I have seen righteous before Me in this generation"), opens: "For the LORD is righteous, He loves righteousness; the upright shall behold his face" (Ps 11:7). Then Psalm 11:7 is related to Genesis 7:1 in the following way:

> R. Tanhuma in R. Judah's name and R. Menahem in R. Eleazar's name said: No man loves his fellow-craftsman, but a sage loves his companion. R. Hiyya loves his fellow-craftsmen and R. Hoshaya loves his. The Holy One, blessed be He, also loves His [in the sense that God is righteous and loves those who are also righteous, and in that respect they are God's fellow-craftsmen]. Therefore, "For the LORD is righteous, He loves righteousness; the upright shall behold his face" (Ps 11:7) applies to Noah, as it is written, ". . . for you I have seen righteous before Me in this generation."

The verse in Psalms is quoted to explicate Genesis 7:1 by showing that God loves the righteous because, like him, they are righteous and are in a sense God's companions. The midrash furthermore echoes Genesis 6:9, "Noah was a righteous man; he was blameless in his age; Noah walked with God."

In addition to verse-by-verse collections of midrashim, such as Genesis Rabbah and Lamentations Rabbah, several collections, like Leviticus Rabbah and Pesikta de Rav Kahana, are arranged homiletically. That is, they are arranged as chapters of homilies that often cluster around a particular topic. The notion that the midrashim are homiletical assumes that we can trace their origins to the synagogue. Recent scholarship, however, has moved in the direction of reading them as literary works.

Case Study in Leviticus Rabbah. Composed around the late fifth century, Leviticus Rabbah (LR) is divided into thirty-seven chapters, each featuring a *petiḥah* (or *petiḥta*) and *gufa*. While the bipartite division holds for all thirty-seven, a messianic peroration at the end of the chapter is found in only twenty-one chapters. Chapters in LR seem to have some thematic unity, while others are organized around a common scriptural verse or topic. LR 23 is a good example of a chapter that addresses the issue of Jewish difference or distinctiveness.

The chapter begins with the following unit:

> "Like the practice of the land of Egypt" (Lev 18:3). Rabbi Isaac opened [expounded the verse]: "Like a rose among the thorns" (Song 2:2). Rabbi Isaac interpreted the verse as referring to Rebecca: "Isaac was forty years old when he took to wife Rebecca, daughter of Betuel the Aramean of Paddam-aram, sister of Laban the Aramean" (Gen 25:20). Why does Scripture state "sister of Laban the Aramean"? Did it not already state "daughter of Betuel the Aramean"? And why does it state, "daughter of Betuel the Aramean"? Does it not already state, "sister of Laban the Aramean?" [Why the superfluity?] Rather, the Holy One Blessed be He said, "Her father is a deceiver [*ramai*] and her brother is a deceiver and the people of her place are deceivers [*rema'im*], and this righteous one emerged from among them. She is like a rose among the thorns." Rabbi Berekhiah in the name of Rabbi Simon makes the point in connection with this verse, "And Isaac sent away Jacob; and he went to Paddan-aram unto Laban, son of Betuel the Aramean" (Gen 28:5), thus labeling them all as practicing deception [*ramma'ut*]. All of them are deceivers.

In this case the proem is Song of Songs 2:2, "Like a rose among the thorns." Through a series of word plays, allusions, and analogies, it is linked to the verse to be explicated—Lev 18:3—the unequivocal prohibition against Israelite assimilation: "Like the practice of the land of Egypt which you dwelled in, you should not practice, and like the practice of the land of Canaan to which I am bringing you, you should not practice, and in their laws you should not go." Given that Leviticus 18 articulates a host of sexual interdictions, it is ironic that Song 2:2 is the intertext.

Positioned between their past in Egypt and their future in Canaan, the Israelites must maintain their distinctiveness and thus avoid taking on the ways of their cultural surroundings. This is illustrated in the midrash, where Rebecca is likened to the rose among the thorns. That is, she is surrounded by deceivers, *ramayim*. By means of a play on the words *arami* (Aramean) and *ramai* (deceiver), the rabbis also draw an analogy between the thorns and members of Rebecca's family, in particular her father Betuel and her brother Laban. But they are not the only thorns; rather the entire town is full of deceivers.

According to the midrash, Rebecca's moral character sets her apart from her kin and townsfolk, from the other Arameans. Later units (4 and 7) of the same *parashah* (chapter), draw on the analogy in this pericope to make a similar claim, but in those instances with respect to Israelite distinctiveness. In fact, one may argue that R. Berekiah's prooftext, Genesis 28:5, "And Isaac sent away Jacob; and he went to Paddan-aram unto Laban, son of Betuel the Aramean," already foreshadows that claim. In other words, Jacob/Israel is now the rose among the thorns, and so, too, are the Israelites in later units of the same chapter. Is the pericope about Jewish difference or should it be read ironically, perhaps as subverting the very notion of difference? Might it reflect uneasiness about the notion of distinction vis-à-vis non-Jews? The midrash complicates the notion of difference, underscoring the extent to which and the ways in which the Jews are set apart.

The prooftext is the linchpin of the entire chapter, and it must be read simultaneously along two vectors, one that hews to audience expectations, and another that upends and devastates those expectations. That is to say, "And Isaac sent away Jacob; and he went to Paddan-aram unto Laban, son of Betuel the Aramean" is a parody that at once supports the notion that Rebecca and by extension the Israelites are unlike the Arameans, and simultaneously subverts that very notion. The midrash at once introduces and traduces the notion of distinction. For indeed, the midrash continues: "All of them are deceivers." But who constitutes "All"? All Arameans? Does "all" include Rebecca and Jacob, and by extension Israel and the Jews?

Leviticus Rabbah 23:1 attempts to set Rebekah, Jacob, and by extension the Jewish people morally apart from other nations, but simultaneously functions to undermine that notion of exceptionalism or distinction. To read it on one plane is to not only lose sight of the midrash's literary richness, but also to limit its theological implications and to ignore rabbinic anxiety and ambiguity about Jewish difference. This is echoed throughout the rest of chapter 23. In fact, LR 23:2 makes the claim that it is only because God vowed to take for himself a nation that Israel is redeemed, not because of its exceptional virtuous behavior or its separation from ambient cultural trappings.

The previous reading of LR 23:1 might lead one to assume that the rabbis were well attuned to the various vectors on which the midrash operates—generally speaking the overt and covert lines of communication. Cognizant of the ludic possibilities of the text, the rabbis were aware of the intertextual connections and ruptures that continually relativize the overt line of communication. In this sense, we draw attention to rabbinic self-reflexivity that is inherent to the rabbinic intertextual enterprise.

General Methods and Literary Devices. Rabbinic exegetical methods employed in halakhic and aggadic midrashim vary, and characteristics of aggadic midrashim in halakhic corpora and vice versa can be detected. The *Qal wahomer* (literally "light and heavy") is an argument established by means of a major or minor premise. "If that is true, how much more is this true!" This form of reasoning is found in both halakhic and aggadic midrashim. The *Gezera Shavah*, however, is more common to halakhic midrashim. By means of analogy, a particular detail of a biblical law in one verse is derived from the meaning of the word or phrase in another. Other rules that characterize halakhic midrashim include the *Binyan av* (a specific law in one verse may be applied to all other similar cases), *Kelal uperat, perat ûkĕlal* (rules of inference between general and specific statements and vice versa), and *Hekkesh* (inference by analogy, whether explicit or implicit between two subjects—not words—within the same or similar context).

These aforementioned rules are used in halakhic exegesis to expound biblical verses and derive halakhic rulings. They are included among the thirteen rules of Rabbi Ishmael enumerated in the introduction of the Sifra, and are in essence amplifications of the seven rules of Rabbi Hillel. The biblical nonlegal passages are often explained by means of philological associations. Wordplay, however, not only provides a lynchpin for rabbis to draw analogies between verses. It also takes the form of *gematria*, whereby the arithmetical value of Hebrew letters is used to interpret a word or verse, and *notaricon*, shorthand writing whereby individual letters are used to signify words. In other words, Hebrew words are understood as acronyms so that each letter stands for another word, which in turn forms a phrase or sentence.

In addition to wordplay, we find scores of stories, maxims, and parables (*meshalim*, sg. *mashal*). The Hebrew parables about kings are the signal form of narrative in rabbinic exegetical literature. Nearly all rabbinic *meshalim* consist of a bipartite structure—the fictional narrative that is the *mashal* proper, and its application, the *nimshal*, which usually concludes with a biblical verse serving as the *mashal*'s prooftext. Formulaic phrases mark the two parts: *mashal le*, "it is like" (also, *mashal lema hadavar dome le*, or simply *le*), and *kak*, "so, too, similarly." Note the king *mashal* in Sifre Deuteronomy 343 previously discussed, and the mashal in Genesis Rabbah 1:1. The following text from Genesis Rabbah 30:10 illustrates the rabbis' use of the *mashal* to explicate Genesis 6:9, "Noah walked with God":

> R. Judah said: This may be compared (*mashal le*) to a prince who had two sons, one grown up and the other a child. To the child he said, "Walk with me," but to the grown son he said, "Walk before me." Similarly (*kak*) to Abraham, whose strength was great, [He said,] "Walk thou before Me" (Gen 17:1); of Noah, whose strength was weak [Scripture says], "Noah walked with God." R. Nehemiah said: He might be compared to (*mashal le*) a king's friend who was sinking in thick mud. When the king looked out and saw him drowning [in the mud], he said to him, "Instead of plunging about in mud, come and walk with me."

The rabbis implicitly ask, "What does it mean that Noah walked with God? How does it differ from the notion that Abraham walked before God?" The use of *meshalim* helps them address the matter and distinguish between the personal qualities of Abraham and Noah. While one may understand walking with God as demonstrating Noah's greater status than that of Abraham who is commanded to walk before God, the rabbis argue the converse. The unit ends with a midrash in which Abraham is likened to one who heralds the prince's arrival. Abraham walks before God in order to glorify him.

Critical Editions. Critical editions for most of the important works of midrash exist. While the list below is not exhaustive, it guides the reader to most of the major critical editions of aggadic and halakhic works of midrash, and it includes recently published editions in paper as well as online. Other critical editions are mentioned *passim*.

Midrash Bereshit Rabbah: Critical Edition with Notes and Commentary, 3 vols. Theodor, Julius, and Chanoch Albeck, eds. (Jerusalem: Wahrmann, 1965). This is the standard edition of Genesis (*Bereshit*) Rabba. It is based on the British Museum MS, but its critical apparatus includes most textual attestations, with the exception of recent Genizah discoveries. Albeck acknowledged that MS Vatican 30 should have been the basis for the edition, and the editors overlooked MS Vatican 60. However, by most accounts the edition is rather impressive and remains the standard scholarly edition of Genesis Rabbah. Reproduction of 1912–1936 (Berlin) edition.

Midrash Vayyiqra Rabbah: A Critical Edition Based on Manuscripts and Genizah Fragments with Variants and Notes, 3 vols. Mordecai Margulioth, ed. (Jerusalem, 1972). First published in five volumes between 1953 and 1960, provides variants in manuscripts and printed editions. The work hews to the basic standards of a critical edition and includes notes, an introduction, and appendices, and thus does not explain the relationship between the textual references.

The online edition of *Leviticus (Vayyiqra) Rabbah*, produced by Milikowsky and Schlueter, http://www.biu.ac.il/JS/midrash/VR. [In Hebrew] Ramat Gan, Israel: Bar-Ilan University, n.d., is an important online resource that allows the users of the critical edition to evaluate textual variants. The project benefits from findings over the past forty years. Textual witnesses are collated together in a line-under-line format.

Pesiqta Rabbati: A Synoptic Edition of Pesiqta Rabbati Based Upon All Extant Manuscripts and the Editio Princeps 3 vols. Rivka Ulmer, ed. (Lanham, Md.: University Press of America, 1997–2009). A synoptic edition of a collection of homilies on the Holy Days and special Sabbaths liturgical Torah-reading cycle, this three-volume work includes an extensive introduction based on all extant manuscripts and the *editio princeps*. The editor presents manuscripts in parallel columns as opposed to adopting a linear or "standard" critical edition technique.

Sifre on Numbers: An Annotated Edition. Menahem Kahana, ed. (Jerusalem: Magnes, 2011). Kahana's three-volume critical edition is the latest development in the study of Sifre. The work is still in progress; the three volumes deal with the first half of the work. The first volume includes a complete critical edition of Numbers 4:21—12:16 (*Naso* and *Beha'alotkha*) and a provisional edition of chapters 13—36. The second volume is devoted entirely to a commentary on *Naso;* volume three is on *Beha'alotkha.* Once complete it will be the definitive critical edition, but even as it stands, the work based on MS Vatican 32 is a major advancement since the last critical edition of Horovitz.

Sifre Deuteronomy (Siphre ad Deuteronomium), Louis Finkelstein, ed. (New York: Jewish Theological Seminary of America, 1993). This eclectic edition was originally published in Germany in 1939 and reissued thirty years later. To date, this is the standard critical edition.

Midrash Shemot Rabbah, Chapters I–XIV: A Critical Edition Based on a Jerusalem Manuscript, with Variants, Commentary and Introduction, Avigdor Shinan, ed. (Tel Aviv: Dvir, 1984). Shinan's edition is an example of the best-text edition, referred to by classicists as the *codex optimus.* It covers the first half of the document and furnishes a good introduction and useful commentary.

Mekhilta de-Rabbi Ishmael, Haim Shaul Horovitz, and Israel Rabin, eds. (Jerusalem: Bamberger and Wahrman, 1960). This tannaitic commentary to the Book of Exodus was first published in 1931. It generally uses Venice 1545 as the base text; contains a critical apparatus and a commentary by Horovitz. It is still considered the standard scholarly edition of the Mekhilta. The Jacob Lauterbach critical edition and translation (reprinted 2004, Philadelphia, JPS) nonetheless offers a thorough, useful introduction in English, a rudimentary critical apparatus, and is accompanied with the Hebrew text. It is far less terminologically consistent than may be desired, but the translation is a pleasure to read and accurately reflects the Hebrew.

Pirqe Rabbi Eliezer Electronic Editing Project, Lewis Barth, ed. (http://www.usc.edu/projects/pre-project/index.html). The goal of this project is to include electronic publication of all *Pirke de Rabbi Eliezer* (*PRE*) manuscripts and fragments in digital facsimile form and transcriptions with hypertextual links. It is an invaluable resource for those working on *PRE,* a medieval midrashic work.

Databases. There are many online databases and catalogs that offer access to midrashic texts in the original, as well as repositories of academic journals on rabbinic literature in general, midrash in particular. The *Bar Ilan Responsa Project* is one of the largest online troves of rabbinic sources, an indispensable tool for those interested not only in midrashic material but all rabbinic works such as the Mishnah, Tosefta, Babylonian Talmud (Talmud Bavli), the Jerusalem Talmud (Yerushalmi). It also includes medieval Bible commentaries, responsa, inter alia. In addition to the Hebrew Bible, the Soncino Midrash Rabbah includes midrashic compilations both in Hebrew and English of the Five Books of Torah, and the Five Scrolls (Song of Songs, Ruth, Lamentations, Ecclesiastes, and Esther). It is searchable and includes footnotes, and while the translation leaves much to be desired it is useful to those who have little or no facility with Hebrew and Aramaic. *Primary Textual Witnesses to Tannaitic Literature* ([http://www.biu.ac.il/js/tannaim/] Ramat Gan, Israel: Bar-Ilan University) currently provides online access to the Mekhilta of Rabbi Ishmael and the Tosefta, but aims to furnish access to all tannaitic literature.

[*See also* Masora and Masoretic Interpretation; *and* Rabbinic Exegesis.]

BIBLIOGRAPHY

Anisfeld, Rachel. *Sustain Me with Raisin-Cakes: Pesikta DeRav Kahana and the Popularization of Rabbinic Judaism.* Supplements to the Journal of the Study of Judaism 133. Leiden, the Netherlands: Brill, 2009.

Bakhos, Carol, ed. *Current Trends in the Study of Midrash.* Leiden, Netherlands: Brill, 2006.

Boyarin, Daniel. *Intertextuality and the Reading of Midrash.* Bloomington: Indiana University Press, 1990.

Dohrmann, N. and D. Stern, eds. *Jewish Biblical Interpretation and Cultural Exchange: Comparative Exegesis in Context.* Philadelphia: University of Pennsylvania Press, 2008.

Fraade, Steven. *From Tradition to Commentary: Torah and its Interpretation in the Midrash Sifre to Deuteronomy.* Albany: State University of New York Press, 1991.

Fraenkel, Jonah. *Darkhei ha'aggadah vehamidrash.* Masada, Israel: Yad Letalmud, 1991.

Hammer, Reuven. *Sifre: A Tannaitic Commentary on the Book of Deuteronomy.* Translated by Reuven Hammer. New Haven, Conn.: Yale University Press, 1986.

Hartman, G. H., and S. Budick, eds. *Midrash and Literature.* New Haven, Conn.: Yale University Press, 1986.

Hasan-Rokem, G. *Web of Life: Folklore and Midrash in Rabbinic Literature.* Translated by B. Stein. Stanford, Calif.: Stanford University Press, 2000.

Heinemann, Joseph. *Aggadot ve-toldotehen.* Jerusalem: Keter, 1974.

Hirshman, Marc G. "Aggadic Midrash." In *The Literature of the Sages*, edited by Shmuel Safrai, Peter J. Tomson, et al. Philadelphia: Fortress, 2006.

Hirshman, Marc G. *A Rivalry of Genius: Jewish and Christian Biblical Interpretation in Late Antiquity.* SUNY Series in Judaica. Albany: State University of New York Press, 1995.

Kessler, Gwynn. *Conceiving Israel: The Fetus in Rabbinic Narratives.* Divinations. Philadelphia: University of Pennsylvania Press, 2009.

Kugel, James L. *In Potiphar's House: The Interpretive Life of Biblical Texts.* 1st Harvard University Press paperback ed. Cambridge, Mass.: Harvard University Press, 1994.

Krauss, Matthew, ed. *How Should Rabbinic Literature Be Read in the Modern World?* Piscataway, N.J.: Gorgias, 2006.

Neusner, Jacob, and Alan J. Avery-Peck, eds. *Encyclopaedia of Midrash: Biblical Interpretation in Formative Judaism.* 2 vols. Leiden, the Netherlands; Boston: Brill, 2005.

Neusner, Jacob, and Alan J. Avery-Peck, eds. *Sifra: An Analytic Translation.* Atlanta: Scholars, 1988.

Neusner, Jacob, and Alan J. Avery-Peck, eds. *Sifre Deuteronomy: An Analytic Translation.* Atlanta: Scholars, 1987.

Porton, Gary. "Rabbinic Midrash." In *History of Biblical Interpretation*, Vol. 1. Edited by Alan Hauser and Duane Watson. Grand Rapids, Mich.: William B. Eerdmans, 2009.

Stern, David. *Midrash and Theory: Ancient Jewish Exegesis and Contemporary Literary Studies.* Rethinking Theory. Evanston, Ill.: Northwestern University Press, 1996.

Stern, David. *Parables in Midrash: Narrative and Exegesis in Rabbinic Literature.* Cambridge, Mass.: Harvard University Press, 1991.

Strack, Hermann Leberecht, Gunter Stemberger, and Markus N. A. Bockmuehl. *Introduction to the Talmud and Midrash.* 2d print., with emendations and updates. Minneapolis: Fortress Press, 1996.

Yadin, A. *Scripture as Logos: Rabbi Ishmael and the Origins of Midrash.* Philadelphia: University of Pennsylvania Press, 2004.

Carol Bakhos

Mimesis Criticism

The word "mimesis" in Mimesis Criticism transliterates the Greek word μίμησις, "imitation"; this methodology attempts to assess if later texts used earlier texts as models. It is difficult for modern readers to appreciate how extensive imitation was in antiquity, especially among Greeks and Romans. For purposes of illustration one might refer to the *Institutio oratoria* of M. Fabius Quintilianus, a contemporary of the Gospel authors (all translations of the *Institutio oratoria* are those by H. E. Butler in Loeb Classical Library).

Selecting Models. In book 10 the famous bilingual rhetorician describes how teachers should equip future orators with literary models to inform their compositions. The goal is to saturate students in exemplary texts so that they will be able to imitate them without having to consult them physically (10.1.5). "For in everything which we teach examples are more effective even than the rules which are taught in the schools, so long as the student has reached a stage when he can appreciate such examples without the assistance of a teacher, and can rely on his own powers to imitate them" (10.1.15). By frequently rereading the models one can adapt them with more subtlety than by rote memorization (10.1.19). "Nor must we study it [the model] merely in parts, but must read through the whole work from cover to cover and then read it afresh" (10.1.20).

Crucial to literary mimesis is the selection of the best models. Here Homer stands alone, the poet "par excellence."

> I shall, I think, be right in following the principle laid down by Aratus in the line, "With Jove let us begin," and in beginning with Homer. He is like his own conception of Ocean, which he describes as the source of every stream and river [in Il. 21.196]; for he has given us a model and an inspiration for very department of eloquence. . . . What can be equal to the prayers which Priam addresses to Achilles when he comes to beg for the body of his son? Again, does he not transcend the limits of human genius in his choice of words, his reflections, figures, and the arrangement of his whole work, with the result that it requires a powerful mind, I will not say to emulate [or rival], for that is impossible, but even to imitate his excellences? But he has in truth outdistanced all

> that have come after him in every department of eloquence. (10.1.46 and 50–51, LCL slightly modified)

After delineating which authors were most worthy of imitation, Quintilian describes mimesis in detail.

> There can be no doubt that in art no small portion of our task lies in imitation, since, although invention came first and is all-important, it is expedient to imitate whatever has been invented with success. And it is a universal rule of life that we should wish to copy what we approve in others. It is for this reason that boys copy the shapes of letters that they may learn to write, and that musicians take the voices of their teachers, painters the works of their predecessors, and peasants the principles of agriculture which have been proved in practice, as models for their imitation. In fact, we may note that the elementary study of every branch of learning is directed by reference to some definite standard that is placed before the learner. (10.2.1–2)

Imitation, however, is only a starting point for a successful composition. Authors also must seek to improve their models by means of "invention, power, and competence" (10.2.12). One way to accomplish this is by borrowing admirable traits from several models, what one might call eclectic emulation. "We shall do well to keep a number of different excellences before our eyes, so that different qualities from different authors may impose themselves on our minds, to be adopted for use in the place that becomes them best" (10.2.26).

Quintilian's instructions on the training of orators apply *mutatis mutandis* to authors of histories and fictions from Herodotus to Lucian. When the first-century B.C.E. rhetorician Philodemus asked, "Who would claim that the writing of prose is not reliant on the Homeric poems?" the answer he expected was "no one" (*On Poetry* 5.30.36–31.2).

Accomplished authors cited apposite lines, embedded allusions, and twisted characterizations or plots confident that their cleverer readers would relish recognizing their transformations.

Criteria for Identifying Literary Connections. It is one thing to acknowledge the importance of mimesis in ancient literary composition, but quite another to identify it. The shores of New Testament scholarship are strewn with the wreckage of failed attempts to prove literary connections, and for this reason many interpreters have abandoned the attempt. Mimesis Criticism, however, provides criteria for identifying such imitations with the goal of minimizing the subjectivity of previous efforts. I have proposed six criteria for identifying dependence of one text on a written antecedent, what I call an "antetext."

Accessibility pertains to the likelihood that the author of the later text had access to the putative model.

Analogy likewise pertains to the popularity of the target. It seeks to know if other authors imitated the same proposed mimetic model.

Density means that the more parallels one can posit between two texts, the stronger the case that they issue from a literary connection.

Order examines the relative sequencing of similarities in the two works. If parallels appear in the same order, the case strengthens for a genetic connection.

Distinction is anything unusual in both the targeted antetext and the proposed borrower that links the two into a special relationship. Often authors used significant names to flag the influence of the targeted text.

Interpretability assesses what, if anything, might be gained by viewing one text as a debtor to another. As often as not, ancient authors emulated their antecedents to rival them, whether in style, philosophical adequacy, persuasiveness, or religious perspective.

Mimesis Criticism Illustrated. Although Mimesis Criticism is a relative newcomer to biblical scholarship, scholars long have noticed how later texts imitate earlier ones. Here I will give an example of Luke's mimesis of two stories, one from Jewish Scriptures and one from the *Odyssey.*

Many scholars have noted striking similarities between Jesus's raising a dead lad in Luke 7:11–17 and Elijah's doing the same in 1 Kgs 17:9–24, a text that surely was available to the Evangelist (criterion 1; Luke actually cites this story in 4:25–26), and an analogous imitation appears in Mark's narration of the raising of Jairus's daughter in 5:35–43 (criterion 2). Furthermore, the similarities are dense, sequential, and distinctive (criterion 3, 4, and 5). Compare the following:

The most distinctive clue that Luke rewrote the story is the phrase "and he gave him to his mother [καὶ ἔδωκεν αὐτὸν τῇ μητρὶ αὐτοῦ]," which is identical in both tales. This phrase appears nowhere else in the Septuagint or the New Testament; it is a distinctive trait (criterion 5).

Luke's narrative clearly improved his model (criterion 6, interpretability). In 1 Kings it was the widow who initiated the resuscitation by berating the prophet: "You came to my house to recall my sins and kill my son." In Luke, Jesus himself initiated the resuscitation. Elijah accused God of injustice and a lack of compassion: "You have done wrong in killing her son." Luke, however, does not blame God for the boy's death and says that Jesus "had compassion" for the widow. Elijah could not raise the dead by his own powers but called on God to do so; Jesus himself raises the dead: "I say to you, arise!" According to 1 Kings only the widow responded to the resuscitation; in Luke "a large crowd" observed the event and acclaimed Jesus as a prophet. For Luke, Jesus was a prophet, but more than a prophet.

The second example of mimesis comes from the Book of Acts and the target for imitation comes not from the Bible but from Homer.

> 20:7 On the first day of the week, when we convened to break bread, Paul spoke to them, and because he intended to leave the next day, he prolonged his speech until midnight.[8] There were plenty of lamps in the upper room where we were gathered.[9] A certain young man named Eutychus was seated at the window and was carried off by a deep sleep, because of Paul's speaking for so long. Carried off by sleep, he fell from the third story and was lifted up dead.[10] Paul went down, lay upon him, embraced him, and said, "Don't raise a ruckus! His soul is in him."
>
> [11] He went back upstairs, broke bread, and once he had eaten and had spoken for a long time, until dawn, he left.[12] Then they took the lad, alive, and were not a little relieved. (Acts 20:7–12)

This peculiar story is Luke's variation on the death of Elpenor in book 11 of the *Odyssey*. In order to return to his home in Ithaca, Odysseus had to consult with the soul of the blind seer Tiresias by conjuring it from the house of Hades. At dawn he summoned his men. Odysseus himself narrates what happened next.

> There was a man, Elpenor, the youngest, not particularly
> brave in battle or gifted in mind.
> Apart from his companions in Circe's sacred home
> he sought fresh air and lay down to sleep, sodden with
> wine.
> When he heard the din and roar of men on the move,
> he jumped up at once. It escaped his mind
> to climb back down on the long ladder,
> and he fell down from the roof. His neck broke from
> the spine, and his soul went down to the house of
> Hades. (10.552–560)

When Odysseus arrived at the edge of the world and called forth the souls of the dead, the first to meet him was that of Elpenor, who asked him to return to Circe's island to care for his corpse. "Burn me in my armor, whatever I had, / and by the shore of the gray sea heap up a mound for me, / a memorial of an unlucky man" (11.74–76). Odysseus agreed and at the beginning of book 12 he describes the burial.

> As soon as early Dawn appeared, rosy-fingered,
> I sent comrades to the house of Circe
> to bring the corpse, dead Elpenor.
> Having felled logs at once, at the point where the land
> ran farthest into the sea
> we burned him, grieving and shedding many tears.
> (12.8–12)

There can be no doubt that this famous story was available to Luke (criterion 1) or that it was a favorite target of imitation. Vergil, for example, has two imitations of Elpenor in the *Aeneid* (Palinurus and Misenus; criterion 2, analogous imitations).

Similarities between this story and Luke's Eutychus are remarkable.

The story of Eutychus is a happy alternative to Elpenor's funeral in *Odyssey.* 12.1–15. Elpenor was buried at dawn, Eutychus revived at dawn. Homer called the young soldier "unlucky," the victim of an "evil doom of a daemon" (*Od.* 11.61, 76, and 80). The name Eutychus, however, means "lucky," from εὐ, "good," and τύχη, "fortune." Surely it is no accident that the raising of Eutychus likewise takes place on the Troad, near where Elpenor spent nine years of his young life. Lucky from Troas is a Christian transform of unlucky Elpenor who fought at Troy. The parallels between Acts 20 and *Odyssey.* 10–12 are too extensive, sequential, and distinctive to be accidental (criteria 3, 4, and 5).

At several points, this story demonstrates emulation (interpretability, criterion 6). Elpenor fell to his death because of a drunken stupor; Eutychus fell while listening to Paul preach. Odysseus was unaware of Elpenor's plight; Paul knew of Eutychus's death and had confidence that his soul had not left him. Elpenor died and his body was buried at dawn; Eutychus died, but at dawn the believers took him up alive. Eutychus truly was Lucky.

Objections to Mimesis Criticism. Although many scholars are willing to acknowledge imitations of Jewish Scriptures in the Gospels and Acts, only a few have done so for imitations of classical Greek poetry, as in this comparison of Homer's Elpenor and Luke's Eutychus. For the most part, New Testament scholars have simply ignored the topic; those who have directly opposed imitations of Homer identify five perceived shortcomings:

(1) Mimesis Criticism when applied to classical Greek poetry slights the influence of Jewish Scriptures;
(2) it requires too much sophistication of the intended readers;
(3) it cannot explain why the Evangelists did not better notify the reader of this intertextual strategy or
(4) why they wanted to imitate Homer in the first place; and
(5) it ignores the failure of two thousand years of interpretation to recognize these points of connection. These are important objections, and each merits a serious response.

The first objection is this: the most apparent antetexts informing the authors of the Gospels and Acts come from Jewish Scriptures, not from Greek classics. This statement, of course, is correct, but it need not disallow imitations of Greek literature as well. Fragments survive of *On the Jews* by a Theodotus and *On Jerusalem* by Philo, dubbed Epicus, both of whom narrated biblical themes in dactylic hexameters (apud Eusebius, *Praeparatio Evangelica* 917–920, 22–24, and 35–38). According to a medieval fragment, "Sosates, the Jewish Homer, flourished in Alexandria" between 142 and 51 B.C.E. (Shaye J.D. Cohen, "Sosates, the Jewish Homer," *HTR* 74 [1981]: pp. 191–196). M. Z. Kopidakis makes a compelling case that Josephus frequently imitated Homer when narrating Jewish history (Kopidakis 1986).

The second objection faults Mimesis Criticism insofar as it "assumes a readership with an in-depth as well as extensive familiarity with the Homeric epics. Ancient education was designed for the upper strata of the population," which would exclude the likes of Mark and Luke (Sandnes, *Challenge*, 249). This objection fails in two respects. First, recent studies of Mark and Luke-Acts demonstrate their literary sophistication; they were no strangers to rhetorical education, and it is reasonable to assume the same for many of their readers. Second, access to Homer was not restricted to elites; even *hoi polloi* were conversant with narrative poetry.

Third, the Evangelists surely did advertise their debts to Greek poetry. For example, Mark's Jesus performs miracles that far surpass anything in Q, such as exorcising an indomitable caveman, sending two thousand demon-infested swine into the sea, stilling the wind and sea, walking on water, multiplying bread and fish to feed thousands, and speaking with the dead. Nowhere in the lost Gospel will one find Jesus insisting that those who witness his miracles keep silent about them; nowhere will one find discoveries of his true identity as God's Son; nowhere will one find feasts, criticisms of the disciples, murderous conspiracies, or Jesus predicting his death. All of this appears in the Homeric epics. Furthermore, Mark repeatedly used significant personal and place names to notify the reader of a classical Greek antetext. None of these significant names appears in the letters of Paul or Q.

The combination of these significant names and epic-like stories not attested in earlier Christian writings should have been sufficient to notify the reader of Mark's revision of Homer. In other words, I agree with Sandnes that "a fundamental step in reading literary contests involving transvaluation is to recognize the body of texts involved" (Sandnes, *The Gospel*, 49). But I adamantly disagree with his claim that Mark did not sufficiently advertise his hypertextuality.

Evidence of Homeric influence is even clearer in Luke-Acts, where one again finds mimetically significant names. For example, one of the two disciples who recognized the risen Jesus on the road to Emmaus was named Cleopas ("All-fame"), a likely pointer to Eurycleia ("Renowned-far-and-wide"), Odysseus's old nurse who recognized him by his scar. Luke gave Lydia of Thyatira (in the provice of Lydia) her name to link her with Maenads, women from Lydia devoted to Dionysus and who accompanied him to Thebes in Euripides' *Bacchae*. As we have seen, Eutychus ("Lucky") of Troas, who died after falling from the second-story window, surely is a contrast to "unfortunate Elpenor," who died after falling from Circe's roof at the end of *Odyssey* 10 and was buried in book 12. The name of the Jewish chief priest in Acts 19, Scevas ("Lefty" in Latin), evokes ambidextrous Asteropaeus whom Achilles slew in book 21 of the *Iliad*.

A fourth objection to proposed examples of mimesis of Greek classics complains that the Evangelists would have had insufficient reason to imitate them. Determining authorial intention always is dicey, but I suspect that Mark and Luke were conscious of Vergil's Homeric imitations in the *Aeneid* and wished to present Jesus as a hero superior to Aeneas and other Greco-Roman heroes. Mark and Luke not only imitated many of the same episodes that caught Vergil's mimetic eye, they were uninteresed in many of the episodes that Vergil was.

A fifth and final objection is the charge that, if Mark and Luke intended their readers to compare their narratives with Homer, they failed miserably insofar as no one for two thousand years has suspected such a connection. Actually Christian and pagan readers of the Gospels at an early date fought over similarities between Jesus and characters in Greek mythological literature.

Not long after the composition of Luke's two-volume work, Justin Martyr wrote a defense of the Christian movement in which he complained that "even though we say things similar to the Greeks, we are hated" (*1 Apol.* 24:1; ca. 156 C.E.). For example, when Christians say that Jesus "is the first offspring of God" and "that he was crucified, died, and after rising ascended into heaven," Justin insists they are "introducing nothing new beyond the sons of Zeus so called by you" (21:1). He then lists various sons of Zeus by mortal women: Hermes, Asclepius, Dionysus, Heracles, the Dioscuri (Castor and Polydeuces), and Perseus. Justin is quick to point out, however, that unlike these sons of Zeus, the conception of Jesus involved no sexual union of a god and a mortal (25:2 and 33).

"And if we say that he [Jesus] made healthy the lame, the crippled, the blind from birth, and raised the dead, we seem to speak things similar to those things performed by Asclepius" (22:6). Jesus's teachings and those of his followers are similar to those of Greek philosophers, especially Socrates and Plato (5, 8, 44, and 59–60); his sufferings resemble those of Heracles; and his ascension into heaven finds analogies in the ascensions of Asclepius, Bellerophon, Ariadne, and even mortals. "What about your dead emperors, whom you always esteem as being rescued from death and set forth someone who swears to have seen the cremated Caesar [Augustus] ascending from the pyre into the sky?" (21:3).

Justin was not alone in recognizing affinities between Jesus and the gods and heroes of pagan antiquity. A north African Christian named Tertullian compared Jesus's ascension in Acts to the ascension of Romulus. After his resurrection, Jesus "spent forty days in Galilee, a region of Judaea [sic!], teaching them what they should teach. Then he appointed them to the duty of preaching throughout the world, and, with a cloud cast about him, he was caught up to heaven—far more truly than any Romulus of yours" (Tertullian, *Apol.* 21.23 [LCL]). Another author similarly argued that his pagan readers had no right to mock the ascension of Jesus insofar as Romans had made the same claim for Romulus (Arnobius, *Nat.* 6.1.41).

Although Justin adduced such similarities between Christian teachings and Greco-Roman mythology to appeal for tolerance, he also viewed these same similarities as a liability insofar as someone could dismiss them merely as mythologies mimetic of pagan prototypes. He therefore went to great lengths to argue that "everybody says what we do because *they* imitate [μιμούμενοι] *us*" (*1 Apol.* 60:10).

His argument goes like this: Moses and the prophets, who lived long before the Greek poets, were inspired by "the prophetic Spirit" to predict things about the coming of the Messiah, so what Christians believe about Jesus actually is older than the Greek writings. Wicked demons then heard these predictions from Jewish writers and imitated them by creating myths about the gods. For example, the presumed prophecy of a birth of a child by a virgin in Isa 7:14 prompted the myth of Perseus's birth to Danae. Psalm 19:5 lies behind the Heracles saga, and Isaiah's predictions of a coming healer caused the demons to invent Asclepius (54:10).

> When they [the demons] heard through the prophets preaching about the coming of Christ . . . , they proposed many so-called sons of Zeus, supposing that they could cause people to think that the things pertaining to Christ were a catalogue of marvels similar to those uttered by the poets. . . . But even though they heard what was said by the prophets, they did not accurately understand them, but they imitated [ἐμιμήσαντο] in error the predictions about our Christ (54:2–4).

In addition to the demons, Homer, Plato, and other Greek authors independently knew something of Jewish Scriptures (44 and 59–60). They sometimes thus espoused true teachings, especially concerning the immortality of the soul. Simply put, when the prophets and the poets disagreed, the poets erred; when they agreed the poets and their Muses had read their Moses. Christian depictions of Jesus thus resemble Greek depictions of the sons of Zeus not because the authors of the Gospels imitated classical Greek literature; *au contraire*, Greek writers imitated Jewish Scriptures.

Obviously Justin would not endorse Mimesis Criticism, but he provides invaluable evidence that early Christians recognized affinities between the Gospels and the writings of Greek poets and philosophers. Furthermore, his polemic suggests that he was aware that non-Christians attributed such affinities to Christian imitation; that is, one can imagine the likes of Porphyry standing Justin's hypothesis on its head: Christians say "what we do because *they* imitate *us*."

Not long after Justin, a pagan intellectual named Celsus attacked depictions of Jesus in the Gospels and, among many other things, attributed Jesus's birth by a virgin to imitations of Greek myths. In response, Origen acknowledged the similarities, as Justin had, but with a caveat.

> It is not out of place with respect to Greeks to refer as well to Greek stories, so that we seem not to be the only ones to refer to such an amazing story. . . . But these stories actually are myths that move people to invent such a notion about a man whom they consider as possessing wisdom and power greater than that of the masses and as having received the initial composition of his body from better and more divine seed, as though they suited those who were greater than merely human. (*Cels.* 1.37)

There can be little doubt that Byzantine Christians heard in the Gospels echoes of Homer. The *Homeric Centos*, which survive in five significantly different versions, were written and rewritten from the fourth century until the twelfth, and possibly beyond. These poems are invaluable, for they provide dozens of examples of Byzantine intellectuals observing similarities between stories in Homer and the Gospels, similarities that often suggest what model the Evangelists originally had in mind. Of course, these poets likely would not have approved of Mimesis Critics attributing these similarities to Mark and Luke imitating Homer, but surely one cannot say that the Evangelists failed at alerting their readers about them.

Mimesis Criticism and Biblical Interpretation. Mimesis Criticism offers New Testament scholars an important new tool with many applications. In the first place it expands the number of texts one should consider as potential models for the composition of the Gospels and Acts. My work suggests imitations not only of the *Iliad* and the *Odyssey*, but also several so-called *Homeric Hymns*, Euripides' *Bacchae* and *Madness of Heracles*, and the Socratic dialogues of Plato and Xenophon. Contrast this with the list of citations and allusions to antetexts in the standard edition of the Greek New Testament (*Novum Testamentum Graece*, Nestle), which contains about three thousand references to the Old Testament and three hundred from other Jewish sources. For all of pagan Greek literature, there exist five references, only two from poetry: one from Menander and one from Euripides. Homer, Hesiod, Aeschylus, and Sophocles are entirely absent, as are all Latin authors. This same silence obtains to virtually all introductions to the New Testament, many commentaries, and even books devoted to locating the New Testament in its ancient literary environment!

Fortunately, a growing number of classicists and New Testament scholars are proposing mimetic connections between the epics and the Gospels, although most of them presume that the Evangelists drew from the epics only indirectly through influence on Greek culture generally (e.g. Bruce Louden) or from Homeric tropes, not from imitations of specific episodes (e.g., Edward P. Dixon). What distinguishes my methodology, what I call Mimesis Criticism, is the reading of narratives in Mark and Luke-Acts as direct, extensive, advertised, and hermeneutically freighted imitations of the epics that invite a comparison of Jesus to the gods and heroes of Greek religion.

Mimesis Criticism also revolutionizes how one understands the role of the Evangelists. Unlike some Form Critics who view Mark and Luke less as authors and more as credulous editors of preexisting traditions and sources, Mimesis Critics view them as creative authors who often invent narratives without the benefit of antecedents other than biblical or classical antetexts. Accordingly, Mark and Luke appear no longer to be unsophisticated transcribers of early Christian folklore but clever mythmakers, who portray Jesus and the apostles as fictional alternatives to the heroes not only of the Bible but also of classical Greek literature.

[*See also* Greco-Roman Context; Inner-biblical Interpretation; *and* Intertextuality.]

BIBLIOGRAPHY

Gilmour, Michael J. "Hints of Homer in Luke 16:19–31." *Did* 10 (1999): 23–33. This brief article identifies several details in Luke's story of the rich man in Hades that suggest literary dependence on Odysseus's visit to the netherworld in *Od.* 11.

Kaiser, Erich. "Odyssee-Szenen als Topoi." *Museum Helveticum* 21 (1964): 109–136 and 197–224. In these two essays a classicist demonstrates how episodes in the Odyssey, especially those concerning Polyphemus and Circe, became popular targets for imitation in ancient literary education and composition.

Kopidakis, M. Z. "*Ιώσηφος ομηρίζων*." *Hell* 37 (1986): 3–25. In this important but seldom cited essay, the author identifies more than a dozen instances in which Josephus embellishes this work with clever imitations of the Homeric epics.

Louden, Bruce. *Homer's Odyssey and the Near East.* Cambridge, UK: Cambridge University Press, 2011. Although this book focuses on possible connections between the *Odyssey* and narratives in the Jewish Bible and other Near Eastern texts, it also devotes attention to the Gospels. Perhaps its most important contribution lies in its discussion of methodology and the dynamic interactions between archaic Greek civilizations and the East.

Lowe, N. J. *The Classical Plot and the Invention of Western Narrative.* Cambridge, UK: Cambridge University Press, 2000. This is a general and beautifully written discussion of the influence of classical plots in Western literature, occasionally including religious texts.

MacDonald, Dennis Ronald. *Christianizing Homer: "The Odyssey," Plato, and "The Acts of Andrew."* New York:

Oxford University Press, 1994. This is one of the earliest attempts at linking Christian literature, in this case the apocryphal *Acts of Andrew*, and Homeric epic. It argues for an extensive and theologically significant use of mimesis to portray the apostle and his God as superior to Greek heroes and deities.

MacDonald, Dennis Ronald. *Does the New Testament Imitate Homer? Four Cases from the Acts of the Apostles*. New Haven, Conn.: Yale University Press, 2003. This book takes a few examples of mimesis from the Acts of the Apostles and shows how Luke's imitations fit comfortably in a tradition of imitations of the same episodes from the *Iliad*.

MacDonald, Dennis Ronald. "The Ending of Luke and the Ending of the *Odyssey*." In *For a Later Generation: The Transformation of Tradition in Israel, Early Judaism and Early Christianity*. Edited by Randal A. Argall, Beverly A. Bow, and Rodney A. Werline, 161–68. Harrisburg, Penn.: Trinity Press International, 2000. This short article suggests that Jesus's recognition by his wounds in the last chapter of the Gospel of Luke imitates Laertes' recognition of Odysseus in the last book of the *Odyssey*.

MacDonald, Dennis Ronald. *The Homeric Epics and the Gospel of Mark*. New Haven, Conn.: Yale University Press, 2000. This book probably is the best known and most controversial contribution to Mimesis Criticism. It argues for massive imitations of the *Odyssey* in the first half of Mark, especially events around the Sea of Galilee, and imitations of Hector's death in *Il.* 22 for Jesus's crucifixion.

MacDonald, Dennis Ronald. "Imitations of Greek Epic in the Gospels." In *The Historical Jesus in Context*. Edited by Amy-Jill Levine, Dale C. Allison, and John Dominic Crossan, 372–84. Princeton, N.J.: Princeton University Press, 2006. This article is a brief introduction to the topic that compares the deaths of Hector and Jesus according to the Gospel of Mark.

MacDonald, Dennis Ronald. "My Turn: A Critique of Critics of 'Mimesis Criticism.'" *IACOP* 53. Claremont, Calif.: The Institute for Antiquity and Christianity, 2009. In this paper the author answers several critics of Mimesis Criticism, including Sandnes.

MacDonald, Dennis Ronald. "Paul's Farewell to the Ephesian Elders and Hector's Farewell to Andromache: A Strategic Imitation of Homer's *Iliad*." In *Contextualizing Acts: Lukan Narrative and Greco-Roman Discourse*. Edited by Todd Penner and Caroline Vander Stichele, 189–203. Atlanta: Society of Biblical Literature, 2003. This paper argues for Luke's imitation of *Il.* 6 in Acts 20.

MacDonald, Dennis Ronald. "Renowned Far and Wide: The Women Who Anointed Odysseus and Jesus." In *A Feminist Companion to Mark*. Edited by Amy-Jill Levine, 128–35. Sheffield, UK: Sheffield Academic Press, 2001. This brief article argues that Mark imitated Eurycleia's anointing of Odysseus when composing Jesus's anointing by an unnamed woman in Bethany.

MacDonald, Dennis Ronald. "Secrecy and Recognitions in the *Odyssey* and Mark: Where Wrede Went Wrong." In *Ancient Fiction and Early Christian Narrative*. Edited by Ronald F. Hock, J. Bradley Chance, and Judith Perkins, 139–153. Atlanta: Scholars, 1998. According to his article, Mark's model for the so-called Messianic Secret was Homer's use of Odysseus's disguise as a beggar when he returned to Ithaca.

MacDonald, Dennis Ronald. "The Shipwrecks of Odysseus and Paul." *New Testament Studies* 45 (1999): 88–107. This detailed article argues for an extensive and strategic imitation of Odysseus's shipwreck in *Odyssey* 5 and Acts 27.

MacDonald, Dennis Ronald. "The Synoptic Problem and Literary Mimesis: The Case of the Frothing Demoniac." In *New Studies in the Synoptic Problem*. Edited by Paul Foster, et al., 509–21. BETL 239. Leuven, Netherlands: Peeters, 2010. This article argues that Mark imitated Euripides' *Madness of Heracles* and that the retelling of the story in Matthew and Luke suggests that these Evangelists failed to see the imitation. Mimesis Criticism in this case supports Markan priority among the Synoptics and Luke's knowledge of Q, Mark, and Matthew.

Sandnes, Karl Olav. *The Challenge of Homer: School, Pagan Poets, and Early Christianity*. LNTS 400. London: T&T Clark, 2009. In this book, Sandnes gives a valuable overview of how early Christians viewed pagan education: from categorical rejection to accommodation. Unfortunately, it ignores many examples of early Christian mimesis such as appear in Clement of Alexandria, Christian apocrypha, and the Byzantine homilies.

Sandnes, Karl Olav. *The Gospel "According to Homer and Virgil": Cento and Canon*. *NovTSup* 138. Leiden, Netherlands: Brill, 2011. This is a valuable and insightful discussion of the Homeric and Vergilian centos. Here he objects to the uses of the centos by Mimesis Critics.

Sandnes, Karl Olav. "*Imitatio Homeri?* An Appraisal of Dennis R. MacDonald's 'Mimesis Criticism.'" *JBL* 124 (2005): 715–32. In this article, Sandnes lays out directly most of his objections to Mimesis Criticism. For a response, see MacDonald, "My Turn."

Schäfer, J. "Zur Funktion der Dionysosmysterien in der Apostelgeschichte: Eine intertextuelle Betrachtung der Berufungs- und Befreiungserägzhlungen in der Apostelgeschichte und der Bakchen des Euripides." *TZ* 66 (2010): 199–222. This is a useful and daring new look at scenes in Acts about prison escapes as imitations of the *Bacchae.* Unfortunately, he does not pursue the influence of Euripides elsewhere in Luke-Acts.

Schembra, Rocco. *Homerocentones.* CCSG 62. Turnhout: Brepols, 2007. This is the authoritative edition of the rewritings of the Gospels by using Homeric verses.

Dennis R. MacDonald

Mythology and Biblical Interpretation

The quest for a single overarching definition having long been given up, "mythology" and "myth" have provided a touchstone for a variety of issues that cut across humanistic and social scientific disciplines, and in certain respects the natural sciences as well. However one approaches the terms, in the context of biblical interpretation the territory includes conceptions of theism, the divine realm, and the fundamental structures of human experience. Such an assessment holds in view of the early use of the term by Plato and Aristotle; the distinction the Greeks made between mythology as the factual recounting of mythological events and myth as visceral impact (Dörrie 1980, p. 109); and its place in patristic polemics and reception among rabbinic commentators. Whatever one's perspective, the terms raise questions of consciousness, the self, and the other.

History and Practitioners. Perceived absurdities of the gods of Homeric tradition and Greek tragedy were resolved in allegory and through other interpretive lenses by Aristotle and commentators like Sallustius. Similarly, fundamental questions of theistic language and of the imagery surrounding the God of the Bible continually occupied those who sought understanding of the notion of one God, a particularly acute problem in view of the "God" of Greek philosophy. These issues included questions of transcendent or immanent, anthropomorphic or abstract, universal or particular, and one or many (for discussion, see S. Cohen, *From the Maccabees to the Mishnah*, esp. pp. 86–87). Michael Fishbane details how Jewish exegesis approached the anthropomorphic and anthropopathic language applied to God in the Bible by qualifying, filtering, and reinterpreting passages in order to rescue the Bible from any semblance of what had come to be understood as irrationality and imaginative excess in myth. These approaches characterize a tradition of interpretation that was averse to mythic language and was thereby given to rescuing from it (often by allegorizing) the God-given truth the community believed it to contain (Fishbane 2003, p. 4).

In addition to allegorizing, patristic writers appealed to Euhemerism (interpreting stories of divine beings as embellished biographies of human rulers or philosophers) in polemic against pagan mythology, and this hermeneutic strategy continued throughout the Middle Ages. Any valuable elements in pagan myths they considered stolen from Judaism ("Plagiarism"), while counting any elements in Judaism that seemed pagan as an intermediate phase in God's plan. Throughout the medieval period, the Christian community avoided applying the term "myth" to its narratives (R. Chase, *The Quest for Myth*, 1949; Scarborough 1994, pp. 4–5).

Eighteenth Century.

The Mythical School. Enlightenment ideas and values produced a view of myth as operating in the absence of modern science, while the rising tide of Romanticism ennobled such thought by valorizing "primitivism." The classicist C. G. Heyne (1729–1812), following Robert Lowth (1710–1787) and J. G. Herder (1744–1803), considered myth the earliest mode of human speech and thought. In his early writing on the topic, Heyne's student J. G. Eichhorn (1753–1827) presents a view of Genesis 2–3 as "historical myths," that is, a mythical portrayal of actual events (Rogerson 1974, p. 3). For Eichhorn, humanity actually descended from an original human pair who lived in a garden and interacted with God. What the present narrative relates as conversations with God, however, were encounters with misunderstood natural phenomena or, in the case of the woman's conversation with the serpent, internal ruminations. In later writings in which he revised his position, Eichhorn considered the narrative an example of philosophical myth, describing the loss of a golden age (Rogerson, p. 4). Other rationalistic interpreters found ways of incorporating the knowledge of the times into theistic discourse. J. P. Gabler (1753–1826), a student of Eichhorn who edited and wrote the introduction and notes to Eichhorn's *Urgeschichte* (1790–1793), argued there that Genesis 2–3 reflects a polytheistic background, evidenced in the compound name *Yahweh Elohim*. The account of Adam's naming of animals, for Gabler, marks the development of speech and reason, and the newly acquired awareness of good and evil is (as Kant argued) a reflection of the rise of reason.

Related Philosophical and Theoretical Issues. Attempts to reconcile Enlightenment rationalism with faith or true religious knowledge increasingly looked to primal human experience, witnessed also in the influential writings of Kant and Schleiermacher. In 1786 and 1793, Kant interpreted the opening chapters of Genesis as a reflection of human beings' relationship to nature and of the rise and consequences of reason, and in the second *Critique* (1788) he relocated the source of religious experience and expression from external revelation to something within humanity. For Kant, the realm of religious truth is the internal sense of duty. Schleiermacher (1768–1834), whose call for a science of understanding established the modern field of hermeneutics, in *Reden über die Religion* (1799) (*On Religion: Speeches to Its Cultured Despisers*) identified "intuitions of the universe" as the essence of religious truth and distinguished the communicative forms that convey these intuitions as "empty mythology" when dissociated from them in any way—that is, divested of the immediate experience of infinity or when extended by speculation. This further placed the Bible alongside other cultural works that pointed to the primordial past.

Nineteenth Century.

Hegelianism and Strauss. A key philosophical development that followed Kant and Schleiermacher came when Hegel's *Phenomenology of Mind* (1831) confronted the ontological and epistemological dualism that dominated philosophy, providing a dialectical model of consciousness in relation to the world and to the idea of history. D. F. Strauss (1808–1874), seeking an authentic approach to theological ideas, incorporated Hegel's approach into New Testament interpretation in *The Life of Jesus Critically Examined* (1835). In it he described myth as the synthesis emerging from the conflict between the ideas of "sacred legends" frozen in writing and the thinking of later generations, who represented "more advanced periods of mental development." Driven by a desire to write from a thoroughly modern perspective that embraced science as the firm ground upon which to build, Strauss invoked Hegel's distinction between *Vorstellung* (representation) and *Begriff* (pure concepts of philosophy), equating myth with pictorial *Vorstellung*. Strauss defined myth as a "representation of an event or of an idea in a *form which is historical*, but at the same time characterized by the rich pictorial and *imaginative mode of thought and expression* of the primitive ages" (Strauss, *Life of Jesus*, 1892, p. 53). The mythical reflected an ongoing "naturalistic process by which legends are originated and developed" through seeking ideas that conform to "the spirit and modes of thought of the people and of the age" (p. 65). In Strauss the struggle over the nature of history and its relation to religion and theology and the question of the historical Jesus versus the Christ of faith came to the fore.

Comparative Mythology. The discovery of the linguistic principle popularized by Jacob Grimm in 1822 as "Grimm's Law" established comparative philology, which reconstructed a proto-Indo European ancestor tongue through a comparative analysis of Germanic and other languages. With it also came comparative mythology, brainchild of the German linguist F. Max Müller (1823–1900), who considered stories of the gods to be the product of misunderstood remnants of crude words and poetic phrases that had belonged to the earliest stages of speech but had fallen into disuse. According to Müller, the earliest stage of language was characterized by "polyonymy" (many terms name a single phenomenon) and a wealth of synonyms, which produced homonyms (one term names many phenomena). In time, language became more efficient by the reduction of terms, and humans began to misconstrue utterances that had originally named or described natural phenomena but whose original meanings were partially forgotten, taking them as the names of beings. Müller espoused a natural religion and related earliest language to a "primordial spark," an intuition of God captured by utterances that diverged as language progressed historically. In this qualified sense, religion emanates from an essential and original human relation to the world or the infinite and proceeded through language development into monotheistic and polytheistic conceptions (Olender 1992, p. 83–84). Natural religion develops through an innate human capacity to perceive the "Infinite" or "Divine," which "manifests itself . . . under three different aspects . . . discovered either in nature, or in man, or in the self" (Stone, *The Essential Max Müller*, New York, 2002, p. 16). Thus Müller's conception of myth as a "disease of language" approximates Schleiermacher's "empty mythology." Ernest Renan regarded comparative philology as "the exact science of the things of the spirit" and described it and comparative mythology as sciences ranking between history and geology with the potential to bring us back "almost to the beginnings of human consciousness." (Olender, p. 636). The philological distinction between Aryan and Semitic languages combined with nationalistic impulses to provide a staging ground for newly forming ideologies of race. Against claims that the Hebrews, despite being recipients of the first spark of religion, were incapable of developing mythology (which had come to be seen as a sign of civilization), Ignaz Goldziher (1850–1921), a Hungarian Jew known primarily as an Islamic studies scholar, endeavored to demonstrate the universality of mythological types, setting forth examples of the mythological expression of solar and other natural phenomena within the Hebrew Bible. Citing the German Idealist and Romantic philosopher Friedrich Schelling, whose ambitious *Introduction to the Philosophy of Mythology* (1854) attempted to provide a systematic philosophical account of myth, Goldziher argued at the outset that all peoples must begin with a mythology, which is the foundation for "a common view of the world," which in turn is the foundation for "community of consciousness between the individuals" that constitutes the people (Goldziher, *Mythology among the Hebrews and its Historical Development*, 1877, p. xxii). Unlike Müller, he argued that the development of myth was governed first by psychological laws shared by all peoples and then by particular cultural histories.

History of Religions, Phenomenology, and the Religionsgeschichtliche Schule. The end of the nineteenth century witnessed sweeping changes in the academy that included the rise of the social sciences and the separation of religion from theology. Already with Hegel (following Hume and Kant), philosophy of religion had emerged as an autonomous modern discipline, separate from its patristic and medieval precursors and Christian theology (Tracy 1990, p. 12–13). In the Netherlands, the writings of P. D. Chantepie de Saussaye (*Manual of the Science of Religion*, 1891) and C. P. Tiele (*Elements of the Science of Religion*, 1897) outlined a comparative historical approach to religion, treating it as a science by focusing on typologies—an approach eventually dubbed both "history of religions" and "phenomenology of religion" (coined earlier by Saussaye). The comparative study of religions broke ties with confessional theology, supplanting its relative authority within the university, and subjecting it to its new "scientific" program of comparative analysis. Religious experience as described by Schleiermacher, and then Rudolf Otto, became central to the movement. Myth became suitable as a concept central to the nascent history of religions owing to its long heritage of use in relation to the phenomena claimed to constitute "religion" (Dubuisson 2003, p. 143).

In Germany, a different variety of comparative study arose in the *religionsgeschichtliche Schule*, the "history-of-religion" school, whose primary interests lay in illuminating the origins of early Christianity against the backdrop of the Hellenistic world and the development of the Old Testament in the context of the ancient Near East. Pioneering figures of the movement included Hermann Gunkel (1862–1932), Hugo Gressmann (1877–1927), and Albert Eichhorn (1856–1926). Gunkel considered religion a matter of piety, the experience that gave rise to the representations and concepts of the texts, and in this sense equated religion with theology, separating it from dogmatics (Ollenburger, in Knight 2004, p. 253). The deciphering of cuneiform and the emerging discipline of Assyriology produced new comparative materials with implications for the study of myth as an interpretive category. Gunkel's *Schöpfung und Chaos in Urzeit und Endzeit* (1894) demonstrated the prevalence of the cosmic battle motif in ancient Near Eastern literature, shedding light on the broader historical and cultural milieu of both the cosmogony of Genesis 1 and the eschatological material of Revelation 12. Gunkel's approach led, most significantly, to the development of Form Criticism. Further, P. Machinist argued that the value of *Schöpfung* lies in part in "demonstrat[ing] the importance of myth as a fundamental category in the religions of the ancient Near East, including that of biblical Israel" (see Gunkel, *Creation and Chaos in the Primeval Era and the Eschaton*, 2006, p. xvii) At the same time, however, we must keep in mind Gunkel's inconsistent use of the term "myth" (see Rogerson, pp. 57–65).

Anthropological Myth. The emergence of disciplinary anthropology in the late nineteenth century through the work of Edward Burnett Tylor (1832–1917) and Lucien Lévy-Bruhl (1857–1939) brought developments that would eventually shape discussions of mythology and biblical interpretation. Tylor defines the source of religious ideas as "by human reason, without supernatural aid or revelation; in other words, as being developments of Natural Religion," stating further, "Animism is the groundwork for the Philosophy of Religion, from that of savages up to that of civilized men" (*Primitive Culture*, 1871, p. 385). Tylor's intellectualist theory, based in the "doctrine of survivals," which ultimately explained belief in God among moderns as a survival of animism, understood myth to be the naïve science of ancients and primitives. Lévy-Bruhl conceived myth as a type of thought, primitive mentality based in mystical participation, the "opposite of scientific thinking ... involv[ing] the projection of mystical qualities onto the world and ... oblivious to contradictions" (Segal 1999, pp. 81–82). The influence of both Tylor and Lévy-Bruhl would later materialize in essays by H. and H. A. Frankfort published in the 1946 volume *Before Philosophy*, through which it passed into discussions of myth in biblical studies.

Twentieth Century.

Astral Mythology. Interest in materials from Mesopotamia also gave rise at the turn of the twentieth century to the relatively short-lived "Astral Mythology" school, represented by H. Winckler, A. Jeremias, and H. Zimmern. The movement is closely associated with the *Babel und Bibel* controversy, sparked by lectures delivered between 1902 and 1904 by Friedrich Delitzsch, who argued the Babylonian origin of monotheism and other religious teachings within the Bible as part of his desire to promote Indo-Aryan superiority through the Babylonians, whom he counted as Indo-Aryan. Critics derided the diffusionist approach, calling the group "pan-Babylonian," and today the school has largely been forgotten. Three items, however, merit attention here. First, its influence contributed to undermining the historicity of patriarchal and early monarchic narratives (see Rogerson, p. 48). Second, its racially informed devotion to the idea of Aryan superiority provides a parade example of the ideological dimensions of myth within scholarship. A third aspect regards the relation of myth to experience. Winckler understood Mesopotamia to be the point of origin not merely of literary myth but of myth as the embodiment of a mystical worldview (*Weltanschauung*), a way of apprehending the world that was shaped by astrological speculation. Within this view, the world of the gods is a macrocosm of human experience. The visible world is an emanation or materialization of the one transcendent God, who manifests in a multiplicity of forms. This knowledge of the cosmos was revealed at the beginning of time and all wisdom comes from the knowledge of the heavens (Parpola 2004, pp. 237–249). Critics, however, dismissed the esoteric interpretation on methodological grounds as a projection of later Hellenistic doctrines and the movement died with Winckler. Its influence on biblical scholarship was restricted to superficial parallels (Rogerson, p. 50) and the experiential dimension of the theory has since gone unexplored.

Rudolf Bultmann. Rudolf Bultmann (1884–1976) reflects a generation of the *religionsgeschichtliche Schule* that arose in the 1920s. In keeping with his interest in Gnostic influence on early Christianity, Bultmann initially used "myth" to denote a particular salvation narrative whose history, geographical locus, and literary qualities could be empirically discerned. Thus one could compare the forms of expression of primitive Christianity with the myths, that is, the religious and philosophical formulations, of Hellenistic syncretism (Roger Johnson, *The Origins of Demythologizing*, 1974, pp. 90–91). Later in his career, Bultmann saw myth as a world picture, a particular view of reality that is shaped by the times, with the Bible's mythological world picture at odds with the scientific world picture of modernity. Starting from this Enlightenment view of myth and drawing upon the existential phenomenology of Heidegger, Bultmann forged a new existentialist interpretation in which this mythological view of the world is obsolete and, in the interest of preserving the truth of the biblical text, must be removed from the text (as opposed to selecting from it or ignoring it). Bultmann argued that the purpose of myth is not cosmic but existential, though it gives rise to its own criticism by addressing fundamentally transcendent issues in the language of the empirical world. New Testament mythology enshrines an understanding of existence whose truth value is a matter of faith. For Bultmann, an existentialist interpretation alone can provide satisfactory answers where other attempts to demythologize the New Testament have failed. As a concrete historical figure presented in mythical terms, Jesus represents a combination of myth and history. The mythological expresses the meaning of the historical. The event of the cross takes on cosmic dimensions and in its redemptive aspect is "not just an event of the past which can be contemplated, but is the eschatological event in and beyond time, in so far as it is an ever-present reality" (Bultmann, *Kerygma and Myth: A Theological Debate*, 1961, p. 36).

Myth and Ritual. The myth and ritual school had its origins in William Robertson Smith's insight in *Lectures on the Religion of the Semites* (1889, 2d ed. 1894) that religion is fundamentally grounded not in belief but in practice. Smith's approach, which Segal (pp. 37–38) calls "behaviorist," found the heart of ancient religion in habitual practices that acquired vague meanings. Robertson Smith called these explanations "myths," distinguishing them from dogma or statements of creedal belief, citing the variety of expression and apparent lack of concern for orthodoxy.

The publication of tablets containing ritual prescriptions and commentary pertaining to the Babylonian *akitu* new year festival, persistent diffusionist influences, and the newly articulated ritual theory of myth in the Cambridge school of Jane Harrison, Gilbert Murray, F. M. Cornford, and A. B. Cook led S. H. Hooke to argue for the presence of a similar ritual pattern in ancient Israel. Scholars of the so-called Uppsala School were the most ardent advocates of the myth and ritual approach in the twentieth century. Ivan Engnell, Sigmund Mowinckel, Geo Widengren, Aage Bentzen, and F. F. Hvidberg saw the rituals as particularly significant in ancient Israel and considered the king to play a special role in securing the welfare of the people. Mowinckel, a student of Gunkel, argued that certain psalms were used in an ancient New Year's festival celebrating and renewing the victory of God over his enemies in the enthronement of the king. An interesting experiential question arises in whether the king simply plays a sacral role or is counted as divine. For some like T. Gaster, myth not only explains the ritual but gives it a spiritual dimension. Gaster, following folklorists like J. G. Frazer, proposed the Ritual Combat as a traditional "rite of invigoration" and mimetic struggle between life and death. The myth of the god's victory over the dragon is a projection of the Ritual Combat, which is historicized in the psalms as the victory of Yahweh over Israel's enemies.

Salvation History. For myth and ritual adherents, myth was an aspect of continuity between Israel and the ancient Near East. Other scholars opposed "myth" to "history" more sharply to define an essentially radical break between Israel and its environment. This history, however, was *Heilsgeschichte*, "salvation history," a concept with roots in the nineteenth century. At the center of these debates lay questions not only of religious experience, worldviews, and modes of consciousness but also of science and theology. Biblical theology attempted to reconcile the myth and history dichotomy by focusing on the interpretation of historical events as divinely guided. George Ernest Wright (1909–1974) upheld the idea of biblical theology as a descriptive enterprise that probed the meaning of events in the biblical record for the original witnesses. "It is . . . the objectivity of God's historical acts which are the focus of attention, not the subjectivity of inner, emotional, diffuse, and mystical experience" (*God Who Acts: Biblical Theology as Recital*, 1952, p. 55). Wright takes great pains to demonstrate the distinctiveness of the Old Testament. Drawing heavily upon the Frankforts (mentioned earlier), he argues Israelite monotheism represented a "radical break" and its literature was "utterly different" from the traditional "mythopoeic" mode of thinking in the Ancient Near East. Unlike Greek philosophical monism derived from speculation, "the experience of their people led them to know it almost intuitively. They recognized their God in the first instance as authoritative and decisive power. And the point where that power was apprehended led them to an entirely different faith from that of the polytheist" (p. 23). The gods of polytheism arose from the experience of power in nature with no distinction drawn "between reality and the force behind it" (p. 17). "The God of Israel has no mythology" and any borrowings were "radically transformed"—myth was historicized to describe actual historical victories, most significantly the exodus event (pp. 26–28).

A position strikingly similar to Wright's from a Jewish perspective is articulated by Yehezkel Kaufmann (1889–1963). "The basic idea of Israelite religion," he argues in *The Religion of Israel: From Its Beginnings to the Babylonian Exile* (Eng. trans. 1960), lies in its "non-mythological" intuition of God as all-transcending or, in less anthropomorphic terms, as "an unfettered divine will" (pp. 60, 121). "Mythological" for Kaufmann means "polytheistic." Ancient Israel's sense of one God was radically different from the pagan conception of many deities who constantly vied for supremacy. Although biblical passages occasionally reflect pagan thought, such fragments were simply the "debris" of myths and not a matter of systematic dogma. References to demons were merely a reflection of the moral world of sin, not of a metaphysical world where God's authority could be subject to challenge. They are "creatures" that entice humans to act but not true gods who could be a metaphysical source of evil. Monotheism was, in fact, a worldview shared by all Israelites, and its disjuncture with the polytheistic worldview of their pagan neighbors was the cause of frequent misunderstanding.

Frank Moore Cross. The approach to myth of Frank Moore Cross in *Canaanite Myth and Hebrew Epic* (1973) stands in stark contrast to the views of those like Kaufmann and biblical theologians, whose systems of theology and metaphysics uphold Israel's religious consciousness as distinctive and unique on dogmatic grounds. Against Kaufmann he writes that "the empirical historian must describe novel configurations in Israel's religion as having their origin in an orderly set of relationships which follow the usual typological sequences of historical change" (p. viii). This statement reflects an orientation to the history of religions and phenomenology of religion, which by this time had come to fruition in the Netherlands under G. van der Leeuw, B. Christensen, and C. J. Bleeker and was becoming established in the United States in the work of J. Wach and M. Eliade at the University of Chicago. To account for Israel's apparent distinctiveness within an empirical model of historical change, Cross begins with the opposition of myth, which is "concerned with 'primordial events' and seeks static structures of meaning behind the historical flux" (p. viii), and history, which features only human actors and precludes divine agency. The religion of Israel, he finds, is based upon the "epic" form that "combines mythic and historical features in various ways and proportions . . . to recreate and give meaning to the historical experiences of a people or nation" (p. viii). Israel's religion stepped forth as distinct from mythopoeic Canaanite tradition when particular historical experiences inspired a new form of expression in the epic cycle, accompanied by covenant rites in the ritual drama of the cult. Later, in the period of the monarchy, a mythopoeic orientation was reintroduced in support of the Davidic dynastic succession. The prophets, however, in their campaign against the influence of the Baal cult, suppressed it, subordinating it to their own visionary experience. In the period of the exile Israel witnessed another recrudescence of myth in proto-apocalyptic visions of Second Isaiah, the Isaianic apocalypse, and Ezekiel. This reconstruction of a "perennial and unrelaxed tension between the mythic and the historical" (p. viii) reconciles problems in the Myth and Ritual desire to emphasize the mythic patterns as primary and the tendency of the *Heilsgeschichte* approach to minimize the presence and importance of Canaanite mythological lore (pp. 79–90). Cross's ideas contributed to Paul Hanson's *The Dawn of Apocalyptic* (1975), which in turn has given rise to numerous treatments of apocalyptic literature in which myth is a central category.

A different approach to the combat myth and to the relation of myth and history is evident in Jon D. Levenson's *Creation and the Persistence of Evil* (1988). Like Cross, he rejects Kaufmann's claim of absolute distinctiveness and, further, takes issue with Kaufmann's argument for the absolute sovereignty of Israel's God. But perceiving more than Cross's mythologizing of historical events, he argues for a dialectic of myth and history, in which the defeat of chaos in the myths is contradicted by an experience of evil in the historical present, with the resulting dissonance resolved through an act of worship. The combat myth was reiterated ritually by the cultic community in a move to counter the experience of evil through the anguished cry that is also a confession of faith (pp. 47–50; see esp. p. 132). Such an instantiating of myth, where myth and history "rise to the level of consciousness" as faith and realism, presents a type of myth and ritual approach that focuses on the religious experience of the individual.

Ideology. In the past two decades, scholars have taken up myth in its political dimensions. Within what has come to be known as the minimalist position, myth becomes a form of expression in the service of (or equated with) ideology. Rejecting what is taken as a theologically motivated acceptance of the general historicity of the biblical materials as given, a number of these works focus on the patriarchal and Exodus narratives as political founding myths (G. Garbini, *Myth and History in the Bible*, 2003; T. Thompson, *The Mythic Past*, 1999). Keith Whitelam integrates scholarly reconstructions of the biblical past with contemporary political realities in *The Invention of Ancient Israel: The Silencing of Palestinian History* (1996). David Rosenberg uses historical fiction in works such as *Abraham: the First Historical Biography* (2006), an imaginative reconstruction that explores mythology and the creation of the present from materials of the past, presenting, for example, biblical Abraham and modern Zionist Theodor Herzl in the context of the Sumerian Dilmun myth as "promised land." Such approaches shade into ideological criticism.

Wendy Doniger observes how scholars in recent decades have become increasingly aware of the extent to which myth theorizing is imbued with the properties of its objects of study, making the student of myth the mythmaker. Doniger, however, finds intellectual merit in "perpetuating the mythical within the confines of contemporary academic life," in which myth theorizing is explored *as myth*, viewed against the political and intellectual context of the theorist toward a "more vibrant conceptual picture" (Patton and Doniger 1996, p. 6).

Phenomenological and Narrative Hermeneutics: Paul Ricoeur. The writings of Paul Ricoeur (1913–2005) embrace many of the fundamental issues of myth: its relation to history, to human behavior (ritual/social), to experience and, perhaps foremost, to language. His work engages a wide variety of approaches, including the philosophical phenomenology of Husserl and the existentialist Hermeneutics of Gadamer but also structuralism and psychoanalysis. His mediating tone, bringing opposing viewpoints into fruitful conversation, is well known. He addresses myth in numerous writings, frequently in the context of biblical texts. Among these are *The*

Symbolism of Evil (1967) and *Essays on Biblical Interpretation* (1980), which contains an essay on Bultmann. His treatment of myth leads in his later writings to the concept of narrative identity.

A relevant example of Ricoeur's thought appears in *The Conflict of Interpretations* (1974), in which he addresses the "war of the myths that invites us to attempt the passage from a simple exegesis of myths to a philosophy through symbols" (p. 296). He subsequently outlines three stages of understanding. The first is the phenomenological, the stage of comparativism, where a symbol is understood in relation to other symbols. The second is the hermeneutical stage, in which "you must understand in order to believe, but you must believe in order to understand." Here he explains hermeneutics as "the expression of modernity's distress and cure for this distress" and "the 'modern' modality of belief in symbols," which constitutes for modernity a "second naïveté" that recovers the Sacred for the modern mind. Being no longer speaks to the individual in the precritical form of immediate belief but as a "second immediacy" which is "the postcritical equivalent of the precritical hierophany" (p. 298). The third stage is the philosophical. Space does not permit us to explore this stage adequately except to point out that Ricoeur cautions that it is not rationalizing—that is, "repeating the symbol in a mime of rationality," which is no more than a "dogmatic mythology"—but neither is it allegorizing, in which "the philosophical meaning rises victorious from its imaginative shell" (p. 299).

Future Directions. The future direction of myth and biblical studies must continue to engage the perennial and overlapping issues of myth and history (see Doniger 2011, pp. xiii–xv), myth and ritual (Weitzman 1997), myth's relation to experience, and its place with respect to ideology (Lincoln 1999). Scholars of myth must continue to raise the question of how language relates to experience and, with respect to experience, must consider more closely the dualism, ontological and epistemological, that has typified Western theological and philosophical thought. As scholars have reconstructed the discourse and world of the Bible, such unexamined dualism has obscured fundamental questions of identity, pervading conceptions not only of the sacred but of the self and of society, with consequences that are only recently being appreciated.

One avenue of this exploration is by way of philosophical phenomenology, particularly as expressed in the work of Maurice Merleau-Ponty, who refined Husserl's phenomenology and whose writings have enjoyed widespread popularity across disciplines. In addition to the phenomenologically informed work of Ricoeur, who also engaged Merleau-Ponty, examples are found in Sanford Krolick (1987), Milton Scarborough (1994), and Gavin Flood (1999). The phenomenological concepts of "life-world," "attitude" and "intersubjectivity" are providing further lines of inquiry into the problematic notion of "worldview" that resonate across disciplines. Such studies of consciousness are no longer the exclusive domain of psychoanalytic and Jungian approaches but belong to the many varieties of "cognitive" studies that have emerged in linguistics, anthropology, and the life sciences.

[*See also* Assyriology and Biblical Interpretation; Cognitive Linguistics and Biblical Interpretation; Folklore and Biblical Interpretation; Form Criticism, *subentry* Hebrew Bible; Genre Criticism; Ideological Criticism; *and* Ugaritology and Biblical Interpretation.]

BIBLIOGRAPHY

Assmann, Jan. *Of God and Gods: Egypt, Israel, and the Rise of Monotheism.* Madison: University of Wisconsin Press, 2008. Discusses conceptions of theism in the ancient world, arguing the translatability of polytheism and its implications and varieties of monotheism, including "Axial Age" developments in ancient Israel, and tendencies to violence. Especially important for the concept of myth is Assmann's concept of "cultural memory," developed in *Religion und kulturelles Gedächtnis* (Munich, 2000; English translation: *Religion and Cultural Memory,* Stanford, 2006).

Csapo, Eric. *Theories of Mythology.* Malden, Mass.: Oxford: Blackwell, 2005. A general treatment of major theories of myth. Especially useful is the scope and clarity of the section devoted to ideology.

Detienne, Marcel. *The Creation of Mythology.* Chicago: University of Chicago Press, 1986.

Doniger, Wendy. *The Implied Spider: Politics and Theology in Myth.* New York: Columbia University Press, 2011.

Dörrie, Heinrich. "The Meaning and Function of Myth in Greek and Roman Literature." In *Yearbook of Comparative Criticism* 9 (1980): 109–31. Reprinted in R. Segal, ed. *Philosophy, Religious Studies and Myth.* New York: Garland, 1996.

Doty, William. *Mythography: The Study of Myths and Rituals.* Tuscaloosa: University of Alabama Press, 2000. Against a one dimensional definition of myth, presents a "polyfunctional" view, effectively developing an approach adumbrated in Percy Cohen's influential 1969 essay "Theories of Myth" in *Man* (n.s. 4/3: 337–353).

Dubuisson, Daniel. *The Western Construction of Religion: Myths Knowledge, and Ideology.* Baltimore: The Johns Hopkins University Press, 2003.

Feldman, Burton and R. D. Richardson, Jr. *The Rise of Modern Mythology: 1680–1860.* Bloomington: Indiana University Press, 1972.

Fishbane, Michael. *Biblical Myth and Rabbinic Mythmaking.* Oxford: Oxford University Press, 2003.

Flood, Gavin. *Beyond Phenomenology: Rethinking the Study of Religion.* London: Cassell, 1999. An important reflection on the phenomenology of religion and philosophical phenomenology. Incorporates hermeneutic and narrative theory, particularly through Ricoeur and Bakhtin and engages of critical studies.

Gunkel, Hermann. *Creation and Chaos in the Primeval Era and the Eschaton: A Religio-historical Study of Genesis 1 and Revelation 12.* Translated by K. William Whitney, Jr. Grand Rapids, Mich: Eerdmans, 2006. The first English translation. Includes complete bibliographic information for the highly abbreviated documentation in the original. Especially useful is Whitney's preface that sheds considerable light on background and arguments, augmented by P. Machinist's foreword.

Hartlich, Christian and W. Sachs. *Der Ursprung des Mythosbegriffs in der modernen Bibelwissenschaft. Tübingen*: J. C. B. Mohr, 1952.

Jensen, Jeppe S. *Myths and Mythologies: A Reader.* Oakville, Conn.: Equinox, 2009. A selection of classic treatments of myth dating back to the mid nineteenth century, along with more recent seminal works, grouped as philosophical, sociological, semiological, and cognitivist approaches. Most selections date from 1946–1997.

Knight, Douglas A., ed. *Methods of Biblical Interpretation.* Nashville, Tenn.: Abingdon, 2004. Contains several excellent historical surveys grouped under "Folklore, Religion, and Myth" with extensive bibliography. Especially useful in the context of the many related approaches surveyed in the volume.

Krolick, Sanford. *Recollective Resolve: A Phenomenological Understanding of Time and Myth.* Macon, Ga.: Mercer University Press, 1987.

LaCocque, A., P. Ricoeur, and D. Pellauer. *Thinking Biblically: Exegetical and Hermeneutical Studies.* Chicago: University of Chicago Press, 2003.

Lincoln, Bruce. *Theorizing Myth: Narrative, Ideology, and Scholarship.* Chicago: University of Chicago Press, 1999.

Oden, Robert. "Myth and Mythology: Myth in the OT," in *The Anchor Bible Dictionary*, Vol. 4. 956–960. New York: Doubleday, 1992. Along with the article "Mythology" in the same volume (946–956), provides a useful survey and exposition of methodological issues.

Olender, Maurice. *The Languages of Paradise: Race, Religion, and Philology in the Nineteenth Century.* Translated by Arthur Goldhammer. Cambridge, Mass.: Harvard University Press, 1992.

Parpola, Simo. "Back to Delitzsch and Jeremias: The Relevance of the Pan-Babylonian School to the Melammu Project." In A. Panaino and A. Piras, eds. *Schools of Oriental Studies and the Development of Modern Historiography.* Milan: Mimesis, 2004.

Patton, Laurie L. and Wendy Doniger, *Myth and Method.* Charlottesville: University Press of Virginia, 1996.

Pongratz-Leisten, Beate, ed. *Reconsidering the Concept of "Revolutionary Monotheism."* Winona Lake, Ind.: Eisenbrauns, 2011. Collected essays from a conference held at Princeton University in 2007 of the same title. Contributors include major voices on the subject in recent decades.

Ricoeur, Paul. *Essays on Biblical Interpretation.* Philadelphia: Fortress Press, 1980.

Ricoeur, Paul. *Figuring the Sacred: Religion, Narrative, and Imagination.* Minneapolis: Augsburg Fortress, 1995. Essays confront the idea of "religious" language, reflections on philosophers including Kant and Levinas and treatments of the Bible and specific biblical passages.

Rogerson, John. *Myth in Old Testament Interpretation.* Berlin and New York: De Gruyter, 1974. An important survey of major movements and theorists of myth as applied to the Old Testament prior to its publication. Rogerson's prescient treatment of Ricoeur called attention to the philosopher's potential impact on biblical studies, which continues to grow.

Scarborough, Milton. *Myth and Modernity: Postcritical Reflections.* Albany: State University of New York Press, 1994. A thorough and engaging treatment of philosophical phenomenology in the tradition of Maurice Merleau-Ponty toward a new vision of myth.

Segal, Robert. *Theorizing about Myth*. Amherst: University of Massachusetts Press, 1999. Segal has written extensively on theoretical aspects of myth. This volume and the essays it contains compare theories of myth in ways that scholars of many fields have found useful.

Smith, Mark. *God in Translation: Deities in Cross-Cultural Discourse in the Biblical World*. Grand Rapids, Mich.: Eerdmans, 2010. Continues his influential work on monotheism that began in earnest in 1990 with *The Early History of God* (2d ed., Grand Rapids, 2002). Fruitfully continues his dialogue with Egyptologist Jan Assmann. Includes a discussion of "academic location," in which argues the need for an intellectual space to facilitate conversation between confessional theological and historical approaches.

Vanhoozer, Kevin. *Biblical Narrative in the Philosophy of Paul Ricoeur: A Study in Hermeneutics and Theology*. Cambridge, UK: Cambridge University Press, 1990.

Vanhoozer, Kevin. *Remythologizing Theology: Divine Action, Passion, and Authorship*. Cambridge, UK: Cambridge University Press, 2010.

Von Hendy, Andrew. *The Modern Construction of Myth*. Bloomington: Indiana University Press. 2002.

Wyatt, N. K. *The Mythic Mind: Essays on Cosmology and Religion in Ugaritic and Old Testament Literature*. London: Equinox, 2005. Includes essays "The Vocabulary and Neurology of Orientation," which discusses cultural experience as a matter of semantic fields related to the structure of human mind and body, and "The Mythic Mind," which presents myth as an archaic yet still present "mind-set" associated with ideology and emotion. Wyatt develops his treatment of myth and history, touched on in the latter essay, in "The Mythic Mind Revisited" *Scandinavian Journal of the Old Testament* Vol. 22.2 (2008): 161–175, 2008.

Dexter Callender, Jr.

N

Narrative Criticism and Narrative Hermeneutics

In 1953 the German-Jewish literary critic Erich Auerbach drew pointed contrasts between a scene in Homer's *Odyssey* and Abraham's near sacrifice of Isaac in Genesis 22. He claimed that Homer's epic reflects traditional oral construction, setting all action in the flat foreground, with nothing happening behind the scenes. In contrast, Genesis constructs a narrative "fraught with background," in which dialogue and action arise from movements occurring within characters, movements the narrator does not directly describe. Readers are forced to wonder about, and to supply, such suggested but unexpressed elements as Abraham's moral reasoning, his love for both God and son, his horror and determination. Thus, as an untold story unfolds simultaneously with the one told, three-dimensionality is constructed and readers are drawn into the gripping mystery of human and divine depths. Such a story "seeks to overcome our reality: we are to fit our own life into its world, feel ourselves to be elements in its structure of universal history" (1953, p. 15).

Biblical narratives portray figures whose voices and viewpoints, unfolding in narrative time, are differentiated from one another's and from that of the story's narrator. Temporal sequence explores causality and allows for changes in circumstance and development in characters. The arrangement of distinct figures, with their viewpoints, allows for the exploration of several perspectives in relation to one another. More than any other form, the narrative genre developed in scripture creates space for ambiguity and change in human experience, vividness in emotional response, and exploration of the limited, contingent, temporal nature of understanding and morality. Narrative replicates, and in fact thematizes, the perspectival experience of human life, both ordinary and extraordinary.

Proponents of narrative hermeneutics assert that narrative meaning differs fundamentally from propositional truth statements. As Hans Frei pointed out in his exploration of the loss of narrative understanding among eighteenth- and nineteenth-century biblical critics, "Narrative form and meaning are inseparable. . . . A great theme in literature of the novelistic type, like a pattern in a historical sequence, cannot be paraphrased by a general statement" (*The Eclipse of Biblical Narrative: A Study in Eighteenth and Nineteenth Century Hermeneutics* [New Haven: Yale University Press, 1974], p. 280). Attempts to distill abstract, universal human truths from biblical narratives, or alternatively to use the narratives as windows through which to reconstruct historical events, "eclipse" narrative meaning itself.

As a subfield of text-eminent literary approaches to biblical exegesis, narrative criticism seeks to take narrative meaning seriously by entering as attentively as possible into the story form. Rather than excavating the text for its historical development and precursors, narrative criticism examines the final form itself on its own terms and according to its own poetics, which are inferred from its recurring patterns of narration, characterization, scene-building, sequencing, gaps, repetitions, and so on. As Robert Alter contends:

> Far from neglecting the Bible's religious character, [narrative criticism] focuses attention on it in a more nuanced way. The implicit theology of the Hebrew Bible dictates a complex moral and psychological realism in biblical narrative because God's purposes are always entrammeled in history, dependent on the acts of individual men and women for their continuing realization. To scrutinize biblical personages as fictional characters is to see them more sharply in the multifaceted, contradictory aspects of their human individuality. (1981, p. 12)

In the Hebrew Bible, narratives are found in Genesis—2 Kings, as well as in 1—2 Chronicles; in parts of Jeremiah, Isaiah, Hosea, and Amos; in Ruth, Esther, Jonah, the beginning and ending of Job, and Daniel 1—6. In the New Testament, narrative is found in the four Gospels and the Book of Acts, as well as the Book of Revelation, which narrates a vision.

Development of Biblical Narrative. In his book *Biblical Narrative and the Death of the Rhapsode,* Robert Kawashima shines light on the development of biblical narrative by drawing a comparison that is similar to Auerbach's, this time of two texts within the Bible: the ancient victory song of Deborah and Barak in Judges 5 and the narrative describing that victory in Judges 4. These stereoscopic renditions provide a nearly unique opportunity to detail the distinctions between epic and narrative. Like traditional oral epics across cultures, the poem is characterized by dense literal repetition. It is highly referential, presupposing—and requiring—a fund of prior cultural knowledge as it rehearses a heroic event. But the prose narrative creates its own world, containing all the explanation and narrative continuity needed to stand on its own, supplying details that derive from, and at some points even appear to misconstrue, the poem. For instance, in 4:21 the author takes the twice-described weapon of Jdg 5:26 to be two different instruments, used in a contrived manner to kill Sisera. But what the narrative might lack in acumen regarding poetic parallelism, it more than makes up in character development, suspense, irony, causality, and narrative completeness. Figures that were merely agents in the poetry spring to life in the story as complex and subtle characters speaking to, acting upon, and ironically paralleling one another. A series of vivid scenes is transformed into a suspenseful narrative flow. By means of the multiple perspectives available not only through the eyes of a single authoritative story teller, but through the competing visions of several players, a complex depth develops that more closely resembles the perspectivally-based world humans negotiate daily.

Poetic epics such as Judges 5 and Exodus 15, as well as Ugaritic, Akkadian, and Greek epics, attest to the early presence and eventual written preservation of an oral genre characterized by language that lent itself to memorization: repetition, word pairs, formulas, unitary viewpoint, and a preponderance of obscurities left unexplained within the poetry. The form of storytelling found in narratives such as Judges 4, by contrast, does not reflect an oral style, but arose as a written genre in a literate culture. Yet a thin line between the oral and the written remained: in a world in which written copies were scarce and many people did not read, even texts composed or compiled first in written form (not only narratives of the Hebrew Bible and New Testament but also non-narrative texts such as Torah laws and the letters of Paul) came to life by being read aloud, often by someone other than the author. Why, how, and precisely when this literate form of storytelling arose in ancient Israel remains a provocative mystery.

Precursors to Narrative Criticism. Since earliest times, readers have experienced the Bible's stories as captivating and compelling. But contemporary narrative criticism arose only in the past four decades, particularly as it became clearer that the biblical storytellers were not simply recording historical events as eyewitnesses, nor merely copying down oral epics, but rather crafting stories with sophistication and skill.

A development in general literary criticism foreshadowed narrative analysis in biblical studies. For decades critics had equated literary meaning with authorial intent, assuming that information from writers' biographies, social circumstances, letters, and other writings might shed light on the meaning of the work at hand (an assumption whose implications are devastatingly explored in Henry James's 1888 novella *The Aspern Papers*). But in a 1946 article entitled "The Intentional Fallacy," revised and republished in a book in 1954, W. K. Wimsatt and Monroe Beardsley declared that "the design or intention of the author is neither available nor desirable as a standard for judging the success of a work of literary art" (*The Verbal Icon: Studies in the Meaning of Poetry* [Lexington: University of Kentucky Press, 1954], p. 4). Since a literary work has its own integrity and meaning quite apart from what the author may have intended, inquiry into the writer's circumstances unjustly circumscribes the work's significance. A movement called "New Criticism" arose, espousing close reading of the literary work's own internal features without undue reference to authors and historical settings.

The quest for historical reconstruction similarly dominated biblical criticism. But while readers of recent literature could seek access to authorial biography, biblical interpreters were forced to reconstruct the historical milieu of passages through archaeology, epigraphy, and clues from the text itself. Using such historical tools, including source, form, and redaction criticism, scholars attempted to reconstruct the ancient world from which the texts emerged, including their assumed written and oral precursors. Meaning was sought not in the text's present form, but in a reconstructed event presumably underlying it. Stories were studied as windows into the life situations reflected in the text.

This approach not only built upon often shaky foundations but neglected claims made upon readers by the narratives themselves. Historical-critical discoveries were invaluable, but interpretation tended to mine, disassemble, and dispose of texts in pursuit of prior texts and circumstances that proved elusive and mostly irrecoverable. The final biblical texts, which for centuries before had been read as unities possessing theological meaning, were bypassed. Dissatisfaction with these weaknesses, coupled with interest in what close "New Critical" readings of scripture might reveal, led to new exegetical emphases.

Literary critic M. H. Abrams (*The Mirror and the Lamp: Romantic Theory and the Critical Tradition*, Oxford: Oxford University Press, 1953) helpfully schematized the variety of potential interpretive approaches in terms of their primary focus on author, reader, text itself, or the world of historical existence. General literary theory before New Criticism was author-centered ("expressive"), while New Criticism encouraged a text-centered ("objective") approach. Historical-critical approaches in biblical exegesis tended to be somewhat author-centered, but even more historically referential ("mimetic"). While early experiments in narrative biblical criticism tended, like New Criticism, to privilege the text itself without appealing to the authorship or history behind the text, the very fact that these texts arose from an ancient world in which customs, language, and mores were shared between authors and readers, but need explanation now, meant that narrative criticism could never detach itself from historical interests. The difference lies in the interpretive goal: clarifying not the world behind the text but the world created by the text.

Development of Narrative Criticism. The 1970s and 1980s saw an explosion of interest in literary analysis of scripture. In studies of the Hebrew Scriptures, both Robert Alter and Adele Berlin sought through close analysis to infer from the narratives themselves the conventions by which they operate, conventions such as the compactness of narrative descriptions, the development of characters through contrasting speech patterns and actions, and the use of the narrator's viewpoint to focus attention on what the narrator wished the audience to observe and infer. Alter's *The Art of Biblical Narrative* (1981) and Berlin's *Poetics and Interpretation of Biblical Narrative* (1983) were preceded in the 1970s by several works examining literary features of particular narratives, especially 1—2 Samuel, and were quickly followed by other programmatic works such as Meir Sternberg's *The Poetics of Biblical Narrative* (Bloomington: Indiana University Press, 1985), David Damrosch's *The Narrative Covenant: Transformations of Genre in the Growth of Biblical Narrative* (1987), and Shimon Bar-Ephrat's *Narrative Art in the Bible* (Sheffield: Almond Press, 1989), which was first published in Hebrew in 1979.

In New Testament studies, Amos Wilder, a poet, literary critic, and biblical scholar, led the way with *The Language of the Gospel: Early Christian Rhetoric* (New York: Harper & Row, 1964), followed by William Beardslee's *Literary Criticism of the New Testament* (Philadelphia: Fortress, 1969), along with several diverse examinations of Jesus's parables, including Robert Funk's *Language, Hermeneutic, and the Word of God* (New York: Harper & Row, 1966), Dan O. Via's *The Parables: Their Literary and Existential Dimension* (Philadelphia: Fortress, 1967), and John Dominic Crossan's *In Parables: The Challenge of the Historical Jesus* (New York: Harper & Row, 1973). Norman Petersen's *Literary Criticism for New Testament Critics* (Philadelphia: Fortress, 1978), Frank Kermode's *The Genesis of Secrecy: On the Interpretation of Narrative* (Cambridge, Mass.: Harvard University Press, 1979), and David Rhoads and Donald Michie's *Mark as Story: An Introduction to the Narrative of a Gospel* (1982) all examined the Gospel of Mark from a narrative perspective as a framework for exploring the poetics of Gospel narratives.

Some early experiments in narrative biblical interpretation tended to assume that a particular text's meaning was stable and embedded and would reveal itself in the same way to any competent reader. But critics soon recognized that the same narrative, rich in potential meanings, was interpreted differently by competent readers in diverse interpretive communities. The role of readers, not only in the discernment of meaning, but in its very making, came to be acknowledged. While focus on the readers' roles is largely the domain of what has come to be called "reader-response criticism" and has informed a wide variety of readings from particular social and geographical locations, narrative critics necessarily have come to incorporate the tools of this sensibility. Reader-response critics have likewise incorporated close literary reading into their practices.

Another text-eminent emphasis that both informs and may be differentiated from narrative criticism is structuralism. French structuralism arose from Russian Formalism, particularly from Vladimir Propp's study of Russian folktales. Its key insights have been helpful starting points for narrative biblical criticism, particularly its communication model, its recognition of language and literature as systems of signs whose meanings are not independent but interrelated, and its assertion that across a variety of oral narratives, certain underlying structures and functions—cultural codes—prevail with predictable regularity.

The term "rhetorical criticism" has sometimes been used interchangeably with "literary criticism," and where this is the case (such as in Phyllis Trible's work), narrative criticism can be seen as a subgenre of rhetorical criticism. Other interpreters, however, see in rhetorical criticism a pragmatic approach focusing on the strategies used to delight, teach, or persuade the audience. Although this understanding is more often associated with texts in which the rhetorical situation in the audience's real world is more discernible, critical readers may in fact discern ways in which biblical storytellers aim to attract readers to the behaviors and beliefs commended, subtly or overtly, by the narrator. This is more obviously the case in the narratives of Kings and Chronicles and the stories of Daniel, as well as in some New Testament narratives, while Genesis and Samuel, for instance, invite readers to engage in more open-ended and variable ways. Feminist critics, joined by other liberationist and post-colonial readers, have been particularly sensitive to the ways in which narratives make their bid to formulate the readers' worldview, and they have engaged in deconstructive readings that resist androcentric interpretation—and in many cases resist androcentrism in the biblical stories themselves.

As narrative criticism and literary interpretation of other biblical genres have matured, not only whole commentaries but entire commentary series have been devoted to narrative readings. As in all commentary series, the quality of individual volumes varies. Notable series include the *Readings* series from Sheffield Phoenix Press and the *Berit Olam* (for Hebrew Bible) and Sacra Pagina (for New Testament) series from Liturgical Press. Three eclectic series that seek to combine older methods with literary interpretation and, especially in the case of the latter, the history of biblical interpretation are the *Interpretation* commentaries (Westminster John Knox), the *New Interpreter's Bible* (Abingdon), and the Smyth and Helwys Bible Commentary (while the Smyth and Helwys "Reading" series combines literary and theological commentary).

Narrative Components. Because narratives function differently from more propositional truth claims, a particular set of tools and questions is needed for exploring them. A story's conclusion is not the whole story, nor is what is explicitly detailed the story's entire scope. As Auerbach pointed out about Genesis 22, "It is not only God's intervention at the beginning and the end, but even the factual and psychological elements which come between, that are mysterious, merely touched upon, fraught with background; and therefore they require subtle investigation and interpretation[;] they demand them" (1953, 15). To enter into the story and experience it properly, it is necessary to recognize ancient narrative strategies.

Many components and customs discernible in biblical storytelling correspond to those of modern fiction, into which implied author and narrator, implied audience and narratee, characters and characterization, dialogue, viewpoint, time and space, repetitions, gaps, and ambiguity all figure. Some of the conventions of biblical narrative differ from the modern, particularly in terms of economy of words, representations of the divine, and chosen stances of the narrator's voice.

Author and Reader, Implied Author and Implied Reader, Narrator and Narratee. Structuralism's communication model, when applied to written narrative, draws attention to the complexity of the layering of both author and reader (see Figure 1). Actual readers encounter, first and foremost, a narrator's voice, distinct in intonation and viewpoint from those of characters who speak and act within the story. Whereas the characters speak to one another, the narrator addresses someone, a "narratee," standing outside the bounds of the story (but inside the bounds of the text or narrative: the larger box in the diagram), the one for whose benefit the story is being told. The book of Jonah, for example, begins with a narrator saying, "Now the word of the LORD came to Jonah son of Amittai" (Jonah 1:1), who then presents in the next verse one character (God) speaking directly to another (Jonah). Within the story, characters may recount narratives to other characters, such as when Jonah says to God, "That is why I fled to Tarshish at the beginning; for I knew that you are a gracious God and merciful . . ." (4:2), but even there their own accounts are framed within the narrative.

Distinctions between narrator and author (both actual and implied), and between narratee and readers (both actual and implied), are sometimes difficult to discern, but they are nevertheless important to distinguish. The narrator depicts a story world that may differ from the world in which author and readers live. The setting may, for instance, be a foreign land, such as Ur or Egypt, or a foreign world where fish swallow and regurgitate prophets, great cities are three days' walk across, and notorious kings repent of evil or, as in other biblical narratives, animals speak to humans, angels are seen and heard, axe heads float, loaves and fishes are multiplied, and four horsemen ride horses of different colors. Or, as in modern fiction, the narrator may be a dolphin-like sea creature living millennia in the future, as in Kurt Vonnegut's *Galapagos*, or may follow children through a wardrobe to a world contested between a lion and a witch, as in C. S. Lewis's fiction. The author presumably knows quite well that these artifices do not describe the world as such, but invites readers to tour an

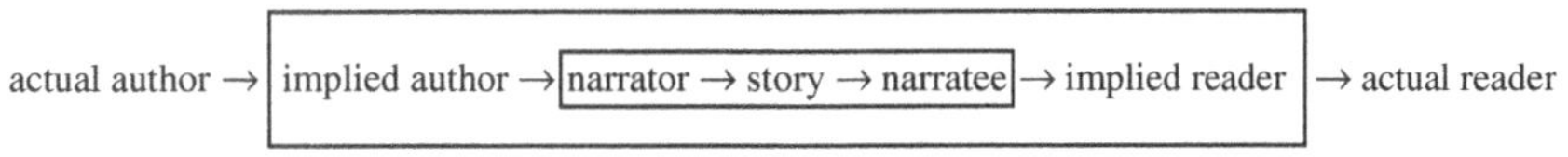

Figure 1.

unfamiliar setting, simultaneously encountering our own world from an unexpected angle. What makes these foreign worlds navigable and instructive is the recognizability of persons. We can follow a prophet, or even a dolphin-like creature with whose reactions we can identify, to the improbable bottom of the sea, but we are not as motivated to spend time even in a familiar setting with a character whose bearing seems contrived.

Similarly, the narrator may invite us to tour the foreign world of someone else's subjectivity by being one of the characters, telling the story in the first person from a limited or even unreliable viewpoint. Here the author, aware of the narrator's idiosyncrasies, likewise expects the reader to see, beneath the story as the narrator tells it, another story positioned at an angle from it. (J. D. Salinger's *The Catcher in the Rye* and Mark Twain's *Huckleberry Finn* are paramount examples). The biblical equivalent of this move is especially evident wherever a character begins to recount a story and his or her reliability is measurable against the perspective of the narrator or other characters (e.g., Potiphar's wife's account of Joseph's assault in Gen 39:13–18 vs. the narrator's account in vv. 7–12).

The implied author may also be distinguished from the actual author. In the process of constructing a narrative, the author has the opportunity to edit out the fits and starts of actual thought to create a voice that sounds more coherent and confident. The implied author is the one we are invited to "hear" and mentally reconstruct as we read. Genesis—2 Kings present an implied author telling a more or less coherent story that begins with creation and ends in exile. Prevailing themes, recurrent motifs, foreshadowings, allusions, and other intertextual devices encourage the illusion of a single, though puzzlingly or delightfully inconsistent, authorial voice responsible for the entire narrative sweep. Since readers are accustomed to fixing mentally an implied author as they read, it is not surprising that scriptural readers have for centuries perceived a single narrator of the Pentateuch and named him "Moses." Nor, since readers are accustomed to suspending disbelief to enter narrative worlds, is it surprising that readers have confused biblical storytelling with the actual history of a remote time period in which, we may become convinced, the rules of nature operated differently than our experience suggests.

The narratee parallels the narrator as the one to whom a story is ostensibly being told (for instance, in the case of Luke's Gospel, "Theophilus"). The implied reader is constructed by, and may be reconstructed from, the implied author's language, as one who shares the implied author's cultural knowledge, catches the allusions, and is able to process the story just as it is told. For instance, when Gen 13:7 states, "At that time the Canaanites and the Perizzites lived in the land," actual readers may infer that the implied reader no longer lived surrounded by Canaanites and Perizzites but was aware that those tribes had once existed. Of all these distinctions, that between the implied reader and actual readers is perhaps easiest to discern—wherever we find gaps between knowledge and assumptions presumed by the author and those we in fact possess.

Narration. Biblical stories are nearly always told in third person. As Robert Alter has pointed out, the narrator exudes greater reliability than the characters and serves as a measuring rod for characters' awareness, knowledge, and truthfulness. In the Hebrew Bible the omniscient narrator even presides over the words, deeds, and thoughts of God, not necessarily presenting the Deity as all good or all knowing. In the Gospels, the narrator shares reliability and authority with the main character Jesus. Yet biblical narrators are also reticent, declining to tell us everything we need or wish to know, demanding that we lean in to participate in the story's unfolding. Timing of disclosures is not moored to temporal sequence. For instance, the fact that Bathsheba was purifying herself after her menstrual cycle is not mentioned when David sees her bathing, but only after he calls her to the palace and sleeps with her—pointedly establishing paternity (2 Sam 11:4). Similarly, Jesus foretells his passion several times, bringing its theme of persecution by the powerful as a risk of serving the powerless to bear on lived discipleship (Mark 8:31; 9:31; 10:32–34).

Narrators serve to move action efficiently to scenes dominated by dialogue, and to communicate actions that accompany dialogue. They mirror, confirm, subvert, and focus characters' words. Narrative repetitions, gaps, sequence, and timing are significant factors in the story's unfolding meaning.

Adele Berlin draws attention to point of view in biblical narrative. No character is perceived by the reader directly, she notes, but rather is filtered through the narrative voice, much as what is viewed in a film is filtered through the camera's eye. And, like the camera's perspective, the narrative perspective may shift attention from one character to another, or from a long shot of the whole scene to a close-up of a detail, or to what one of the characters is seeing. This shifting focus gives biblical narrative a sense of multidimensionality. "Point of view" can refer not only to perception but also to conception or worldview. The biblical presentation of so many differing viewpoints forces readers to negotiate the tangle of perspectives to establish his or her own understanding, much as we must do when confronting the multiplicity of viewpoints in the world around us. Careful readers find that discerning the narrative viewpoint is one crucial step in interpretation, but not its totality, since in a perspectival world we too may see things differently. Though the narrator of ancient stories appears to have been presumed morally reliable, modern readers may in fact, and often do, differ with the narrator's (and implied author's) sensibilities. We may, for instance, take exception to the commendation of Jehu (2 Kgs 10:30), or to Gospel portrayals of Pharisees and Sadducees.

Characters and Dialogue. Literary artistry underlies the vividness of biblical characters who—especially in classical biblical narratives—are not provided detailed descriptions. Sparse but often metaphorically salient details introduce and accompany them. Esau, for instance, is identified from birth as red and hairy, and later as a skilled hunter. All three of these characteristics come back to haunt him, as he first trades his birthright for "that red stuff" (literally, "this red red," Gen 25:30) and later, while he is away hunting, he is cheated out of his blessing by means of animal skins that replicate his hairiness (Gen 25; 27). The painful irony characterizing Judas in Mark's Gospel is even more obvious: when the twelve disciples are appointed, the last in the list is "Judas Iscariot, who betrayed him" (3:19), and when this narrator's comment is fulfilled in the passion narrative, Judas is always spoken of as "one of the twelve" (14:10, 20, 43).

Beyond such terse external descriptions, the narrator allows readers to come to know the characters just as we come to know people in real life, through inference rather than direct information. Alter posits a range of explicitness in presentation of characters. At the top of this range, rarely, the narrator may pronounce a direct judgment: Eli's two sons are dismissed as scoundrels with no regard for God or for their own priestly duties (2 Sam 2:12–13), before their tasteless actions and brutish words are sampled. Any doubts about Job's character are, by contrast, summarily dismissed by a narrator introducing him as blameless and upright, fearing God and turning away from evil (Job 1:1). These are the exceptions. More often readers must negotiate a range of glimpses into a person's motives and character through his or her speech or thoughts, through the comments of other characters, through appearance, gestures, posture and costume, and through actions. Often these glimpses yield ambiguous results. When, for instance, David reacts to Goliath's challenge with, "What shall be done for the man who kills this Philistine, and takes away the reproach from Israel? For who is this uncircumcised Philistine that he should defy the armies of the living God?" (1 Sam 17:26), we are left wondering just what mix of opportunism and piety informed this speech—and we later see both qualities competing in his moral structure. Elizabeth Struthers Malbon perceives tension in the characterization of Jesus in Mark's Gospel, manifest by the contrast between what is said by the narrator and other characters and what is said by the character Jesus, all under the control of the implied author, who is not to be merged with the narrator (2009). While the narrator and other characters speak about Jesus, the Markan Jesus speaks about God, consistently deflecting attention and honor from himself to God. The implied author communicates both narrative strains to the implied audience without resolving them.

Berlin points out characters' variety in complexity. Stock characters, or "agents," do not emerge with their own personalities but only serve supporting roles as messengers, servants, sons, daughters, and so on. Flat characters, or "types," may have lines to speak and individual actions to perform, but their depths are not plumbed and they do not change. Often stock or flat characters may be crowds or groups who all speak in one voice. Round or "full-fledged" characters are provided ample room to show inconsistency and ambiguity, to develop over time and even off stage, to emerge as three-dimensional persons possessing all the familiarity and mystery of people we know intimately but never quite figure out. While Mark's narrative presents both negative "flat" characters (e.g., most, although not all, Jewish leaders) and positive "flat" characters (e.g., the hemorrhaging woman and the Syrophoenician woman), the disciples are more "round." The disciples are portrayed dialogically under negotiation—they may at times get it right and at other times, despite all they see and hear, miss the point, letting themselves be upstaged in proper speech or action by a minor character. Implied readers stand somewhat in the place of the disciples, well meaning but prone to similar mistakes, and by the disciples' examples being warned away from erroneous assumptions and unfaithful actions. Threats toward those thinking the things of God, and temptations to side with powerful but corrupt human ways, create drama and draw readers to ponder their own loyalties. (See Malbon 2000.)

Biblical narratives strikingly prefer dialogue over action and direct discourse over indirect, allowing readers, as it were, to "see" characters, and without overt guidance to explore possible discrepancies between self-presentation and actual motives or thoughts. Biblical dialogue generally occurs between only two parties at a time. Contrastive speech patterns are used to convey personality distinctions. In the books of Samuel, for instance, women's speech patterns tend to be syntactically and semantically more complex than men's, and David's speeches tend to be longer and more rhetorically forceful than Saul's. The speech of elders may display more formal patterning than that of youths. More effectively than dialects or other affects, such distinctions keep characters from functioning simply as mouthpieces for the narrator and allow readers the impression that each personality emerges from a distinct consciousness.

Time and Space. Since narrative emphasizes not historical chronicle but vivid story, and scenes are preferred over synopsis, many years between events can pass in a single line, but a single scene may take as much time to narrate as the event would take to occur, or even more. An event may be recalled or predicted more than once, as when Abraham's servant prays that Isaac's future bride will offer to water the camels (Gen 24:14), and then the narrator has the girl say, "I will draw water for your camels" (v. 19), after which the servant recounts to her family his prayer about watering the camels (v. 44) and her words, "Drink, and I will also water your camels" (v. 46). Finally, upon returning home, "he told Isaac all the things that he had done" (v. 66), recalling without again relating the servant's conscientious participation in Abraham's God-given destiny.

Sometimes repeated sequences will unfold into one story that breaks the repetition, as when Hannah's yearly suffering at Shiloh prompts her to make one history-altering pledge in the sanctuary (1 Sam 1:3–11). At other times one story will be inserted within another, with readers left to ponder the relationship between them. Such intercalation occurs frequently in Mark: the healing of a woman suffering from a twelve-year-long hemorrhage interrupts the healing of a synagogue leader's twelve-year-old daughter (5:21–43), and the beheading of John the Baptist is narrated as a flashback between the sending out and returning of Jesus's disciples (6:7–30). In Genesis 38, a story spanning many years of Judah's life improbably occurs as Midianites are transporting his brother Joseph to Egypt, but one parallel motif after another joins the stories.

Geographical settings figure into the drama, particularly in New Testament narratives. Abraham and Sarah's journey to and from Egypt foreshadows that of their descendants (Gen 12:11–20; 46:3–7; Exod 3:7–8), and, in Matthew, Jesus's family reenacts the journey once again (2:13–23), traveling both to and from Egypt. The Jordan River does for Joshua what the Sea had done for Moses a generation before (Exod 14:21–22; Josh 3:15–17), marking both a miracle and a boundary. For Jesus, the Sea of Galilee serves not as a boundary between lands but as a miraculous bridge uniting them. On the night of Jesus's arrest, the location on the Mount of Olives recalls the pathos of his ancestor David's flight from Jerusalem (Mark 14:26; 2 Sam 15:30). In fact, in Mark the Jordan River, the desert, the sea, and the mountain all function as intertextual evocations of motifs of transition, testing, and divine presence and power in the Hebrew Scriptures, while the regions of Galilee and Jerusalem, and the journey between them, mark particular points of tension and threat.

Much more can be said about the biblical narratives' uses of gaps, ambiguities, and repetitions, about the functions of readerly knowledge and lack of knowledge in relation to characters' knowledge, about the uses of humor and irony. Though readers continue to find the narratives and the people populating them vivid and compelling, there is without doubt much going on in them that earliest readers would have recognized but modern readers miss or only catch in glimpses. Narrative criticism offers a means and a motive to slow down and pay close attention to stories that have significantly shaped western sensibilities, stories that still continue not simply to populate, but even to create, readers' worlds.

[*See also:* Deconstruction; Formalist Interpretation; Literary Criticism, Literary Theory, and the Bible; Performance Criticism; Poststructuralist Interpretation; Reader-Response Criticism; Reception Criticism and Theory; Rhetorical Criticism; Structuralist Interpretation; *and* Synchronic Interpretation.]

BIBLIOGRAPHY

Alter, Robert. *The Art of Biblical Narrative.* New York: Basic Books, 1981. This classic must-read combines detailed discussion of narrative poetics with refreshingly original examples of narrative analysis at work.

Auerbach, Erich. *Mimesis: The Representation of Reality in Western Literature.* Princeton, N.J.: Princeton University Press, 1953.

Bechtel, Carol M. *Esther.* Interpretation. Louisville, Ky.: Westminster John Knox, 2002. Granted, Bechtel had wonderful material to work with in Esther, but still, it is not many serious biblical commentaries that are composed with such incisive wit and refreshing style as to compel readers at times to laugh out loud, as this one does.

Berlin, Adele. *Poetics and Interpretation of Biblical Narrative.* Sheffield, UK: Almond Press, 1983. Still one of the classic detailed descriptions of narrative in the Hebrew Bible, well worth reading.

Damrosch, David. *The Narrative Covenant: Transformations of Genre in the Growth of Biblical Narrative.* San Francisco: Harper & Row, 1987. Besides being a delightfully well-written book, this study by a scholar of English and comparative literature remains a classic example of sensitive exploration of the relationship between historical and literary concerns, employing careful attention to genre and offering close readings particularly of the David narratives.

Darr, John A. *On Character Building: The Reader and the Rhetoric of Characterization in Luke-Acts.* Louisville, Ky.: Westminster John Knox, 1992. Based on literary-critical and reader-response critical theory, a careful interpretation of the role of the reader in understanding three representative characters: John the Baptist, the Pharisees, and Herod the Tetrarch.

Day, Linda M. *Esther.* Abingdon Old Testament Commentaries. Nashville, Tenn.: Abingdon, 2005. Following up on her innovative earlier analysis of Esther's character as presented in the three different extant Hebrew and Greek versions of the book (*Three Faces of a Queen: Characterization in the Books of Esther*, Sheffield: Sheffield Academic Press, 1995), Day offers a full commentary that deftly combines literary analysis with other exegetical approaches.

Exum, J. Cheryl. *Tragedy and Biblical Narrative.* Cambridge, UK: Cambridge University Press, 1992. Brings the dimension of tragedy to a close reading of the narratives of Jephthah, Saul, and David, raising questions of human choice and fate as they are explored through the stories of these ambiguous figures.

Gunn, David, and Danna Nolan Fewell. *Narrative in the Hebrew Bible.* Oxford: Oxford University Press, 1993. A lively introduction to narrative analysis in the Hebrew Bible, taking a more deconstructionist stance than

Alter does, interweaving theory with examples from Genesis, Jonah, and Daniel.

Howell, David B. *Matthew's Inclusive Story: A Study in the Narrative Rhetoric of the First Gospel.* Journal for the Study of the New Testament Supplement Series 42. Sheffield UK: Sheffield Academic Press, 1990. From the point of view of an eclectic reader-response paradigm, an exploration of plot, point of view (especially of the implied author/narrator), and the implied reader.

Kawashima, Robert S. *Biblical Narrative and the Death of the Rhapsode.* Bloomington: Indiana University Press, 2004. Drawing on critical theory, linguistics, Hebrew grammar and syntax, and comprehensive knowledge of comparative literature both ancient and modern, Kawashima builds on Auerbach's early observations concerning distinctions between narrative and epic genres, showing particularly biblical narrative's innovative representations of narrative time, human consciousness, and monotheism.

Kuhn, Karl A. *The Heart of the Biblical Narrative: Rediscovering Biblical Appeal to the Emotions.* Minneapolis: Fortress, 2009. Redressing the long-held resistance of biblical exegesis to affective dimensions of biblical narratives, Kuhn offers an approach to both the Hebrew Bible and the New Testament that especially attends to the ways in which the stories seek to move and persuade audiences. He illustrates his suggestions with a close reading of Luke 1 and 2.

Malbon, Elizabeth Struthers. *In the Company of Jesus: Characters in Mark's Gospel.* Louisville, Ky.: Westminster John Knox, 2000. A collection of essays on characters in Mark (women, crowds, disciples, Jewish leaders, minor characters), introduced by an overview of narrative criticism with Markan examples.

Malbon, Elizabeth Struthers. *Mark's Jesus: Characterization as Narrative Christology.* Waco, Tex.: Baylor University Press, 2009. A detailed examination of the characterization of Jesus on the basis of his words and actions and the words and actions of other characters and the narrator in relation to him, which also points out the importance of maintaining a clear distinction between narrator and implied audience.

Moore, Stephen D. *Literary Criticism and the Gospels: The Theoretical Challenge.* New Haven, Conn. and London: Yale University Press, 1989. Incorporating the critical theories of deconstructionists such as Stanley Fish, Jacques Derrida, and others, this volume offers a lively discussion of narrative and reader-response criticism and includes an extensive bibliography.

Powell, Mark Allan. *What Is Narrative Criticism?* Guides to Biblical Scholarship. Minneapolis: Fortress, 1990. This important introduction relates New Testament narrative criticism to other critical approaches and offers a guide to narrative elements such as story and discourse, events, characters, and settings.

Rhoads, David, and Donald Michie. *Mark as Story: An Introduction to the Narrative of a Gospel.* Philadelphia: Fortress, 1982. The second (1999) and third (2012) editions add Joanna Dewey as an author. This groundbreaking examination of Mark's narrative has been thoroughly revised from the first edition, incorporating insights from recent scholarship. It includes a fresh English translation of Mark and an afterword on the ethics of reading.

Stibbe, Mark W. G. *John as Storyteller: Narrative Criticism and the Fourth Gospel.* Society for New Testament Studies Monograph Series 73. Cambridge, UK: Cambridge University Press, 1992. An eclectic integration of literary, theological, structuralist, historical critical, and sociological questions in relation to narrative criticism, resulting in practical criticism, genre criticism, a look at social function, and a narrative-historical approach to John's story, with a detailed application to John 18–19.

Trible, Phyllis. *Texts of Terror: Literary-Feminist Readings of Biblical Narratives.* Philadelphia: Fortress, 1984. Feminist perspectives and literary methods are skillfully interwoven to explore violent aspects of male/female interactions in four terrifying biblical stories: those of Hagar the slave of Sarai, King David's raped and abandoned daughter Tamar, the sacrificed daughter of Jephthah, and the concubine who was gang-raped, murdered, and dismembered as the narrative of Judges dissolved into wanton violence.

Walsh, Jerome T. *Old Testament Narrative: A Guide to Interpretation.* Louisville, Ky.: Westminster John Knox, 2009. A recent introduction to narrative analysis, this volume is able to incorporate the insights of three decades of scholarship. It includes many biblical illustrations of the concepts discussed.

Yamasaki, Gary. *Watching a Biblical Narrative: Point of View in Biblical Exegesis.* London: T&T Clark, 2007. Drawing from literary and linguistic theory, particularly the work of Boris Uspensky, assesses the use of point of view in Old and New Testament exegesis and offers guidance for sophisticated analysis of point of view.

Patricia K. Tull

New Historicism

Some have observed that there is something inherently odd if not outright contradictory about the label "New Historicism." The word "history" conjures up images of what is old, what has come before now, what is past. The concept of "new," on the other hand signals the novel, what is to come, what we can expect in the future. To complicate matters further, New Historicism arose among a group of literary critics who claimed to be committed to making a difference in the present. So what is the New Historicism? (See Hens-Piazza 2002, from which portions of this article have been taken with permission of the publisher.)

During the first half of the twentieth century, traditional historical criticism held sway in biblical studies as the dominant mode for the interpretation of texts. Here, factors external to the text were considered integral in the production of meaning. Authorial intention, context, sources, editorial process, and literary form constituted the locus of study. A host of historical approaches developed for systematic analysis of these factors in the service of interpretation. Many of these methods are still practiced today. Specialization in historical studies continued to grow, reaping important gains. Biblical scholars regularly began to rub shoulders and collaborate with colleagues in other areas of the humanities. These influences and exchanges became especially evident in the second half of the twentieth century.

Mirroring shifts in the larger academy, historical methods of interpretation eventually gave way to literary approaches in the biblical field. The rise of various methods from schools of literary criticism created what some termed a "paradigm shift" and what others labeled as a "revolution" in biblical interpretation. Meaning, once tied to the text in relation to its context, was now consigned to the text alone. Analysis of the biblical stories for literary coherence, rhetorical elements, narrative design, deep structures, poetics, and all other kinds of literary pursuits challenged the sovereignty of historical critical inquiry. In 1992 Mark Allan Powell's anthology of modern literary studies on the Bible attested to the burgeoning status of the literary field. Cataloging research from the 1970s to 1990s, Powell identified well over a thousand studies on biblical texts that employed a vast array of literary methods. And these studies were matched in number by other explorations that discussed the theoretics of literary approaches to the Bible by biblical scholars and literary critics alike. Given the dramatic shift from historical explorations to a literary focus, the rise of a literary school called New Historicism on the campus of the University of California at Berkeley in the late 1980s was somewhat of an anomaly at first glance. Even more disconcerting was the lack of agreement about what to call it.

While the term New Historicism can be traced to an essay by Michael McCanles in 1980, Stephen Greenblatt, the *chef d'école* of the movement in the United States, claims to have coined the label somewhat arbitrarily (Greenblatt 1982, pp. 3–6). Earlier, in his *Renaissance Self-Fashioning*, which is generally taken as the programmatic work in this area, Greenblatt described his way of working as a "poetics of culture" (Greenblatt 1980. p. 5). Others had other labels. "The new history," "historical-materialist criticism," "cultural materialism," and "critical historicism" were among the candidates. Lee Patterson even went so far to observe that "no single label can be usefully applied to the historicist enterprise as a school, least of all the already assigned, hotly contested, and irredeemably vague 'New Historicism'" (Patterson 1990, p. 1).

This reticence about what to call it was not the only oddity about the new literary activity. There was an intrinsic resistance among its practitioners to setting forth an operational definition that might domesticate this literary nova for straightforward public consumption. Greenblatt referred to New Historicism as a "trajectory" rather than a "set of beliefs" (Greenblatt 1990, p. 3). Louis Montrose called it an "orientation" rather than a prescription of practices in interpretation (Montrose 1986, p. 6). Joel Fineman defined it as an "intellectual posture" (Fineman 1989, p. 52). And Catherine Gallagher described it as a "phenomenon of apparent political indeterminacy" (Gallagher 1989, p. 37). Yet a common thread runs through all this reticence. At the start, New Historicism is best comprehended as less a theory and certainly not a method of interpretation. Adopting Daniel Boyarin's suggestion, New Historicism might be aptly understood as a sensibility or perspective on literature (Boyarin 1996, pp. 118–141). It views texts as caught up in the social processes and contexts out of which they emerge. Though identified with a single author, texts are generated by a community. One community produces a text while another community interprets the text. Hence the text is constantly under production.

As a sensibility rather than a method, New Historicism views literature (including the biblical texts) as integrally tied to and identified with other material realities—cultural practices, relics, data from a context, and the like—that make up social contexts. Of interest here is how historical, social, economic, biographical, sexual, aesthetic, and psychological forces are disclosed by this material evidence. New Historicism investigates these forces by crossing disciplinary boundaries, venturing into such territories as economics, medicine, and psychology to offer its interpretations.

As sensibility, New Historicism views literature and history as essentially the same. Traditionally, a constructed history formed the stable backdrop against which unstable literary texts were read and interpreted. New Historicism abandons these distinctions between literature and history. It views both as story and involved in the fashioning of each other. Hence, distinctions between foreground and background, superstructure and substructure, cultural reality and mirror image no longer function to delineate the boundary between a story and its context. Instead, literature and social context are thought to reside in a dynamic relationship of mutual shaping and defining of one another. How literature impacts the construction of social context on the pages of history and how social context impacts the production of literature defines New Historicism's interests.

Finally, as sensibility, New Historicism presumes that all constructions of the past are intimately tied to the present. Thus, it resists hard and fast distinctions that separate now/then, author/reader, what the text meant/what the text means, and even composition/interpretation. All these long-standing categories that separate and reinforce distinctions between the past and present begin to erode in the New Historicist's view.

Antecedents of a New Historicism. Tracing the development of New Historicism crafts one of many stories that could be told about it. If an identifiable theoretical base could be established for the tenacious resistance to theory among New Historicists, it would most certainly be the work of Michel Foucault (Sheridan 1980). In the years immediately preceding its identification in the Department of English Literature of the University of California at Berkeley, Michel Foucault, a reluctant theorist himself, was a visiting professor there. Foucault laid the basis for a New Historicism with his emphasis on literature as discourse, his insistence on history as made up of numerous discourses, and his explorations of the relationship between discourse and power (Poster 1979, p. 93). New Historicists also manifest a theoretical kinship with Marx. The frequent preoccupation with struggle, contestation, and power relations in texts and the social processes that produced them suggests the Marxist influence (Althusser 1971, pp. 123–173; Eagleton 1976; Machery 1978). Moreover, this turn toward the social processes involved in a history's production suggests a great deal of anthropological torque. The influence of anthropologist Clifford Geertz and his approach to culture with "thick description" echoes resoundingly across essays by New Historicists (Geertz 1973, pp. 3–30). As Geertz studies culture as text, New Historicists study texts as culture.

Finally, this movement acknowledges the influence that feminists and voices of the tri-continental world (a term sometimes used to refer to Africa, Latin America, and Asia) have had in their persistent attention to articulated hierarchies of value and power resident in texts. These currents nudge New Historicism to attend to voices excluded from the texts. It investigates the fragmentary elements of a story. It takes seriously a passing comment of a character. It fixes its gaze upon unanswered questions and the places in the text that lack cohesion.

Consequently, as New Historicism gained momentum across the academic terrain of the 1980s, it hosted a range of practitioners that extended beyond the confines of departments of literature. It included those interested in feminism, Marxism, ethics and cultural studies, and history as well as literature. Though separated by different disciplines, what joined together this loose if not aberrant confederacy of critics was their return to history after a long exile and their lively production of a *new* historicism.

Recurring Features of a New Historicism. Unlike a method of interpretation, no blueprint or set of steps exists for how to proceed in conducting a New Historicist study of a biblical text. Still, the situation is not hopeless. In the New Historicist's studies on Renaissance literature several features recur often enough to suggest characteristic proclivities of the enterprise. Three of them are discussed here.

First, New Historicist studies frequently involve ways of reading and interpreting that look less at the center and more at the borders of a story or literary work. Instead of pursuing rhetorical integrity or literary unity, New Historicism attends to the cracks, the undersides, and signs of disarray latent in a work. Convinced that whole readings are but a self-satisfying illusion, New Historicism opts for more fragmentary kinds of considerations. Resisting the tendency to integrate dominant images, dialogues, and characters into a single master discourse, it attends to fleeting references, incongruities, or unanswered questions resident at the edges or margins of the text. For example, instead of focusing on whether King Josiah's religious reform (2 Kgs 24) was religiously grounded or politically motivated, New Historicism might wonder about the peasants who lost their jobs when the king ordered the dismantling of the local shrines. Instead of being captivated by the details of this king's centralization of cult, it would inquire about how hierarchical forms of power become the enabling conditions of such detailed representations. Attention to such borders often discloses a complicated past that resists the coherence of reigning historical reconstructions, while unaddressed questions lurking in the margins disrupt the artificial integrity of unified reading. Rather than producing an outcome that conforms to the monological tendencies of traditional historical or even literary interpretations, New Historicism uncovers "a past of competing voices, values and centers of power. . . ." (Rosenberg 1989, p. 376).

This focus on the edges or more fragmentary elements of a text leads easily to a second recurring feature—a focus on the tensions and struggles in text. New Historicism theorizes the relation between the material/political world on the one hand and the textual/representational world on the other and the way they closely and mutually fashion one another. Influenced by Foucault, New Historicism assumes a concept of discourse that comingles the linguistic, cultural, sociopolitical, and material realms. And it is within this comingling that echoes of struggle, contestations, and tension can be heard. All texts are caught up in the complex and contestatory processes by which a society defines and maintains its organization and its institutions, as well as its self-understanding. All societies are caught up in the struggles whereby one segment of culture defines itself as dominant. In the process, segments of culture construct discourses that distinguish themselves from a subservient segment defined as "the other."

For example, a story that celebrates a monarch's wisdom such as the tale of Solomon and the Two Mothers (1 Kgs 3:16–28) probably represents reality in a way that serves the interests of dominant culture. Girded with the gift of wisdom bestowed by none other than God, the king adjudicates between two women subjects arguing before him. In contrast to the one woman's frantic, wordy oration and the forensic deadlock evoked when both women speak, the king practices an economy of words. In Hebrew, his two-worded command, "Bring me the sword" (3:24), not only elicits immediate obedience but also ruptures the impasse of the women's wordy exchange. While the women speak more words than the king, his words count more in the story. While the women are portrayed as incapable of resolving their differences, the king dislodges the deadlock. Thus, this contrast in characterization between the women and the king suggests the tension. The depiction of these subjects as women and then as harlots contrasts sharply with and distances them from the depiction of the sovereign as male and as "wise king." Here, the biblical texts participate in constructing and reinforcing a version of reality that represents a dominant culture within which members of a subservient culture understand themselves. Furthermore, a New Historicist reading might inquire why the women here and elsewhere in the biblical tradition are depicted at odds with one another in stories that address and illustrate the sovereignty of kings, especially those whose rule is questionable (for example, Jehoram and the Two Cannibal Mothers 2 Kgs 6:24–33). Or to put it another way, New Historicists might inquire whether women working together pose a threat to maintaining the hierarchical elevation of sovereigns (Hens-Piazza 1998, pp. 91–104). But the struggle in the texts is not confined to the works themselves. Those who read, interpret, and preach the biblical texts down through the ages participate in these contestations.

Third, New Historicist studies are marked by their attention to the interests, voices, and forces that crisscross and rebound across cultures and across generations. New Historicism recognizes that the questions we ask of the past are invariably tied to the questions we ask about the present as we make our way toward the future. In fact, the crux of our orientation toward texts resides within this explicit entanglement of past, present, and future. Hence, New Historicism investigates the multitude of forces, the myriad of voices, the variety of interests and concerns that traverse and synapse along the continuum of history and within the web of culture. Attention to these exchanges as we read and write about the past in the present enables us to envision change in the future. As Daniel Boyarin notes, while we cannot change the past, we can change our understanding of the past. This in turn enables us to live differently in the present and "puts us on a trajectory of empowerment for transformation" for the future (Boyarin 1986, pp. 118–141).

With this orientation, biblical texts are not identified with one particular group or author in the past. Instead, they are viewed as acts of engagement with a vast and ever-changing reality made up of different and even opposing beliefs, values, biases, and investments. As representations of such a reality, a text both bears witness to, and is imprinted with, the complexity of its fashioning. When a text arrives in our lap, it bears the accumulation of effects from its own production as well as all of its former receptions. Needless to say, these two processes are difficult to separate. As the text moves across generations, cultures, and even religious traditions, it absorbs the amalgam of these influences. For example, as the tradition of the Exodus/Settlement in the Land has made its way across generations, it has narrated the liberation of the Israelites from bondage at one time, the early Christians' escape from the enemy of death at another, and most recently the release of Latin Americans from political oppressors. At the same time, it has attested to the terrible fate of the Canaanites, the anti-Judaic strands that helped fuel contempt for the Jews, and even the fate of the Native Americans in the face of Manifest Destiny.

Gradually, the complexity of these interchanges spans spatio-temporal webs of time, place, peoples, and culture in the ongoing production and reception of a text. Subjectivity in the production thus spills over into subjectivity in reception. This slippage not only obscures the distinction between production and reception but also between text and reader and between past and present.

Perils and Prospects of a New Historicism. For some, the machinations of a New Historicism and other such orientations (Post Modernism, Cultural Studies, etc.) signal perils. Collapsing the distinction between the world of the text and the world of the reader risks abandoning the long hallowed distinction between "what the text meant" and "what the text means." It allows for the comingling of what some still assume to be the objective investigation of historical studies with the subjective bias of the reader's contemporality. It risks tainting the exegesis of the text with what might become an exegesis of the reader and the reader's context.

For others, the perils of a New Historicism lie in the boundaryless disciplinary horizons of inquiry that such an orientation allows. Instead of confining history's lens to matters of the past and its constructions, a New Historicism risks broadening the scope of investigation to include such questions as: Whose history does criticism relate? What transactions take place in the ancient and contemporary context in history's production? How does that history get told? Who is empowered to do the telling? What changes in the social fabric does biblical studies effect or fail to effect? For those who sense peril on the horizon of a New Historicism, anything beyond a one-dimensional totalizing explanation of history, context, or even the biblical text itself becomes suspect.

Unlike the justifications for the rise of many new methods or approaches, the prospects and interests in New Historicism do not stem from the assessment of how past and current methods have failed. The harvest from traditional historical methods and the harvest from the variety of literary approaches in biblical studies have been richly successful. But as the parameters of individual historical methods are defined and the theoretical boundaries of newer literary and cultural approaches are sketched, the gap between these two arenas widens. The possibility of arriving at an integrated grasp of our subject fades. Synchronic approaches seem at odds with diachronic methods. A focus on context contrasts with a focus on text. Literary analysis frequently involves setting aside the research and conclusions of historical critics. Different approaches to interpretation engender polarization as to the determinacy or indeterminacy of meaning. While such disagreements can be productive, they can also encourage fragmentation. Methodological specialization in biblical studies often seems to have bred methodological ghettos. Even during this first decade of the twenty-first century, biblical studies still appears to be a profession of specialists, refining and defending their methods, parsing these sophisticated approaches further into subspecialties.

Along with other newer orientations, New Historicism resists such specialization. It crosses boundaries separating the different disciplinary specializations and ignores the dividing line between the world of the text and the world of the reader. It invites critics to address the political consequences, economic ramifications, social functions, and the ethical import of the texts in both their historical and their contemporary contexts. It assumes that any social historical construction that one might compose is not only founded upon a production of the past but also resulting in a production about and by a reader. Consequently, such a construction must be seen in relation to the ancient writing and the contemporary reading as well as the ideological and institutional agendas that lie behind the writing and the reading practices.

One final explanation looms large explaining the appeal and the need for a New Historicism. Whether in the biblical guild or at the level of the institutions where biblical studies is taught—colleges, universities, communities, seminaries—a sea change has taken place in how business is conducted. The homogenous character of these institutions has all but vanished. Under the banner of cultural diversity, the curricula, pedagogy, administrative models, and even financial packages have had to undergo major renovation. Globalization has given way to world systems, world economy, global frames of knowledge, and a demand for new ways of knowing and understanding. The emphasis on specialization has been supplanted by the urgent need to prepare persons to participate in this global setting. Educational institutions themselves have become "markets of exchange." Whether engaged in the study of complex moral issues, questions of doctrine, or a challenging biblical passage, students are constantly exchanging information across national, ethnic, cultural, sexual, and class borders and attending to the cultural transactions at the heart of these exercises. Instead of mastering a specialized pool of knowledge, students learn how religious knowledge transmutes into forms of political power and back again. In concert with appreciating the biblical text as a confessional or an aesthetic work, students must learn how these texts can also function as oppressive or hegemonic forces.

The appeal of a New Historicism in biblical studies is thus more than the product of a theoretical argument in literary studies. Rather, its rise is seeded by changes in the very institutions where it is being practiced. Exchange and negotiation across the cultural histories and identities of seminary and university population concerning the very cultural histories and identities in the biblical writings are at the heart of our efforts. We cannot do otherwise in a world where boundary crossing has become requisite not only for economics, politics, and communication, but for ministry, for biblical and theological understandings, and for knowledge itself.

Conclusions. Described here as a sensibility, New Historicism motivates a reclaiming of history but with an awareness of the entanglements of the present embedded in every account of the past. Literature, as a medium for this return to the historical, is scrutinized as a site of struggle both in its production and in its reception. This rivets attention upon the diverse and contentious rather than upon the uniform and coherent within texts. For example in the programmatic tale of Abraham and the Three Visitors at Mamre (Gen 18:1–16), New Historicism might fix upon the question left unanswered in that narrative, "Why did Sarah laugh?" In the account of Solomon's business dealings with Hiram, it might turn attention away from these major players and wonder about the residents of the towns that were given away by this king in exchange for bronze and gold (1 Kgs 9:10–14). In the conflict between kings and prophets, it investigates the passing mention of those very minor characters, for example servants, laborers, virgins, daughters, the crowd, and others whose stories are never told. In the process, New Historicism discloses the widest variety of ways for speaking about the past as well as accommodates the greatest number of possible strategies for conducting these orations. Along these lines, New Historicism not only charts new territory but shares this space as common ground with other movements within and outside the biblical field. Feminist studies, postcolonial studies, cultural studies, and ideological investigations partake in some of New Historicism's interests and strategies, as well as approach texts with similar sets of assumptions. Moreover, they define themselves more readily as orientations rather than codified methods that objectively operate on texts.

Resisting the fracturing that has so characterized the biblical field, New Historicism refuses identification with any method or even any explication of itself as method. Understanding the complexity of the past, New Historicism resists any historicizing of itself that would tie it solely to any one theoretical base or align itself with a single founding figure and his or her work. Aside from a fairly fluid litany of recurring features, New Historicism provides no creed for its practitioners to avow. And as those working with Renaissance studies would readily affirm, New Historicism's overarching feature is its resistance to definition.

So is New Historicism a mirage? Or is it, in all its variety and non-specificity, a refreshing and optimistic commentary about a growing shift both in the academy and in biblical studies—a shift away from the splintering of methodological specialization that has so characterized the discipline over the past century? As noted, New Historicism readily shares concerns and features with other taxonomies. And while it practices a discourse analysis of literature bent on emancipating voices, highlighting overlooked people and practices, and producing other histories, it seems not to expend much discussion distinguishing itself from these other movements.

No, New Historicism is no mirage. Rather the appeal for a New Historicism in biblical studies at this juncture is symptomatic of another condition. Biblical studies itself is becoming a montage with New Historicism as part of the display. Across this postmodern manifestation of interpretive practices, a growing number of critics have become less interested in distinguishing and defending what they do from the work of other critics. Abandoning the high degree of specialization, they are more interested in crossing methodological and disciplinary borders. They are producing hybrid studies. And while their participation in this market of exchange results in an ever-increasing number of lenses with which to read and interpret the biblical text, they find themselves united not so much by a sameness in their outcomes or methods as by a growing consensus about what they are up to.

Increasingly, critics working on the biblical texts have begun to recognize and claim the political import of what they do when they interpret texts. They understand that there are social consequences tied to the outcomes of their work. Hence, a commitment to work in biblical studies increasingly enjoins a commitment to social change on the part of those who would participate in this practice. Given the recognized influence of the Bible on culture in the past and in the present, a cadre of critics (whether practitioners of New Historicism, postcolonial studies, feminist studies, cultural studies, and so on) determined to be influential on humanity's future by virtue of what they do with these texts in the present is not a bad prospect for the next era in biblical studies.

[*See also* Class Criticism; Cultural-Historical Criticism; Cultural Studies; Diachronic Interpretation; Feminist Biblical Interpretation; Historical Criticism, *subentry* Hebrew Bible; Historical Criticism, *subentry* New Testament; Ideological Criticism; Literary Criticism, Literary Theory, and the Bible; Materialist Criticism; Narrative Criticism and Narrative Hermeneutics; Postcolonial Biblical Interpretation; Postmodern Interpretation; Race, Ethnicity, and Biblical Criticism; Rhetorical Criticism; *and* Synchronic Interpretation.]

BIBLIOGRAPHY

Althusser, Louis. "Ideological State Apparatuses." *Lenin and Philosophy and Other Essays.* Translated by Ben Brewster. New York: Monthly Review Press, 1971.

Boyarin, Daniel. "*Carnal Israel: Reading Sex in Talmudic Culture.*" In *The New Historicism: Studies in Cultural Poetics* 25. Berkeley: University of California Press, 1993.

Boyarin, Daniel. "Rabbinic Resistance to Male Domination: A Case Study in Talmudic Cultural Poetics." In *Interpreting Judaism in a Postmodern Age*, edited by Steven Kepnes, 118–141. New York: New York University Press, 1996.

Eagleton, Terry. *Criticism and Ideology: A Study in Marxist Literary Theory.* London: New Left Books, 1976.

Gallagher, Catherine, and Stephen Greenblatt. *Practicing New Historicism.* Chicago: University of Chicago Press, 2000.

Geertz, Clifford. "Thick Description: Toward an Interpretive Theory of Culture." *The Interpretation of Cultures.* New York: Basic Books, 1973.

Greenblatt, Stephen. *Learning to Curse: Essays in Early Modern Culture.* New York: Routledge, 1990.

Greenblatt, Stephen. *Renaissance Self-Fashioning: From More to Shakespeare.* Chicago: University of Chicago Press, 1980.

Greenblatt, Stephen, ed. *Forms of Power and the Power of Forms.* Norman, Okla.: Pilgrim, 1982.

Hens-Piazza, Gina, "Forms of Violence and the Violence of Forms: Two Cannibal Mothers before a King (2 Kgs 6:24–33)," *Journal of Feminist Studies in Religion* 14, no. 1 (1998): 91–104.

Hens-Piazza, Gina. *The New Historicism.* Guides to Biblical Scholarship: Old Testament Series. Minneapolis: Augsburg Fortress, 2002.

Machery, Pierre. *A Theory of Literary Production.* Translated by Geoffrey Wall. London: Routledge & Kegan Paul, 1978.

McCanles, Michael. "The Authentic Discourse of the Renaissance," *Diacritics* 10 (1980): 85.

Montrose, Louis. "Renaissance Literary Studies and the Subject of History," *English Literary Renaissance* 16 (1986): 5–12.

Moore, Stephen D., ed. "Biblical Studies and the New Historicism," *Biblical Interpretation* 5:4 (thematic issue), 1997.

Patterson, Lee, ed. *Literary Practice and Social Change in Britain, 1380–1530.* Berkeley: University of California Press, 1990.

Poster, Mark. "The Future According to Foucault: The Archaeology of Knowledge and Intellectual History." In *Modern European Intellectual History: Reappraisals and New Perspectives*, edited by Dominick LaCapra and Steven L. Kaplan. Ithaca, N.Y.: Cornell University Press, 1979.

Powell, Mark Allan. *The Bible and Modern Literary Criticism: A Critical Assessment and Annotated Bibliography.* New York: Greenwood, 1992.

Rosenberg, Brian. "Historicizing the New Historicism: Understanding the Past in Criticism and Fiction," *Modern Language Quarterly* 50 (1989): 375–392.

Schipper, Jeremy. *Disability Studies and the Hebrew Bible: Figuring Mephibosheth in the David Story.* London: T&T Clark, 2006.

Sheridan, Alan. *Michel Foucault: The Will to Truth.* London: Tavistock, 1980.

Sherwood, Yvonne. *A Biblical Text and Its Afterlives: The Survival of Jonah in Western Culture.* Cambridge, UK: Cambridge University Press, 2000.

Veeser, H. Aram, ed. *The New Historicism.* New York: Routledge, 1989.

Gina Hens-Piazza

O

Orality Studies and Oral Tradition

[*This entry contains two subentries,* Hebrew Bible *and* New Testament]

Hebrew Bible

The study of oral traditions has been influenced by various schools, including the "ethnopoetics" of Dell Hymes and Dennis Tedlock, the study of orality and literacy by Walter Ong and Jack Goody, and the study of living oral traditions and orally derived texts by Milman Parry and Albert Lord. Of these, the most influential in biblical studies has been the Parry/Lord approach.

Nineteenth century classists argued over the Homeric question—that is, whether the *Iliad* and the *Odyssey* were written by one Homer (the Unitarians) or many Homers (the Analysts). The Analysts had philology on their side, because Homer's language contained grammatical forms from multiple historical periods, suggesting multiple redactions.

In the 1920s and 1930s, Parry entered this debate with a compromise that accepted the Analysts' philological arguments but argued with the Unitarians that the Homeric epics could be composed by a single individual. His initial insight came from the fieldwork of Vasilii Radlov with the Turkic traditions of Central Asia, which suggested that the Homeric question could be addressed not only by textual study but also by comparative study with living oral traditions. Thus, in 1934–1935 Parry and his student Lord visited the former Yugoslavia and recorded performances by Serbo-Croatian *guslari.* Their fieldwork demonstrated that the traditional idiom used by these oral bards included both archaisms and neologisms, thereby undercutting the argument for multiple redactions.

After Parry's death in 1935, Lord refined Parry's work and applied it to other literature, including *Beowulf,* the *Song of Roland,* and the Bible. Lord defined formulas as "a group of words which is regularly employed under the same metrical conditions to express a given essential idea" (1960, p. 30). Lord also defined themes as "groups of ideas regularly used in telling a tale in the formulaic style of traditional song" (p. 68)—for example, preparing for battle. With these basic observations—formula and theme—the Parry/Lord approach to orally derived literature demonstrated that the type of formulaic language found in, for example, the decasyllable of Homer or the alliterative verse of *Beowulf* could be composed orally.

The foremost successor to Parry and Lord is John Miles Foley. Foley has written the definitive history of the school, five other monographs, and numerous articles and essays. He has edited and translated a performance of a Serbo-Croatian epic. He has encouraged the use of the Parry/Lord approach in other areas of literature and has refined earlier understandings of formulas and themes. For example, in *Teaching Oral Traditions*, he included essays by scholars in the following living oral traditions: Native American, African, Hispanic, Jewish, Indian, Chinese, Japanese, Arabic, South Slavian, and British American, as well as essays by scholars in the following textual traditions with "roots in oral tradition": the Hebrew Bible, New Testament, Homer, *Beowulf*, Chaucer, Middle English, Old French, the Icelandic sagas, and medieval frame narratives. A greater diversity is evident in the journal *Oral Tradition*, which he founded in 1986 and edited until his recent death. Foley has had a significant impact in biblical studies. He has directed three National Endowment for the Humanities Summer Seminars that have included biblical scholars as participants; he has participated in annual meetings of the Society of Biblical Literature; he coedited a *Festschrift* for Werner Kelber (Horsley, Draper, and Foley 2006); and he edited the Blackwell *Companion to Ancient Epic*.

One significant revision that the increased comparative work has required is a rejection of "the Great Divide thesis." Based on early studies of orality versus literacy—for example, Ong's *Orality and Literacy*—many scholars imagined a tremendous gulf between orality and literacy. It was as if, when an oral epic was written down, it was completely removed from its traditional culture, never again to be influenced by that culture, and even the earliest readers of this new text were ignorant of its traditional culture. Furthermore, it was as if the very act of writing changed the idiom of oral discourse. More recent studies, however, discuss an oral-literate continuum, thereby narrowing the supposed gap between oral and literate cultures, especially as it relates to the interaction of orality and literacy in transitional cultures like ancient Greece and medieval Europe (Clancy 1979; Stock 1983; Thomas 1989). Therefore, not only can the traditional idioms of orally composed epics be preserved in dictated texts, but also texts that are produced in a scribal environment removed from oral performance can nevertheless be influenced by the traditional oral idioms. In fact, the traditional idioms can continue to influence the texts after their composition—that is, during their scribal transmission. Thus, although some earlier studies assumed that the mere presence of formulas and themes strongly suggested oral composition, this assumption has been widely abandoned (Foley 1990, pp. 3–5).

Oral Tradition and the Hebrew Bible. The most influential early applications of the Parry/Lord approach to the Hebrew Bible can be found in the work of Robert Culley, Robert Coote, and David Gunn (see Culley 1986). Although some biblical scholars have too easily succumbed to the "Great Divide thesis" (for example, Polak 1998), Culley, Coote, and Gunn were somewhat more cautious. More recent studies extend this more cautious approach with regard to the value of formulas and themes as evidence of oral origins and rather begin with the growing consensus that ancient societies were primarily oral societies in which writing was limited to a small elite. Thus, within primarily oral societies, even written texts were produced within the framework of those oral societies—that is, written texts drew from the oral aesthetics of the society and were often mnemonic aids. These studies are informed by archaeological studies and comparative studies that strongly suggest that writing in ancient Israel was not widespread and that for the vast majority of ancient Israelites the act of learning to read and write would have been far too costly (for example, Jamieson-Drake 1991; van der Toorn 2007). When one starts from this position, one begins to understand the composition, transmission, and reception of ancient texts quite differently. Below, the work of four scholars who have made significant contributions to discussions concerning oral traditions and the Hebrew Bible in the last twenty years—Susan Niditch, Raymond Person, David Carr, and Martti Nissinen—will be summarized.

Susan Niditch. Niditch earned her doctorate at Harvard, where she studied under Lord. Her two most significant contributions are her 1996 monograph *Oral World and Written Word* and her 2008 *Judges* commentary.

In *Oral World and Written Word*, Niditch provided a nuanced argument for understanding all Israelite writing within the context of a primarily oral society.

> Our position throughout this study is not that ancient Israelites knew little of writing, but rather that Israelite literacy in form and function is not to be confused with modern literacy and that ancient Israelite literacy has to be understood in the context of an oral-traditional culture. Literacy and orality are part of an ongoing continuum even in the latest biblical period. (1996, p. 99)

She drew from comparative studies of literacy in the ancient world and discussed how the logistics of writing—that is, archives, education, and writing materials—strongly suggested that few Israelites were literate. Although she concluded that we cannot prove that any particular biblical text was composed orally, she nevertheless insisted that all biblical texts belong within an "oral register"—that is, regardless of the mode of composition, biblical texts were composed under the influence of the dominant oral traditional style. Thus, "an oral aesthetic infuses the Hebrew Scripture as it now stands" (1996, p. 24). This oral traditional style is evident in the use of repetition, formulas, and conventionalized patterns, which she illustrated with Genesis 1, Genesis 2—3, and Ezekiel 28.

Niditch explored what she considered to be at the literate end of the continuum—that is, the references to writing in Deuteronomy 6:4–9; Deuteronomy 17:14–20; 2 Kings 23; selected passages in Jeremiah; and Nehemiah 8—and still concluded that an oral aesthetic was present.

> Thus even at the literate end of the continuum, the oral mentality is present and active, informing the way writing is used. Exploring the interplay between orality and literacy is essential to understanding the social contexts of reading and writing in a traditional culture. (1996, p. 98)

Niditch acknowledged that understanding ancient Israel as a primarily oral society "forces us to question long-respected theories about the development of the Israelite literary traditions preserved in the Bible" (1996, p. 134)—especially source criticism. As a proposal to understanding better "the genesis of the Hebrew Bible," she proposed four models:

> (1) the oral performance, which is dictated to a writer who preserves the text in an archive, creating a fixed text out of an event;
> (2) the slow crystallization of a pan-Hebraic literary tradition through many performances over centuries of increasingly pan-Israelite tales to audiences with certain expectations and assumptions about shared group identity; late in the process authors write down the shared stories;
> (3) a written imitation of oral-style literature to create portions of the tradition;
> (4) the production of a written text that is excerpted from another written text by a writer who deftly edits or recasts the text in accordance with his own view of Israelite identity. (1996, p. 130)

For the majority of "the large narrative threads" she preferred model 2, the slow crystallization of oral performances (1996, p. 127). However, she noted that even those texts composed according to model 4—that is, based on a written *Vorlage*—nevertheless reflect the oral traditional style. For example, even though Chronicles is a late rewriting of Samuel–Kings and despite their multiple variants, the tradition preserves both works in their multiformity.

Niditch's *Judges* commentary is the first commentary that reflects a concerted effort to apply the Parry/Lord approach. She wrote:

> The present commentary . . . offers an exciting opportunity to study closely one rich collection of biblical tales from the perspective of the field of early and oral literatures. The conviction that Judges reflects a traditional-style culture has important implications for the way one goes about doing a commentary, touching upon text-critical approaches, translation, format, and the exegesis itself. (2008, p. vii)

In her introduction, she laid out the implications for how this perspective influenced her analysis and the format of her commentary. For example, rather than describing the redaction history of Judges in the standard manner, she identified three voices: the "epic-bardic voice" (pre-Deuteronomistic sources), the "voice of the theologian" (Deuteronomistic redactors), and the "voice of the humanist" (post-Deuteronomistic). She also included a brief but excellent discussion of "epic language" (for example, "And it was in those days" and "And it was in the days of X") and the oral-traditional register in Judges.

Throughout the commentary itself, Niditch provided insights from oral traditional studies. For example, in her discussion of the Song of Deborah (Judg 5), she wrote:

> The style of the song is characterized by parallel constructions typical of the most poetic of Israelite literature, with oral-style variation upon formulaic expressions and phrases, the use of an economical or limited vocabulary, and frequent chant-like refrains. (2008, p. 77)

Niditch ended her commentary with a second English translation, this one much more literal, even to the point of preserving the verb-subject word order of the Hebrew. Her division of the verses into lines also appears to be influenced by the ethnopoetics of Tedlock by dividing the verses up into smaller units of meaning, thereby attempting more accurately to reflect the oral register of the Hebrew text.

Raymond Person. Person participated in the National Endowment for the Humanities Summer Institute directed by John Miles Foley in 1992. His significant contributions are his 1998 *Journal of Biblical Literature* article "The Ancient Israelite Scribe as Performer," his 2002 monograph *The Deuteronomic School*, and his 2010 monograph *The Deuteronomic History and the Book of Chronicles*.

In "The Ancient Israelite Scribe as Performer," Person concluded as follows:

> The ancient Israelite scribes were literate members of a primarily oral society. As members of a primarily oral society, they undertook even their literate activity—that is, the copying of texts—with an oral mindset. When they copied their texts, the ancient Israelite scribes did not slavishly write the texts word by word, but preserved the texts' meaning for the on-going life of their communities in much the same way that performers of oral epic re-present the stable, yet dynamic, tradition to their communities. In this sense, the ancient Israelite scribes were not mere copyists, but were also performers. (1998, p. 602)

As support for this conclusion, he reflected on the definition of "word" in oral traditions in contrast to our modern notion and then examined selected text critical variants. When he asked "What is a word?" he found answers in both the Serbo-Croatian tradition and in the semantic range of the Hebrew word *dabar*. Within Serbo-Croatian epic, a word is understood as a line, a stanza, or even the entire epic. The semantic range of the Hebrew word *dabar* can be translated as "word" but also "speech" and "utterance." Thus, what the ancient Israelites understood as a "word" included much more than what we moderns typically understand as a "word." Even if the scribes did not copy their texts "word for word" from our perspective, from their perspective they very well may have copied them "word for word."

Person then turned to a discussion of text critical variants, beginning with "synonymous readings"—for example, "against this place" (2 Kgs 18:25) and "against this land" (Isa 36:10). He then discussed the type of common variants found between Masoretic Text (MT) of Jeremiah and Septuagint (LXX) of Jeremiah (the MT pluses are given in italics): such as "And Jeremiah *the prophet* said to Hananiah *the prophet*"(Jer 28:5), "Baruch *son of Neriah*" (Jer 36:8), and "Thus says the Lord *of Hosts, God of Israel*" (Jer 29:21). He noted that what the ancients understood as "word for word" may allow for this kind of multiformity—for example, the reading "Jeconiah" (LXX Jer 28:4) and "Jeconiah, *son of Jehoiakim, king of Judah*" (MT Jer 28:4) may be understood as the same "word," since both clearly refer to the same individual.

In *The Deuteronomic School*, Person understood the redactional process behind the Deuteronomic History as one that introduced numerous "changes" (that is, from our modern perspective) each time the text was copied by the Deuteronomic scribes as performers, a process that continued into the Persian period. He included a survey of scribes and scribal schools in the ancient Near East as an analogy to the Deuteronomic school as a scribal guild. He then provided fresh readings of selected passages in the Deuteronomic History in the Persian period.

In *The Deuteronomic History and the Book of Chronicles*, Person extended his earlier arguments to critique the consensus model of the relationship between Samuel–Kings and Chronicles—that is, the idea that Chronicles is a late rewriting of the earlier tradition, with Samuel–Kings as its main exilic source. That is, if the redaction of the Deuteronomic History extended into the Persian period, the consensus model required reassessment and was found insufficient. As an alternative, he imagined both Samuel–Kings and Chronicles as contemporary historiographies descended from a common source produced by the same exilic scribal guild—that is, the Deuteronomic school. With the return to Jerusalem under Zerubbabel, the scribal guild divided into two groups: the Deuteronomic school in Yehud and the Chronistic school in Babylonia. With the return of Ezra, the two schools came into contact with each other, eventually leading to the demise of the Deuteronomic school as a scribal institution.

Based on his survey of both the Deuteronomic History and Chronicles–Ezra–Nehemiah, Person concluded that the portrayal of scribes and writing in these works strongly supports Niditch's notion of the interplay between orality and literacy. He then discussed multiformity as an important characteristic in oral traditions and literary texts with roots in primarily oral cultures. Such multiformity is found within the Deuteronomic History (for example, between the MT and LXX versions of the story of David and Goliath in 1 Sam 16–18) and the book of Chronicles (for example, the various source citations, many [if not all] of which probably refer to the same source). He noted that the idea of multiformity in oral traditions parallels well the notion of textual plurality in text criticism, especially in Julio Trebolle's assertion of "the co-existence of parallel editions" (2006, p. 98). He then discussed the multiformity between Samuel–Kings and Chronicles in both the synoptic and non-synoptic material.

Drawing from the work of memory in oral traditions, including that of Carr, Person concluded that, despite their apparent differences, these two contemporary historiographies from competing scribal schools nevertheless faithfully represent the broader tradition.

> In an oral tradition, no one performance can be understood as the primary authoritative performance that must be replicated verbatim. All performances are simply one instantiation of the tradition, such that past and future performances may represent more or less of the tradition but none of them can alone represent the tradition in its fullness. Likewise, no one text in a primarily oral society can fully represent the broader tradition in its fullness. Therefore, no one text is determinant for future texts. In a primarily oral society a constant interplay between literary texts and the broader oral tradition preserved in the community's memory occurs. Thus, co-existing parallel editions of texts, despite their apparent differences, can nevertheless equally re-present the tradition, and the broader tradition is best understood by the collective re-presentation of the texts in all of their multiformity. (2010, p. 169–170)

Thus, for example, even the "unique" readings in Samuel–Kings and Chronicles may faithfully represent the broader tradition in ways that those in the competing scribal guild may still find acceptable.

> We must, therefore, practice great caution when reconstructing theological differences on the basis of what from our modern perspective are variant readings but what may be from the ancient perspective a faithful representation of the tradition. (2010, p. 170)

Thus, he concluded that his study had implications for how the composition, transmission, and reception of biblical texts in general should be imagined. We must avoid the assumption of a unilinear process with one definitive, original text. Rather we must take seriously the textual plurality of the extant texts and understand this plurality with reference to the characteristic of multiformity as found in primarily oral societies.

David Carr. Carr's most significant contributions are his 2005 monograph, *Writing on the Tablet of the Heart*, and his 2011 monograph, *The Formation of the Hebrew Bible: A New Reconstruction.*

In *Writing on the Tablet of the Heart*, Carr drew extensively from comparative data. He provided chapters on ancient Mesopotamia, ancient Egypt, and ancient Greece as precursors and/or contemporary cultures to ancient Israel and chapters on Hellenistic culture in Egypt, Israel, and the Jewish Diaspora as later comparands. He concluded that "many ancient texts were not written in such a way that they could be read easily by someone who did not already know them well" (2005, p. 4). Many manuscripts have no spacing between the words. The Mesopotamian cuneiform, Egyptian hieratic script, and the consonant-only Semitic alphabets are limited in their representation of how the texts should be pronounced, thereby requiring a high degree of familiarity with their content. In fact, an early Hebrew manuscript (Oxford Ms Heb e 30) provides the first word of each verse and then simply the first letter of subsequent words in that verse. Thus, he concluded,

> [T]his element of visual presentation of texts is but one indicator of the distinctive function of written copies of long-duration texts like the Bible, Gilgamesh, or Homer's works. The visual presentation of such texts presupposed that the reader already knew the given text and had probably memorized it to some extent. (2005, p. 5)

Carr then concluded that these texts were composed and transmitted in educational settings in which they were used as mnemonic aids for the internalization of the tradition.

> [S]uch written copies were a subsidiary part of a much broader literate matrix, where the focus was as much or more on the transmission of texts from mind to mind as on transmission of texts in written form. Both writing and oral performance fed into the process of indoctrination/education/enculturation. (2005, p. 5)

Since texts were used as a means of teaching oral recitation, "written texts are intensely oral" (2005, p. 7). "Orality and writing technology are joint means for accomplishing a common goal: accurate recall of the treasured tradition" (2005, p. 7).

When he discussed education, Carr noted that, due to various forms of evidence, the educational system in which these texts would have been used would be limited to a small minority of elites. Epigraphic data and the material conditions of writing as well as the biblical portrayal of writing and reading as belonging to the realm of literate professionals all suggest that the majority of ancient Israelites were illiterate, having no formal education. He illustrated this by his reading of various texts, especially in wisdom literature and the Deuteronomistic History. Being literate primarily meant more than the ability to read or write; it meant having "an oral-written mastery of a body of texts" (2005, p. 13)—that is, the kind of formal education limited to elites. However, even the literati approached texts differently from educated modern Westerners.

> Rather than juggling multiple scrolls or having one scribe take dictation from two or three others, this model suggests that Israelite scribes most likely would have drawn on their verbatim memory of other texts in quoting, borrowing from, or significantly revising them. Of course, as in other cultures, Israelite scribes probably visually copied certain texts that they wished to reproduce precisely. Yet, as in other cultures, Israelite scribes probably did not work with cumbersome scrolls when they needed to produce something new, something not bearing the claim of being a precise visual copy of an earlier document. (2005, p. 161)

Carr extended his earlier arguments on memory in *The Formation of the Hebrew Bible*. He introduced the term "memory variants," which are "the sort of variants that happen when a tradent modifies elements of texts in the process of citing or otherwise reproducing it from memory" (2011, p. 17) such as "exchange of synonymous words, word order variation, [and] presence and absence of conjunctions and minor modifiers" (2011, p. 33). He provided numerous examples from the Gilgamesh epic, the Temple Scroll, parallels between Samuel–Kings and Chronicles, and parallel proverbs.

Carr undertook various case studies of "documented cases of transmission history" such as the Gilgamesh epic and the Temple Scroll in order to provide a more empirically based model of transmission. He concluded that "three main trends of revision" are evident:

> (1) ancient scholars who were producing a new version of an ancient tradition (or portion of an ancient tradition) either preserved it unchanged (aside from memory or graphic variants) or expanded it. . . .
> (2) Conversely . . . ancient scribes rarely appropriated earlier compositions in their entirety. In particular, they often eliminated their beginning and/or end in the process of strategically redirecting them. . . .
> (3) the tendency of many ancient scholars to harmonize and/or otherwise coordinate ancient written traditions with themselves and other texts. (2011, pp. 99–100)

Carr noted that from the perspective of the ancients such revisions are meant to preserve the tradition.

> In cases of memory variants, the shifts probably were seen as reproductions of what was essentially the "same" tradition. In cases of harmonization/coordination, the tradition was being made more true to itself. In cases of expansion, the bulk of the tradition was preserved, but enriched through additional exclusively oral traditions, theological updates, and other elements perceived as enhancements to the sacred deposit of more ancient material. (2011, p. 100)

Carr's methodological reflections led him to conclude that much of the past and present scholarly consensus concerning the formation of the Hebrew Bible must be revised, especially when such models posit the isolation of multiple redactional layers. The bulk of the volume then contains his "modest" but systematic reconstruction of the formation of the Hebrew Bible, working backwards from the Hasmonean period to the tenth and ninth centuries. Most of his reconstructions closely follow earlier more traditional approaches, although reaching more minimalistic conclusions. Notable exceptions are his dating of Proverbs, Qoheleth, and Song of Songs to the early monarchal period.

Martti Nissinen. Nissinen has established himself as one of the top scholars concerning the comparative study of prophecy in the ancient Near East. He has edited the 2003 collection of primary sources in English translation, *Prophets and Prophecy in the Ancient Near East*, and a related 2000 collection of essays, *Prophecy in Its Ancient Near Eastern Context*, as well as authored a variety of essays and articles. Although he may not be familiar with the Parry/Lord approach directly, he has accepted many of the conclusions of Niditch and Carr.

Nissinen defined prophecy as containing four elements: the divine sender, the message, the messenger/prophet, and the recipient. Thus, the prophetic process consists of two phases: the transfer of the message from the divine being to the prophet and the transfer of the message from the prophet to the recipient. Furthermore, the prophetic process was a communal event that often occurred within institutional settings, especially temples. He concluded as follows:

> [A]ncient Near Eastern prophecy was basically oral performance, that is, delivery of verbal messages spoken by a prophet. The message could be transmitted orally by one or several go-betweens all the way through, from prophet to destination. Occasionally, but never quite systematically, the spoken word ended up in written form, for different purposes and under varying circumstances. Writing was used, not only as an aid for memory, but also either (a) to make the divine message communicable if the addressee was not reachable by means of oral communication, or (b) to preserve the oracles for posterity, thus enabling its subsequent quotation and interpretation. (2000b, p. 268)

These two uses of writing are illustrated well in the Mari letters, which contain reports of prophetic oracles to the king, and the Neo-Assyrian prophetic collections, which were probably compiled from other written records.

In "How Prophecy Became Literature" Nissinen dealt with the Hebrew Bible and how an oral phenomenon like prophecy became a unique genre of literature—that is, "[t]he Hebrew Bible forms a special case, since it includes the only extant collection of prophetic books, a genre otherwise unknown in the ancient Near East" (2005, p. 172). He asserted that prophecy was a strictly oral phenomenon.

> From the point of view of the process of communication, . . . the communication was considered finished when the message was received and heard. (2005, p. 169)

Anything beyond that must be considered interpretation of the prophetic message.

> The physical restrictions alone—the writing speed, the dimensions of the writing material, etc.—prevented the verbatim memorization of the spoken words of the prophet, and this was not even attempted. Hence, and according to the usual laws of communication, the interpretation began immediately when the word came out of the prophet's mouth. (2005, p. 169)

Nissinen distinguished between "ancient Hebrew prophecy"—that is, the phenomenon of prophecy behind the literature—and "Biblical prophecy"—that is, the biblical portrayal of prophecy. Although "ancient Hebrew prophecy" was an oral phenomenon, "Biblical prophecy" included a greater use of written texts—for example, references to the prophets themselves as writers (Isa 8:16; 30:8; Hab 2:2). He rejected such portrayals of literate prophets—at least as a general phenomenon—and he suggested that Jeremiah 36 provides a more "historical" perspective concerning how prophecy became literature, even though his interpretation does not require the historicity of the specific events narrated in the passage.

In Jeremiah 36, God tells Jeremiah to write a scroll of prophecy. Jeremiah dictates the prophetic oracles to the scribe Baruch, who writes the scroll and then reads it aloud in the temple. When he receives the scroll, King Jehoiakim rejects its contents and burns the scroll. God then commands Jeremiah to write another scroll with all of the earlier content plus much more. Nissinen noted that this passage illuminates the literarization of prophecy in four ways. First, the reason for the writing of the prophecy is religiopolitical—"It may be that when the house of Judah hears of all the disasters that I [God] intend to do to them, all of them may turn from their evil ways, so that I may forgive their iniquity and their sin" (Jer 36:3). Second, it suggests that even some prophecies that were written down may have been judged to be false and were therefore destroyed. Third, the prophets did not write down their own prophecies, but professional scribes were involved. Fourth, it hints at the redactional process of the prophetic books themselves, including rewritings with additional materials. Thus, he concluded, "Irrespective of its historicity, then, the story . . . serves as a paragon for the emergence and legitimation of the prophetic books" (2005, p. 164). He also concluded that, like the Neo-Assyrian collections, the story suggests that the redactors of the prophetic books probably had sources from archives.

Nissinen considered the proposal that materials from the ancient Hebrew prophets may have been preserved orally by their disciples. Especially since there is no comparative evidence for the oral transmission of prophetic materials or such prophetic schools, he remained skeptical of the proposal.

> As it is easier to assume than to prove, the assumption of oral transmission may be used as an emergency solution to circumvent some difficult historical questions concerning the prophetic origin of the texts. (2005, p. 172)

Noting that prophecy in the ancient Near East was located in temples, he concluded that ancient Hebrew prophecy occurred in institutional settings.

> If there were oral prophetic traditions, their carrier groups must have been close enough to the literate circles to have their traditions accepted into the corpus of authoritative literature. (2005, p. 172)

Here Nissinen hinted at a possible interplay between the oral and written in the preservation of prophetic oracles, even though he preferred written preservation of an oral phenomenon.

[*See also* Folklore and Biblical Interpretation; *and* Orality Studies and Oral Tradition, *subentry* New Testament.]

BIBLIOGRAPHY

Carr, David M. *The Formation of the Hebrew Bible: A New Reconstruction*. Oxford: Oxford University Press, 2011.

Carr, David M. *Writing on the Tablet of the Heart: Origins of Scripture and Literature*. Oxford: Oxford University Press, 2005.

Clancy, M. T. *From Memory to Written Record: England, 1066–1307*. Cambridge, Mass.: Harvard University Press, 1979.

Culley, Robert. "Oral Tradition and Biblical Studies." *Oral Tradition* 1 (1986): 30–65.

Foley, John Miles. *The Theory of Oral Composition: History and Methodology*. Bloomington: Indiana University Press, 1988.

Foley, John Miles. *Traditional Oral Epic: The* Odyssey, Beowulf, *and the Serbo-Croatian Return Song*. Berkeley: University of California Press, 1990.

Foley, John Miles, ed. *A Companion to Ancient Epic*. Oxford: Blackwell, 2005.

Foley, John Miles, ed. *Teaching Oral Traditions*. New York: Modern Language Association, 1998.

Horsley, Richard A., Jonathan Draper, and John Miles Foley, eds. *Performing the Gospel: Orality, Memory, and Mark: Essays Dedicated to Werner Kelber*. Minneapolis: Augsburg Fortress, 2006.

Jamieson-Drake, David W. *Scribes and Schools in Monarchic Judah: A Socio-Archeological Approach*. Sheffield UK: Almond, 1991.

Lord, Albert B. *The Singer of Tales*. Cambridge, Mass.: Harvard University Press, 1960.

Niditch, Susan. *Judges: A Commentary*. Louisville, Ky.: Westminster John Knox, 2008.

Niditch, Susan. *Oral World and Written Word. Ahcirent Irralite Literature*. Louisville, Ky.: Westminster John Knox Press, 1996.

Nissinen, Martti. "How Prophecy Became Literature." *Scandanavian Journal of the Old Testament* 19 (2005): 153–172.

Nissinen, Martti. "Spoken, Written, Quoted, and Invented: Orality and Writtenness in Ancient Near Eastern Prophecy." In *Writings and Speech in Israelite and Ancient Near Eastern Prophecy*, edited by Ehud Ben Zvi and Michael H. Floyd, 235–271. Atlanta: Society of Biblical Literature, 2000b.

Nissinen, Martti, ed. *Prophecy in Its Ancient Near Eastern Context: Mesopotamian, Biblical, and Arabian Perspectives*. Atlanta: Society of Biblical Literature, 2000a.

Nissinen, Martti, ed. *Prophets and Prophecy in the Ancient Near East*. Atlanta: Society of Biblical Literature, 2003.

Ong, Walter. *Orality and Literacy: The Technologizing of the Word*. New York: Methuen, 1982.

Person, Raymond F. Jr. "The Ancient Israelite Scribe as Performer." *Journal of Biblical Literature* 117 (1998): 601–609.

Person, Raymond F. Jr. *The Deuteronomic History and the Book of Chronicles: Scribal Works in an Oral World*. Atlanta: Society of Biblical Literature, 2010.

Person, Raymond F. Jr. *The Deuteronomic School: History, Social Setting, and Literature*. Atlanta: Society of Biblical Literature, 2002.

Polak, Frank. "The Oral and the Written: Syntax, Stylistics and the Development of Biblical Prose Narrative." *Journal of Ancient Near Eastern Studies* 26 (1998): 59–105.

Stock, Brian. *The Implications of Literacy: Written Language and models of Interpretation in the Eleventh and Twelfth Centuries*. Princeton, N.J.: Princeton University Press, 1983.

Thomas, Rosalind. *Oral Tradition and Written Records in Classical Athens*. Cambridge, UK: Cambridge University Press, 1989.

Toorn, Karel van der. *Scribal Culture and the Making of the Hebrew Bible*. Cambridge, Mass.: Harvard University Press, 2007.

Trebolle, Julio C. "Samuel/Kings and Chronicles: Book Divisions and Textual Composition." In *Studies in the Hebrew Bible, Qumran, and the Septuagint Presented to Eugene Ulrich*, edited by Peter W. Flint, Emanuel Tov, and James C. VanderKam, 96–108. Leiden, Netherlands: Brill, 2006.

Raymond F. Person, Jr.

New Testament

In his 1989 presidential address to the Society of Biblical Literature (SBL), Paul Achtemeier issued a challenge. He noted that while scholars had researched a plethora of dimensions of the social, anthropological, and historical world in which the New Testament took shape, one aspect neglected by all but a small cadre of scholars was the fact that these writings arose in a world that had high levels of residual orality. In this address he urged that biblical scholars recognize in all their work the oral environs within which the New Testament took shape. Serious reflection was needed regarding the nature of this media world and how awareness of this neglected dimension of the ancient world might reshape biblical interpretation. This new mindset would demand that many assumptions then current in biblical scholarship would need intense reexamination and reformulation. Scholars would need to abandon the anachronistic projection of our own print world back onto New Testament texts; they would need to take seriously the complex interface between orality and writing that existed at the time of the composition of New Testament literatures.

Several scholars have joined forces with that small cadre of early researchers so that, two decades later, sessions at the SBL now abound in which presenters take seriously one dimension or another of Achtemeier's challenge. Since much of the work that addresses this challenge has begun with research of the Gospel of Mark, that will provide the focus for much of what follows, so that a broad spectrum of the issues raised by a particular text may be examined. The bibliography will help orient the audience to how awareness of orality has shaped other elements of biblical interpretation.

Early Precedents. Interest in oral dimensions of the biblical text is not new to biblical studies. Johannes Gottfried Herder made claims about the oral nature of the Gospels as long ago as the eighteenth century. The most influential figure in twentieth-century biblical criticism, Rudolph Bultmann, constructed his system of form criticism on the assumption that oral traditions were incorporated into each of the synoptic Gospels. He envisioned these oral traditions as brief fragments and discrete units that the author gathered together and steered toward his own purposes. The trained scholar sees the stitching that holds together the author's additions as well as the other multiple layers of tradition that preceded the final received form.

Bultmann downplayed the difference between oral and written sources and their use by the evangelists, believing that oral and written traditions functioned under similar evolutionary laws. Drawing upon what happened to the tradition as it passed from Mark's Gospel into Luke's and Matthew's, Bultmann sought to formulate the rules or laws that had governed the transmission of materials within oral processes as well as in the shift from oral to written narrative. This quilt of multiple sources could be disassembled, and the scraps could be sorted according to the phase at which their contribution appeared, using the laws Bultmann had formulated. In the end, this process would help separate that which authentically could be traced back to the historical Jesus from strata that accumulated during the evolutionary process. Bultmann formulated his understanding in dialogue with secular scholars who explored other folk traditions. He imagined an analogous process within the biblical witness.

Secular Studies on Orality. The small cadre of scholars that Achtemeier mentioned in his address had been influenced by the work of secular scholars. Milman Parry, an expert in Homeric studies, was concerned with the performance of Homer's epic poetry. Parry explored the level at which ancient performances of the epics was dependent upon prior written sources. He concluded that the epics were constructed in the act of performance, with the storyteller weaving together blocks of material using standard themes and formulaic phrases. He drew upon contemporary oral performances in Yugoslavia as an analogy for the ancient performances. Upon his death, his work was continued by his student Albert Bates Lord and finally published in *The Singer of Tales* (Cambridge, Mass.: Harvard University Press, 1960). These theorists made a clear distinction between the improvisational work done by the storyteller using traditional materials and the fixed control asserted by written texts.

Walter Ong's *Orality and Literacy: The Technology of the Word* (1982) added to the understanding of the interface between subsequent media. He formulated an understanding of the different ways that consciousness is shaped in the transition from primarily oral to primarily literate cultures. He argued for particular features that distinguish the two modes of organizing thought. Orality is additive and aggregative in its organization of thought as opposed to literacy, which inclines toward subordinative and analytic modes. Orality is drawn toward lived experience in the world as opposed to abstraction from the world. It is profoundly interested in the agonistic dimensions of reality and portrays those in ways that encourage empathetic responses and participation. Written discourse, on the other hand, pushes the reader back, creating distance from the material at hand. Words in oral performance do things to their hearers. They do not simply reference reality; they create reality for those listening. Thus the different modes of discourse actually create different habits of the mind, different ways of knowing, and different ways of socially organizing life; they are not simply generative of different pools of knowledge, but have different currents to be navigated by those who swim in their waters.

The Small Cadre. A solid overview of seminal work in this field is best explored through an examination of several of the scholars that Achtemeier may have had in mind in his address when he spoke of a small cadre of scholars. Thomas Boomershine, Werner Kelber, and Joanna Dewey were among the primary pioneers in this field and have continued to lead in reflections to this day.

Thomas Boomershine. Fifteen years before Achtemeier issued his challenge, a biblical student at Union Theological Seminary in New York was already addressing the task in that most difficult medium of all to express innovation, his doctoral dissertation, "Mark, the Storyteller: A Rhetorical-Critical Investigation of Mark's Passion and Resurrection Narrative" (1974). Here Boomershine lays the foundations for a lifelong examination of how attention to oral dynamics in this literature transforms basic assumptions held by biblical scholars. Boomershine argues that the Markan narrative was intended for oral performance in its entirety. Ears listening to a storyteller, not eyes scanning a page, were the original filters through which almost all people would have received this story in its ancient context. Thus, common scholarly references to "readers" of a text must be replaced with "hearers" of the story. Sound, not silence, situated the story. Drawing upon the dynamics observed by Ong, Boomershine argues that this medium invited empathetic engagement rather than the detachment that scholars in the twentieth century had come to prize.

Boomershine argues that the oral medium of the story is essential to understanding how it made an impact on ancient audiences. Following Ong, Boomershine claims that the form in which the Gospel narratives were produced shapes narrative meaning in an essential and not merely instrumental way. For example, "verbal threads," Boomershine's term for repeated words and phrases, are more easily registered with the ears than with the reader's eyes. When Jesus's prediction of betrayal is repeated at the point of Peter's actual denial (Mark 14:72), it is recognized as an echo by the audience's ears. The passion predictions and their fulfillment also share in this dynamic. These repeated phrases stitch together major motifs throughout the Gospel, create emphasis within specific episodes, and provide an audio structure for the narrative as a whole.

The narrator tells the story in a way that also puts in play levels of distance and nearness between the audience and various characters. The audience is caught up in the tensions of the Jesus story in such a way that they must sort the issues out for themselves. Through this dynamic, the norms of the story are transmitted to the audience, shaping and forming not only the audience's immediate response but also their on-going self-understanding. Boomershine shows that the structure of the passion narrative causes the audience to participate in the passion of Jesus, empathetically sharing his suffering.

This focus on what the narrative does to those hearing it persists throughout the monograph. Boomershine shows how the particular form of an episode moves the audience toward desired responses. For example, when accusers of Jesus in the Sanhedrin utter false testimony against Jesus, those who have heard the whole story know for themselves that lies are spoken. They find themselves thinking that Jesus said no such thing. Often in the performance, the audience is cast as characters in the story; the questions addressed to crowds throughout the trial scenes are also addressed to the audience members, demanding their own response. Boomershine is very attentive to the level of identification that the narrative creates between the audience members and various characters. The dance between identification and distance is carefully choreographed. In the end, Mark's telling recreates the tensions inherent in the crucifixion itself—and points the audience toward a faithful resolution of them.

Boomershine's most radical claim for interpretive methodology is that actually hearing the performance of the Gospel narratives must be an integral part of all biblical research. Even more radical is the fact that Boomershine put into practice this claim with his dissertation by submitting an audiotape in which he performs the passion narrative in Greek. While scholars have not always had ears to hear this proposal, Boomershine has taught thousands of ordinary interpreters of the biblical narrative to engage in this practice and has had a dramatic impact through this expanding interpretive practice.

Werner Kelber. Werner Kelber has been the most publicly recognized head of Achtemeier's cadre. If Boomershine conceives of Mark in the oral orbit, Kelber's book *The Oral and Written Gospel* (1983) draws heavily upon the other side of Parry, Lord, and Ong, emphasizing the shift that occurred when the Gospel was committed to writing. He admits that, in this shift, Mark's author carries forward elements of the Gospel's oral provenance. Kelber sees that Mark's Gospel is closely aligned with oral traditions and that it carries forward an oral legacy. Signs of orality remain embedded in the text, including heroic stories of healing that work with established forms like those the form critics identified. Yet despite the similarities within forms (heroic stories, polarization stories, parables), Kelber notices how similar forms are put into different service for a multiplicity of effects. The healing of the leper introduces the secrecy motif (Mark 1:40–45); the healing of the paralytic (Mark 2:1–12) creates the controversy regarding the authority to forgive sins. These stories are marked by concreteness, with individual, personalized characters receiving the focus. Other stories bring to light orality's penchant for the agonistic dimensions of life. The stories of demoniacs especially exhibit this characteristic. Parables also invite audience engagement, speaking out of commonplace experiences but infusing the known with radical surprises. These parables embody the heart of oral speech dynamics, drawing in the audience to a plethora of reflective possibilities.

Likewise, the Gospel's grammar has not shed itself of key components from its oral roots. The excessive use of the additive conjunction "and" links otherwise disjointed events into a stream of urgent proclamation. Words spoken by the main characters do things, as Ong suggested, leaving reality in a different state. Triadic repetition typical of folklore appears throughout the text: three passion predictions, three denials by Peter, three times Jesus enters Jerusalem. Progressive duplication introduces a theme only to revisit it immediately, bestowing on it even more complex meaning. The stories are action driven rather than character driven. Verbs in the historical present tense create immediacy with the story told. Clearly in the oral event, the bond that develops between storyteller and audience is part and parcel of the message. There is no original form of the story from which all others were born. Bultmann and the others were calling forth a phantom imagined within the confines of literacy. Every telling was original as the storytelling, shared by performer and audience, came together in a way without precedent and without hope of antecedent. Each performance was an original.

Yet, argues Kelber, the oral remnants within the written Gospel should not blind us to the fact that something tremendous has happened once this Gospel is written down. Kelber identifies the literacy side of the equation developed by Parry, Lord, and Ong and therefore sees what later critics dubbed a "great divide" between the oral and written accounts. The early flow of oral traditions became frozen once the story was written down. Writing down the story changed everything, or perhaps, better, stopped the flow of continual change from occurring. The living and lively voice of the storyteller is silenced as the narrative passes into print. Kelber accuses the author of the Gospel of remembering past voices in order to silence them. Speech is abandoned in favor of the new medium. Therefore, Mark's use of the oral traditions should be approached with suspicion. He has claimed the tradition only to destroy its life. Mark's act of recording the Gospel breaks the speaker/hearer bond, distances readers from the narrative's impact, and crucifies the word in order to bring to life a new textuality. This move by the author claims authority for a particular version of the story in order to destroy the lively multiplicity inherent in the oral forms. Lively performance gives way to the author's preferred, static account.

Joanna Dewey. Joanna Dewey, also from the cadre of those early explorers of biblical orality, maps out a proposal that understands with Kelber the long oral life that the basic framework of the Gospel of Mark enjoyed before it was written down. Yet she also argues for the continuation of this active oral life even after the scribal work was done. She argues that the account written after the Roman-Jewish War did not halt the oral performance of the story. Storytellers continued to tell it with little or no use of the recorded manuscript. The level of authority that Kelber seeks for Mark's account forgets that the original writing of the Gospel did not confer upon it status as "scripture"; that was not given until much later in the canonical process. While Dewey admits that claiming a long, dynamic oral life for Mark alongside and at times independent of its manuscript presence is a hypothesis that cannot be definitively proven, she does construct a framework that makes this possibility credible.

Dewey notes that the Gospel of Mark works well when performed as a story. It has an appropriate length for such performance. Both storyteller and audience would find it easily remembered. Like Boomershine and Kelber, Dewey sees the markers of orality that were identified by Parry, Lord, and Ong throughout the entire narrative. Mark contains short narratives, repetitive patterns, sets of three, and other devices most at home in oral performance.

Dewey notes that, since storytelling was a popular practice virtually everywhere in the ancient world, in all likelihood Mark's Gospel enjoyed a presence in that medium. Writing need not be conceived of as the correcting of an oral process, since these two forms of publication (performance and manuscript) often operated in support of each other. She argues that the oral patterns and practices so deeply embedded in Mark's writing make it likely that it was composed orally.

The content of Mark's Gospel also suggests a rural audience, which would have an even lower level of literacy than more urban areas. Since these communities would lack basic literacy as well as the financial means to acquire manuscripts, the audience the narrative seems to assume requires that communication happened in performance.

Especially interesting in Dewey's proposal is her examination of data extraneous to the narrative itself that may be found through text critical observations. First, critical editions of the New Testament indicate that Mark's text has a significantly higher presence of textual variants than the other canonical Gospels. Since transmission through orality is known to be more variable than transmission through successive written versions, this evidence points to orality. Second, extant Markan manuscripts are relatively scarce compared to the other three Gospels, with only one known manuscript prior to the end of the third century. If this Gospel was primarily encountered via performance, this would explain the absence of manuscripts. Third, citations of Mark's Gospel by early Christian writers drop precipitously from the second to the third century. These elite authors quoted Mark as a popular source early on, but then this practice declined as Mark's Gospel was overshadowed by the more literary Gospels in the move toward canonization. Given Mark's lively and popular oral life in the earlier century, it could not be ignored even by those who may have preferred the other Gospels. Dewey has responded well to the question posed in her article title, "The Survival of Mark's Gospel: A Good Story?" (Journal of Biblical Literature 123 [2004]: 495–507).

Further Developments. Since the work of these early pioneers, many scholars have deepened the understanding of New Testament texts as themselves oral traditions. We will explore a sample of the issues that arise: the role of sound in the ancient world, the style of performance in that place, the role of social memory in relation to the Gospels, and, finally, how competing social visions are noted even within a given Gospel.

Sound. One of the important elements of the early proposals is the importance of sound in the ancient world. Leading the research on this front are Margaret Ellen Lee and Bernard Brandon Scott with their book, *Sound Mapping the New Testament* (2009). For most people in the ancient world, words were not markings on paper or tablet, but sound. Even in urban areas, literacy broadly defined was not possessed by more than 15 percent of the population; in Palestine the number would be more like 3 percent. Even by literate groups, words were typically vocalized during both reading and writing. The dominance of declaration was true for pedagogical, economic, and pragmatic reasons. Schooling in the ancient world stressed recitation and memory. Writing existed to be at the service of this pedagogy. Economically, the material and processes that led to the production of manuscripts were expensive, and so even a single text would be a luxury in a given educational community. Students were not instructed to turn to a passage in their own personal copy of a text, but listened as it was read aloud. Finally, with low literacy rates, the primary form of publication was oral recitation. Manuscripts were at the service of this form of publication. Manuscripts were not first thought of as repositories of concepts and ideas; they first and foremost captured the linear stream of sound so that it could be vocalized at a later date. Lee and Scott have done important work exploring the grammar of sound. They have created a method for discerning and analyzing sound patterns in the New Testament that opens up new dimensions of the text. Conclusions about narratives and discourses can be based on ancient understandings of how particular sounds and sound patterns organized emotional and tonal effects in a discourse.

Performance. Whitney Shiner has mapped out the cultural ideal of performance in the ancient world in his book, *Proclaiming the Gospel: First-Century Performance of Mark* (2003). Shiner has argued that the four Gospels as well as many other parts of the New Testament would likely have conformed to the norms implicit in the performance ideals of antiquity. Drawing upon rhetorical handbooks as well as descriptions of public performance from the ancient world, he offers a framework for understanding how the Gospel of Mark would have been presented. Mark is of a length that was fully capable of being memorized in the ancient world. The Gospel as we have it would take approximately two hours to perform. The performer would have some freedom to shrink or expand the material in light of audience need, while maintaining the accepted contours of the tradition. The performance would be lively, with the storyteller using vivid gestures, variation in tone and speed, and different voices to distinguish the characters from one another. The style would often be bombastic by modern standards, with an emphasis on agonistic dimensions of the story. This is especially true when the venue is large and subtlety would be lost on those farthest from the performer. The narration would drive toward making an impact on the audience's emotions and motives rather than simply teaching about events or presenting doctrinal understanding. Performance contributed to community formation not only the conveyance of information. The narration would create a primary experience of the story world for the audience. The audience in return would play an active role in the performance. They would respond openly, loudly, and physically to the performance.

Social Memory. Holly Hearon has written an article whose title expresses another dimension of the work on oral traditions, "The Construction of Social Memory in Biblical Interpretation" (*Encounter* 67 [2006]: 343–359). In this work she explains how performance functions to create a social memory that gives a people a solid sense of communal identity. This social memory weaves a connection between individuals using an interpretive narrative that draws upon the past in order to make sense of the present. Additionally the past is pressed into the service of mapping out a preferred future for the community. In the process of constructing this shared memory, personal memories are taken up into a larger narrative and find their place within it. While this may often occur consciously, just as likely this creative activity happens on an unconscious level.

This growing focus on social or collective memory differs from some of the ways memory has been thought about in earlier biblical approaches. Memory is understood not simply as a technique for storing and passing on the tradition, but is itself a generative process that synthesizes the past into meaningful directions in the present. In this understanding, memory is a constructive tool in the quest for identity that is not wielded by a lone individual but comes into being through communal dynamics. Historical events and elements of material culture are taken up into memory and are morphed to serve the challenges facing the community. The community condenses, conflates, marks the boundaries of, and even invents details so that the whole process of remembering what happened maintains a tension between the historical and the fictive.

Because memory in this process serves particular interests, it does more than preserve remembrances of social conflicts from the past; it is itself a participant in and product of such tensions. The construction of identities happens in a site of contending interpretations by different elements of a society or a community negotiating traditions in light of the exigencies and desires of their time and location (Holly E. Hearon, "The Construction of Social Memory in Biblical Interpretation"). The first-century performance of the Gospel of Mark played precisely this role. The performed Gospel draws upon the history of Israel and the life of Jesus in order to map out the direction for the community who have identified with him.

Contending Memories. Richard A. Horsley in his book, *Hearing the Whole Story: The Politics of Plot in Mark's Gospel* (Louisville, Ky.: Westminster John Knox, 2001), has applied this framework in order to observe contending interpretations of Israel's past within the Gospel of Mark. He notes that the central conflicts in Mark's Gospel pit the Galilean Jesus against the Pharisees and scribes. Horsley claims that Jesus's opponents in the narrative do not represent a normative Judaism preoccupied with the law, as common interpretations often assume. Rather, what is on display are contending versions of what it means to be an Israelite. These versions were in conflict during Jesus's time and in the time the memories of him were constructed.

Horsley notes that scholars often assume that both Jesus and the religious elite of his day appeal to the same scriptures, but offer different interpretations of those traditions. Horsley sees the conflicts flowing out of different social locations and the variant traditions about key figures from Israel's narrative that were constructed within those different locations. Following James C. Scott, he sees at play within Mark's narrative world an elite or great tradition of Israel that contains memories that run counter to the popular or little tradition of Israel's memory upon which Jesus relies. Mark's story is shaped by particular oral scripts that remember Israel's traditions in ways that occasionally parallel the official, written version but at other times demonstrate extraordinary twists that resist the inscribed telling of its own history. So while not accepting Kelber's conclusions regarding the divide between written and oral versions of Mark, Horsley does see a different written/oral conflict playing out within the narrative. He takes pains to remind us that even among the literate elite, the primary mode of teaching their traditions was oral. In fact, he will not allow us to forget that even when written texts are invoked by the elite, no authoritative version of the Torah yet exists.

In Horsley's reconstruction, Jesus is interpreted through and draws upon oral scripts or memories of Moses, Elijah, and David as prophetic figures. For example, not regal David, but subversive David is used by Jesus to drive home his points. When this occurs, clearly the oral script differs from the written official versions that eventually became part of the canon. One example may suffice to illustrate his point. Horsley looks at Jesus's appeal to David in the controversy over plucking grain on the Sabbath (Mark 2:23–28). He notes that the story Jesus draws upon to express David's actions differs in significant ways from the version we have in the later canonical form from 1 Samuel 21:1–6. The priest's name is different; David has companions with him; they are identified as hungry; he actually enters the house of God and does not wait at the door; and they all eat the bread. Jesus is drawing on a popular Israelite tradition that holds a memory of David as supporting the right of people to address their real hunger rather than respecting laws that set aside such rights for the religious elites alone ("which it is not lawful for any but the priests to eat," Mark 2:26). Through the invoking of such popular memory, Jesus initiated a movement of renewal among rural Israelites that appealed to the needs and aspirations of Galilean villagers. The Gospel of Mark that we possess was originally heard as good news when performed orally to communities of subjected people.

A Name of its Own. In light of multiple emerging trends that take seriously the role of orality in biblical texts such as the Gospel of Mark, David Rhoads, one of the scholars we have yet to engage from the original cadre, has proposed a name for this collection of interests in his two-part article, "Performance Criticism: An Emerging Methodology in Second Temple Studies" (*Biblical Theology Bulletin* 36 [2006]: pp. 1–16 and 164–184). In this decisive article, Rhoads draws together the concerns of those whom we have already explored as well as many others that space has not allowed us to pursue. He claims that the New Testament writings were like the fossil remains of living oral performance. Orality played a role in composition, transmission, and publication of them all. Performers of the texts and communities who heard them were always present in the original proclamation of these narratives and discourses. Concrete performances rooted in particular communities were always involved in the reception of what scholars think of in strictly textual terms. Frequently, perhaps more often than not, these written remains of the lively event were not even present during the memorized performance. In light of this he wonders why the performance realities of the ancient world have played so small a role in much of biblical scholarship.

Rhoads argues that given the way that biblical texts were performed, the typical method of interpreting texts privately and silently is like musicologists studying musical scores without ever hearing the music played. Like Boomershine, Rhoads advocates for contemporary performances as a necessary tools for understanding the textual remains of earlier performances. Performance will shift attention to several neglected elements of the ancient Christian context. The performer him or herself must be taken into account as must the audience that would have heard the performance. The shift from text to performance makes clear the relational nature of what is conveyed through biblical narratives. Likewise the physical place and social location of a telling shifts its meaning. All this leads to an analysis of the impact that the story would have made on various audiences. Rhoads argues that the performance in all its dimensions contributes in incarnate ways to the impact that the audience experienced. The narrative carried much more than a neatly packaged set of beliefs and ideas. The narrative created a relationship between the audience and the performer through which transformation could occur. The story that took on flesh in performance became the means to propel the hearers into lives of particular forms of faithfulness.

While Rhoads advocates for a brand new paradigm for biblical interpretation based on performance, he recognizes that many already established approaches have important contributions to make to this emerging discipline. Joining hands with these disciplines will not lead to a definitive interpretation of an original performance, since, as Kelber has noted, every performance is an original and no single, pristine specimen ever existed. Rather these disciplines can aid in the construction of credible performance scenarios that are generative in understanding the multiplicity of ways the narrative may have made an impact in the ancient world.

Rhoads gathers a broad list of areas of biblical studies that might assist in creating credible scenarios and in interpreting the impact of performance within those contexts. Historical criticism helps in the reconstruction of social and media context; form and genre criticism call attention to patterns that play into performance. Narrative criticism offers means to interpret plot, setting, and conflicts.

Reader-response criticism guides reflection on possible audience responses. Rhetorical criticism helps us understand how ancient forms of argumentation play a role in the narrative. Orality criticism helps in reflection on media impact. Social scientific criticism helps unpack the social dynamics at play in the narrative. Areas outside the field of biblical scholarship, particularly in the fields of theatre and performance studies, make essential contributions as well. Rhoads envisions a broad convergence of resources. With this initiative, it is safe to say that Achtemeier's dream has become a reality.

[*See also* Folklore and Biblical Interpretation; Form Criticism, *subentry* New Testament; Genre Criticism; Narrative Criticism and Narrative Hermeneutics; Performance Criticism; Reader-Response Criticism; Reception Criticism and Theory; Rhetorical Criticism; Social Sciences, *subentry* New Testament; Socio-rhetorical Criticism; *and* Speech-Act Theory.]

BIBLIOGRAPHY

Achtemeier, Paul. "Omni Verbum Sonat: The New Testament and the Environment of Late Western Antiquity." *Journal of Biblical Literature* 109 (1990): 3–27. Achtemeier's Society of Biblical Literature presidential address that challenged scholars to take account of the oral environment of the New Testament's creation.

Bailey, Kenneth E. "Informal Controlled Oral Tradition and the Synoptic Gospels." *Asia Journal of Theology* 5:1 (1991): 34–54. Offers an important understanding of how the oral tradition may have been regulated by the community. Bailey's extensive experience in the Middle East shapes his understanding. His article and Bauckham's work (following) provide an alternative to Kelber's understanding of the relationship between oral traditions and written word.

Bauckham, Richard. *Jesus and the Eyewitnesses: The Gospels as Eyewitness Testimony.* Grand Rapids, Mich.: Eerdmans, 2006. A detailed account that seeks to demonstrate that the Gospels are rooted and controlled by eyewitnesses to the events recounted.

Boomershine, Thomas E. *Story Journey: An Invitation to the Gospel as Storytelling.* Nashville, Tenn.: Abingdon, 1988. A primer on elements of narratives that a storyteller should take into account when performing Gospel accounts. For those interested in learning to do performance of biblical texts, this is the definitive book.

Dewey, Joanna, ed. "*Orality and Textuality in Early Christian Literature.*" *Semeia* 65 (1994). A collection of essays examining various aspects of orality and textuality in Early Christian literature.

Harvey, John D. *Listening to the Text: Oral Patterning in Paul's Letters.* Grand Rapids, Mich.: Baker, 1998. The most thoroughgoing exploration of how orality shapes the Pauline corpus.

Hearon, Holly E. *The Mary Magdalene Tradition: Witness and Counter-Witness in Early Christian Communities.* Collegeville, Minn.: Liturgical, 2004. Helpful reconstruction of the role of storytelling that complements Shiner's work with special attention to the role of women.

Hearon, Holly E., and Philip Ruge-Jones, ed. *The Bible in Ancient and Modern Media.* Biblical Performance Criticism Series 1. Eugene, Ore.: Cascade, 2009. Collection of essays by leaders in the field who communicate their central insights in a way that is accessible to beginners in biblical studies.

Horsley, Richard A., and Jonathan A. Draper. *Whoever Hears You, Hears Me: Prophets, Performance and Tradition in Q.* Harrisburg, Pa.: Trinity Press International, 1999. The most important volume to explore orality in relation to Q.

Horsley, Richard A., Jonathan A. Draper, and John Miles Foley, ed. *Performing the Gospel: Orality, Memory, and Mark.* Minneapolis: Fortress, 2000. Continued exploration of dynamics and issues identified by Kelber.

Juel, Donald. "The Strange Silence of the Bible." *Interpretation* 51 (1997): 5–19. An experiential account by a fine biblical scholar about the insight he gained by watching someone perform a Gospel.

Kelber, Werner H. *The Oral and the Written Gospel: The Hermeneutics of Speaking and Writing in the Synoptic Tradition, Mark, Paul, and Q.* Philadelphia: Fortress, 1983. The book that started the scholarly conversation about orality in relation to the New Testament. In addition to the work on Mark discussed earlier, Kelber addresses Paul's commitment to the oral gospel.

Lee, Margaret Ellen, and Bernard Brandon Scott. *Sound Mapping the New Testament.* Salem, Ore.: Polebridge, 2009. Explains the material aspects of ancient media and the centrality of sound as an organizing principle in rhetoric. This work provides a method to analyze and interpret biblical texts using sound maps.

Maxey, James A. *From Orality to Orality: A New Paradigm for Contextual Translation of the Bible.* Biblical Performance Criticism Series 2. Eugene, Ore.: Cascade, 2009. Demonstrates the challenges and possibilities encountered when translating the Bible's orality for contemporary oral communities.

Ong, Walter. *Orality and Literacy: The Technology of the Word.* New York: Methuen, 1982. A classic work exploring the ways that different media result in different ways of structuring and understanding and society.

Ruge-Jones, Philip. "The Beginning of the Good News." Select Multimedia Resources, 2009. A DVD recording of a live performance of the whole Gospel of Mark.

Shiell, William David. *Reading Acts: The Lector and the Early Christian Audience.* Biblical Interpretation Series 70. Boston: Brill Academic, 2004. Does work similar to Shiner's (following) but with a focus on the Acts of the Apostles.

Shiner, Whitney Taylor. *Proclaiming the Gospel: First-Century Performance of Mark.* Harrisburg, Pa.: Trinity, 2003. Documents the expectations for performance in the antiquity and how that informs interpretation of Mark's Gospel.

Swanson, Richard. *Provoking the Gospel: Methods to Embody Biblical Storytelling Through Drama.* Cleveland: Pilgrim, 2004. Great pedagogical resource to create engagement with the text through theatrical improvisation techniques.

Thatcher, Tom, ed. *Jesus, the Voice, and the Text: Beyond the Oral and Written Gospel.* Waco, Tex.: Baylor, 2008. Appreciative volume of essays that examines the work of Kelber in terms of oral and written interfaces as well as the role of memory in contemporary research.

Wire, Antoinette Clark. *The Case for Mark Composed in Performance.* Biblical Performance Criticism Series 3. Eugene, Ore.: Cascade, 2011. The most thoroughgoing attempt to demonstrate that Mark was composed for and lived in performance. Wire provides an interesting possible reconstruction of the role of women in preserving Mark's Gospel.

Philip Ruge-Jones

Orthodox Jewish Interpretation

The term Orthodox has been applied to several manifestations of Judaism since approximately 1800, which suggests that only interpretations of the Bible composed since then qualify for consideration under this designation. Yet, these latter-day compositions represent but a small fraction of the interpretative efforts used by contemporary Orthodox Jews to study and explain the Bible; many are centuries, even millennia older. Generally, the authority of interpretations increases with age, the most binding of them having been composed in Hebrew or Aramaic and attributed to the rabbis of Late Antiquity; those even older expositions, many originally Jewish but often preserved by Christians in Greek or in other languages no longer used regularly by Jews, are excluded from consideration here because they were unknown to or ignored by most rabbinic writers.

The pre-Orthodox rabbinic literature is replete with different exegetical trends, schools, and compositions that provide a rich variety of interpretative models and specific expositions from which Orthodox Jews may choose, on which they may build, and in response to which they may offer new, complementary interpretations. These include early rabbinic expositions (talmudic, targumic, and midrashic); the scientific, philosophical, and linguistic contributions of medieval Judeo-Arabic literature; the literalist interpretations produced in medieval France, Germany, Spain, and Italy; the mostly medieval Jewish philosophical and mystical literatures; the contributions of the halakhic literature (Jewish law); numerology and related interpretative conceits; and many others, as well as their later developments. All are potentially available to the contemporary Orthodox interpreter, and they can render Orthodox hermeneutics highly varied, complex, and multifaceted. Potentially they can serve non-Orthodox Jewish interpreters also, as demonstrated by the *JPS Torah Commentary*, which is largely a product of writers affiliated with the Conservative Movement (and arguably the best original Jewish commentary on that text published in our time), and by many of the other Jewish commentaries composed over the past century or two, but rarely are they as compelling to these writers as they are to the Orthodox ones. Only in the most extraordinary circumstances will the Orthodox Jew explore alternative interpretations without first examining a selection of traditional, pre-Orthodox ones, and many will not explore them at all.

Moreover, just as every pre-Orthodox exegetical movement has reacted positively or negatively to the contemporary intellectual contexts in which it evolved, Orthodox efforts can and must be measured contextually. Even if its affiliated writers eschew all involvement with external efforts or interpretative interests, that in itself qualifies as such interaction; indeed, according to the Vilna Gaon, avoidance of scientific information in this context is an extreme and embarrassing case of isolationism.

By the time the Orthodox label could be applied to Bible study and related exegetical work, these numerous ancient, medieval, and early modern interpretative approaches had coalesced into three.

1. The midrashic/zoharic approach to the Bible included some Talmud, but in place of its dialectics and complexities, this hermeneutical model stressed kabbalistic and midrashic myths and related sources, issues, and interpretations. Though produced largely in the thirteenth century, the Zohar was attributed to Rabbi Shimon bar Yohai and treated in many rabbinic and Christian circles as if more than a millennium older; it therefore competed with the Mishnah and the Talmud for authority and influence. Midrashic/zoharic interpretations were universally respected, but ultimately they became primarily the domain of Hasidim, as the Zohar lost most of its appeal in other Orthodox circles. Still, in works produced in the seventeenth, eighteenth, and nineteenth centuries, the treatment of *Parashat Mishpatim*, for example, often serves as a simple test that differentiates between works that follow the Zohar's treatments and others that stress the Talmud's.

2. The second approach, perhaps best classified as talmudic/midrashic, combined two Late Antique literatures possessing great rabbinic authority and their interpretations. Both were pre-medieval and reportedly contained the interpretations of the Bible received by Moses and transmitted to his followers. The Talmud reportedly contained the best of that tradition, and the midrashim, though less binding as practice and dogma, were only slightly less authoritative. Midrashic and talmudic interpretation became the stock in trade of Orthodox rabbis, and synagogue goers were influenced continually by their expositions of the Torah. The rabbinic group that adopted this approach most thoroughly was that of the Mitnaggedim, "opponents," so named for their rejection of Hasidism.

3. The third group is primarily rational scientific in outlook. Not anti-talmudic, but less positively disposed toward the Zohar and its mystical hermeneutics, this approach depended largely on the literalist exegetes and the philosophers from within the medieval classes of rabbinic writers (e.g., Rashbam, Ibn Ezra, and Maimonides). In terms of eighteenth and nineteenth-century politics, they were represented as the Maskilim, followers of the Enlightenment.

Initially all three groups consisted of believers in and practitioners of Rabbinic Judaism, and they maintained both traditional lifestyles and rabbinic intellectual postures, coupled with strong commitment to Talmud and Halakhah. But eventually that changed, and many Maskilim began to develop in new and more modern ways, particularly regarding openness to external intellectual trends. In many cases these postures would be considered the antecedents of Reform, Conservative, and secular forms of Judaism, even if their leaders emerged via other paths. But groups of learned individuals affiliated with Orthodox institutions also share much with them, and traditional publishing efforts from the early eighteenth century (e.g., the Rabbinic Pentateuch from Berlin, 1705) confirm the authenticity and propriety of such attitudes. Eventually the two other groups (talmudic/midrashic and midrashic/zoharic) grew closer to each other, and they now function more or less as one (known as Haredim), even if they maintain some distinctive ideological, literary, and political commitments. Thus contemporary Orthodox Bible study is largely an amalgamation of the first two types of rabbinic exegesis, despite the fact that some institutions—Yeshiva University in New York, Bar-Ilan University in Ramat-Gan, and even a few Israeli yeshivot—and some individuals struggle daily with integrating the desired elements of rational/scientific exegesis into their Bible study. Generally they have little or no difficulty with the medieval contributions; modern ones often require further consideration.

Because Orthodoxy is a term applied to or adopted by numerous independent individuals and groups that either flourished in early modern times or continue to do so, one must consider how its adherents' lifestyles and aspirations relate to Orthodox Bible study, which therefore consists not merely in the study of books (as would be the treatment of medieval Ashkenazi or Renaissance Italian Bible study) but remains a contemporary manifestation of Judaism that maintains strong links with the past and competes with other contemporary groups for legitimacy and influence.

Orthodox Bible Study. Orthodox treatment of the Bible normally develops within multiple contexts, but it tends to be largely homogeneous, due largely to the conservative policies of the institutions and the teachers they employ. Also, like all Jewish movements, it tends to draw a significant percentage of its leaders and teachers from more traditional movements and sends its teenage students to study in more conservative institutions of higher learning, thus maintaining a strongly conservative religious influence within its midst, at least when they are successful, which is far from always.

(1) Elementary level Orthodox Bible study stresses understanding the scriptural text (primarily the Torah) and the commentary of Rashi, who died in early twelfth-century France. Rashi encouraged a significant refinement in the use of midrash, but as preserved most of his commentaries incorporate a large amount of it, and therefore schools that use his work extensively usually follow suit.

(2) As Bible study progresses through high school, post-pentateuchal scriptural books are added, and the selection of commentaries found in various Rabbinic Bibles broadens, primarily for female students; male students are streamed into classes that stress Talmud. (Talmud study includes examination of some passages from the Bible, but often those tractates studied have other priorities and their Bible-related discussions often develop either hyper-literal or non-literal expositions of it.) Advanced schools for women continue to treat the Bible as a major subject and broaden the selection of commentaries. It is no accident that the most prominent Orthodox Bible teacher of the twentieth century was a woman, Nehama Leibowitz.

(3) Enrollment in post-secondary institutions varies widely, but females tend to be exposed to more Bible study, especially in the better schools, while males often are not, though that is changing in some places.

(4) Study of the weekly Torah reading begins before children can read and continues throughout adulthood. Thus weekly review of a few chapters read seriatim every Saturday in the synagogue, discussed at the Sabbath table, and interpreted or highlighted by the rabbi in the weekly sermon becomes the primary exposure of the Orthodox Jew to that scriptural book. These practices have kept its contents and messages in constant public view, and after a lifetime of such exposure, many individuals have been deeply influenced by the rabbis' messages; indeed, they often believe that these homiletical treatments are the primary if not the only legitimate way to understand the text. This is not true of the non-pentateuchal books, whose exposure often is minimal.

(5) Other practices include the study of the weekly Torah portion with Onkelos (a talmudic requirement) or with a different commentary each year (obviously a later one as commentaries originated in medieval times), as well as the following: the daily study of a chapter of the Bible; attendance at adult education classes devoted to one or more biblical texts or issues; and personal study. Rarely will these activities engage any interpretation more critical or more modern than the study of the recent Israeli commentary *Da`at Miqra* (which is modern but not critical), yet to a large extent that will depend on the instructor's comfort with the modern interpretative literature. In most cases these activities will be based on one or more editions of the Rabbinic Bible or its sub-units.

(6) Some ritually Orthodox individuals pursue advanced academic degrees in one or more aspects of Biblical Studies. Those who concentrate on textual matters of necessity will meet many contemporary critical issues, but others who prefer to study the history of Bible interpretation; ancient Semitic languages and literatures; the cultures, history, or geography of the Ancient Near East; archaeology;

comparative literature or law; and the like may, for the most part, avoid direct confrontation with them. A few individuals who are well educated in both the history of Rabbinic Bible interpretation and modern Biblical Studies attempt to contribute to a new Orthodox hermeneutic, but no serious, word-by-word commentary worthy of being so identified has appeared in the United States (the closest is perhaps the recent Torah exposition of the Sefaradi rabbi, Moshe Shammah – *Recalling the Covenant* (Jersey City: Ktav, 2011); and the only Israeli product is *Da`at Miqra*, a group project of more than thirty volumes written by Orthodox Israelis that has stepped into the breach between the pre-Orthodox rabbinic tradition and the contemporary critical world by using much recent scholarly material and some of its methods but by carefully avoiding most related critical issues.

In short, Orthodox Bible study is a highly conservative affair. The interpretations of the text are generally rooted in Late Antique midrashim or in medieval commentaries, and while many subsequent interpretations have been composed, rarely do they share the authority of the earlier works. Even so, it is impossible to describe all pre-Orthodox rabbinic works as fundamentalist and the range of opinions they offer is far more varied, more creative, and more liberal (if I may use that overworked word) than many contemporary readers – Orthodox and non-Orthodox – imagine. Even so, accusations of heresy are quickly associated with those believed to overstep the boundaries of propriety, which can be drawn in a plethora of ways and in accord with widely disparate early modern or modern expectations, even when they have been aligned with the thinking of other authoritative traditionalists.

Some Individual Orthodox Contributions to Bible Study. It is substantially easier to identify biblical interpretations as rabbinic than as Orthodox, because rabbinic works appear so through the sources they cite and the general postures they adopt. Usually they were composed in Hebrew, and often they contain approbations from other Orthodox rabbis that confirm their ideological propriety. The Orthodox label is substantially more complex to assign. Rarely does an author identify his work accordingly, and one cannot rely only on the date of publication, though it is useful. Some Orthodox readers accept as Orthodox books that others emphatically reject. Being Orthodox cannot be subject to whimsical politics, and the marginal cases are the most interesting and often the most challenging. The following group includes individual works and group projects; all are generally recognized as Orthodox, but they are far from uniform in method, focus, or ideology.

1. *Meir Leb Malbim* (1809–1879) was one of the few well known rabbinic writers who composed commentaries on almost all books of the Bible. He served as rabbi in many communities of Russia, Poland, and Romania, and was staunchly committed to understanding the text according to its straightforward meaning. Though later generations did not find him totally successful, the fact that he suffered at the hands of his liberal opponents and hostile governments endeared him to many traditionalists. His Torah commentaries are closely linked to the halakhic midrashim, which he understood to share the antiquity and authority of written Scripture. His hermeneutical attitudes negated the recognition of repetitions of any sort. He wrote on synonyms in an attempt to demonstrate that they really do not exist. Though most subsequent Orthodox writers are not close to Malbim in methods or results, he is considered by many to be the last great traditional interpreter of the Bible.

2. *David Tzvi Hoffman* (1843–1921) was an Orthodox writer of a very different sort. Also an ordained rabbi, Hoffman was a professor at and later rector of Hildesheimer's rabbinical seminary in Berlin. His scholarly output was substantial, and he wrote full commentaries on Leviticus and Deuteronomy and partial ones on Genesis and Exodus. Hoffman engaged the contemporary critics head-on, especially Julius Wellhausen's documentary hypothesis, and he used its own critical assumptions to challenge its treatment of the Torah. He also made important contributions to the scholarly analysis of early

rabbinic texts, wrote numerous halakhic *responsa*, and made other contributions to Orthodox Judaism.

3. *Umberto Cassuto* (1883–1951) represents an open trend in Bible study that has antecedents in a series of medieval and post-medieval Italian writers. Aware of critical issues and willing to use them when he found them appropriate, Cassuto, who migrated to Israel after being educated in Italy and writing a number of studies on Italian Jewry, reportedly was a rabbi, and maintained a strictly Orthodox lifestyle. He wrote extensively on Genesis and Exodus and served as the editor of *Entziqlopedia Miqra'it.* He also wrote several volumes on Ugarit and the Bible and a book-length critique of the documentary hypothesis.

4. The Soncino Books of the Bible is a set of commentaries produced in the middle of the twentieth century by a group of British writers. The Soncino Torah commentary is based on those in many Rabbinic Bibles and seems to stand as a direct alternative to that of Hertz, a modern work published by the same press. The Soncino commentary on the rest of the Bible is based largely on traditional rabbinic writers but interspersed with modern comments. While not critical, it did acknowledge the links between some modern, scholarly approaches to the Bible and parallels or antecedents in the tradition. It minimized midrashic interpretation and, while it remains on the market, was effectively replaced by the Artscroll commentaries, which were written largely with that purpose.

5. *Nehama Leibowitz* (1905–1997) was educated in Europe and migrated to what would become Israel in 1930. A slight woman with broad religious and educational goals, she began to teach in numerous Zionist and Orthodox institutions and created something that resembled a personalized correspondence course with hundreds of interested students who could not attend her classes. Eventually the question sheets that provided the base of this correspondence turned into a series of books, and today most Orthodox Israeli Bible teachers pride themselves on having been her students. Nehama's approach to the Bible essentially compared several classical rabbinic interpretations on each passage. It stressed careful reading and isolation of the problem (even if not articulated by the commentator) that stimulated each of his comments. Thus her work often led to comparing a half-dozen or so traditional commentaries and sometimes the work of Martin Buber, Umberto Cassuto, Benno Jacob, and others in search of the problems that lay behind their comments and the best solutions to them.

6. *Da'at Miqra'* is a series of commentaries on the entire Bible that runs over thirty volumes in length. It was produced by a group of Orthodox Israeli writers in the last quarter of the twentieth century, but it does not dwell on the previously existing rabbinic interpretations. Rather it establishes the meaning of the text using its original combination of classical and modern philological tools and whatever it can exploit from contemporary scholarly sources. It contains numerous maps and pictures of contemporary artifacts to explain the text, and it leaves the reader with the impression that the Bible is an authentic description of ancient realities. Since most Rabbinic Bibles leave a two-century gap between their dates of publication and the latest commentaries they contain, this commentary can be seen as the rabbinic product of those intervening years.

7. Artscroll is the name of a publication revolution that began with a commentary on Esther in 1976 and has taken over much of the Orthodox world. It has produced numerous Bible commentaries and parts of them, but it seems not to have completed any series, though it has published a translation of the entire Scripture. Artscroll claims to be totally based on earlier rabbinic sources, and while it has added many books to those generally cited, it has chosen what to cite in a tendentious way. This means that an isolationist philosophy determines the sources used and the way they are usually interpreted and applied. Despite its routine claims to express the rabbinic tradition, it actually presents a distorted picture of it by limiting what is cited and discussed and effectively denying that anything else exists. Many unsuspecting readers accept this line of thought, and for many Artscroll has actually become *the* rabbinic tradition, an

attitude emphasized by downplaying the identities of the individual authors of the Artscroll books and stressing their corporate identity. Artscroll Bible commentaries are important to many Orthodox Jews, but most of them remain unaware of the extent to which they misrepresent the pre-Orthodox rabbinic tradition. When joined with the numerous errors it contains—mis-citations, partial citations, misrepresentations, and simple mistakes—it cannot be seen to represent the Jewish tradition. The fact that many people choose to believe otherwise is a serious problem that seems not about to be corrected any time soon and reflects their sincere but erroneous expectations of the tradition.

8. *Moshe Shammah*, author of *Recalling the Covenant* (Jersey City: Ktav, 2011), is a new and unusual Sefaradi attempt to grapple with both classical rabbinic and modern critical issues in Bible study. No theme or challenge is beyond his reach, and while he has not produced a line-by-line commentary, in many places his inclusion of such considerations is revolutionary and represents a new wave of Orthodox writing about the Torah.

9. *Lord Jonathan Sacks* is Chief Rabbi of the British Commonwealth. Educated at Oxford and Cambridge, as well as a number of Jewish institutions in England and in Israel, he is one of the most prolific Orthodox writers alive and both Jews and non-Jews in England consider him one of the country's most respected thinkers. Though Sacks has issued independent books on Genesis and Exodus, he cannot yet be counted among the authors of a contemporary Orthodox Torah commentary, but they, his weekly on-line pieces, and numerous discussions in his many books allow him to be considered with this group of writers. His most recent book, *The Great Partnership: God, Science, and the Search for Meaning*, is more a study of the relationship of science and religion than a Torah commentary, but it serves as an important hermeneutical forerunner, particularly insofar as it discusses the initial chapters of Genesis, as do many of his previously published monographs.

A Brief Comparison of Rabbinic and Orthodox Hermeneutics. It is now useful to explore some of the interpretative outcomes of Orthodox hermeneutical policies and to compare them to rabbinic ones and to many of those writers just described. It is impossible to do justice to all Orthodox policies and practices, and exceptions can be found for virtually every example, but these seem typical of the way most Orthodox readers approach the Bible.

1. Orthodox Jews believe the Torah was given on Sinai by God to Moses and that it has been transmitted perfectly ever since. This means the text has not changed, that the script remains as it was then, and that the orthography (spelling) is equally old and intact. Similar claims often are made for the rest of the Bible.
2. Orthodox Jews usually read biblical narratives as if they are history, with all the implications of their being divinely revealed history. They are treated as correct and accurate. Expansions derived from them are treated as part of them.
3. Recognizing the numerous multifaceted ways the Bible has been read by authoritative rabbinic leaders over the millennia, Orthodox Jews generally accept the polyvalent nature of the Bible text: virtually every passage is subject to multiple meanings and theoretically all are correct.
4. Details in the text regularly are assumed by Orthodox Jews to be perfect. Numbers, names, spellings, predictions, and similar details are and must remain inviolate. These details are omni-significant (to borrow a term coined by Professor James Kugel); no element in the text is superfluous or without meaning.
5. Orthodox Jews believe that the patriarchs and other pre-Mosaic characters conducted their lives in accord with Mosaic and even rabbinic standards, including the expectations articulated in the Talmud. Unless presented as sinners and sometimes even then, post-Mosaic ones are assumed to have followed the Torah, and deviations from such practice are interpreted in ways that accommodate the previous assumption.
6. Orthodox Jews believe that the biblical books were written by the individuals listed in talmudic tractate Baba Batra (14b–15a).

7. Orthodox Jews generally prefer a closed approach to Bible study and opt to think about it in isolation from other cultures, values, and texts, particularly insofar as it may have been influenced by them,

All of these positions and many others have been adopted by Orthodox Jews from ancient or medieval rabbinic writers, and all may be legitimate expressions of their beliefs. See Ben Zion Katz, *A Journey Through Torah: A Critique of the Documentary Hypothesis* (Jerusalem: Urim, 2012) for other examples. But alternative rabbinic positions, essentially the opposite of those expressed here, are equally authentic and, in many cases, were articulated clearly by the same rabbinic writers who popularized these or by equally authoritative colleagues. They also have parallels in contemporary scholarly treatment of the Bible, so one who opts for one or more of the alternatives of necessity approaches what are generally considered foreign, hostile, or critical ideas. One therefore must conclude that, in some very significant areas, rabbinic and Orthodox hermeneutical values are not identical; in some cases they are diametrically opposed, and the extent of that opposition raises serious doubts about the ways in which some aspects of Orthodoxy have developed the rabbinic tradition during the past two centuries. Simply put, rabbinic hermeneutics and Orthodox hermeneutics are not always interchangeable; often they are quite different, as can be seen from some of the works briefly described earlier.

Moreover, two thousand years of attacks alleging careless preservation, infidelity in transmission, active manipulation of the text, and willful distortion of its interpretation and application have taken their toll. Arguably in response to the Holocaust and numerous other anti-Semitic attacks, many Orthodox individuals have adopted a hermeneutical position that is more defensive than accurate, designed to counter challenges imagined to be encountered on the ideological slippery slope of contemporary Jewish life rather than to represent the real exegetical issues that have been addressed by the spokesmen for the tradition and their actual contents.

Rabbinic Bibles. One of the best ways to envision the ideological differences between Orthodox and rabbinic treatments of the Bible is to examine the recent evolution of the Rabbinic Bible, which at first glance seems to be somewhat immune to such ideological considerations. The first full Bible with rabbinic commentaries was published in Venice in 1517. Others appeared from the sixteenth through eighteenth centuries, but the most extensive publication spree occurred in the nineteenth century and later in the twentieth. Rabbinic Bibles and their parts (Rabbinic Pentateuchs, Megillot, etc.) have become symbolic of Orthodox Bible study and the primary tool used in it. Examining some of the details of their evolution demonstrates what Orthodoxy attempts to accomplish with the Bible, how it imagines that reality, and what changes it is prepared to support.

In the sixteenth and seventeenth centuries, the Rabbinic Bibles were published in four volumes, Torah, Former Prophets, Latter Prophets, and Hagiographa. As they evolved, they often contained a dozen or more volumes, sometimes close to two dozen. As might be expected, initially almost all of the commentaries were composed by the fourteenth century; most, several centuries earlier. Today that is no longer true, but roughly two centuries separate the dates of the latest contributors from the dates of publication. Tradition thus maintains a significant gap between the authors and their inclusion, therefore between the contexts of the commentaries and those of their readers. Even so, almost every book in every Rabbinic Bible except the first contains more than one commentary on every biblical book. Whatever else one may suggest about these editions, they all reflect a multiplicity of ways to understand the sacred text.

Initially the Rabbinic Bibles were printed as large folios and proudly exhibited the grandeur of sacred scripture. Subsequently they were reduced in size to quartos, and in the nineteenth century they shrank to octavos. While they became more portable, they also lost much of their prestige to the Talmud, originally published in volumes somewhat smaller than the early Rabbinic Bibles but later much larger than the new sizes.

Initially the Rabbinic Bibles contained Rashi's commentary on the Torah, Radak's on the rest of the Bible, and little else. By the second edition (1524), that list was expanded to include more of Rashi and much of Ibn Ezra and Gersonides; gradually dozens of other writers were added. Even so, with the exception of Rashi, little of midrashic quality was included, and almost nothing zoharic (it was centuries before Rambam's Torah commentary, though printed independently, was added). By the end of the nineteenth century, all sorts of midrashic and zoharic works were excerpted for inclusion (primarily but not exclusively in Pentateuch editions), and the focus had evolved from literal reading to non-literal; full commentaries often were replaced by excerpts from many dozens of rabbinic writers, and the fabric of what these books contained changed; interest was now focused almost exclusively on the Torah and on its homiletical treatment.

Some contemporary editions have eliminated the use of the distinctive font known (erroneously) as Rashi script, while other subsequent ones have restored it. Some have improved on the editions of the commentaries by checking early printings and manuscripts; others have eschewed all such evidence. And still others have admitted to introducing numerous textual and editing changes in order to make the texts more readable and usable. In each case, specific ideological stances have been accommodated, but that in itself is not new. Previous centuries saw the publication of Ashkenazi, Sefaradi, and Oriental Rabbinic Pentateuchs, and editions that are closer to the intellectual models valued by Hasidim, Mitnaggedim, and Maskilim have made their marks. Even the two popularly reprinted Rabbinic Pentateuchs, one from Vienna (1858) and the other from late nineteenth-century Poland, represent major ideological alternatives. While both contain the Torah text, Onkelos' translation, Rashi, and Ibn Ezra, the latter also offers *Or Ha-Hayyim* and *Keli Yaqar*, while the former omits both but includes Norzi's *Minhat Shai*. The evolution of this trend is at least as old as the edition of Berlin (1705), which included mostly peshat commentaries and omitted most midrash and kabbalah. This was the first edition of Rashbam, a medieval iconoclast who was Rashi's grandson and staunch critic.

All of these editions can be claimed as "Orthodox," particularly those published after 1800, and no Orthodox reader would deny the value of the 1705 edition, which in some way may have anticipated the Haskalah, but they evidence a wide range of ideological preferences and potential directions for practitioners of latter-day Rabbinic Judaism. Initially and for several centuries, one version sufficed for everyone; this has evolved into several dozen Orthodox versions. Contemporary reprints reflect this, and though it may appear trivial, it would be remiss to omit the observation that the JTS Library seems to prefer the "Western" Vienna Rabbinic Pentateuch to the "Eastern" Polish one.

Conclusion. Orthodox Bible interpretation is more than two centuries old and has to its credit numerous individual and group products that simultaneously integrate traditional and modern interpretative elements into its orbit. The next decade or two will witness the development of new and even more iconoclastic attempts to integrate more scholarly treatments into the fiber of Orthodox Bible study, even as others will articulate and encourage even more restrictive alternatives. Where and how, as well as the extent to which they will be accepted, rejected, or merely ignored, remains to be seen.

[*See also* Conservative Jewish Interpretation; Historical Criticism, *subentry* Hebrew Bible; Masora and Masoretic Interpretation; Midrash; Rabbinic Exegesis; Reconstructionist Interpretation; *and* Reform Jewish Interpretation]

BIBLIOGRAPHY

Angel, Hayyim. *Creating Space Between Peshat and Derash.* Hoboken, N.J.: Ktav, 2011.

Angel, Hayyim. *Through an Opaque Lens.* New York: Sephardic Publication Foundation, 2006.

Angel, Hayyim. *Revealed Texts, Hidden Meanings: Finding the Religious Significance in Tanakh.* Hoboken, N.J.: Ktav, 2009.

Breuer, Edward. *The Limits of Enlightenment: Jews, Germans, and the Eighteenth-Century Study of Scripture.* Cambridge, Mass.: Harvard University Press, 1996.

Carmy, Shalom, ed. *Modern Scholarship in the Study of Torah: Contributions and Limitations.* Northvale, N.J.: Aronson, 1987.

Dresner, Samuel H. *The Zaddik: An Inspired Study of the Mystical Spiritual Leader of Eighteenth-Century Hasidism.* London: Abelard-Schuman, 1960.

Green, Arthur. *Devotion and Commandment: The Faith of Abraham in the Hasidic Imagination.* Cincinnati: Hebrew Union College Press, 1989.

Lamm, Norman. *The Religious Thought of Hasidism.* Hoboken, N.J.: Ktav, 1999.

Levenson, Alan T. *The Making of the Modern Jewish Bible: How Scholars in Germany, Israel, and America Transformed an Ancient Text.* Lanham: Rowan and Littlefield, 2011.

Levenson, Jon D. *The Hebrew Bible, The Old Testament, and Historical Criticism.* Louisville, Ky.: Westminster John Knox, 1993.

Levy, B. Barry. "Artscroll: An Overview." In *Approaches to Modern Judaism,* edited by M. L. Raphael, 111–140, 157–162. Chico, Calif.: Scholars Press, 1983.

Levy, B. Barry. *Fixing God's Torah: The Accuracy of the Hebrew Bible Text in Jewish Law.* New York: Oxford University Press, 2001.

Levy, B. Barry. *Jewish Masters of the Sacred Page: A History of the Rabbinic Bible and a Reader's Guide to Rabbinic Bible-Interpretation.* Jerusalem: Urim, forthcoming.

Levy, B. Barry. "Judge Not a Book by Its Cover." *Tradition* 19 (1981): 89–95.

Levy, B. Barry. "Our Torah, Your Torah, and Their Torah: An Evaluation of the Artscroll Phenomenon." In *Truth and Compassion: Essays on Judaism and Religion in Memory of Rabbi Dr. Solomon Frank,* edited by Howard Joseph et al., 137–189. Waterloo: Wilfred Laurier University Press, 1983.

Levy, Ze'ev. *Hermeneutica Ba-Mahashavah Ha-Yehudit Ba-Et Ha-Hadashah.* Jerusalem: Magnes, 2006.

Magid, Shaul. *From Metaphysics to Midrash: Myth, History, and the Interpretation of Scripture in Lurianic Kabbala.* Bloomington: Indiana University Press, 2008.

Magid, Shaul. *Hasidism on the Margin.* Madison: University of Wisconsin Press, 2004.

Saebø, Magne, ed. *Hebrew Bible / Old Testament: The History of Its Interpretation—The Middle Ages,* Vol. 2. Goettingen: Vandenhoeck and Ruprecht, 2008.

Shavit, Yacov, and Mordechai Eran. *The Hebrew Bible Reborn: From Holy Scripture to the Book of Books – A History of Biblical Culture and the Battles over the Bible in Modern Judaism.* Berlin: De Gruyter, 2007.

Simon, Uriel, ed. *Ha-Miqra' Va-Anahnu. The Bible and Us.* Tel-Aviv: Devir, 1979.

Soloveitchik, Menahem and Zalman Rubeshoff (Shazar). *Toledot Biqqoret Ha-Miqra'.* Berlin: Devir-Miqra', 1925.

Sperling, David, ed., with contributions by Baruch Levine and B. Barry Levy. *Students of the Covenant: A History of Jewish Biblical Scholarship in North America.* Atlanta: Scholars Press, 1992.

Stolow, Jeremy. *Orthodox by Design: Judaism, Print Politics, and the Artscroll Revolution.* Berkeley: University of California Press, 2010.

B. Barry Levy

P

PATRISTIC INTERPRETATION

The Christian Bible was being interpreted before there was a Christian Bible. That is to say, before there was anything like an "official" Christian canon of Holy Scripture, certainly no sooner than the fourth century, there was a repertoire of sacred texts that Christian teachers and bishops already considered *virtually* canonical (Barton 1997, pp. 1–34). At least prior to Marcion of Sinope and his *apostolicon*—a controversial selection and edition of authoritative Christian writings intended to supplant the Hebrew Scriptures save as a foil for the gospel—churches were preoccupied less with closing a biblical canon than with the immediate exigencies of Christian identity and self-definition. Justin Martyr's report that in early worship services Christians heard readings from "the prophets" and the "memoirs of the Apostles" (*1 Apology* 67) indicates that "Scripture" at this point was the Hebrew Bible/Septuagint, whose "prophets" (Moses, David, Isaiah, Jeremiah, et al.) gave witness to the Christian dispensation, together with "Apostles" whose own gospel memoirs of Jesus laid claim to those ancient prophetic witnesses. More than fixed lists of authoritative scripture, churches needed a "past" and the connecting links between Israel's sacred history and the advent of Christ. Probably the earliest functional "canon" was what Irenaeus and others called the "canon of truth" or "rule of faith," an epitome of sacred revelation that set out, in variable wording, its definitive contents: the one God; divine creation of the world; the incarnation, death, and resurrection of Christ, and the like (cf. Irenaeus, *Against Heresies* 1.10.1; 1.22.1; 3.4.2; *Epideixis* 3, 6; Tertullian, *On the Prescription of Heretics* 13.1–6; *On the Veiling of Virgins* 1; *Against Praxeas* 2.1–2; Origen, *On First Principles* 1, Pref. 1–8; *Comm. on John* 32.16; *Comm. on Matthew*, ser. 33). This rule in turn provided a criterion for determining both what texts qualified as "New Testament" scripture and their normative relation to the "Old Testament." As well, the rule served as a touchstone and framework for the interpretation of scriptures being authorized within Christian communities (see Kugel and Greer 1986, pp. 155–199).

Prophecy and Typology in Earliest Patristic Interpretation. Patristic interpretation of the Bible thus began with a mandate, as it were, to expound the overarching narrative of salvation that tied together God's revelation to Israel and God's revelation in Jesus Christ to all the gentiles. The archetypal pattern in earliest Christian exegesis, already obvious within the New Testament writings themselves and in the Apostolic Fathers, was that of prophecy and fulfillment. Not only apologetic and polemical works like Justin's *Apologies* and *Dialogue with Trypho*, Irenaeus's *Against Heresies*, or Origen's *Against*

Celsus, but also sermons like Melito of Sardis's *On Pascha* and theological treatises like Tertullian's *On the Resurrection of the Flesh* demonstrated how the Old Testament—Genesis and other narratives of the Torah, the prophetic books, and not least the Psalms—teemed with adumbrations of, even explicit vectors toward, the mystery of Christ (see Skarsaune 1987).

This was more than a pattern of ancient prophetic voices predicting future events that had their ultimate fulfillment or outcome (*ekbasis*) in Christ, such as in the pervasive appeal to Isa 9:6–7 ("For unto us a child is born, unto us a son is given. . . .") as a prophecy of divine incarnation and nativity. There were variations. One such was prosopology ("impersonated speech"), where a certain statement from the Old Testament was ascribed to God the Father or to Christ himself. Already in the New Testament, Davidic enthronement psalms were interpreted as the Father speaking honorifically to Christ at the completion of his earthly ministry (e.g. Ps 2:7 in Acts 13:33 and Heb 1:5, 5:5; Ps 110:1 in Acts 2:34 and Heb 1:13); and Christ himself was understandably accredited ultimate authorship of the lament in Psalm 22 that he uttered from the cross (Mt 27:46 and parallels). Justin details not only the Father's routine declarations through the Prophets (e.g. Isa. 66:1) but also the Son's foretelling of his own scourges and redemptive passion (Isa 50:6; 65:2) and even the Holy Spirit's distinctive announcement that "out of Zion shall go forth the law, and the word of the Lord from Jerusalem" (Isa 2:6), referring to the future mission of Christ's apostles (*1 Apology* 36–53).

Not just prophetic discourse properly speaking, but also events, characters, images and symbols, and unique literary or lexical features within the ancient texts could all prophetically foreshadow or suggest future developments in the economy of salvation. All could serve as "types" (*typoi*; *figura*). And yet "typology" was not in patristic interpretation a single "method" of exegesis per se, one allegedly more respectful of *historical* correspondences and less subjective than allegory, though a functional distinction between typology and allegory can be useful in analyzing early Christian exegesis (cf. Young 1997, pp. 152–157, 161–185; O'Keefe 2000; O'Keefe and Reno 2005, pp. 69–113; Martens 2008). Types, after all, were hardly transparent in the biblical text. Jesus's own claim that "as Moses lifted up the serpent in the wilderness, so must the Son of man be lifted up" (John 3:14; cf. Num 21:9) appears an innocent comparison unless one explores the larger analogy between the elevation of the serpent and the elevation of Christ on the cross as representations of the giving of life, and unless one considers the rich overlapping senses of the Son's "lifting up" in John's Gospel.

Similarly, in the figural interpretation of the relation between the ancient Passover and the new Christian Passover (Pascha) inaugurated through Christ's death, the second-century bishop Melito of Sardis indicates how Jesus's passion was adumbrated not only in the events of Israel's Passover but in vivid narrative types throughout the Hebrew Scriptures:

> For indeed the law has become word,
> and the old new . . .
> and the commandment grace,
> and the model (*typos*) reality (*alêtheia*),
> and the lamb a Son,
> and the sheep a Man,
> and the Man God . . .
>
> He is the Pascha of our salvation.
> It is he who in many endured many things:
> It is he that was in Abel murdered,
> and in Isaac bound,
> and in Joseph sold,
> and in Jacob exiled,
> and in Moses exposed,
> and in the lamb slain,
> and in David persecuted,
> and in the prophets dishonoured.
> (Sermon on Pascha 7, 69; trans. Hall 1979:5, 37)

The intelligibility of the connection between types and antitypes in Melito's sermon rested not on natural historical correspondences but on their mutual orientation to a higher comprehending truth. Even if Melito and other early Christian apologists wanted to suggest that such correspondences were self-evident, it required the lens of the Christian rule of faith truly to make sense of them. What Melito calls the "reality" (*alêtheia*) seems at first sight to represent a simple hermeneutical closure, whereby the *typos* gives way to a superior event (antitype) within the forward advance of salvation history. More than once, Melito refers to the type being rendered obsolete or perishable by its superior antitype. And yet there can be no "fulfillment" without referring both type and antitype to a larger, overarching economy, what Origen later called the "Eternal Gospel" (*On First Principles* 3.6.9; 4.3.13; see de Lubac 2007, pp. 247–259). Within this scheme, the integrity of the *typos*, the original historical referent, was guaranteed, and its original sense, though rendered "useless," could not be utterly evaporated since type and reality each has its "proper season" (Melito, *On Pascha* 37–38). But in the unfolding divine plan a type had always to yield to a horizon of new significance.

"Spiritual" Interpretation and the Negotiation of Scripture's Literal Sense. For Origen and other patristic devotees of the Alexandrian hermeneutical tradition, that horizon of new significance was boundless, since the mystery of Christ, the reality of realities, was infinitely polyvalent. Indeed, Origen says, the scriptures provide the primary launching-points for knowledge of divine things, but "once they have been accurately understood, we must go from them up to Jesus, that he may grant us the spring of water that leaps unto everlasting life (John 4:14)" (*Comm. on John* 13.5.37). The mature Christian must transcend not only the literal sense of texts but all "types, shadows, and indications" (*Comm. on John* 13.24.146) en route to the higher revelation intimately communicated to the soul or to the church by Christ himself—a theme Origen prolifically develops in his *Commentary* and *Homilies on the Song of Songs.* Since, however, all revelation is accommodated through the constraining features of human discourse, those features have to be relentlessly analyzed. Precisely in negotiating the "letter" (*gramma; littera*) of scripture, or in exploring the "thickness" or complexity of the mimetic relation between a scriptural type and its fulfilling truth, Origen and his heirs moved into the terrain of various forms of "spiritual" interpretation aimed at uncovering moral (tropological), doctrinal (allegorical), and mystical (anagogical) dimensions of biblical texts. Here, indeed, typology gave way to multiple senses, a legacy of Origen that endured in medieval exegesis (see de Lubac 2007, pp. 159–171; de Lubac 1998, 2000). In his homily on Noah's ark (*Hom. 2 in Gen.*), for example, Origen works with the basic typological correspondence between the ark and the church as vessels of salvation, with Christ as the "spiritual Noah;" but he discerns in those connections all manner of symbolic and allegorical nuances as well. The dimensions and tiered decks of the ark, scaled to humans and beasts, bespeak the diversity of persons in the church and the hierarchy of ascent from immaturity to maturity in the faith. Indeed, the decks signal the different levels of spiritual interpretation, with all readers called to ascend from lower to higher insights.

Even the animal dung at the bottom of the ark had spiritual significance in Origen's homily. Extremes like this in turn prompted his critics, particularly those associated with the fourth- and fifth-century "Antiochene school" of interpretation (Eustathius of Antioch, Diodore of Tarsus, Theodore of Mopsuestia, John Chrysostom, Theodoret of Cyrus, et al.), to assail such allegorization as extravagant and exotic, and most importantly, as ignoring or violating the literal sense of biblical texts. Drawing on disciplines of literary analysis appropriated from rhetorical and grammatical studies, these exegetes proved far more guarded about the coherence of texts in their original context and suspicious of allegedly hidden senses (see Schäublein 1974; Young, pp. 76–96, 161–185).

And yet the radical polarization between Alexandrian and Antiochene approaches, or even more dubiously between "spiritualizing" and "literalist" approaches, has often been exaggerated in studies of patristic hermeneutics. For one thing, already in the fourth century there were mediating exegetes like Eusebius of Caesarea and Jerome, both of whom became prolific biblical commentators, who combined a strong focus on biblical *historia* with the disciplined use of allegorical exegesis. Eusebius, who in the early Constantinian age reenergized the prophetic-typological reading of the Old Testament, remained very protective of Origen's exegetical methods. Before turning against his theological legacy, Jerome too thoroughly emulated Origen's technical philological and grammatical analysis of the Bible and sanctioned allegory where it was invited by the texts themselves. For another thing, just as the Alexandrians like Origen, or later Cyril (fifth century), still retained genuine respect for the literal meaning (*historia*) of texts (see de Lubac 2007: 103–158), Antiochenes demonstrated their own resistance to literalism and openness to a broader vision (*theôria*) of the spiritual horizon of biblical texts. Diodore of Tarsus, who seminally influenced the Antiochene hermeneutical tradition, affirmed *theôria* as rooted in the purview of the scriptural authors themselves.

What is more, to patristic exegetes Scripture's "literal" meaning in its own right proved hardly to be monolithic, let alone straightforward. Not only were there linguistic, syntactical, and rhetorical issues in its determination, there was the sheer foreignness and obscurity of much of what Scripture recounted, especially the Old Testament (see Kannengiesser 2004, 1:167–205; Young, pp. 187–189). Underlying all these considerations, however, was the issue of God's own intention (*skopos*) in and for the text. As Charles Kannengiesser rightly observes, "a first principle of the literal meaning of the Bible, underscored again and again in patristic exegesis is that *the biblical 'letter'... had its own status, originating from a divine source in a supernatural way; therefore it admitted no neutral reading devoid of the appropriate kind of religious faith.* For the exegetes of the early church the correct interpretation of the *littera* was in itself a spiritual exercise, because for them the materiality of the written text itself was filled with divine mysteries" (Kannengiesser 2004, 1:168). In other words, the literal meaning had to do not just with the original author's intention or with historical context, but with its ultimate theological meaning for the church, in which case it invariably intersected with "spiritual" interpretation. The literal meaning was not frozen in the past but alive and well in the Christian community (see Williams 1991).

Theological Interpretation of the Bible and the Shaping of Christian Doctrine. The "literal" or "plain" sense of Scripture was from the outset central to expounding Christian doctrine. A case in point was doctrine concerning divine creation. Some gnostic interpreters employed the creation story in Genesis 1 to develop myths of a demented creator of the material world working in opposition to the divine First Principle, while Marcion ignored this story altogether since it was irrelevant to his gospel of the benevolent "alien" God revealed solely through Jesus and the apostles. Most pagan critics, meanwhile, scoffed at any cosmogony that claimed a chronological "beginning" of the world or that something could be created "from nothing" (*ex nihilo*). From the second century on, patristic interpreters scrambled to explain the "literal" meaning of the phrase "in the beginning" (Gen 1:1) and of the details of the six-day creation account. Theophilus of Antioch, Origen, and later Basil of Caesarea, Ambrose, and Augustine opted to interpret the true "beginning" (*archê*; *principium*) as Christ himself, through whom God created all things (cf. John 1:3, 10; Col 1:16; Heb 1:2). Eventually, Basil and others stressed the chronological "beginning" of the world as well, especially to protect the pure eternity of the Creator from pagan claims of the coeternity of matter. The christological and chronological readings of Genesis 1:1 were not, however, considered mutually exclusive. Together they represented the pliability of the "literal" sense which could accommodate both.

Augustine pioneered a virtual science of the literal sense in his various commentaries on Genesis. He makes clear from the outset of his *Commentary on the Literal Meaning of Genesis* (*De Genesi ad litteram*) that the *sensus litteralis* is complex, not simple, especially in the case of an event like creation, which was historically incomparable and admitted of different phases and of intelligible and sensible dimensions. Not only were there anthropomorphisms to be overcome in explaining how God "spoke" creation into being (Gen 1:3ff.), how he "rested" from his labor (2:2), or how he "walked about" in the garden (3:8), but there were also physical and metaphysical issues concerning creation *ex nihilo* and the stuff out of which spiritual and material creatures respectively were made. As well, a literal interpretation, to be theologically responsible, had to address the role of the entire Trinity in the creative act, as, for example, in explaining Genesis 1:26 ("Let *us* make humanity in *our* image and likeness") as the shared counsel of Father, Son, and Holy Spirit. Literal interpretation elucidated the ways that the Christian gospel of new creation, and even moral instruction for the Christian life, were already nascent in the original Genesis creation story. Augustine treated these and other themes in exploring the literal sense. His ultimate concern in literal interpretation of Genesis 1–3 was less the apologetic task of establishing the fact of divine creation of the world than the pastoral and catechetical concern to explicate its full significance for Christian understanding of the ways of the Creator and Redeemer of the world.

The *theologically* literal sense also proved crucial for expounding trinitarian and christological doctrine in the early church. The Arian controversy of the fourth century showcased debate over the literal meaning of a number of key texts in which both Arian and pro-Nicene theologians laid heavy stakes. For instance, with a text like Colossians 1:15, which designates Christ (the Son) as "firstborn of creation," Arians took its plain sense to be that the Son of God was himself a created being, albeit the most exalted of creatures or even the agent of divine creation. Athanasius and the Cappadocians brought other considerations into play in order to argue exactly the opposite. Athanasius takes his cue from the larger flow of the passage. How, logically, could the one "in whom" and "through whom" all things were created (Col. 1:16) and "in whom all things hold together" (1:17) be a creature himself? Athanasius takes as self-evident "that neither for himself as a creature, nor as sharing in the same essence with all creation, has he been dubbed 'firstborn' of it, but because the Logos, when at the beginning he formed creatures, condescended to created things to enable them to come into existence" (*Orations against the Arians* 2.64). The other option—and here we see the pliability of the literal sense—was to interpret "firstborn of all creation" in reference to the Son's incarnation, his *created* humanity, which was the archetypal model for all human beings (cf. Athanasius, *Orations against the Arians* 2.61–4; Gregory of Nyssa, *Against Eunomius* 1.573; 3.2.45–57; Hilary of Poitiers, *On the Trinity* 8.50; Theodore of Mopsuestia, *Comm. in Col.* 1.15). The context of Colossians 1:15–20 could accommodate this meaning as well, since Christ is also called "firstborn from the dead" (Col. 1:18), just as in Romans 8:29 he is the "firstborn among many brothers and sisters."

Proverbs 8:22—"God created me the beginning of his ways, for the sake of his works"—commanded attention because both Arian and pro-Nicene interpreters took it literally (and prosopologically) as an utterance of the Logos himself, *qua* Wisdom. Arians predictably assumed that the Logos here attested his own creaturely status, but Athanasius, Gregory of Nyssa, and others considered such a reading simplistic and superficial. Some referenced the follow-up in Proverbs 8:24–25, where Wisdom says that the Creator "begets me" (present tense) before having created the earth, as an affirmation of the "eternal generation" of the Son (Athanasius, *Defense of the Nicene Definition* 26; *Orations against the Arians* 2.80; Hilary, *On the Trinity* 12.37). Several writers famously referred Proverbs 8:22 to the incarnate Son's created humanity (Marcellus of Ancyra, *Fragments* 26–9; Athanasius, *Orations against the Arians* 2.44–82; Gregory of Nyssa, *Against Eunomius* 2.110–113; Gregory Nazianzen, *Oration* 30.2; Ambrose, *On the Faith* 1.15.96). Pro-Nicenes consistently beheld a pattern within Scripture interweaving *theologia* (the mystery of the Trinity) and *oikonomia*, the historical outworking of the Trinity's salvific initiatives.

On the whole, patristic theological interpretation of Scripture operated not according to a strict regimen of "senses" of Scripture but by a larger "deductive" reasoning and by "reading strategies" designed to understand the whole of Scripture in relation to its overarching divine intentionality, or *skopos* (Young, pp. 40, 117, 200, 247, 299). A true master of this strategic approach was Cyril of Alexandria, especially in his *Commentary on John*, where each pericope of the ministry of Jesus is treated as a tableau of the mysterious divine economy. For example, in the miracle at Cana (John 2:1–11), Cyril, true to his exegetical habit, integrates literal and spiritual interpretation. The miracle is, at one level, a straightforward demonstration of the Son of God's power to transform a material that he had already created. But its context within a nuptial celebration signals the mystery of the Bridegroom (the Son) uniting himself with the bride (human nature) so as to renew and resurrect it (as the miracle happened on "the third day") (*Comm. on John* 2; see Margerie 1993, Vol. 1, pp. 241–270).

Scriptural Interpretation and Religious Devotion. Modern standards of academic interpretation, whereby critical exegesis of the Bible needs to be strictly segregated from use of the sacred texts in devotional and liturgical settings, could not be more foreign to the conventions of patristic hermeneutics. We need look no further than the two most influential hermeneutical treatises of the early church, Origen's *On First Principles* (Book 4), and Augustine's *On Christian Doctrine.* Origen's principles (*archai*) of interpretation have more to do with the whole economy of biblical revelation than with exegetical methods per se (see Daley 1998). The Holy Spirit, he avers, has providentially disposed all of scripture, including its difficulties and obstacles (*skandala*), to advance souls toward higher spiritual truth (*On First Principles* 4.2.7–4.3.15). Augustine, in his scrupulous analysis of the nature of biblical language, distinguishes between scriptural "signs" (*signa*)—both straightforward and ambiguous signs—and the realities (*res*) to which they refer, and insists that the ultimate *res* of all scripture is the mystery of the Trinity, which can be approached and "enjoyed" only by those who are being purified, maturing in their journey of faith, and exercising the love of God and neighbor (*On Christian Doctrine* 1.5.5–1.40.44; see Markus 1996). Like Origen, Augustine maintains that the Holy Spirit has designed scripture to motivate and satisfy spiritual hunger (*On Christian Doctrine* 2.6.8). For both authors, the Bible is a book of enigmas and mysteries embedded in the texts to goad the lazy and reward the diligent.

Patristic devotion to the Psalms—the book on which we have the most abundant commentary in the early church—is an extraordinary demonstration of the crucial religious and liturgical function of scripture. Not only did the psalter become the hymnbook of churches and monasteries, it was also a work of spiritual consolation and of vicarious repentance, confession, and worship (cf. Athanasius, *To Marcellinus*; Augustine, *Confessions*; John Cassian, *Conference* 10; see Daley 2003). Within the psalms, doctrine and spirituality were already thoroughly fused. Read in a christocentric key, the psalter was a rich testament to the economy of salvation and a guide to Christians' spiritual and ecclesial formation. Gregory of Nyssa explored how individual psalms, and the overall ordering of all the psalms, reflected a "sequence" (*akolouthia*) drawing the interpreter/singer onward and upward, in the trajectory of the divine *skopos* of cultivating virtue (*On the Titles of the Psalms* 2.11, 14). Augustine, in his *Explanations of the Psalms*, treated many of the psalms as witnesses to the "whole Christ" (*totus Christus*), that is, the deep solidarity between Christ and his church through the storms and stresses of its earthly pilgrimage.

Patristic interpreters discovered spiritual riches in texts often ignored or marginalized in later Christian tradition. The Song of Songs enjoyed a prolific afterlife in the early church and well into the Middle Ages. Commentators like Origen and Gregory of Nyssa set an example for their medieval counterparts (e.g., Bernard of Clairvaux and William of St. Thierry) of reading the Song as an allegory dramatizing the "erotic" love between Christ (the Bridegroom) and his bride (the soul, or corporately the church). The eroticism of this ode, amplifying the elusiveness of the Bridegroom and enflaming of the bride, needed not scandalize the pious once *erôs* was redefined in its true mystical idiom as the deep-seated desire of the soul/church for union with God. Indeed, the Song was in many respects an allegory of the process of interpretation itself, a relentless chasing after the elusive Logos hiding behind every word of the biblical text. From a different scriptural genre, Ecclesiastes, with its sober musings on the vanity of human existence, was reimagined by Gregory of Nyssa (*Homilies on Ecclesiastes*) and the monastic exegete Evagrius Ponticus (*Scholia on Ecclesiastes*) as a deep insight into the paradox wherewith the monotonous cycles of nature and human striving prove to be the medium whereby the Creator providentially converts the creature to the deeper beauty and salvific order of things. Both Gregory and Evagrius, moreover, prosopologically interpret the Ecclesiast, or "Preacher," as Christ himself, the very Wisdom of God.

Numerous patristic interpreters wittingly or unwittingly perpetuated Origen's axiom that *all* of scripture, even its seemingly most repulsive elements, carried spiritual utility or "benefit" (*ōpheleia*). In early monastic tradition, with its combination of fierce pragmatism and contemplative devotion in the use of the Bible, the elder sages, even those resistant to Origen's kinds of interpretive techniques, thoroughly embraced the idea that scripture was an inexhaustible resource of wisdom on the ascetical and spiritual life (see Burton-Christie 1993). In the West, Ambrose of Milan appropriated Origenian hermeneutics in his strongly pastorally-oriented commentary on biblical texts in his homilies and exegetical treatises. He reinforced Origen's conception of three dimensions of biblical wisdom—the "natural," "moral," and "mystical" (otherwise called "rational")—respectively coordinated with Ecclesiastes, Proverbs, and Song of Songs in the Wisdom literature and Genesis, Deuteronomy, and Leviticus in the Pentateuch (*Comm. on Twelve Psalms* 36.1–2; *Comm. on Luke*, Prol.; cf. Origen, *Comm. on Song of Songs*, Prol. 3.1, 6). These were not strictly segregated because the various aspects of divine wisdom embedded in biblical texts were all organically interconnected and mutually edifying.

In addition, Ambrose carried forward the longstanding *exempla* tradition, identifying and amplifying biblical saints as worthy objects of moral and spiritual imitation, whether the audience be clergy, as in his *On the Duties of Ministers*, or catechumens and others, as in his treatises on the Patriarchs (*On Abraham*, *On Isaac and the Soul*, *On Jacob and the Happy Life*, *On the Patriarchs*, and *On Joseph*). Literal, moral, and allegorical exegesis all functioned in these works to construct profiles of the individual patriarchs as models of Christian virtues. This same *exempla* tradition also thrived in Christian hagiography, where the literary icons of martyrs and monastic saints were often fashioned as reminiscences of heroic biblical figures or of Jesus himself in the Gospels (e.g. the *Life of Daniel the Stylite*). Indeed, hagiography became a crucial literary medium through which the early church was able to dramatize its own life as both a mimesis and continuation of the sacred biblical history, bolstering Christians' confidence that God was still in contemporary times raising up extraordinary exemplars of allegiance to the Christian gospel who were also mediators of supernatural healing grace.

So far as biblical interpretation and religious devotion were concerned, the Syriac Fathers developed a distinctive tradition on Christianity's eastern frontier. Especially Ephrem, but also a cadre of later exegetes under his sway, including, in the sixth century, the great Syro-Byzantine hymnist Romanos the Melodist and the prolific preacher Jacob of Serug, plumbed the latent beauty and mythopoeic power of biblical texts (see Brock 2006). In his prose *Commentary on Genesis*, for example, Ephrem proved he could undertake disciplined analysis of the literal sense of the creation story, including its physical and metaphysical difficulties, but in his *Hymns on Paradise*, he broke through to the rich tapestry of symbols, images, and metaphors in the opening chapters of Genesis. In contemplating "Paradise" itself, Ephrem spiritually envisioned, not a mere terrestrial garden, but a grand mountain of primordial and eschatological significance, a haven of the righteous defying the constraints of space and time (Ephrem 1990).

Conclusion. Though much diversity prevailed in patristic hermeneutics, certain principles remained fairly axiomatic in both East and West. First is the conviction of the internal unity and harmony (*symphonia*) of the Bible, discernible solely through careful attention to the letter and to hidden meanings, and through assiduous inter-scriptural interpretation. As Origen states succinctly, all the sacred writings are "one Word that consists of abundant ideas, each of which is part of the whole Word" (*Comm. on John* 5.5). Second, the divine Word is semantically inexhaustible and polyvalent, with any text admitting of multiple legitimate meanings, allowing for the possibility of fresh insight, an ever "fuller sense" (*sensus plenior*). Exegesis must accordingly adapt to the texts' sophistication and pliability. Third, the church is the primary hermeneutical matrix, since interpretation functions foremost to shape Christian identity, doctrinal consistency, liturgical and sacramental practices, and ethics. Finally, scripture is *sacramental* communication, a medium of the presence of Christ the Logos, in which case interpretation itself demands the abiding presence and aid of the Holy Spirit.

[*See also* Allegory and Allegorical Interpretation; Canon of the Bible; Catholic Biblical Interpretation; Eastern Orthodox Interpretation; Exegesis; Theological Interpretation; *and* Translation Techniques, *subentry* Ancient Versions.]

BIBLIOGRAPHY

Barton, John. *Holy Writings, Sacred Text: The Canon in Early Christianity.* Louisville, Ky.: Westminster John Knox Press, 1997.

Blowers, Paul M., ed. and trans. *The Bible in Greek Christian Antiquity.* Notre Dame, Ind.: University of Notre Dame Press, 1997.

Brock, Sebastian. *The Bible in the Syriac Tradition.* Piscataway, N.J.: Georgias Press, 2006.

Burton-Christie, Douglas. *The Word in the Desert: Scripture and the Quest for Holiness in Early Christian Monasticism.* New York: Oxford University Press, 1993.

Canévet, Mariette. *Grégoire de Nysse et l'herméneutique biblique.* Paris: Études Augustiniennes, 1983.

Daley, Brian. "Finding the Right Key: The Aims and Strategies of Early Christian Interpretation of the Psalms." In *The Psalms in Community: Jewish and Christian Textual, Liturgical, and Artistic Traditions,* edited by Harold Attridge and Margot Fassler, 189–205. Leiden: Brill, 2003.

Daley, Brian. "Origen's *De Principiis*: A Guide to the Principles of Christian Scriptural Interpretation." In *Nova et Vetera: Patristic Studies in Honor of Thomas Patrick Halton,* edited by John Petruccione, 3–21. Washington, D.C.: Catholic University of America Press, 1998.

Ephrem the Syrian. *Hymns on Paradise.* Translated by Sebastian Brock. Crestwood, N.Y.: St. Vladimir's Seminary Press, 1990.

Fontaine, Jacques and Charles Pietri, eds. *Le monde latin antique et la Bible.* Paris: Beauchesne, 1985.

Heine, Ronald. *Origen: Scholarship in the Service of the Church.* Oxford: Oxford University Press, 2010.

Heine, Ronald. *Reading the Old Testament with the Ancient Church: Exploring the Formation of Early Christian Thought.* Grand Rapids, Mich.: Baker Academic, 2007.

Kannengiesser, Charles, ed. *Handbook of Patristic Exegesis,* 2 vols. Leiden, the Netherlands: Brill, 2004.

Kugel, James, and Rowan Greer. *Early Biblical Interpretation.* Louisville, Ky.: Westminster John Knox, 1986.

La Bonnardière, Anne-Marie, ed. *Saint Augustin et la Bible.* Paris: Beauchesne, 1986.

Lubac, Henri de. *History and Spirit: The Understanding of Scripture according to Origen.* Translated by Anne Nash. San Francisco: Ignatius Press, 2007.

Lubac, Henri de. *Medieval Exegesis: The Four Senses of Scripture,* 3 vols. Translated by Mark Sebanc. Grand Rapids, Mich.: Eerdmans, 1998, 2000, 2009.

Margerie, Bertrand de. *An Introduction to the History of Exegesis,* 3 vols. Petersham, Mass.: St. Bede's, 1993–1995.

Markus, Robert. *Signs and Meanings: World and Text in Ancient Christianity.* Liverpool: Liverpool University Press, 1996.

Martens, Peter. *Origen and Scripture: The Contours of the Exegetical Life.* Oxford: Oxford University Press, 2012.

Martens, Peter. "Revisiting the Allegory/Typology Distinction: The Case of Origen." *Journal of Early Christian Studies* 16 (2008): 283–317.

Melito of Sardis. *"On Pascha" and Fragments.* Greek text edited and translated by Stuart Hall. Oxford: Oxford University Press, 1979.

O'Keefe, John. "'A Letter that Killeth': Toward a Reassessment of Antiochene Exegesis, or Diodore, Theodore, and Theodoret on the Psalms." *Journal of Early Christian Studies* 8 (2000): 83–103.

O'Keefe, John, and R. R. Reno. *Sanctified Vision: An Introduction to Early Christian Interpretation of the Bible.* Baltimore: Johns Hopkins University Press, 2005.

Rondeau, Marie-Josèphe. *Les commentaires patristiques du Psautier (IIIe-Ve siècles).* Rome: Pontificium Institutum Studiorum Orientalium, 1982.

Schäublein, Christoph. *Untersuchungen zu Methode und Herkunft der antiochischen Exegese.* Cologne: Peter Hanstein, 1974.

Simonetti, Manlio. *Biblical Interpretation in the Early Church: An Historical Introduction to Patristic Exegesis.* Translated by John Hughes. Edinburgh: T&T Clark, 2001.
Skarsaune, Oskar. *The Proof from Prophecy: A Study in Justin Martyr's Proof-Text Tradition.* Leiden, the Netherlands: Brill, 1987.
Williams, Rowan. "The Literal Sense of Scripture." *Modern Theology* 7 (1991): 121–134.
Young, Frances. *Biblical Exegesis and the Formation of Christian Culture.* Cambridge, Mass.: Cambridge University Press, 1997.

Paul M. Blowers

Pentecostal Interpretation

Pentecostal biblical interpretation describes the emerging approaches being employed by Pentecostal biblical scholars in their study of scripture.

Origins of Pentecostalism. Pentecostalism as a movement is just over one hundred years old, with two locations playing significant roles with regard to its origins. On 1 January, 1901 at a Bible School in Topeka, Kansas, a female student named Agnes Ozman was reported to be the first person in the twentieth century to experience Spirit Baptism accompanied by speaking in tongues in accordance with the teaching of Charles F. Parham, an itinerate teacher and preacher. Later that decade in 1906, an African American student of Parham's, William Seymour, traveled to Los Angeles, California to become pastor of a small congregation. Having been turned out of the congregation to which he was called, owing to his preaching Spirit Baptism with the evidence of speaking in tongues, Seymour began to preach in a home that was opened to him. The response to these meetings was significant, necessitating a move to an old rented building on Azusa Street that had formerly been used as a stable. Here an interracial revival of phenomenal proportions took place, repercussions being felt globally with numerous missionaries passing through the revival meetings, quickly taking the message of Pentecost to every continent save Antarctica. The theological heart of this emerging movement would be identified as the Full or Fivefold Gospel that proclaims Jesus is Savior, Sanctifier, Holy Spirit Baptizer, Healer, and Soon Coming King. Other significant revivals would break out around the world almost simultaneously, but Azusa Street would come to be regarded by most as the home of the modern day Pentecostal movement. Though the movement would later be scarred by divisions over race, sanctification, and an understanding of the godhead, by the turn of the twenty-first century, there would be over six hundred million individuals who would identify themselves with the Pentecostal and charismatic movements worldwide. Of this constituency, the majority are young (under twenty), female, illiterate, southern hemisphere, and persons of color. While it is not uncommon for Pentecostals to be thought of as fundamentalists who speak in tongues, a comparison of the movement with other groups by means of the Fivefold Gospel reveals its differences from fundamentalism and its points of commonality with the holiness, Orthodox, and even Roman Catholic traditions. By the same token, though most Pentecostals have a very high view of scripture, it is not a static understanding, but one that sees scripture in dynamic and active ways. Though in North America Pentecostalism would later be influenced by evangelical approaches, at its heart there are major differences. To illustrate this point, for years the denominational statement on scripture for the Church of God was, "We believe in the whole Bible rightly divided. . . ." with no explicit statement on inspiration itself until the denomination joined the National Association of Evangelicals decades later. Rather than studying the Bible to derive theological principles by which to live, most Pentecostals approach scripture as a way to encounter the living God as the text is read. In fact, it would not be going too far to say that there is a sense in which scripture has a sacramental function for Pentecostals. Ignoring the artificial division between texts that are deemed "didactic" and those that are deemed "illustrative," Pentecostals avoid a canon within the canon approach by taking seriously the theological dimension of all scripture, especially narrative, believing that scripture interprets scripture and is, not surprisingly given the

Fivefold Gospel, christologically oriented. Generally speaking, Pentecostals take scripture as an invitation to enter into and participate in the biblical world itself alongside the biblical characters.

Development and Prominent Figures. While Pentecostalism and Pentecostal interpretation of the Bible have been influenced by numerous individuals, and its story can be told by several narrative trajectories, below is a discussion of some of the most seminal figures who shaped the more reflective approach to self-understanding and interpretive praxes.

Gerald T. Sheppard. The first scholar to call for intentional reflection about the need for and shape of a distinctively Pentecostal approach to scripture was Old Testament scholar Gerald T. Sheppard, who in 1978 published a two-part series in *Agora*, an Assemblies of God (USA) periodical. Citing extensive historical research into early Pentecostal (Assemblies of God) literature, Sheppard argues that Pentecostals had a literal (though not historical-critical) sense of the text that was informed by their religious experience. Not interested in choosing sides between liberal or conservative uses of historical criticism nor canonizing authorial intent, they were interested in a "spiritual criticism" that resulted in a theological interpretation of their Pentecostal experience. Calling for an approach to scripture that is more consistent with the instincts of early Pentecostalism rather than following a modernist paradigm, Sheppard urges the development of a Pentecostal approach that is based upon spiritually informed discernment and intuition.

Howard M. Ervin. If Sheppard anticipates the development of a Pentecostal hermeneutic, Oral Roberts University Old Testament scholar Howard M. Ervin appears to be the first person to propose a concrete Pentecostal hermeneutic in a 1981 *Pneuma* article. Informed by the hermeneutical trends of the day, Ervin offers an evaluation of existentialism, historical-critical exegesis, and the new hermeneutic. He argues that a pneumatic epistemology provides a way forward that can bridge the dichotomy between faith and reason (existentialism), serves as an antidote to the destructive rationalism that sometimes accompanies historical critical exegesis, and provides rational accountability for mysticism. Such an approach would seek to give priority to the text of scripture itself, offer space for an appreciation of the numinous within scripture, and offer a much needed revisioning, if not jettisoning, of what is and is not acceptable to "the modern mind," which is itself an artificial construct. Since the Holy Spirit as divine hermeneut is needed for an understanding of scripture, an experience of the Spirit on the order of apostolic experience allows one to interpret "from within" resulting in a pneumatic continuity in experience, faith, and doctrine for the Pentecostal interpreter within both scripture and the experience of the historical church.

Mark D. McLean. Three years (1984) after Ervin's article, Assemblies of God Bible scholar and philosopher, Mark D. McLean, warns that the development of a Pentecostal hermeneutic is an inescapable necessity if the movement is to engage in effective ministry in the "modern" world, rather than wither after the deaths of a variety of charismatic leaders. Specifically, he calls upon Pentecostals to pay attention to the hermeneutical and theological differences between themselves and their evangelical and neo-orthodox counterparts owing to their view of the place and role of the Holy Spirit in their diverse communities. Pentecostalism's conviction of the continuity of the Spirit's activity from creation to the last days, as well as the continuity of presence among biblical writers and contemporary believers, leads to the conclusion that a Pentecostal witness must be accompanied by the gifts of the Spirit. Such a different worldview makes the need for the exploration and development of a Pentecostal hermeneutic absolutely essential.

Russell P. Spittler. Though his work is not described as a proposed model for a Pentecostal hermeneutic, New Testament scholar Russell Spittler (1985) provides a testimony of sorts about his own interpretive approach to scripture as a Pentecostal devoted to Evangelical options in the study and use of the Bible. Drawing upon early Pentecostal models of doing theology, his own formative churchly influences, and the impact of the schools he attended, Spittler offers a theological sample of his approach by examining 1 Corinthians 11:2–16. His approach includes some background information on the city of Corinth, a brief description of the context of the chosen passage, attention to structure of the text, as well as an application of his reading. His concluding theological reflections include the idea that scripture serves to nourish personal piety, that a convergence of a variety of methodological approaches can result in interpretation that is life-changing, that while exegesis can bring one to the "vestibule of truth," the Holy Spirit must open the inner door, and that historical critical approaches are inadequate without being enhanced by faith, hope, and love.

Rick D. Moore. One of the most significant figures in the call for and development of a Pentecostal hermeneutic is Old Testament scholar Rick D. Moore. As early as 1987, Moore not only argues that those in the tradition have no choice but to work toward the development of a distinctively Pentecostal approach to scripture, but he also offers an outline of the contours of such a hermeneutic. Central for Moore are: (a) the role of the Holy Spirit that addresses the interpreter in ways that transcend reason; (b) the role of experience where knowledge and lived-experience mutually inform one another in the believer's response to the transformative invitation of scripture; (c) the Pentecostal understanding of the prophethood of all believers where all believers are expected to integrate their calling as witnesses to "walk in the light" and to bear witness to those within and beyond the community's borders; and (d) the inseparable connection between knowledge of the truth and "active membership in the localized Body of Christ," for it is here that the Spirit speaks as nowhere else, Acts 15 being an example of such a phenomenon. Two of Moore's subsequent studies are devoted to explorations of the Book of Deuteronomy. In the first (1992) he discovers that the dialectical elements of inscripturated word and prophetic utterance are not only found within the book, in the form of "the God so near" and "the law so good" (Deut. 4:5–8), but also the way these elements are to function in the believing community. Later (1995), Moore discerns the central role Horeb and the fire of God play in the book by exploring Deuteronomy from the internal vantage point of divine encounter where the interpreter not only makes a claim about the text, but is claimed by the God of the text. The fact that the significance of the Horeb event has received so little scholarly attention reveals that such an internal starting point has had little place in the world of critical scholarship, suggesting that such biblical criticism is not critical enough! Later, however, Moore's approach would lead him to an engagement with the prophets that results in an articulation of a taxonomy of the prophetic calling, an assessment of the role of prophet as mentor in the presentations of Moses, Elijah, and Elisha, and analyses of these figures and writings that take into account the role of prophetic passions (Jonah). The Writings too are the object of Moore's Pentecostal approach where there is a clear appreciation in the interpretive process for the dialectical dimensions of the text as well as for the role the affections play in interpretation.

John McKay. In 1994, a significant article by British Old Testament scholar John McKay appeared. McKay sought to set out the impact of his Spirit Baptism—experienced while he was a university lecturer—upon his approach to biblical interpretation. Arguing that "academic biblical study" (whether liberal or conservative) and prophetic Christianity function on two different levels, McKay uses the analogy of the theater, suggesting that biblical scholars function much like the critics who review the play, while prophetic Christians actually go onto the stage and act in the drama! McKay claims that his Spirit Baptism resulted in numerous new insights into the Book of Deuteronomy in particular, insights that had not come earlier despite considerable previous academic attention given to the book. As prophetic people, or at least as those who have prophetic sympathies, Charismatic readers approach the scripture by means of a basic "shared experience" with the characters in the biblical text, whether they be prophets, apostles, or even Jesus. This awareness of such biblical similarities naturally leads to an appreciation for spiritual gifts, for example, rather than a dismissal of the phenomena as legend or myth. Rather, Pentecostals experience scripture as prophetic literature or charismatic biographies. Thus, the approach to scripture for prophetic readers is as witnesses, not analysts. They are called upon to have the courage to leave aside their role as critic and actually step onto the stage of the biblical drama.

J. C. Thomas. Published alongside McKay's essay was J. C. Thomas's first formal attempt at helping to construct a Pentecostal hermeneutic. Acts 15, a text that reflects the debate about whether or not gentile believers in Jesus must first convert to Judaism to be considered fully-fledged Christians, was the starting point for which a close narrative reading was offered. The reading revealed three component parts of the implicit hermeneutical paradigm modeled in the passage: the role of the community, the role of the Holy Spirit, and the role and place of scripture. The community is the place where testimonies are given and discerned and the context in which the leader speaks. The role of the Holy Spirit is unexpectedly significant, as it is the experience of the Spirit that has created the context and the need for the discernment of this issue. The Spirit then leads James and, in turn, the community to a specific biblical text deemed most appropriate for the context, and is instrumental in reaching the final decision that "it seems good to us and the Holy Spirit" (Acts 15:28). Scripture's place in this process is surprising for several reasons. The deliberations do not begin with scripture but move from the context of divine activity to the text. The choice of the scripture, which seems to be at odds with a variety of other Old Testament texts with regard to the place of gentiles among the redeemed community, seems to have been heavily influenced by the community's experience of the Spirit in their midst. The scriptures also contribute to the temporary stipulations with regard to the admission of gentiles. Thus, in this text, the function of scripture is dynamic rather than static and contextual rather than propositional. These hermeneutical findings were then tested on the issue of women in ministry, where the Pentecostal experience of women being called to a variety of ministries should lead the community to identify with those scripture texts that testify to the involvement of women in ministry rather than focusing only on the passages advocating silence. Thomas's other contributions to Pentecostal hermeneutics have come in the form of distinctive approaches to introductory courses to the teaching of the New Testament, approaches to commentary writing, and engagement with previous generations of Pentecostals as well as those from the broader Christian tradition by utilization of *Wirkungsgeschichte* (reception history).

Larry R. McQueen. The first Pentecostal treatment of a single biblical book comes in the form of Larry McQueen's volume devoted to *Joel and the Spirit.* His dialogical approach (a) combines his Pentecostal pre-understanding, which highlights aspects of the text often not observed by other readers, with "a fresh critical reading of Joel" that results in a clearer articulation of both Pentecostal eschatology and ecclesiology; (b) respects both the historical and literary significance of the text as well as its character as living word of God; and (c) seeks a deep communal knowledge of God. McQueen's initial examination of the text of Joel highlights three dominant themes—lament, salvation, and judgment—all of which are connected to the promise of the Spirit in Joel. These themes are traced in the New Testament and then in early Pentecostal periodical literature. Focusing upon the revisioning of Pentecostalism in the light of his study, McQueen calls upon the movement to be intentional about the need for its eschatological context, the recovery of lament, and its need to function prophetically as both a sign of salvation and judgment.

Kenneth J. Archer. In 2005, the first full scale study devoted to Pentecostal hermeneutics appeared in the form of a monograph by Kenneth J. Archer. From the time of its publication, it has been considered something of a "state of the art" study. Contextualizing his study by means of his own narrative journey as a Pentecostal, Archer locates early Pentecostal practice within other nineteenth century approaches. Gleaning data from early Pentecostal sermons, testimonies, and the like, Archer proposes that the method used in this period is what he calls "The Bible Reading Method," which illustrates the approach by means of early Pentecostal discussions of Spirit Baptism and controversies that developed around baptism in the name of Jesus. Proposing that the Pentecostal story and identity are understood through the hermeneutical filter of what he terms the "Central Narrative Convictions" that Jesus is Savior, Sanctifier, Holy Spirit Baptizer, Healer, and Soon Coming King, Archer goes on to offer a withering critique of the historical-critical method used by many evangelicals. Informed by semiotics, narrative analysis, and reader-response criticism, Archer builds constructively upon Thomas's earlier proposal arguing for a triadic negotiation of the biblical text, the Pentecostal community, and the Holy Spirit from which meaning emerges.

Robby Waddell. The next major contribution to Pentecostal hermeneutics comes in the form of the first monograph length treatment of the pneumatology of the Apocalypse from Robby Waddell. In an overview of the history of research on this topic, Waddell reveals both the fault lines along which interpretations fall as well as the way the context of the individual interpreters impacts the interpretations that they propose. This overview is followed by a highly nuanced and sophisticated chapter on the origins, history, and development of intertextuality and its appropriation within Apocalypse studies. Seeking to engage the pneumatology of the Apocalypse intertextually from his context as a Pentecostal, Waddell sets forth what he calls "the profile of a Pentecostal reader of the Apocalypse," which has four component parts. First, the initial word in the text, "Apocalypse," would encourage the reader to expect an experience of Jesus Christ in which Jesus would unveil the text's meaning for the reader. Second, the status of scripture revealed in Revelation 1:3 underscores the relationship between written and spoken word, interpreting and keeping the prophetic word, and the communal text for interpretation. Third, the dynamic interplay between "Word" and "Spirit" that exists for Pentecostals would lead to the expectation that such interpretation should take place within a community that appreciates and practices "the prophethood of all believers." And fourth, the Pentecostal's approach to scripture is informed by the fear of God in worship and the reading of scripture. In the last chapter Waddell offers a reading of Revelation 11:1–13, concluding that in the Apocalypse, the Spirit inspires "the prophetic witness of a pneumatic church" so that the church functions prophetically in a hostile world.

Lee Roy Martin. In the most recent major contribution to the field of Pentecostal hermeneutics, Old Testament scholar Lee Roy Martin, offers a literary and theological reading of the book of Judges from a Wesleyan-Pentecostal perspective. Martin describes the goal of his own Pentecostal approach, informed by the biblical studies guild and the emerging discipline of Pentecostal hermeneutics, as "A Pentecostal 'Hearing' of Judges" owing to the prominence of the term "hearing" in the biblical canon, the oral nature of both the biblical and Pentecostal contexts, the implicit connection between hearing and obedience and transformation, and the submission implied in the term. Martin's careful hearing of the speeches of Yahweh, the narrative's main character, leads Martin to the conclusion that there is within the Yahweh of Judges a dialectic between his anger and his compassion, which leads to risk and vulnerability on his part, an unresolved tension in which the hearer is called upon to live and discern.

Major Characteristics. The preceding approaches share for the most part a conviction and attempt to think through a Pentecostal hermeneutic from the ground up, an approach that is not beholden to existing theological grids but one that is representative of the ethos and practice of the Pentecostal movement. As such, these attempts are distinct from a number of fundamentalist or even evangelical approaches, but rather make use of a wide range of dialogue partners spanning the interpretive and theological landscape. Although diverse in starting points and methodological approaches, certain central components surface in not a few of the proposals put forward. The three elements that appear most often are a robust expectation of the Spirit's involvement in the interpretive task, a concrete and defined role for the interpretive community, and a dynamic view of the role and function of the text of scripture. Though there is considerable overlap between these elements, each of them will be treated individually in the attempt to make as clear as possible their distinct contributions.

The Role of the Spirit. It almost goes without saying that Pentecostal interpreters share with a number of other Christian interpreters a belief in the inspiration of scripture by the Spirit. However, in contrast to approaches that have no distinct role for the Spirit in the interpretive process or those who reduce the Spirit's role to rather vague talk about illumination, the Spirit's role in a Pentecostal biblical hermeneutic is deemed to be concrete and discernible at most every step in the hermeneutical process.

Formation of the Interpreter. As evident from the models surveyed, for many, the role of the Spirit in the interpretive process is thought to begin as early as the formation of the individual interpreter within the Pentecostal community. It would appear quite evident that it is well nigh impossible to be a Pentecostal interpreter if one is not part of a worshipping Pentecostal community, for it is within this context that one comes to know the "full gospel" not simply as a catechism but as a narrative way of life. The experiential journey of coming to know Jesus as Savior, Sanctifier, Spirit Baptizer, Healer, and Soon Coming King by means of the Spirit's activity, results both in the transformation of one's affections or dispositions and in a degree of appreciation for the dynamic role experience plays in the interpretive process. At the same time, the experience of the Spirit in the community serves to cultivate within the community and individual interpreter an appreciation of a hermeneutical worldview that includes an expectancy of the Spirit's direct involvement and intervention. Among other things, this expectation serves to create within the interpreter an openness to a variety of aspects of the biblical text that are often ignored or downplayed by other interpreters—phenomena such as exorcisms, miracles, healings, prophecy, and other activities of Spirit, for example. This openness to the biblical text also creates a sensitivity within the Pentecostal interpreter both to the function of "passions" within the biblical text as well as to their role in the Pentecostal hermeneutical process. Thus, an interpreter sensitive to the prayerful, passionate, and prophetic dimensions of the text of scripture would be prepared to explore the ways in which these "passions" might be incorporated into the interpretive process—for instance, how the practice of lament prepares one to interpret biblical lament (as in McQueen's work on Joel). The Pentecostal interpreter is also formed by means of participation in the practice of pneumatic discernment, opportunities which present themselves at most every turn in Pentecostal life and worship. One such example is the practice of offering, hearing, and discerning testimonies given by various members of the community about God's activity in their lives. The offering of such "sacred stories" is not restricted to the "professional clergy" but may come from any member of the community, including children. Likewise, the community learns to engage in pneumatic discernment of the words offered and the lives that lie behind the words, as not everyone who speaks in the name of God actually speaks for God. Whether admonition, confirmation, or correction, the communal responses reveal the depth of the discernment practiced and, as such, encourage individual members to become more and more experienced at discerning reflection about the intersection of testimony, the text of scripture, and the broader Christian story. Such discerning reflection also prepares the Pentecostal interpreter for assessing other more distant "testimonies" that come in the form of voices from the past, both inside and outside of the Pentecostal community, so that for the Pentecostal interpreter, the practice of *Wirkungsgeschichte* becomes an opportunity for active dialogue with living voices from the past, rather than a survey of artifacts from a distant time. Specifically, for a number of Pentecostal interpreters, the testimonies of the first twenty years of the Pentecostal movement's existence have borne much fruit, not only as a helpful bridge between the biblical text and the interpreter, but also by means of the depth and clarity of insight into a variety of topics of relevance for the community.

Formation of the Community. The role of the Spirit in Pentecostal interpretation is, however, not limited to the formation of the interpreter but is also believed to play a role in the interpretive process by creating the communal context in which interpretation takes place. Such creative work includes the Spirit's establishment of the discerning community, often, by means of dynamic divine intervention and activity. Thus, the specific interpretive context is not seen as outside the domain of the Spirit's involvement but, rather, as its production.

The Role of the Community. It is within this interpretive community that the Spirit's concrete activity is placed into dialogue with the text of scripture to discern the way forward on a variety of issues. As in the example from Acts 15, it is here that the testimonies of brothers and sisters with regard to the Spirit's activity is discerned as scripture and is examined and reexamined in the light of the Spirit's work. Such matters may range from significant to more mundane aspects of doctrine, practice, and mission. On this approach, the community offers a safe place to explore the experience of the people of God in the light of scripture and, as such, offers a check to rampant individualism and subjectivism, on the one hand, while providing space for all members of the community to be active members in such discerning work on the other hand. Thus, the communal context for interpretation is a living reminder of the biblical mandate that interpretation is no private matter, while at the same time, offering concrete expression of the way in which the diverse gifts of the Spirit function within the body of Christ.

The Role of Scripture. The third rather obvious component in this triadic approach to interpretation is the role of scripture itself. While it is clear that scripture functions authoritatively for Pentecostal interpreters, it is just as clear that Pentecostal approaches to scripture are not concerned with reducing the text to orderly propositions, nor are they overly concerned with what lies behind the text as in historical-critical approaches. Rather, the authority of scripture is understood much more dynamically—it is regarded as a living voice that can still be heard by means of the activity of the Spirit within the discerning community. As such, Pentecostal interpreters give pride of place to the text itself on the text's own terms, often utilizing narrative approaches as the method of choice, owing in part to the fact that story has figured so prominently in testimony, sermon, and song in the movement. Such approaches encourage active participation by the interpreter in the biblical story itself. This approach allows Pentecostal interpreters to gauge the authenticity of their experience as they see within the pages of scripture accounts of the same kind of Spirit inspired phenomena they have experienced. This means that not only the broad strokes of the biblical accounts are important, but even smaller details can also serve to confirm their experiences. At the same time the text can function as boundaries, revealing that certain experiences do not "line up" with the text and, as a result, are not to be seen as legitimate in faith and practice. Thus, hearing the individual voices of scripture proves to be very important indeed. At the same time, there is an appreciation for the diversity of the scriptural witness. Rather than trying to play one voice in the scripture choir over against another one, the Pentecostal interpreter is more concerned to hear the entire scripture choir with all its dissonances. This reflects the importance of hearing the individual voices of scripture, while not dismissing the collective sound these voices generate in all their diversity, resulting in what might be called "diverse voice in one accord." The practice of worshipping in community where a diversity of gifts exist, prepares the Pentecostal interpreter to value the individual, even smallest, voice while keeping one's ear attuned to the whole choir. Such an approach allows the interpreter to pick up on the singular contributions of the individual voice, while at the same time, to hear and discern the meaning of the new sounds, the blue notes, when voices that do not sing in unison sing together. Far from being a static or frozen word, scripture is a dynamic, inviting word that confirms, leads, and directs the Spirit-inspired interpreter and community in the light of the Spirit's activity, which often generates new ears to hear dimensions of the biblical witness that heretofore have not been recognized.

The Future of Pentecostal Biblical Interpretation. While the emerging academic discipline of Pentecostal hermeneutics is a relatively recent phenomenon, it is already generating exciting results that have been well received within the movement as well as by major biblical scholars outside the tradition who have served as influences and dialogue partners. The field for future exploration would appear to be wide open. An especially important project would be a detailed examination of early Pentecostal hermeneutics. To date, most of the relevant data has been generated by tracing the effective history of specific texts or as a result of examinations of texts relevant to a specific theological topic. Some work has been done on the interpretive approaches of individual early leaders and no doubt more will follow. The development of additional Pentecostal reading strategies and actual readings of a variety of texts will no doubt continue. A recent but growing trend is the development of interpretive approaches that are intentionally interdisciplinary. Owing to Pentecostalism's global constituency, one could well expect that contextual contributions from a variety of locations around the world will be forthcoming.

[*See also* Authority of the Bible; Evangelical Interpretation; Exegesis; Historical Criticism, *subentry* Hebrew Bible; Historical Criticism, *subentry* New Testament; Intertextuality; Literary Criticism, Literary Theory, and the Bible; Narrative Criticism and Narrative Hermeneutics; Reader-Response Criticism; Reception Criticism and Theory; *and* Theological Interpretation.]

BIBLIOGRAPHY

Archer, Kenneth J. *A Pentecostal Hermeneutic: Spirit, Scripture and Community.* Journal of Pentecostal Theology Supplement Series 28; London: T&T Clark, 2005, now Kenneth J. Archer, *A Pentecostal Hermeneutic: Spirit, Scripture and Community.* Cleveland, Tenn.: CPT Press, 2009. State-of-the-art study of Pentecostal hermeneutics.

Ervin, Howard M. "Hermeneutics: A Pentecostal Option." *Pneuma* 3, no. 2 (Fall, 1981): 11–25. First actual proposal for a Pentecostal hermeneutic.

Martin, Lee Roy. *The Unheard Voice of God: A Pentecostal Hearing of the Book of Judges.* Journal of Pentecostal Theology Supplement Series 32; Blandford Forum, UK: Deo, 2008. Most detailed examination of an Old Testament book from a Pentecostal perspective.

McKay, John. "When the Veil Is Taken Away: The Impact of Prophetic Experience on Biblical Interpretation." *Journal of Pentecostal Theology* 5 (1994): 17–40. Reflections of an Old Testament scholar on the impact of his Spirit Baptism upon his biblical interpretation.

McLean, Mark D. "Toward a Pentecostal Hermeneutic." *Pneuma* 6, no. 2 (Fall 1984): 35–56. One of the earliest calls for the construction of a Pentecostal hermeneutic.

McQueen, Larry R. *Joel and the Spirit: The Cry of a Prophetic Hermeneutic.* Journal of Pentecostal Theology Supplement Series 8. Sheffield, UK: Sheffield Academic Press, 1995. See now Larry R. McQueen, *Joel and the Spirit: The Cry of a Prophetic Hermeneutic.* Cleveland, Tenn.: CPT Press, 2009. First treatment of an entire book by means of a Pentecostal approach.

Moore, Rick D. *The Spirit of the Old Testament.* Journal of Pentecostal Theology Supplement Series 35. Blandford Forum, UK: Deo, 2011. Best collection of hermeneutical studies by a leading Pentecostal Old Testament scholar.

Sheppard, Gerald T. "Word and Spirit: Scripture in the Pentecostal Tradition—Part One." *Agora* 1, no. 4 (Spring 1978): 4–5, 17–22. First call and rationale offered for a distinctively Pentecostal approach to scripture.

Sheppard, Gerald T. "Word and Spirit: Scripture in the Pentecostal Tradition—Part Two." *Agora* 2, no. 1 (Autumn 1978): 14–19.

Spittler, Russell P. "Scripture and the Theological Enterprise: View from a Big Cano." In *The Use of the Bible in Theology: Evangelical Options,* edited by Robert K. Johnson. Atlanta: John Knox, 1985, 56–77. Early reflections on Pentecostal interpretation by a leading New Testament scholar.

Thomas, John Christopher. *The Spirit of the New Testament.* Blandford Forum, UK: Deo, 2005. Collection of important essays on a variety of topics related to Pentecostal approaches to scripture.

Thomas, John Christopher. "'Where the Spirit Leads': The Development of Pentecostal Hermeneutics." *Journal of Beliefs and Values* 30, no. 3 (2009): 289–302. Extensive chronological survey of the most significant developments in Pentecostal biblical interpretation.

Waddell, Robby C. *The Spirit of the Book of Revelation.* Journal of Pentecostal Theology Supplement Series 30. Blandford Forum, UK: Deo, 2006. The first monograph length study of the pneumatology of the Apocalypse. Utilizes intertextuality, constructs a profile of a Pentecostal reader of the Apocalypse, and offers a detailed reading of Revelation 11:1–13.

John Christopher Thomas

Performance Criticism

Performance criticism is an interpretive method that seeks to understand the biblical texts within an oral/aural milieu. A relatively new approach in the field of biblical studies, its aim—broadly conceived—is to appreciate how orality and performance shaped the composition, presentation, transmission, and reception of the biblical traditions.

Origins of Performance Criticism. Within the broader academy, performance criticism (or performance studies) has been an established discipline for over thirty years. Representing a wide and intellectually diverse constellation of perspectives and ideologies, including theories of dance, anthropology, theatre, literature, philosophy, and cultural studies, performance studies transcends any one field of inquiry and, by nature, is an interdisciplinary enterprise. With multiple stories of origin and no univocal perspective, "performance" is thus a complex and far-reaching term that encompasses a broad range of activities from theatre and dance to ritual and play (Crane 2001).

In the domain of biblical studies, the concept of "performance" has a more restricted field of meaning. In general, the term is used in reference to the events associated with the practice of oral delivery—the "performance" of a biblical tradition. The critical study of performance and its implications is an emerging discipline, but the contours of the discussion are tied to other developments in the field of biblical studies.

Historical Roots. The impetus for performance criticism is dependent upon hermeneutical shifts in the broader discipline and beyond. In some respects, the rise of performance criticism can be traced to form-critical studies in the early twentieth century and the movement to push beyond questions of source criticism to the pre-textual traditions of the Bible. However, while a primary motivation of the form critics was to understand the oral traditioning process (e.g., Gunkel, Bultmann), scholars were unable to disentangle themselves from a literary mindset. Though the form critics were poised to establish a paradigm shift, they were unable to imagine an oral milieu that adequately accounted for the social realities of the ancient world. Instead, in the field of biblical studies, advancements in disciplines such as anthropology and folklore had a more pronounced effect on the understanding of orality.

No study was more influential than the work of Milman Parry and Albert Lord. Through their pioneering research on the Homeric epics, Parry, who has been called the "Darwin of oral literature," and Lord, his protégé, single handedly ushered in a new awareness of orality and performance. Some of the conclusions of the "Parry-Lord theory" are no longer accepted—notably the rigid bifurcation between oral and written traditions—but the findings sparked a reappraisal of orality across a host of disciplines. Scholars such as Eric Havelock, Walter Ong, Jan Vansina, Jack Goody, Ruth Finnegan, and John Miles Foley built on the work of Parry-Lord and advanced the conversation still further, propelling the scholarly world to reconsider the relationship between orality and literacy.

As orality studies were gaining momentum in other disciplines, the field of biblical studies was experiencing the rise of a different hermeneutical approach that eventually laid the groundwork for the advent of performance studies. Beginning in the 1970s, a handful of scholars began experimenting with the Gospels as storytelling events. Drawing from the work of scholars such as Wayne Booth, Seymour Chatman, and Gérard Genette, some began applying secular literary theory to the study of the biblical narratives (e.g., Alter, Rhoads and Michie, Culpepper, Kingsbury). Narrative criticism, as the movement was termed, was in many respects a response to traditional historical-critical approaches and attempted to bring renewed focus on the final form of the biblical texts, arguing that the scriptural narratives were creative and unified stories. Although narrative critics wed themselves to contemporary literary theory and ironically fell victim to many of the same shortcomings as the form critics, the strategy did much to reinvigorate discussion of the biblical stories as literary creations.

Influential Biblical Scholars. By analyzing the biblical narratives using literary tools, narrative criticism unwittingly set the stage for the reappraisal of the biblical stories as oral events. Indeed it is not surprising that many of the same scholars who were instrumental in the early discussion of narrative criticism have become significant voices in performance studies. One of the first to champion this perspective was Werner Kelber. His 1983 publication, *The Oral and Written Gospel: The Hermeneutics of Speaking and Writing in the Synoptic Tradition, Mark, Paul, and Q*, was not the first to probe oral hermeneutics in the field of biblical studies, but was a pioneering work that offered a penetrating critique of Bultmann's form-critical assumptions and attempted to move beyond the print-centric perspective that had dominated the study of biblical texts. Drawing upon a wealth of research spawned from the work of Parry, Lord, Havelock, Ong, and others, Kelber argued that the biblical narratives must be understood in their oral contexts—as events in sound rather than words on a page. Indeed, Kelber (1983, p. 14) concluded that "the circumstances of performance, the composition, and the transmission of oral versus written materials are sufficiently distinct so as to postulate separate hermeneutics." Recognizing that the biblical texts arise out of a fundamentally different media context than written documents, Kelber argued that scholars must reorient themselves to the reality of ancient performance.

In addition to Kelber's influential work, one of the more significant figures in the rise of performance criticism has been Thomas Boomershine. Both in the academy and the church, Boomershine has been a leading figure in the discussion of biblical storytelling. In 1988 Boomershine published *Story Journey: An Invitation to the Gospel as Storytelling* (Nashville: Abingdon, 1988), a volume that was intended to provide "a journey into the gospel tradition in its original medium, oral narrative" (p. 17). Outlined around ten scenes from the gospel traditions, the study charted a practical guide to the art of biblical storytelling, including issues ranging from how to discern (audibly) the structure of a story to the use of gestures. Rich with insight, *Story Journey* laid out the first methodological program for the telling of gospel stories. Likewise, in 1985 Boomershine was instrumental in helping establish "The Bible in Ancient and Modern Media," a Society of Biblical Literature group that for many years has considered the implications of media culture, as well as offering an opportunity for scholars to interact and engage around questions of orality and performance. To reach an even broader audience, Boomershine helped found the "Network of Biblical Storytellers," an international organization designed to provide a forum for scholars, ministers, and laypersons to exchange ideas and become more effective storytellers.

Notwithstanding the contributions of Kelber and Boomershine, the individual who is perhaps most widely associated with performance criticism is David Rhoads. A trailblazer in the field of narrative criticism (1982), Rhoads has become one of the leading voices in the discussion of performance criticism. He has written extensively on the subject (2006) and is the first to argue that performance criticism is a distinct and emerging discipline within the field of biblical studies. As well, Rhoads is the editor of a monograph series entitled Biblical Performance Criticism and is an active performer. He has performed the Gospel of Mark over 200 times, along with other books in the NT, including Galatians, Philemon, James, 1 Peter, and Revelation.

Distinguishing Characteristics. Performance criticism has its roots in various hermeneutical approaches and thus draws from an array of methodologies. What distinguishes the strategy is a pursuit to understand how orality impacts the dynamics of biblical interpretation.

Critical Assumptions. Although scholars have long noted that many of the biblical traditions—particularly the Jesus story—originated in an oral context, the implications of this observation have been widely neglected. As many scholars have observed, approximately 5 percent of the population was literate around the period of the first century. The question that naturally follows is how the vast majority of individuals could have participated in communal activities, which presumably featured instruction from the biblical texts. Performance critics argue that the answer to this query lies in the act of performance, which Rhoads (2006, p. 119) defines as "any oral telling/retelling of a brief or lengthy tradition—from saying to gospel—in a formal or informal context of a gathered community by trained or untrained performers—on the assumption that every telling was a lively recounting of that tradition."

Rhoads's definition is particularly helpful and underscores three elements that are generally shared by performance critics. First, a key assumption is that performance constitutes a form of oral delivery. Not only were most individuals unable to read, but it is presumptuous to assume that many possessed copies of the scriptures. Moreover, contrary to modern ways of thinking, the most trusted means of instruction was through the medium of oral communication. Exactly how oral delivery was performed is a matter of debate. Some argue that the biblical texts were memorized and delivered without the use of mnemonic aids (i.e., texts). Others, however, affirm that ancient performers physically held and directly read from the ancient manuscripts. While the distinction between the two perspectives is not unimportant, it is crucial to recognize that both theories rest on a shared assumption. In either case, it is postulated that the biblical traditions were transmitted through oral media and received in the context of an aural event.

Second, in concert with oral delivery, performance criticism assumes that the biblical traditions were experienced in communal settings. Though this observation is shared by any number of interpretive approaches, traditional methods of interpretation have uncritically adopted literary perspectives that have minimized this foundational assumption. Rather than appreciating the texts as part of a communicative process between performer and audience, the biblical texts have frequently been analyzed using the methods derived from the practice of silent reading. Not only does this perspective overlook the oral nature of private reading in the ancient world (e.g., Acts 8:27–30), it minimizes the unique dynamics at play in the communal reception of an oral tradition, which ultimately demand a very different set of interpretive strategies.

Third, performance criticism assumes that the performance arena was a lively and evocative atmosphere. Those responsible for performance typically embodied the characters they presented and employed a full range of verbal and nonverbal techniques, including gestures, vocal inflection, facial expressions, and more. Likewise, audiences were not passive in the communicative process. It was not uncommon for audiences to become active participants through the use of applause, verbal response, and gestures. In this sense, performance critics have sought to understand how the use of emotion impacted all facets of communication between storyteller and audience—an issue that has been largely overlooked by biblical scholars.

These underlying assumptions may not appear to warrant a new hermeneutical approach. Indeed, many of the insights have been acknowledged in previous scholarly discussion; however, only infrequently have these observations been reflected upon in concert with one another and rarely have the full implications of these presuppositions been addressed. At the center of performance criticism is a call to reorient biblical studies, to shift the scholarly discussion from a print-centric approach to one that considers how orality and performance alter the interpretive process. What this requires is a rethinking of the biblical methods that have been based on the practice of silent reading. At the most foundational level, performance criticism necessitates a paradigmatic shift—a challenge for biblical scholars to alter their angle of vision. Even more broadly, an understanding of performance necessitates an appreciation of the full spectrum of verbal and nonverbal techniques that enrich the aesthetic exchange between performer and audience. This reorientation ultimately requires the implementation of new interpretive tools that can facilitate an understanding of performance and its various dimensions. Accordingly, performance critics have begun incorporating findings from disciplines as broad as media studies, theatre, speech act theory, orality, and the social sciences.

Relation to Ancient Media Studies. Given the recent development of performance criticism, it is perhaps easier to define the general assumptions of the discipline than the fixed parameters of the approach. At this stage, performance criticism is a discipline whose boundaries remain pliable. Nonetheless, it is important to consider how performance criticism is related to what has been termed "ancient media studies." Some have argued that "ancient media studies" constitutes an umbrella concept that encapsulates three related interests: orality, performance, and memory studies (Le Donne and Thatcher 2011, p. 1–8). According to this schematization, performance criticism is an interpretive subset of a broader field of inquiry, namely, ancient media studies. Others scholars, however, seem to imply the opposite relationship, suggesting that the discipline of performance criticism is the overarching concept that links the various components associated with ancient media studies (Rhoads 2006). The distinction between the two approaches hinges on the conceptual breadth that one assigns to the notion of performance, and whether performance can be reduced specifically to the act of delivery or whether it also includes the elements and activities *associated with* performance. A resolution to this conceptual dilemma will depend on the evolution of the disciplines. What remains relatively clear is that the two concepts enjoy considerable overlap as both emphasize the ancient media culture from which the biblical texts emerged.

Interpretive Implications. It might be argued that performance criticism, though based upon legitimate and accepted assumptions, is overly subjective and beyond the reach of modern interpreters. Since scholars do not have recourse to ancient biblical performances, attempts at reconstruction are therefore futile. It should be acknowledged that every performance is—to a certain extent—an irretrievably, unique communicative event, dependent upon a number of factors ranging from the disposition of the performer to the setting of the communicative event. However, that performances of a given tradition varied does not mean that the biblical texts are devoid of performative clues, including illocutionary details.

Recognizing the performance context through which the biblical traditions emerged is only one aspect of the hermeneutical shift. Scholars have already identified consequences that enlighten many traditional exegetical conclusions, particularly in relation to the ways in which narratives are understood. Two examples will suffice.

First, one of the standard practices in Gospel scholarship has been to describe the respective plot lines of the individual evangelists. Typically, this practice is carried out through the construction of outlines, which are intended to provide an orderly account of the various shifts in the narrative. But as Joanna Dewey (1991, p. 221) has observed, a retrospective examination of these works suggests that there is little scholarly consensus and that "of the making of outlines . . . there is no end." The reason for this perplexing array of interpretations is that scholars have been working with the wrong assumptions. Rather than approaching the Gospels as performance events whose contents are arranged for the listening ear, scholars have operated under the presumption that the Gospels were arranged for literary purposes. Differentiating between the two is significant. Dewey argues that, unlike written texts, the Gospels reflect an oral pattern of structuring. Scholars have often assumed that the gospels unfold in a linear fashion around the geographical, thematic, or historical features of the narrative, but Dewey maintains that the practice of oral structuring is similar to a fugue or interwoven tapestry, where themes are blended together in a more complex and interlocking fashion. Unlike print media, texts written for performance are characterized by "multiple overlapping structures and sequences" (Dewey 1991, p. 224) that are composed around the acoustic principle of the echo. The purpose of this rhetorical technique is to facilitate the audience's understanding by forecasting what is to come through what has already occurred. In this respect, Dewey points to a new way of understanding biblical stories, simultaneously accounting for the absence of linear plots and providing an explanation for the use of overlapping and interwoven structures that characterize biblical traditions.

Second, in the history of biblical interpretation it has sometimes been assumed that the concern for the reader was "a commercial blemish on an otherwise spotless face of art" (Booth 1983, p. 90). More recent hermeneutical trends, including narrative and reader-response criticisms, have taken a more favorable view toward the role of the reader and the impact that narratives have upon audiences (implied or real). These attempts, despite offering a corrective in many respects, have nonetheless been wed to literary approaches with limited theoretical means of articulating how this interaction occurs. Performance critics have shown that in oral discourse audiences are not merely outside observers to whom the narrator subtly attempts to communicate. Instead, in the performance arena, audiences actually become participants in the telling of the story. As the performer depicts the events, the storyteller is not simply an "implied" narrator but an individual who is physically present in the performative arena. What is more, as the story is narrated, the performer naturally takes on the role of the characters. For example, Doan and Giles (2005) have argued that in the prophets, the storyteller takes on the authority of the prophet, thereby creating a powerful interplay with the audience. Likewise, in the Gospels, the storyteller frequently becomes the mouthpiece of Jesus (Boomershine 2011). The effect of this phenomenon is that the storyteller is able to engage the audience directly and to reorient the audience within the horizons of the story world. As the performer becomes a character in the drama, the audience is invited to take on the role of the character to whom the address occurs. The performative context allows the storyteller to blur the interpretive boundaries in order to facilitate audience participation in the narrative and to engage in direct audience address. Only by appreciating the dynamic interchange between the audience and performer is the interpreter able to explain adequately how the storyteller is able to appeal to the audience in such a powerful and evocative manner.

Approaches to Performance Criticism. Performance critics do not speak of a formal classification scheme, but there appear to be three trajectories set in motion by the discussion. The following explication charts the various approaches and provides examples of the scholarly insights generated from these studies. To date, the majority of research in the discipline has focused on the Gospel narratives, in particular the Gospel of Mark. Despite the significant overlap between the approaches, each offers a particular focus under the rubric of performance criticism.

Enacted Performance Criticism. Because performance entails something that is beyond the experience of silent reading, some have argued that in order to appreciate the paradigm shift, interpreters must experience the biblical texts in performance. Just as it would be inconceivable to study Beethoven's 7th Symphony without hearing a musical rendition of the piece, so too it is inherently reductionistic to consider the biblical traditions apart from an enacted performance. To do so is to neglect an array of rhetorical and storytelling features that are brought to life in performance and enliven an understanding of the biblical stories.

Holly Hearon demonstrates the importance of oral performance by analyzing Mark 5:21–43 using both narrative and performance criticisms. Hearon explores dimensions of the text such as setting, conflict, character, and narrator in order to show how performance criticism is distinguishable from traditional literary approaches. Most significantly, Hearon (2011, p. 211) argues that "the oral nature of the written text changes everything" by evaluating the performative elements as depicted in two contemporary, dramatic presentations of Mark's Gospel.

Among Hearon's numerous observations is the suggestion that many foundational assumptions about Mark are based on theories derived from literary perspectives. For example, Hearon examines the setting in Mark's intercalated stories of the hemorrhaging woman and Jairus's daughter. Whereas narrative approaches highlight the descriptive elements of the contextual backdrop, including the temporal and spatial markers that situate the account in Jesus's ministry, along with the memorial clues that draw connections to the story of Israel (e.g., the number 12), these features are typically analyzed as textual or, at best, verbal cues within the narrative. Hearon suggests that in performance the spatial setting of an episode takes on a physical dimension. The implications of this are twofold. First, a performer is able to designate certain areas of the "stage" for particular kinds of events (e.g., miracles) or types of space (e.g., synagogues). Although this is a seemingly pedantic observation, the use of physical space allows the performer to establish connections between (seemingly) disparate episodes in a more powerful way (as compared to literature) by drawing upon visual and verbal cues. Second, Hearon argues that the narrative setting is ultimately embedded within a performative setting that exerts a controlling influence on the reception of the story. For example, it makes a significant difference whether the story of Jesus is performed in a church setting that frames the Gospel in a liturgical context or whether it is performed in a prison setting that accents the Gospel's claim to set people free. As Hearon observes, the "physical setting of the audience both determines the performance space that can be used and creates an interpretive lens though which the performance is experienced" (Hearon 2011, p. 216).

In light of the performance dimension, Philip Ruge-Jones (2009) offers a similar reassessment but in relation to the role of the narrator. Stemming from his work as a performer and participant in the Network of Biblical Storytellers, Ruge-Jones argues that literary critics have confused how the narrator functions in the telling of a story. It is often assumed that the narrator represents an omniscient and omnipresent entity that stands over and above the narrative—a detached, unidentified noncharacter who is responsible for the telling of the story. In performance, however, the narrator is never a transcendent, internalized voice. Rather the narrator is a living person that is embodied in the act of performance, a special kind of character that takes on physicality, even participating in the narrative. This fundamental distinction, Ruge-Jones argues, is the reason scholars have proposed the notion of an omniscient narrator, mistakenly assuming that the narrator is an otherworldly being rather than a living person. While this might be viewed as a limiting feature of performance, in actuality it is a key to the rhetorical power of storytelling. Through the dynamic interaction between the narrator and audience, the performer functions as a guide that leads the audience through the story. Ruge-Jones (2009, p. 40) concludes that the "storyteller's authority and reliability do not lie in the illusion of being invisible or neutral or above it all, but in being present and attentive to, perhaps even partisan with, the audience and their concerns."

While Hearon and Ruge-Jones emphasize different elements of performance, both do so from a shared methodological perspective. The resulting conclusions are derived from an analysis that recognizes that it is possible to "experiment with twenty-first century performances as a way to help . . . understand the meaning and rhetoric of the biblical texts in their historical context" (Rhoads 2009, p. 95).

Idealized Performance Criticism. The concept of performance introduces an inherently broad and elastic class of components into the interpretive process, including features such as voice intonation, facial expression, and gestures. While it is true that these elements complexify the hermeneutical process, some maintain that it is possible to recreate an ideal performance scenario. Whitney Shiner (2003, p. 4) argues that, although scholars may not have immediate access to ancient performances, it is nonetheless possible to envision an ideal performance based upon the Gospel text and what is known about rhetorical techniques and the ancient world in which the Gospels took shape. In this respect, the practice is similar to other historical reconstructions and, most importantly, attempts to account for the media context in which the Gospels emerged.

Shiner's work on the subject is the most important to date, and though it focuses on the Gospel of Mark, the discussion offers a host of insights for performance criticism in general. For example, Shiner discusses the importance of gesture and movement. Unlike the act of silent reading where words and gestures are divorced from one another, performance is a multifaceted enterprise that draws on an array of communicative tools, including gestures. Shiner provides an extensive discussion of the subject from the works of Plato, Philostratus, Siculus, Quintilian, and Cicero, as well as the Terence manuscripts. Shiner discusses numerous examples—many of which are quite unusual from a contemporary perspective—including stereotypical movements in the Greco-Roman world used for activities such as reproaching, exhortation, and insistence. Additionally, Shiner points out how Mark's Gospel includes various stage directions to guide performers in the use of gestures. At various points in the story, the narrator deliberately includes statements supplying some type of hand (e.g., 1:31, 41) or body movement (e.g., 3:5; 5:31; 7:33–34). Not only does the use of gestures flow naturally from the telling of the story and accentuate the performer's delivery and rhetoric—what Demosthenes described as the most important element of speaking—but understanding how speakers use nonverbal communication has interpretive implications as well. Shiner argues that the repeated use of gestures can help to link scenes and themes that might otherwise be overlooked.

Utilizing a similar conception of performance in order to hypothesize about an idealized presentation of the biblical narratives, others have focused on exploring the interaction that takes place between audience and performer. It has been shown that some features of the Gospels that have caused interpretive debate are actually performative tools that enhance the audience's participation in the narratives. Iverson (2011), for example, argues that, despite the widespread attention generated by the secrecy motif in Mark's Gospel, scholars have largely neglected the rhetorical effect of the device. Although Mark reveals the identity of Jesus in the opening verses of the Gospel, and thus the notion of secrecy pertains only to the characters in the story, the use of the device nonetheless has a powerful effect on the audience's experience of the story, particularly when delivered in a performance setting. Contrary to others who have suggested that the presence of secrecy in the Second Gospel is a reflection of the strategies employed by the Markan community to demarcate themselves from hostile forces, Iverson suggests that the device functions in an altogether different capacity. Utilizing the social sciences, Iverson demonstrates that the secrecy motif functions as a rhetorical tool to invite audience sympathy toward the performer and the message of the Gospel. Instead of operating as a narratological device that is leveraged for the sake of insulating the community, Mark employs the secrecy motif to attract outsiders to the community. Through the principle of the disclosure-liking relationship—a term used by sociologists to refer to the relational synergy generated by revelatory discourse—the performer is able to exploit the rhetorical device to encourage the positive reception of the Gospel.

What is notable about these latter approaches is the attempt to situate performance within the context of the first century (or other appropriate period). Thus, rather than deriving their conclusions primarily from modern performances, these scholars have focused attention on what is discernable about ancient performance as a means to help theorize and better understand the biblical traditions.

Discipline-Inspired Performance Criticism. Although the appreciation of biblical traditions as performance has sparked an emerging discipline, just as important are the tangential effects of the paradigm shift. The extent of the movement can also be observed in the scholarship of those working with the traditional methodologies, such as source, form, and textual criticism. However, whereas the majority of those working within performance studies are focusing on the dynamics of performance for the sake of performance, others are concerned to show how performance sheds new light on longstanding discussions within the field of biblical studies.

The recently launched Biblical Performance Criticism series contains several volumes that fall into the category of discipline-inspired performance criticism. For example, James Maxey (2009) examines how an understanding of ancient orality and performance challenges modern conceptions of Bible translation as it relates to African nations. Whereas Bible translation often operates as a subtle means to exert linguistic, social, and theological control over developing churches, Maxey argues that ancient performance establishes a basis for translation contextualization. In addition, the discussion elevates a whole new set of questions. The issue is not merely how to translate the written text into a host language. In a region of the world where epics, proverbs, and folktales are celebrated, the rich appreciation of verbal art demands that translators also consider how biblical performances might be "translated."

In another volume in the Biblical Performance Criticism series, Antoinette Clark Wire (2011) engages traditional questions regarding the composition of Mark's Gospel. While it has been widely assumed that the evangelist constructed the Gospel as a literary act—with some reliance on source materials—Clark takes an altogether different perspective. Utilizing a variety of techniques, Clark argues that Mark's Gospel was composed in performance. Clark suggests that Mark's textual artifact bears the imprint of storytelling techniques that collectively point to an orally derived composition. In particular, Clark analyzes the text of Mark to show that the Gospel evidences a kind of special speech, or short "intonation units," that characterize oral rather than written communication.

Though these examples outline specific contributions of performance theory, they demonstrate that the discussion of performance has far-reaching implications across the field of biblical studies. Quite naturally, scholarly inquiry has gravitated toward the Gospel narratives, but the analysis of performance might be applied to a broader range of biblical and nonbiblical material, including but not limited to the Hebrew Bible and New Testament letters. Given this untapped potential, although performance criticism is a relatively new discipline, the approach is sure to have a pronounced effect in the years to come. Indeed, many would argue that in order to understand the context in which the biblical traditions emerged, the study of performance is crucial. It may be hyperbolic to suggest that performance criticism reveals "why everything we know about the Bible is wrong" (Fowler 2009, p. 3), but the assertion may be far more accurate than many acknowledge.

[*See also* Form Criticism, *subentry* New Testament; Narrative Criticism and Narrative Hermeneutics; Orality Studies and Oral Tradition, *subentry* New Testament; Reader-Response Criticism; Reception Criticism and Theory; Rhetorical Criticism; Speech-Act Theory; *and* Synchronic Interpretation.]

BIBLIOGRAPHY

Boomershine, Thomas E. "Audience Address and Purpose in the Performance of Mark." In *Mark as Story: Retrospect and Prospect*, edited by Kelly R. Iverson and Christopher W. Skinner, 115–142. Atlanta: SBL, 2011. A detailed examination of how Mark uses the character of Jesus to engage directly the audience of the narrative.

Booth, Wayne C. *The Rhetoric of Fiction*. 2d ed. Chicago: University of Chicago Press, 1983. A classic work detailing the methods and techniques used in narrative, many of which remain helpful for understanding the dynamics of storytelling.

Crane, Mary Thomas. "What Was Performance?" *Criticism* 43, no. 2 (2001): 16–87. An excellent introduction to the discussion of performance by a leading scholar in the field.

Dewey, Joanna. "Mark as Interwoven Tapestry: Forecasts and Echoes for a Listening Audience." *CBQ* 53 (1991): 221–236. An early effort to demonstrate the importance of orality for the interpretation of the Gospels.

Doan, William and Terry Giles. *Prophets, Performance, and Power: Performance Criticism of the Hebrew Bible*. London: T&T Clark, 2005. An informative volume that provides a methodological introduction to performance criticism along with a detailed analysis of Amos.

Foley, John Miles. *How to Read an Oral Poem*. Chicago: University of Illinois Press, 2002. Written by one of the leading theorists in orality studies, this monograph demonstrates how extra-textual features of oral poems can be interpreted.

Fowler, Robert M. "Why Everything We Know About the Bible is Wrong: Lessons from the Media History of the Bible." In *The Bible in Ancient and Modern Media*, edited by Holly E. Hearon and Philip Ruge-Jones, Biblical Performance Criticism 1, 3–18. Eugene, Ore. Cascade, 2009. An article that traces the media history of the Bible, exposing several popular fallacies regarding biblical texts.

Hearon, Holly E. "From Narrative to Performance: Methodological Considerations and Interpretive Moves." In *Mark as Story: Retrospect and Prospect*, edited by Kelly R. Iverson and Christopher W. Skinner, 211–232. Atlanta: SBL, 2011. Detailed examination of Mark 5:21–43 that compares and contrasts the exegetical insights of narrative and performance criticisms.

Iverson, Kelly R. "'Wherever the Gospel Is Preached': The Paradox of Secrecy in the Gospel of Mark." In *Mark as Story: Retrospect and Prospect*, edited by Kelly R. Iverson and Christopher W. Skinner, 181–210. Atlanta: SBL, 2011. An analysis of Mark's messianic secret using performance criticism.

Kelber, Werner H. *The Oral and the Written Gospel: The Hermeneutics of Speaking and Writing in the Synoptic Tradition, Mark, Paul, and Q*. Philadelphia: Fortress, 1983. A pioneering work in the field of NT studies, arguing that scholars have widely neglected the oral/aural context in which the Gospels emerged.

Le Donne, Anthony and Tom Thatcher, eds. *The Fourth Gospel in First-Century Media Culture*, Library of New Testament Studies 426. London: T&T Clark, 2011. A collection of essays that offers one of the first attempts to explore the intersection between ancient media studies and the Fourth Gospel.

Maxey, James A. *From Orality to Orality: A New Paradigm for Contextual Translation of the Bible*. Biblical Performance Criticism 2. Eugene, Ore. Cascade, 2009. Includes excellent background sections on the nature of orality and further demonstrates the broad implications of performance for Bible translation.

Miller, Robert D. II, SFO. *Oral Tradition in Ancient Israel*. Biblical Performance Criticism 4. Eugene, Ore. Cascade, 2011. Given that the majority of work on performance has been in NT studies, this volume's tracing of orality in ancient Israel and discussion of orality in the OT is especially helpful.

Rhoads, David. "Performance Criticism: An Emerging Methodology in Second Temple Studies—Part I." *Biblical Theology Bulletin* 36 (2006): 118–133; "Performance Criticism: An Emerging Methodology in Second Temple Studies—Part II." *Biblical Theology Bulletin* 36 (2006): 164–184. An excellent introduction to performance criticism by a key figure in the field.

Rhoads, David. "What is Performance Criticism?" In *The Bible in Ancient and Modern Media: Story and Performance*, edited by Holly E. Hearon and Philip Ruge-Jones, Biblical Performance Criticism 1, 83–100. Eugene, Ore. Cascade, 2009. Provides an overview of performance criticism and posits a similar trajectory for the discipline as the one outlined here.

Rhoads, David, and Donald Michie. *Mark as Story: An Introduction to the Narrative of a Gospel*. Philadelphia: Fortress, 1982. The first volume to introduce narrative criticism to the NT and the first to apply the methodology to Mark's Gospel.

Ruge-Jones, Philip. "Omnipresent, Not Omniscient: How Literary Interpretation Confuses the Storyteller's Narrating." In *Between Author and Audience in Mark: Narration, Characterization, Interpretation*, edited by Elizabeth Struthers Malbon, New Testament Monographs, 29–43. Sheffield UK: Sheffield Phoenix, 2009. Applying a performance-critical perspective to the role of the narrator, the essay demonstrates how literary theories potentially confuse the dynamics of oral narratives.

Shiner, Whitney Taylor. *Proclaiming the Gospel: First-Century Performance of Mark*. Harrisburg, Pa. Trinity Press International, 2003. A groundbreaking volume that explores ancient rhetorical practices for the purpose of understanding the performance of Mark's Gospel.

Swanson, Richard W. *Provoking the Gospel: Methods to Embody Biblical Storytelling Through Drama*. Cleveland: Pilgrim, 2004. Provides a methodological handbook for biblical storytelling and is a part of the *Provoking the Gospel* series, which also includes performance-specific volumes for Matthew, Mark, Luke, and John.

Wire, Antoinette Clark. *The Case for Mark Composed in Performance*. Biblical Performance Criticism 3. Eugene, Ore. Cascade, 2011. To date, the most comprehensive and thorough argument that Mark's Gospel was composed through repeated performance.

Kelly R. Iverson

Phenomenological Interpretation

The term "phenomenological interpretation," in the fields of both literary and biblical criticism, is of limited usefulness as the designation for a specific interpretive method. Indeed, although there was a school of analysis in literary critical studies named "phenomenological criticism" (more on this later), the views and methods of this school constituted only one subset of the broader impact that assumptions arising from the philosophical school of "phenomenology" have had on hermeneutical theory and literary analysis. Phenomenological claims regarding the nature of human perception, knowledge, and communication have influenced a wide array of reading strategies, from "phenomenological criticism" to various forms of literary criticism, including reception theory and even deconstruction. In the arena of biblical studies, the term is not widely employed, and ambiguity often accompanies its use.

Consequently, this entry will not attempt to define detailed parameters of what constitutes "phenomenological interpretation" within the field of biblical studies. Nor will it offer hard and fast criteria for determining which works should be categorized with this designation. Instead, the entry will review the main tenets of phenomenology, and discuss how those tenets influenced certain assumptions, objectives, and movements in literary criticism and, in turn, biblical studies.

The Basic Tenets of Phenomenology. According to Robert Sokolowski (*Introduction to Phenomenology* 2000, p. 2), phenomenology is, at its most basic, "the study of human experience and of the way things present themselves to us in and through such experience." Its founder was the German philosopher, Edmund Husserl (1859–1938), and the system he established was taken up and advanced in the works of Husserl's student Martin Heidegger (1889–1976) and the Frenchmen Emmanuel Levinas (1906–1995), Jean-Paul Sartre (1905–1980), Maurice Merleau-Ponty (1907–1960), and Paul Ricoeur (1913–2005) among others.

Phenomenological Reduction. As a starting point, Husserl agreed with Descartes that we cannot assume the independent existence of things. However, he argued that we can be sure of how objects appear to us in our conscious minds. This is the so-called "phenomenological reduction" that is at the root of his method and most forms of phenomenology: "everything not 'immanent' to consciousness must be rigorously excluded; all realities must be treated as pure 'phenomena,' in terms of their appearances in our mind, and this is the only absolute data from which we can begin"(Terry Eagleton, *Literary Theory: An Introduction.* Rev. ed.; Minneapolis: University of Minnesota Press, 2008, p. 48). It is from this phenomenological reduction that phenomenology gets its name. The name also points to the focus of the Husserl's philosophy: a systematic analysis of the phenomena—or the manifold appearances of objects—in our conscious minds.

How does such analysis differ from how we commonly perceive things? Husserl distinguished between the "natural attitude" and the phenomenological reduction he proposed by claiming that the natural attitude perceives through the senses. It is inclined to discern and test the appearance of the objects in view. In the natural attitude, our focus is on the qualities and nature of the object itself. The focus of phenomenology is an examination of how we go about "intending" objects (i.e., holding them in consciousness) when engaged in the natural attitude. It is the study of how we as rational creatures engage in propositional thinking. It is not concerned with assessing the empirical validity of that thinking, but with how we go about it and construct images of objects in our minds.

> When we move into the phenomenological attitude, we become something like detached observers of the passing scene or like spectators at a game. We become onlookers. We contemplate the involvements we have in the world with things in it, and we contemplate the world in its human involvement. We are no longer simply participants in the world; we contemplate what it is to be a participant in the world and in manifestations (Sokowlowski, p. 48).

Eidetic Reduction. This starting point and focus of phenomenological reduction was paired with another important claim and pursuit. Husserl argued that when we examine human consciousness and intending, we find that humans typically engage in sophisticated, imaginative reflection that analyzes the components of phenomena as they appear to us. Phenomenology pursues the possibilities and limits of such intentionality, and finds that when we freely and imaginatively vary the components of the phenomena being studied, we are able to determine which are their essential, and which their conditional, features. This process is called "eidetic reduction" or "eidetic intuition." In other words, by engaging in such analysis, we can discern what is essential and unchanging about the appearances of phenomena we consider and come to understand the relations between those appearances. Furthermore, phenomenology does not simply maintain that such cognitive constructions of the things we intend provide us with the mental images and concepts we need to speak meaningfully about the world. When these essential predicates have been identified (of a human being, for example), then we have immediate (unmediated), certain knowledge of the actual, fundamental qualities of the objects we hold in consciousness. In short, our careful and repeated observations of the ways in which objects appear to us enable us to penetrate the very essence of the things we observe.

Phenomenology and Ontology. Although phenomenology focuses on the appearances of objects in our conscious minds, it does not maintain that such appearances are unconnected to external reality. To the contrary, the appearances manifested in our minds are themselves real and public, meaning that they can be shared among those intending an object.

> What phenomenology does through its doctrine of the intentionality of consciousness is to overcome the Cartesian and Lockean bias against the publicness of mind, which is also a bias against the reality of the appearance of things. For phenomenology, there are no "mere" appearances, and nothing is "just" an appearance. Appearances are real; they belong to being. Things do show up. Phenomenology allows us to recognize and to restore to the world that seemed to have been lost when we were locked into our own internal world by philosophical confusions. Things that had been declared to be merely psychological are now found to be ontological, part of the being of things. Pictures, words, symbols, perceived objects, states of affairs, other minds, laws, and social conventions are all acknowledged as truly there, as sharing in being and as capable of appearing according to their own proper style (Sokolowski, p. 15).

Yet when it comes to the relationship between the objects intended and the external objects themselves, the phenomenological reduction does not permit the philosopher to go any further down the ontological path (at least not as a phenomenologist). That is the domain of the natural attitude as it inclines toward propositional thinking. At the same time, most forms of phenomenology are not inimical to the natural attitude. To the contrary, phenomenology depends on the natural attitude for its existence and purpose.

> The most important contribution phenomenology has made to culture and the intellectual life is to have validated the truth of the prephilosophical life, experience and thinking. It insists that the exercises of reason that are carried out in the natural attitude are valid and true. Truth is achieved before philosophy comes on the scene.... Phenomenology is parasitic on the natural attitude and all the achievements thereof. Phenomenology has no access to the things and disclosures of the world except through the natural attitude and its intentionalities. Phenomenology comes only later (Sokolowski, p. 63).

The Analysis of Appearances. As mentioned earlier, phenomenology examines the ways in which we perceive and categorize the appearances of phenomena. Basic to this exercise is the recognition that objects we "intend" (hold in consciousness) can appear to us in a multitude of ways. Thus, as we intend objects, we can perceive and explore their various dimensions and through such reflection discern basic features of their identity. The three interrelated, formal structures that guide the phenomenological analysis of objects are: (1) the structure of parts and wholes, (2) the structure of identity in manifold, and (3) the structure of presence and absence. There are two different kinds of parts that can make up a whole. "Pieces" are parts that can exist and appear apart from a whole and present themselves as individual entities (such as apples apart from their tree). "Moments," however, cannot be presented apart from the whole to which they belong. The redness of an apple, for example, cannot be separated from the apple (or at least its skin). Musical pitch cannot exist except as blended with sound. The structure of identity in manifolds maintains that any object can only appear to us as a series or collection of manifold appearances. And yet, it is through such manifold appearances that we can come to discern the identity of an intended reality. Even so, that identity is distinct from its appearances.

> The identity that is given through its manifold of appearances belongs to a dimension different from that of the manifold. The identity is not one member of the manifold: the cube is not one of the aspects or profiles, the proposition is not one of the uttered sentences, the play is not simply one of its performances. The identity transcends its manifolds of presentations, it goes beyond them (Sokolowski, p. 30).

Finally, presence and absence refer to the different ways we may intend phenomena depending on our proximity to them. By engaging phenomena in their modes of presence and absence, we learn more about how we consciously intend such phenomena and how their proximity may alter our perception and reaction to them.

The Use of Phenomenological Concepts in Literary Criticism. As mentioned at the start of this entry, key elements of phenomenology have played an important role in shaping literary critical assumptions and methods, but have done so in rather variable fashion. There is a particular approach critics commonly label as "phenomenological criticism." However, the reach of phenomenology extends beyond this method to influence in varying degrees other literary approaches and their assumptions regarding human perception and the construction of meaning. For this reason, it may be best to use "phenomenological" as an adjective to describe certain features of a literary perspective rather than as a label indicating a specific methodology. What follows are three features of phenomenological thought that have played an important role in shaping what is often referred to as phenomenological criticism and other interpretive endeavors.

Phenomenological Reduction and the Bracketing of Context. A key dimension of what most critics refer to as phenomenological criticism is the application of something like Husserl's phenomenological reduction to a literary text. Among the tendencies of phenomenology that have influenced modern literary theory, this is the one most consistently manifested in works described as "phenomenological."

> As with Husserl's "bracketing" of the real object, the actual historical context of the literary work, its author, its conditions of production and readership are ignored; phenomenological criticism aims instead at a wholly "immanent" reading of the text, totally unaffected by anything outside of it (Eagleton, p. 51).

What becomes the focus of such an approach, then, are the ways in which the author embodied in the text (not the actual author) engages, construes, structures, and interacts with the word the text conveys—how the author, in other words, presents his or her own "manifold of appearances" and "eidetic reduction." The text itself "is reduced to a pure embodiment of the author's consciousness," the deep structures of which "can be found in the recurrent themes and patterns of imagery" presented within the literary work (Eagleton, 51). This approach was the focus of the Geneva school of criticism during the 1940s and 1950s, including the work of Georges Poulet, Jean Rousset, Jean-Pierre Richard, and Emil Staiger. This school explored, in varying ways, the text's internal testimony to the how the author as subject perceived and construed the object of the narrative world.

Whereas the Geneva school focused its analysis on the author embodied in the text, others sought to push against the margins of this phenomenological reduction. Heidegger, followed by Hans-Georg Gadamer and others, argued that human beings are unable to engage any object apart from their own rootedness in a particular context. They rejected the confidence of the Geneva school that a reader can offer an objective, dispassionate account of the author as subject and the text as object. In fact, they set aside the author altogether. Instead, they came to focus on how readers in a given time and place can fuse their horizons with the horizon of a literary work and create a meaning that is coherent but also contingent. Indeed, there is still a reduction in force here. There is no effort to get behind the text to the actual author or the author's historical context or setting; the focus is on the immanent reading experienced by a reader rooted in a particular context. For Gadamer, "all interpretation is situational, shaped and constrained by the historically relative criteria of a particular culture; there is no possibility of knowing the literary text 'as it is'" (Eagleton, p. 62). It is our particularized encounter with the world of the text that is to be the focus of hermeneutics.

The attention Gadamer placed on the role of the reader was taken up by the advocates of reception theory, such as Wolfgang Iser. Iser developed sophisticated accounts of how readers encounter literary works and the role they play in construing meaning from them. From his works and those of others arose the exploration of such concepts as implied readers and authors, gaps of indeterminacy, the horizon of the reader, the repertoire of the reader, and the dialogic nature of interpretation. At the same time, by drawing attention to the techniques, devices, and forms that guide the reader's construal of literary meaning, Iser's work, and that of other "uniformist" reader-response critics, were also very much text centered. Their work reflects a degree and type of bracketing similar to that of the Geneva school's phenomenological criticism, and is the kind of analysis most commonly associated with "phenomenological" interpretation in both the fields of literary-critical and biblical analysis.

Other reader-response critics, such as French critic, Rolland Barthes, and the American critic, Stanley Fish, shift the phenomenological bracket so that the reader stands even more solidly at its center, and the text at its periphery. They argue that readers are the primary if not sole creators of meaning. Jacques Derrida and the proponents of deconstruction take this even a step further, adopting something like Husserl's reduction not only as a methodological starting point but as a guiding maxim. All acts of reading, and perception, are immanent and contingent to the extreme: "In order to learn from deconstruction, we need to suspend our assumption that our words refer to things, that our expressions mean things, that there are, in fact, 'things' at all—including ourselves" (A K. M. Adam, *What is Postmodern Biblical Criticism?* Guides to Biblical Scholarship Series. [Minneapolis: Fortress, 1995] p. 27).

Eidetic Reduction and the Unity of the Literary Text. As noted earlier, phenomenology argued that intended objects, through careful analysis, will eventually reveal consistent and coherent patterns of manifestation to our conscious minds. When carried over to literary analysis, this claim of "identity in manifolds" led phenomenological critics to presume the unity of literary texts and the publically accessible cohesion of the narrative world they depict. This prejudice toward cohesion continues on through the hermeneutics of Heiddeger, Gadamer, and into the uniformist school of reception theory. Here too it is presumed that texts form organic wholes, and it is the role of readers to eventually discern the harmony coursing throughout and binding together the various features of the text. Such analysis frequently begins with an openness to the various ways in which a text might speak to a reader.

> But at the same time the "openness" of the work is something which is to be gradually eliminated, as the reader comes to construct a working hypothesis which can account for and render mutually coherent the greater number of the work's elements. Textual indeterminacies just spur us on to the act of abolishing them, replacing them with stable meaning. They must, in Iser's revealingly authoritarian term, be "normalized"—tamed and subdued to some firm structure of sense (Eagleton, pp. 70–71).

The idea that the text presents coherent meaning, or any particular meaning *apart from a reader*, would be challenged by Barthes and Fish. The idea that the text presents coherent and stable meaning *at all* would in turn be challenged by Derrida and deconstructive criticism. Phenomenology, in its attempt to find meaning and the nature of things through the examination of our intentions, is essentially *logocentric*: it is committed to the principle that there is finally some metaphysical thread connecting words and their referents, signifiers, and signified. Likewise, most forms of reception theory and reader-response criticism advocate the view that there is something essential, and coherent, that the text as intended object conveys to a reader. Deconstructionists, however, contend that the contingent and shifting nature of both texts and readers resist eidetic reduction. There is no universal, no essential character of the things we intend. There is, in short, no identity in manifolds to discover. All is appearances—at least when viewing it through a deconstructive lens.

Focus on Human Perception and Understanding. As previously stated, one of the primary aims of phenomenology is to analyze and explain the ways in which humans interact with and understand phenomena. This endeavor soon spread beyond the sacred hallows of philosophers and began to permeate the halls of academia. It eventually informed, if not spurred, the onset of modern literary criticism, concerned with the only slightly more narrowly focused objective of discerning how humans interact with and understand *literary* phenomena. According to William Ray, phenomenology introduced to literary criticism a basic paradigm that has become programmatic for that discipline: every instance of consciousness, or intention, presumes both a subject and an object, reciprocally constituting one another as act and structure (*Literary Meaning: From Phenomenology to Deconstruction* [Oxford: Basil Blackwell, 1984], p. 3).

> This deceptively simple paradigm of consciousness and its objects has, under a variety of guises, served to justify a wide range of critical theories or programs. Since it authorizes viewing the literary work as an act of consciousness and as a structure, intentionality can be used to underwrite reader-response criticism and "author intention" readings as well as formalistic close reading and structural approaches that objectify the text. And because the same work of literature can exist in the consciousness of both author and reader—indeed of many readers—one can postulate a single intentional object for many intentions and use this postulate to ground a theory of objective literary knowledge (pp. 8–9).

It is for this reason that parallels, if not direct connections, can be seen between the basic concerns of phenomenology and many forms of modern literary criticism. Beyond inserting this basic paradigm of consciousness into the fields of epistemology and literary theory, phenomenology also uncovered a conundrum that has continued to vex widely diverse forms of hermeneutical theory.

> From roughly the beginning of the period when phenomenologists started looking closely at literature to the current post-structuralist project, the major theoreticians have all been grappling with the same problem: namely that "meaning," as it pertains to literature, always seems to have at least two meanings, each of which entails a different, and frequently contrary, theory of the literary work, as well as a distinct critical practice. The clearest example of this can be found in the tension between our two common-sense intuitions of meaning, as both historically bound act, governed by a particular intention at a particular moment, and permanent textual *fact*, embodied in a word or series of words whose meaning transcends particular volition and can be apprehended in its structure by any individual possessed of the language (pp. 1–2).

While not all later literary theory, according to Ray, is simply a development of phenomenological thought, phenomenological criticism began the process of identifying and trying to address the dichotomy of meaning that every text presents. In Ray's view, nearly all recent forms of literary criticism have tended to emphasize one form of meaning while suppressing the other. But even more basic than this, phenomenology also endeavored to explore the nature of human perception and understanding itself. Therefore, postmodern approaches that problematize or even deny the existence of a "permanent textual fact" also share a kindred spirit with Husserl and other phenomenologists. One common thread to all of these various tapestries of hermeneutical theory is that they are all trying to figure out how texts, and readers, mean.

Phenomenological Tendencies in Biblical Studies. Several of the reading strategies discussed earlier have been adopted and adapted by biblical critics, leading to the integration of phenomenological tendencies in the reading of biblical texts. The practice of bracketing historical concerns from consideration and pursuing a detailed account of how the text guides readers' understanding eventually influenced a new wave of biblical critics, many of whom were seeking alternatives to historical criticism. Early attempts to apply secular literary-critical modes of reading to biblical texts were pursued by Robert W. Funk, Dan O. Via, and John D. Crossan in their study of the parables.

Phenomenology, Reader-Response, and Narrative Criticism. Eventually, a new brand of biblical interpretation dubbed "narrative criticism" arose, drawing from several literary-critical strands, but most prominently from the reception theory of Iser and literary critics Seymour Chapman and Wayne Booth. Pioneers in this field include David Rhoads and Don Michie, Jack Dean Kingsbury, R. Alan Culpepper, Richard Edwards, and Robert C. Tannehill, all of whom applied this approach to the Gospels (and in Tannehill's case, also Acts). Their work was joined by that of secular literary critics who engaged their reading strategies to demonstrate how biblical texts function as literature, including Frank Kermode, Robert Alter, and Meir Sternberg. While many elements of the "uniformist" reader-response approach of Iser and others became the basis of narrative criticism, the reader centered theories of Fish and Derrida were adopted by a select few wishing to introduce deconstruction into the rapidly diversifying field of biblical interpretation. Some of the more important engagements of this form of analysis were offered by Stephen Moore. All together, these works marked a surging interest in the application of literary criticism to the biblical texts, which in turn inspired other notable attempts to introduce biblical critics to these reading strategies, such as those offered by Edgar McKnight, Robert Fowler, Mark Allan Powell, Stephen Moore, and A. K. M. Adam among others.

Among the relatively few biblical critics who label their colleagues' work or their own as "phenomenological," most take that modifier to mean a mode of investigation focused on a detailed account of how the biblical text is engaged or experienced by a reader, while unconcerned with questions of historical context or authorial intent. Some, in fact, explicitly identify uniformist reader-response strategies as "phenomenological" (e.g., Robert Detweiler and Mark Allen Powell), though the term might apply equally well to most forms of narrative criticism, which build upon Iser's form of reception theory and the works of literary critics influenced by him. Yet, as I cautioned earlier the term is probably best used as an adjective to modify certain strategies and perspectives rather than as a label designating a specific methodology or even a closely related set of approaches. As with literary criticism, there are several forms of reader response, narrative criticism, and deconstruction making use of phenomenologically inspired strategies, and not all in the same way.

Phenomenology and N. T. Wright's Critical Realism. One further caution seems in order. The association of "phenomenological" with only modes of inquiry unconcerned with historical context and authorial intent may obscure the contribution phenomenology has made to other forms of critically inquiry (as noted by Ray earlier), including historiography. One such example in the arena of biblical studies may be the "critical realist" approach articulated and pursued by N. T. Wright in his multi-volume study of Jesus and the early church. Wright emphasizes at the outset of his introduction to his approach the impossibility of pure, objective analysis, using language that would lead most advocates of postmodern "phenomenological" approaches to nod in agreement.

> The legacy of positivism often seduces us into imagining that a "fact" is a "purely objective" thing, unalloyed by the process of knowing on anybody's part. But in reality what we call "facts" always belong in a context of response, perception, and interaction—a process which is both complex and continuing (*The New Testament and the People of God* [Minneapolis: Fortress, 1992] p. 83).

In offering this critique of positivism, Wright places himself in the long lineage of thinkers who have made the phenomenological pursuit their own, attempting to ferret out the complex relationship between humans and the objects they intend and recognizing that this relationship is more sophisticated and problematic than the natural attitude would assume. Yet, this does not mean, for Wright, that historical inquiry is a lost cause. Despite the fact that we can only encounter objects through the interpretive matrixes of our own sense perceptions and worldviews, that does not mean we are shut off from external reality or our ability to speak meaningfully about it.

> There is no need, despite the assertions of many empiricists of a former age and some phenomenalists in more recent times, to reduce talk about objects external to ourselves to talk about our own sense-data, so that instead of saying "this is a desk" I should really only say "I am aware of sensations of hardness, flatness and woodenness such as I usually have when I sit here", or possibly, to get rid of the suggestion that I have illicitly imported a reference to an actual object, namely myself, "there is here a sensation of hardness, flatness, and woodenness"—or perhaps, more simply, "hardness—flatness—woodenness!" (p. 89).

In making this assertion, Wright clearly steps back into the natural attitude and outside of the phenomenological reduction, but not in a way and for a purpose that Husserl and many others after him would find problematic. The phenomenological reduction was intended as a suspension of the natural attitude which it presupposed, not a denial of its validity.

[*See also* Deconstruction; Literary Criticism, Literary Theory, and the Bible.; Narrative Criticism and Narrative Hermeneutics; *and* Reader-Response Criticism.]

BIBLIOGRAPHY

Adam, A. K. M. *What is Postmodern Biblical Criticism?* Guides to Biblical Scholarship Series. Minneapolis: Fortress, 1995. Helpful introduction to postmodern literary theory and its use in biblical studies.

Alter, Robert. *The Art of Biblical Narrative.* New York: Basic Books, 1981. An application of modern literary theory to the Hebrew Bible.

Anderson, Janice Capel and Stephen D. Moore, eds. *Mark and Method: New Approaches in Biblical Studies.* 2d ed. Minneapolis: Fortress, 2008. A collection of essays applying postmodern literary theory to Mark's Gospel.

Beardslee, William A. "Saving One's Life by Losing It." *Journal of the American Academy of Religion* 37 (1979): 57–72. An example of a "phenomenological-literary" analysis to the saying about finding one's life.

Booth, Wayne. *The Rhetoric of Fiction.* 2d ed. Chicago: University of Chicago Press, 1983. Now a classic introduction to fiction, the text explores how fictional form works, how authors make novels accessible, and how readers recreate texts, using concepts and terms—such as "the implied author," "the postulated reader," and "the unreliable narrator"—that have become part of the standard critical lexicon and important to narrative critics.

Chapman, Seymour. *Story and Discourse: Narrative Structure in Fiction and Film.* Ithaca, N.Y.: Cornell University Press, 1978. Provides a comprehensive approach to a general theory of narrative, in both verbal and visual media. The distinction he makes between story and discourse has become a standard concept in narrative criticism.

Crossan, John Dominic. *The Dark Interval: Towards a Theology of Story.* Salem, Ore.: Polebridge, 1988. First published in 1974, applies modern literary theory to the study of the parables.

Culpepper, R. Alan. *Anatomy of the Fourth Gospel: A Study in Literary Design.* Philadelphia: Fortress Press, 1983. An early narrative critical study of John's Gospel.

Derrida, Jacques. *Speech and Phenomena: and Other Essays on Husserl's Theory of Signs.* Translated by David B. Allison. Evanston, Ill.: Northwestern University Press, 1973. An important introduction to Derrida's thought and deconstruction.

Detweiler, Robert. "What is a Sacred Text?" *Semeia* 31 (1985) 213–230. A phenomenological examination with a reader-response analysis of passages speaking to the authority and character of sacred tradition.

Ebree, Lester et al., eds. *Encyclopedia of Phenomenology.* Boston: Kluwer, 1997. A collection of articles that treat the major concepts in phenomenology. It is commonly regarded as one of the most authoritative reference works on phenomenology.

Edwards, Richard Alan. *Matthew's Story of Jesus.* Philadelphia: Fortress, 1985. An early narrative critical study of Matthew's Gospel.

Fish, Stanley. *Is There a Text in This Class? The Authority of Interpretive Communities.* Cambridge, Mass.: Harvard University Press, 1980. A good source as an introduction to Fish's version of reception theory.

Fowler, Robert M. *Let the Reader Understand: Reader-response Criticism and the Gospel of Mark.* Minneapolis: Fortress, 1991. An early reader-response study of Mark's Gospel that created within biblical studies a more focused close-reading of the biblical texts.

Funk, Robert W. *Language, Hermeneutic and the Word of God: The Problem of Language in the New Testament and Contemporary Theology.* New York: Harper, 1966. An early investigation of recent developments in hermeneutical theory and how they might contribute to the understanding of the Bible as scripture.

Funk, Robert W. *The Poetics of Biblical Narrative.* Sonoma, Calif.: Polebridge, 1988. An application of modern literary theory to biblical narrative.

Gadamer, Hans-Georg. "The Phenomenological Movement." In his *Philosophical Hermeneutics*, edited and translated by David E. Linge. Berkeley: University of California Press, 1976, 130–181. A review of the main themes in the history of phenomenology.

Gadamer, Hans-Georg. *Truth and Method.* Rev. ed. New York: Continuum, 2004. First published in 1960, a now classic work in hermeneutical theory.

Guigon, Charles, ed. *The Cambridge Companion to Heidegger.* Cambridge, UK: Cambridge University Press, 1993. Ten essays on Heidegger's thought with introductory overview and extensive bibliography.

Heidegger, Martin. *Being and Time.* SUNY Series in Contemporary Continental Philosophy. Translated by Joan Stambaugh. Albany: State University of New York Press, 2010. English translation of Heidegger's most famous work, *Sein und Zeit*, first published in 1927.

Hirsch, E. D. *Validity in Interpretation.* New Haven, Conn.: Yale University Press, 1967. One of the best-known attempts to re-establish the author's meaning as the normative principle of interpretation.

Husserl, Edmund. *The Idea of Phenomenology.* Translated by L. Hardy. Boston: Kluwer, 2010. English translation of five lectures Husserl offered in 1907.

Husserl, Edmund. *Logical Investigations.* International Library of Philosophy. Dermot Moran, ed. Translated by J. N. Findlay. 2 vols. English translation of Husserl's most famous work, first published in 1901.

Ingarden, Roman. *The Literary Work of Art: An Investigation on the Borderlines of Ontology, Logic, and Theory of Literature.* Northwestern University Studies in Phenomenology & Existential Philosophy. Evanston, Ill.: Northwestern University Press, 1973. First published in 1931, presents Ingarden's version of reception theory.

Iser, Wolfgang. *The Implied Reader: Patterns of Communication on Prose Fiction from Bunyan to Beckett.* Baltimore: Johns Hopkins University Press, 1974. An introduction to Iser's form of reception theory and the concept of the implied reader, both important to narrative critical and reader-response treatments of biblical narrative.

Kermode, Frank. *The Genesis of Secrecy: On the Interpretation of Narrative.* Cambridge, Mass.: Harvard University Press, 1979. An application of modern literary theory to the Gospels.

Kingsbury, Jack Dean. *The Christology of Mark's Gospel.* Philadelphia: Fortress, 1983. An early narrative critical study focusing on Mark's use of the secrecy motif. Widely read as an example of narrative critical method and considered a key work in the study of Mark's Christology.

Kockelmans, Joseph J. *Edmund Husserl's Phenomenology.* West Lafayette, Ind.: Purdue University Press, 1997. Biographical sketch and an overview of the salient features of Husserl's thought.

McKenna, William R., and J. Claude Evans, eds. *Derrida and Phenomenology.* Dordrecht, the Netherlands: Kluwer, 1995. A review of the relationship between phenomenology and deconstruction.

McKnight, Edgar. *The Bible and the Reader: An Introduction to Literary Criticism.* Philadelphia: Fortress, 1985. An introduction to the use of literary critical theory and the role of the reader in the study of the Bible.

Moore, Stephen. *Literary Criticism and the Gospels: The Theoretical Challenge.* New Haven, Conn.: Yale University Press, 1992. A survey of new literary criticism of the Gospels, tracing its emergence and development, and providing an introduction to the works of critics such as Fish, Derrida, Tannehill, Kelber, and Moore.

Moore, Stephen. *Mark and Luke in Post-Structuralist Perspective.* New Haven, Conn.: Yale University Press, 1991. An excellent introduction to reading Mark and Luke, applying the poststructuralist techniques of Derrida, Lacan, and Foucault.

Newing, Edward. "The Rhetoric of Hope: The Theological Structure of Genesis–2 Kings." *Colloquium* 17 (1985): 1–15. An argument for using the term "phenomenological" to refer to a synchronic, literary analysis of the text in its final form.

Powell, Mark Allen. *What is Narrative Criticism?* Guides to Biblical Scholarship Series. Minneapolis: Fortress, 1990. A helpful introductory guide to narrative criticism and its relationship to modern literary theory and reader-response criticism.

Rhoads, David, Joanna Dewey, and Donald Michie. *Mark as Story: An Introduction to a Narrative of a Gospel.* 2d ed. Minneapolis: Fortress, 1999. The first narrative critical study of an entire Gospel, first published in 1982. This work is widely cited and read as a helpful introduction to narrative criticism.

Roth, Wolfgang. "You are the Man! Structural Interaction in 2 Samuel 10–12." *Semeia* 8 (1977) 1–13. An exploration of 2 Samuel 10–12 using a "phenomenological-structural" method.

Smith, Barry, and David Woodruff Smith, eds. *The Cambridge Companion to Husserl.* Cambridge, UK: Cambridge University Press, 1995. Collection of essays on Husserl's thought with introductory overview and extensive bibliography.

Sokolowski, Robert. *Introduction to Phenomenology.* Cambridge, UK: Cambridge University Press, 2000. Helpful introduction to the main features of phenomenology.

Sternberg, Meir. *The Poetics of Biblical Narrative: Ideological Literature and the Drama of Reading.* Bloomington: Indiana University Press, 1985. An application of modern literary theory to the Hebrew Bible.

Tannehill, Robert C. *The Narrative Unity of Luke-Acts: A Literary Interpretation.* 2 vols. Philadelphia and Minneapolis: Fortress Press, 1986 and 1990. An early narrative critical study of Luke-Acts.

Via, Dan O. *The Parables: Their Literary and Existential Dimension.* Philadelphia: Fortress, 1967. An application of modern literary theory to the study of the parables.

Karl Allen Kuhn

Pop Culture and the Bible

The study of the reciprocal relationship between the Bible and popular culture is fairly new to the academic field of biblical studies, having arisen in the 1980s. It was made possible by the explosion of new disciplinary approaches in higher education—such as sociology, anthropology, and, more broadly, cultural studies—as well methodologies/hermeneutics that had their origin in the academic (and societal) discontent of the 1960s, most notably feminism, reader-response criticism, and post-structuralism. Currently, the predominant method of interpretation employed by scholars examining how the Bible has been interpreted in, and how it has been shaped by popular culture, is Reception History (RH). In what follows, I will offer a definition of "popular culture," delineate some basic assumptions and questions commonly found in RH, provide a brief summary of important work in this field, and raise some issues for its future.

Defining "Popular Culture." One of the most difficult issues in the study of the Bible and popular culture is how one goes about defining "popular culture." Generally, there has been little to no controversy in this area of study about how to understand "Bible," but defining "popular culture" has been more complex, especially since many scholars simply avoid the issue altogether. For simplicity, I will offer two examples of definitions: one propositional, and one open.

Chandra Mukerji and Michael Schudson posit a propositional definition of "popular culture," writing that it is "the beliefs and practices, and the objects through which they are organized, that are widely shared among a population. This includes folk beliefs, practices, and objects rooted in local traditions, and mass beliefs, practices, and objects generated in political and commercial centers. It includes elite cultural forms that have been popularized as well as popular forms that have been elevated to the museum tradition" (1991, pp. 3–4). This definition allows us to see clearly our object of study, in that it includes emotional, performative, material, and critical (or metadiscursive) components. However, in our postmodern age, any propositional definition is suspicious insofar as it attempts to confine, circumscribe, and clarify a wide array of phenomena into a more coherent and comprehensible form.

In his standard work on popular culture, John Storey explores a variety of historical definitions, yet finds that they share little in common aside from the mutual acknowledgement that popular culture is a relatively recent phenomenon, one that appeared in the wake of "industrialization and urbanization" (2009, p. 12). Due to the absence of definitional agreement, Storey argues that popular culture is "an empty conceptual category," (p. 1), and reminds his readers that what one researcher means by "popular culture" is both variable and created by the methods employed to study it (p. 14). The remainder of Storey's introductory text discusses various disciplines and approaches that have studied popular culture, yet it does not advocate a specific definition. As such, Storey ultimately leaves open the question of how to define "popular culture."

As is obvious even from these two examples, defining "popular culture" is an arduous task. On the one hand, one needs to have a sense of what one is studying. On the other hand, when dealing with a malleable object of study like popular culture, one needs a definition that is flexible enough to compensate for new forms and new technologies. As I note, most scholars who study the Bible and popular culture simply do not address the issue of how to define the latter (or for that matter, the former). So, for our purposes we may make two observations: (a) within works that perform RH there is usually a pragmatic focus on specific genres within what we might call popular culture, such as film, novels, television, comic books, and the like, so that in-depth theoretical discussions of how to define popular culture are absent in favor of a more focused examination of its ingredients or manifestations; and (b) much like religion itself, popular culture is not objective or inherent such that it can be defined definitively for all time, so if we were to engage in a detailed theoretical examination of it, perhaps it would be best to think of it as a discourse, in the sense that Michel Foucault and others have defined that term. As I note, though, this theoretical discussion is rare in the field of biblical studies, and because of this lack of focus we will move on to more useful issues.

Assumptions and Questions. To understand how scholars engage in the study of the Bible and popular culture, especially through the lens of RH, it is important to understand not only how they proceed, but also some of the general questions they ask about the phenomenon of popular culture as well as about a specific interpretation. Greater clarity with regards to these two starting points will hopefully allow us to be less ambiguous about this scholarly approach.

Assumptions. It is useful at this point to outline some of the basic assumptions found in most works on Bible and popular culture and in RH in general. I will list these in no particular order, as the following list is not a checklist of mandatory presuppositions, but rather some of the common assumptions made by scholars who work in this area.

- There is no distinction between "high" and "low" cultural forms. Mukerji and Schudson make two important points in this regard. First, oftentimes this distinction is more political or ideological than substantive; and second, there is a remarkable fluidity between these two assumed domains (pp. 1, 35–36). A corollary observation: this lack of distinction opens up for study of ordinary, everyday objects and phenomena, so that scholars can, and have, examined popular cultural renderings like tchotchkes, action figures, video games, and even comic strips for how they interpret and transmit biblical texts.
- Texts are "multivocal." That is, there is a carnival of voices resounding behind, in, and beyond texts. The subsequent question is, in which voice does meaning reside? Does the text itself contain meaning? Do readers create it based on their background, context(s), etc.? Or is meaning constructed out of the creative interplay between text and reader? Theorists call this issue "textual determinacy," that is, the determination of textual meaning, and it is often addressed through a type of methodology called Reader-Response Criticism (see *The Bible and Culture Collective* 1995, pp. 20–69, 130–131). The assumption of the majority of scholars who work in Bible and popular culture is that meaning is (a) created through the

cooperative encounter of text and reader; and (b) transient. In this view, there is no inherent Meaning in texts—be they literary, cinematic, musical, artistic, material, etc.—that interpreters, through the proper application of a proper method, can access. For example, one audience at one time in one place may view a particular film very differently than another audience (or indeed themselves) at a later point in time. As such, scholars who investigate examples of "Bible" in/and popular culture are not seeking a specific, timeless message in those examples. Rather, they remain open to a variety of contextual meanings and, in fact, sometimes these various meanings tell us more about the examples and, by extension, how the Bible has been interpreted, than more traditional biblical interpretive methods. This approach to interpretation is rightfully characterized as "postmodern," and the meaning(s) and implication(s) of such an approach have been explored by scholars such as A. K. M. Adam and the contributors to *The Bible and Culture Collective*. One important result of this assumption is to de-privilege "authorized" interpretations as a primary source of meaning. Put differently, when scholars seek to understand how a particular biblical text has been understood historically, they no longer are bound specifically to Patristic or Rabbinic readings, however illuminating those may be. Rather, now common or ordinary interpretations can be examined as being just as meaningful, especially those from disenfranchised groups.

- "Interpretive communities" play an essential role in promulgating, not creating, interpretations. This emphasis recognizes the role communities play in both validating and transmitting interpretations they find meaningful as well as neglecting and obfuscating readings with which they disagree or find foreign to their experience. The implication of this claim for scholars of the Bible and popular culture is obvious: renderings of Bible in popular culture only achieve lasting stature and thus have the possibility of affecting the way(s) in which the Bible is widely understood if those renderings find support through the acquiescence of an interpretive community (Adam 1995, p. 68). Practically, this means that the object of scholarly inquiry will, in most cases, have already been accepted by an interpretive community for the simple reason that if it were not, it would not be available to scholars as an object of study, either because it would not be seen as a significant rendering or because it would not exist in a material form.
- Both texts and interpretive communities exist in a state of intertextuality. No text exists in a vacuum; all creative aesthetic endeavors rely on prior creations to some degree. Every text refers to and is in some sort of relationship with other texts (*The Bible and Culture Collective*, p. 129). By extension, the same is true for individuals and communities. That is, since meaning is not inherent but constructed, not permanent but constantly negotiated, how an individual and a community understand the texts they encounter always involves referring to other texts. Much in the same way that dictionaries explain the lexical meanings of words by referring to other words, individuals and communities engage texts based on their engagement with previous texts. The implication of this constant state of intertextuality was best stated by Clifford Geertz when he noted that "man is an animal suspended in webs of significance he himself has spun [and] I take culture to be those webs," (Geertz 1973, p. 5). In essence, Geertz's webs consist of multiple texts from various genres as well as our attempts to make sense of them as well as our place within them. As such, intertextuality as described here always serves an identity function, that is, much of our human existence can be seen as a striving to cogitate and ruminate on who we are as a node or nexus within this textual web of significance(s).
- Interpretation functions as "myth-making." Scholars of religion have long focused on

myths because they function to explain, endorse, and/or empower the beliefs and/or practices of communities through aesthetic creativity. Both Mary Callaway (2004, pp. 13–14) and John F. A. Sawyer (2004, pp. 9–10) note that one of the hallmarks of RH is to ask how biblical texts have *affected* readers, communities, and/or culture(s). I take this to mean that RH broadly understands the interpretation of biblical literature to represent an attempt to explain ourselves to ourselves. Put differently, if we grant the preceding presupposition of an intertextual existence and we acknowledge that for a majority of religious adherents in the world today the Bible is maximally determinative for identity and behavior, then the activity of interpreting the Bible assumes a mythic function as well. And one of the most pregnant, ponderous, and principal arenas in which this interpretation can be found is popular culture, which has been described as "a society thinking out loud about itself" (Mukerji and Schudson, p. 26).

Questions. Again, this list should not be seen as a necessary checklist that must be filled out prior to engaging in research of the Bible and popular culture. Rather, these questions are culled from the examinations of scholars in this area of study.

- How does this particular example/object of study interpret the Bible? Which biblical text is it using? And why does it use it this way?
- How is the Bible changed, rewritten, or refashioned through this example/object of study?
- Is the interpretation of the Bible in this example/object of study isolated or idiosyncratic, or is it part of a larger trend of interpretation?
- How important is this example/object of study for the way in which a group, location, movement, or time period understands the Bible?
- How important is this example/object of study for the way in which a group, location, movement, or time period understands itself?
- Is it the case that this interpretation of the Bible is more meaningful for a group, location, movement, or time period than the biblical text itself? If so, why? And how would one demonstrate this?
- Is it possible to chart the history of the development of this idea, theme, character, book, or verse through a group, location, movement, or time period?
- What can this example/object of study and the way(s) it renders the Bible tell us about the culture(s) in which it was created and transmitted?
- What does this example/object of study demonstrate about the impact or effect biblical literature has had on consumers of the text(s), be they individuals or a community?

History of Interpretation and Reception History. Before discussing some of the important works and scholars who have examined issues of the Bible and popular culture, it will be necessary to discuss RH in more detail. Scholars have long been interested in the way(s) in which biblical literature has been interpreted, as is evinced not only by the late medieval anthological commentary by Rashi, but also by the more recent *Ancient Christian Commentary* series published by InterVarsity Press. This scholarly discussion of the way other, usually ancient, prominent scholars or important scriptural interpreters have engaged the biblical texts and how those engagements influenced the interpretations of various religious communities is usually referred to as the History of Interpretation (HI). Two of the more important practitioners of HI are Brevard Childs and James L. Kugel. This approach has undoubtedly increased our understanding of how the Bible has been interpreted in various communities by various scholars. However, by and large this approach focuses on well-known or acknowledged scriptural readers, and examines almost exclusively written scriptural exegesis. In essence, the majority of HI works retain, knowingly or not, the dichotomy between "high" and "low" culture mentioned earlier. Furthermore, as Mary Callaway notes, HI often underscores its investigations with a religiously edifying tone as well as the notion that various readings are ultimately underscored by one biblical Truth, which was the intention of the author to convey (Callaway, p. 4–13).

In contrast, RH affirms a more constructed understanding of truth, dispenses with authorial intent, focuses more on history and culture rather than theology, collapses the "high"/"low" dichotomy, and casts its net wider in order to probe the manifold ways in which Bible has been received in culture more generally (see Callaway, p. 12). In his work, Ulrich Luz notes the diversity of targets that RH investigates, and comments that the goal of such a wide array of study is to point out that educated, literate, recognized masters of scriptural interpretation are not the only, and perhaps not even the most important, readers of biblical literature (2006, p. 130). In keeping with the assumptions listed previously, RH presumes that these diverse targets include more than simply written scriptural interpretations, and should, for the purposes of scholarly investigation, be considered "texts" in that they can be (a) read or interpreted as carrying cultural significance; and (b) they can be seen as "multivocal," that is, possessing various meanings for various individuals and communities. Some examples of these "texts" include film, music, art, drama, television, opera, comic strips, comic books/graphic novels, fiction, fashion, video games, body art/modification, public rituals/spectacles, pieces of material culture, and many others. These various examples of possible objects of study can be probed, according to RH, in an attempt to determine not only *how* the Bible has been rendered, but also *why* certain communities accept and transmit specific readings and not others. In doing so, RH not only accepts the importance of interpretive communities, but also presupposes that readings and communities may be influenced by one another in an intertextual web of meaning. Finally, one of the goals of RH is to try to understand how communities negotiate and maintain their identities in conversation with the Bible and its interpretation(s), that is, the "myth-making" function of interpretation. Since one of the hallmarks of our culture is an increasing fragmentation of social community and subsequently shared meaning that is best exemplified through social network sites such as Facebook and the individual technologies used to access such sites, popular culture, in all its sundry semblances, its multifarious malleability, its byzantine bricolages, its assorted assemblages and motley modes, has become an ideal discourse in which to locate and interrogate how, when, where, and why this negotiation and maintenance occurs.

Brief Survey of Reception History Scholarship. To provide a detailed history of scholarly examples of RH is beyond the scope of this entry. However, I will try to offer a broad sense of RH in the discourse of biblical studies by mentioning three trends in recent scholarship: (a) a focus on specific characters; (b) a focus on specific biblical books; and (c) a more general focus on biblical themes or issues. Two caveats: (a) this treatment is necessarily brief and selective; and (b) several of these works do not claim to practice RH, but their assumptions, foci, and examples overlap with RH to such an extent that I feel justified in including them.

Specific Characters. First, and most commonly, one finds RH examinations of specific biblical characters in which historical and cultural understandings/manifestations are charted through time and/or geography. Some of these examinations address various themes in the way(s) in which a specific character has been read. Others engage the fibrous influence a character has had in various ideological, social, or even political arenas and movements. Some works seek to interrogate readings and texts in a specific time period to determine how a character was rendered in different genres in a particular time frame/historical moment, as I do in my work on Susanna (Clanton 2006). Finally, some scholars attempt to understand how popular cultural interpretations of female biblical characters have affected the way(s) in which those characters have been received in various contexts. An example of this trend is J. Cheryl Exum's *Plotted, Shot, and Painted.* The character that is the most obvious and common target of RH examinations, though, is Jesus.

Reception History work on Jesus started early on, with Jaroslav Pelikan's 1985 *Jesus through the*

Centuries, in which Pelikan deliberately addresses not simply "what poets, philosophers, and artists create," but rather a larger swath of interpretations in order to determine how Jesus has impacted Western culture in general (p. 6). In a similar vein, Stephen Prothero, in his *American Jesus*, examines the way(s) in which Jesus has been understood by various religious and racial groups through what he calls "the kaleidoscopic character of American culture" (2003, p. 7). These two works are both engaged in RH analysis in that they seek to understand and graph the reception and use of Jesus in various milieus—cultural, political, religious, literary, racial, scriptural, etc.—and this in spite of the fact that neither of them frame their work as RH. More recent work on Jesus shows a more specific focus, both in terms of genre and communities. The former is illustrated nicely in a work that examines filmic Jesuses, Adele Reinhartz's *Jesus of Hollywood*. She organizes her work not around specific films, but rather around specific characters from the Jesus stories and how they have been presented in various films. Her orientation is attuned to RH, even though she does not claim to be doing RH. For example, she notes in her introduction that the Jesus films use "the past as a vehicle for contemplating the present," and that the films speak to various issues current at the time of filming (2007, p. 7). As such, Reinhartz reads the films as (a) biblical interpretations composed of multivocal texts that are obviously intertextual; and (b) readings that engage in myth-making, all of which mark her work as reflecting many of the assumptions of RH. Finally, I have recently tried to begin a more deliberate RH exploration into Jesus by examining two specific trends in current American popular cultural renderings of Jesus: "the Biblical/Devotional Christ" and "Jesus in Elseworlds" (Clanton 2010). The former refers to popular cultural products designed to inculcate piety and/or religiosity through restatements of Jesus; the latter signifies readings of Jesus that place him into strange, spastic, side-splitting, or satirical settings. My main assertion in this work is that Jesus functions as an empty vessel, waiting to be filled with meaning by individuals and communities engaged in identity formation and myth-making, much like Storey's aforementioned claim regarding popular culture.

Specific Books. In addition to the emphasis on particular characters in much RH, there are also examples of engagements with entire biblical books. These works obviously are selective, for the following pragmatic reasons: (a) no one can hope to probe every nook and cranny of either a biblical book or the multifarious renderings of it in popular culture; and (b) not everything within a biblical book has been equally influential. Having said that, there are two towering examples of this type of RH, and both of them stem from across the pond.

In 2000, Yvonne Sherwood published *A Biblical Text and Its Afterlives*, her monograph on the reception and influence of the book of Jonah in Western culture. Taken as a whole, this work shares virtually all of the assumptions listed earlier. In the introduction, Sherwood even notes, "In this study, interpretation comes first, indeed interpretation overwhelms my text, as if to demonstrate how it also overwhelms, eclipses, *and always precedes* the biblical 'original.' My premise is that biblical texts are literally sustained by interpretation, and the volume, ubiquity, and tenacity of interpretation make it impossible to dream that we can take the text back through some kind of seductive academic striptease, to a pure and naked original state" (p. 2). Obviously, Sherwood's writing style is as effective as her inquiry, which takes the reader through what she terms "the Mainstream approach"—a masterly and quirky survey of the reception of Jonah in traditional scriptural interpretation and academic biblical exegesis—and an approach she characterizes as "Backwaters and Underbellies," which tracks both Jewish and popular cultural readings of the book. In her conclusion to this section, she not only suggests that Jonah could be understood as an example of Richard Dawkins's "meme" (what a gene is to genetics, a meme is to culture) (p. 196), but also argues for an extension of what we mean by "religious" so it will be possible to examine biblical literature within (popular) culture without limiting that examination to the authorized and recognized scriptural interpretations found within specific traditions (p. 208). In so doing, Sherwood opens up space for an increased engagement with popular cultural manifestations of Bible disentangled from traditional arenas of religious authority, and provides what, in my opinion, is a watershed moment in the development of RH.

To date, the most sustained enterprise in RH is the Blackwell Bible Commentary series from the Wiley-Blackwell publishing house. Beginning in 2004, volumes began to appear whose aim is stated on the series' website. That aim "is based on the premise that how people have interpreted, and been influenced by, a sacred text like the Bible is often as interesting and historically important as what it originally meant," and includes "the conviction that what people believe a sacred text means, and how they actually use it can be studied with the same degree of sensitivity and rigour as its 'original meaning.'" For example, in his commentary on Judges, David M. Gunn reviews not just films and music. Alongside ancient renderings, he also pays attention to how the widespread availability of affordable and mass distributed family Bibles and tracts devoted to women affected how biblical characters and stories were received in the eighteenth and nineteenth centuries. In so doing, Gunn and, by extension, the Blackwell Bible Commentaries provide readers with a plethora of interpretations, as well as discussions on how these interpretations have impacted communities and the perceived and received meaning(s) of specific biblical texts. As such, they offer the most comprehensive example of RH thus far.

Specific Themes/Issues. Finally, there are works that address broader issues and themes found in biblical literature, and their manifestations in popular culture. For example, Terry Ray Clark uses the framework of apocalyptic and prophetic literature to analyze the popular and influential DC Comics graphic novels *Kingdom Come* and *Watchmen.* In understanding these texts as reflecting an apocalyptic worldview yet functioning as prophetic voices, Clark blends these prominent biblical outlooks with specifically modern stories of superheroes not only to demonstrate the vitality of biblical themes, but also to expose graphic novels as a possible source of religious meaning.

In keeping with Clark's emphasis, the most commonly examined broad biblical theme is "apocalypse." A chronologically continuous curiosity in this theme is evident from Sheffield Phoenix Press's wide-ranging series dedicated to exploring the influence of apocalyptic language and imagery in various popular cultural genres. Titled "The Apocalypse and Popular Culture Series," it includes engagements with film, the Internet, the *Left Behind* series of novels, and comics and graphic novels. A more specific engagement of the book of Revelation can be found in Brian K. Blount's fascinating study of the function of the book's hymnic material and how it parallels the function of traditionally African American musical genres, such as spirituals, blues, rap, and hip-hop. By adopting this functional emphasis, Blount can address the issue of effect or impact that both Callaway and Sawyer see as integral to RH studies.

This emphasis on how "apocalypse" has impacted or affected culture(s) and/or readers lies at the heart of one of the most innovative and interdisciplinary approaches to the topic: Tina Pippin's 1999 work *Apocalyptic Bodies.* In this work, Pippin uses a variety of theoretical approaches to examine a number of interpretations—ranging from films such as *Nightmare on Elm Street* to Tom Robbins's *Skinny Legs and All* to medieval art to biblical snow globes—in order to interrogate how the Apocalypse and apocalyptic literature understand God, women, bodies, etc., and, by extension, how her own postmodern and feminist reading can alert, allay, and alter these emphases and traditional readings. By doing so, Pippin not only adopts the assumptions of RH mentioned earlier, but she also seeks to counter claims that such assumptions (and postmodern approaches in general) lead both to relativism and an ignoring of ethical issues. She is obviously and intently interested in discerning a way to read Revelation in a constructive way, as her analysis reveals the disturbing ideologies of power and gender in the Apocalypse that have wormed their way into both popular and biblical culture. Through this revelation, Pippin hopes to illuminate the possibility of change, even a new creation (1999, p. 77).

Future Issues. As should be obvious by now, the study of how the Bible and popular culture intertwine and interpret one another is a relatively new approach in the discipline of biblical studies, yet it draws upon a plethora of methods and theories and their presuppositions. The boon of such an approach lies in its ability to (a) reveal the mutual influence of the Bible and popular cultural products and genres, so that (b) one may observe/analyze the continuing and tendrilous influence of biblical literature in multiple discourses and ideologies, with the hope that (c) one will be able to see more clearly the impact or effect biblical texts, language, imagery, and themes have had on individual readers, interpretive communities, and/or culture(s).

Both HI and RH continue to be utilized to achieve the aforementioned goals, even in new and inventive ways through new series and new technologies. There are still areas to be explored, though. Some questions that may be addressed in future iterations of this approach, or some future projects, might include:

- As more work appears that addresses the relationship between the Bible and popular culture, will it be necessary or possible to maintain the distinction between HI and RH that Callaway posits? As an example, there are works that could be considered RH that take a "backwards" or "from the bottom up" approach in that they begin with a specifically delimited popular cultural product and then inquire as to how it reflects, engages, or interprets biblical literature. A series that consistently employs this method is the "Gospel according to" series from Westminster John Knox Press. With topics ranging from Oprah to the *Twilight* series to the Beatles, these volumes operate from the premise that popular cultural products can be used as a resource in Christian spiritual development. That is, while popular culture used to be considered a rampant secular wasteland, opposed to the values of the church or religion in general, these authors instead find spiritual value in these examples of popular culture. By doing so, they problematize Callaway's claim that RH differs from HI because of the latter's religiosity. They also reject several of the assumptions previously mentioned as well, including a constructed and conditioned view of truth. So, are these works HI or RH or perhaps some new type of criticism?
- How do factors such as race, gender, sexual orientation, social location, religious affiliation, etc., affect popular cultural interpretation? Work has been done on this issue generally in the field of biblical studies, but given the traditional hegemonic nature of mass media and the fragmenting of that hegemony due to new technologies and media, this would seem to be a ripe area for study.
- How are the interpretations of Bible in popular culture performed, enacted, and/or consumed? How do the genres or mediums affect the interpretation? In essence, how does Marshall McLuhan's oft-quoted claim that "the medium is the message" apply to popular cultural renderings of biblical literature?
- How has the rise in literacy and/or the availability of Bible through various technological boulevards affected the way(s) in which popular culture has interpreted the Bible?
- How do popular cultural interpretations of Bible and the material culture they foster serve to create, sustain, and/or bond social structures and/or communities? Similarly, how are interpretations affected by the collective social groupings that shape and/or transmit them?
- What does the rendering of Bible in ritual(s), celebration(s), and/or other public spectacle(s) tell us about which interpretations and which biblical texts are meaningful for specific groups?
- In keeping with my earlier comments on mythmaking, how do interpretations of Bible in a popular cultural context or medium explain us

to ourselves? That is, is there an element of mythmaking or identity formation inherent in popular cultural renderings of biblical literature? Do these interpretations tell us who we are by the way(s) in which they read and render certain biblical texts and ignore others? In essence, these questions build on Geertz's aforementioned assertion that humanity is ensconced in a self-made network of meaning, which he understands to be culture, and attempt to probe how and why rewriting(s) of Bible not only help us understand our suspension but also the resulting significance(s).

Because of the continuing presence of/interest in new offerings, genres, and approaches in popular culture—not to mention the assumed longevity of biblical literature and its influence in various discourses—these methods have the potential to be longstanding avenues of inquiry in biblical studies.

[*See also* Cultural-Historical Criticism; Intertextuality; Literary Criticism, Literary Theory, and the Bible; Postmodern Interpretation; Reader-Response Criticism; *and* Reception Criticism and Theory.]

BIBLIOGRAPHY

Adam, A. K. M. *What is Postmodern Biblical Criticism?* Guides to Biblical Scholarship Series. Minneapolis: Augsburg Fortress, 1995.

The Bible and Culture Collective. *The Postmodern Bible.* New Haven, Conn.: Yale University Press, 1995. An important introduction to (post)modern methodologies such as Reader-Response, Poststructuralist, and Feminist/Womanist criticisms.

Blount, Brian K. "The Rap against Rome: The Spiritual-Blues Impulse and the Hymns of Revelation." In *Can I Get a Witness? Reading Revelation through African American Culture,* 91–117. Louisville, Ky.: Westminster John Knox, 2005.

Callaway, Mary Chilton. "What's the Use of Reception History?" Paper presented at the annual meeting of the Society of Biblical Literature. San Antonio, Tex., 21 November 2004; available online at http://bbibcomm.net/files/callaway2004.pdf.

Childs, Brevard S. *The Book of Exodus: A Critical, Theological Commentary.* The Old Testament Library. Philadelphia: Westminster, 1974. A classic example of HI, Childs's work was one of the first commentaries to examine the afterlives of texts, but these afterlives were confined to how scriptural interpreters read the texts in question.

Clanton, Dan W., Jr. *The Good, the Bold, and the Beautiful: The Story of Susanna and Its Renaissance Interpretations.* Library of Hebrew Bible/Old Testament Studies 430. New York: T&T Clark, 2006.

Clanton, Dan W., Jr. "'Here, There, and Everywhere': Images of Jesus in American Popular Culture." In *The Bible in/and Popular Culture: A Creative Encounter,* edited by Philip Culbertson and Elaine M. Wainwright, 41–60. Semeia Studies 65. Atlanta: Society of Biblical Literature, 2010.

Clark, Terry Ray. "Prophetic Voices in Graphic Novels: The 'Comic and Tragic Vision' of Apocalyptic Rhetoric in *Kingdom Come* and *Watchmen.*" In *The Bible in/and Popular Culture: A Creative Encounter,* edited by Philip Culbertson and Elaine M. Wainwright, 141–156. Semeia Studies 65. Atlanta: Society of Biblical Literature, 2010.

Exum, J. Cheryl. *Plotted, Shot, and Painted: Cultural Representations of Biblical Women.* Journal for the Study of the Old Testament: Supplement Series 215/Gender, Culture, Theory 3. Sheffield, UK: Sheffield Academic, 1996. An important work in which Exum analyzes how stories of women like Naomi and Delilah have been understood in art, music, and film.

Foucault, Michel. *The Archaeology of Knowledge and the Discourse on Language,* translated by A. M. Sheridan Smith. New York: Pantheon Books, 1972 [1969]. A classic but difficult text in which Foucault outlines his methodological approach to studying discourses.

Geertz, Clifford. "Thick Description: Toward an Interpretive Theory of Culture." In *The Interpretation of Cultures: Selected Essays,* 3–30. New York: Basic Books, 1973. A foundational text of modern sociology.

Gunn, David M. *Judges.* Blackwell Bible Commentaries. Malden, Mass.: Blackwell, 2005.

Kugel, James L. *The Bible As It Was.* Cambridge, Mass.: Harvard University Press, 1999. Kugel's masterpiece, this book identifies ambiguities and aporiae in numerous biblical texts and then demonstrates how later scriptural interpretations attempt to address those questions and problems.

Luz, Ulrich. "The Contribution of Reception History to a Theology of the New Testament." In *The Nature of New Testament Theology: Essays in Honour of Robert Morgan,* edited by Christopher Rowland and Christopher Tuckett, 123–134. Malden, Mass.: Blackwell, 2006.

Mukerji, Chandra and Michael Schudson. "Introduction: Rethinking Popular Culture." In *Rethinking Popular*

Culture: Contemporary Perspectives in Cultural Studies, edited by Chandra Mukerji and Michael Schudson, 1–61. Berkeley: University of California Press, 1991. A learned survey of various disciplinary approaches to popular culture.

Pelikan, Jaroslav. *Jesus through the Centuries: His Place in the History of Culture*. New Haven, Conn: Yale University Press, 1985.

Pippin, Tina. *Apocalyptic Bodies: The Biblical End of the World in Text and Image*. New York: Routledge, 1999.

Prothero, Stephen. *American Jesus: How the Son of God Became a National Icon*. New York: Farrar, Straus and Giroux, 2003.

Reinhartz, Adele. *Jesus of Hollywood*. New York: Oxford University Press, 2007.

Sawyer, John F. A. "The Role of Reception Theory, Reader-Response Criticism and/or Impact History in the Study of the Bible: Definition and Evaluation." Paper presented at the Biennial Meeting of the authors of the *Evangelisch-Katholischer Kommentar* series. Germany. 21–23 March 2004; available at http://bbibcomm.net/files/sawyer2004.pdf.

Storey, John. "What is Popular Culture?" In *Cultural Theory and Popular Culture: An Introduction*, 1–15, 5th ed. Essex, UK: Pearson Education Limited, 2009.

Dan W. Clanton, Jr.

POSTCOLONIAL BIBLICAL INTERPRETATION

Like many "isms," postcolonialism pursues a particular grievance—the impact of European colonialism. The mention of postcolonialism raises the spectre of empire, conquest, slavery, racism, sexism, and orientalism, and it is seen as being implicitly critical. Postcolonialism, at its simplest, can be seen in two ways. One is historical, marking the dismantling of the empire and its attendant instruments of power; and the other is an intellectual project that searches for "alternative sources, alternative readings, alternative presentation of evidence" (Viswanathan 2001, p. 222). In the latter sense, it pays much attention to the intricate relations between the native and invader societies and cultures, wrestles with questions of identity and representation, and invests much in theories of indigeneity and diaspora. In this sense, essentially, postcolonialism identifies the dominant power, exposes it, and engages critically with it.

Empires and colonization—that is, the control of another people by power and force—have existed in all historical periods. Current postcolonial study began its career by investigating the modern colonization, which started with the European conquest of overseas countries in the sixteenth century and culminated in the nineteenth century. This subjugation was unique in its scope, scale, and style, and its cultural and political reverberations are still with us. Later, the same scrutiny was extended to other empires and other forms of colonization.

Postcolonial theory, like any critical category, has evolved over the years (see Ato Quayson, *Postcolonialism: Theory, Practice or Process?* [Cambridge: Polity Press, 2000]; Nicholas *Postcolonial Criticism, History, Theory and the Work of Fiction* [Cambridge: Polity Press, 2003]; Justin D. Edwards, *Postcolonial Literature: A Reader's Guide to Essential Criticism* [Basingstoke: Palgrave Macmillan, 2008]; Ania Loomba, Suvir Kaul and Bunzl Matti, eds. *Postcolonial Studies and Beyond* [Durham: Duke University Press, 2005]). The initial, primary phase consisted of textual analysis dense with new theoretical categories. This gave way to conceptual and disciplinary challenges posed by globalization, environmentalism, religious fundamentalism, and terrorism. The current phase confronts the contemporary neo-imperial practices of market economy and humanitarian intervention—the new form of the "White man's burden" assumed on behalf of humanity. A new class of politicians, bureaucrats, corporate entrepreneurs, disaster-experts, and the like takes upon itself the task of civilizing and developing the uncivilized and underdeveloped. A noticeable example is that of Western trauma experts parachuting into disaster areas like the Asian tsunami and the Haiti earthquake. In the name of humanistic intervention, Western solutions are applied to health and psychological problems that could have been solved by indigenous resources (O'Hara 2011, p. 5). Postcolonialism has opened up a metropolitan canon dominated by English, French, and Spanish texts, to include literature produced in Swahili, Hindi,

Chinese, Tamil, and so on. It has now come to embrace a larger set of conceptual and ideological positions and interests. It has also moved from the earlier hostile Occident-Orient binary division to cross-cultural contact and dialogue between the once colonized and the colonizer.

The nature of colonialism has also changed. External colonialism has been replaced by an internal type. Initially imperialism was an overseas venture and a European mercantile project procuring luxury goods for the aristocracy from foreign lands, later becoming a nationalist project where the economic benefits began to reach the working class. Now colonialism has turned inwards and the post-independence nationalist governments wage war against their own civilians, grabbing the lands, minerals, and other indigenous resources in the name of developing them.

Postcolonial Preoccupations. Like many critical theories, postcolonialism reached biblical studies late in the 1990s. (see Fernando Segovia, *Decolonizing the Biblical Studies: A View from the Margins* [Maryknoll, NY: Orbis Books, 2000]; Musa W. Dube, *Postcolonial Feminist Interpretation of the Bible* [St. Louis: Chalice Press, 2000]; R. S. Sugirtharajah, *The Bible and the Third World: Precolonial, Colonial and Postcolonial Encounters* [Cambridge: Cambridge University Press, 2001]; *Postcolonial Criticism and Biblical Interpretation* [Oxford: Oxford University Press, 2002]; *Postcolonial Reconfigurations: An Alternative Way of Reading the Bible and Doing Theology* [London: SCM Press, 2003]; *The Bible and Empire: Postcolonial Explorations* [Cambridge: Cambridge University Press, 2005]; *Exploring Postcolonial Biblical Criticism: History, Method, Practice* [Oxford: Wiley-Blackwell, 2012]; and Stephen D. Moore and Fernando F. Segovia, eds. *Postcolonial Biblical Criticism: Interdisciplinary Intersections* [London: T&T Clark, 2005]). The academic climate of the time played a critical role. Postcolonial biblical criticism was an inevitable progression from the then prevailing interpretative practices that went under the name of contextual, vernacular, or liberation hermeneutics. While these interpretative approaches were rightly preoccupied with questions of economic exploitation and victimhood, postcolonialism was able to add another increasingly problematic issue—the cultural implications of living in diverse religious and racial communities in a globalized society. This was also the time when the biblical "orient" was re-discovered by those biblical scholars, especially in America, who were trying to apply social-science and anthropological approaches to biblical texts. In their attempt to wrestle with and give a form to the biblical orient, these scholars unwittingly regurgitated the old Orientalist stereotypes, thus forcing those from the Orient to investigate both the Orient itself and the Orientalist practices of these biblical scholars.

Postcolonial biblical criticism has several textual functions. Firstly, it pays attention to the presence of the empires of the biblical world. The ancient Israelites were under the control of the Egyptian empire. The Judean scribes, priests, and prophets, who shaped the Pentateuch and prophetic books of the Hebrew Scriptures, were confronted with Persian and Assyrian empires. The books of the New Testament emerged during the Roman empire. In studying the Bible, a postcolonial critic interrogates the texts with a series of questions such as: How are these imperial powers portrayed? Do the biblical authors support or challenge them? Where does their allegiance lie—with the subjugated people or the dominating power? Secondly, it asks how, in their examination of biblical texts, biblical commentators interpret these empires? Do they support or oppose them? How do they represent the "other"? What kind of oriental images appear in their work? Do they unwittingly re-orientalize the orient? Thirdly, it examines the role played by the Bible in colonial expansion and its veneration and degradation in the colonies. Fourthly, it engages in a work of retrieval. This involves (a) bringing to the fore forgotten, sidelined, and often maligned biblical figures and texts; (b) reclaiming the resistant literature of the 'natives' themselves as they talk back to the master using the very texts provided by them; and (c) recovering the hermeneutical work of a few missionaries and Orientalists who, though invariably compromised with the ideals of empire, were at the same time ambivalent about its usefulness Fifthly, it pays scholarly attention to Bible translation projects and their positive and negative contributions to indigenous languages. Finally, it addresses issues which have arisen in the aftermath of colonialism—migration, multiculturalism, nationhood, and diaspora.

Postcolonial biblical criticism has a number of allies that share its concerns. One of these is Feminism. (For examples of postcolonial feminist biblical reading, see Musa W. Dube, *Postcolonial Feminist Interpretation of the Bible* [St. Louis: Chalice Press, 2000]; Judith E. McKinlay, *Reframing Her: Biblical Women in Postcolonial Focus* [Sheffield: Sheffield Phoenix Press, 2004]; and Caroline Vander Stichele and Todd Penner, eds. *Her Master's Tools? Feminist and Postcolonial Engagements of Historical-Critical Discourse* [Leiden: Brill, 2005]). While both oppose hierarchical and patriarchal systems and resist the political, economic, and cultural nature of colonialism, feminists point to the sexual character of colonialism and the supremacy of male power and authority. Another ally is Queer studies. Both recognize the struggles and stigmatization of the 'other,' and the hegemonic power of heterosexism and homophobia, and are involved in rethinking the conventional societal patterns and often present positions on behalf of the "othered." (See Jeremy Punt, "Queer Theory Intersecting with Postcolonial Theory in Biblical Interpretation," *The CSSR Bulletin* 35 [2] [April 2006]: pp. 30–34; "Intersections in Queer Theory and Postcolonial Theory, and Hermeneutical Spin-Offs," *The Bible and Critical Theory* 4 [2] [2008]: pp. 24.1–24.16; see John C Hawley, ed., *Postcolonial, Queer: Theoretical Intersections* [Albany: State University of New York Press, 2001]).

A New Reading Practice. One of the reading practices which postcolonialism can claim as a major contribution to reading strategies is contrapuntal reading. This is the re-reading of the approved sources and documents in conjunction with other texts. The aim is not to downgrade or disparage, or replace the former with the once marginalized texts as a revisionist reading would encourage. It is rather to question and expose some of the cultural, racial, and "oriental" suppositions of mainstream discourse with alternative texts and experiences. At its simplest, it makes connections between texts. As Edward Said explained, its function is to "read what is there or not there, above all, to see complementarity and interdependence instead of isolated, venerated, or formalized experience that excludes and forbids the hybridizing intrusions of human history" (Said, 1993 p. 115). It not a matter of one text incorporating another, but of allowing dissident voices to dialogue with the governing discourse with a view to relativizing it. The object is to read a variety of texts in juxtaposition in order to facilitate the interpretative process. Contrapuntal reading creates, as Said puts it, an "atonal ensemble." It constitutes a polyphony rather than a symphony. (For how contrapuntal reading works in biblical studies, see Alissa Jones Nelson, *Power and Responsibility in Biblical Interpretation: Reading the Book of Job with Edward Said* [Sheffield: Equinox Publishing, 2012]; and Sugirtharajah 2012, 143–52.)

Empire Studies and Postcolonial Biblical Criticism. Recently a new disciplinary division has emerged under the name of Empire Studies. Such studies arose mainly in the USA at a time when American hegemony was unsurpassed. The literature is voluminous, and includes Richard Horsley, ed. *Paul and Politics: Ekklesia, Israel, Imperium, Interpretation: Essays in Honor of Krister Stendahl*, (Harrisburg, Pa: Trinity Press International, 2000); Richard Horsley, *Jesus and Empire: The Kingdom of God and the New World Disorder* (Minneapolis, Minn.: Fortress Press, 2003); John Dominic Crossan, *God & Empire: Jesus Against Rome, Then and Now* (San Francisco: HarperSanFrancisco, 2007); *Jesus: A Revolutionary Biography* (San Francisco: Harper, 1994); and Warren Carter, *Matthew and Empire: Initial Explorations* (Harrisburg, Pa.: Trinity Press International, 2001); *The Roman Empire and the New Testament: An Essential Guide* (Nashville, Tenn.: Abingdon Press. 2006); *John and Empire: Initial Explorations* (New York: T&T Clark, 2008). There is one common interest among those who practice postcolonial biblical criticism and empire studies. Both go beyond reading the biblical texts exclusively as intra-religious documents and view them as the literary products of empires, to be read over against Assyrian, Babyonian, Persian, and Roman imperial history.

Besides this shared aspiration, there are a number of differences. Empire studies largely uses historical-criticism and still work under the illusion of detached scholarship. The motivation for such work is not colonial or postcolonial concerns, nor are its investigations spurred on by colonial discourse analysis, but, largely, as a "consequence of new archaeological and epigraphic discoveries" (Harry O Maier, "A Sly Civility: Colossians and Empire," *The Journal for the Study of the New Testament* 27/ 3 [2005], 323). A further spur is the American experience of the attack. In situating the New Testament in the Roman imperial context, one can see roughly four positions emerging. One is that the New Testament is not an anti-imperial text and not in conflict with Roman ideology (Mark).

A second, in the face of Roman supremacy, accommodates the message of Jesus as a religious reformer rather than as a political agitator (Luke). A third is critical of the imperial power, but the anti-Roman rhetoric is camouflaged in a series of visions and images set in an imaginary universe and invites readers to recognize themselves in the ongoing battle between good and evil (Revelation). (For explication of these positions, see Werner H. Kelber, "Roman Imperialism and Early Christian Scribality" in *The Postcolonial Biblical Reader,* R. S. Sugirtharajah, ed. [Oxford: Blackwell Publishing. 2006], 96–111.)

A fourth offers an alternative to the imperial power—Christ's rule replaces Caesar's rule. Those who opt for this last category argue that the politically charged imperial language is borrowed and adapted in order to describe the triumph of Christ (Harry O. Maier, "A Sly Civility: Colossians and Empire," *The Journal for the Study of the New Testament* 27 [2005] 323–49). Christ's rule is described as incorporating all humanity and providing peace and prosperity to the people. Christ's work is described as a universal reconciliation brought about by the death of Christ on the cross. This reign brings together every ethnic, national, and religious group, not through the Roman idea of the sword but through sacrifice and love. These studies acknowledge that at the heart of the Roman empire is its "imperial theology," which proclaims the emperor as not only divine but also as the prince of peace. This, however, is a peace built on conquest and compulsion, whereas there is another empire, also ruled by a prince of peace, but his peace comes with love and justice. It is this kingdom that one should advocate. Humankind is freed from one subjection and put under another, as it submits itself to the love of Christ.

Empire studies is largely risk-averse and concentrates on imperial cult and idolatry, and engages in philological discussion on words like *arché* (rule), *exousia* (authority), *dynamis* (power), and *basileu* (rule). There is a refusal and reluctance among its practitioners to consider the political implications of such studies. As with traditional historical critics, the ideological stance of the interpreter is rarely revealed. These scholars, largely white Americans, ceaselessly talk about the impact of, for instance, the imperial cult in the Mediterranean world, but shy away from discussing the implications for the contemporary world. Most of them avoid raising disturbing questions on the role of the US in imperial expansion. Rare exceptions here are Norman Gottwald ("Early Israel as an Anti-Imperial Community," in *In the Shadow of Empire: Reclaiming the Bible as a History of Faithful Resistance,* edited by Richard A Horsley [Louisville Ky.: Westminster John Knox Press, 2008], pp. 9–24; and in that same book edited by Richard Horsley pp. 1–8, pp. 75–96).

Empire studies is marked by two characteristics. One is that some of its practitioners project the church as an alternative to the empire. They are deeply concerned about the church and its message of the kingdom of God. The concluding sentence in Dominic Crossan's book *God & Empire* illustrates this: "In the challenge of Christian faith, we are called to cooperate in establishing the Kingdom of God in a transformed earth. In the challenge of human evolution, we are called to Post-Civilization, to imagine it, to create it, and to enjoy it on a transfigured earth" (p. 242). The other characteristic is that those who practice Empire Studies are, like any revisionist movement, in the business of rescuing the text from its tainted colonial uses and presenting it is anti-imperial. As Roland Boer put it, the whole enterprise is "a deeply confessional effort" and, to this, one could add it has a hint of Christian triumphalism.

Biblical Scholarship and Orientalism. The emergence of biblical criticism is complicated. The popular perception is that it was Protestant Christianity and the Enlightenment ideals which led to the development of the field. But there are two other factors that are often overlooked. One is that biblical studies emerged at a time when Europe was gaining economic and political ascendancy on a global scale. This provided an opportunity to obtain, along with spices and cotton, a large number of Oriental texts from Egypt, India, and China which challenged the uniqueness of the Bible, its chronology, and its historical authenticity. A second is that it evolved in Germany in the second half of the nineteenth century in the field of theology where theology was a sub-speciality discipline of Oriental studies. This was the time when Europe's understanding of the Orient was being shaped. The work and motivation of the Orientalists is a complex one. Was it simply a scholarly venture or in part political? Although there was a genuine interest among the European Orientalists in looking for spiritual and intellectual information in the East, the debate continues as to whether they were not also providing data that supported imperial policies.

Orientalism may not have been motivated by imperial policy, but what it did was to classify the "other" in ways that facilitated conquest. Even Suzanne Marchand, who had questioned Said's link between knowledge production and imperial power, has conceded such a connection. Even though Oriental scholarship developed before Germany had any imperial ambitions, later, when it began to join the imperial race, it, too, Marchand admits, used Oriental scholarship to aid collaboration with the Ottomans and to "acquire colonies in Africa, in the Pacific, and in China" (Suzanne L. Marchand, *German Orientalism in the Age of Empire: Religion, Race, and Scholarship* [New York: Cambridge University Press, 2009], 158).

Biblical scholars who worked under the aegis of Oriental studies saw the Old Testament and the New Testament as Oriental scriptures worthy of study. Adolf Deissmann called the New Testament the "book of the East," and, more pertinently, characterized Jesus and Paul as "sons of the East." Much of the Orientalist project was concerned with Christianity's early relationship with Judaism and cultural and theological aspects of the Middle East. As participants in Oriental studies, these biblical critics shared such earlier marks of Orientalism as treating the Orient as static, reducing culture to certain essentials, and contrasting people as "us" and "them."

It was these scholars who schematized the relationship between the Old and New Testaments and privileged Greek philosophy and culture. Their work led to the creation of a binary perception of the Jews and Greeks—Jews as primitive, poetical, and pragmatic, the Greeks as sophisticated, rational, and judicious. Jewish and Christian faith were framed similarly. The former was seen as primitive, provincial, morally low, and ritualistic, whereas the later was seen as progressive, universal, cerebral, and morally superior. These typecasts enabled and encouraged later biblical scholars to come up with their own tendentious pigeonholing of the "other" (see Marchand, chapter 3).

Orientalist impulses continue, especially among some biblical scholars who apply social-scientific and anthropological methods in their work. Unlike the earlier Orientalists who showed little interest in the contemporary East and were concerned only with ancient cultures, some modern day scholars are interested in highlighting a contemporary East/West divide. For instance, commenting on Jesus's refusal to accept the drink on the cross, John Pilch remarks that this action "stands in contrast to mainstream US citizens who seek alleviation for pain" (Pilch, *Introducing the Cultural Context of the New Testament: Hear the Word,* Vol. 2 [New York: Paulist Press, 1991], p. 217).

The Christian Bible and Colonizing Tendencies. In their attempt to situate the Bible in its various imperial contexts, interpreters often overlook the colonialist character of the Christian Bible. The New Testament writings are a striking example of persistent seizure of other peoples' gods and theological tenets. While some Jewish ideas were taken over, others were denied any continuing legitimacy or efficacy. The Christian Bible not only took over the God of the Jews, their prophets, and their sacred books, but also incorporated basic theological tenets of Judaism—the chosen people of God, salvation, eschatology, the concept of the Messiah, the suffering servant. In doing so, it claimed that its interpretation was accurate, effective, and final. In the colonizing imagination, the ideas and resources of other people belong to those who are best able to exploit them. There are many such requisitions by the New Testament writers which radically transform these Jewish concepts. A conspicuous case in point is the way the concept of the Messiah was reconfigured by the early Christains: among the Jews there was a wide range of ideas and expectations about the concept of the Messiah. These images of the Messiah, depending on the religious and political needs of the time, included being a king, priest, prophet, the one hidden and unrecognized, and the Messiah who would be slain on an eschatological battlefield (Jacob Neusner, William S. Green, and Ernest Frerichs, eds., *Judaisms and Their Messiahs at the Turn of the Christian Era* [Cambridge: Cambridge University Press, 1987]).

These varied images were replaced with one final and fixed understanding of the Messiah whose theological properties were unrelated to the prevalent perceptions of the anticipated savior. In order to appeal to the Gentiles, Paul tweaks the existing expectations of the Messiah, going beyond the conventional notions. Among the New Testament writers, it is Paul who uses the word *Christos* most. The conferring of the title was shaped by the death and the resurrection of the historical Jesus. The resurrection was understood as the beginning of the eschatological act of the raising of the dead. In envisioning Jesus as the Messianic leader ushering in the end, Paul went beyond "the concept of Messiah as traditionally known" (George MacRae, "Messiah and Gospel," in *Judaisms and Their Messiahs at the Turn of the Christian Era*, ed. MacRae, 172). No Jew would recognize what Paul was saying about Jesus: he created a wholly new definition of the Messiah, something that few or no Jews recognized. A variety of earlier images were made redundant and Paul introduced a fixed content to the term.

In the history of religion, it is the Christian faith that has relentlessly summoned the principal themes of other peoples' religious ideas and transformed them for its own purposes. In doing so, it has simultaneously disallowed the abiding spiritual strength these precepts have provided to those to whom they belonged, and contended that their reading is true and valid. No other religion has engaged in such a colonization of other peoples' beliefs and doctrines. The Buddha incorporated a number of brahmanical ideas, but the Buddhist scriptures that record the Buddha's thinking never claimed that they superseded the Hindu Vedas. These hermeneutical practices of the New Testament writers show that other peoples' heritage and resources are treated as potential sites for the realization of Christian beliefs.

Colonialism is not simply restricted to the actual domination of another country. A comparable impulse can be seen in the way a dominating personality tries to control others. The obvious example is Paul. In his letters, he is very assertive and domineering. He demands absolute obedience in a number of ways. Firstly, he interlinks his faith and belief in God to instil submission: "And we have confidence in the Lord concerning you, that you are doing and will go on doing the things that we command" (2 Thess 3:4). Secondly, Paul gains his authority by identifying himself with Christ and his death: "I have been crucified with Christ; and it is no longer I who live, but it is Christ who lives in me" (Gal 2:20). Such an identification in the eyes of his admirers makes Paul equal to Christ and creates difficulties for his congregation to oppose his authority. Thirdly, the churches he established were manipulated by the self-esteem of the founder and deceived into submission by false privileges.

The following verse is characteristic of Paul: "with such yearning love we chose to impart to you not only the gospel of God but our very selves, so dear had you become to us" (1 Thess 2:8). He demands compliance and surrender. Fourthly, this submission is solicited through a mixture of disclaim and granting of status to himself. In the first letter to the Corinthians, he begins with modesty and humility, and disowns any eloquence and articulation. He tells them that when he came to them he did not have any lofty words or wisdom: "And I came to you in weakness and in fear and in much trembling" (1 Cor 2:3). Then suddenly the message changes and he asserts his authority. "But we speak God's wisdom, secret and hidden, which God decreed before the ages for our glory" (1 Cor 2:7). Fifthly, subordination is achieved through urging his followers to imitate him. Paul often offers himself as an example to be followed by his congregations (2 Thess 3:7).

Elizabeth Castelli has shown how Paul uses the language of imitation as a powerful tool. Such language "identifies the fundamental value" of Paul's own privileged position in relation to the "gospel, the Christian communities he founded and supervises, and Christ himself" (Castelli, *Imitating Paul: A Discourse of Power* [Louisville: Westminster John Knox Press, 1991], 87). To go against what the apostle stands for is virtually to stand against Christ. What Paul does is to use the gospel of freedom and reconciliation to mask aggressive self-assertion. The conformity he insists upon makes criticism impossible. Internal critique and debate are ruled out by appealing to his bearing bodily the brand marks of Jesus. Paul's branded body becomes both a token of his authority and a shield against opposition: "Let no one make trouble for me" (Gal 6:17).

The colonialist tendencies of the Bible are evident in its promotion of a single religion and culture. It tends to oppose social and cultural diversity—realties of a postcolonial condition. It encourages the collapse of ethnic differences and encourages conformity under Christ's headship. Although the Bible emerged out of multicultural contexts there is no evidence of its supporting diversity and plurality. Paul, who himself was a product of diverse cultures, advises his converts that if possible they should refrain from mixing socially and culturally with the non-believing Gentiles. For Paul, these Gentiles are "slanderers, God-haters, insolent, haughty, boastful, inventors of evil (Rom 1:30)." They commit all kinds of sexual transgressions. Their heinous traits include envy, deceit, malice, insolence, covetousness, malignity, haughtiness, and boasting. They are generally foolish, heartless, and ruthless (Rom 1:28–32 cf. also 1 Cor 5:9–13). In this context, the term "Gentile," like the colonialist "Paki" and "Nigger," is a term of abuse for Paul. He accuses Peter of being a Jew living like a Gentile and readily equates Gentiles with "sinners" (Gal 2:14–15). Equally he is scathing about Gentile piety. His savage comments should be seen against what he has to say about Christian devotion. Christians (in this case, Gentiles who believe in Paul's message) are people of God who serve "a living and true God" (1 Thess 1:9), whereas others are idol worshippers blinded by the god of the world (2 Cor 4:4).

On reading Paul one gets the impression that he often viewed those who were not part of his community as lesser human beings and sometimes even worse. If the meat offered to idols is to be served at public banquets or private homes and this is going to cause a problem to the young in faith, then keep away from such occasions (1 Cor 8:1–13; 10:22–23). If a spouse who is not a Christian wants a separation, "let it be so" (1 Cor 7:15). To his Thessalonian readers, Paul says "live quietly" and "mind your own affairs" (1 Thess 4:11). Paul's attitude to non-Christians is summed up in the words he quotes from Isaiah. He wrote to the Corinthians: "Therefore come out from them, and be separate from them says the Lord, touch nothing unclean" (2 Cor 6:17). Since the ways of the Gentiles are to a larger extent corrupt and polluted, social integration with them is not merely inadvisable, but even impossible for the newly converted. The simple message was that the followers of Jesus should not live as the non-believing Gentiles do.

There are friendly references to the Gentiles but this is conditional upon their submission to the gospel. They have followed the examples of the converted and have turned from idols "to serve a living and true God" (1 Thess 1:9). Those who have not, are seen as given over to lust and drunkenness (1 Thess 4:5; 5:7). Given such a view of the entire non-Christian world, the occasional references to showing love to them lack conviction (1 Thess 3:1; 5:15).

The traditional and popular image of Paul is that he supported and encouraged multicultural, multireligious communities. As evidence of this, the famous passage from his Galatians letter is routinely cited: "There is no longer Jew or Greek, there is no longer slave or free, there is no longer male and female; for all of you are one in Christ Jesus" (3:28). A closer reading will reveal that what Paul envisaged here was not equality but inclusion by the dissolving of all cultural and racial specificities. To borrow a phrase from Daniel Boyarin, what Paul had in mind was "identicalness" or "coercive sameness" (Boyarin, *A Radical Jew: Paul and the Politics of Identity* [Berkeley: University of California Press, 1994], p. 236). Such a melting down of various differences was the result of Paul's passionate desire that humanity be One under the sign of One God. As Boyarin put it: "For Paul, the only possibility for human equality involved human sameness. Difference was the threat" (ibid., p. 156). Differences must be erased for the sake of harmony and order. Paul's apparent tolerance "deprives difference of the right to be different, dissolving all others into a single essence in which matters of cultural practice are irrelevant and only faith in Christ is significant" (ibid., p. 9). Paul's colonialist intentions are unambiguous in this statement: "One Lord, one faith, one baptism, One God and Father of all, who is above all, and through all, and in you all" (Eph 4:5, 6). Such a hard-line approach rules out any possibility of pluralism or diversity. Paul's vision of the unity of humankind under the headship of Christ serves to nullify and discredit other voices. This leads conveniently to our next point.

The concept of the cosmic Christ enshrined in the letters of Paul, especially in Colossians, is another case of colonial intention. The classical marks of colonialism can be seen in Paul's threefold description: the enthronement of the exalted Christ who "disarmed the rulers and authorities and made a public example of them, triumphing over them in it" (Col 2:15); the worldwide proclamation of the gospel; and the incorporation of humankind into the "kingdom of his beloved son" (Col 1:13). Such an image is very well suited to the imperial dominion of a Christian empire, and history has shown how the admirers of empires and emperors have reminted this image to validate the imperial idea that it is "in the monarchs of this earth that Christ as a 'heavenly monarch' was considered to be manifested and revealed" (Saúl Trinidad, "Christology, Conquista, Colonization," in *Faces of Jesus: Latin American Christologies*, edited by Jose Miguez Bonino [Maryknoll, NY: Orbis Books, 1983], p. 52). There are examples from antiquity to modern empires. Eusebius, the church historian, hailed Constantine as the earthly representative of Christ who, like Christ himself, overcame pagan religions and extended the Christian empire to include the Greeks and the barbarians. Constantine, in the words of Eusebius, "graced by his heavenly favor with victory over all his foes, subdues and chastens the open adversaries of the truth in accordance with the usages of war" (*Oratio* II, p. 4; see IV, p. 2). During the Spanish conquistador days, the royal pair Ferdinand and Isabella were seen as the celestial representation of Christ and Mary. They were glorified as "lord and master" and "lady and mistress." Their portraits were framed with gold and had halos. Those who venerated the image of Christ were in fact honoring and accepting "the earthly representative of these glorified beings" (Trinidad, p. 52).

The Future of Postcolonial Criticism. Postcolonialism has produced a whole host of phrases that no interpreter can ignore today: "Orientalism," "knowledge and power," "third space" (an ambivalent and contradictory state which has the ability to traverse and transcend both vernacular and metropolitan cultures), "hybridity" (cultural exchange which disrupts the culture and language of the colonizer and the colonized while mediating both affinity and difference), "interrelated histories" (histories that go beyond the ideological oppositions of East and West and see cultures, histories, and memories as intermingled and interdependent), and "speaking truth to power" (the intellectual's role in questioning received histories). None of these concepts would have their current purchasing power if Edward Said, Homi Bhabha, and Gayatri Spivak—the supposed pioneers of the field—had not supplied their intellectual energy and achieved reputations.

Postcolonialism has its share of weaknesses and defects which have been well documented. Some of the oft-repeated accusations are that: it reinforces Western colonialism as the dominant experience, thus sidelining other experiences; it recycles the binary mode of production—colonial literary productions supplying the raw material and the West providing the vocabulary and criteria in the form of a neat theory; it depends excessively on Western theoreticians, is preoccupied with Western audiences, and is associated with expatriate academics whose credentials are open to question; it fails to engage with Marx; it is monotonous in its veneration of hybridity; its resistance discourse, bordering on triumphalism, is self-righteous in tone; by its dense style it distances the practitioners from the ordinary people whose interest it is supposed to serve; it is over-reliant on theory and acts of theorization. There is an element of truth in these accusations and, in the present writer's opinion, the last of these is critical. If postcolonalism loses its ethical edge and political vigor in pursuit of theoretical finesse, its reason for existing is questionable.

What about the future of postcolonialism? Will it lose its usefulness as time goes on? Will it suffer from theory fatigue? Unlike other theories, postcolonial criticism does not depend on the whims and impulses of disciplinary fashions. Colonial impulse never goes away. The nature of colonialism may change but postcolonialism will have an important role to play as long as there are colonizing opportunities. As long as there are (a) markets to explore and exploit; (b) cultures which believe that their way of life is superior and that others should conform; and (c) sacred scriptures interpreted to promote the idea of an elected a chosen people of God and sanction conquest and conversion, postcolonialism will have a critical role to play.

Finally, the future utility of postcolonial criticism will not depend on the excellence of its theoretical framework. Its future lies in turning back to its earlier practice of producing imaginative literature where anti-colonial rhetoric first emerged and the study of historical texts. As Said has suggested, a historical study of the text is much more interesting than the "massive, intervening, institutionalized presence of theoretical discussion." Historical textual studies facilitate many "more opportunities for genuine discovery" and make political and cultural issues "much clearer in terms of comparable issues in our times" (*Power, Politics, and Culture*, p. 216). It is both the creative literature and the study of these which can "dramatize oppositions, present the alternative voice" (Ibid., p. 223).

[*See also* Empire Studies and Biblical Interpretation; Feminist Biblical Interpretation; Queer Criticism and Queer Theory; Social Sciences, *subentry* Hebrew Bible; *and* Social Sciences, *subentry* New Testament]

Bibliography

Dube, Musa W. *Postcolonial Feminist Interpretation of the Bible*. St. Louis, Mo.: Chalice Press, 2000. Illustrates with biblical examples the intricate relationship between patriarchy and imperialism.

Liew, Tat-Siong Benny. *Politics of Parousia: Reading Mark Inter(con)textually*. Leiden, Netherlands: Brill, 1999. Argues that Mark's Gospel reinstates colonial ideology even as it tries to defy it.

Moore, Stephen D. and Fernando F. Segovia, eds. *Postcolonial Biblical Criticism: Interdisciplinary Intersections*. London: T&T Clark, 2005. Examines postcolonial biblical criticism from a number of important political and theoretical currents such as feminism, Marxism, and poststructuralism.

O'Hara, Mary. "Western Plague," *Society Guardian* 6/4 (2011): 5.

Said, Edward W. *Culture and Imperialism*. London: Chatto & Windus, 1993.

Segovia, Fernando and R. S. Sugirtharajah. *The Postcolonial Commentary on the New Testament Writings*. London: T&T Clark, 2007. Thematic commentary on each book of the Bible.

Sugirtharajah, R. S. *The Bible and Empire: Postcolonial Explorations*. Cambridge, UK: Cambridge University Press, 2005.

Sugirtharajah, R. S. *The Bible and the Third World: Precolonial, Colonial and Postcolonial Encounters*. Cambridge, UK: Cambridge University Press, 2001.

Sugirtharajah, R. S. *Exploring Postcolonial Biblical Criticism: History, Method, Practice.* Oxford: Wiley-Blackwell, 2012. All these volumes offer a concise and multifaceted overview of the origins, development, and application of postcolonial criticism to biblical studies.

Sugirtharajah, R. S. *Postcolonial Criticism and Biblical Interpretation.* Oxford: Oxford University Press, 2002.

Sugirtharajah, R. S. ed. *The Postcolonial Bible, The Bible and Postcolonialism.* Sheffield, UK: Sheffield Academic Press, 1998. Interrogates colonial assumption embedded both in biblical texts and biblical interpretation.

Sugirtharajah, R. S. ed. *The Postcolonial Biblical Reader.* Oxford: Blackwell Publishing, 2007. A collection of essays by the leading practitioners in the field. Assembled under four headings: "Theoretical practice," "Empire Old and New," "Empire and Exegesis," and "Postcolonial concerns."

Vuswanathan, Gauri. ed. *Power, Politics, and Culture: Interviews with Edward W. Said.* New York: Pantheon Books, 2001.

R. S. Sugirtharajah

POSTMODERN INTERPRETATION

The term "postmodernity" refers to the historical period usually dated from around 1965 to the present; the term "postmodernism" refers to the cultural expressions characteristic of the period. These cultural expressions involve various assumptions that reject or problematize earlier obsolete or ill-founded ideas and values that postmodern critics view as philosophical residue of the eighteenth-century European Enlightenment (e.g., the autonomous self, unity and harmony of nature, human reason, human progress, objective knowledge, universal absolutes, transparency of language, and totalizing systems). Postmodern criticism, then, is an umbrella term for a group of interpretive approaches that position the reader *before* a text under the pressure of one or more of the assumptions that we may describe as philosophical and political positions with respect to interpretation.

Philosophical and Hermeneutical Positions. While the following list is not exhaustive, it does reflect some of the most important philosophical/hermeneutical assumptions that position literary critics before texts in interesting ways. These concepts are not distinct, but they are interrelated in terms of human understanding.

The Problem with Objective Knowledge. According to Linda Hutcheon, postmodernism "challenges all forms of totalizing thought that do not acknowledge their role in the very constitution of their objects of study and in the reduction of the heterogeneous and problematic to the homogeneous and transcendental" (Hutcheon, p. 98). All human activity that involves thought takes place within a matrix of contexts (historical, social, political, aesthetic, and theological). As a result, human knowledge is radically contextualized. Knowledge, then, is always context bound. Many postmodern critics have embraced Martin Heidegger's concept of *Dasein*, a "being-there," meaning that whatever constitutes human beings is inextricably linked to *being* in the world as contextualized, historical creatures. No ontological being exists—no human essence or nature. Everything that humans think, decide, know, and interpret is from within a "fore-structure" consisting of a "fore-having, fore-sight, and fore-conception" (Heidegger, p. 191). Consequently, this radical embeddedness precludes objective human knowledge. Humans always know and understand from *within*; they are always *inside* looking in, not outside looking in from some position of Cartesian cleanness or Baconian precision.

Social Location. The problem with objective knowledge is related to a concept current in both literary and philosophical discussions—social location—which refers to the contexts within which human beings structure their lives, or the contexts that structure humans. Social location is a matrix or convergence of a number of thought systems that define a community and its reality. This matrix includes political, theological, social, linguistic, aesthetic, literary, scientific, educational, and other systems that constitute a community's symbolic world. From within this social location, a person values, makes judgments and decisions, and knows as far as the conventions of the system allows. All human activity (including the construction of systems, the creative arts, writing, reading, and interpreting) occur *within* contexts. Critical approaches, such as Ideological, *Mujerista*, feminist, Asian/Asian American, liberation, postcolonial, queer, psychoanalytic, new historicism, transactive, social scientific, reception theory, and the like. proceed from the premise that all interpretation happens *within* a variety of contexts from which the interpreter cannot escape. Contemporary literary and cultural critics argue that because authors write and readers interpret from *within* their social locations, objective knowledge is not inscribed within a text nor is it generated in the reading of a text.

Truth. From the time of Plato, in the Western philosophical tradition, truth was defined as a body of content (e.g., physical laws, natural laws, and knowledge), which exists in the structure of the universe in specific areas such as morality, politics, economics, and science. This truth exists independently of human action and thought, but it is accessible to humans. It is a universal, coherent, unified body of content. However, philosophers like Heidegger and Nietzsche began to question the existence of such universal truth or truths, and later philosophers like Jacques Derrida, Geoffrey Hartman, Paul de Man, Michel Foucault, Richard Rorty, and Jean-François Lyotard posit a world in which communities create systems through which they process experience. Communities then substitute these systems—moral, aesthetic, scientific, religious—for truth.

In his *The Postmodern Condition: A Report on Knowledge*, Jean-François Lyotard argues that postmodernism marks the end of appeals to legitimating narratives whatsoever. Postmodernism is the demise of the metanarratives that claim to represent truth. We are left with local narratives, stories that can define personal identity and give purpose and shape to social experience. Reality is the convergence of these local narratives. Richard Rorty suggests a similar idea in his brief work on ethics, *An Ethics for Today: Finding Common Ground between Philosophy and Religion.* Borrowing the idea of language games from Wittgenstein, Rorty claims that every sector of our existence speaks an idiom, and the truth or falsity of a proposition depends on the rules of the idiom in which it is enunciated. Gianni Vattimo observes in his introduction to the Rorty text, "If you start singing hymns to the Virgin Mary in the tavern, the lads will probably laugh you out of the place, just like churchgoers will chase you out of their place if you start singing tavern songs there" (Rorty, p. 3). Ultimately, only local truths exist.

Objective Historical Knowledge. The issue of reliable historical knowledge also relates to the postmodern claim that objective knowledge is obtainable. Traditionally, modern historians have assumed that they have unmediated access to the past, that they stand above the pressures of agenda, bias, and ideology, just to mention a few possible influences. The assumption that historians can recreate the circumstances surrounding past events has met with formidable challenges from postmodern critics. Modern critics of the Bible, for example, have assumed a correlation between a writer's purpose and the events that surrounded the writing of the text. The more knowledge an interpreter has about the world of the author, the more likely that person is to get at the author's meaning. As a result, the more "the reader knows about Paul's Corinthian audience and the generative circumstances of the Corinthian correspondence, the more accurately that reader is able to configure a plausible understanding of the letters" (Tate, p. 168).

Postmodern critics, however, have challenged the assumption that accurate historical reconstruction is possible by discussing the issue of access to the past. Indeed, the only access to the past is *textual,* which postmodern critics argue means that something must be *interpreted.* Our primary access to the past is through texts—artifacts—that historians must interpret. The texts were written within one social location and are now being read within a different one. New historicists refer to this dilemma as the textuality of history and the historicity of texts. Both the author's and the reader's contexts are affected by various assumptions, biases, purposes, and methodological and ideological concerns.

Consequently, postmodern critics jettison the possibility of historical reconstruction in favor of historical construction. Historiography is not a re-presentation of the past but a presentation of an *interpreted* past. The historian then becomes more an interpreter of the past than a recorder of it.

History and Historiography. The distinction between history (past events) and historiography (writing about those events) is an important one. A historiographer always selects certain events to discuss while excluding others. What determines that selection? Postmodern critics assume that the writer's *agenda*—political, theological, and so on—is partially responsible for the selection, perhaps even subconsciously. Two historiographers may present differing versions of the same period based on which events are included or excluded, and how events are weighted. History, then, becomes the narrative of past events. One does not have to be keenly observant to note that the authors of the historical narratives of the Hebrew Bible selected and arranged materials from a variety of sources. The primary focus was not to merely record the past but to communicate a theological, ideological message for the present. A postmodern critic also investigates the *intentions* of contemporary interpretation of these historical narratives.

Other problems facing historians are the availability and types of materials that exist. In past eras, records were kept about things that were sanctioned by the political and religious authorities. Consequently, historians may know more about rulers, wars, and political and religious issues than they know about the concerns and lives of ordinary people, the activities and roles of women and minorities, or popular culture. Even where this information is available, historians must interpret it. Even when historians claim objectivity, their ideology inevitably predisposes them to find some portions of the surviving evidence significant and other parts less important. Assumptions or ideological stances shape authors' interpretations of the evidence they choose to discuss. To add to the problem, an author's interpretation of the past is only one among many possible interpretations that may exist. For example, Martin Bernal argues that the contributions to European culture from Egypt, Africa, and the Near East were systematically distorted during the nineteenth century based upon racial attitudes:

> The paradigm of "races" that were intrinsically unequal in physical and mental endowment was applied to all human studies, but especially to history. . . . To be creative, a civilization needed to be "racially pure." Thus it became increasingly intolerable that Greece—which was seen by the Romantics not merely as the epitome of Europe but also of its pure childhood—could be the result of the mixture of native Europeans and colonizing Africans and Semitics. (Bernal, p. 29)

Metanarratives and Metalanguage. Thought systems that emphasize social location may be called metanarratives—systems that undergird a civilization. Postmodern thinkers often see these systems as "legitimizing myths" because they are human constructs that are accepted over time as universal by members of a community, and they provide the means by which the community legitimates itself (Grenz, p. 44). In addition, postmodernists claim that no universal narratives exist that represent reality *as it is.* Narratives that communities accept as reflecting the way things *are* amount to human constructs, each with its own set of conventions. While postmodernists view such systems as useful tools by which humans organize and understand the world, they reject them as a means of accurately representing the nature of things.

According to Jean-Francois Lyotard, these systems become life defining for communities, and eventually, the communities assume that the systems are universally valid. Lyotard suggests that in the hands of the Western world, the systems have actually led to the oppression of large parts of the world. He further claims that these systems can exist only by excluding other possibilities by demonizing or marginalizing them. The Neo-pragmatist Richard Rorty advocates replacing epistemology with hermeneutics, which he defines as the ongoing conversation *between* local systems or metanarratives.

> Regarding the critical analysis of texts, postmodern critics assume that in varying degrees, texts reflect their underlying metanarratives. Consequently, readers/critics should approach any text with a sense of resistance to the pressure of these metanarratives. For biblical studies, this positioning "means that the social structures, institutions, systems of valuing, prescriptions for lifestyles, and the like which have their origins in the biblical texts and have been declared as universally valid need to be reconsidered as local, limited, and not universal." (Tate, p. 212)

Metalanguage is a language "game" about language. The practitioners of a metalanguage assume that they can somehow perform critical examination that is completely objective and disinterested. Examples are seen in structuralism, semiotics, and linguistics, which examine the ways sign systems (e.g., a poem, a narrative, a myth, a folk tale, or a natural language) function. Consequently, any critical theory or interpretive approach is a metalanguage because it uses a technical vocabulary in the critical analysis of its object. The ultimate issue here is *meaning*. Because a metalanguage (approaches like formalism, new historicism, postcolonialism, narrative criticism, reader-response criticism, and rabbinic hermeneutics) creates the categories and parameters within which the critic analyzes the object, many critics claim that these categories actually dictate the configuration of meaning (i.e., the critical language game is constitutive of meaning). A structuralist's configuration of meaning of a particular text will differ from that of a formalist or new historicist. Meaning is not something *in* the text but something the critic *creates* through the analytical structures of the metalanguage. Objective meaning is a myth. For example, postcolonialists read with a certain sensibility toward the historical reality of imperialism and its influence upon literature. The imperialist culture wrote the literature and decided what literature would be canonized, and this literature affected society by propagating the differentiation and subsequent oppression of the colonized people (Hall, pp. 268–269). Consequently, postcolonial critics set as one of their tasks the reinterpretation of texts with an awareness of the authors' underlying imperialist assumptions. In biblical studies, postcolonialists such as R. S. Sugirtharajah urge that third-world readers adopt a discourse of resistance by which they use their own cultural identities to examine biblical texts (Sugirtharajah, p. 7). Although postcolonialists may focus on the reality of ancient Assyrian, Babylonian, and Roman imperialism and how these cultures influenced the writing of biblical texts, they extend their focus to the modern interpretations of texts. They examine the ways in which Western readers position themselves (assuming that Western readers are products of an imperialist mentality) before the biblical texts and then compare those readings to those of marginalized people. Interpretation is then partly a function of metanarratives and metalanguages.

The Nature of Language. The nature and function of language have become rallying points for postmodern critics. Discussions usually center on the relationship between language usage, social structures, and totalizing systems. A brief review of the enlightenment view of the nature of language will serve as a setting for the postmodern critique of the modernist view of language.

Postmodernists argue that since Plato, Western philosophy has proceeded under what Derrida refers to as "metaphysics of presence," the foundational assumption that an objective world of realities exists independent of humans and human thought. Otherwise stated, truth and meaning are transcendental signifieds that are present *prior to our discovery of them*. They are always already present in the structure of things, waiting for humans to use their reason to discover them and present them to the world using the objective structures of language. Such a re-presentation is possible if language is a transparent medium, and Western metaphysics assumes transparency as a property of language. "As objects present themselves to the mind, humans are capable of making objective assertions about those objects. If that language is subsequently analyzed, humans can fully know that object because the logical structures of the universe (or object) are revealed in the assertions, which are themselves the meaning of the object" (Tate, 277). However, postmodern thinkers challenge all three assumptions—(1) that there is an objective world of knowledge, (2) that language is transparent, and (3) that language can objectively re-present the world. Neither reality nor language is transcendental. Languages are conventional social constructs that map reality in a variety of ways, shaping the way humans experience the world. Rather than re-presenting or reconstructing the world, languages construct the world:

> Languages are world-creating rather than world-describing systems. This means, then, that rather than an already-existing objective body of knowledge or truth, or even an objective world waiting to be discovered, there are only potential worlds and many truths. These worlds, each with its own truth, are symbolic worlds that we construct through languages. So postmodernists refuse to split language from reality: they assume that there is no direct access to the world that is unmediated by language. (Tate, p. 277)

Language, Totalizing Systems, and Structures of Power. Postmodern critics such as Derrida and Foucault expand the issue of language beyond representation to claim that language or discourse is inseparable from totalizing systems and the power structures within the systems. If language constitutes or creates that which it represents, discourses are far from being value-neutral (e.g., science, philosophy, literary criticism, theology). If every act of knowing is the function of the self within a language game, then this knowledge expression is or may be an assertion of power. Humans employ discourse to gain and maintain control over others. Both Derrida and Foucault have argued that practices within discourses determine controls, qualified members, accepted procedures of expression, the production of objects, and the rules of legitimation. All institutions, according to Lyotard, are based on a language game that establishes the limits of legitimate thought, expression, and action.

While a discourse allows some possibilities, however, it excludes others. Any discourse, totalizing system, or metanarrative exists through exclusion. A player within the game can make certain moves but not others. If a player wants to make a novel move, that person runs the risk of being censored by the institution, which is generally more interested in conformity than in creativity. According to Lyotard, an institution has many ways to encourage or enforce conformity—the simplest being "conform or else." These controls or well-defined limits reside at the heart of every system—theological, philosophical, scientific, academic, social, and aesthetic.

In the Western metaphysical tradition, exclusion is based on what postmodern thinkers refer to as "binary oppositions." A binary opposition refers to two terms—the first term is privileged while the second is subordinated or marginalized. Examples include white/black, light/dark, masculine/feminine, spirit/flesh, heaven/hell, Western/Eastern, and so on. The Western concept of reality relies on oppositions. The recognition of and search for such exclusionary oppositions have become mainstays in many postmodern readings of texts, including biblical ones. Some oppositions that regularly occur in the Bible are God/Satan, light/darkness, Jew/Gentile, spirit/flesh, man/woman, and husband/wife. By examining these underlying structures, a critic can determine how a community defined itself to some extent. For example, when the apostle Paul addresses problems involving women in the church at Corinth, he appeals to the second account of creation in Genesis 2—3 to argue his case. In 1 Corinthians 11:2–9, he argues that the "husband is the head of his wife," and that the man "is the image and reflection of God, but the woman is the reflection of man." He also says that the woman was created "for the sake of man." In a similar fashion, the author of 1 Timothy subordinates the woman to the man: "Let a woman learn in silence with full submission. I permit no woman to teach or to have authority over the man; she is to keep silent. For Adam was formed first, then Eve; and Adam was not deceived, but the woman was deceived and became a transgressor" (1 Tim 2:11–14). The binary opposition, man/woman, underlies both of these cases in which the first term "man" is privileged while the second term "woman" is marginalized. Neither Paul nor the author of 1 Timothy could have supported their arguments by using the first account of creation because subordination is not an issue there. That the two writers chose the *second* account, which *does* support their argument, posits a worldview based on binary oppositions. David W. Odell-Scott suggests that "the identities of this oppositional pair are elaborated by their associations with other oppositional pairs, in which identifications are made with other concepts which are also defined in dyadic sets: Man-Woman, First-Second, God-World, Sacred-Profane, Soul-Body" (Odell-Scott, p. 60).

The pattern is clearly discernible. In each binary, the first term is invested with value while the second one is divested of value. Thus, the associations line up as follows:

> Because man is created from the earth, he is nearer to God, is identified with God, and is, therefore, more sacred. Furthermore, because the soul is associated with God, the man is identified with soul.
>
> Because woman is created second and is created from the man and not directly from God, she is associated with the world and is, therefore, profane. The woman is identified with the body, the opposite of the soul, reinforcing her marginalization.

Meaning, Method, Interpretation, and Contexts. Obviously, postmodern critics spend a lot of time examining the issue of the *locus* of meaning, especially literary meaning. What is the source of meaning? Is it the same as the reader understands? What is the role of method in interpretation? Do methods themselves establish meaning? How does the reader's context influence interpretation? The issue of context is perhaps most vital in current critical discussions, including biblical studies. Context becomes the frame through which interpreters process a text. Biblical authors communicated through cultural filters, and readers interpret through theirs. A reader's context is a matrix of thought systems that create a social location, the framework within which a person values, makes assumptions and judgments, and interprets texts. The reader can never escape from this location or assume an objective stance from which to interpret an artifact.

Similar to literary studies, however, current biblical scholarship focuses much energy on examining the relationships between meaning, method, and context. Each interpretive method presupposes a context or a set of questions that focuses the interpreter's examination of the text. Because each method asks certain questions and not others, the interpretive results vary. Clearly then, method is constitutive of meaning, if meaning involves interpretive results or understanding. In his *Contexts for Criticism*, Donald Keesey has identified seven primary contexts within which critics examine texts—author, text, audience, language, literature, reality, and culture. Each of these contexts serves as a category for individual methods. Some approaches fit well into more than one of these categories, while others fit uncomfortably in any category. In addition, not all the current approaches are mentioned here. Thus, we begin to see the complexity of current biblical studies and the fluidity of *meaning* when it is tied closely to context.

Author as Context. Approaches that focus on the author as the source of meaning may rightly be called "genetic." The task of most genetic approaches is to recognize the author's OIO (original intentional object). Because meaning is the product of an author's mind, any information that assists in recovering that product should be examined (e.g., sources that the author may have used, current social, political, religious, and scientific institutions, original language, etc.). In biblical studies, critics continue to publish and read works that deal with the worlds that existed during the writing of the Hebrew Bible and the New Testament—assuming that the more interpreters know about the Greco-Roman and Judaic worlds, the more plausible their interpretations will be. Although these approaches are not specifically postmodern (postmodern approaches actually challenge the assumption that we can recover the author's intention), they continue to attract many biblical scholars. Among the critical methods that fall under this paradigm are form, historical-critical, Marxist, psychoanalytic, social-scientific, source, and tradition. Again, postmodern critics find it problematic to assume that interpreters can somehow bracket out their social locations and examine artifacts from a completely objective perspective. To postmodern critics, every object that presents itself to human consciousness must be interpreted from a perspective and contextualized. In addition, an understanding of a past is only partially recoverable because interpreters have only limited access to the worlds in which texts were given birth.

Text as Context. Theories that view the actual text as the primary source of meaning usually examine the structures, rhetorical strategies, and conventions of the text. These critical approaches include archetypal, composition, formal, genre, mimetic, myth, narrative, redaction, rhetorical, speech act, socio-rhetorical, performance, and structuralist. As with the author as context, postmodern critics reject a basic assumption of most of the preceding methods—the assumption that meaning resides in the structures of the text waiting for a competent reader to recover it. Typically, a postmodern critic is suspicious of any claim that meaning is present in an object, whether the object is the author's mind or the text. A text means nothing until someone picks it up and means something by it. In other words, meaning is inextricably bound to the interpretive context that includes the interpretive approach involved.

Reader/Audience as Context. Several critical approaches assume in varying degrees that the context for meaning is the reader/audience. Meaning is not necessarily in the text or in the mind of the author; it is created through the interaction of the creative reader and the enabling structures of the text. Meaning is then the function of the activities and responses of readers. This group includes approaches along a continuum, depending on the degree of privilege allowed the text or the reader. For example, the phenomenological criticism of Wolfgang Iser, the reader-response criticism of Umberto Eco, and the approach of biblical scholars like Robert Fowler (*Let the Reader Understand: Reader-Response Criticism and the Gospel of Mark*) are relatively close to the text, while the objective criticism of David Bleich and the transactive criticism of Norman Holland focus almost entirely on the activities of the reader. In biblical studies, this critical group includes canonical, reader-response, autobiographical, and tendenz (authorial intention).

With the recognition of the creative role of the reader in determining meaning, the world of biblical studies experienced its own Copernican revolution. The paradigm shift was such a thoroughgoing one because once meaning was linked to the activities of readers, it was only a matter of time before concerns about interpretive communities and their language games, legitimizing procedures, structures of exclusion, as well as the reader's social location (including gender, ethnicity, politics, race, religion, education, language, etc.) were center stage. Each of the four contexts is an expression of this paradigm shift. First, postmodern critics recognize that communities have different realities and are, thus, situated to see the world through their own unique ideologies. The claim to objectivity is simply superfluous. Second, some postmodern critics extend the interpretive context to include the entire world of literature in which authorial uniqueness is called into question. Certainly meaning is context bound, but the context is boundless. Third, if humans are forced to talk about a linguistic text through a linguistic sign system, then meaning is inseparable from the conventions of that system. Readers are prisoners of their languages. And fourth, authors and readers do their work within cultures that have structured them. Consequently, any attempt to escape the pressures of these cultures is destined to fail.

Reality as Context. Another approach is reality, which focuses on interpreting texts from *within* particular worldviews or theories of reality. For example, if Marxism truly describes the way history and societies work, then any text should reflect that reality. If the human psyche is constructed as Freud claims and literature is a means of coping with inherent neurosis, then any text can be examined as an expression of that psyche. As a result, critics can make either a Freudian or a Marxist out of Job or the author of Job. The same observations apply to Lacanian, Jungian, and Aristotelian views of reality. Psychoanalytic approaches may focus on the psychoanalysis of the reader, the author, or a character in the piece. The interpretive results of these theories of reality are a direct function of the questions the theories apply to the text. (A Marxist defines and understands reality differently from an Aristotelian or a Freudian, and so forth.) Postmodern critics assume that every person who reads a text does so under the pressure of an ideology (political, theological, etc.). Thus, this critical category includes approaches that biblical scholars recognize as ideological, including race, class, gender, feminist, political, ecological, and socioeconomic as well as psychoanalytic and Marxist.

Literature as Context. Still another context for meaning is the text's relationship to and interaction with other texts. This approach is based on the assumption that no text is unique, but that each builds upon prior texts and literary conventions. Therefore, a person who has read the epics of Homer, Dante, and Virgil is better prepared to read Milton or, for that matter, better equipped to read the Gospels. Reciprocally, the person who has read Milton is better prepared to read Homer, Dante, and Virgil. The same holds for all types of literature. Critical approaches of this nature include archetypal, genre, myth, and intertextual.

Language as Context. The assumption here is that in discussing meaning, humans are forced to talk about language *through* language, which is itself a system of signs that functions according to codes. Meaning is impossible except *within* a system of signs. Some critics see language as a transparent means of communication, while others think that language is characterized by ambiguity, its signifiers pointing only to signifieds that are *themselves* signifiers resulting in unlimited semiosis. Consequently, language does not have extralinguistic objects to which it points. Meaning does *not* reside in these objects; rather, language always suggests more language. Meaning is fluid—like attempting to contain a drop of water on a table by pressing down on it with the thumb. Included in this critical group are deconstruction, new historicism, and structuralism.

Culture as Context. The last group of approaches is varied, but each assumes somehow that the context for meaning is culture, both that of the author and that of the reader (though most of the approaches focus on the culture of the reader). Both authors and readers reflect their social locations. The only access interpreters have to the past is text (any object that claims to represent the past and, thus, must be interpreted), which is itself an interpretation of something of the past. Since texts are produced, read, and valued within a variety of contexts, the objectivity of writing and reading is open to dispute. Included in this critical group are new historicism, cultural materialism, cultural, feminist, postcolonial, postcolonial feminist, African/African American, Asian/Asian American, and *Mujerista* and womanist interpretation.

Projection. In some form or other, the path that biblical studies will take in the future seems to be a hermeneutic of *suspicion.* This will most likely occur because of the explosion of critical methods that are suspicious of closed systems, absolutes, objectivity, institutionalized truth claims, the validity of interpretive approaches that ignore the role of culture, ideology, and interpretive agenda in all respects (political, theological, academic, social). In light of this, along with structures of legitimation that marginalize individuals and groups, the discipline of biblical studies (even if it is appropriate to speak about "the" discipline) will inevitably attract a much broader field of scholars and without doubt a more inclusive dialogue about the extent, nature, and ultimate goal of biblical interpretation. Globalization will become the Ground Zero that transforms biblical studies into a multivoiced discipline, ensuring an ongoing conversation marked by unforced agreement and tolerant disagreement.

[*See also* African American Interpretation; African Biblical Interpretation; Class Criticism; Cultural Studies; Deconstruction; Feminist Biblical Interpretation;

Ideological Criticism; Intertextuality; Lesbian, Gay, Bisexual, and Transgender Interpretation; Materialist Criticism; Performance Criticism; Postcolonial Biblical Interpretation; Poststructuralist Interpretation; Queer Criticism and Queer Theory; Race, Ethnicity, and Biblical Criticism; Reader-Response Criticism; Reception Criticism and Theory; Structuralist Interpretation; *and* Womanist Interpretation.]

BIBLIOGRAPHY

Adam, A. K. M., ed. *Handbook of Postmodern Biblical Interpretation.* St. Louis, Mo.: Chalice, 2000.

Anderson, Janice Capel, and Stephen D. Moore, eds. *Mark and Method: New Approaches in Biblical Studies.* Minneapolis: Fortress, 1992.

Bernal, Martin, ed. *Black Athena: The Afroasiatic Roots of Classical Civilization*, Vol. 1. New Brunswick, N.J.: Rutgers University Press, 1989.

Cahoone, Lawrence, ed. *From Modernism to Postmodernism: An Anthology*, 2d. ed. Malden, Mass.: John Wiley and Sons, 2003.

Derrida, Jacques. *Writing and Difference.* Translated by Alan Bass. London: Routledge and Kegan Paul, 1978.

Exum, J. Cheryl, and Stephen Moore, eds. "Biblical Studies/Cultural Studies: The Third Sheffield Colloquium." *Journal for the Study of the Old Testament: Supplement Series* 266. Gender, Culture, Theory 7. Sheffield, UK: Sheffield Academic Press, 1998.

Grenz, Stanley J. *A Primer on Postmodernism.* Grand Rapids, Mich.: Eerdmans, 1996.

Hall, Donald. *Literary and Cultural Theory: From Basic Principles to Advanced Applications.* Boston: Houghton Mifflin, 2001.

Hayes, J. H., ed. *Dictionary of Biblical Interpretation.* 2 vols. Nashville: Abingdon, 1999.

Heidegger, Martin. *Being and Time.* Translated by John Macquarrie and Edward Robinson. New York: Harper and Row, 1962.

Helmer, Christine, ed. *Biblical Interpretation: History, Context, and Reality.* Atlanta: Society of Biblical Literature, 2005.

Hutcheon, Linda. *A Poetics of Postmodernism: History, Theory, Fiction.* New York: Routledge, 1988.

Jobling, D., and S. D. Moore, eds. "Poststructuralism as Exegesis." *Semeia* 54 (1991).

Keesey, Donald, ed. *Contexts for Criticism*, 4th ed. Boston: McGraw Hill, 2003.

Lyotard, J.-F. *The Postmodern Condition: A Report on Knowledge.* Minneapolis: University of Minnesota Press, 1984.

Odell-Scott, David. "Deconstruction." In *Handbook of Postmodern Biblical Interpretation*, edited by A. K. M. Adam, 55–61. St. Louis: Chalice, 2000.

Phillips, G. A., ed. "Poststructural Criticism and the Bible." *Semeia* 51 (1990).

Porter, Stanley E., ed. *Dictionary of Biblical Criticism and Interpretation.* London: Routledge, 2007.

Ray, William. *Literary Meaning: From Phenomenology to Deconstruction.* New York: Blackwell, 1984.

Rorty, Richard. *An Ethics for Today: Finding Common Ground between Philosophy and Religion.* New York: Columbia University Press, 2011.

Segovia, F. F., and M. A. Tolbert, eds. *Social Location and Biblical Interpretation in the United States.* Vol. 1, *Reading from This Place.* Minneapolis: Fortress, 1995.

Sugirtharajah, R. S. *The Bible and the Third World: Precolonial, Colonial, and Postcolonial Encounters.* Cambridge: Cambridge University Press, 2001.

Tate, W. Randolph. *Interpreting the Bible: A Handbook of Terms and Methods.* Peabody, Mass.: Hendrickson, 2006.

Thiselton, Anthony. *Interpreting God and the Postmodern Self: On Meaning, Manipulation, and Promise.* Grand Rapids, Mich.: Eerdmans, 1995.

W. Randolph Tate

Poststructuralist Interpretation

Poststructuralism is a postmodern form of semiotics, which is the study of signs. Its primary concern is with the relationship between reading and text. "Reading" here refers to any perception and comprehension of a text, and a "text" may be any meaningful thing or event. Texts include not only writings but oral utterances and electronic media, as well as anything else that signifies, such as architecture, artifacts of every kind, social institutions, human or nonhuman behaviors, and even natural phenomena (such as the movement of stars) insofar as they are taken by someone to be meaningful.

What distinguishes poststructuralism from structuralism or other ways of reading is rejection of "logocentric" understandings of texts, according to which the reality of a text is a single meaning or *logos* that defines its "truth" (Derrida). Poststructuralists believe that "difference" or multiplicity is prior to logical or ontological unity and disrupts the text's significance. They engage in close readings that are suspicious of any alleged unity or wholeness within the text, and they are more concerned with signifying mechanisms than with signified meanings. There are always many possible interpretations of any text. This has philosophical consequences: poststructuralists do not seek one universal Truth, but instead they expect many local, transitory, partial truths.

There are many differences of emphasis and terminology among poststructuralist critics. The following is necessarily a general survey.

Roots. Poststructuralism derives most directly from structuralism, which emerged from the linguistic theories of Ferdinand de Saussure and Charles Sanders Peirce, and was further developed by Vladimir Propp, Roman Jakobson, and Claude Lévi-Strauss, among others. A second source of poststructuralism is the philosophy of language as developed by thinkers such as Gottlob Frege and Ludwig Wittgenstein. A third source is philosophical phenomenology. Phenomenology and the philosophy of language have been combined with semiotics in various ways by poststructuralist thinkers such as Paul Ricoeur, Jacques Derrida, and Gilles Deleuze. Other sources include the writings of Friedrich Nietzsche and Karl Marx (and later Marxist thinkers such as Theodor Adorno and Walter Benjamin), as well as the writings of Sigmund Freud (especially as developed by Jacques Lacan). From Nietzsche, Marx, and Freud, poststructuralism derives its approach of suspicion and its attention to that which has been systematically excluded or suppressed.

Poststructuralism also derives from postmodern literature and art, as well as precursor movements such as Symbolism, Dada, and existentialism. An important focus has been the field of popular culture, including cinema, television, popular and experimental music, and comic books.

Poststructuralism is implicit in the semiotic roots of structuralism, and any clear distinction between the two will inevitably break down. In the 1950s and 1960s, scholars who were well versed in Saussure's theories, such as Deleuze and Michel Foucault, began to challenge and surpass structuralist thought "from within," drawing upon the theories of Peirce as well as phenomenology and Marxism. This shift in understanding is sometimes described as the move from structural to textual analysis.

Poststructuralism appeared in biblical studies almost as soon as structuralism did, perhaps most notably in many articles in the journal *Semeia*, which played an active role from 1974 until 2002 in promoting both structuralist and poststructuralist analyses of biblical texts. Even earlier, Roland Barthes published poststructural readings of Genesis 32 and Acts of the Apostles 10–11 (see the following.) Many other poststructuralists, including Derrida, Deleuze, Umberto Eco, and Julia Kristeva, have also discussed biblical texts, as well as various theological topics. For poststructuralism, even God is constrained by imperfections inherent in sign-systems, and the divine word simulated in the Bible brings with it of necessity its own misunderstandings and transgressions.

Theory. Semiotics regards texts as mechanisms composed of signs. For Saussure, a sign unites a signified (an idea or nonmaterial meaning) to a signifier (formed matter, such as spoken or written words). The meaning of a text derives not only from the arrangement or sequence of signs that make up the text (the syntagm) but also from the relations between those signs and other signs in the reader's linguistic repertoire (the paradigm).

Poststructural semiotics accepts these concepts, but it also claims that every text invites and even demands the breakdown of its own sign-system, and that the points where such systems break down say a great deal about them. The semiotic connection between signifier and signified is neither tight nor exclusive, and it is entirely artificial. Breakdowns occur when this connection is disrupted by physical features within the text itself. As a result, meaningful reading must be shaped and directed by extra-textual supplements that repair or correct the disruption. In other words, the signifier both supports and resists meaning; the very mechanism that makes meaning possible also disrupts meaning. Just as meaning depends on differences between signifiers (as for Saussure), so it also is influenced by differences within each signifier, between its sheer meaningless materiality and its semiotic potential.

The signified has primary importance for structuralist semiotics, and connotation (or "sense") is secondary to denotation (or "reference"). In contrast, poststructuralism regards the signifier as more important than the signified, but it does not simply invert the logocentric privileging of meaning. Semiotics is given a postmodern twist when Saussure's binary sign-system is profoundly transformed by the addition of Peirce's concept of the "interpretant," the third element of the sign. Nearly all linguistic signs (which Peirce calls "symbols") consist not only of a signifier ("representamen") and a signified ("object"), but also require an interpretant, which connects the other two elements. The interpretant is the connoted sense of the signifier, as distinct from its denoted object. Therefore denotation depends upon connotation.

This implies that no text can be read purely by itself, as though it were a self-contained system. The connection produced by the interpretant must itself be explained, and this requires yet other signs that must also be explained, and so on. Every signifier may be signified, and every signified may itself be the signifier of yet another signified. There is no final signified or first signifier: the connotative chains between one text and another extend endlessly—and multidirectionally. "Unlimited semiosis" (Eco) is always a vertiginous and bottomless abyss, while the physical text itself is a surface that forestalls decisive signification. Meaning is elusive and fluid, and connotations run wild in the flux of signification. Although flows of semiosis characterize every text, they are particularly apparent both within the Bible (for example, in the appropriation and transformation of the Jewish scriptures in the New Testament) and in the many "afterlives" of biblical texts in extra-canonical cultural products such as works of art, literature, and cinema.

In order to understand a text, the reader brings to it other similar or different texts that she has read. The interpretant arises from the signifier's relation to signifiers in these other texts, and it is finally inseparable from this interplay of signifiers, or "intertextuality" (Kristeva). Intertextuality lies in spaces between texts that are formed by tensions between signifiers and occupied by readers. Each reader is a living repository of texts, a network of potential connections, and thus each reader is both product and event of intertextuality, the point at which an intertextual network comes to bear upon a text. Culturally-determined codes (Barthes 1974) filter the reader's experience of the text and generate its semiotic articulation. Themselves usually unconscious, these codes control and limit the text's semiosis, defining the text's meaning for the reader. They are the means through which the signifiers become meaningful. However, the codes also define the reader. The codes involved are not necessarily the same from one reader to another, or from one text to another, and thus no two readings are exactly alike. Different readers—different intertextualities—will attach different signifieds to the same signifiers.

In other words, reading connects the semiotic machine that is a text to the intertextual machine that is a reader, and it limits the flows of semiosis by means of an intertextual interruption. The reader wants the text to convey a single coherent meaning—that is, she wants the potentially endless flows to stop. She attaches meaning to the text through an act of interference, which is reading. Every reading involves a decision to curtail semiotic flows by selecting one potential intertext and rejecting others, thereby "breaking" the flow (Deleuze and Guattari 1983). Apart from such reading, the text has no meaning, but through that reading, the text is in effect rewritten. Thus the intertextual network that produces the reader also controls or limits the text's hermeneutical possibilities for that same reader. The meaningful text and its reader are not two independent things, but they are both products of the same semiotic mechanisms.

Ideology is an irrational factor introduced by the interpretant into the production of meaning. It connects reader to text, and it controls that connection through linguistic structures that inevitably involve exclusions or omissions that cannot be justified rationally. Ideology appears in intertextual controls over semiosis, such as codes of reading through which acceptable or "natural" readings are generated. Such readings join the reader to other like-minded people. Ideology also appears in fundamental linguistic structures, "discursive formations" (Foucault), which are ways of thinking and speaking that are usually unconscious, but which control the possibility or impossibility of saying any particular thing at some particular time.

This explains why some texts are easier to read than others. The flow of semiosis resists intertextual control, but this resistance is much more evident in some texts than it is in others. The "readerly" text (Barthes 1974) appears to be fully and naturally meaningful. It speaks for itself, and its meaning is "obvious" to the reader—that is, the text's semiosis is safely limited by the reader's ideology, and the intertextual machine works smoothly and unconsciously to control it. In contrast, the "writerly" text is enigmatic and makes the reader conscious of her struggles to make the text meaningful. The opacity of the signifier resists the workings of the intertextual machine, and unlimited semiosis becomes explicit. As a result, instead of a well-managed channel of meaning there is a flood of possibilities, and the text's meaning is deconstructed. Both texts require the reader to make choices to determine meaning, but the writerly text makes the reader's active involvement in the formation of meaning evident, while the readerly text conceals it. However, not only are some texts more resistant to the reader's control than others, but some readers are more attuned to possible codes than are others.

Intertextuality and unlimited semiosis stand in reciprocal relationship to one another. Semiosis produces and disperses texts, and therefore it makes intertextuality possible. Nevertheless, for a coherent message to be received, the potential for excessive or multiple connotations must be controlled. Because texts only mean in intertextual juxtaposition to other texts, settled meaning is never located within a single text. There is no absolute anchor to which proper meaning can be attached: no single true meaning or deep structure in any text. Although these interrelated concepts are already implicit in structuralism, when either or both of them become explicit in the analysis of a text, that analysis becomes poststructuralist.

Poststructuralism and Biblical Studies. Poststructuralist studies of biblical texts typically feature serious engagement with relevant theoretical concepts, combined with close readings of biblical texts. Intertextual juxtapositions of biblical and nonbiblical texts is also often (but not always) involved in the analysis. Two examples are noted here.

Close Readings. Roland Barthes's essay "The Structural Analysis of Narrative: Apropos of Acts 10–11" (1988) was written in 1969 and first appeared in the journal *Exégèse et Herméneutique* in 1971. Barthes retains the structuralist distinction between the syntagm and the paradigm, but he uses this to engage Kristeva's concept of intertextuality and its relation to ideology through the production of meanings through codes, the "counter-text" (p. 227), and the question of readability. Barthes later raised all of this to a much higher degree in his book *S/Z* (1974). He adopts the ancient practice of biblical scholarship by breaking the text into small units, which he calls "lexias" (1988, p. 229). The division of the narrative into lexias is arbitrary and practical, to reduce the text to a size that may be analyzed in terms of the codes that are employed. Each lexia will have one or more codes operating in it. The codes are abstractions from the total field of the paradigm that the reader engages in order to decipher the text, filters through which the reader's experience with other texts is brought into play. The codes produce the range of possible meanings that may be attached to the lexia, and hence, through the overall arrangement of lexias, they generate the semiotic articulation of the entire text.

The goal of Barthes's reading of Acts of the Apostles 10–11 is not to determine the one correct meaning of the text. Instead, he questions the possibility of any final signified in a "limitless" text (pp. 244–245). He seeks to lay out as clearly as possible the actual movements of a reading, to dissect the text and also the reading of that text into the smallest possible units, and then to reassemble these units so that it is clear how they fit (or do not fit) together. In short, Barthes deconstructs the semiotic mechanisms of the text and of the reader. He shows that the meaningful text and its reader are not two different things, but in fact they are both produced by something else.

Yvonne Sherwood's book *A Biblical Text and Its Afterlives: The Survival of Jonah in Western Culture* (2000) draws upon Barthes's concept of the "perpetual signifier." Sherwood traces the ways in which Jonah's "mongrel text" (p. 236) has reproduced itself, both within and outside of the Bible, in a wide variety of written, graphic, and televised texts. Many of these rewritings of Jonah were produced by Christians or Jews, but others have come from beyond any canonical or creedal context. Sherwood argues that the interpretive afterlife "overwhelms, eclipses, and *always precedes* the biblical 'original'" (p. 2; her emphasis); it is a translation, moving its precursor through time and space and reanimating but also transforming and betraying it, recreating signifiers or signifieds, sometimes in radically different form. Sherwood demonstrates in detail how relatively marginal readings can be influenced by readings from the centers of power, and also how mainstream readings become infected by themes that appeared originally on the margins.

The book's final chapter presents Sherwood's conclusions, including her own reading of Jonah. Because this reading draws on the numerous interpretive voices that she has already acknowledged, it is more anti-commentary than commentary, an explosion of semiosis in which Jonah's range of potential meanings becomes infinite. The reader's ideology plays a crucial role in all of this, as do larger cultural, economic, political, and even geophysical forces, including shifts of intertextuality. The book suggests a new model for the commentary, which, instead of controlling and domesticating the text as traditional commentaries do, liberates the text from all canonical and other orthodox constraints, producing a "mutable canon" (p. 287). It raises the question of how far these semiotic flows can extend or stretch. In other words, what is *not* an afterlife of Jonah?

Implications. In addition to providing valuable critical tools for the close reading of any biblical text, poststructuralist thought offers substantial implications for topics of more general importance for biblical studies, including the following.

History. Intertextuality describes how *readers* understand texts, and it comes most evidently into play at points where meaning breaks downs. It is *not* limited to or primarily concerned with a search for historical sources or textual citations or allusions or parallels. No intertextuality could ever yield a text's "true meaning," and the intertextual context of any text, even the most ancient or authoritative ones, is always finally the here and now of the living reader. Readers may have some knowledge of historical circumstances (such as an author's intentions, gender, or social class) under which texts were produced or how other readers (including the first ones) understood or understand those texts, but each reader's awareness of any such circumstances or other readings is itself always conditioned by her own contexts, interests, and commitments.

In other words, the act of reading is always anachronistic and local. Ancient or foreign readings of texts always stand at a disadvantage to contemporary, local readings through which they are inevitably filtered. Intertextuality is undoubtedly also a factor in the historical production of texts, but the reconstruction of a text's genesis will always reflect the modern reader's intertextual position, and with that the modern desire for an origin that makes the text intelligible. For these reasons, poststructuralism is highly suspicious of historical speculations that attempt to reconstruct the "original" or true meaning of a text. It regards history neither as an objective, linear sequence lying behind texts nor as an external, impartial standard that justifies critical judgment and to which the critic must be responsible. Instead history is always a "partial object" (Deleuze and Guattari) that is itself assembled or produced here and now by subjective forces of signification and desire.

Translation. In relation to the Bible, translation is inescapable, for even the most accomplished scholar stands at some linguistic distance from the ancient texts. The interplay between semiosis and ideology that appears in any translation is perhaps even more potent in translations of the biblical books, beginning with differences between Greek and Hebrew texts of the Jewish scriptures, but also including modern translations. Due to unlimited semiosis, any text has many different possible meanings, some of which may even be contrary to one another. The translator inevitably favors some meanings over others in the process of recreating the text in another language. In this way semiosis flows through translation but is also directed by it.

The ideal of a "literal" translation is to reproduce the signifiers of the "source" or original text in the "target" or translated text "word by word" and without regard for meaning. This approach places more importance on the signifier than the signified, and therefore many poststructuralists favor it. Because the signifier itself can never be translated, extremely literal translations approach incoherence, and they are of value primarily to those who can also read the source text. According to this ideal, the task of the translator is not to transfer a signified message from the source to the target text, but to create an intertextual tension between the two texts, so that the target text "supplements" and becomes an "afterlife" of the source (Benjamin). Differing translations of the same source text supplement that text in different ways.

In contrast, a "dynamic equivalence" translation seeks to identify the signified meaning of the source text and to recreate something like that meaning in the target text. This requires that the translator must identify one among the many possible meanings of the text as the preferred meaning, and the target text will then limit semiosis in this way. The priority and importance of the immaterial *logos* is stressed, and the physical, textual material that encloses it is treated as secondary and dispensable, of value only insofar as it transports its cargo without damage. Such translations are more reader-friendly than literal translations, and they often replace the source texts entirely in the usage of ordinary readers, who may have no knowledge of ancient Hebrew or Greek.

Widespread acceptance of dynamic equivalence translations suggests that this is not a serious concern for many scholars, perhaps because theological factors continue to play an important role in much critical study of the Bible. The topic of Bible translation is of particular importance due to Christian desire to make "the Word of God" readily available, and translations of the Bible have been and still are instruments of political and economic power. However, histories of Bible translation as well as studies of translation theory and practice rarely acknowledge that the different approaches to translation correspond to different ideological positions and yield different practical results.

The semiotic implications of interlingual translation also apply to "translation" between media. Not only does any English text of a biblical book mean differently than the Hebrew or Greek text does, but even the earliest Hebrew or Greek writings, if they were transcribed from oral traditions in those languages, necessarily transformed those traditions. Likewise, modern digital transcriptions of biblical texts do not signify in the same ways that earlier printed or manuscript codexes do.

Canon. Unlimited semiosis characterizes every text, and intertexts are as common and as numerous as are readers themselves. However, in a "scripture" or written text that is believed to transmit the "Word of God," the unlimited flow of semiosis becomes a serious challenge to the reader's desire for definitive and authoritative meaning. Because no text can ever conclusively define its own meaning, some intertexts are institutionalized or given authoritative status for and within communities of readers. An important instance of such institutionalized intertextuality is the Christian canon of the scriptures, better known as the Bible. There is also a Jewish canon of scriptures, but the Tanakh is not identical to the Christian Old Testament, nor do Jews generally have the same relation to their own canon that Christians have to theirs.

The Christian canon was formed in order to unify and regulate Christian belief, once the church had been approved by the Roman emperor Constantine. Like dynamic equivalence in translation, the Christian concept of canon is deeply logocentric. Without the canon there is no Bible, but merely an assortment of more or less unrelated texts. Despite the fact of many different translations, as well as denominational differences regarding which books belong in the canon, many people, even nonbelievers, often speak as though there is just one Bible, a single book with a single message. As the Word of God, the Bible is supposed to be a communication either directly from or inspired by God, and just as the Christian God is believed to be unique and single, so the divine Word must be one. In other words, no matter how diverse and plurivocal the many books of the Bible actually are, they must all convey a single, coherent message.

The canon privileges the Bible over other intertextual networks that might be chosen for the reading of biblical texts. It makes those texts appear familiar and normal, as though they belonged together. Canonical pressure toward harmonization channels the semiosis of the texts into approved "orthodox" readings, in which the various texts illuminate one another and speak as one. The larger canonical context helps the reader to identify appropriate semiotic codes and to decipher the message. The control of meaning does not occur in the individual texts themselves but rather in the ways that they are juxtaposed with one another in the interpretive practice of readers. One can gauge the power of the canon's control by reading a biblical text in a non-canonical context—that is, apart from the Bible and in conjunction with non-canonical texts.

However, just as no single text can explain itself, so no collection of texts can explain itself. Even binding the canon into a single physical codex cannot guarantee that the reader will assemble the various texts in the "proper" way. Although the canon deeply influences the deciphering of its component texts, its control over those texts has always been loose and incomplete, and lively and significant disagreement over the meaning of the Bible frequently occurs. Additional assistance is continually required in the form of extra-canonical commentaries, introductions, sermons, catechisms, and other guides that describe "how to read the Bible."

Technologies of Text. Apart from text-critical and paleographical studies, where the focus has been almost entirely historical, biblical scholars have not until recently been interested in the physical production, mediation, or dissemination of the text. Again, this may be due to the prevalence of logocentric thinking and Christian theology, for which the physical matter of the text is relatively unimportant.

Any written text escapes its author's control as soon as it falls into the hands of a reader. The Christian canon was developed to standardize and control the extent, dissemination, and semiosis of the recognized scriptures. With the appearance of print technology five hundred years ago, control over reproduction of the Bible passed into the hands of commercial publishing houses, freeing the dissemination of biblical texts from control by the churches. The decline in canonical authority begins with the printing of Bibles for, since the print revolution, the Bible has functioned less and less as the communal property of Christian congregations and more and more as the private property of individual readers—that is, as a commodity to be bought and sold. The recent proliferation of Bibles addressed to particular groups of readers or in different print formats (such as magazines or children's versions) advances this trend.

As a mass-produced text that is readily available and often read in private, the printed Bible makes the reader more aware of its semiotic unruliness, even as the printing process replaces ecclesiastical, canonical assurances of its authority. Furthermore, ever since the Protestant Reformation and the Renaissance—which occurred at the same time as, and were deeply involved in, the print revolution—readers have become more aware of the multiplicity of the Bible: multiple canons and multiple translations, as well as the multiplicity of books that has always been there within the Bible.

The dissemination of the Bible in digital form on computers or the World Wide Web exacerbates the effects of printing. Stored in databases that make the texts easier to retrieve but that also decontextualize them, the canonical texts are fragmented and made available for uncontrolled recontextualizations. Recorded on storage media that are accessible only through sophisticated electronic technology, digital texts add to the reader's consciousness of the frailty of the medium, reminding her of the physical stuff of text and the tenuous connections between signifier and signified.

It is hard to distinguish the digitized Bible from the huge amounts of other digital material, for it no longer appears as a distinct, single codex, and it is easy to juxtapose biblical texts with nonbiblical texts when they are all accessed on a computer. At the same time, digitization gives the reader greater control both over individual texts, which can easily be rewritten, and over the extent and structure of the canonical collection, for whole texts can easily be added or deleted. The reader becomes more conscious as well that reading and writing are artificial technologies, and of her own need for meaning and the constructed character of meaning.

Under such circumstances, the tension between intertextuality and semiosis becomes more evident, and the canon is even less able to control the reading of its constituent texts. The canon of the scriptures becomes just one of many possible intertexts, no more important than any other. Different sorts of play with or upon the biblical texts in cultural products that include novels, movies, music and video recordings, comic books, and electronic games, channel the semiosis and suggest remarkably different readings of the texts. The Bible's texts are recycled and recontextualized, and their semiotic potential is played out in a wide variety of ways.

Exegesis. For poststructuralism, meaning is never neatly packaged in a text, to be unwrapped and displayed by careful interpretation. Any text by itself, as an assemblage of signifiers, cannot signify—that is, it cannot really be a text—until it is read by someone. This reader is necessarily "in front" of the text. By itself the text means nothing, and there is nothing "behind" it. Meaning is intertextual, stretched between texts as they are brought together in the understandings of readers, and it is always attached to the text through an ideological act. No matter how careful or scholarly, each reading adds meaning to the text that it would not have apart from such reading.

Therefore poststructuralism rejects the concept of "exegesis," which is widespread in biblical studies. According to this concept, signified meaning is already there in the text, securely enclosed within its signifiers, and this meaning can be uncovered by careful, "valid interpretation." This meaning can then be restated using a different set of signifiers, such as a commentary or some other statement of concepts or values, to clarify or otherwise improve the reader's understanding. The concept of exegesis is thus closely related to the dynamic equivalence approach to translation and to the Christian concept of canon, and it shares with both of them a strong commitment to logocentrism.

Some biblical scholars distinguish between exegesis and hermeneutics, which is regarded as a more overtly theological form of interpretation, but both exegesis and hermeneutics are always deeply "interested" in the text. This is perhaps especially true in relation to the Bible, which for many Christians is crucial to their understanding of themselves and the world. For Christian belief, God is in effect the real author of the scriptures, and biblical exegesis is a profoundly theological enterprise, uncovering God's intentions.

In contrast, for poststructuralism, meaning is always produced through eisegesis. "Eisegesis" is often used as a pejorative term in biblical studies, for it implies that meaning has been read into the text, or in other words, that the reading is not true to the text. Yet according to the poststructuralists, this is precisely what reading always does; every reading plays with the text and its meanings. Meaning is always something that the reader brings to and imposes upon the text—that is, she always "reads into" the text. Since all reading is inherently intertextual, all so-called exegesis is really eisegesis.

Conclusion. One consequence of the poststructuralist shift is that any illusion of control from within the text over its own interpretation evaporates. Instead, responsibility is placed on the reader to acknowledge the ideological interests that guide her reading. Biblical texts are not easily interpreted—after all, their meanings and values have been disputed for thousands of years, and they still are. This is not because readers have been ignorant, careless, or ill willed. It is because readers always read biblical texts—just as they read any other texts—in highly specific contexts, and they always bring to those texts their own particular individual and communal interests and experience.

[*See also* Deconstruction; Formalist Interpretation; Reader-Response Criticism; Semiotics; Structuralist Interpretation; *and* Synchronic Interpretation.]

BIBLIOGRAPHY

Aichele, George. *Sign, Text, Scripture: Semiotics and the Bible.* Sheffield, UK: Sheffield Academic, 1997. This book presents a brief introduction to semiotics, with examples from the Gospel of Mark.

Bal, Mieke. *Death and Dissymmetry: The Politics of Coherence in the Book of Judges.* Chicago: University of Chicago Press, 1988. Bal's book unites feminist and poststructuralist suspicion of narrative coherence.

Barthes, Roland. *The Semiotic Challenge.* Translated by Richard Howard. New York: Hill and Wang, 1988. This book collects several of Barthes's early essays, including his groundbreaking studies of Genesis 32 and Acts 10–11. Note also the essay "Introduction to the Structural Analysis of Narratives."

Barthes, Roland. *S/Z.* Translated by Richard Miller. New York: Hill and Wang, 1974. This is still arguably the finest example of poststructuralist analysis of a text, rich with theoretical detail and close reading.

Benjamin, Walter. *Illuminations.* Translated by Harry Zohn. New York: Schocken, 1968. Benjamin is an important precursor to poststructuralism; note especially the essays "The Task of the Translator" and "The Work of Art in an Age of Mechanical Reproduction."

Bible and Culture Collective. *The Postmodern Bible.* New Haven, Conn.: Yale University Press, 1995. This is an introductory survey of several postmodern approaches to biblical studies and includes chapters on structuralism and poststructuralism.

Castelli, Elizabeth. *Imitating Paul: A Discourse of Power.* Louisville, Ky.: Westminster John Knox, 1991. Castelli's exploration of the relevance of Foucault's understanding of "pastoral power" to Paul's letters is perhaps the first and still one of the best of the burgeoning field of poststructuralist studies of Paul.

Deleuze, Gilles, and Félix Guattari. *Anti-Oedipus: Capitalism and Schizophrenia 1.* Translated by Robert Hurley, Mark Seem, and Helen R. Lane. Minneapolis: University of Minnesota Press, 1983.

Deleuze, Gilles, and Félix Guattari. *A Thousand Plateaus: Capitalism and Schizophrenia 2.* Translated by Brian Massumi. Minneapolis: University of Minnesota Press, 1987. Deleuze and Guattari's two volumes subtitled "Capitalism and Schizophrenia" include a critique of Freud (Vol. 1) and several studies relating to biblical texts (Vol. 2).

De Man, Paul. *The Resistance to Theory.* Minneapolis: University of Minnesota Press, 1986. This book is of value not only for de Man's deconstructive readings of literature but for the essay "Conclusions: Walter Benjamin's 'The Task of the Translator.'"

Derrida, Jacques. *Speech and Phenomena.* Translated by David B. Allison. Evanston, Ill.: Northwestern University Press, 1973. Derrida's work is a crucial point at which Edmund Husserl's phenomenology enters poststructuralist thought; see the essay "Differance."

Eco, Umberto. *The Role of the Reader.* Bloomington: Indiana University Press, 1979. Eco played an important role in popularizing the thought of Peirce and developing the concept of unlimited semiosis. Note also the essay on Genesis 2–3.

Foucault, Michel. *The Archaeology of Knowledge and the Discourse on Language.* Translated by A. M. Sheridan Smith and Rupert Sawyer. New York: Harper and Row, 1972. This small and very difficult book is perhaps Foucault's most direct challenge to structuralism.

Kermode, Frank. *The Genesis of Secrecy: On the Interpretation of Narrative.* Cambridge, Mass.: Harvard University Press, 1979. Kermode's study of secrecy in the Gospel of Mark in relation to a variety of modern literary texts is one of the earliest poststructural studies of a Gospel.

Kristeva, Julia. *Revolution in Poetic Language.* Translated by Margaret Waller. New York: Columbia University Press, 1984. In this book, Kristeva draws upon Husserl, Frege, and Louis Hjelmslev to develop the theoretical concept of intertextuality.

Miscall, Peter D. *Isaiah 34–35: A Nightmare/A Dream.* Sheffield, UK: Sheffield Academic Press, 1999. Miscall's study of poetic ambiguity in Isaiah draws upon the fantasy theory of Tzvetan Todorov.

Moore, Stephen D. *Mark and Luke in Poststructuralist Perspectives: Jesus Begins to Write.* New Haven, Conn.: Yale University Press, 1992. Moore's readings of Mark and Luke are influenced by Derrida and James Joyce, among others.

Pyper, Hugh S. *An Unsuitable Book: The Bible as Scandalous Text.* Sheffield, UK: Sheffield Phoenix, 2005. Pyper's book explores a wide range of biblical texts as commodities and cultural objects.

Sherwood, Yvonne. *A Biblical Text and its Afterlives: The Survival of Jonah in Western Culture.* Cambridge, UK: Cambridge University Press, 2000. Sherwood studies the reception and transformations of the book of Jonah in Judaism, Christianity, and popular culture.

George Aichele

Psychological Biblical Interpretation

Psychology is the study of human behavior—both external, observable actions and internal mental processes such as perception, evaluation, memory, and consciousness. Every aspect of the Bible—whether related to its origins, its shape and content, or its impact on readers and communities—involves and is shaped by human behavior, and thus offers a potentially rich ground for psychological examination. Psychology itself involves interpretation in seeking to identify the factors that shape human activity and awareness. Those factors are multiple, ambiguous, and many-faceted, and are themselves affected by cultural, familial, and environmental context. Different psychologists make different decisions about what behaviors count for study, how phenomena are to be measured and interpreted, and what implications they hold. There are nearly as many forms of psychological biblical interpretation as there are theories about the patterns and roots of human behavior.

Definition. Psychological biblical criticism is an approach to reading and interpreting biblical texts that is critically sensitive to psychological factors and effects evidenced in all aspects of the Bible—the composition and development of the texts, the personalities, themes, and relationships described in them, and the effects of the Bible on individual readers and communities engaged in preserving, translating, sharing, interpreting, and expressing those texts. Psychological interpretation is not a single perspective, but encompasses many different approaches. In its various manifestations, psychological biblical criticism brings together insights into human behavior, consciousness, will, and intention, and the critical study of the biblical tradition.

Since both psychology and biblical studies encompass so many diverse methods and perspectives, it is always important to consider which psychological framework, theory, or assumptions are being used for any given study, and how well they fit the chosen aspect of the biblical text. Psychological interpretation may draw on theoretical approaches such as depth psychology, cognitive learning theory, or family systems, and employ that framework as a lens through which to explain or interpret the text. Despite wide variation in methods, all these approaches share the fundamental assumption that the Bible shows the effects of the human psyche, and that a psychologically informed exploration can reveal and illuminate those dimensions.

Several names have been used for the approach; these may reflect the particular psychological orientation used (e.g., Freudian interpretation, Jungian interpretation, psychoanalytic approach) or the focus of the study (e.g., psychological exegesis, psychological hermeneutics, psychological reading). Psychological biblical criticism has come into general acceptance as an overall term, as it allows for a plurality of approaches and aims, while making it clear that biblical phenomena form the specific focus of investigation and setting the field firmly within the biblical critical tradition.

History and Development. The relationship between psychology and the Bible is not new. Long before psychology emerged as a field of study, folk wisdom carried information and admonitions based on observations of human behavior. The Bible includes innumerable examples of such wisdom, for example, in the words to a young student in the book of Proverbs. Psychology as a systematic discipline developed out of philosophical speculation about the nature of the human soul, known in Greek as the *psyche.* The Greek philosopher Aristotle wrote extensively concerning the soul and its relationship to the body, reason, and will. The early church theologian Tertullian (ca. 160–220 C.E.) used Aristotle's own title *De Anima* (Concerning the Soul) as the title of his major work exploring the biblical description of the human soul. While drawing on classical Greek theories, Tertullian argued against them when they departed from his understanding of the Bible. Augustine of Hippo (354–430 C.E.) considered the importance of studying the human soul to be second only to the importance of knowing God. His writings include *De anima et eius origine* (Concerning the Soul and Its Origin), *De duabus animabus* (Concerning the Two Souls), *De Immortalitate Animae* (Concerning the Immortality of the Soul), and *De Quantitate Animae* (Concerning the Greatness of the Soul). The specific term *psychology* to describe a field of study emerged in 1530 in the work of systematic theologian Philipp Melanchthon, the reformer and colleague of Martin Luther. *Psychology* was his term for the study of the human soul to distinguish it within the wider field of *pneumatology*, study of spirits.

The beginnings of modern scientific psychology are usually traced to Wilhelm Wundt, who established a school for experimental psychology at Leipzig in 1879. From that time on, psychology began to move out of the realm of philosophy and theology into the world of scientific investigation. As the field began to shift, the study of biblical psychology likewise changed. One of the last major efforts at developing a biblical psychology was produced in 1855 by Franz Delitzsch, a widely-known and respected professor of Hebrew and Old Testament at the University of Leipzig. In *A System of Biblical Psychology*, Delitzsch carefully explored the biblical understanding of the soul as a field of study distinct from general theology. Incorporating insights and vocabulary from the newly-developing field of psychology, he sought to relate and critique biblical viewpoints, and argued that biblical psychology was a necessary expression of the human capacity for self-examination.

By 1912, when M. Scott Fletcher published his Oxford dissertation, *The Psychology of the New Testament*, the newly-established discipline of psychology had begun to develop. Fletcher sought to correlate new concepts and terms of psychology to the language and experiences in the Bible. The three sections of Fletcher's work included his discussion of terminology, investigations into psychological experience, and comparisons of Greek, Jewish, and Christian understandings of personality and their relation to the newer psychological theories. Bringing together historical critical methods with psychological reflection, Fletcher suggested that psychology had much to offer biblical studies in helping to enrich understanding of biblical spiritual experience, recovering the psychodynamic value of biblical language, illuminating biblical personality, and studying the psychological effects of early Christianity.

Not everyone was as enthusiastic as Fletcher about the value of psychology for biblical interpretation. Many early attempts to apply psychological theories to the Bible involved studying biblical figures like the prophets, Jesus, or Paul as if they were case studies. They accepted the Bible as historically reliable and gravitated toward unusual or remarkable behavior as crying out for psychological explanation. Often they concluded that these behaviors were pathological. Several efforts to explain Jesus as an epileptic, a paranoid, or otherwise pathological at last drove Albert Schweitzer to denounce them in *The Psychiatric Study of Jesus* (1913), the dissertation for his M.D. degree. In much the same way as he had previously criticized the historical Jesus studies of his day, Schweitzer roundly condemned four psychiatric studies of Jesus and demonstrated how they were neither medically nor historical-critically valid. Schweitzer's work rightfully highlighted the dangers of uncritical application of psychological theory to the text, but his critique was to discourage psychological approaches within the field of biblical criticism for much of the early part of the twentieth century.

Psychologists, for their part, were similarly cautious about mixing with religious matters. Perhaps desiring to affirm their discipline as being truly scientific and seeking to distance themselves from their philosophical and theological origins, many psychologists were openly hostile to religion, considering it at best a delusion and at worst pathological. There seemed little reason to bring the two disciplines together.

Freud and Jung. The early part of the twentieth century was notable for the development of depth psychology, that branch of psychology which concerns itself with unconscious factors that shape behavior. The work of Sigmund Freud, C. G. Jung, and others provided vocabulary, concepts, and methods that have had a lasting impact on biblical studies.

Although Freud touched on biblical issues in *Totem and Taboo* (1913) and in his final book *Moses and Monotheism* (1939), his theories about the origins of biblical texts and stories were generally disregarded. His theories of the unconscious and how it affects human behavior had far greater impact. His investigations suggested that unconscious dynamics were constantly at work within the human psyche using protective mechanisms like repression, sublimation, denial, projection, and displacement that distorted experience and understanding. Persons and situations in the dreams of individuals and, by extension, the myths and stories shared within a culture were seen as symbolic representations of psychic dynamics, and required careful interpretation. It did not take long before Freud's theories were applied to the Bible. Not only was the Bible the product of human beings in whom unconscious factors were at work, its stories and symbols were the stuff of myth, and could be analyzed and interpreted much like a patient in psychoanalysis. Psychoanalytic or Freudian approaches are distinguished in that they employ Freudian models or Freudian methods to investigate the text. They may focus on the mind of the author, the minds of characters in the biblical stories, or on the minds of the readers in the present. Among those who have applied Freudian approaches to the Bible are F. Dolto, D. Halperin, D. Merkur, S. Moore, I. Rashkow, R. Rubenstein, R. Scroggs, G. Theissen, M. A. Tolbert, W. Wuellner, and D. Zeligs.

The Bible was a uniquely important book for C. G. Jung. In his work spanning the first half of the twentieth century, Jung wrote extensively on biblical texts, themes, and symbols. In his *Collected Works* (1953–1979), Jung refers to all but thirteen of the sixty-six books of the Protestant canon, including 120 references to the Gospel of John. In "Answer to Job" (1952), his only work focused specifically on interpreting a biblical text, he described the Bible as "an utterance of the psyche," an expression of the deepest parts of the soul.

Jung developed four key concepts that proved especially significant for biblical studies: archetypes, amplification and active imagination, individuation, and personality types. According to Jung, archetypes are inborn, unconscious structures or prototypes in the psyche that serve to shape human experience, perceptions, responses, and behavior. Archetypes are part of the collective unconscious, that is, unconscious material shared by everyone. Archetypes cannot be observed directly, but instead are manifested through symbols found in dreams, myths, and culture. The Bible's stories, personalities, interactions, and symbols all carry archetypal dimensions that operate beyond consciousness. The processes of "amplification" and "active imagination" are techniques for getting at this hidden archetypal material. Amplification involves expanding the symbols and images by examining them in detail and identifying other images, experiences, or memories, both personal and collective, to which they might be associated. Active imagination involves imaginatively reentering a dream, story, or myth and allowing it to unfold further. Jung was convinced that archetypal images would continue to develop if allowed to do so; active imagination allowed for new insights to emerge by way of art, movement, or active fantasy.

Individuation is the process by which a person becomes a distinct individual. Each stage of the developmental process of individuation presents specific challenges for encountering archetypes and integrating conscious and unconscious elements of the psyche into a whole.

Jung's personality theory considered how people differ from one another in how they relate to the world around them. He identified two main mental processes: perception (how one takes in information) and judging (how one makes decisions). Some people prefer to take in information through their physical senses (sensing), while others rely on hunches or intuition (intuition). In decision making, some may prefer to work from objective, logical principles (thinking), while others prefer to apply values and relationships (feeling). In addition, Jung noted, individuals may prefer to focus on the outside world or their inner world. Different combinations of these preferences result in differing personality types.

Jung's insights have proved quite useful for interpreting the Bible. For example, Jungian interpretation may focus on identifying and illuminating archetypal symbols and dynamics within the text, on patterns of individuation in biblical figures, or on the effects of personality type on reading and preaching. Among those who have used Jungian approaches are S. Brown, A. Y. Collins, E. Edinger, H. Efthimiadis-Keith, D. A. Kille, R. S. Kluger, F. Kunkel, D. McGann, G. Theissen, M. W. Newheart, J. Sanford, W. Wink, H. Westman, and W. Wuellner.

Other Approaches. The earliest examples of psychological biblical criticism draw predominantly on the depth psychologies of Freud and Jung, but scholars were soon finding useful concepts in other schools of psychological study. Behavioral Psychology and Learning Theory, which explore how behavior can be modified through systems of reward and punishment or by an individual's desire to imitate a valued model informed work by Bufford (1981) and was one of the approaches used by Theissen (1987). Theissen also drew on Cognitive Psychology for understanding how individuals frame their understanding of experience, as did P. Anderson in studies of the Gospel of John and R. P. Carroll in examining reactions to prophecy that did not come to fulfillment.

Developmental Psychology, which describes common stages of psychological and social maturation, has been used by P. Anderson, L. Bechtel, J. Miller, and W. Vogels to interpret the stages of Christology in John, the myth of Genesis 3, Jesus, and Job. Viktor Frankl's Existential Psychology provided the lens for R. Leslie and W. Wuellner to interpret New Testament stories. Object Relations Theory, which attends to psychic relationships developed in early childhood as the root of later interactions with the world, has been applied to the interaction of the interpreter with the text by P. Pruyser and R. Underwood. Fritz Kunkel, influenced by Freud, Jung, and Adler, wrote a commentary on the Gospel of Matthew, *Creation Continues* (1987), based on his own "We" psychology. J. Sanford carried Kunkel's work forward in his own commentaries on biblical stories.

The work of J. Lacan, L. Irigaray, and J. Kristeva represent post-Freudian developments of psychoanalytic approaches that have entered biblical studies through Structuralism, Deconstruction, and Feminist criticism. Today, a host of new models including Family Relations Theory, Terror Management Theory, Identity Theory, and studies in memory, is emerging with potential value for interpreting biblical texts.

Changing Attitudes. In *Jung and the Bible* (1983), Wayne Rollins not only introduced biblical scholars to Jung's deep engagement with the Bible, but laid out a systematic argument for why psychological approaches were now essential. The long-standing separation between psychology and biblical studies was beginning to break down. Key factors leading to changes in attitude included the development of newer and more sophisticated psychological theories; the increasing "psychologization" of Western culture in which formerly technical concepts and terms such as "the unconscious," "projection," or the "Oedipus complex" had now become part of daily life; and new methods of biblical criticism that went far beyond traditional historical-critical methods. Interpreters were no longer limited to psychological theories that focused on individuals and pathology, but could draw on social psychology, family systems theories, cognitive psychology, or studies in memory, perception, and brain function for ways to understand interactions with the Bible. Nor were the boundaries of biblical interpretation limited any longer to uncovering the historical world behind the text; there was a sudden expansion of interpretational strategies that concerned themselves with language, structure, narration, rhetoric, and the process of reading. Social sciences like anthropology, linguistics, and sociology were now being integrated as tools for interpretation.

The shift in biblical studies was signaled by scholars like F. C. Grant, who envisioned an entirely new field of depth psychology and psychoanalysis that would go beyond conventional historical and exegetical methods and represent "a new kind of Biblical criticism" (1968). An article published in *Christian Century* in 1982 by New Testament scholar R. Scroggs was titled "Psychology as a Tool to Interpret the Text." W. Wink's essay critiquing the dominance of historical-critical methods, *The Bible in Human Transformation* (Philadelphia: Fortress, 1973), declared that it was time for biblical scholars to look at the readers of the text and to exercise an "archaeology of the subject," informed by psychoanalytic perspectives. Soon after, Wink presented the rationale and methods for such study in *Transforming Bible Study: A Leader's Guide* (1980).

New journals began to appear—the *Journal of Psychology and Theology* (1973), the *Journal of Psychology and Christianity* (1982), *Biblical Interpretation: A Journal of Contemporary Approaches* (1993)—joining *Pastoral Psychology* (1950) in publishing articles on the integration of psychological perspectives into study of the Bible.

In 1991, Wayne Rollins proposed a new group for the Society of Biblical Literature (SBL) that would focus on psychological approaches to scripture. The goals of the group would include tracing and critiquing the development and usefulness of psychological biblical criticism and offering a forum for further expansion of the field. Several well-established biblical scholars who were themselves working with psychological methods made up the original steering committee: Marcus Borg, Adela Y. Collins, James Dittes, David Halperin, Mary Ann Tolbert, Walter Wink, Wilhelm Wuellner and Andre Lacocque. "Psychology and Biblical Studies" quickly became established as a section within the SBL, and continues to serve as a key resource for advancing and refining psychological approaches. Other program units within the society also have begun to include papers that employ psychologically informed perspectives in their own areas of specialization.

Many of the papers presented in the Psychology and Biblical Studies section have been published so as to make them more accessible to those interested in the field. *Psychology and the Bible: A New Way to Read the Scriptures*, a four-volume collection edited by J. Harold Ellens, the founding editor of *Journal of Psychology and Christianity*, and Wayne Rollins, appeared in 2004. The subtitles of each volume suggest the breadth and diversity of psychological criticism: "From Freud to Kohut" centers on fourteen schools of psychology and how their perspectives address the Bible; "From Genesis to Apocalyptic Vision" deals with the Hebrew Bible, while "From Gospel to Gnostics," features psychological perspectives on the New Testament. Finally, "From Christ to Jesus" highlights contemporary research on Jesus and the Gospels.

An important introduction to psychological biblical criticism is Wayne Rollins's *Soul and Psyche: The Bible in Psychological Perspective*, published in 1999. The book presents a comprehensive history of the relationship of psychology and the Bible, and explores the usefulness of psychology for exegesis and hermeneutics. It was followed by D. Andrew Kille's *Psychological Biblical Criticism* (2001), a volume in the *Guides to Biblical Scholarship* series, which offered a briefer introduction to the discipline and a comparative evaluation of interpretations of Genesis 3 from Freudian, Jungian, and Developmental perspectives. Rollins and Kille collaborated on *Psychological Insight into the Bible: Texts and Readings* (2007), an annotated reader in psychological criticism that included excerpts from forty-four sources, many of them previously difficult to find, which illustrated the development of the field, the diversity of methods and subject matter it involves, and suggested extensive additional readings.

The International Society for Biblical Literature now includes a program unit on "Psychological Hermeneutics of Biblical Themes and Texts." Two German scholars in particular deserve note for their contributions to the field. Gerd Theissen, already well known for his use of sociological models in New Testament research, employed three psychological approaches—Learning Theory, Psychodynamic Analysis, and Cognitive Psychology—to explore selected Pauline texts in *Psychological Aspects of Pauline Theology* (1987). Using more than one approach allowed Theissen to compare the usefulness of each, and he suggested that together they offer a fuller understanding of the texts. Eugen Drewermann's massive two-volume work *Tiefenpsychologie und Exegese* (Depth Psychology and Exegesis), published in 1984, worked from a Jungian perspective to explore the psychological truth communicated by way of dreams, myths, tales, sagas, and legends, as well as by actions and teachings, including miracle stories, visions, wisdom sayings, apocalyptic texts, history, and parables.

Increasingly, psychological criticism is being noticed within biblical studies at large, being included in dictionaries, encyclopedias, and works that showcase different methods of biblical interpretation. Psychological biblical criticism has taken an indispensible place among tools available for exegesis and hermeneutics.

Psychological Approaches: Three Worlds of the Text. It is possible to think of the biblical text as "three-dimensional," reflecting three interrelated, but slightly different, "worlds" of experience. The world "behind" the text is the context in which the text originally came to be. It is the long-ago world inhabited by the historical authors and their communities. The world "of" the text is where the structures and language of the text reside—narrative, characterization, rhetoric, and action as described in the text. The world "in front of" the text is the world that is imaginatively created in the process of reading; it is where the reader interacts with the text intellectually, emotionally, and psychologically in the effort to understand it. Like the physical dimensions of length, width, and height, these three dimensions all exist within the text, and are interconnected. However, it is possible to focus more closely on one or another. Various psychological theories will prove more or less helpful depending upon which dimension of the text one seeks to study.

The World Behind the Text. Historical-critical approaches to the Bible focus on the world behind the text, seeking to recover the original life setting in which the text came to be written, the original audience to whom it was addressed, its original form, and so on. For over a century, this was the dominant model for biblical studies, and so it is not surprising that early efforts at psychological criticism attempted to psychoanalyze the writers of the texts or the characters in the text, dealing with them as though they were historical individuals. Psychology is not, however, a particularly effective tool for recovering the mind of the original author. Biographical information is scarce in the Bible, and what little information there is has been filtered through several stages of composition and editing. Biblical characters themselves have been shaped by literary conventions and culturally-regulated modes of expression. There is no way to question the "patient" further to get more information or to check a diagnosis. Early attempts at analyzing biblical figures as historical individuals deserved much of the scorn they received. Still, if exercised with care to sift through the evidences of textual development, literary conventions, and cultural understandings, psychological criticism has potential to illuminate ancient personalities. Significant examples include David Halperin's study of Ezekiel (1993) and studies of Paul by Richard Rubenstein (1972) and Robin Scroggs (1977). Psychology can, however, be very useful in investigating such biblical phenomena as glossolalia or conversion, or in understanding how memory and language affect the transmission of oral traditions.

The World of the Text. Biblical figures as we have them are part of the world of the text. One reason that we respond to such characters is that, however literary they may be, on a certain level they are recognizable as human beings. They behave, move, speak, and interact in ways that reflect human behavior. Psychological criticism can certainly analyze the qualities of the figure presented in the text, but must be cautious not to confuse the figure with a historical person and must resist the temptation to fill in details about the character that are not there. Too often, such elaborations reflect a desire to fit the text more closely to a chosen theory.

Even without such elaborations, it is clear that the actions and interactions of characters in the Bible reflect family relationships, conflicts between individuals and communities, social pressure, defense mechanisms, and psychological development. These dimensions, as well as psychological experiences of emotion, cognition, and intention, are not described in modern psychological language, but in the Bible's own way. Sensitivity to psychological issues and dynamics can enable one to tease out the implications of biblical descriptions.

Jesus presents a special case of a biblical figure, and newer efforts have addressed the previous weaknesses of methods that failed to evaluate the reliability of the Gospel accounts. Historical Jesus study in particular has proved a vital tool for grounding contemporary psychological studies of Jesus by D. Capps, J. W. Miller, A. van Aarde, and B. van Os. Van Os's work, *Psychological Analyses and the Historical Jesus* (2011) represents a quantum leap forward in Jesus studies. Rather than looking to the Gospel accounts for hints about Jesus's childhood experiences, van Os instead turns his attention to exploring how Jesus might have the impact that he did on the development of early Christianity, using discrete approaches of attachment theory, rational choice theory, anthropological psychology, and role theory to address specific issues in Jesus's life.

The world of the text also is the setting for the symbols and images that reflect and stimulate archetypal dimensions of the human psyche. Again, with careful attention to cultural context and historical development, psychological approaches can enable amplification of symbols not only by comparison to other ancient Near Eastern cultures, but as part of the archetypal inheritance of humanity.

The World in Front of the Text. It is in the world in front of the text that psychology makes its strongest contributions, for here it is possible to examine the interaction of readers and the text and observe how the text affects real readers. One may have access to the readers themselves and can ask them about their experience or can be examining one's own process of reading and reflecting on what takes place.

Readers are personalities. Hermeneutic theory has long recognized the importance of presuppositions that an interpreter brings to the process of interpreting. Those expectations, experiences, worldviews, and attitudes that the reader brings shape the reading and may be in turn changed by the process. Psychological criticism can alert us to additional unconscious presuppositions and predispositions carried in the personality. Cedric Johnson (1983) observed how personality type, cognitive styles, psychological defense mechanisms, and social dynamics can shape reception. Leslie Francis and his colleagues have used Jungian personality theory to illuminate the ways different individuals might react to lectionary readings (1997) and how an understanding of personality types might shape preaching.

Where historical-critical methods were interested in recovering the original setting of the text in historical and cultural context, psychological criticism enables study of the effects of the text on readers and communities, identifying both pathological and therapeutic dimensions. It further allows for examination of how individuals and communities move the tradition forward, expressing the symbols and themes of the Bible in new ways.

Relation to Other Methods. With so many dimensions of study and so many theories it is not strictly possible to speak of psychological biblical criticism as a method. Each theoretical framework and each level of the text demands particular tools and approaches. In this sense, psychological biblical criticism is not a method, or even a cluster of methods. Rather, it is a way of reading that is sensitive to psychological dynamics within the text. In this way it is similar to feminist criticism, which employs a variety of exegetical and hermeneutical tools, but always with an eye to issues related to the role and status of women.

As one of the social sciences, psychological criticism shares common ground with social-scientific criticism. Social-scientific criticism focuses on group behavior, while psychology tends to concentrate on individual behavior. More socially-informed psychologies overlap concepts and dynamics studied in sociology, such as the development of symbolic worlds, construction of identity, and deviance theory.

Several other interpretive strategies often incorporate implicit psychological assumptions. Structuralism, rhetorical criticism, and reader-response theory all make assumptions about how individuals encounter and process texts. Psychological analysis can help to make those models explicit, rather than implicit, by suggesting how texts "work" on readers.

Challenges and Concerns. The two criticisms most often leveled against psychological criticism are reductionism and "psychologizing." In the past, interpreters were often prone to deal with a text as if it were only a psychological phenomenon. They might dismiss anything about it that might not fit their preferred theory, or they might read into the text what they want to see. It is indeed proper to reject such readings. But to dismiss any psychological insight as merely psychologizing is to deny significant dynamics within the text and its interpreters. Psychological readings cannot replace historical-critical methods and other ways to open up the text, but when used in a multidisciplinary approach with interpretive tools for understanding language, structure, styles, history, and social context, they offer insights that are not otherwise accessible.

Psychological approaches raise some of the same concerns as social-scientific criticism—whether the text is a reliable description of the phenomenon or has been altered by literary convention and transmission; whether the interpreter is sufficiently competent in the models of his or her chosen discipline, knowing the strengths and weaknesses; and to what extent models developed in the modern era are valid when applied to the phenomena under study.

The very nature of language makes multiple interpretations not only likely, but inevitable. Nevertheless, there are some criteria for a more adequate psychological interpretation: (1) Recognize that the text is a text, and not a person. It is not possible to analyze a text as if it were a patient on the couch with whom the analyst can check perceptions or confirm intuitions. (2) Understand the literary and historical context and conventions that might shape the text. (3) Seek a good fit between the chosen theoretical framework and the dimensions of the text under consideration. (4) Remember that the text is determined by a number of factors, not just the psychological. An interdisciplinary approach will help counter psychologizing.

Contribution. Despite the diversity of methods and the cautions about applying psychological theory to the interpretation of biblical texts, psychological biblical criticism continues to be an important way to investigate the Bible. It is not possible for an interpreter to avoid psychological interpretation in our psychological age, for we now understand the many ways in which human psychology touches on the biblical tradition. Every step of the journey from religious experience to text to canon, and of the Bible's movement from oral tradition to written scripture that included the tasks of composing, gathering, selecting, and preserving the sacred texts, involves human beings with human psyches, acting and interacting with inspiration, community, and tradition.

Psychological biblical interpretation offers unique tools to enable us to be more conscious of the many dimensions of that interaction.

[*See also* Feminist Biblical Interpretation; Historical Criticism, *subentry* Hebrew Bible; Historical Criticism, *subentry* New Testament; Historical Jesus, Quest for the; Reader-response Criticism; Rhetorical Criticism; Social Sciences, *subentry* Hebrew Bible; Social Sciences, *subentry* New Testament; *and* Structuralist Interpretation.]

BIBLIOGRAPHY

Bufford, Rodger K. The Human Reflex: Behavioral Psychology in Biblical Perspective. San Francisco: Harper & Row, 1981.

Delitzsch, Franz Julius. *A System of Biblical Psychology.* Translated by A.E. Wallis. 2d. ed. Grand Rapids, Mich.: Baker Book House, 1966. Originally published in 1855, the work represents one of the last examples of biblical psychology.

Drewermann, Eugen. *Tiefenpsychologie und Exegese.* 2 vols., Olten: Walter-Verlag, 1984. Not available as yet in English translation, this is a foundational example of psychological criticism from a Jungian perspective.

Edinger, Edward F. *The Bible and the Psyche: Individuation Symbolism in the Old Testament.* Studies in Jungian Psychology by Jungian Analysts. Edited by Daryl Sharp. Toronto: Inner City Books, 1986. Edinger has written several volumes of interpretation from a Jungian perspective.

Ellens, J. Harold, and Wayne G. Rollins, eds. *Psychology and the Bible: A New Way to Read the Scriptures.* 4 vols. Westport, Conn.: Greenwood-Praeger, 2004. A collection of essays written by members of the Psychology and Biblical Studies Section of the Society of Biblical Literature.

Francis, Leslie J. *Personality Type and Scripture: Exploring Mark's Gospel.* London: Mowbray, 1997. Looks at the readings for the first year of the lectionary cycle from the perspective of Jungian personality types.

Grant, Frederick C. "Psychological Study of the Bible." In Religions in Antiquity: Essays in Memory of Erwin Goodenough, edited by Jacob Neusner. 107–24. Leiden: Brill, 1968.

Halperin, David J. *Seeking Ezekiel: Text and Psychology.* University Park: Pennsyvania State University Press, 1993. An excellent analysis of a biblical figure that sheds light on problematic aspects of the book of Ezekiel.

Johnson, Cedric B. *The Psychology of Biblical Interpretation.* Grand Rapids, Mich.: Zondervan, 1983. A delineation of unconscious factors that can affect biblical interpretation.

Jung, C. G. "Answer to Job." Translated by R. F. C. Hull. In *The Collected Works of C.G. Jung,* edited by H. Read, M. Fordham and G. Adler. Bollingen Series 20, 355–470. Princeton, N.J.: Princeton University Press, 1952. An extended essay that begins with the book of Job but ranges through much of the biblical text.

Kille, D. Andrew. *Psychological Biblical Criticism.* Guides to Biblical Scholarship, Old Testament Series. Edited by Gene M. Tucker. Minneapolis: Fortress Press, 2001. A brief introduction to the field, with comparison of three psychological models for interpreting Genesis 3.

Kunkel, Fritz. *Creation Continues: A Psychological Interpretation of the Gospel of Matthew.* New York: Paulist, 1987. A full psychological commentary on the Gospel of Matthew from the perspective of Kunkel's "We" psychology.

Os, Bas van. *Psychological Analyses and the Historical Jesus: New Ways to Explore Christian Origins.* Library of New Testament Studies. Edited by Mark Goodacre. London: T&T Clark, 2011. A solid exploration of Jesus through examination of the impact he had on people around him, using several psychological models.

Psybibs. http://www.psybibs.org (accessed January 1, 2012). The official website of the Psychology and Biblical Studies Section of the Society of Biblical Literature includes the history of the group, information on annual meeting sessions, and book reviews of significant works in psychological biblical criticism.

Rollins, Wayne G. *Jung and the Bible.* Atlanta: John Knox Press, 1983. A foundational book for the discipline of psychological biblical criticism.

Rollins, Wayne G. *Soul and Psyche: The Bible in Psychological Perspective.* Minneapolis: Fortress Press, 1999. A comprehensive survey of the history, methods, and theories of psychological biblical criticism with an exhaustive bibliography of examples.

Rollins, Wayne G, and D. Andrew Kille, eds. *Psychological Insight into the Bible: Texts and Readings.* Grand Rapids, Mich.: Eerdmans, 2007. A collection of original sources for psychological biblical criticism with commentary and suggestions for further reading.

Rubenstein, Richard. *My Brother Paul. New York:* Harper & Row, 1972. An examination of Paul from a Freudian perspective.

Scroggs, Robin. *Paul for a New Day.* Philadelphia: Fortress, 1977. An examination of Paul from a Freudian perspective.

Theissen, Gerd. *Psychological Aspects of Pauline Theology.* Philadelphia: Fortress, 1987. Three theoretical approaches—Learning Theory, Psychodynamic Theory, and Cognitive Psychology—applied to selected texts in the Pauline writings.

Wink, Walter. *Transforming Bible Study: A Leader's Guide.* Nashville, Tenn.: Abingdon, 1980. A rationale and guidebook for an approach to Bible study for lay people, based on a Jungian model.

Wuellner, Wilhelm, and Robert Leslie. *The Surprising Gospel: Intriguing Psychological Insights from the New Testament.* Nashville, Tenn.: Abingdon, 1984. Several texts in the New Testament interpreted by Wuellner, a biblical scholar, and Leslie, a pastoral psychologist.

D. Andrew Kille

Q

Queer Criticism and Queer Theory

Queer criticism of the Bible attempts to read biblical texts in light of the interdisciplinary studies known as queer theory. Queer theory is a body of academic writing that emerged during the 1990s in the context of feminist and lesbian and gay studies. Although closely associated with the study of homosexuality, queer theory also investigates the assumptions and practices that allow certain norms, such as those that privilege heterosexuality and fixed gender identities, to be created, maintained, and challenged in both academic and popular representations of sex, gender, and sexuality. In particular, queer theory is associated with a critical analysis of the organization of sexual and gendered meanings and identities around binary distinctions, including those between male and female, and heterosexual and homosexual. Queer criticism brings the critical analyses associated with queer theory to bear on the interpretation of biblical texts.

Origins of Queer Theory. The emergence of queer theory and queer criticism as terms for academic analysis was made possible by the increased attention given to gender and sexuality during the 1970s and 1980s, particularly by feminist and gay and lesbian activists and scholars. Such attention long preceded the appearance of the phrase "queer theory." However, during the late 1980s and early 1990s, the word "queer" began to be used frequently by lesbian, gay, bisexual, and transgendered activists inside and outside of the academy to refer to themselves, their movements, and their cultural products. This usage contrasted with what had previously been a more common deployment of the term "queer" as an insult. While the word "queer" was therefore reclaimed as a rallying term for political organizing and community formation, its inclusion of otherwise diverse groups of people (lesbians, gay men, bisexuals, transsexuals, intersexed persons, sex radicals, etc.) made it apparent that the populations who were identified or who identified themselves as "queer" often lived their lives quite differently from one another as well as from mainstream culture. Thus, recognition of multiplicity was often implied by the use of the term. Still today the word "queer" is frequently used in this way to refer both to a wide range of individuals or groups of people whose sexual and gender identities and practices depart from the heterosexual mainstream, and to their activities or cultural products.

Picking up on this colloquial use of the word "queer," feminist theorist Teresa de Lauretis coined the phrase "queer theory" in 1990 in an essay titled "Queer Theory: Lesbian and Gay Sexualities" (*differences* 3/2: iii–xviii). One of her goals in proposing this unusual terminology was to take seriously the differences that exist between lesbians, gay men, and others who are marginalized on the basis of sexual practices or desires. The differences that concerned her included differences of gender, race, and class. By the mid-1990s, however, her phrase "queer theory" was being applied more widely to a growing body of interdisciplinary intellectual work that included influential writings by professors of Modern Language and Literature such as Eve Kosofsky Sedgwick, Michael Warner, and Leo Bersani; philosophers such as Judith Butler; classicists such as David M. Halperin; and social scientists such as anthropologist Gayle Rubin. Many of these early queer theorists were influenced not only by feminism and lesbian and gay studies, but also by the philosophical-historical work of the French poststructuralist thinker Michel Foucault, who attempted to rethink the relationships among sexuality, power, and discourse. As the influence of Foucault indicates, much of academic queer theory fit within a wider set of intellectual trends during the late twentieth century that were associated with poststructuralist thought.

Subsequently, the projects carried out under the phrases "queer theory," "queer studies," and "queer criticism" have grown even more diverse. Indeed, it is difficult to give a description of queer theory that accurately captures all of these projects, partly because queer theorists themselves often resist summary and classification as academic norms. Nevertheless, several recurring themes or analytical moves can be said to characterize much queer criticism.

Queer Theory and Sexuality. Most queer critics emphasize sexual practice and gender as crucial lenses for the interpretation of societies and texts. With respect to sexual practice, in particular, this emphasis marks a shift in comparison to earlier forms of scholarship that sometimes downplayed sexuality as a minor or "private" matter that served merely as background for more important objects of study.

Although associated with the study of homosexuality, queer theorists call into question the universal relevance or stability of the binary distinction between heterosexual and homosexual identity categories. In modern Western societies, it is now widely assumed that sexual desire for a member of the opposite sex rules out desires for members of one's own sex and that sexual desire for a member of one's own sex rules out desires for members of the opposite sex. Such fixed desires are understood to be constitutive of a key component of modern individual identities, called "sexual orientation," that is thought to be closely related to one's biological sex and one's gender identification (though the exact nature of these relations is often vague). However, historical and cross-cultural research indicates that, even though same-sex desires and practices can be documented in most cultures, the tendency to organize such desires and practices around distinct heterosexual and homosexual identities or psychological orientations is a fairly recent phenomenon, originating in modern Western societies. In some ancient Greek and Roman societies, for example, a man who married a woman and sired children was still considered capable of desiring and pursuing sexual contact with other males, though the protocols for such contacts were structured by rigid assumptions about status and penetration (e.g., an adult male citizen should play the active role with subordinate males, who in turn normatively played the passive role for their social superior). Similarly, anthropological research indicates that, in some non-Western cultures, young males are initiated into manhood through rituals of oral intercourse and semen ingestion with other males, rituals that Western society might label as homosexual. Yet most of these males go on to participate in opposite-sex sexual intercourse and father children. Attention to specific case studies such as these led to an increasing emphasis on the social and historical construction of sexuality by the late 1980s and early 1990s.

Moreover, in his influential *History of Sexuality, Volume I*, Foucault attempted to historicize the emergence of the new category of identity, the "homosexual," in the nineteenth century. Foucault interpreted this new understanding of the "homosexual" as a "species" of human to be a consequence of both the classifying ambitions of sexologists and psychiatrists, on the one hand, and the attempts by those who identified with the category to reverse the relations of power in which they were engaged, on the other hand. For queer theorists, all of these case studies denaturalize absolute distinctions between homosexuals and heterosexuals as two ontologically different types of people. Even within modern Western industrialized societies, such experiences as bisexuality cast doubt on rigid versions of the opposition between heterosexual and homosexual.

While some gay and lesbian activists fear that these attempts to destabilize modern heterosexual and homosexual identities will undermine the political struggle for gay civil rights, queer theorists argue that dualistic distinctions between heterosexuality and homosexuality actually reinforce the belief that heterosexuality is a fixed, coherent category. In order for heterosexuality to exist as a stable concept, it must be differentiated from homosexuality. Heterosexuality comes to be understood as the norm, and homosexuality as the deviation. To undermine the distinction between these categories is consequently to call into question the assumed normalcy of heterosexuality. Thus, in spite of its origins in lesbian and gay studies, queer theory devotes as much energy to a critical reexamination of heterosexuality and the power relations and norms that support it as it does to homosexuality. Such power relations and norms produce what queer theorists call "heteronormativity," a widespread bias in favor of heterosexual relations and binary gender roles as primary organizing principles of society. Queer theory is therefore misunderstood if it is thought to be relevant only for individuals or communities who self-identify or are identified by others as "queer." Its relevance extends to the wider set of social meanings and practices that necessarily inform anyone's experiences of sex and gender in a heteronormative society. Heteronormativity is not precisely identical to heterosexuality, however, since heterosexual relations could, in principle, be organized in ways that do not privilege heterosexuality over homosexuality or alternative sexual practices.

One of the primary sites for reproducing heteronormativity is the nuclear family. Thus, queer theory builds upon historical and anthropological investigations of kinship structures to point out that the modern nuclear family is only one among several possible ways of organizing affective and communal life. Even within modern society, alternative kinship structures exist.

So too, modern heteronormativity frequently entails the assumption that sexual practice properly takes place only as a private expression of romantic love between monogamous partners. Thus queer theorists tend to examine alternative forms of sexual practice such as sex with multiple partners (whether same-sex or opposite-sex partners), public sex, prostitution, pornography, and sadomasochism. Many queer theorists insist that such practices need to be studied or understood as examples of what Gayle Rubin refers to as "benign sexual variation" rather than dismissed out of hand or interpreted in the worst possible light. Queer theory does not discount the need for sexual ethics, of course; but, following Rubin and other sex radicals, it tends to suspect that sex is too often overlaid with an excess of meaning and moralism surpassing that applied to other human practices that also require ethical deliberation, such as eating.

Queer Theory and Gender. Partly because norms for sexual activity and assumptions about sexual desire are tied closely to beliefs about the two biological sexes, queer theorists also reexamine ideologies of sex and gender. Much contemporary research starts from a distinction between biological sex and gender, the latter of which is understood as the cultural interpretation of biological sex. Queer theory tends to emphasize a very wide scope of possibilities for gendered behavior. Indeed, the assumption that all bodies fit neatly into only two biological sexes is itself challenged by some queer writers who note, for example, that certain bodies are born with ambiguous sexual markers and others are modified sexually over time. Even when bodies can be fit into one of two sexed categories, "male" and "female," there is no automatic correlation between sexed bodies and gendered behavior or dispositions. Many individuals with biologically male bodies exhibit so-called "feminine" behaviors or self-identify in "feminine" ways, and many individuals with biologically female bodies exhibit so-called "masculine" behaviors or self-identify in "masculine" ways. However, there is no precise correlation between these multiple behaviors, identifications, and sexual preferences.

The classification of particular behaviors as "masculine" or "feminine" itself varies widely across cultures. Some societies include additional gender classifications, such as a "third sex," to handle the fact that binary distinctions between male and female cannot account for all gendered practice. Individuals of the "same" sex within a single society also exhibit gender characteristics to variable degrees; and this variability is sometimes used to allot prestige and shame differentially to members of the "same" sex, as when certain men are deemed more or less "manly" than others.

As all of these examples indicate, the binary distinction between male and female, though assumed as common sense throughout Western societies, is not taken for granted by queer theorists. Rather, it is subjected to critical analysis. For some queer theorists, particularly those writing under the influence of feminist philosopher Judith Butler, such binary systems of sex and gender are considered "performative" effects of bodily practices rather than naturally occurring phenomena or cultural interpretations of fixed biological sexes. That is to say, our repeated attempts to conform our bodies and our practices to norms for sex and gender over time produce the illusion of a stable, absolute distinction between male and female. Yet these attempts to embody norms for male and female behavior are only more or less successful imitations of earlier performances. Thus, queer theorists emphasize the many differences that exist between repeated performances of sex and gender as part of a larger project of challenging the stability and success of the norms that inform those performances. On the one hand, queer studies may call attention to transgender lives and practices, which often subvert norms for sex and gender intentionally. On the other hand, queer theorists also argue that even more conventional or "normal" lives fail to conform completely or in a uniform way to dominant gender norms.

Queer Theory and Ethnicity. One of the most significant developments in queer theory in recent years has been the attempt to study in greater detail how sexual and gendered meanings and practices are structured in relation to race, ethnicity, nation, colonialism, class, and religion. Beliefs about "manly" or "womanly" behavior, including accepted sexual behavior and kinship norms, vary according to the racial, ethnic, and class backgrounds of both the individuals whose behavior is being evaluated and the individuals who make evaluations. In addition, racism, class prejudice, and colonial relations are often structured through sexual stereotypes. In pursuing such issues, queer theory will sometimes make use of "intersectional" analyses of gender, race, class, and nation that have been important for feminist and postcolonial studies. At the same time, the tendency to "queer" categories by demonstrating their mobility and fluidity rather than assuming their fixed or essential nature can be applied not only to gender and sexual practice but also to race, which is sometimes structured through binary oppositions (e.g., "white" versus "black"), and ethnicity, which relies upon the creation of boundaries between self and other.

The Bible and Heteronormativity. Because queer theory devotes much of its attention to the analysis of modern societies, its relevance for biblical interpretation might appear to be limited. Indeed, the use of queer criticism has been less common to date among biblical scholars than among scholars elsewhere in the humanities. It is important to recall, however, that one crucial influence on queer theory's critique of modern ways of organizing sex and gender was the demonstration that ancient societies, and particularly Greek and Roman societies, organized relations of sex and gender in quite different ways than modern societies. The queer point taken from such historicizing demonstrations was not to romanticize patriarchal societies of the ancient world by claiming them as models (though this has occasionally been done), but rather to undermine the assumption that modern systems of sex, gender, and kinship are either natural or universal.

One possible agenda for queer criticism of the Bible, then, is to explore or emphasize the gap between modern heteronormative assumptions and the ancient literature found in the Bible. To be sure, it is conventional for contemporary advocates of so-called traditional family values to insist or imply that such values are directly grounded in the Jewish and Christian traditions that utilize biblical texts as religious resources. A few biblical texts are frequently cited in support of this claim, such as the declaration of God in Gen 1:27–28 that humankind, "male and female," will "be fruitful and multiply and fill the earth." Yet many more biblical texts indicate that the writers of biblical literature held views about gender and sexual practice that stand in some tension with modern heteronormative assumptions. Queer criticism may emphasize such texts rather than simply acknowledging them as social background.

It is clear, for example, that marriage in ancient Israel (if "marriage" is even the right word for the ancient household) was not organized around heterosexual monogamy. Numerous biblical male characters are represented as having multiple wives and concubines, including Abraham, Jacob, Elkanah, Saul, David, and possibly Moses. None of these characters is criticized for taking multiple women. Indeed, in the case of David, we are even told explicitly that God gave the women of other men to him (2 Sam 12:8). While Solomon does receive criticism in connection with his multiple wives and concubines, the criticism appears to be aimed not at the number of his women but rather at the fact that, having taken many foreign wives and concubines, he promotes the worship of their non-Israelite deities. Even the legal prohibitions against adultery do not enforce monogamy in as strict a way as many readers imagine. If a man had sexual relations with the wife of another man, both partners could be killed; but there do not seem to be many restrictions on sexual activity between a married man and a woman other than his wife who was available sexually, such as a prostitute or a slave. The sexuality of women, on the other hand, seems to be more narrowly restricted than that of men so long as a woman falls under the authority of a father or husband. Indeed, as feminist scholars have noted, adultery is understood in the Hebrew Bible as something akin to a property offense. The Ten Commandments even list women alongside houses, slaves, animals and fields as objects that one man has which another man might want (Ex. 20:17; Deut. 5:21).

Significantly, marriage is almost never associated in the Hebrew Bible with companionate love, as it is in modern Western societies. The recognition of physical desire between partners and a longing to be together is clear in the Song of Songs; but, as scholars of the Song have long recognized, the speakers in the Song are not married. Among men of stature such as Israel's kings, the ability to collect multiple wives and concubines appears to have been interpreted as an indication of wealth, prestige, and "manly" leadership.

A number of New Testament texts, on the other hand, take a more ambivalent or even negative view of marriage and family. Neither Jesus nor Paul is represented as being married. In the Gospel of Luke, Jesus states that "Whoever comes after me and does not hate father and mother, wife and children, brothers and sisters, yes, and even life itself, cannot be my disciple" (Luke 14:26). Although the Gospel of Matthew nervously tones down that saying, all three synoptic Gospels recount an incident in which Jesus learns and responds to the fact that his mother and brothers are outside asking for him: "And he replied, 'Who are my mother and my brothers?' And looking at those who sat around him, he said, 'Here are my mother and my brothers! Whoever does the will of God is my brother and sister and mother'" (Mark 3:33–35; cf. Matt 12:46–50; Luke 8:19–21). Paul, while clearly allowing for marriage, also states just as clearly that his preference would be for those who are unmarried to remain that way (1 Cor 7:8). These and other biblical passages served as reference points for early Christian figures who emphasized virginity and chastity while discouraging marriage and childbirth.

If queer criticism is understood as being focused solely on same-sex relations, most of these observations are beside the point. Because queer criticism is also aimed at the wider context of heteronormative society, however, such observations potentially challenge the attempt to ground heteronormative assumptions in biblical literature.

Much queer criticism of the Bible accepts that a few biblical passages condemn at least some forms of same-sex sexual relations. Queer critics will generally note, however, that same-sex sexual relations were not conceptualized in the world that gave us the Bible in the same way that homosexuality is understood today. As in other ancient societies, the writers of both Testaments almost certainly interpreted same-sex eroticism in terms of a politics of penetration that understood intercourse to involve an active, penetrating social superior and a passive, penetrated social subordinate. The model for this understanding was, precisely, heterosexual intercourse in a patriarchal society. For example, the levitical proscriptions of male same-sex intercourse are explicitly articulated in terms of gender differentiation, inasmuch as such intercourse is referred to by comparison with lying with a woman (Lev 18:22; 20:13). Thus, there is little direct correlation between such passages and contemporary debates about homosexuality, which are informed by very different notions of sexual practice on all sides of the issue.

Queer Readings of the Bible. However, relatively little queer criticism is actually devoted to debates about the handful of texts that are usually cited against homosexuality. Such contemporary debates normally entail assumptions about biblical authority and textual meaning that historical criticism and studies of reading and reception have undermined, and that queer criticism usually rejects. Instead, queer criticism takes other approaches that intentionally stand outside more conventional approaches to the Bible and ethics.

It is possible to make a rough distinction between two different types of queer criticism of the Bible. Some queer critics build upon the use of the word "queer" as a term for a range of individuals or groups who depart from norms of sex and gender (lesbians, gay men, bisexuals, transgendered, etc.) and understand "queer" as a social location from which contemporary readers can interpret the Bible. According to this approach, new meanings are generated from the biblical texts when they are read from the perspectives or concerns of queer readers or queer communities. Some of these readings can be quite popular in orientation, while others are more academic. Many of these queer readings understand the Bible as a theological resource for queer religious communities, though the use of this resource is often quite nontraditional; and so they may be aimed at queer audiences as well as emerging from queer communities.

Another type of queer criticism places less emphasis on the social location of readers and gives more explicit attention to the interpretive questions found in academic queer theory. These queer readings of the Bible are usually more closely related to queer criticism as it can be found in academic disciplines outside of biblical or theological studies; and the assumed audience tends to be academic rather than popular. Questions and influential texts from queer theory can be integrated with various methods and figures from biblical scholarship, but this is accomplished in a wide variety of different ways.

Although this manner of distinguishing among queer readings is useful to some degree, the distinction cannot be applied in a dogmatic fashion. The lines between academic and popular approaches are often fluid rather than fixed, as are the lines between ancient and contemporary meanings; and the influence of academic queer theory can be present even when appeals to it are less explicit. Indeed, consistent with the queer emphasis on blurring boundaries, a queer reading of a text may set out intentionally to contravene normative assumptions about the form that queer criticism "ought to take."

Regardless of where it fits in terms of the distinction just made between two types of queer reading, queer criticism will frequently focus on texts in which assumptions about proper gender behavior seem to be undermined or transgressed. Such texts illustrate the queer point that the binary opposition between male and female is less stable than is often assumed. Examples of individual characters who have attracted or might attract this type of queer attention could include Jacob, who becomes Israel's eponymous ancestor in spite of being more closely associated with his mother, cooking, and the domestic space of the tents than his brother (Gen 25:27–34); Lot and his daughters, or Joseph and the wife of Potiphar, who reverse the normative assumption that men will be sexual subjects and women will be sexual objects (Gen 19:30–38; 39:1–23); Jael and the woman of Thebez, who each kill men in scenes with significant phallic overtones (Judg 4:17–22; 10:50–54). The representation of an assumed male Israelite audience as a woman in the controversial sexual and marital images used by such prophets as Jeremiah, Ezekiel, and Hosea arguably creates queer gender dynamics in the relations between text, original audience, and contemporary reader. Eunuchs have received a lot of attention from queer critics, and the Ethiopian eunuch in Acts 8 has proven to be an especially fruitful object of queer interpretation. Paul's apparent dissolving of gender distinctions in Galatians 3:28 may lay the groundwork for a queer reading of Christianity, though it sits uneasily alongside other Pauline statements. Even the complex gender protocols used to represent Jesus, both in the New Testament and among later interpreters, have been analyzed by queer criticism.

Of course, other approaches to biblical interpretation, such as feminist criticism, gender studies, or masculinity studies, have also emphasized some of these same texts and figures. However, queer criticism will often blur the boundaries between identified methods of biblical interpretation, just as it blurs boundaries that concern gender and sexuality. The distinctiveness of its perspective from some of the other approaches to gender in the same texts will lie in queer criticism's consistent preference for fluid and mobile notions of gender over fixed gender roles and static gender models. Indeed, a queer reading may attempt to demonstrate that even a character, image, or text that seems on the surface to represent a more stable notion of gender (e.g., the story of the Garden of Eden, or Paul's Corinthian correspondence) can in fact be read in a more dynamic fashion. A queer reading can also focus on queer gender dynamics in the history of a text's reception, as in Stephen Moore's work on readers of the Song of Songs.

Queer criticism also looks for biblical examples of sexual activities or symbolism that stand in tension with heteronormative conventions. In some cases this may involve homoerotic readings of the interactions between two characters of the same sex, such as David and Jonathan, Ruth and Naomi, or Jesus and the beloved disciple. However, other sorts of nonconventional sexual matters also attract attention. The figures of prostitutes in both Testaments are sometimes interpreted as queer figures, since prostitutes participate in stigmatized sexual activities while, in certain texts, displaying significant agency. A few queer critics have used sadomasochism, with its dynamics of pain, pleasure, and domination, to interpret dynamics in the relationship between Israel and God. The public use of sex in such passages as 2 Samuel 16 challenges modern notions of sex as a private matter. The widespread sexual use of slaves in the ancient world may also shed light on both the Hebrew Bible (e.g., the story of Hagar) and the New Testament (e.g., the letter to Philemon). These are only examples of a number of textual figures and symbols that are emphasized by queer criticism because of the ways in which their sexual images transgress heteronormative assumptions.

Consistent with the emphasis in queer theory on the intersections of sex, gender, race, ethnicity, class, and nation, queer criticism also reexamines biblical texts in which such intersections appear to be at work. While numerous passages in the Hebrew Bible represent ethnic difference in terms of gender and sexual practice, queer criticism focuses in particular on passages in which the links between ethnicity, gender, and sexual practice involve some sort of transgression of norms or conventions. Examples might include, from the Hebrew Bible, the story of Lot's sexual unmanning by his daughters; or, from the New Testament, the story of the Ethiopian eunuch.

Contribution. As the brief examples given above indicate, queer criticism of the Bible is a heterogeneous enterprise. It does not provide, and in fact tends to avoid, any agreed upon set of methodological steps that its practitioners all follow consistently. It is usually characterized by an emphasis on the dynamics of sex, gender, and sexual practice in biblical texts and biblical interpretation, dynamics that are also studied by other approaches to the Bible. However, the specific contributions of queer criticism to the study of such dynamics include an emphasis on the fluidity and multiplicity of gender and sexual practice as well as the inextricability of sex and gender from matters that are often kept separate from it, such as ethnicity, race, nation, and religion. Just as significantly, queer criticism carries out its interpretations of biblical texts with a view toward queer challenges to contemporary heteronormativity.

Queer theory outside of biblical scholarship, which has had an influence on queer criticism within biblical scholarship, continues to evolve. Many of the practitioners of queer theory have begun to focus on issues that are not always associated with sex and gender, including race, globalization, international conflict, economics, the changing shape of the public sphere, and theories of affect and emotion. Although it is too soon to know what the implications of these more recent developments in queer theory might be for biblical scholarship, it is likely that queer criticism of the Bible will continue to evolve, at least in the near future, in order to take such developments into account.

[*See also* Feminist Biblical Interpretation; Ideological Criticism; Lesbian, Gay, Bisexual, and Transgender Interpretation; Masculinity Studies; *and* Race, Ethnicity, and Biblical Criticism]

BIBLIOGRAPHY

Queer Theory

Butler, Judith. *Bodies That Matter: On the Discursive Limits of 'Sex.'* New York: Routledge, 1993. Further development and clarification of Butler's performative theory of gender as well as engagement with issues of race and queerness.

Butler, Judith. *Gender Trouble: Feminism and the Subversion of Identity.* 2d ed. New York: Routledge, 1999. Includes an early articulation of Butler's influential performative theory of gender as well as her critique of the sex/gender distinction.

Halley, Janet, and Andrew Parker, eds. *After Sex? On Writing Since Queer Theory.* Durham, N.C.: Duke University Press, 2011. A collection of essays that reflect on some of the most recent trends in queer theory, including those dealing with race and affect.

Halperin, David M. *Saint Foucault: Towards a Gay Hagiography.* New York: Oxford University Press, 1995. Uses an engagement with the work of Michel Foucault to develop a theory of queer politics.

Jagose, Annamarie. *Queer Theory: An Introduction.* New York: New York University Press, 1996. A helpful overview of the texts and issues that shaped the emergence and early years of queer theory.

Rubin, Gayle S. *Deviations: A Gayle Rubin Reader.* Durham, N.C.: Duke University Press, 2011. A collection of writings by the anthropologist whose essay "Thinking Sex," included in the volume, was especially influential in the development of queer theories of sexuality.

Sedgwick, Eve Kosofsky. *Epistemology of the Closet.* Berkeley: University of California Press, 1990. Notable for its critical examination of the binary distinction between homosexuality and heterosexuality.

Sullivan, Nikki. *A Critical Introduction to Queer Theory.* New York: New York University Press, 2003. An overview of queer theory that includes attention to issues of race and transgender.

Warner, Michael, ed. *Fear of a Queer Planet: Queer Politics and Social Theory.* Minneapolis: University of Minnesota Press, 1993. A collection of essays from the early years of queer theory that includes Warner's influential articulation of "queer" as resistance to heteronormativity.

Queer Criticism and the Bible

Armour, Ellen T., and Susan M. St. Ville, eds. *Bodily Citations: Religion and Judith Butler.* New York: Columbia University Press, 2006. A collection of essays on the relevance of Butler's theories for religious studies that includes two contributions by biblical scholars and a response from Butler.

Guest, Deryn, et al., eds. *The Queer Bible Commentary.* London: SCM Press, 2006. Examines each book of the Bible in the light of queer perspectives and issues.

Hornsby, Teresa, and Ken Stone, eds. *Bible Trouble: Queer Reading at the Boundaries of Biblical Scholarship.* Atlanta: Society of Biblical Literature, 2011. A diverse collection of essays by biblical scholars who

bring queer and other theories to bear on biblical interpretation.
Macwilliam, Stuart. *Queer Theory and the Prophetic Marriage Metaphor in the Hebrew Bible.* Abingdon, UK: Equinox, 2011. An examination of the relevance of queer theory for biblical scholarship that uses queer theory to reconsider the role of sex and gender in the biblical prophetic marriage metaphor.
Martin, Dale B. *Sex and the Single Savior: Gender and Sexuality in Biblical Interpretation.* Louisville, Ky.: Westminster John Knox Press, 2006. A collection of essays by the author on sex, gender, and the interpretation of the New Testament, combining historical criticism with queer theory and contemporary theories of reading and rhetoric.
Moore, Stephen D. *The Bible in Theory: Critical and Postcritical Essays.* Atlanta: Society of Biblical Literature, 2010. Includes essays on queer theory and biblical interpretation as part of the author's larger project of re-reading biblical texts with the aid of poststructuralist literary theories.
Moore, Stephen D. *God's Beauty Parlor: And Other Queer Spaces In and Around the Bible.* Palo Alto, Calif.: Stanford University Press, 2001. A collection of essays by the author that directly engage queer theory as a lens for interpreting both biblical texts and the history of biblical interpretation.
Stone, Ken. "Gender Criticism: The Un-Manning of Abimelech." In Gale A. Yee, ed., *Judges and Method: New Approaches in Biblical Studies*, 2d ed., 183–201. Minneapolis, Minn.: Fortress Press, 2007. A methodological overview that locates queer criticism of the Bible within a larger set of approaches to gender studies.
Stone, Ken. *Practicing Safer Texts: Food, Sex and Bible in Queer Perspective.* Edinburgh: T&T Clark, 2005. Uses queer theory, anthropology, and biblical scholarship to reexamine a number of texts from the Hebrew Bible in which food and sex both appear.
Stone, Ken, ed. *Queer Commentary and the Hebrew Bible.* Sheffield, UK: Sheffield Academic Press/Pilgrim Press, 2001. An early collection of essays bringing queer theories and perspectives to bear on biblical interpretation.

Ken Stone

QUR'ANIC AND ISLAMIC INTERPRETATION OF THE BIBLE

Islamic interpretation of the Bible for more than a millennium has been mainly outside characterization of the Bible according to Muslim categories on the one hand, and polemical use of actual quotations from the Bible on the other.

One can speak of "Qur'anic" interpretation of the Bible because the Qur'an repeatedly refers to three "writings" understood to be part of the Bible. Explicit references to these three books in the Qur'an are consistently positive and respectful. During the first three centuries of Islam, most Muslim exegetes and other scholars seem to have referred to the earlier scriptures in the same respectful way. In spite of this, the best-known "interpretation" of the Bible among Muslims today is that the Bible is corrupted and falsified.

In the centuries between, Islamic intellectual history offers a number of notable Muslim encounters with the content of the Bible itself. These include a famous metaphorical interpretation of the Gospel's description of the deity of Jesus, and a lesser-known project to interpret the Qur'an through the Bible.

The Qur'an on the Bible. Both Christianity and Judaism and their scriptures were firmly established in the Middle East when Islam arose during the seventh century. Therefore one should not be surprised to find references to the earlier scriptures, or to their contents, in the Muslim scripture. Because of the strong faith of Muslims that the Qur'an is the Word of God, Muslim perceptions of the Qur'anic interpretation of the Bible influence all other areas of Islamic interpretation of the Bible as well.

Three particular books are mentioned by name in the Qur'an, which we identify as substantial parts of the present-day Bible: the *tawrāt* (Torah), the *injīl* (Gospel), and the *zabūr* (Psalms). The term *tawrāt* appears eighteen times in the Qur'an, mostly in the third and fifth *suras* or chapters. The term *injīl* appears twelve times. Its pattern of occurrence is similar to that of the term *tawrāt*. In fact, in all but two of its occurrences the term *injīl* appears in tandem with *tawrāt*.

The singular noun *zabūr* appears only three times in the Qur'an. Its pattern of occurrence is quite different from that of the other two books. *Zabūr* never appears together with the other two names of earlier scripture. In addition to the particular names of scriptures, the Qur'an also refers many times to these books through other expressions such as "the book of Moses" (Q 11:17) and "the book that Moses brought" (Q 6:91).

The verses in which these books are mentioned by name provide some basic information about the Qur'anic approach to them. Progressing canonically, the reader first learns that God "sent down the Torah (*tawrāt*) and the Gospel (*injīl*)" (Q 3:3). The Torah and the Gospel were revealed after the time of Abraham (Q 3:65). Subsequently, God taught Jesus the Torah and the Gospel (Q 3:48), and Jesus in turn confirmed the truth of the Torah (Q 3:50).

Perhaps more interesting for the Qur'anic interpretation of the Bible are the characterizations that the Qur'an uses to describe the earlier scriptures. A striking, though typical, example is found at Q 6:155: "Then we gave Moses the book, complete for him who does good, and distinguishing every thing, and as a guidance and a mercy." These and other expressions are repeated throughout the Qur'an. The Torah is characterized as containing "guidance and light" (Q 5:44). The same phrase is used to describe the contents of the Gospel at Q 5:46. The Gospel is also called "a guidance and an admonition to the godfearing" (Q 5:46). The Torah is said to contain "the judgment of God" (Q 5:43).

The Qur'an also characterizes the earlier scriptures by way of actions that often seem to be related to polemical situations. For example, Q 3:93 contains the command, "Bring the Torah now and read it, if you are truthful." The context seems to be a dispute about what foods were permitted to the Children of Israel. In another polemical passage, at Q 5:43, the Torah is said to be "with" the Jews and to contain God's judgment. Another verse says, "If you are in doubt regarding what we have sent down to you, ask those who read the book before you" (Q 10:94). The verse follows a substantial story about Moses, Pharaoh, and the Children of Israel. The impression given by these and other verses (Q 16:43; 21:7) is that the Qur'an sees the earlier scriptures as intact, available sources of authority.

This impression is born out in the language of "confirmation" that the Qur'an uses to portray the relationship between the earlier scriptures and what is conceived of as being "sent down" in the present. A typical statement of this relationship comes in a polemical speech to the Children of Israel: "And believe in that I have sent down, confirming (*muṣaddiqan*) that which is with you. . . ." (Q 2:41). This active participle occurs some eighteen times in the Qur'an. The object of the participle is generally one of a number of indistinct phrases that could be understood to refer to earlier scriptures. These "confirmation verses" portray the present recitation as aligning with what God has revealed in the past, and perhaps also as gaining authority from past revelations. The frequent repetition of phrases like "what is with you" (Q 3:81; 4:47) and "what is with them" (Q 2:89, 101) also suggests a concept of intact copies of the earlier scriptures in existence at the time of the recitation.

The Qur'an contains several passages that either quote or resemble expressions from the Bible. Q 7:40 has the phrase, "until the camel passes through the eye of the needle," though there is no apparent awareness in the context that this may come from the Gospel (Matt 19:24). At Q 5:45, immediately after two references to the Torah (Q 5:43–44), we read, "And therein we prescribed for them: 'A life for a life, an eye for an eye, a nose for a nose, and ear for an ear, a tooth for a tooth. . . .'" (cf. Exod 21:23–25). At Q 48:29 the Qur'an seems to claim to offer a quotation from either the Torah or the Gospel: "as a seed that puts forth its shoot, and strengthens it, and it grows stout and rises straight upon its stalk, pleasing the sowers, that through them he may enrage the unbelievers." This also seems to be the approach to the Psalms at 21:105: "For we have written in the Psalms, after the remembrance, 'the earth shall be the inheritance of my righteous servants'" (cf. Ps 37:29). The only time that the Qur'an claims that the Torah, the Gospel, and the Qur'an hold a specific content in common is at Q 9:111. The common content is said to be a promise binding upon Allah in those three scriptures: that believers "fight in the way of Allah; they kill and are killed."

Stories of the Prophets. In the Qur'an we find a kind of interpretation of Bible stories without any certain awareness of the Bible's contents. Stories involving biblical characters are told not as if they came from the Bible or could be found in the Bible. The Qur'an seems to show no actual familiarity with the text of the Bible. The stories are told as if overheard.

The stories are often presented in a kind of homiletic fashion, using selected details and differing versions evidently for the teller's own purposes. Some of the details of the Qur'anic stories are also found in the Bible. Other details are extra-biblical and familiar from rabbinic or apocryphal sources, and some details match no known source.

The Qur'an presents stories of many biblical characters, including Adam, Noah, Abraham, Lot, Joseph, David, and Solomon. In some suras the stories are told in a formulaic fashion. Allah sends his messenger to a particular people. The messenger delivers Allah's message, but the people do not accept the message. The messenger warns the people of the consequences of resisting Allah, and the people begin to manhandle the messenger. Before any harm can come to the messenger, Allah delivers the messenger and his family and destroys the people. However, in other cases the Qur'an offers carefully-presented stories, for example the story of Joseph in sura 12. In the Qur'anic telling (described as "the best of narratives" at Q 12:3), the Joseph story lacks details such as the names of Joseph's brothers, while providing extra-biblical details such as an episode in which the friends of Potiphar's wife cut their hands when they first see Joseph. But the Qur'anic story follows the general biblical outline and indeed claims to be a "confirmation" of the existing narrative (Q 12:111).

Of all the biblical figures mentioned in the Qur'an, Moses receives by far the most attention. His name appears some 136 times, in 50 separate pericopes in 36 of the Qur'an's 114 suras, totaling more than 500 verses. Even more striking than the abundance of material is the special profile that the Qur'an seems to give to Moses. In the Qur'an, God speaks directly with Moses (Q 4:164), and says to him, "Moses, I have chosen you above humankind by my messages and my word" (Q 7:144). In five extended versions of the Moses story, the Qur'an relays different elements of the narrative in different sequences, with differences in the details among the narrative elements. These many Qur'anic versions—characterized by John Wansbrough as "variant traditions" (1977: 22–23)—contain elements that are familiar from the Hebrew Bible. Other details in the Qur'anic narratives match the details found in extra-biblical tellings such as in Midrash, Mishnah, and Talmud.

The Qur'anic material on Jesus—called *ʿĪsā* in the Qur'an—mostly concerns the circumstances of his birth, some of which resemble those of the first chapter of the Gospel according to Luke. Again, the material on Jesus is not offered as from the Gospel, or as matching what is in the Gospel, but simply as an independent telling (Q 3:62). Jesus is presented briefly in two verses as a miracle worker who heals the blind and the leper, and who raises the dead "by permission of Allah" (Q 3:49; 5:110). The Qur'anic report in the same verses that Jesus created a bird from clay and blew life into it resembles a story in the apocryphal Gospel of Thomas the Israelite.

When it approaches the death of Jesus, the Qur'an appears ambiguous, ranging from verses that seem to assume his death (Q 3:55; 5:117; 19:33) to an explicit denial that the Jews killed Jesus (Q 4:157). However, there is little ambivalence in the Qur'anic denial of Jesus's deity. The Qur'anic Jesus is emphatically not God, not the Son of God, not to be "associated" with God, and not the "third of three." Most Muslims have understood the Qur'anic interpretation of these central New Testament affirmations to be an unequivocal denial. On the other hand, Jesus is given the name "Messiah" (Q 3:45) and is mysteriously called the "word" of God and "a spirit" from God (Q 4:171).

Readers of the Qur'an evidently had a strong desire to know more about the biblical characters mentioned in the Qur'an, because many details are supplied in Muslim works of commentary, history, and a special genre called *qiṣaṣ al-anbiyāʾ* (Stories of the Prophets). Two of the best-known works of this genre are the *ʿArā ʾis al-majālis fī qiṣaṣ al-anbiyāʾ* of Aḥmad ibn Muḥammad Thaʿlabī (d. 1035), and the

Qiṣaṣ al-anbiyā' of al-Kisā'ī, written around 1200 C.E. These works drew on a variety of sources, among them information provided by Jews and Christians from the biblical narratives.

A good example of a key biblical detail missing from the Qur'an is the name of Abraham's intended son of sacrifice in the single Qur'anic telling of the story at Q 37:102. Abraham says, "My son, I see in a dream that I shall sacrifice you; consider, what do you think?" However, the name of the son is not provided, either in the verse or in the context. Early commentators such as Muqātil ibn Sulaymān (d. 767) immediately specified the son as *Isḥāq* (Isaac), and even at the end of the third Islamic century the great classical exegete al-Ṭabarī (d. 923) argued that the son was Isaac. Later Muslim commentators such as Ibn Kathīr (d. 1373) eventually reached a doctrinaire understanding that the son of intended sacrifice was Ishmael, but it is interesting that prior to al-Ṭabarī, Ibn Qutayba (d. 885) wrote that he preferred Isaac because he had found it so in the Torah. Tha'labī, on the other hand, was certain the son was Ishmael: "the Jews claim it was Isaac; but the Jews lie."

The Bible as a Source of References to Muhammad. At various points in Muslim intellectual history, Muslim scholars have treated the Bible as a source of prophecies about Muhammad. Muslim writings from the early centuries of Islam are full of stories of Jews and Christians reading references to Muhammad in their scriptures and then responding in Muslim terms either appropriately or inappropriately. There are also two verses in the Qur'an that, according to some Muslims, state that prophecies about Muhammad are found in the earlier scriptures. At 7:157 the Qur'an says that readers of the Bible find references to the "*ummī*" prophet "written down with them in the Torah and the Gospel"; while at 61:6 'Īsā is portrayed as "giving good tidings of a messenger who will come after me whose name is *aḥmad* [more praised]."

The earliest example of the Bible being treated in this way is the quotation of a Syriac version of John 15:23–16:1 in the *Sīrat rasūl Allāh* of Ibn Isḥāq (d. 767). Muslims interpreted Jesus's words about the Comforter to mean a prophecy of Muhammad. Other biblical texts that have frequently been used in this way include Deuteronomy 18:15, 18; Isaiah 42:1–4 and—more surprisingly—Isaiah 21:7. The most famous example of a Muslim work written expressly for this purpose is *The Book of Religion and Empire* of 'Alī ibn Rabban al-Ṭabarī (d. 855). Ibn Rabban offered many examples out of a preconversion knowledge of the Bible. While citing these examples, Ibn Rabban was treating the earlier scriptures as intact texts, and did not in fact accuse them of textual corruption or falsification.

But the practice of interpreting the Bible as a source of prophecies of Muhammad has remained popular with Muslim scholars throughout Islamic history and up to the present day. The claim of intact prophecies and the accusation of corruption continued on parallel tracks—often in the same works.

The Understandings of the Muslim Interpretive Tradition. In addition to verses that explicitly mention one or both of the earlier scriptures, there is a series of verses in the Qur'an that some Muslims have understood to refer to a variety of "tampering" actions related to the earlier scriptures. These verses generally do not specify actor or object, and the verbs seem to indicate a range of indistinct actions that are seldom clarified by context. Taken on their own, it is difficult to say what the verses mean. However, Muslim exegetes have offered their interpretations.

One example from this group of verses is Q 2:75: "Are you then so eager that they should believe you, seeing there is a party of them that heard God's word, and then tampered with (*ḥarrafa*) it, and that after they had comprehended it, wittingly?" Of this particular verse, Muslim exegetes wrote that it referred to an incident in the time of Moses, when Israelite leaders heard God's word from Moses but reported it to the Children of Israel incorrectly. In most other cases, however, Muslim exegetes told a story of encounter between the Jews of Medina and Muhammad. In this narrative, the Jews have in their possession the Torah that contains the description of Muhammad. The Jews do not want to acknowledge the authority of Muhammad because of envy that he is from the line of Ishmael rather than Isaac, and therefore they hide the references, misinterpret or mispronounce the verses, or otherwise "tamper" with the word of God.

The chart of verbs, terms, and expressions related to the "tampering" theme in the Qur'an shows a series of repeating verbs in suras 2–7. Most significant of these verbs are those associated with alteration (*ḥarrafa, baddala*) and with concealment (*katama, asarra, akhfā*). Because verses of concealment outnumber verses of alteration, Muslim exegetes provided much more narrative material about a lively scenario in which the Jews of Medina know the prophecies of Muhammad in the Torah in their possession, but hide the prophecies in order not to have to submit to Muhammad.

CHART OF ARABIC ROOTS RELATED TO "TAMPERING" THEME

VERSE	*TERM/VERB*	*SUBJECT*	*OBJECT*
2.41	CONFIRMING	what I revealed	what is with you
	sell for small price	children of Israel (C of I)	signs of God
2.42	*labasa* (confound)	C of I	truth with vanity
	katama (conceal)	C of I	truth
2.59	*baddala* (substitute)	evildoers of C of I	a saying
2.75	*ḥarrafa* (tamper)	hearers of God's word	the word of God
2.77	*asarra* (conceal)		
2.79	write with hands	the book (*kitāb*)	
	sell for small price		what they have written
2.89	CONFIRMING	a book from God	what is with them
2.91	CONFIRMING	truth	what is with them
2.97	CONFIRMING		what was before it
2.101	CONFIRMING	a messenger from God	what is with them
	throw behind backs	those given the book	the book of God
2.106	*ansā* (cause to forget)	God	a verse
2.140	*katama* (conceal)	people of the book (P of B)	testimony from God
2.146	*katama*	those given the book	truth
2.159	*katama*		evidence and guidance
2.174	*katama*		what God sent down
	sell for small price		
2.211	*baddala* (substitute)	C of I	the blessings of God
3.3	CONFIRMING	God/the book	what was before it
	TORAH & GOSPEL		
3.48	TORAH & GOSPEL		
3.50	CONFIRMING	Jesus	Torah
	TORAH		
3.65	TORAH & GOSPEL		
3.71	*labasa* (confound)	P of B	truth with vanity
	katama (conceal)	P of B	truth
3.77	sell for small price		covenant of God
3.78	*lawā* (twist)	a sect of P of B	tongues with the book
3.81	CONFIRMING	a messenger	what is with you
3.93	TORAH (x2)		
3.187	*katama* (conceal)	those given the book	
	throw behind backs	those given the book	the book
	sell for small price	those given the book	
3.199	sell for small price	P of B	signs of God
4.37	*katama* (conceal)		bounties God gave
4.46	*ḥarrafa* (tamper)	some of the Jews	words from places

Continued

CHART OF ARABIC ROOTS RELATED TO "TAMPERING" THEME

VERSE	*TERM/VERB*	*SUBJECT*	*OBJECT*
	lawā (twist)	some of the Jews	tongues
4.47	CONFIRMING	what we have sent down	what is with you
4.163	PSALMS		
5.13	*ḥarrafa* (tamper)	C of I	words from places
	nasiya (forget)	C of I	what reminded of
5.14	*nasiya*	Christians	what reminded of
5.15	*akhfā* (conceal)	P of B	much of the book
5.41	*ḥarrafa* (tamper)	Jews	words from places
5.43	TORAH		
5.44	TORAH		
	sell for small price	Jews	signs of God
5.46	CONFIRMING (x2)	God, Jesus	Torah
	TORAH (x2)		
	GOSPEL		
5.47	GOSPEL		
5.48	CONFIRMING	We/the book in truth	what was before it
5.66	TORAH & GOSPEL		
5.68	TORAH & GOSPEL		
5.110	TORAH & GOSPEL		
6.92	*akhfā* (conceal)		much
6.93	CONFIRMING	a book we sent down	what was before it
7.157	TORAH & GOSPEL		
7.162	*baddala* (substitute)	evildoers of C of I	a saying

This trend in the commentaries on the Qur'an is also followed by other Muslim genres, such as *sīra* and *maghāzī* (biography of Muhammad), *ḥadīth* (sayings attributed to Muhammad), and *asbāb al-nuzūl* ("occasions of revelation"). In all of these works the overarching narrative is of Jewish (rarely Christian) obstinacy in the face of clear descriptions of Muhammad in their scriptures. Accusations of textual corruption or falsification appear seldom, if at all. The tone is sometimes free of any sense of confrontation, such as in the *ḥadīth*, "the people of the book used to read the Torah in Hebrew and then explain it in Arabic to the Muslims." In this tradition Muhammad says, "Do not believe the people of the book, nor disbelieve them, but say, 'We believe in Allah and whatever is revealed to us, and whatever is revealed to you.'"

One of the best-known stories of this type is the story about the "verse of stoning" that many Muslim exegetes tell to interpret Q 5:41 ("...the Jews...tampering with words out of their places...."). A group of Jews brings a pair of adulterers to Muhammad in Medina for a ruling on their punishment. Muhammad proceeds to the Jewish study center and determines from their best Torah scholar that the punishment for adultery in the Torah is stoning. In some versions of the story, a Jewish teacher actually hides the "verse of stoning" with his hand until a Jewish convert to Islam removes it from the verse. Muhammad then commands that the two adulterers be stoned. This story reflects, on the one hand, a concept of the authority of the Torah and an understanding of its intact state. On the other hand, the story reflects a deep Muslim uncertainty about the ruling itself: though Muslim scholars are convinced that it was the *sunna*, or custom, of Muhammad to stone adulterers, there is no verse in the Qur'an that supports this ruling (but cf. Q 24:2).

This anomaly became one of the major flashpoints of Muslim discussion on Islamic Law.

Interpretation of the Bible for Polemic. Cut loose from their Qur'anic context, a number of verses from the Qur'an have been used by Muslim polemicists to support their accusations of corruption and falsification against the Bible. In the early centuries of Islam, accusations of falsification seem to have been related to contemporary testimony of Jews and Christians that they did not find any references to Muhammad in their scriptures. If there truly are no references to Muhammad in the Torah and Gospel when the Qur'an says they certainly will be found (Q 7:157), reasoned some Muslim polemicists, then the Jews and Christians must have erased the references. Once they made these accusations, however, some polemicists undertook a reading of the Bible in order to search for materials that they then claimed provided proof of the Bible's corruption.

To interpret the Bible merely for the sake of polemic involves first of all a decision made prior to studying the text: that the earlier scriptures are corrupt or falsified. The aim is to attack and discredit the bases of Judaism and Christianity in the Bible. From there the search proceeds to find passages that could be judged by predetermined criteria to be unworthy of the word of God.

The two Qur'anic verses that have drawn the highest number of accusations of biblical falsification from Muslim exegetes and other scholars are Q 2:79 and 3:78. These verses are typically vague about subject and object, and the scriptures themselves are not named. The focus of Q 2:79 is "those who write the book with their hands, then say, 'this is from God.'" At Q 3:78, "there is a sect of them who twist their tongues with the book, that you may suppose it part of the book, yet it is not part of the book." In spite of their lack of clarity, these verses have drawn the accusation that the Jews of Medina erased references to Muhammad from the Torah in an attempt to avoid having to acknowledge the authority of Muhammad. Most exegetes have limited the accusation to the Jews' encounter with Muhammad in Medina and to alleged biblical materials related to Muhammad. However, Muslim polemicists have extrapolated from those beginnings of the accusation to include other time periods and other biblical materials.

The earliest extant work of Muslim anti-Christian polemic to contain a substantial passage from the Bible is the *Radd 'alā al-naṣārā* (Refutation of the Christians) of Abū Muḥammad al-Qāsim ibn Ibrāḥm al-Ḥasanī (d. 860). Al-Qāsim did not accept the integrity of the Gospels, so he freely changed the wordings of the text to suit Muslim beliefs about Jesus. In his rendering of Matthew 1—8, for example, al-Qāsim removed references to "Father" and "Son of God" as well as teachings of Jesus in the Sermon on the Mount that 'Īsā—according to Islam—could not possibly have delivered. A later polemical work that contained a quantity of biblical material unseen in earlier writings was the *Tathbīt dalā'il al-nubuwwa* (Confirmation of the Proofs of Prophecy) of the Mu'tazila Qāḍī 'Abd al-Habbār (d. 1025). 'Abd al-Habbār quoted from all four Gospels, the book of Acts, and also the epistles of Paul and of John. The intent was negative—that is, to attack Christian belief in line with earlier works of Mu'tazila polemic. However, in some of his arguments he used passages from the Bible to defend Islamic beliefs about Jesus, implicitly relying on the Bible's authority. His acceptance or rejection of the authority of the Bible depended, of course, on the particular argument he was making.

The first Muslim to develop the accusation of the corruption of the Bible in a major and systematic way was the Spanish scholar Ibn Ḥazm (d. 1064). In his *Kitāb al-fiṣal fī 'l-milal wa 'l-ahwā' wa 'l-niḥal* (Book of Separation Concerning Religions, Heresies, and Sects) he wrote of what he considered to be chronological and geographical inaccuracies, theological impossibilities, and preposterous behavior of prophets in the Hebrew Bible. Ibn Ḥazm did the same with the Christian Gospels. These "proofs" that the Bible was corrupted were determined, of course, according to Islamic doctrines such as the sinlessness (*'iṣma*) of prophets. Islam judged unworthy of the Word of God statements about God that it had determined were impossible (for example, that God wrestled with Jacob in Genesis 32).

Biblical reports of the behavior of figures considered prophets in Muslim thought that show them sinning (for example the adultery of David with Bathsheba) were cited as examples of biblical corruption. The Muslim doctrine of prophetic sinlessness took root even though the Qur'an, too, provides examples of the sins of prophets and has them asking God for forgiveness (including David, at Q 38:24f.)

The polemical approach of Ibn Ḥazm was picked up in a major way by Muslim scholars in the wake of the Mongol incursions into the Middle East and especially the destruction of Baghdad in 1258. The Egyptian jurist Aḥmad ibn Idrīs al-Qarāfī (d. 1285) drew heavily on Ibn Ḥazm, as did Ibn Qayyim al-Jawziyya (d. 1350), the student of the famous Ibn Taymiyya. Some western scholars have suggested reasons for the harshness of this anti-Bible polemic: that Ibn Ḥazm was enraged by a rumored attack on the Qur'an written by a Jew in Spain; that there was a mood of "religio-political competition" in the century following the Mongol onslaught; or that a letter by Paul of Antioch in the early 1200s provoked Muslim scholars to counterattack.

A Muslim text on the Bible in the tradition of Ibn Ḥazm that has been very influential in modern times is the *Izhār al-ḥaqq* (Demonstration of Truth) of Mawlana Raḥmat Allāh Kayrānawī (1818–1891). The book grew out of material that Raḥmat Allāh had collected for a public debate with a European missionary in Agra, India in 1854. Raḥmat Allāh made use of traditional Muslim accusations as well as the arguments of Ibn Ḥazm. However, Raḥmat Allāh started a new trend in Muslim anti-Bible polemic by bringing in the writings of western critics of the Bible in the middle of the nineteenth century. This polemic, too, was undoubtedly complicated by political tension during this period of British rule. Three years after the debate the Indian soldiers' "Mutiny" occurred, and Raḥmat Allāh himself was forced to flee India.

Muslim arguments against the Bible have not progressed much beyond Raḥmat Allāh's book, published in Arabic in 1864 and still widely distributed in an Urdu translation in South Asia. In recent decades, Muslim writers who "interpret" the Bible solely for the sake of polemic will make use of any popular western material judged to support the traditional Muslim accusations, including the speculations of the Jesus Seminar or the thesis of "orthodox corruption" from Bart Ehrman. Such Western materials have become very popular among some Muslims, especially in the era of the Internet, simply because they seem to give scholarly support to the traditional Muslim accusations against the Bible.

In a recent survey of Muslim popular literature on Christianity, Kate Zebiri reports that all of the authors who write on the subject of scripture claim that the text of the Bible is corrupt (1997, p. 50). She adds that among contemporary Muslims the doctrine of the textual corruption of the earlier scriptures is "virtually unchallenged" (p. 6). On a more anecdotal level, one London group surveying YouTube contents in 2006 found more than 43,000 videos attacking Christianity, many of them from well-known Muslim polemicists such as Ahmad Deedat, Shabir Ally, Jamal Badawi, and Zakir Naik.

Notable Exceptions in Islamic Interpretation. Though polemic against the Bible is by far the most common method of Islamic interpretation past and present, Muslim intellectual history also offers a number of notable encounters with the text of the Bible that strike a different tone.

One work that has caught the fascination of many scholars is *al-Radd al-jamīl li-ilāhiyyat ʿĪsā bi-ṣarīḥ al-Injīl* (The Fitting Refutation of the Deity of Jesus through the Evidence of the Gospel). The work is widely attributed to Abū Ḥāmid al-Ghazālī (d. 1111), though some scholars dispute this. *Al-radd* processes several Gospel texts about the deity of Jesus through an interesting hermeneutical grid: if such passages are opposed to reason or seem to resist a rational explanation, asserts the author, they should be interpreted through *ta'wīl*, that is, metaphorically. Therefore, the author's refutation of the Christian belief in the deity of Jesus rests on giving metaphorical interpretations to many passages from the Gospels that either clearly present or strongly imply the deity of Jesus.

Unique in the history of Muslim interpretation of the Qur'an is the commentary of Burhān al-Dīn al-Biqāʿī (d. 1480). Al-Biqāʿī's massive *Naẓm al-durar fī tanāsub al-āyāt wa-al-suwar* (String of Pearls Concerning the Harmony of the Verses and the Suras) is the only known commentary to contain extensive verbatim quotations from the Bible. The exegete used the Bible not only for polemical purposes, but primarily as scripture to elucidate the Qur'an. He quoted a chapter or more at a time from the Bible, and the purpose of many of his quotations was simply that of learning from the Bible. For example, in the process of showing that Q 21:105 is a quotation of Psalm 37:29, al-Biqāʿī quoted from fourteen other Psalms before he offered Psalm 37. Of the various reasons why al-Biqāʿī provided these frequent and extensive quotations from the Bible, the most common was to provide more details for a laconic or elliptical Qur'anic reference to biblical content. For example, where the Qur'an first provides a version of the creation of Adam, al-Biqāʿī quoted the full first three chapters of Genesis.

One Muslim attempt to interpret the Bible by actually writing a commentary on it is the *Mohomedan Commentary on the Holy Bible* by Sayyid Aḥmad Khān (d. 1898), written in India during British rule. Sir Sayyid wrote in Urdu on Genesis 1–11 and Matthew 1–5. His approach to scripture was Modernist, and his writing is free of polemic. Even more unusually, Sir Sayyid proposed that the Bible could have a positive role in Muslim life as long as it was read in the light of the Qur'an. In this way, he wrote, any distortions from Jewish and Christian misinterpretation could be corrected. Sir Sayyid did not accuse the Bible of having a corrupted or falsified text.

A recent event in Islamic interpretation of the Bible shows what is possible in the age of the Internet. In October 2007 a group of Muslims associated with King Abdullah II of Jordan posted to the internet a statement titled, "A Common Word between Us and You." The statement proposed as a basis for Muslim-Christian dialogue that Christians and Muslims share "in common" a belief in love for God and love for neighbor. The Muslim authors quoted the words of Jesus in Matthew 22:37–40 about love for God and neighbor in answer to a question about "the greatest commandment in the Law." This is similar, said the authors, to materials in Muslim scripture and tradition. Therefore they claimed that this is the "common word" referred to in Q 3:64, a place where Muslims and Christians can meet for dialogue.

This recent Muslim initiative seems to show a willingness to read both the Bible and the Qur'an and to take their contents seriously. The Qur'an itself certainly appears to hold the previous scriptures in high regard. In between, however, Islamic interpretation of the Bible has generally not shown this willingness to treat the Bible as the word of God.

BIBLIOGRAPHY

ʿAbd al-Habbār. *Critique of Christian Origins* (parallel English-Arabic text from *Tathbīt dalāʾil al-nubuwwa*). Translated by Gabriel Said Reynolds and Samir Khalil Samir. Provo, Utah: Brigham Young University Press, 2010.

Accad, Martin. "The Gospels in the Muslim Discourse of the Ninth to the Fourteenth Centuries: An Exegetical Inventorial Table." *Islam and Christian-Muslim Relations* 14 (2003): 67–91, 205–220, 337–352, 459–479.

Adang, Camilla. *Muslim Writers on Judaism and the Hebrew Bible from Ibn Rabban to Ibn Hazm.* Leiden, Netherlands: Brill, 1996.

Goldziher, Ignaz. "Über muhammedanische Polemik gegen Ahl al-kitāb. *Zeitschrift der Deutschen Morgenländischen Gesellschaft* xxxii (1878): 341–387.

Hirschfeld, Hartwig. "Mohammedan Criticism of the Bible." *Jewish Quarterly Review* 13/2 (1901): 222–240.

Lazarus-Yafeh, Hava. *Intertwined Worlds: Medieval Islam and Bible Criticism.* Princeton, N.J.: Princeton University Press, 1992.

Massignon, Louis. "Le Christ dans les Évangiles selon al-Ghazālī." *Revue des Études Islamiques* 6 (1932), 523–536.

McAuliffe, Jane Dammen. "The Qur'ānic Context of Muslim Biblical Scholarship." *Islam and Christian-Muslim Relations* 7 (1996), 141–158.

Michel, Thomas F., ed. and trans. *A Muslim Theologian's Response to Christianity: Ibn Taymiyya's Al-Jawab Al-Sahih.* Delmar, N. Y.: Caravan, 1984.

Nickel, Gordon. *Narratives of Tampering in the Earliest Commentaries on the Qur'ān.* Leiden, Netherlands: Brill, 2011.

Pulcini, Theodore. *Exegesis as Polemical Discourse: Ibn Ḥazm on Jewish and Christian Scriptures.* Atlanta: Scholars, 1998.

Rippin, Andrew. "Interpreting the Bible through the Qur'ān." In *Approaches to the Qur'ān*, edited by G. R. Hawting and Abdul-Kader A. Shareef. London: Routledge, 1993, 249–259.

Royal Aal al-Bayt Institute for Islamic Thought, "A Common Word between Us and You," posted at http://www.acommonword.com/index.php?lang=en&page=option1. (Accessed May 30, 2012)

Saleh, Walid. *In Defense of the Bible: A Critical Edition and an Introduction to al-Biqā'ī's Bible Treatise.* Leiden, Netherlands: Brill, 2008.

Schirrmacher, Christine. *Mit den Waffen des Gegner: Christlich-muslimische Kontroversen im 19. und 20. Jahrhundert.* Klaus-Schwarz-Vig, 1992.

Sweetman, J. Windrow. *Islam and Christian Theology*, Vol. 1. London: Lutterworth, 1955.

Ṭabarī ʿAlī ibn Rabban al-. *The Book of Religion and Empire.* Translated by A. Mingana. Manchester, UK: Manchester University Press, 1922.

Thomas, David. "The Bible in Early Muslim Anti-Christian Polemic." *Islam and Christian-Muslim Relations* 7 (1996), 29–38.

Wansbrough John. *Quranic Studies: Sources and Methods of Scriptural Interpretation.* Oxford: Oxford University Press, 1977.

Watt Montgomery. "The Early Development of the Muslim Attitude to the Bible." *Transactions of the Glasgow University Oriental Society* 16 (1955–56), 50–62.

Zebiri Kate. *Muslims and Christians Face to Face.* Oxford: Oneworld, 1997.

Gordon Nickel

R

Rabbinic Exegesis

For reasons of space and because of the other entries available in this Encyclopedia, this article will focus on Rabbinic exegesis in the Middle Ages, which was formative for later Jewish interpretation. For medieval Jews, much as for their ancestors, the Bible was a sacred text that was studied for religious edification, as a source of law and a guide to ritual practice, and that was read aloud in synagogue for the community to hear. Much of the literary creativity of the period, including biblical commentaries, sermons, legal responsa, treatises on Jewish thought, philosophy, mysticism, and liturgical compositions, resulted from serious engagement with scripture. Consequently, a discussion of medieval Jewish biblical interpretation could draw from a variety of genres and sources. The following discussion is limited to a particular genre, the formal running commentary on a biblical book as it took shape among Jews between the late ninth and fourteenth centuries—thus traveling a chronological path between the end of the rabbinic period and the crystallization of the major trends in Jewish exegesis that would carry on into modernity.

During the period from the birth of Christianity until the rise of Islam, most Jewish biblical exegetes had their teachings preserved in collections of midrash. Although commenting on an entire biblical book was a popular practice in Christian circles as early as the third century, Jewish scholars did not begin to do so until the ninth century, when they were living in the Islamic world.

Islam posed a different set of challenges for Jews than did Christianity. The former offered the idea of a replacement revelation, while the latter at least acknowledged the importance of the Hebrew Bible/Old Testament. Muslim commitment to the perfection of Arabic as the holy tongue led its scholars to approach the text of the Qur'an by developing a sophisticated linguistic and philological method that was also influenced by the rationalism of Islamic Kalam philosophy. The claims made about the perfection of the Arabic language and the Qurʾanic text left Jewish scholars on the defensive regarding Hebrew and the text of the Torah. In order to respond, Jews appropriated the tools of Muslim scholarship and began to explore and study the Bible in similar ways. This led to the advanced study of Hebrew grammar and the compilation of dictionaries of biblical Hebrew. These contrasted with the midrashic method, which interpreted individual words or phrases out of context, by relying on a new set of assumptions: among them that language is constructed according to identifiable conventions by which it conveys meaning and that words have a semantic range delimited by their context.

Karaite Biblical Commentary. In the eighth century, Jews began translating the biblical text into the Arabic vernacular much as their predecessors had done with the Aramaic Targumim. However, in contrast to the Targumic literature that could be paraphrastic and that often introduced rabbinic exegesis into the translation, these new efforts consisted of finding appropriate and accurate Arabic equivalents for each Hebrew word. These translations were precursors to a new genre of Jewish biblical exegesis, individually authored commentaries. A political shift in the Jewish community further catalyzed the move to this new form of biblical interpretation. In Iraq the Karaites (Scripturalists) arose in opposition to rabbinic authority and challenged the traditional type of biblical study among Jews. The authority of rabbinic "oral law," which often relied on apparently far-fetched interpretations and could contradict the written Torah, provoked some Jews of more rationalist leanings to question rabbinic exegesis, particularly in matters of halakhah (Jewish law). Daniel Frank has argued, "It was unquestionably the Karaites who moved biblical exegesis to center stage. Abandoning Rabbinic midrash while championing philology, they perfected a new form. The Bible commentary was born in the Islamic East" (2004, p. 257). The earliest Jewish Bible commentary to survive from the Middle Ages is Daniel al-Qumisi the Karaite's (ninth c., Iran, later Palestine) commentary on the Minor Prophets, although fragments of earlier commentaries are extant. Karaite exegesis blossomed in the tenth and eleventh centuries and numerous commentaries on the Bible are preserved from their community in Jerusalem (e.g., Yefet ben Eli [second half of the tenth c.] composed commentaries on the entire Bible, although no witness to Lamentations has been found).

The Karaite commentaries, composed primarily in Arabic, follow biblical verse order and are exceptionally concerned with the literary qualities of the Bible, and the contextual relationship between verse, pericope, and biblical book in particular. They include lexical glosses from Arabic and other languages (e.g., Persian), and are sensitive to grammar and syntax. Despite their Scripturalism the Karaites occasionally turned to midrashic or homiletical explanations (especially when the lemma was poetic or prophetic), but only after the primary contextual meaning was highlighted. Although the rabbis were committed to a multivalent biblical text and maintained that individual words could be polysemous (i.e., could have multiple meanings), the Karaites countered that biblical texts had only one legitimate meaning. In later works the Karaites's interests expanded to historical-literary and redaction issues (e.g., the historical setting of a particular narrative and how it aids understanding; typical patterns of expression in biblical Hebrew; and the editorial process).

Saadiah Gaon and Early Medieval Rabbinic Biblical Commentary. The rise of Arabic grammatical thought and the influence of rationalism that inspired Karaite scholars did not go unnoticed by the rabbinic Jewish elite, nor did the Karaite threat to their authority. Saadiah ben Yosef al-Fayyumi (882–942, Egypt and Iraq) was the Gaon of the Talmudic academy in Sura. His preserved oeuvre includes liturgical poetry, a commentary on the esoteric work *Sefer Yetsira*, studies of grammar and linguistics (e.g., *Agron*), works on the Talmud and rabbinic hermeneutics, responsa, anti-Karaite polemics, a major work of Jewish philosophy (*The Book of Beliefs and Opinions*), an Arabic translation of the Bible (*Tafsir*), and commentaries on the Torah, Isaiah, Daniel, Psalms, Proverbs, Job, and the Five Scrolls (although not all are complete).

Saadiah's study of the rabbinic tradition, his embrace of Arabic language theory and the encounter with Kalam philosophy, and his stark opposition to Karaite teachings shaped his exegesis. In the *Book of Belief and Opinions* (treatise 7, chapter 2) and the introduction to his commentary on Genesis he makes clear that the Bible should be understood literally except when it contradicts (1) what is observed through the senses; or (2) reason; or (3) another biblical verse; or (4) a reliable rabbinic exegetical tradition. The last is the most conservative element of Saadiah's approach, but he granted significant autonomy for the individual exegete to judge the value of any teaching. Saadiah draws on midrash in all sorts of exegetical matters without any distinguishable system for deciding what to include. His general approach was adopted by his successor Samuel ben Hophni (d. 1013), but already in his time the rabbinic school of exegesis had begun a move to al-Andalus and North Africa.

The Grammarians in Spain. Perhaps no innovation had as siginificant an influence on Jewish Bible commentary as did the arrival of the biblical Hebrew dictionary. Although not a biblical commentary per se, it was composed using systematic philological study of the Bible and became an essential tool in the hands of exegetes. The act of producing a dictionary concretized the new assumptions of Jewish interpreters that words had meanings in context, that they shared roots (in the earlier theory bi-literal, and later tri-literal), and that Hebrew followed rules which could be deduced. The earliest of the dictionaries, Menahem ibn Saruq's *Mahberet* (notebook, mid tenth c.), was composed in Hebrew, which later facilitated its transmission to communities in France and elsewhere where Jews lived under Christian rule and were not fluent in Arabic. The Karaite community likewise produced such dictionaries, although in Arabic (e.g., David ben Abraham al-Fasi's *Kitab Jami' al-Alfaz* [Book Containing a Collection of Words, tenth c.]). Ibn Saruq was followed in the late tenth century by Judah Hayyuj, and in the eleventh century by Jonah ibn Janah. The former wrote three treatises on Hebrew grammar and a biblical commentary preserved in fragmentary form and perhaps never completed. The fragments preserve an introductory essay (it may be the first in a Jewish commentary to discuss philological exegesis) and interpretations of verses from Joshua, Judges, 1 and 2 Samuel, 1 Kings, Isaiah, Jeremiah, Ezekiel, and Malachi. Hayyuj was the first to advocate for the tri-literal roots of Hebrew verbs, and the commentary was novel in putting these grammatical theories into practice in biblical interpretation.

Ibn Janah wrote several grammar books in an effort to refine Hayyuj's theories but, from the perspective of biblical interpretation, his major innovation was the application of rhetorical analyses to biblical texts. This was especially important since midrashic exegesis assumed that each biblical word was significant while ibn Janah's theory suggested that some words were mere rhetorical flourishes. He also paid significant attention to biblical *realia* and sought to properly identify toponyms, flora and fauna, implements, and tools.

The significance of the growth of a school of Hebrew grammarians for encouraging the shift from midrashic exegesis to literary-contextual exegesis cannot be overemphasized. The students of Ibn Janah and Hayyuj quickly translated their theoretical concepts into full-blown biblical commentaries in Spain. These new schools took Jewish biblical interpretation in radical directions, which left them open to rather significant criticism from more conservative members of the rabbinic elite.

Peshat Exegesis in Northern France. In the eleventh and twelfth centuries northern French rabbis participated in a revolutionary change in biblical studies. The community of scholars who primarily devoted their attention to Talmud study moved away from traditional biblical studies that relied on studying scripture with midrash. In essence, they complemented and then replaced this approach with a new methodology termed *peshat* exegesis. Generally, *peshat* refers to a contextual reading of biblical text, but a precise definition is not possible because medieval exegetes likely understood and applied it in different ways.

The rise of *peshat* exegesis was intimately tied to an explosion of Jewish literary creativity in northern France. Three contributing factors help explain its rise: Spanish-Jewish cultural influence; the twelfth-century Renaissance in Christian Europe; and Jewish-Christian polemics. Scholars typically agree that these factors encouraged the development of *peshat* exegesis, but they debate the degree to which each component acted as a catalyst. The exact route of the Spanish influence is not entirely clear, but that Ibn Saruq is cited by name in Rashi's commentaries helps to seal this argument. That *peshat* grew naturally out of a similar approach to Talmud study that was already well-established in northern France has also been suggested. The move to *peshat* biblical exegesis was, in part, an application of an old method to a new text. The Jewish-Christian polemic as the source of *peshat* also has merit since Jews and Christians would have debated scripture at the *peshat* level because they could not have convinced their opponents by citing proofs from confessional works. Jews and Christians could agree on the rules of Hebrew grammar in a far more substantial way than they could agree that the Talmud understood the text correctly or that a verse typologically foreshadowed Jesus. The renaissance of literary activity in twelfth century Christian Europe as it encountered the difficulties of reconciling issues of scriptural authority, reason, and faith is evident in the writings of Jews of northern France in particular. The increased activity of both Christians and Jews was apparently simultaneous, but as with the other factors, demonstrating actual influence is not easily done. Certainly, Jews and Christians interacted, but demonstrating that they explicitly discussed scripture is much harder to do. However, economic and business ties almost certainly led to cultural interchange.

The stand-out figure of the *Peshat School* is Solomon ben Isaac (Rashi, 1040–1105), whose commentary on the Bible continues to be the primary one studied by traditional Jews today. Rashi wrote commentaries on almost every book of the Bible (and most likely intended commentaries on all the books). Those attributed to him on Ezra–Nehemiah and Chronicles almost certainly are the work of other authors. Rashi nowhere provides a systematic description of his approach to scripture. On occasion, as in his comment on Genesis 3:8, he notes his intention to explain the text according to its *peshat* and that when necessary he will turn to midrash to clarify a lemma. Whether this should be understood as a general statement or something more limited has been regularly debated. Although Rashi is clearly concerned with *peshat*, he frequently cites midrash, sometimes offering a *peshat* and midrashic explanation together on a single lemma. Thus, his method for selecting when and what to cite from midrash remains obscure. Often these midrashic sources are rephrased or exclude parts of the original text, changing the meaning of the teaching in order to meet his needs.

Rashi had access to Ibn Saruq's *Mahberet*, but much of the Spanish Jewish grammar oeuvre was only available in Arabic. As a result, Rashi, although sensitive to the nuances of biblical language, could not frame his interpretations with the sophistication of his Spanish contemporaries. Rashi glosses more than 1000 biblical terms with Old French (and occasionally German and Slavonic), compares words to Mishnaic Hebrew usage, relies on the Aramaic Targums, sometimes refers to his contemporary circumstances and realia (his commentary on Psalms written after the Crusades of 1096 shows significant anti-Christian polemic), and uses the cantillation accents in the Masoretic text as a source of information about the meaning of the text.

Although Rashi set the tone for the next century of biblical exegesis in northern France, he was not the first concerned with these methods or with *peshat*. The early eleventh century saw a group of unidentified Jewish scholars, the *poterim*, teaching the Bible using the vernacular in northern France, and Rashi refers explicitly to them (e.g., Lev 14:14). By the mid-eleventh century Menahem bar Helbo had likely produced commentaries on the entirety of the Prophets and Hagiographa (only fragments remain). They show some of the same traits as Rashi (e.g, the use of Old French glosses, *peshat* comments, and citations of midrash). However, Helbo was more aware of the connection between Hebrew and Arabic. He had significant influence on later generations of northern French exegetes, particularly via his nephew Joseph Kara who may later have studied with Rashi.

The phenomenon of *Peshat* exegesis was almost entirely the product of the circle around Rashi and his students. His colleague Shemaiah (1060–1130) may have composed a biblical commentary, but only a manuscript of his glosses on Rashi's commentaries is extant. Like Rashi, he used midrashim to reinforce literary-contextual readings and was attentive to biblical realia (e.g., weights, measures, construction methods).

Whether Joseph Kara (1050–1125) was actually Rashi's student is unclear but they cite each other's work and likely knew one another. Rashi's grandson, Samuel ben Meir (1080–ca. 1160), identifies Kara as a colleague. Kara, who may have written commentaries on the entire Bible (fragments of his Torah commentary are preserved, as are commentaries on the Prophets, Psalms, Job, and the Five Scrolls), was more systematic in his *peshat* exegesis than Rashi. He sometimes used midrashic explanations, but precisely why is unclear. Although he relied on Rashi's commentary, often quoting him, he disputed his explanations. Kara used Old French and German to explain biblical words, compared biblical terms to similar ones found in Rabbinic Hebrew and Aramaic, relied on cantillation notes to aid exegesis, and suggested that information that seemed irrelevant in context could be necessary for understanding material later in the biblical narrative.

Samuel ben Meir (Rashbam, ca. 1085–ca. 1158), like Rashi his grandfather, was a biblical exegete and a prominent Talmudist and legal authority. Given that *peshat* exegesis could undermine rabbinic traditions, it is noteworthy that Rashbam was committed to the idea that the text operated simultaneously on two interpretive levels: the primary one being the rabbinic legal tradition, and the secondary one being literary-contextual. His own exegesis was devoted to the latter, and because he occasionally interpreted verses in opposition to rabbinic interpretations his defense of their complementary nature is important. Rashbam was likely the most ardent *peshat* exegete and was remarkably consistent in distinguishing between *peshat* and *derash*, even challenging Rashi's explanations when they disagreed with the former. According to Rashbam, he even did this in discussions with his grandfather (Rashbam to Gen 37:2). Rashbam's commentary might be seen as a commentary on Rashi; he offers interpretations when he disagrees with him but offers no comment when he is apparently in agreement. Despite his lack of knowledge of developments in biblical exegesis among Spanish Jews because of the Arabic disconnect, Rashbam's method with regard to grammar was the most highly developed of the northern French school, he even composed a work on the topic (*Sefer Dayekut.*) He was also remarkably sensitive to the rhetorical and literary aspects of the biblical text.

Eliezer of Beaugency (mid-twelfth c.), who wrote commentaries on most of the Bible (only commentaries to Isaiah and the Minor Prophets survive), may have been Rashbam's student, although this cannot be demonstrated conclusively. His commentaries contain very few references to midrash; he was especially focused on using context to explain terms, and many interpretations are offered as paraphrases rather than explicit comments. Rashbam's brother, Rabbenu (Jacob) Tam (1100–1171), and their pupil, Joseph Bekhor Shor (1130–1200), also wrote biblical commentaries. The former's on Job is preserved, as are the latter's on the Torah. In essence, Bekhor Shor was the last true member of the *peshat* school and his work evidences a return to midrashic concerns. Although his interpretations are literary-contextual (in contrast to his predecessors he knew the work of Hayyuj and ibn Janah, whom he identifies by name [e.g., former Deut 11:26; latter Gen 30:8]), midrashic comments are found throughout and he uses rabbinic numerology, which was by then returning to vogue. Bekhor Shor offered numerous interpretations revealing significant insight into the nature and character of biblical figures.

The Spanish School. In al-Andalus in the latter half of the eleventh century the two most important commentators were Moses ben Samuel Chiquitilla and Judah ben Samuel ibn Bal'am. The former's biblical commentaries have only survived in fragmentary form (he wrote on the Pentateuch, Isaiah, the Book of the Twelve, Psalms, Job, and Daniel). The influence of ibn Janah on him is apparent. He also translated Ibn Hayyuj's grammar works into Hebrew. Chiquitilla was a rationalist who attempted to demonstrate that biblical miracles did not deviate from the natural order and that many of the prophecies referred to events that had already happened rather than to things that would transpire in the messianic era.

Ibn Bal'am was a biblical commentator, halakic scholar, and Hebrew grammarian who lived in Toledo and then Seville. He wrote a complete Bible commentary in two parts: *Kitāb al-Tārjih* (The Book of Decision) on the Pentateuch, and *Nuqat al-Miqra* (Glosses to the Scripture) on the Prophets and

Hagiographa. Although much influenced by Ibn Janah, Ibn Bal'am was an independent thinker who actively disagreed with his forerunners. Some have suggested that he only offered a comment on a verse when he was explicitly challenging an earlier interpretation. Many of his comments are uniquely grammatical, although occasionally he commented on the subject matter of a particular Bible text (e.g., theology, history, philosophy, geography, the character of biblical figures). Digressions of this sort are more common in his Torah commentary. Ibn Bal'am described his method in his introduction to the commentary on the Prophets as explaining difficult words by translating them into Arabic, then comparing them to related words in the Bible, and then to Rabbinic Hebrew, Aramaic, and Arabic, and by studying syntax and morphology. He was also concerned with issues of *realia* and toponyms, frequently disagreeing with his predecessors' conclusions in these matters but not always providing alternative renderings.

The preeminent representative of the twelfth century Spanish School is Abraham ibn Ezra (1089–1164), who, although he lived in Spain for more than fifty years, spent his last twenty-five traveling in Italy, France, and England. Although Ibn Ezra is famed as a neo-platonic thinker, liturgical and secular poet, grammarian, and astrologer, he composed biblical commentaries on the Torah, Isaiah, the Book of the Twelve, Psalms, Job, the Five Scrolls, and Daniel. He did not begin these until after he left Spain. Once in Christian Europe, he was commissioned by patrons to compose commentaries, and for some biblical books (e.g., Exodus, Esther) he wrote two commentaries, one while in Rome and another once he arrived in France. As a result, long and short versions of some commentaries are extant.

Ibn Ezra was well read in the work of the Spanish grammarians, earlier Spanish exegetes, the Karaites, and Rashi. His approach was shaped primarily by his encounter with grammar and linguistics. Saadiah and the grammarians were his primary influences. He says little positive about Rashi noting that only one in one thousand of his comments provided a true *peshat* interpretation (*Safah Berurah* 5a). Ibn Ezra probably did not know of Rashi's works before reaching Italy. He delineates five types of exegesis in the introduction to his Torah commentary: (1) extensive commenting that treats issues of content and subject matter beyond the simple meaning of the words (as represented by the *Geonim*); (2) the Karaite approach, which rejects the authority of the rabbinic oral tradition; (3) allegorical interpretation (e.g., as promoted by Christian exegetes); (4) midrash, or fanciful interpretation (as practiced by the early rabbis in non-halakhic discourse); and, (5) grammatical exegesis. Of these five, he endorses only the last. In contrast to the northern French *peshat* commentators, he did not allow grammatical readings to contradict rabbinic legal traditions. In this he agreed with Saadiah, as he also did with respect to reason as the sole guide for the exegete. Ibn Ezra's *peshat* exegesis was concerned primarily with philology and grammar as compared to those in northern France who, given their lack of access to the Spanish grammarian's works, were more interested in the literary-contextual reading.

Traveling in the opposite direction, Isaac ben Samuel Al-Kanzi (1065–1140) went from Spain to Egypt (or was perhaps born there to a Spanish father). Although he composed a commentary on the Former Prophets, only parts of 1 and 2 Samuel and Kings survive. The commentaries are primarily an Arabic word-for-word translation inserted following Hebrew trigger words. Al-Kanzi cites all the major authorities including Saadiah, Hayyuj, ibn Janah, ibn Bal'am and Chiquitilla, as well as Karaites. He consistently explains passages as supporting halakhic tradition, but adheres to contextual readings otherwise. Al-Kanzi had three exegetical objectives: realistically reconstructing historical events, properly explaining character's motives, and expounding on ethical-religious behavior and the Divine reward.

Moses Maimonides, the *Guide for the Perplexed*, and Philosophical Exegesis. In approximately 1191, Moses ben Maimon (Maimonides; Rambam; 1138–1204) the Cordoba-born head of the Cairo Jewish community completed his philosophical work *The*

Guide for the Perplexed. Although composed in Arabic it was quickly translated into Hebrew (once by Samuel ibn Tibbon, and slightly later by Judah al-Harizi) and from the start attracted significant attention (not all of it positive). Maimonides never produced a systematic commentary on the Bible (although a work on Esther was incorrectly attributed to him), but there can be no doubt that he was an exegete and that the *Guide* is a biblical commentary, arranged by theme rather than by biblical book or verse. Maimonides produced the work for a specific student and those like him, who were religiously knowledgeable and committed to Jewish practice but who had studied the sciences and philosophy and were perplexed by apparent contradictions between the two bodies of knowledge. In an attempt to deal with these contradictions, Maimonides interpreted the Torah through a philosophical lens. In order to resolve the contradictions Maimonides accepted that the Torah communicated on multiple levels according to the intellectual ability of the reader. The simple-minded would read the narratives and laws as just that, while the philosophically-minded individual would see that these were parables intended to reveal philosophical (particularly Aristotelian) truths. Apparent contradictions between revelation and reason could be resolved by accepting the biblical language was deliberately equivocal and had been revealed by God to Moses, the greatest of the philosophers.

Maimonides laid out a method for biblical exegesis that triggered a short lived Middle Eastern school of interpreters. His influence on exegesis became far more significant elsewhere.

Joseph ben Judah ben Jacob ibn Aknin (ca. 1150–1220), whose family originated in Barcelona, took refuge in Fez during the Almohad invasions and may have met Maimonides there. His commentary on the Song of Songs *Inkishāf al-asrār wa-ṭuhūr al-anwār* ("The Divulgence of Mysteries and the Appearance of Lights") explains the text as an allegory of the cravings of the rational soul for the active intellect. Although ibn Aknin states that he was the first to read the biblical book in this way, his work appears to build on Maimonides's description in his *Mishneh Torah* (The Laws of Repentance 10:3) and the *Guide for the Perplexed* (3:51).

In Egypt, Maimonides's son Abraham (1186–1237) completed commentaries in Arabic on Genesis and Exodus. These were heavily influenced by Sufi mysticism and offer a diverse range of comments including grammatical and literary interpretations, rhetorical analysis, philosophical teachings, and pietistic lessons. He quotes from Saadiah and Samuel ben Hofni, as well as ibn Janah, Rashi, and ibn Ezra, among others, and draws richly from the writings of his father and grandfather.

The Jewish-Sufi circle that developed gave rise to several commentators, including Abu Sulayman Abraham ibn Abi r-Rabia he-Hasid (d. 1223), whose commentary on Song of Songs (preserved only in quotations in the writings of Abraham Maimonides) is an allegory of a dialogue between a mystical devotee and the Divine object of his desire. Hanan'el ben Samuel (1180–1250), who was Abraham Maimonides's father-in-law, is believed to have composed a commentary on the Torah and Haftarot. These are preserved in fragmentary form but reveal that he used an allegorical method of interpretation that offered a mystical-philosophical reading of the text influenced by Moses Maimonides and Sufi thought. The last significant exegete in this tradition was Tanhum ben Joseph Yerushalmi (1220–1291), who died in Egypt although he was from the land of Israel. Though not an original thinker, he was a remarkably successful anthologizer of the work of the great masters of Spanish, North African, French and Karaite traditions. He was influenced by Maimonides and Sufism and composed an Arabic commentary on the whole Bible (only parts of the Former and Latter Prophets, the Five Scrolls, Daniel, and Psalms are preserved) that was primarily concerned with grammatical and rhetorical analysis but also uses philosophical and mystical allegory.

From Muslim Spain to Christian Europe: The Provençal School. Around 1150 Joseph Kimhi (1105–1170) left Spain with his eldest son Moses (1127–1190) for Narbonne in Provence, where another son David was born (1160–1235). By the time of his arrival, Provencal Jewry focused on the midrashic approach to Bible, and because of the absence of Arabic literacy continued to rely on outdated scholarship on grammar. Joseph composed commentaries on the Pentateuch, Prophets, Proverbs, and Job (only the last two are extant). In addition, he wrote a Hebrew work on grammar that challenged the theories of Ibn Saruq and others on whom the earlier *peshat* exegetes had relied. As might be expected, Joseph was guided by reason in his exegesis and made clear that commentary without proper grammatical understanding could not be *peshat*. To explain the biblical text he used comparisons with rabbinic Hebrew, Aramaic, and Arabic as well as knowledge of poetry and poetic formulations, and he explicitly challenged midrashic traditions. In so doing, he set the groundwork for a shift in Provençal exegesis that was reinforced by his sons.

Moses Kimhi composed commentaries on Proverbs, Job, and Ezra–Nehemiah. He is almost uniquely concerned with issues of grammar and philology, likely a response to the Provencal scholars' preference for midrash. Although his commentaries do address some historical and philosophical concerns, his primary commitments are clear, especially with regard to the workings of Hebrew syntax.

David Kimhi (Radak) lost his father when only ten years old and was primarily educated by his brother. Of the members of his family, he gained the most renown, particularly for his biblical commentaries (Genesis, Former and Latter Prophets, Psalms, Proverbs, and Chronicles), a grammar (*Sefer Mikhlol*), and a dictionary (*Sefer Shorashim*). Although steeped in the knowledge of grammar and philology, Radak (unlike his brother) also studied the rabbinic Talmudic-Midrashic tradition. He was influenced significantly by the rationalism of ibn Ezra and Maimonides. For example, his commentaries include philosophical insights on issues of providence, miracles, and prophecy. He is clear to distinguish between *peshat* and *derash*, but both are a significant presence in his works. Although some of his discussion blatantly dismisses the value of midrash as merely homiletical, he was influenced by its creativity and synthesized it in his own approach (e.g., reading passages as if prophetically referring to the events of his day), thus setting a new trend that differed from the Spanish legacy of his father and brother and from the Provençal milieu in which he was raised and educated.

Nahmanides and Mystical Exegesis. Nahmanides (1194–1270) was born in Gerona in Christian Spain. A rabbi and scholar, he made contributions to philosophy, mysticism, biblical commentary, and poetry. Although he earned his living as a medical doctor he was among the leading Talmud commentators of the Middle Ages. He was born into the Jewish intellectual and economic elite and was the descendant of significant scholars and a relative of high status officials in the community of Gerona. Early in life he studied Talmud with the method of the Tosafists of northern France along with those current in Provence. During the Maimonidean controversy (which began in France in 1232) Nahmanides attempted to act as mediator between the two camps despite the fact that he disagreed with the radical philosophizing that had developed as a result of Maimonides's work. So great was his reputation that in 1263 he was drawn into a public dispute with the apostate Pablo Christiani by King James I. Although he was victorious in the dispute, after the publication of the contents he was ultimately forced to leave Spain. He fled to the Land of Israel, arriving at Acre in 1267.

Nahmanides wrote commentaries on the Torah and the book of Job (believing all to be "authored" by Moses). These appear to have been written later in his life and although he began composing them in Spain he continued them after fleeing to Israel. As a product of Christian Spain, he was an heir to the exegetical traditions of al-Andalus and the traditions of Ashkenaz (France and Germany). His commentaries frequently cite rabbinic material, and Nahmanides devoted significant space to analyzing midrash and its relation to the biblical text. For Nahmanides the Bible operates on a number of levels. It is both a record of the past and a sign of things to come. Nahmanides often quotes earlier exegetes, including Rashi (whom he especially esteems), Ibn Ezra, Saadiah, and Maimonides, and frequently challenges their respective interpretations. Nahmanides was learned in grammar and was concerned with the literary structure of biblical narratives. He also uses typological reading, a method generally rejected by Jews because of its use by Christians, and sees the events of later Israelite history foreshadowed in the actions of the patriarchs. Perhaps most significantly, Nahmanides was among the earliest commentators who applied kabbalistic methods to interpret the text. This is especially noticeable in the introduction to his Torah commentary, where he describes the entire Torah text as the Names of God. The text can be subdivided into these names rather than the words of the narrative. Nahmanides was committed to the notion of what has come to be called "omnisignificance," (i.e., even the slightest of details of the biblical text were deliberate and must be appropriately interpreted). For Nahmanides the Torah texts contains hidden secrets (*sod*) that have been transmitted from teacher to student since antiquity; that is, the Bible as a whole has both an exoteric and an esoteric meaning. These secret interpretations do not trump the contextual readings but complement them, the text being able to sustain multiple interpretations simultaneously. A commentary on Song of Songs was attributed to him, although it was the work of fellow Geronese exegete and mystic Ezra ben Solomon (d. 1238 or 1245). If anything, this demonstrates the growth of Nahmanides's reputation and the productivity of mystical exegetes in this period.

In the Torah commentary of Nahmanides's student Bahya ben Asher (Saragossa, d. 1340), the idea appropriated from Christian circles of a fourfold interpretation of scripture in which all were correct exegesis at once was given the name *Pardes.* Although *pardes* was a real word originally meaning orchard, in this context it is an acronym for the exegetical approaches: *Peshat* (the contextual reading), *Remez* (philosophical or typological allegory), *Derash* (midrashic tradition), and *Sod* (mystical teachings). Bahya rarely applies all four methods to any one verse and this is true generally of the exegetes to follow. Most used one, two, or three methods in combination.

The most significant work of medieval exegesis, the *Zohar* (Book of Radiance or Splendor), is more accurately described as a mystical "midrash" on the Torah using the frame story of the relationship between the second century sage Simeon bar Yochai and his students. Although its composition was begun in the circle of Moses de Leon in Castile in the mid-thirteenth century, it did not take on its form and organization until the rise of printing. For much of its history it was attributed to Simeon and treated as ancient sacred wisdom. Its composition in Aramaic gave it the appearance of age, but a close study of the language reveals many late elements that are inconsistent with rabbinic period Palestinian Aramaic. Kabbalistic exegesis relies on decoding the biblical text as an allegory about the interaction of the *sefirot* (the ten emanations of God). The *Zohar*'s influence can be seen in the Torah commentary of Menachem Recanati (1250–1310) where it is cited explicitly (although only the then available sections).

The Maimonidean Exegetical Tradition in Europe. Despite anti-Maimonidean concerns among French and Spanish rabbis and even the banning of the study of philosophy by those under twenty-five by Solomon ibn Adret of Barcelona in mid-1306, biblical commentaries shaped by Maimonides's philosophy were composed in significant numbers during the thirteenth to fifteenth centuries in Provence, Spain, and Italy. In Provence three important figures were Joseph ibn Kaspi (1279–1331), Nissim ben Moses of Marseilles (works composed in the 1320s), and Levi ben Gershom (Ralbag, Gersonides, 1288–1344). Others include Samuel ibn Tibbon (1165–1232), who translated the *Guide* into Hebrew, composed a Maimonidean-type commentary on Ecclesiastes, and a philosophical-exegetical treatise *Ma'amar Yiqqawu ha-Mayim* (*Let the waters be gathered* [Gen 1:9]) in which he includes extensive philosophical discussion of Genesis, Isaiah, Ezekiel, Job, and the Book of Psalms, and Abba Mari ben Eligdor (fourteenth c.), whose commentary on Job relies heavily on Maimonides.

Joseph ibn Kaspi was a grammarian, philosopher, and biblical exegete. So committed was he to the study of Maimonides's philosophy that he traveled to Egypt to study with his grandchildren and then to Fez where the *Guide* was studied in Muslim philosophical schools. Ibn Kaspi wrote on the works of Abraham ibn Ezra and Maimonides, in addition to commentaries on the Torah (modeled on Rashi and Ibn Ezra), the Prophets, Proverbs, Job, Song of Songs, Ruth, Lamentations, Ecclesiastes, and Ezra–Nehemiah. The commentaries focused on *peshat* exegesis (with regard to grammar he was especially influenced by Ibn Janah), but also contain philosophical explanations. In the case of Job his commentary is devoted to challenging Maimonides's interpretation as offered in the *Guide* 3:22–23. In general, Ibn Kaspi agreed with Maimonides that a *peshat* meaning of a verse was true while it simultaneously had an esoteric philosophical meaning. However, in contrast to Maimonides, who described supernatural events in the Bible as sometimes taking place in a character's prophetic vision, he asserted that they really happened as the *peshat* of a narrative described.

Nissim ben Moses of Marseilles composed a commentary on the Torah (*Ma'aseh Nissim*) primarily concerned with providing naturalistic explanations for all supernatural and miraculous depictions of events. Miracles could be explained by the superior intellectual or prophetic ability of the prophet, or by the fact that events took place in a vision. In this respect he was significantly influenced by Maimonides. The commentary shows a thorough knowledge of rabbinic sources and Abraham ibn Ezra.

Levi ben Gershom was a polymath who composed significant works on Talmud and Jewish law, philosophy and logic, astronomy, and mathematics. He wrote commentaries on the Torah, Former Prophets, the Five Scrolls, Proverbs, and Job. In organizing his commentaries, Gersonides divided the text into sections, first offering an explanation of key words according to the rules of grammar and available lexical knowledge, then a paraphrase of the text including more extensive explanatory glosses, and finally a collection of ethical-moral and philosophical lessons. For Gersonides, who was very much influenced by Maimonides, the Torah is a book of both revelation and philosophy. It functions to direct the learned reader to philosophical and moral perfection. In contrast to Maimonides, who saw philosophical lessons hidden in the biblical text, Gersonides held that the philosophical meaning of a passage is its *peshat*, and he revealed philosophical explanations that Maimonides kept hidden in his *Guide*.

In Spain, the Maimonidean tradition was perpetuated by scholars like Isaac Arundi (fourteenth c.). He likely originated from Ronda, Spain, and lived in Italy and perhaps Provence. His commentary on the book of Job is extant and was clearly influenced by Maimonides and Gersonides although it also contains quotations from the rabbis, Plato, Aristotle, and Averroes.

In Italy, Immanuel of Rome (1261–1335) composed commentaries on the entire Bible. Those extant include all or parts of the commentaries on the Torah, Habbakuk, Psalms, Proverbs, Job, Song of Songs, Ruth, Lamentations, and Esther. By his own description Immanuel culled the "pearls of wisdom" from other sages, dividing his comments up according to grammar, *peshat* interpretations, his original interpretations, and the hidden and allegorical meanings. The last often includes material from Maimonides's *Guide* and from his halakic work, *Mishneh Torah*. In the commentary on Job, Immanuel is explicit in stating that his work is based on Maimonides, and he may be the first to have written a verse-by-verse commentary on Job in the Maimonidean vein.

Conclusion. By the late fourteenth and early fifteenth centuries the major trends in Jewish biblical exegesis had been established. What followed were commentaries that synthesized these various perspectives and that were largely in conversation with the previous sages, especially Rashi, ibn Ezra, Maimonides, and Nahmanides. New developments were in certain ways a return to older styles, e.g., the anthologizing of midrash and homiletical exegesis. Later generations could not escape the influence of the methodologies established by the *peshat*, philosophical, and mystical exegetes who had preceded them. This was reinforced in the early sixteenth century with the printings of *Biblia Rabbinica* (*Miqraot Gedolot*) in Venice in 1517 and 1524–1525. These printed Hebrew Bibles typically included on the page the biblical text, an Aramaic Targum, and in the earlier edition one and occasionally two medieval biblical commentaries, with many more per page in the second edition. The most frequently included commentaries were those of Rashi, Ibn Ezra, Radak, Nahmanides, and Gersonides. Of particular importance is that for all the rabbinic Bibles produced until 1619 the only commentators included were those who lived between the eleventh and fourteenth centuries. In so doing, the act of printing created a canon, or at least reinforced the importance of particular commentators. This influenced the methods and approaches of future biblical exegetes who began with this recognized stable of commentaries. Simultaneously, the inclusion of multiple commentaries on a single page showed the dialogic and varied nature of Jewish biblical commentary in the Middle Ages.

[*See also* Midrash; Orthodox Jewish Interpretation; Qur'anic and Islamic Interpretation of the Bible; Reconstructionist Interpretation; *and* Reform Jewish Interpretation.]

BIBLIOGRAPHY

Berlin, Adele. *Biblical Poetry through Medieval Jewish Eyes*. Bloomington: Indiana University Press, 1991. A study of Jewish exegesis of biblical poetry as a window on scholars' knowledge and application of grammar, linguistics, and literary analysis.

Berlin, Adele, and Marc Z. Brettler, eds. *The Jewish Study Bible*, Oxford: Oxford University Press, 2004. The Jewish Publication Society translation and commentary on each biblical book, with fifteen essays on the place of the Bible in Jewish life and thought. Those by Barry D. Walfish ("Medieval Jewish Interpretation," 1876–1900), Hava Tirosh-Samuelson ("The Bible in the Jewish Philosophical Tradition," 1948–1976), and the editors and Elliot Wolfson ("The Bible in the Jewish Mystical Tradition," 1976–1990) provide an excellent survey of medieval Jewish exegesis along with extended overviews of individual scholars and examples from their works.

Carasik, Michael. *The Commentators' Bible: The JPS Miqra'ot Gedolot*. Philadelphia: Jewish Publication Society, 2005–ongoing. The first major attempt by a single author to translate major medieval commentaries on the Torah in the style of the *Biblia Rabbinica*. It includes translations of Rashi, Rashbam, Ibn Ezra, and Nahmanides, along with selections from others. The translation excludes comments made redundant by the translation, the repetition of one exegete cited in another's commentary, and occasionally condenses long comments. It successfully provides an experience akin to reading the Hebrew original, but the individual commentaries have been translated by others (e.g., Martin Lockshin's translations of Rashbam on Torah).

Cohen, Menachem. *Mikraot Gedolot Ha-Keter* (Hebrew). Ramat Gan, Israel: Bar-Ilan University Press, 2000–ongoing. The preliminary results of an effort to produce a Rabbinic Bible with accurate texts of the commentaries. Currently available are volumes on Genesis, Exodus, Numbers, Deuteronomy Joshua, Judges, 1–2 Samuel, 1–2 Kings, Ezekiel, Isaiah, Jeremiah, the Minor Prophets, the Five Scrolls, and Psalms.

Cohen, Mordechai Z. "Biblical Exegesis: Rabbanite." In *Encyclopedia of Jews in the Islamic World* edited by Norman Stillman, et al. Vol. 1, 442–457. Leiden, the Netherlands: Brill, 2010. The most up-to-date survey of Jewish exegesis by rabbinic Jews in North Africa, the Middle East, and Muslim Spain by an author engaged in cutting-edge work on the influence of Islamic scholarship on Jewish intellectual enterprises. Includes many articles on individual exegetes.

Cohen, Mordechai Z. *Three Approaches to Biblical Metaphor: From Abraham Ibn Ezra and Maimonides to David Kimhi*. Leiden, the Netherlands: E. J. Brill, 2003. Explores the hermeneutical methodology used by three major exegetes to reconcile the literary contextual meaning of the biblical text with reason (i.e., when should a text be taken literally and when should it be read as metaphorical?). An essential text for understanding Jewish philosophical exegesis.

Eisen, Robert. *The Book of Job in Medieval Jewish Philosophy*. Oxford: Oxford University Press, 2004. A case study of medieval Jewish philosophical exegesis on Job, especially as practiced by Maimonideans. Includes discussion of Saadiah, Maimonides, Samuel Ibn Tibbon, Gersonides, Immanuel of Rome, and others.

Frank, Daniel. *Search Scripture Well: Karaite Exegetes and the Origins of the Jewish Bible Commentary in the Islamic East*. Leiden, the Netherlands: Brill, 2004. A recent study of Karaite exegesis and the origins of the single author verse-by-verse biblical commentary by Jews.

Frank, Daniel. "Biblical Exegesis: Karaite." In *Encyclopedia of Jews in the Islamic World* edited by Norman

Stillman, et al. Vol. 1, 457–461. Leiden, the Netherlands: Brill, 2010. A survey of key developments in Karaite exegesis in the Middle Ages based on the most current research.

Grossman, Avraham. *The Early Sages of France: Their Lives, Leadership and Work* (Hebrew). Jerusalem: Magnes, 1996. An intellectual biography of the major exegetes in the *peshat* school by the premier scholar of the field.

Harris, Robert A. "Biblical Interpretation, Medieval French." In *Encyclopaedia of Judaism* edited by Jacob Neusner, Alan J. Avery-Peck, and William Scott Green. 2d ed. Vol. 1, 234–251. Leiden, the Netherlands: Brill, 2005. An extremely thorough survey of Jewish exegesis in medieval France, including descriptions of a number of exegetes who made more modest contributions.

Harris, Robert A. *Discerning Parallelism: A Study in Northern French Medieval Jewish Biblical Exegesis.* Providence, R.I.: Brown University, 2004. Presents the literary sense of the *Peshat* school of exegetes by exploring its members' analysis of the phenomenon of biblical parallelism.

Harris, Robert A. "Medieval Jewish Biblical Exegesis." In *A History of Biblical Interpretation: The Medieval through the Reformation Periods*, edited by Alan J. Hauser and Duane F. Watson, 141–171. Grand Rapids, Mich.: Eerdmans, 2009. An effective overview with a focus on Rashi and Rashbam, Abraham ibn Ezra, Radak, Ramban, Ralbag, and Isaac Abarbanel. Includes examples from their commentaries.

Kalman, Jason. "Medieval Jewish Commentaries and the State of Parshanut Studies" Religion Compass 2, no. 5 (2008): 819–843, http://onlinelibrary.wiley.com/doi/10.1111/j.1749-8171.2008.00099.x/full (accessed January 9, 2012). A survey of the major trends in the study of medieval biblical exegesis, current debates and disputes, and bibliographic references to the best available editions of many medieval commentators and European language translations thereof.

Katznellenbogen, Mordechai Leib, ed. *Torat Haim* (Hebrew). Jerusalem: Mossad Ha-Rav Kook, 1986–ongoing. Mossad Ha-Rav Kook has for almost fifty years been a premier publisher of quality editions of medieval commentaries. This Rabbinic Bible reproduces many of them without the editorial comments and textual variants found in the original editions. Included are brief but helpful notes on each commentary. Currently available are volumes on the Torah and the Five Scrolls.

Howard Kreisel. "Philosophical Interpretations of the Bible" in *The Cambridge History of Jewish Philosophy*, edited by Steven Nadler and Tamar M. Rudavsky, 88–120. Cambridge, UK: Cambridge University Press, 2009. A survey of Jewish philosophical exegesis from Saadiah through Maimonides, into Provence and the Renaissance, concluding with Spinoza. It is especially important for its treatment of Nissim of Marseille who otherwise is rarely discussed.

Levine, Michelle J. *Nahmanides on Genesis: The Art of Biblical Portraiture.* Providence, R.I.: Brown University, 2009. A treatment of Nahmanides's exegesis and knowledge of biblical poetics. Explores the influence of other commentators on his commentary on Genesis and more generally.

Levy, B. Barry. 1991 "Rabbinic Bibles, *Mikra'ot Gedolot*, and Other Great Books," *Tradition* 25 (1991): 65–81. An overview of the development of *Biblia Rabbinica*, along with descriptions of their contents and discussion of the commentators included in various editions.

Polliack, Meira. *The Karaite Tradition of Arabic Bible Translation.* Leiden, the Netherlands: Brill, 1997. A study of Torah translation and exegetical concerns of Karaties in tenth and eleventh century Jerusalem with significant comparisons to the translation of Saadiah.

Polliack, Meira. "Major Trends in Karaite Biblical Exegesis in the Tenth and Eleventh Centuries." In *Karaite Judaism: A Guide to its History and Literary Sources*, edited by Meira Polliack, 363–413. Leiden, the Netherlands: Brill, 2003. A thorough survey of the exegetical methods of the major Karaite exegetes.

Saebø, Magnes, ed. *Hebrew Bible/Old Testament, Vol. 1, pt. 1, From the Beginnings to the Middle Ages: Antiquity.* Göttingen, Germany: Vandenhoeck & Ruprecht, 1996.

Saebø, Magnes, ed. *Hebrew Bible/Old Testament, Vol. 1, pt. 2, From the Beginnings to the Middle Ages: The Middle Ages.* Göttingen, Germany: Vandenhoeck & Ruprecht, 2000.

Saebø, Magnes, ed. *Hebrew Bible/Old Testament, Vol. 2, From the Enlightenment to the Renaissance.* Göttingen, Germany: Vandenhoeck & Ruprecht, 2008. Collectively these volumes (along with a forthcoming one) survey Jewish and Christian Interpretation from antiquity to modernity. Vol. 1, pt. 2 is devoted to the Middle Ages and includes many articles written by an international group of the best scholars on each individual exegete or interpretive trend. It is the finest available material on Jewish biblical exegesis in one place and includes important English articles by scholars who primarily publish in Hebrew (e.g., Avraham Grossman on *Peshat* in France).

Signer, Michael. "Bible, Jewish Interpretation of." In *Medieval France: An Encyclopedia*, edited by William Kibler and Grover Zinn, et al., 123–126. Oxford: Routledge, 1995. A survey of medieval Jewish exegesis in France. Signer is effective here, as in his other works, in comparing Jewish interpretation to the practices of contemporary Christian scholars.

Simon, Uriel. *Four Approaches to the Book of Psalms.* Albany: State University of New York Press, 1991. A comparison of the approaches of Saadiah, the Karaites Solomon ben Yeruham and Yefet ben Eli, Moses Chiquitilla, and Abraham ibn Ezra. By comparing their views of the same texts the similarities, differences, and influences are highlighted.

Targarona, Judit. "Biblical Exegesis: In al-Andalus." In *Encyclopedia of Jews in the Islamic World,* edited by Norman Stillman, et al. Vol. 1, 461–462. Leiden, the Netherlands: Brill, 2010. A brief overview of the major developments and primary exegetes in Muslim Spain.

Walfish, Barry D. *Esther in Medieval Garb: Jewish Interpretation of the Book of Esther in the Middle Ages.* Albany: State University of New York Press, 1993. A survey of all the medieval Jewish commentators on Esther, along with biographical information and descriptions of their exegetical methods.

Jason Kalman

RACE, ETHNICITY, AND BIBLICAL CRITICISM

Ethnicity and race are important modes of group social organization that draw on various elements, including a sense of common origin and destiny, religion, language, homeland, or customs. Groups emerge and reemerge at different periods and are able to adapt their mode of organization as a response to changes in the environment, which can include migrations, responses to warfare, and other intergroup conflict. While ethnicity has been an important mode of human organization and socialization from the early third millennium B.C.E. to today, the vast majority of scholars maintain that race is a wholly modern phenomenon arising during the European Age of Discovery in the sixteenth to seventeenth centuries. It was during this period of conquest and colonization that the early modern light-skinned peoples from Europe encountered the dark-skinned peoples of Africa.

Theorizing Ethnicity and Race. In the late 1960s, Fredrik Barth's work in ethnic studies broke new ground by proposing that ethnic groups are organized by variable and socially defined ethnic boundaries and not strictly through shared culture, as was most often assumed. Subsequently, scholars began to focus their analysis on the construction and maintenance of ethnic boundaries with greater attention to the external and internal forces that influence the shape, durability, and permeability of group boundaries as well as the nature of the relationships between majority and minority groups.

Though ethnic studies focused first on culture and later on boundaries, race, on the other hand, was most often associated with skin color in the nineteenth to twentieth centuries. The earliest discussions about race included commentary about other physical characteristics in defining racial difference, among them cranial capacity and phrenological mapping, measurement of facial angles and forearm lengths, analysis of the position of the navel, configuration of the ear, as well as differences in eye and hair color (Kidd). In recent decades, however, biologists and geneticists have dismantled all of these earlier suggestions, insofar as mappings of genetic difference conclusively show more variation within socially constructed racial or ethnic populations than they do between one population and another. Indeed, consistent with archaeological evidence that suggests that modern humans originated in Africa, scientists note that there is more genetic variation in that continent than in the rest of the planet put together, facts that demolish the notions of blood purity at the center of most constructions of race in contemporary society.

The most important component of racialized group identity is the permanent nature of phenotype as a marker of identity, and the generally negative mental, moral, and personality characteristics that accompany modern constructions. The earliest English uses of the word "race" occur in sixteenth to eighteenth century discourse about cultural character that tether the temperament of a people to their national origin. The negative epithets from this period about so-called inferior peoples, like the Irish or Teutons or Jews, would soon be applied to the blacks and Natives in the American context. Thus, race rhetoric in the modern period was saturated with beliefs about the ingrained psychological characteristics of groups. Though many view ethnicity as an ascribed characteristic based on physical descent, it is often still possible to change ethnicity through intermarriage, assimilation, conversion, or even concealment. Such change is of course impossible when skin color or facial features identify group membership, as in the case of race. When these physical characteristics hinder acquisition of vitally needed resources, the permanence of race has catastrophic social and economic repercussions.

There is considerable debate about the difference between the concepts of race and ethnicity. Some maintain that race is entirely different from ethnicity, while others hold that ethnicity is an ancient, perennial, and primordial characteristic of human society, viewing race as a subset of ethnic identification. This debate is responsible, no doubt, for the frustrating theoretical overlap between the ideas of race and ethnicity. Much of the problem stems from the fact that in the pre-modern period and stretching into the eighteenth and nineteenth centuries, "race," "nation," and "ethnic group" were synonyms that referred to groups of people who held a belief in a common origin and/or heritage. If some theorists now emphasize the territorial components of common origin while others stress kinship and common ancestry, the emphasis on common descent constitutes the most pervasive definition of ethnic identity in the most recent discussions. Though some maintain that race is a stigmatized identity that is a subset of ethnicity and others insist that race is wholly imposed, all agree that the two are socially constructed without a basis in biological fact. Indeed, the social construction of race and ethnicity leaves room for the idea that either set of theorists may be right in a given time period, perspectival posture, or social context. The discursive ambiguities in theorizing difference over time has given rise to use of the term "ethnoracial" as a way of pointing to the shifting definitions of these socially constructed concepts (Buell).

The rejection of essentialized subjects most characterizes contemporary scholarship in ethnic and racial studies. Theorists see essentialism as the act of violently imputing a fundamental, basic, and necessary constitutive quality to a person or group, or enumerating characteristics that are assumed to define the essence, boundaries, or nature of the group in question (Werbner). The key word in this definition of essentialism is "violent" and points to the difference between imposed vs. independent determinations of identity. There is a clear difference between a minority group's own description of itself and the violent imposition of group characteristics and boundaries by powerful outsiders who want to maintain the status quo. Postmodern studies of identity are thus hostile to the kinds of rigid, biologically-based notions of shared origin or common descent found in modern conceptions of race.

This rejection of rigid categories of group identity gives rise to two other trends in research on ethnicity and race: a priority on hearing the voices of the oppressed, and attention to the fluidity and complexity of group identification processes. The emphasis on retrieving the previously muted voices of the oppressed seeks to reverse one of the most tragic results of the modern era—the silencing of categorized and stigmatized population groups who previously only existed as written about, and pressed into assimilation. The proliferation of hermeneutical strategies that focus on these marginalized voices in biblical studies is the most visible and important payoff of interdisciplinary work in ethnic and racial studies and biblical criticism.

The second consequence of scholarship that minimizes essentialism is an emphasis on fluidity and hybridity, which theoretically offers resistance by highlighting the implicit and explicit boundary crossings associated with mixed identities. This resistance is perhaps most visible in the demands that led to the inclusion of a multiracial category in the US census data and elsewhere. Yet even this improvement may subtly contribute to reifying existing hierarchies. On the one hand, the new multiracial category does deconstruct rigid racial categories, but on the other hand, the new category simply functions as a "non-black" placeholder that does nothing to destabilize the fictional notion of a "pure" whiteness at the top of the racial hierarchy.

In other words, as a theoretical construct the notion of hybridity challenges the status quo only to the degree that it problematizes any conception of purity—be it racial, ethnic, or national. An emphasis on hybridity must interrogate the social structures that continue to operate to maintain inequalities, recognizing that culture, ethnicity, and race continue to be utilized as political resources.

Thus, we may define an ethnoracial community as one that believes it shares a common descent, place of origin, and a common destiny, as well as a common set of values, practices, or personal traits, which may include emotional, mental, or moral characteristics. An ethnoracial group is one that believes that its traits or characteristics are transmitted within the self-defined boundaries of the group, through either descent or culture. This definition acknowledges that kinship is an important and crucial element of ethnicity in multiple social and historical contexts. Yet further, this definition acknowledges that values or personal characteristics play a significant and sometimes determinative role in constructions of group identity across history.

Ethnicity and Race in the Biblical Period. One frequently encounters the claim that ethnicity and race did not exist in antiquity, whether articulated as an observation about the lack of a word that corresponds to the modern concept of ethnicity or encountered in the assertion that race is a wholly modern invention. However, ancient texts reflect a confluence of ideas similar to those associated with the modern idea of ethnicity, despite the fact that the ancients lacked a particular word, as is the case with the related ideas of culture, class, or even gender (Hall, *Hellenicity*). Consider, for example, evidence of a Greek ethnic consciousness as revealed in a passage from the fifth-century B.C.E. historian Herodotus, who comments on Athenian resistance to the Persians in the War of 480–479 B.C.E:

> There are many important reasons that would prevent us from doing this [i.e., surrender] even if we wanted. First and foremost, there are the statues and temples of gods that have been sacked and destroyed; it is necessary for us to avenge these with all our might rather than come to an agreement with the man who did this. In addition, there is the matter of the Greek nature (*to Hellenikon*)—that is, our common blood (*homaimon*), common tongue (*homoglosson*), common shrines and altars (*theōn hidrymata te koina kai thysiai*) and similar customs and habits (*hēthea te homotropa*); it would not be good for the Athenians to betray these things. (Herodotus, *History* 8.144, my translation)

The word "ethnicity" does not appear in this selection, but the passage has several features associated with it, including religion, common blood, language, ways of life, and even "national character" (also see Dionysius, *Roman Antiquities* 1.29–30).

Ethnicity is communicated over time through particular conventions that shape the experience of a people, conventions residing in myths, memories, values, and symbols. Premodern ethnic groups are populations with common ancestry and a set of common myths, histories, and culture. They are named communities who have a sense of group solidarity and an association with a particular homeland (Smith, pp. 22–32). Though most ancient peoples were largely unaware of their cultural distinctiveness—or at best, an ethnic sentiment only resided among the elites—ancient Israelites/Second Temple Jews are perhaps the parade example of the persistence of ethnic sentiment. In the biblical material this people had well-preserved and well-known narratives of common descent and shared history. The stories about origins were reinforced by the distinctive culture promoted in the materials, and were supplemented by narratives of group conflict in the tradition. Given that conflict is perhaps the most effective stimulus of ethnic sentiment, narratives about Egyptian slavery and the conquest of Canaan, defeat by a succession of ancient near-eastern empires, the Hasmonean revolt, and the wars with Rome all served to build and sustain Jewish ethnic sentiment. Even if the intensity of ethnic sentiment waxed and waned, we have evidence in the historical record for a strong sense of group solidarity that likely transcended social and class divisions in Jewish society throughout much of the biblical period.

With respect to the question of whether race exists in antiquity, it should be noted at the start that even though translators commonly render the Greek word *genos* with the English "race," the ancient concept had little to do with skin color or physical appearance. Generally lacking color prejudice against dark-skinned people like that which accompanies modern racism, images and portrayals of blacks in classical antiquity bear little of the pejorative and negative associations of Enlightenment-era color prejudice against dark skin (Snowden). Similarly, the biblical authors do not make use of the modern racial categories that associate blackness or other physical characteristics with pejorative psychosocial traits. In the Hebrew Bible, for example, Ethiopians (Cush) are not depicted as racially inferior, beyond the presence of an Israelite ethnocentric bias that values many other peoples less than their own (Sadler). It is true, however, that early Christians were deeply conscious of difference, and engaged in rhetorical othering of blacks/blackness, Egypt/Egyptians, and Ethiopia/Ethiopians in negative and sometimes positive ways, building and reinforcing their own boundaries and symbols of Christian virtue by defining themselves over and against the Egyptian and Ethiopian other (Byron). These observations are important in tracing the evolution of modern color consciousness, but we should note the direction of these conclusions, that they implicitly assume the connection between color and race found in modernity and do not interrogate ancient constructions of race on their own terms.

If racism is the ideology which assigns negative psychosocial traits to certain permanent physical features and is thus a key component of the modern idea of race, then it is possible that there are analogous processes in antiquity that correspond to modern ethnoracial dynamics even in the absence of color prejudice in those societies. In fact, the climatological determinism in classical literature does appear to correlate with the "scientific" racism of the seventeenth and eighteenth centuries. Classical texts show that the ancients combined geographic determinism with the belief that progeny inherit acquired traits as well as physical ones from their parents (Isaac 2004). For example, climatological determinism would hold that a people living in a temperate climate have agreeable natures, while hostile climates produce warlike peoples (e.g., Strabo, *Geography*, 2.5.26). If a racial group is a group of people who are believed to share imagined physical, mental, or moral characteristics that are entirely determined by unchangeable factors, then the ancients exhibit "proto-racism" when they assume that personal characteristics come from an association with the geography of their birthplace and the climate associated with that territory (Isaac 2004).

By understanding racism via the key element of determinism, we are able to correlate determinism in antiquity as ideologically analogous to the racialist determinism of modernity, despite the fact that the former uses geography and climate as a focal point while the latter revolves around biology. Thus, racism occurs when a group is the object of imagined attributed characteristics determined by immutable forces. This transhistorical framework for race and racism thus accommodates the definition of the "Jewish race" in Nazi Germany as well as the situation in contemporary American society in which blacks and other people of color are racialized vis-à-vis whites. Though the mechanisms of determinism vary by epoch, the similarities in the intergroup identity processes are nevertheless clearly discernible.

Turning, then, to a consideration of what ancients meant when they identified themselves as a *genos* (race, people, clan) or an *ethnos* (nation, people, gentile), we cannot provide an exhaustive description of these concepts given the difficulties in defining ethnicity and race in the modern period and the fragmentary nature of the historical data. We can note, however, the nature of the ancient usage in the texts in which the words appear. *Ethnos* appeared in a broad variety of contexts in antiquity, some going well beyond what we mean by "ethnicity" or "ethnic group," the words most closely aligned etymologically with the Greek word. The word describes swarms of bees and flies and flocks of birds in Homer's *Illiad* in the eighth century B.C.E. (*Iliad* 2.87; 2.469; 2.459), elsewhere referring to warriors, the dead, and groups of young men (*Iliad* 2.92; 3.33; *Odyssey* 10.526). Romans in the empire would use *ethnos* for the provinces outside Italy (Appian, *Civil Wars* 2.13). The word *ethnos* was sometimes a virtual synonym for *barbarous* (barbarian) and used to designate other in a way analogous to Jewish and Christian denigration of non-Jews, and reminiscent of the modern use of "tribe" to designate primitive groups who are deficient in civilization (Aristotle, *Politics* 1324.b.10; cf. 3 Macc. 6.9 and Gal 2:15).

The Greek words *genos* and *ethnos* often functioned as synonyms in antiquity much as the analogous terms race and ethnicity do in contemporary thought (1 Pet 2:9; Jer 38:35–37; Diodorus, *Library of History* 2.46.4). Nevertheless, analysis reveals differences in usage: later second temple Greek writers who are neither Jewish nor Christian construct ethnic identity primarily in terms of territory or homeland, and racial identity in this context is overwhelmingly associated with common descent. The dual emphasis on racial kinship and ethnic homeland in constructions of identity results in the kind of boundary rigidity and permanence that is analogous to popular racial understandings in the modern era. Further, given the way that ethnocentric endogamous marriage practices and geographic constraints on travel produced a high degree of kinship within confined territories, we can see that homeland was the central organizing principle of identity for these writers.

Just as views about ethnoracial identity in the contemporary period differ by culture and/or nationality—whites and blacks for instance think about race in very different ways—Jewish constructions of identity differed from non-Jewish concepts, primarily based on the differing importance of religion in the respective societies. In the Hebrew Bible Israelite ethnicity was more clearly dependent on religion than on language, kinship, physical appearance, or any of the other markers of ethnic identity, though the authors of the Hebrew Bible do not all espouse the same religious ideologies (Sparks). For example, while Hosea used his religious sentiments in support of a "mono-Yahwist" agenda, Amos and Isaiah preferred a "Yahwistic universalism." Religious identity—not kinship—is a principal concern of the Deuteronomist and Jeremiah, but in Ezekiel, practices such as observance of the Sabbath and circumcision become criteria distinguishing the Judeans from others (Sparks). Likewise, in the second temple Jewish literature, religion is the central organizing principle in ethnicity, and there is a deemphasis on territory compared to contemporaneous Greco-Roman constructions because religion saturated most aspects of Jewish life. This implies that the lack of a territorial homeland had a negligible effect on social and religious identification in the Jewish Diaspora. In Jewish texts about race, on the other hand, the dominant element is group consciousness or awareness of being a certain people, a sense fostered by religious customs and values and buttressed by kinship claims.

The prominence of religion in developing the ideas of ethnicity and race in biblical literature produces a porousness of ethnoracial identity that is deeply at odds with modern popular constructions of race with their permanent boundaries marked by skin color. When religion is a central component of identity, conversion can result in a change in race or ethnicity, as seen in Philo's views on the standing of proselytes vis-à-vis native Jews. In Philo, Jews warmly embrace proselytes, honoring them as much as the native-born because their change in life marks them as superior (*Special Laws* 1.51–52). For Philo, God gives precedence to proselytes, helping them because they have forsaken their false and vain ancestral customs, rewarding them for having crossed over to serve the true and living God (*Special Laws* 1.309). For Philo and others, outsiders who worship the God of Abraham, Isaac, and Jacob could become members of the Jewish people. Thus, those who insist that it is inappropriate to identify "gentile" as an ethnic category in Christian literature are right only insofar as they have in mind definitions of ethnicity that privilege kinship and territory in Greco-Roman and modern western discourse.

Further, constructions of peoplehood that center religious faith and practice also characterize some postbiblical early Christian thought about identity (Buell). Likewise, the New Testament exhibits similar dynamics where it juxtaposes Gentile inclusion and participation in the Jesus movement with familial language and claims about Christian kinship (Matt 12:47–49; Gal 3:6–9).

There is thus a contrast between ancient and modern constructions of identity regarding the way "race" functions over time. In antiquity, "race" was a term that peoples used of themselves and others, and it did not necessarily convey a sense of otherness or alienness, as it frequently does now; ancient Jewish and non-Jewish Greek-speakers used different terms to convey this sense of otherness. While non-Jews used the word *barbaros* to exclude the alien outsider, Jews used *ethnos* as a term for exclusion and often used *genos* to convey a sense of shared origin and heritage (e.g., Phil 3:5). This situation has been completely inverted in the contemporary world: now theorists are trying to promote the idea that ethnicity is a ubiquitous property of people groups, while the word "race" most often communicates deviance and exclusion. Though antiquity lacks the association with marked physical characteristics that dominates modern race rhetoric, both race and ethnicity nearly always appeal to common descent across time, even though religion dominates the biblical materials as the major factor in ethnoracial identity.

The fluid and sociohistorical nature of ethnic and racial identity means that we cannot discuss these phenomena in a given period without attending to the contextual parameters that shape the ideas in that period. As mentioned earlier, no study or dataset will ever be able to calculate definitively the nature of race or ethnicity for an era given the fluidity of the concepts, and especially not in a case so far removed from our own. Nevertheless, just as there are factors in current discourse about identity that influence the prevailing ideas about race, so too were there contextual features that contributed to the construction of race in antiquity. More attention is required in investigating the nature of constructions of ethnicity, race, prejudice, and racism across time, analysis that will help all readers of ancient documents better understand the horizons of the texts as well as the social perceptual lenses through which they read those texts.

Engaging Ethnicity and Race in Biblical Scholarship. Perhaps the earliest work in biblical studies that engaged modern ideas about ethnoracial identity emerged in scholarship about the African presence in the Bible, which challenged Eurocentric silence and/or assumptions about black characters, themes, or interests in the narratives. One of the foremost voices in this area was Hebrew Bible scholar Charles B. Copher. In "The Black Presence in the Old Testament," Copher's investigations identified blacks in the narratives by locating adjectives and names used to describe black or dark-skinned people (*Šaḥor, ḥām/ḥūm, Kūš, Pīneḥas, Qēdār*). In the same collection featuring Copher's work, Randall Bailey describes a systematic "de-Africanization" of ancient near-eastern studies, maps of the Near East, and discussions about the location of Cush, especially when considering important Cushite characters in the narratives. Bailey builds on this program in a different essay with a re-reading of Exodus 2:1–10, arguing that the oldest layer of the traditions on Moses's biography depicts him as an Egyptian, and that later additions correct his biography in order to account for the lawgiver's Egyptian name, ultimately giving him a Jewish identity.

Several passages in the Hebrew Bible have been at the center of discourse about race in modern society deep into the nineteenth and twentieth centuries. The so-called "Curse of Ham" (Gen 9:18–27) and Ham's traditional association with African peoples has been an important bulwark in the construction of race. Assuming the "whiteness" of Noah and his family, early modern interpreters often identified blackness as that which arises from the curse on the descendants of Noah's son Ham, despite the fact that the text identifies Canaan as the recipient of the curse. Several scholars have engaged in understanding how interpretation of the passage contributed to the construction of race and the justification for black slavery in the modern period, investigating interpretations in Christian, Jewish, and Muslim traditions (e.g., Goldberg). In the *Forging of Race,* historian Colin Kidd reviews the way that biblical interpretation has been deeply intertwined in the construction of race, and describes how conflicts between racist ideology and scripture gave rise to a "crisis of faith" among Christian interpreters. Those who wanted to assert the naturalness of black inferiority in Anglo/American slave debates found themselves at odds with the Adamic and Noachic narratives of monogenesis in the Hebrew Bible.

Unable to hold these two impulses in tension, some interpreters turned to Gen 4:15 as a mediating narrative to account for blackness, interpreting the mark of Cain as the origin of blackness. Others questioned Adam's race and skin color—white, black or red—or maintained that blacks originated from a pre-Adamite race, holding that two different races emerge from the two creation narratives in Gen 1–2. Thus, many white southern Protestants who wanted to claim a biblical sanction for slavery but reject polygenesis could rely instead on the Curse of Ham as an explanation for black slavery.

Kidd's work powerfully depicts how biblical interpretation and theology contributed to the construction of race in the Anglophone west, resisting the trend among scholars in modern race theory to ignore these theo-political contributions. His larger thesis that Protestant theology did as much to inhibit racialized thinking as it did to promote it founders especially in light of more recent work on the topic of race-as-theology, particularly in the work of theologian Willie James Jennings' *The Christian Imagination: Theology and the Origins of Race.*

In the latest research at the intersection of ethnicity, race, and biblical criticism, scholars explore the way that biblical themes and stories promote, sustain, or resist ethnic prejudice and racism as they appear in modern society. Vincent Wimbush's body of work in African American biblical hermeneutics has been influential in this arena, especially in helping to move scholarship away from concerns about biblical rhetoric about Africans. Highlighting agency in engaging the Bible, his particular concern is with analysis of African American interpretation, interrogating appropriations of scripture in African American spirituals, sermons, and speeches. In a recent essay, for instance, Wimbush uses Fredrick Douglass' 1883 speech "The United States Cannot Remain Half-Slave and Half-Free" to explore the rhetoric of nation and scripture in building US public policy. In the speech, Douglass recasts the major charac-ters of the exodus story so that post-slavery/post-Lincoln America is a "mixed rabble" of whites and peoples of color, lacking a modern Joshua to lead the wandering peoples out of the wilderness of debate about the status of blacks in a pluralistic nation. Wimbush sees in Douglass' work an example of an African American hermeneutic that seamlessly blends biblical imperatives with the political, as Douglass' speech casts blacks' political hopes for justice in larger-than-life eschatological and apocalyptic terms. In a different register, Brian Blount's work in *Can I Get a Witness?* sees an analogy between the African American struggle for civil rights and the anti-imperialism of the Apocalypse. Here Blount gains critical leverage by connecting the biblical text to African American political resistance, instead of Wimbush's use of African American interpretations of scripture.

Reader response criticism from Asian, African, Latino/a, and postcolonial hermeneutics likewise engages racial and ethnic studies. Book length treatments in these areas include a collection of Fernando Segovia's essays on postcolonial methods in *Decolonizing Biblical Studies,* ethicist Miguel De La Torre's *Reading the Bible from the Margins,* and Tat-siong Benny Liew's *What is Asian American Hermeneutics,* where he deftly deploys race and ethnic studies from Japanese, Chinese, and Korean perspectives in reading the New Testament. Tat-siong Benny Liew, Fernando Segovia, and Randall Bailey's edited collection *They Were All Together in One Place: Towards Minority Biblical Criticism* opens up an exciting new avenue in biblical scholarship, as it seeks to move toward cultural exchange among scholars working in African American, Latino/a, Asian American, and feminist hermeneutics.

According to the editors, the double-consciousness of bicultural fluency in minority and dominant cultures that are coincident with the social location of minority scholars may yield political and interpretive practices that have particular transformative potential.

Womanist biblical scholars such as Renita Weems and Clarice Martin, who explore the interaction of feminist theory, race, and biblical scholarship, were on the forefront of intersectional analysis and biblical studies, and attorney and biblical scholar Cheryl Anderson's *Ancient Laws and Contemporary Controversies* continues this rich tradition through her accent on inclusive biblical interpretation. First coined by legal scholar Kimberlé Crenshaw in the late 80s, "intersectionality" refers to the way that multiple identity modalities such as race, gender, sexual orientation, class, and religious bigotry, intersect to create a network of oppression rather than acting independent of each other; this kind of analysis is the hallmark of womanist biblical criticism. Outside of womanist scholarship, in *Prejudice and Christian Beginnings,* editors Laura Nasrallah and Elisabeth Schüssler Fiorenza bring together a collection of essays that explores the intersectionality of race, gender, class, sexuality, and imperialism in early Christian studies, and several of the contributions in the volume directly or indirectly engage biblical interpretation. For example, Joseph Marchal's essay builds on Homi Bhabha's concept of colonial mimicry to analyze the theme of imitation in 1 Corinthians, while Cynthia Baker explores the multinational/multiethnic diversity of ancient Jews in Philo and in Acts.

Scholarship on anti-Semitism in the New Testament also features work that engages the topics of ethnic and racial identity. Shawn Kelley's *Racializing Jesus* argues that racialized Enlightenment valuations of cultures deeply saturated the thought of two of the most important modern philosophers Martin Hegel and Martin Heidegger, and that these two thinkers shaped the discipline of biblical scholarship through their influence on Ferdinand Christian Baur and Rudolph Bultmann. Kelley argues that the influence of Hegel's racialized schemas of history and civilizations on a cultural continuum (primitive Africans, despotic Orientals, free and enlightened Greco-Romans/Europeans) are subtle but still perceptible in later thinkers such as Conzelmann, Käsemann, and the parable scholarship of Funk and Crossan. Daniel Boyarin and Caroline Johnson Hodge represent other work in this arena that explicitly addresses the topic of anti-Semitism through the categories of racial and ethnic identity. Daniel Boyarin locates the genesis of aspects of modern Christian identity politics in the Pauline corpus in *A Radical Jew: Paul and the Politics of Identity,* where he maintains that Pauline theology is supersessionist, obliterates the legitimacy of Jewish difference, and normalizes white, male, European identity. In *If Sons Then Heirs: A Study of Kinship and Ethnicity in the Letters of Paul,* Caroline Johnson Hodge explores ethnic constructs in Paul's arguments about Christian identity, and forcefully challenges the view that Christianity is a religion that transcends ethnicity and eschews markers of culture and human practice. Hodge argues that in Paul kinship and ethnicity are not metaphorical, but that the concepts of lineage, paternity, and peoplehood are central to his arguments; according to Hodge, they are the preeminent categories for understanding status before God. Thus, the categories of ethnicity and race are becoming more important in both historical and ideological biblical criticism.

[*See also* African Biblical Interpretations; Asian American Biblical Interpretation; Chinese Interpretation; Cross-Cultural Exegesis; Cultural Studies; Feminist Biblical Interpretation; Latina/o Interpretation; Postcolonial Biblical Interpretation; Postmodern Interpretation; Reader-Response Criticism; *and* Womanist Interpretation]

BIBLIOGRAPHY

Anderson, Cheryl. *Ancient Laws and Contemporary Controversies: The Need for Inclusive Biblical Interpretation.* New York: Oxford University Press, 2009.

Bailey, Randall C. "Beyond Identification: The Use of Africans in Old Testament Poetry and Narratives." In *Stony the Road We Trod: African American Biblical*

Interpretation, edited by Cain Hope Felder, 165–186. Minneapolis: Fortress, 1991.

Bailey, Randall C. "Is That Any Name for a Nice Hebrew Boy: Exodus 2:1–10: The De-Africanization of an Israelite Hero." In *The Recovery of the Black Presence: An Interdisciplinary Exploration*, edited by Randall C. Bailey and Jacquelyn Grant, 25–36. Nashville, Tenn.: Abingdon Press, 1995.

Bailey, Randall, Fernando Segovia, and Tat-siong Benny Liew, eds. *They Were All Together in One Place: Towards Minority Biblical Criticism*. Atlanta: Society of Biblical Literature, 2009.

Barth, Frederick, ed. *Ethnic Groups and Boundaries: The Social Organization of Culture*. London: Allen and Unwin, 1969.

Blount, Brian. *Can I Get a Witness? Reading Revelation through African American Culture*. Louisville, Ky.: Westminster John Knox, 2005.

Boyarin, Daniel. *A Radical Jew: Paul and the Politics of Identity*. Berkeley: University of California Press, 1997.

Buell, Denise Kimber. *Why This New Race: Ethnic Reasoning in Early Christianity*. New York: Columbia University Press, 2005.

Byron, Gay. *Symbolic Blackness and Ethnic Difference in Early Christian Literature*. London: Routledge, 2002.

Copher, Charles B. "The Black Presence in the Old Testament." In *Stony the Road We Trod: African American Biblical Interpretation*, edited by Cain Hope Felder, 146–164. Minneapolis: Fortress, 1991.

De La Torre, Miguel. *Reading the Bible from the Margins*. Maryknoll, N.Y.: Orbis, 2002.

Goldberg, David M. *The Curse of Ham: Race and Slavery in Early Judaism, Christianity, and Islam*. Princeton: Princeton University Press, 2005.

Hall, Jonathon. *Hellenicity: Between Ethnicity and Culture*. Chicago: University of Chicago Press, 2002.

Hays, J. Daniel. *From Every People and Nation: A Biblical Theology of Race*. Downer's Grove, Ill. IVP Academic, 2003.

Hodge, Caroline Johnson. *If Sons Then Heirs: A Study of Kinship and Ethnicity in the Letters of Paul*. New York: Oxford University Press, 2007.

Isaac, Benjamin. *The Invention of Racism in Classical Antiquity*. Princeton N.J.: Princeton University Press, 2004.

Jennings, Willie James. *The Christian Imagination: Theology and the Origins of Race*. New Haven, CT Conn.: Yale University Press, 2010.

Kelley, Shawn. *Racializing Jesus: Race, Ideology and the Formation of Modern Biblical Scholarship*. New York: Routledge, 2002.

Kidd, Colin. *The Forging of Races: Race and Scripture in the Protestant Atlantic World, 1600–2000*. Cambridge, UK: Cambridge University Press, 2006.

Liew, Tat-siong Benny. *What is Asian American Hermeneutics? Reading the New Testament*. Intersections: Asian and Pacific American Transcultural Studies. Honolulu: University of Hawai'i Press, 2008.

Martin, Clarice J. "Womanist Interpretations of the New Testament: The Quest for Holistic and Inclusive Translation and Interpretation." In *Black Theology*. 2 vols., edited by James H. Cone and Gayraud Wilmore, 225–244. Maryknoll, N.Y.: Orbis, 1993.

McKenzie, Steven L. *All God's Children: A Biblical Critique of Racism*. Louisville, Ky.: Westminster John Knox, 1997.

Nasrallah, Laura, and Elisabeth Schüssler Fiorenza, eds. *Prejudice and Christian Beginnings*. Minneapolis: Fortress Press, 2009.

Sadler, Rodney Steven, Jr. *Can A Cushite Change His Skin: An Examination of Race, Ethnicity, and Othering in the Hebrew Bible*. London: T&T Clark, 2005.

Sechrest, Love. *A Former Jew: Paul and the Dialectics of Race*, LNTS 410. London: T&T Clark, 2009.

Segovia, Fernando F. *Decolonizing Biblical Studies: A View from the Margins*. Maryknoll, N.Y.: Orbis, 2000.

Smith, Anthony. *The Ethnic Origin of Nations*. Oxford: Blackwell, 1986.

Snowden, Frank. *Before Color Prejudice: The Ancient View of Blacks*. Cambridge, Mass.: London: Harvard University Press, 1991.

Sparks, Kenton. *Ethnicity and Identity in Ancient Israel: Prolegomena to the Study of Ethnic Sentiments and Their Expression in the Hebrew Bible*. Winona Lake, Ind.: Eisenbrauns, 1998.

Renita Weems, "Womanist Reflections on Biblical Hermeneutics," in *Black Theology*, James H. Cone and Gayraud Wilmore, eds. 2 vols., 2:216–224. Maryknoll, N.Y.: Orbis, 1993.

Werbner, Pnina. "Essentialising Essentialism, Essentialising Silence: Ambivalence and Multiplicity in the Construction of Racism and Ethnicity." In *Debating Cultural Hybridity: Multicultural Identities and the Politics of Anti-Racism*, edited by Pnina Werbner and Tariq Modood, 228–230. Los Angeles: University of California Press, 1985.

Wimbush, Vincent. "'No Modern Joshua . . .' Nationalization, Scriptures, and Race." In *Prejudice and Christian Beginnings*, edited by Laura Nasrallah and Elisabeth Schüssler Fiorenza, 259–278. Minneapolis: Fortress Press, 2009.

Love L. Sechrest

Reader-Response Criticism

Rather than a unified method, reader-response criticism is best described as a spectrum of diverse and sometimes opposing methodologies focusing on the reader. More specifically, these methodologies focus on the one who encounters the text and the meaning produced by the dynamic process of that encounter. Complications arise when reader-response critics variously define the characteristics of the reader, the text, the process of reading, and the meaning produced. This mutivalency applies even within the specific field of biblical studies.

Summary of the History of Reader-Response Criticism. Dissatisfaction with a focus on the author (historical criticism) and a focus on the text (New Criticism) eventually shifted focus to the reader. The historical criticism of the nineteenth and early twentieth centuries demonstrated a preoccupation with ancient authors, origins, and cultures that often failed to allow the text to speak in the present. Historical-critical form and source methodologies in particular were criticized for atomizing or disassembling the text without putting it back together again and for looking behind the text so intently as to neglect the text itself.

As a result, the largely Anglo-American New Critics of the 1930s through the 1950s were impelled to rescue the text from oblivion. The New Critics insisted that the objective text itself was the autonomous locus of meaning, and the historical background of a text should not influence the text's interpretation. Likewise, once the text was written, the historical author had no control over its meaning. The "intentional fallacy" was laid bare by New Critics who argued that the author's private intent was not only irretrievable but also irrelevant to interpretation.

In the mid-twentieth century, structuralists began to study the text as a system of symbols and codes compiled by the author. The meaning of a text was inherent in the signifiers. Early structuralists argued that the communication system between the text and the reader was closed. But an element was missing: a reader was necessary for the decoding or translation of the message. Poststructuralists soon began to champion an open system, which allowed the reader more control (and so more freedom) in the interpretive process.

This critical evolution lays the framework for the birth of modern reader-response in the mid-twentieth century. Reader-response criticism began, of course, in literary critical circles before being incorporated into biblical studies. I. A. Richards (1920s), D. W. Harding, Louise Rosenblatt (1930s), and Walker Gibson (1950s) were forerunners of reader-focused methodology who began to discuss the responses of the reader, both emotional and cognitive. Wayne Booth's *The Rhetoric of Fiction* (2d ed., University of Chicago Press, 1983) explored the roles of implied authors and readers, and Gerald Prince (e.g., "Introduction to the Study of the Narratee," *Poetique* 14 [1973]: pp. 177–196) declared that a critical focus on the reader introduced a new set of analytical tools, including the identities of the real reader, the virtual reader, and the ideal reader. As reader-centric analysis continued to mature, Wolfgang Iser identified the reader as the "co-creator" of the text but maintained that neither the text nor the reader contained meaning. Instead, the meaning of a text was found in the ever-changing gap between text and reader.

Stanley Fish's early work focused on the moment-by-moment experience of the reader, completing the shift to the reader as the source of meaning and literary value. Fish's now well-known question, "Is there a text in this class?," emphasized the plurality of meaning not only in an entire text, but in any phrase or sentence at any given time. David Bleich's work (e.g., *Subjective Criticism*, Johns Hopkins University Press, 1978) specified that interpretation proper is the work of a subjective individual reader's response, but that the interpretation only becomes a form of knowledge when that response is mediated by the reader's community. Fish's later work (e.g., "Interpreting the 'Variorum'," *Critical Inquiry* 2.3 [1976]: pp. 465–485) also involved the "interpretive community," which influences the way a reader perceives and responds to a text.

Reader-Response Criticism and Biblical Studies. The interpretive community has typically played an important role in biblical reader-response criticism because it provides a more plausible manner by which to describe an ancient reader. While some biblical critics have embraced fully subjective reader constructs, most have used reader-response criticism more conservatively, choosing to accept the limitations of the ancient culture and text. Because of this procedure, this form of reader-response has shared much in common with redaction and narrative criticism. Robert Tannehill's essay on the disciples in Mark inaugurated New Testament reader-response criticism by examining the effect the Markan disciples have on the reader. He writes that what the Gospel's author "reveals about the disciples may become a revelation about the readers and so enable them to change" ("The Disciples in Mark: The Function of a Narrative Role," *Journal of Religion* 57, no. 4 [1977]: pp. 386–405).

Since Tannehill's foray, reader-response criticism has been employed by many biblical critics including Robert Alter, Janice Capel Anderson, Jouette Bassler, Alan Culpepper, John Darr, Eryl W. Davies, Joanna Dewey, Elisabeth Schüssler Fiorenza, Robert Fowler, Susan Gillingham, John Paul Heil, Donald Michie, K. L. Noll, James Resseguie, David Rhoads, Bernard Brandon Scott, Gerrie Snyman, Phyllis Trible, James Watts, and A. L. H. M. van Wieringen.

Some have suggested that reader-response criticism is an echo of an older method with roots in Greco-Roman, Jewish, and ancient Christian practice. Without doubt, the audience held great importance for ancient Greek and Roman rhetoricians and performers. Aristotle's entire philosophy of rhetoric is based on the idea that the hearer determines a speech's end and object (*Rhet.* 1.1.10; 1.3.1), and he taught his students to adjust their rhetoric according to their audience and the audience's response. He remarks in *Poetics* that "the poets follow the wish of the spectators" (*Poet.* 8.10). In fact, if the audience objected to the performance of a play, Aristotle considered that play to be a failure (*Poet.* 17.4).

Like Aristotle, Cicero recognized the importance of assessing the audience. He likens the importance of gauging the identity of an audience to the task of "a careful physician who, before he attempts to administer a remedy to his patient, must investigate not only the malady of the man he wishes to cure, but also his habits when in health, and his physical constitution" (*De Or.* 2.44.186). An oration, of course, is not constrained by the form of written text, and so the rhetoricians recommended changing the oral "text" to fit the identity and responses of the audience. The ancient rhetoricians believed that language had transformative power, a perception shared by modern reader-response criticism. For modern critics a reader's response is a way of arriving at meaning, while for the ancients it was a form of political and moral behavior. Nevertheless, a preoccupation with the response of the reader or the audience remains constant.

Second Temple rabbinical interpretation may also prove a forerunner to reader-response. Carol Newsom observes that midrash in particular accepted "multiple, even contradictory, interpretations of the same text" that demonstrated little regard for historical influence ("The New Biblical Critics Probing Scripture," *Christian Century* 118, no. 1 [2001]: pp. 21–28). In his work on midrash, Alan Avery-Peck notes that the rabbis used the Hebrew Bible as a "foundation for explaining and making sense of the contemporaneous experience of the Jewish communities out of which the rabbinic literature itself emerged" ("Midrash and Exegesis: Insights from Genesis Rabbah on the Binding of Isaac," in *Method Matters* [Resources for Biblical Study 56, edited by Joel M. LeMon and Kent Harold Richards; Atlanta: Society of Biblical Literature, 2009], pp. 441–457). Such midrashic interpretations intentionally read scripture through the lens of the interpreting community for the purpose of discovering the contemporary relevance of the text for the community.

Finally, Michael Cahill argues that reading precritical allegorists in the context of reader-response reveals that the allegorists were not randomly applying meaning to texts. They were reading as professional theologians who experienced the Bible in the context of the Church's tradition. He writes that "allegorizing readers are colleagues, members of the reading club, perhaps not to be admired nor indeed imitated, but certainly not to be disowned" ("Reader-Response Criticism and the Allegorizing Reader," *Theological Studies* 57 [1996]: pp. 89–96).

Ancient or modern, reader-response criticism has been embraced by biblical scholarship in the late twentieth and early twenty-first centuries. Discussions of the modern reader, the ancient audience, and the response of both are readily found in the form of articles, essays, and monographs.

Biblical reader-response has been critiqued by those outside the discipline as being too conservative. Readers constructed by biblical critics appear to be merely idealized and abstract reflections of the text itself. Others have charged biblical reader-response critics with possessing ideological commitments that are too strong to allow for the transformative power of a textual encounter.

Those within the guild have also criticized the adoption of reader-response criticism. On the one hand, some deem reader-response criticism too akin to eisegesis. Due to its focus on the reader, reader-response silences the voice of the (human and/or divine) author in favor of the subjective interpretation of individual readers who may unrestrainedly appropriate the biblical text. If historical context is ignored, critics of the methodology argue, the original meaning cannot be determined, and so the authoritative message of the text is lost in relativity. George Montague warns that "without controls, reader-response can become totally subjective and can be used for unhealthy political, myopic, egoistic, even oppressive ends" (2007, p. 107).

On the other hand, Stephen Moore has criticized biblical scholars for remaining too "close to shore" (1989, p. 73). By remaining tied to author-oriented, historically-bound methodologies, those attempting to use reader-response within biblical studies are limiting the usefulness of the methodology. Conservative use of reader-response criticism breaks no new ground, charge the critics of conservative scholarship. Such attempts provide only disappointingly tame readings of the text. Critics must be willing to explore new territory boldly if reader-response criticism is truly to come into its own within biblical scholarship.

Assumptions Made by Reader-Response Criticism. Reader-response criticism requires several assumptions about the process of reading. Reading is assumed to be a dynamic process. Rather than a one-way, punctiliar event during which a text impresses meaning onto a reader, the reading is a transactional process between the text and reader. The reader, already possessing preconceptions and preunderstandings, encounters the text, is changed by the text, creates a world in response to the text, and then returns to encounter the text again. Each subsequent encounter results in a reader further transformed by the meaning he creates, organizes, and reorganizes. Reading is a dialog that spirals forward, never quite reaching an end.

The reading process is also ethical in nature. If the meaning of a text is realized in the transformation of a reader, it will affect the world of the reader. Booth (*The Company We Keep: An Ethics of Fiction*, University of California Press, 1989) writes that reader-response is a type of ethical criticism that reveals connections between the reader's life and the text. In her 1988 address to the Society of Biblical Literature ("The Ethics of Biblical Interpretation: Decentering Biblical Scholarship," *Journal of Biblical Literature* 107, no. 1 [1988]: pp. 3–17), Elisabeth Schüssler Fiorenza called for biblical critics to accept the responsibility of reading scripture for the sake of informing and transforming social and ecclesial actions in the modern world, particularly by exploring the power/knowledge relationship in the biblical text and contemporary interpreting communities. The process of reading, then, does not end with a reader encountering a text. Reader-response criticism assumes that the process is dynamic, complex, and ongoing.

Reader-response criticism also assumes that the reader is the primary source, even the creator, of the meaning of a text. During the reading process, the reader is highly self-conscious, using her immediate context as a framework through which to produce the meaning of a text. Iser writes, "It is in the reader that the text comes to life" (1978, p. 19).

Even from this powerful position, however, reader-response critics assume that the reader can never arrive at the ultimate meaning of a text. As the dialogical spiral of encounter continues, one reader may arrive at various meanings of a text, depending on the reader's situation and the stage in the conversation. When several kinds of readers are added to the numerous individual meanings, interpretations multiply exponentially. Gaps left in a text are filled by readers in different ways, creating various meanings. The multiplicity of interpretations is not considered a problem but a boon. The inexhaustible depths of a text testify to the richness of both text and reader.

Techniques Used by Reader-Response Critics. In general, reader-response critics read synchronically rather than diachronically, subjectively rather than objectively, and dynamically rather than statically. While a multitude of techniques have been used by biblical reader-response critics, two systems may be helpful when attempting to understand readers and readers' reading. Kevin Vanhoozer (2010) divides reader-response techniques into two groups: Conservative Reader Response and Radical Reader Response. The former group assumes "obedient readers" who remain responsible for considering the dynamics and direction of the text. These readers are likely to respect the author's intentions, as far as they can be discerned, and may, for instance, study the effect rhetorical devices in the text have on a reader. The latter group, however, assumes "resisting readers." These readers consider the text as a tool for pursuing their own interests, and they undermine traditional interpretations by exposing underlying institutional agendas.

A. L. H. M. van Wieringen likely falls into Vanhoozer's "obedient reader" category. He proposes five reader-oriented strategies, which may be signaled by the text at various points. In Strategy I, the reader is simply an observer. The narrative is being presented in the third person, allowing the reader to lean back, needing only to wonder "How will it all end?" Strategy II invites the reader closer by using discursive language. The narrative no longer takes place independently of the reader, but the reader "seems to receive the information himself due to the occurrences of a second person in the text." The third strategy involves "we-texts," which draw the reader even further into the unfolding of the text. Strategy IV occurs when the text speaks directly to the reader, immediately and explicitly involving the reader. Finally, Strategy V leaves the text and enters the world of the reader. An open-ended text, for example, will require the reader to engage the meaning of the text in the world outside the text (2011, p. 50).

Other techniques used by reader-response critics include determining the identity of the reader and the constraints under which that reader reads. Critics may choose to focus on an ancient reader, constructed as much as possible from ancient sources. Others choose to focus on a modern reader—perhaps even the critic herself—who exists in a particular situation with contemporary philosophies, values, and experiences in full play. Texts may be read from the standpoint of a first encounter with the text, or through the eyes of a reader enriched or jaded by long-term exposure to the text, with positive or negative effects.

Key Issues. The key issues in reader-response criticism revolve around the components of the preceding concise definition: the nature of the reader, the text, the reading process, and the meaning produced by reading. The many possible definitions of the nature of each element may create methodological difficulties for reader-response critics unless each is carefully described at the outset.

Reader-response critics may describe the one encountering the text as "the ideal reader, the informed reader, the implied reader, the narratee, the authorial reader, the hypothetical reader, the optimal reader, the intended reader, the competent reader, the superreader, the composite reader, the average reader, the encoded reader, the actual reader, the flesh-and-blood reader" (Fowler 1991, p. 26), the ancient reader—including in that context the Jewish/gentile reader, the wealthy/poor reader, the male/female reader, the virginal reader, the jaded reader, the later reader, the modern reader, the virtual reader, the fit reader, the hearer, the audience, and so on. Psychological, social, and cultural factors in the reader's experience are welcomed as essential components of the reading process. Readers may take different positions relative to the text, resulting in multiple interpretations. One may read from within the text, another from a position over the text, and yet another may read alongside the text. Each reader's experience of the text, to one degree or another, is recognized as valid, and each critic must define "the one who encounters" and the characteristics that validate the competency of one's appropriation of the text's meaning.

The reader's identity should, however, be clearly distinct from that of the critic. The critic is a member of an interpretive community who stands in a particular context of critical interpretation and tradition. While the reader may create meaning from the text, the critic is responsible for the text's analysis. The reader works to get as close to the text as possible; the critic maintains distance, acting as observer of the reader, the text, and the reading process. Fowler notes that most biblical critics were readers of the text before they were critics, and they then attempt to reconcile the "reader" and the "critic" within. Paul Ricoeur's process of pre-critical, critical, and post-critical reading, particularly as employed by Walter Brueggemann (e.g., "Psalms and the Life of Faith," *Journal for the Study of the Old Testament* 17 [1980]: pp. 3–32), relates directly to this process of evaluating one's position in relation to the text.

Though the text plays a vital role in reader-response criticism, it has lost the objective autonomy granted by the New Critics. The text is viewed as a stable whole, but meaning is not found exclusively in the text. Indeed, the meaning of a text is completely reliant on the activity of the reader. A text cannot effectively communicate or even exist before it is realized by a reader, and its actualization is, at least to some extent, at the mercy of the reader and the reader's identity and context. The reader-response critic may or may not dismiss the text's historical context, formation, and transmission, but the focus remains on the reader's contemporary experience, how the reader perceives the rhetoric and language of the text, and how that perception influences the reader's thought and behavior.

Perhaps one of reader-response's greatest contributions has been the rediscovery of reading as a variegated, dynamic, temporal experience. The communicative encounter between the reader and the text has been described as an unpredictable dialog, a temporal (as opposed to static) process, a phenomenological union, and a performative interpretation. However the encounter between reader and text is described, it cannot be objective; the reader necessarily reads subjectively, from a particular context. Thus the reader's perception is central to interpretation, yet all power does not reside with the reader. The text also affects the reader. Encountering and engaging the text requires the reader to create a world in response to the text, an activity that changes the reader in various ways, be it ethically, ideologically, or epistemologically.

The meaning produced as a result of the reader encountering the text is at the same time discovered and created by the reader. The text itself contains some meaning, represented by signifiers encoded by the author, but reader-response critics maintain that this meaning is not realized or complete. The full meanings of a text cannot be understood apart from the encounter between text and reader and the effect that encounter has on the mind of a reader. The meaning of a text is multivalent, even in its definition: it may or may not be constrained by the "intended" meaning of the text; it may or may not be identified with the response of an individual reader; it may reside at least partially in the text, the reader, or even the gap between the two.

Todd Davis and Kenneth Womack suggest that reader-response criticism deals with three basic questions: "do our various responses to literary works produce the same (or similar) readings?; can literary texts genuinely enjoy as many meanings as readers are able to create?; are some readings essentially more valid and justifiable than others?" (2002, p. 51). Answers to these questions depend largely on a predetermined definition of the reader, the text, the process of reading, and the meaning produced by reading. While critics adopting particular definitions may arrive at defensible conclusions to the questions of Davis and Womack, the multivalency of the method precludes overall definitive answers.

Other Approaches/Disciplines with Comparable/Shared Perspectives. Reader-response criticism is connected with other methodologies from several interpretive traditions. While the focus of this methodology rests upon the reader, reader-response shares ground with historical redaction critics who explore the way authors compiled texts and the effects produced by those compilations. Points of similarity can also be found within various fields of literary criticism, including narrative, rhetorical, and audience-oriented methodologies.

Advocacy criticisms have strong connections to reader-response, reading biblical texts through the eyes of liberation activist readers (e.g., Carlos Mesters), feminist readers (e.g., Carol Newsom [2001], A. C. Thiselton), queer readers (e.g., Randall C. Bailey, Jeremy Punt), black readers (e.g., Michael Joseph Brown), Latino/a readers (e.g., J. Severino Croatto [1987]), and so on. Reader-response criticism is linked to postmodern hermeneutics as well, in which interpretation is seen "as the translation . . . of aspects of meaning uncovered in an experience of the reader into some sort of language and conceptuality shared by a community of contemporaries" (McKnight 1988, p. 267).

Illustrations of the Method in Action and its Interpretive Payoff. As can be expected, a multivalent methodology produces multivalent interpretations. In addition to the critics previously mentioned, only a few of the myriad of examples are included in the following.

In 1985, *Semeia* devoted a volume to "Reader Response Approaches to Biblical and Secular Texts" (R. Detweiler, ed., 1985). The essays in this volume include Hugh White's reading of the Joseph Story ("The Joseph Story: A Narrative Which 'Consumes' Its Content," pp. 49–69), which involves van Wieringen's Strategy V. White concludes that the reader's perception of the story as a whole overrides even the narrator's structure within the text. By the end of the story, the crisis of estrangement between Joseph and his brothers is not fully resolved, despite the passing on of the divine promise in Genesis 50:24. White proposes that the reader experiences the promise as the strongest determiner of the future of the story, not the narrative system the narrator has put in place.

In the same volume, Janice Capel Anderson's essay on doublets and triplets in Matthew reveals the rhetorical effect that redundancy has on the reader ("Double and Triple Stories, the Implied Reader, and Redundancy in Matthew," pp. 71–89). Repetition sets up an expectation of a pattern. Subsequent variations of that pattern stand out to the reader. Anderson offers the example of the blind men stories in Matthew 9 and 20. The first men disobey Jesus's command to remain silent (they do not fully "see"); the second set of men follow Jesus (presumably because they truly "see"). Readers first recognize the pattern and then are invited to interpret the variation of the pattern.

Gary Phillips's *Semeia* essay also considers Matthew, this time focusing on the parables in Matthew 13 ("History and Text: The Reader in Context in Matthew's Parables Discourse," pp. 111–138). By applying reader-response methodology, Phillips de-monstrates that the reader becomes a living interpreter not only of Jesus's words, but of the prophets before him and ultimately the word of God. Once a reader becomes a "living interpretant," he participates in God's revealing action in the world.

Keith Bodner's *JSOT* essay ("Is Joab a Reader-Response Critic?" *Journal for the Study of the Old Testament* 27, no. 1 [2002]: pp. 19–35) takes the interesting approach of applying reader-response criticism to a biblical character. Bodner explores the interpretive license that Joab takes after reading David's letter regarding the fate of Uriah in 2 Samuel 11. He concludes that Joab's creative interpretations of the king's words ultimately lead to the general's death after Solomon's succession.

In 1989, John Paul Heil used reader-response to study irony in Luke, specifically using the story of Jesus before the Sanhedrin ("Reader-Response and the Irony of Jesus before the Sanhedrin in Luke 22:66–71," *Catholic Biblical Quarterly* 51, no. 2 [1989]: pp. 271–284). Heil's study demonstrates that the evidence offered by Jesus in this trial causes

Jesus to be condemned as a false messiah, the Sanhedrin to be condemned for failing to recognize the Messiah, and the reader to believe that Jesus is truly God's Messiah. Held in ironic tension, these ideas lead the reader to conclude that "the self-condemnation of Jesus is also his self-revelation as the messianic Son of Man and Son of God" (p. 283). The tragedy in the story is also its triumph.

Mark Allan Powell's 2000 essay ("The Magi as Kings: An Adventure in Reader-Response Criticism," *Catholic Biblical Quarterly* 62, no. 3 [2000]: pp. 459–480) explores the identity of the magi from Matthew's Gospel and their popular and persistent identification as "kings." By clarifying the perception of the original reader, and then tracing the development of later readers, Powell demonstrates how the magi, perhaps originally understood as servants, came to be viewed as kings. This reader-response exercise reveals that over time, readers shifted God's preference for the powerless to God's support of the powerful.

James A. Metzger's 2007 volume (*Consumption and Wealth in Luke's Travel Narrative*, Brill, 2007) applies a reader-response approach to the four Lukan Travel Narrative parables, which address issues of consumption and wealth. He explicitly reads from the perspective of a real reader: a citizen of the United States, a location characterized by "rampant overconsumption and unprecedented personal wealth," and as a Christian who "is encouraged to prioritize dialogue with the canonical books of the First and Second Testaments when reflecting critically upon and formulating a response to our present situation in the world" (p. 56). As a result of his reading, Metzger hears Jesus's message as a "perspective on wealth and consumption, forged among and for the benefit of a disenfranchised plebeian majority under the early Roman Empire," which is "an invaluable, representative protestation 'from below' to an unjust, extractive economy" (p. 193). Jesus's critique speaks directly to the Christian in the United States who possesses great wealth in the midst of a world experiencing severe inequality and "offers a challenge to current global economic structures, but also encourages readers to explore new social and economic relationships that are more just and humane" (p. 196).

In a final example, Teresa Okure ("Jesus and the Samaritan Woman [Jn 4:1–42] in Africa," *Theological Studies* 70 [2009]: pp. 401–418) studies Jesus and the Samaritan Woman in John 4:1–42 through the eyes of an African reader. She concludes that by identifying himself as one of the poor, and by crossing the boundaries of societal prejudice, Jesus gives the Samaritan woman her voice, allowing her to discover the potential within herself. Okure proposes that while Christians should also identify with the marginalized and give them their voices, God has already done so. God sent Jesus to be a human being, who proclaims good news to the poor.

Recognizing and appreciating the reader's horizon, be it ancient or modern, sheds light on the interpretive process. Use of reader-response criticism provides insight into the nature of the text, the characters in the narrative, and the relevance of the biblical message for contemporary communities.

Present and Future Impact on Current Intellectual and Cultural Environment. Reader-response methodologies have had and will continue to have a profound impact on readers of the biblical text and the communities in which they live. Reader-response accounts for differing interpretations of the biblical text. The context of both text and reader may shape the interpretive process. Emphasis on reading as a communal, performative, and transformative act provides a method through which readers of the biblical text can ethically interact with the text and their world, engaging the fields of political, gender, psychological, and ethnic studies.

At the end of the matter, any act of interpretation is in some way a reader's response. Although critics may choose to be more or less constrained by other factors (genre of the text, intent of the author, historical situation of the original message), reader-response criticism serves to bring the identity of the reader to the fore. Whether or not a critic gives complete control to the reader, the reader's situation is a recognized element in the interpretive process. Acknowledging the reader helps guard against blindness to presuppositions and at the same time opens new avenues of interpretation and application of the biblical text. Despite multivalent meaning and the privileging of any and all readers, reader-response remains a critical method. In order to preserve this nature, careful and cooperative work must continue to develop a critical apparatus that further defines the methodology and ensures dialog between readers and communities.

[*See also* Literary Criticism, Literary Theory, and the Bible; Narrative Criticism and Narrative Hermeneutics; Postmodern Interpretation; Poststructuralist Interpretation; Redaction Criticism, *subentry* Hebrew Bible; Redaction Criticism, *subentry* Apocrypha and Deuterocanonical Books; Redaction Criticism, *subentry* New Testament; Rhetorical Criticism; *and* Structuralist Interpretation.]

BIBLIOGRAPHY

Croatto, J. Severino. *Biblical Hermeneutics: Toward a Theory of Reading as the Production of Meaning.* Maryknoll, N.Y.: Orbis, 1987. Example of reader-response from a Latino, liberation theologian perspective.

Davis, Todd F., and Kenneth Womack. *Formalist Criticism and Reader-Response Theory.* New York: Palgrave, 2002. Provides an overview and history of formalist and reader-response methodologies with the intent of encouraging their inclusion in an eclectic hermeneutic.

Detweiler, Robert, ed. *Semeia* 31. Decatur, Ga.: Scholars, 1985. Essays utilizing reader-response to read biblical and secular texts.

Exum, J. Cheryl, and David J. A. Clines, eds. *The New Literary Criticism and the Hebrew Bible.* Journal for the Study of the Old Testament: Supplement Series 143. Sheffield, UK: JSOT Press, 1993. Essays focusing on eclectic poststructuralist approaches to the Hebrew Bible.

Firth, David G., and Jamie A. Grant, eds. *Words and the Word: Explorations in Biblical Interpretation and Literary Theory.* Downers Grove, Ill.: IVP Academic, 2008. Collection of essays applying literary theory to biblical hermeneutics from a generally confessional standpoint.

Fish, Stanley. *Is There a Text in This Class? The Authority of Interpretive Communities.* Cambridge, Mass.: Harvard University Press, 1980. Collection of essays that trace Fish's evolution from a critic who asked if interpretation and meaning were to be *found in* the (existing and stable) text or the reader, to a critic who concludes that the text, reader, and author are all *products of* interpretation.

Fowler, Robert M. *Let the Reader Understand: Reader-Response Criticism and the Gospel of Mark.* Minneapolis, Fortress Press, 1991. Seminal work discussing the experience of reading Mark's Gospel by taking up "critical comments made by generations of biblical critics as disguised reports of the critics' own experience of reading biblical texts" (p. 1).

Haner, Philip. *Relation Analysis of the Fourth Gospel: A Study in Reader-Response Criticism.* Lewiston, N.Y.: Mellen, 1993. A close examination of the relationships between the characters of the Fourth Gospel and the narrative world those relationships create for the implied reader.

Iersel, Bas M. F. van. *Mark: A Reader-Response Commentary.* Journal for the Study of the New Testament: Supplement Series 164. Sheffield, UK: Sheffield Academic, 1998. A synchronic commentary on the Third Gospel by an accomplished Markan scholar that uncovers a myriad of literary connections and concentric structures, interacts with other scholars, and finally encourages a fresh reading of the text.

Iser, Wolfgang. *The Act of Reading: A Theory of Aesthetic Response.* Baltimore: Johns Hopkins University Press, 1978. Introduction to the active process of reading, including the relationship between text and reader, the gap between the two, in which meaning is realized, and the multivalent impact of the text on the world of the reader.

McKnight, Edgar V. *Post-Modern Use of the Bible: The Emergence of Reader-Oriented Criticism.* Nashville, Tenn.: Abingdon Press, 1988. Traces development of pre-critical to critical to contemporary interpretive methodologies. Includes examples of a reader-oriented approach to hermeneutics, with emphasis on the Bible as a unified literary work.

Montague, George T. *Understanding the Bible: A Basic Introduction to Biblical Interpretation.* New York: Paulist, 2007. Introduction to hermeneutics that situates a helpful chapter on reader-response (163–174) within the larger field of biblical interpretation.

Moore, Stephen D. *Literary Criticism and the Gospels: The Theoretical Challenge.* New Haven, Conn.: Yale University Press, 1989. Excellent introduction to reader-response approaches in New Testament studies. Includes survey of reader-response works, as well as a glossary of technical terms.

Noble, Paul R. "Fish and the Bible: Should Reader-Response Theories 'Catch On'?" *Heythrop Journal* 37 (1996): 456–467. Response to Stanley Porter's question, "Why hasn't reader-response criticism caught on in New Testament studies?"

Poirier, John C. "Some Detracting Considerations for Reader-Response Theory." *Catholic Biblical Quarterly* 62, no. 2 (2000): 250–263. Critique of reader-response theory that demonstrates that two of the methodology's major premises are not logically consistent.

Porter, Stanley E. "Why Hasn't Reader-Response Criticism Caught on in New Testament Studies?" *Journal of Literature and Theology* 4 (1990): 278–292. Discusses why, apart from advocacy criticisms, reader-response rarely is used by New Testament scholars.

Tompkins, Jane P. "An Introduction to Reader-Response Criticism." In *Reader-Response Criticism: From Formalism to Post-Structuralism*, edited by Jane P. Tompkins, ix–xxvi. Baltimore: Johns Hopkins University Press, 1980. An excellent collection of essays introducing the literary critical development of reader-response criticism.

Utzschneider, Helmut. "Text—Leser—Autor: Bestandsaufnahme und Prolegomena zu einer Theorie der Exegese." *Biblische Zeitschrift* 43, no 2 (1999): 224–238. Explores the state of interpretation in the Hebrew Bible, concluding that while biblical exegesis is primarily a literary discipline, it also will remain a historical discipline that should be used in service of theological application.

Vanhoozer, Kevin J. "The Reader in New Testament Interpretation." In *Hearing the New Testament: Strategies for Interpretation*, 2d ed., edited by Joel B. Green, 259–288. Grand Rapids, Mich.: Eerdmans, 2010. Examines the way readers approach the text and the ethical responsibility of the reader. Includes examples of the methodology and suggestions for further reading.

Vorster, Willem S. "Readings, Readers, and the Succession Narrative: An Essay on Reception." *Zeitschrift für die Alttestamentliche Wissenschaft* 98 (1986): 351–362. Illustrates the thesis that reading is an active process that produces meaning by exploring various actualizations of readings of the Succession Narrative.

Wieringen, A. L. H. M. van. "Assur and Babel against Jerusalem: The Reader-Oriented Position of Babel and Assur within the Framework of Isaiah 1–39." In *"Enlarge the Site of Your Tent": The City as Unifying Theme in Isaiah*, edited by A. L. H. M. van Wieringen and Annemarieke van der Woude, 49–62. Boston: Brill, 2011. Compares Assur, Babel, and Jerusalem as "characters" in Isaiah in order to determine the comparison's effect on the implied reader.

Kathy Reiko Maxwell

Reception Criticism and Theory

Reception criticism or reception theory is an approach to biblical study interested in the "afterlife" of biblical texts: how they have been received and appropriated by diverse readers across time and in a variety of media. Given its focus on reception by audiences, it could be viewed as a form of reader-response criticism. The terms "reception theory" and "reception criticism" come initially from literary studies, and especially from the literary critic of the Konstanz School, Hans Robert Jauss (1921–1997). The former term emphasizes the theoretical underpinning of the discipline. Those more interested in its practical outworking in the history of how specific texts (including biblical texts) have been received prefer the terms reception criticism or reception history (what Jauss calls *Rezeptionsgeschichte*).

The latter term is a reminder that attention to the reception of texts is a historical discipline. Indeed, it is a more truly *diachronic* approach than the historical criticism usually designated by this epithet, in that reception history is concerned with the reception of biblical texts through the centuries and regards such reception as key rather than accidental to their interpretation. It also challenges the notion that exegesis of biblical texts should be restricted to written explication—as opposed, for example, to visual exegesis—or to the writings of academic exegetes or magisterial interpreters such as the early Fathers, the medieval Schoolmen, or the Protestant Reformers.

Closely related to reception criticism or reception history are the terms "history of interpretation" and *Wirkungsgeschichte*. The latter is derived from Jauss's teacher Hans-Georg Gadamer (1900–2002). It first appears in his classic work *Wahrheit und Methode* (1960; English trans. *Truth and Method*), and is variously translated "history of effects," "history of effect," "history of influence," and "effective history."

Further precision is possible, however. "History of interpretation" (*Auslegungsgeschichte*) is perhaps best understood as a subcategory of reception history or *Wirkungsgeschichte*. It concerns how professional biblical scholars in commentaries and academic monographs have interpreted a text. The history of interpretation of the book of Revelation, for example, would include the commentaries of Victorinus, Andreas of Caesarea, Bede, and Luis de Alcázar, as well as the modern critical works of R. H. Charles, George Caird, and Richard Bauckham. By comparison, reception history or reception criticism does not restrict its interests to professional interpreters, but is open to a wide range of interpreters (marginal and even maverick as well as magisterial) and to the broader dimensions of reception: in art, music, poetry, liturgy, and community living.

Although the terms reception history and *Wirkungsgeschichte* overlap in content (and in practice are often used interchangeably), a logical distinction may still be made between them. The focus of the former is on the readers: how they have received the text in their different contexts and via different media. The emphasis of *Wirkungsgeschichte* (whether translated as "history of effects" or "history of influence") is rather on the text and its effects, its ability to influence human lives.

In a seminal article published in 1992, the Finnish New Testament scholar Heikki Räisänen (1941–) offered an alternative definition of the difference between history of reception and "effective history." For Räisänen, the latter term should be restricted to interpretations in a range of media where the text is allowed to be "effective." Reception history would then be something broader: covering all receptions in various media, including "misreadings" of the text (he gives the example of the use of a biblical text in a sermon that amounts to its suppression: Räisänen 1992, p. 311). Räisänen's definition may be too optimistic about our ability to distinguish clearly between good and bad effects and underestimates the dynamic relationship between reader and text.

History and Leading Practitioners.

Hans-Georg Gadamer. As noted already, Gadamer is often regarded by biblical scholars as the father of reception history. Certainly, its philosophical underpinning and some of its key terminology (notably *Wirkungsgeschichte* and "historically effected consciousness" or *wirkungsgeschichtliches Bewußtsein*) derive from him. However, Gadamer is clear that he is not proposing a new method of exegesis to be placed alongside or as an alternative to existing scholarly approaches. Indeed, fundamental to his writing is a critique of empirical methodologies or claims to scientific objectivity typical of many historical approaches. Rather, Gadamer's *Wirkungsgeschichte* is a form of philosophical hermeneutics, describing how we understand and what our relationship to history really is. As he expresses it in his foreword to the second edition of *Truth and Method*, it describes "not what we do or what we ought to do, but what happens to us over and above our wanting and doing" (Gadamer 1989, p. xxvi; see Mark Knight in Roberts and Rowland, eds., 2010, p. 139). The English translation of *Wirkungsgeschichte* that best conveys this is "effective history." It acknowledges that, far from standing outside history so as to analyze it objectively, we are firmly within history. Following Martin Heidegger and Paul Ricoeur, Gadamer thus emphasizes the crucial role of the interpretative subject in the hermeneutical process:

> In fact history does not belong to us; we belong to it. Long before we understand ourselves through the process of self-examination, we understand ourselves in a self-evident way in the family, society, and state in which we live. The focus of subjectivity is a distorting mirror. The self-awareness of the individual is only a flickering in the closed circuits of historical life. *That is why the prejudices of the individual, far more than his judgements, constitute the historical reality of his being* (Gadamer 1989, pp. 276–277; italics in original).

In a similar vein, *wirkungsgeschichtliches Bewußtsein* has a twofold meaning, as Gadamer explains: "it is used to mean at once the consciousness effected in the course of history and determined by history, and the very consciousness of being thus effected and determined" (Gadamer 1989, p. xxx). History is that in which all humans are necessarily embedded. Moreover, against the "naive assumption" of historicism, the temporal distance between "now" and "then" is not a problem for the historian, a gulf to be overcome, so much as "a positive and productive condition enabling understanding. It is not a yawning abyss but is filled with the continuity of custom and tradition, in the light of which everything handed down presents itself to us" (Gadamer 1989 p. 297).

Hans Robert Jauss. Jauss comes closer than Gadamer to treating reception history as a method, outlining seven theses for literary studies in his *Toward an Aesthetic of Reception* (Jauss 1982, pp. 20–45; see Parris 2009, pp. 128–147). This explains his particular attraction for the theologian and biblical scholar, and indeed how Jauss's appropriation of Gadamer has set the agenda for much reception history. So, for example, his "summit dialogue" of authors (*der Gipfeldialog der Autoren*) underlines the importance of what are considered "defining moments" of the contours of a tradition (see Parris 2009, pp. 216–222). Such a dialogue would give particular consideration to those interpreters who represent "peaks" or significant "summits" in the reception of a particular text, given their impact on contemporaries or later readers, or the innovative character of their readings. David Paul Parris provides an example of such a summit-dialogue in relation to Matthew's parable of the wedding banquet (Parris 2009, pp. 222–274).

Jauss's reception of Gadamer is not without its critics, however. For some, it risks domesticating Gadamer's potentially subversive hermeneutic by supposing that most of us actually work in some neatly packaged tradition, which may be more a figment of our imagination than the reality that actually conditions our lives. Actual interpreters are formed by traditions much more diverse and eclectic than can be easily encapsulated by this or that theological label. It is a crucial insight to acknowledge the extent to which we are formed, socially, culturally, and psychologically, but that which is handed down, "tradition," is extremely varied. Though many religious traditions make an attempt to form those who will lead them by a process of inculturation, most readers of biblical texts are not so formed and that which we receive is a much more complex amalgam that is peculiarly historically contingent.

Ulrich Luz. One of the most important pioneers of *Wirkungsgeschichte* in biblical scholarship is the Swiss New Testament scholar Ulrich Luz (1938–). His Matthew commentary for the ecumenical *Evangelisch-Katholischer Kommentar* (EKK) series is noteworthy for the significant amount of space it devotes to *Wirkungsgeschichte* or the "history of influence" (Luz 1989, 2001, 2005), particularly in the later volumes. He has subsequently articulated his approach in a number of books and articles (e.g. Luz 1994, 2006). As well as noting his indebtedness to both Gadamer and Jauss, Luz also hails his teacher Gerhard Ebeling (1912–2001) as an early pioneer of reception history for his conviction that church history is the history of the interpretation of scripture (Ebeling 1968).

As well as Luz's robust commitment to *Wirkungsgeschichte* as integral to biblical interpretation, his project shares with the wider EKK series a strongly ecclesial dimension (albeit one that is ecumenically broad). This contrasts strongly with the historical-critical suspicion of dogmatic or ecclesially committed dimensions of the text. One of Luz's criteria for selection of passages to focus on and material to include in the first volume of his commentary is whether they have been especially "effective" in the Protestant and Catholic traditions (Luz 1989, p. 96). In later volumes, this criterion is broadened. Thus his discussion of the "history of influence" of the "Parable of the Sheep and the Goats" (Matt 25:31–46) includes not only Origen, John Chrysostom, Luther, and Calvin, but also Tolstoy, Gutiérrez, and the Korean poet Kim Chi Ha (Luz 2005, pp. 267–274). This goes some way toward addressing the criticism that Luz's ecclesial sympathy excludes more marginal and even maverick receptions of the text.

The Blackwell Bible Commentaries. The EKK project (at least in terms of its format) separates out the "history of influence" from exegesis or analysis. This risks treating the latter as a kind of foundation on which the former is built as a second-stage superstructure, thus falling foul of the Gadamerian critique. By contrast, the authors of the Blackwell Bible Commentaries (BBC) prioritize reception history. This important series for reception history in the English-speaking world is under the general editorship of John Sawyer, Christopher Rowland, and Judith Kovacs. As the editors note, the series is "based on the premise that how people have interpreted, and been influenced by, a sacred text like the Bible is often as interesting and historically important as what it originally meant" (Kovacs and Rowland 2004, p. xi). Like Luz's definition of *Wirkungsgeschichte*, the parameters of reception-historical focus in the BBC are as broad as possible, incorporating art, music, film, literature, and religious and political praxis, and engaging with patristic, medieval, and (in the case of Old Testament books) rabbinic exegesis as well as more familiar historical-critical readings.

Multivalency and Multiple Receptions. What are the main contributions of reception criticism? First, it insists that texts are multivalent and thus do not simply convey one single meaning. In other words, it refuses to prioritize authorial intention, or the meaning assigned to a text by its first readers (both features of historical criticism). Rather, it invites a broader understanding of meaning: one that engages directly with the subject matter of the text, and the potential of meaning inherent in the text, rather than getting side-tracked into *prolegomena*, such as questions of sources, origins, and background.

In part this springs from Gadamer's conviction that historical consciousness is itself determined by history, such that a historian cannot examine a biblical text as though it were simply an object for examination. Luz uses the metaphor of a river or the "stream of history" of which historical texts are a part, and which "carries the boat" in which the interpreter of the text sits (Luz 2006, p. 125). Nor should the biblical scholar imagine that the historical enterprise is an attempt to leap across an "ugly ditch" between the first century and the twenty-first. (Luz's use of the phrase differs from Lessing's gulf between the contingent truths of history and the necessary truths of reason). Rather, to change the metaphor to one drawn from his own Swiss context, Luz likens reception history to a rich landscape that frames the original meaning of the text:

> As a Swiss living in Berne, I know that no view of the summit of a distant high mountain like the 'Jungfrau' is possible without looking at all the hills, valleys and smaller mountains in the foreground. Even more: it is only this foreground, the frame of the surrounding landscape, which makes the beauty of the high mountain visible. A 'naked' Jungfrau would be ridiculous. In the same way a 'naked' biblical text, not viewed from a specific point of view and not 'framed' by a specific reception history, would be meaningless (Luz 2006, p. 128).

In other words, reception-historical study facilitates a more profound understanding of biblical texts. On the one hand, it enables readers to understand where they have come from, how their vision of history is "framed," and how far they are standing on the shoulders of giants in their receptions of the text. On the other, it also exposes them to the readings of other reading communities (both ancient and modern) of which they may hitherto have been unaware. This ecumenical dimension of reception history is one consciously embraced by the EKK, albeit largely restricted to Catholic and German Protestant traditions. However, even this is in danger of prioritizing an alternative canon of "classic" receptions. Reception history in its widest extent has the potential to expose interpreters to popular, marginal, and even eccentric receptions of the text alongside the centrist and magisterial readings. Whilst rehabilitating a sense of the importance of tradition for those reading communities that have hitherto eschewed it, it also holds within it the capacity to critique particular accounts of what that tradition entails through exposure to the receptions of those who have stood outside the dominant interpretative traditions.

Ambiguities and Spaces. Another of reception history's greatest contributions to biblical study is its demonstration of how later interpreters deal with problems posed by the text or exploit the space offered by the text. A prime example is the enigmatic and suggestive reference to Enoch in Genesis 5:24. This was the basis for a welter of speculation throughout Jewish and Christian history, whose importance for the emergence of beliefs about Jesus has been a significant feature of modern New Testament study.

Genesis 5:24 reads in NRSV: "Enoch walked with God; then he was no more, because God took him." On the basis of comparison with other biblical passages, interpreters exploited the space offered by the text to interpret what "God took him" means. On the one hand, via a comparison with 2 Kings 2:9–11, Enoch was compared with Elijah who was "taken up" to heaven (2:9: "Tell me what I may do for you, before I am taken up from you"—the same Hebrew word is used in both). Enoch then became a member of the divine court, a heavenly scribe, and even the heavenly Son of Man, in the Ethiopic *Apocalypse of Enoch* 71. On the other hand, other references to the Hebrew "take" are explored and a very different conclusion is reached. Thus, in Ezekiel 24:16 the verb is used of the *death* of Ezekiel's wife ("Mortal, with one blow I am about to take away from you the delight of your eyes"). The later Jewish rabbinic teachers, who were suspicious of extravagant speculation about Enoch's role, favored an interpretation of Enoch being taken that referred to his death, removed from life before he sinned any more.

Both traditions, via the usual canons of interpretation, had sought to elucidate the ambiguity and the interpretative space offered by the passage. This is a reminder that there is a rich tradition of interpretation in both Judaism and Christianity (neglected in historical criticism's focus on contemporary "parallels" to the biblical books) exploring the interpretative space offered by the biblical text. For example, the Jewish Targumim, Aramaic paraphrases of the Bible, and especially the Targum known as *Pseudo-Jonathan*, demonstrate this to the full. The story of Abraham's near sacrifice of Isaac becomes the bedrock of a tradition of righteous suffering, the Akedah. In Christianity the ignorance about the early life of Christ was explored from an early date in a text like *The Protoevangelium of James* and exploited to the full with infancy narratives and tales of Jesus's precocious behavior as a child.

We find a similar wrestling with problems posed by the text, and exploitation of the space it offers, in William Blake's 1825 *Illustrations of the Book of Job.* One of the problems posed by the Book of Job is the role of Satan. He functions as an agent of God, who is to a degree complicit in Job's torments by permitting the "testing" to take place by Satan. However, Satan disappears from the narrative after Job 2. Blake explores God's collusion with Satan in Job's suffering (Job 1:12; 2:3) in a remarkable image, Plate 11 of the series. Here Blake depicts Job's nightmare, in which the divinity is seen as a mix of God and Satan tormenting him. Nor does Blake ignore Satan's disappearance from the story of Job. So, in Plate 16, Satan is depicted falling from heaven, picking up a well-known biblical theme, being judged by God for his behaviour toward the hapless Job.

There is another feature of this image, however, that shows us the way in which a close reader of the biblical text like Blake could exploit the space offered him by the text. Job 7:13–14 reads: "When I say, 'My bed will comfort me, my couch will ease my complaint,' then you scare me with dreams and terrify me with visions." What the content of those terrifying dreams and visions is not given in the biblical text. Blake the artist exploits the opportunity offered by this deficiency in these verses and depicts the nightmare apparition, a mixture of God and Satan terrifying him.

Similarly, Job 42:5 ("I had heard of you by the hearing of the ear, but now my eye sees you") tells us nothing about what Job *saw* of God. Indeed, in the light of the preceding theophany (Job 38–41) there are only the words of the inscrutable Almighty. Blake understands this moment as one of vision and then interprets this vision christologically, juxtaposing the vision of God to Job and his wife in Plate 17 with a vision of Christ, as is evident from the marginal references to the Gospel of John (especially John 14:9).

Debates. Sufficient has been said to show differences of opinion between practitioners of reception theory, reception history, and *Wirkungsgeschichte* regarding the task in which they are engaged, its purpose, principles, and parameters.

Purpose. Is reception history, for example, primarily a task of collating or cataloging neglected or unfamiliar receptions of the text? The concern that reception history simply adds to the existing body of knowledge at the risk of creating yet more areas of specialism is a real one. In response, one may point to the "historical" nomenclature of both reception history and *Wirkungsgeschichte*: a "history" or *Geschichte* presupposes an interpretative framework, an ordered account that does more than simply collate material or facts, but locates them in an interpretative frame that explores inter-relationships and causal links. Similarly, the creation of a catalog (such as a catalog for a museum or art exhibition) involves selection, categorization, and analysis. Furthermore, broad reception-historical catalogs are indispensable for opening up possibilities that subsequent scholars can follow up in more detail. This latter task is a complementary aspect of the discipline, and there are a growing number of fine examples covering specific biblical books and passages and exploring their reception in a variety of media, including visual art. These include Yvonne Sherwood's study of the afterlives of the book of Jonah (Sherwood 2000), Rachel Nicholls's monograph on the *Wirkungsgeschichte* of Matthew's "Walking on the Water" narrative (Nicholls 2008), Martin O'Kane's exploration of the artist as biblical interpreter (O'Kane 2007), and Natasha O'Hear's examination of interpretations of the Apocalypse in late medieval and early modern art (O'Hear 2011).

Parameters. Second, there is disagreement concerning the appropriate limits of reception history. Some practitioners prefer the limitations of what we have defined as "the history of interpretation," or a focus on the "peaks" of reception implied by Jauss's "summit-dialogue." Luz's particular interest in significant receptions in Catholic and Protestant traditions, albeit within a growing appreciation of wider reception embracing poetry, art, and music, is too broad for some and too narrow for others. This debate is reflected in the various volumes of the Blackwell Bible Commentaries, whose individual answers are related in part to questions of genre. In his BBC commentary on Galatians, John Riches opts for in-depth engagement with a small number of classic interpreters in order to elucidate this difficult Pauline letter (Riches 2008). Given the very different elusiveness (and allusiveness) of the Apocalypse, Judith Kovacs and Christopher Rowland adopt a more inclusive approach, which embraces lesser known interpreters and receptions in nonverbal media. The justification for the latter is their conviction that artists may engage the subject matter of this visual and visionary text more effectively than those who write verse-by-verse commentaries (Kovacs and Rowland 2004).

But adopting such a broad approach to reception history immediately confronts the interpreter with the enormity of the task at hand and the need to create some kind of boundary to what may seem to be a potentially limitless task. Thus, the Kovacs-Rowland Revelation commentary seeks to order the vast amount of material it discusses via a relatively simple hermeneutical model (which identifies a spectrum between allegory or "decoding" and analogy or actualization) for shaping the plethora of material from outside, as well as inside, the mainstream Christian tradition. Other Blackwell authors adopt different strategies. Engagement with the problems posed by those very different approaches (also evident to some extent in the differences evident in the EKK series) is necessary to explore the problematic nature of the reception history task.

Adjudicating among Interpretations. A third area for debate concerns the question of validity or truth in interpretation (see Sawyer 2004). Are there bad as well as good receptions, false as well as true interpretations, and what are the criteria for assessing between them? Historical criticism tends to prioritize "original meaning" as virtually synonymous with authorial intention (a "historical" version of the patristic and medieval interest in the "literal sense"). Many sympathetic to reception history would still wish to assess interpretations according to their correspondence to the original meaning, albeit acknowledging the difficulties inherent in articulating such a meaning. Others make judgments less on authorial grounds than on textual: they point to clues within the text that constrain what may be considered a valid reading.

With the "history of influence" of New Testament texts particularly in mind, Ulrich Luz proposes two converging and functional criteria for making judgments, one historical and the other ethical. The first he calls "correspondence with the essentials of the history of Jesus," in which the historical dimension prevents it from being a criterion excluding the receptions of those outside the churches. The second draws both upon the Matthean insight that "you shall know them by their fruits" (Matt 7:20) and the Augustinian concern that interpretations tend toward the building up of the divine kingdom of love (Luz 1994, pp. 82–97; Augustine, *De Doctrina Christiana* 1.36). Yet critics of the ethical criterion point to the difficulty of establishing "love" as a universal criterion, or even as at the heart of the New Testament witness. Others adopt a broader ethical criterion, which can critique even readings approximating to the perspective of the original author: readings promoting unjust or immoral actions, such as genocide, should be rejected.

Impact, Relevance, and Prospectus. The impact of reception theory and reception criticism/history on biblical studies is increasingly acknowledged, even if its implications for the wider discipline, and particularly the extent of its challenge to the hitherto dominant historical-critical paradigm, remain contested. Seminars on the history of influence are now integral to academic conferences, such as the Society of Biblical Literature Annual Meeting and the British New Testament Conference. Other signs of its contemporary relevance include the Oxford-based Centre for the Reception History of the Bible and the ongoing *Encyclopedia of the Bible and its Reception* (EBR) project, published by De Gruyter.

Interdisciplinary Dimension. The wide focus of reception history, and its interest in biblical reception in a variety of media, encourages interdisciplinary collaboration between biblical scholars and those working in other disciplines in the humanities. The influence of Gadamer and Jauss is felt strongly in these other disciplines, where the centrality of reception theory offers promising possibilities for cooperation. Some practitioners (e.g. William John Lyons in Roberts and Rowland, eds., 2010, pp. 207–220) have suggested that this capacity for interdisciplinary bridge-building may be crucial to the continuing survival of biblical studies in a time of economic crisis.

Theology. Within theology specifically, the turn to reception history offers an opportunity to overcome the increased specialization and therefore fragmentation of the subject into discrete disciplines. There is an obvious synergy with the rediscovery by the academy of neglected patterns of exegesis, especially the polyvalent readings of patristic and medieval interpretation of scripture. This is reflected in a number of commentary and monograph series and offers potential for greater collaboration between biblical studies, historical and systematic theology, and church history.

Nor is this potential restricted to academic theologians or to the humanities more generally. A crucial dimension of reception history, identified in Luz's work, is its serious attention to the reading of scripture in distinctive religious communities. Professional biblical scholars could be criticized for having replaced one *magisterium* (that of the Church or the rabbinic tradition) with another (that of the academy) that is not always sympathetic to the theological subject matter of the Bible. Reception history's potential openness to non-magisterial and especially popular receptions of scripture, alongside a rediscovery of magisterial interpretations from the "pre-critical" period, offers a way for re-engagement with the concerns and agendas of the churches.

On the other hand, it could follow in the footsteps of the historical-critical method and replace the latter's "received wisdom" with an alternative *tradition* of "classic readings," instead of viewing tradition as an inevitably fluid constellation of ideas and events at a particular time and place that condition particular readings of biblical texts. Interpreters may indeed have been prompted by earlier readings, but that quest for influence is one that comes too readily to the hand of the interpreter. Anyone who has scrabbled round in the byways of biblical interpretation, not least in the work of poets and artists who might not make it to "the summit dialogue," will be aware that their impact on "tradition" might be every bit as significant for a modern reader as Origen, Aquinas, Calvin, or Augustine. This warns us of the danger of reducing the enterprise of reception history either to an expert's playground or to the neat application of an aesthetic methodology.

Interpretation in its totality is a telling of a story about what the text means, and we need to find a way to tell a new story of the text that includes voices from the past and also non-dominant voices past and present, e.g. the rich tradition of women's appropriation of the Apocalypse. The methodological pattern is going to be different for each biblical text. Our task, however, is to make that idiosyncratic account one that can also embrace readers as they craft their own stories of interpretation.

Biblical Studies. Within biblical studies, a number of challenges present themselves. The discipline may still have a long way to go in convincing historical critics of the necessity or even value of reception history. Careful reception-historical analysis of modern as well as ancient receptions may be necessary in order to illuminate the extent of (often unconscious) dependence of critical commentaries on specific strands of reception history in the questions they pose, to the neglect of others. To look at the challenge from another angle, reception history could offer historical critics a paradigm for the future that is in fact more thoroughly historical, in that it traces receptions of the text through history, illuminating the changing "horizons of expectation" (Jauss's *Erwartungshorizont*) with which readers in different contexts have approached the text.

One particular avenue, which may help reinvigorate the future of biblical studies, is to view reception history less as another "criticism" (one possible translation of the German *Geschichte*) alongside source, form, redaction, or narrative criticisms, and more a way of engaging the text that impacts a range of historical, literary, and theological methods. Markus Bockmuehl's stimulating discussion of the current state and future prospects of New Testament study (Bockmuehl 2006) points precisely to the potential of *Wirkungsgeschichte* for bringing together in a shared focus subdisciplines as diverse as textual criticism, narrative criticism, and liberationist deconstruction.

Two particular contributions could usefully be noted in conclusion. The first is the invitation reception history issues to textual participation, an invitation found in both scholarly and popular readings. It is particularly rooted in the conviction that the subject matter of the texts is fundamentally theological and that it has the capacity to transform the lives of readers. This contrasts sharply with the nonparticipatory character of much historical criticism, with its focus on information rather than transformation.

Second, it raises awareness of the key role of the imagination in interpreting texts, which is in fact widely shared. Although more obvious in figurative and allegorical readings typical of patristic and especially medieval exegesis, imaginative reconstruction is no less present in historical-critical readings. The capacity to reconstruct intended audiences, or illuminate study of the Gospels of Matthew and John by appeal to "Gospel communities," is not qualitatively different from the imaginative (and equally text-grounded) receptions found in pre-critical predecessors. Rather, the use of the imagination, like reception history itself, is integral to the task of finding meaning in biblical texts.

[*See also* Historical Criticism, *subentry* Hebrew Bible; Historical Criticism, *subentry* New Testament; Patristic Interpretation; *and* Reader-Response Criticism.]

BIBLIOGRAPHY

Bockmuehl, Markus. *Seeing the Word: Refocusing New Testament Study*. Studies in Theological Interpretation. Grand Rapids, Mich.: Baker Academic, 2006. A proposal for future directions in New Testament studies advocating a greater role for reception history.

Ebeling, Georg. *The Word of God and Tradition*. Translated by S. H. Hooke. London: Collins, 1968. English translation of *Wort Gottes und Tradition*, first published in 1964. A book that argues for a re-imagining of church history as the history of the interpretation of the Bible and that is considered by Luz to anticipate the *Wirkungsgeschichte* of biblical texts.

Gadamer, Hans-Georg. *Truth and Method*, 2d rev. ed. Translated by J. Weinsheimer and D. G. Marshall. London and New York: Continuum, 1989. English translation of *Wahrheit und Methode*, first published in 1960. Gadamer's major text on hermeneutics, which is the point of reference for all modern discussions of *Wirkungsgeschichte*.

Jauss, Hans Robert. *Toward an Aesthetic of Reception*. Translated by T. Bahti. Minneapolis: University of Minnesota Press, 1982. An English collection of Jauss's seminal writings; an influential attempt to systematize Gadamer's discussion of hermeneutics and provide a methodological framework.

Knight, Mark. "*Wirkungsgeschichte*, Reception History, Reception Theory." In Roberts and Rowland, eds., 2010, 137–146. An introduction to the relationship between these terms in recent discussion and the different ways in which Gadamer's ideas have been appropriated by biblical scholars.

Kovacs, Judith, and Christopher Rowland. *Revelation: The Apocalypse of Jesus Christ*. Blackwell Bible Commentaries. Malden, Mass., Oxford, and Carlton: Blackwell, 2004. A broad engagement with the reception history of the Apocalypse, including popular, marginal, and artistic receptions.

Luz, Ulrich. "The Contribution of Reception History to a Theology of the New Testament." In *The Nature of New Testament Theology*, edited by C. Rowland and C. Tuckett, 123–34. Malden Mass., Oxford, and Carlton: Blackwell, 2006. A more recent outline of Luz's approach, which examines the relationship between *Wirkungsgeschichte* and reception history, the ecumenical impact of a reception-historical approach, and what it might contribute to a theological interpretation of the New Testament for today.

Luz, Ulrich. *Matthew in History: Interpretation, Influence, and Effects*. Minneapolis: Fortress, 1994. A seminal discussion of Luz's engagement with the "history of influence" of Matthew's Gospel.

Luz, Ulrich. *Matthew 1–7: A Commentary*. Edinburgh: T&T Clark, 1989. *Matthew 8–20: A Commentary*. Hermeneia. Minneapolis: Fortress Press, 2001. *Matthew, pp. 21–28: A Commentary*. Minneapolis: Fortress Press, 2005. Luz's EKK commentary, which pays particular attention to *Wirkungsgeschichte*.

Lyons, William John. "Hope for a Troubled Discipline? Contributions to New Testament Studies from Reception History." In Roberts and Rowland, eds., 2010, 207–220. A proposal for re-labeling historical-critical methodologies with the terminology of reception history, with a view to ensuring the survival of biblical studies within the academy.

Nicholls, Rachel. *Walking on the Water: Reading Mt 14:22–33 in the Light of its Wirkungsgeschichte*. Leiden, Netherlands: Brill, 2008. An application of Gadamer's concept of *Wirkungsgeschichte* to one specific gospel narrative.

O'Hear, Natasha. *Contrasting Images of the Book of Revelation in Late Medieval and Early Modern Art*. Oxford Theological Monographs. Oxford: Oxford University Press, 2011. An in-depth study of visual exegesis of the Apocalypse in selected manuscripts, tapestries, altarpieces, and woodcuts.

O'Kane, Martin. *Painting the Text: The Artist as Biblical Interpreter*. Bible in the Modern World 8. Sheffield, UK: Sheffield Phoenix Press, 2007. An exploration of the role of art (mainly from the fifteenth to seventeenth centuries) as biblical exegesis, in which nuances and subtleties in the biblical narrative are highlighted by the artist, revealing aspects of the text of which viewers may have hitherto been unaware.

Parris, David Paul. *Reception Theory and Biblical Hermeneutics*. Princeton Theological Monograph Series. Eugene, Ore.: Pickwick, 2009. A study of the impact of Gadamer and Jauss specifically on biblical studies, with worked examples of interpretation following Jauss' method.

Räisänen, Heikki. "The 'Effective History' of the Bible: A Challenge to Biblical Scholarship?" *Scottish Journal of Theology* 45 (1992): 303–324. An article assessing the scope, impact, and limits of "effective history" and reception history for the interpretation of biblical texts.

Riches, John. *Galatians Through the Centuries*. Blackwell Bible Commentaries. Malden Mass., Oxford, and Carlton: Blackwell, 2008. A reception-historical commentary on this Pauline letter that engages in depth with a selected group of "classic" commentaries, including Augustine, John Chrysostom, Thomas Aquinas, Luther, and Calvin.

Roberts, Jonathan, and Christopher Rowland, eds. *Journal for the Study of the New Testament* 33/2 (2010). An issue of the journal specifically dedicated to reception theory and reception history; in addition to the articles mentioned in this bibliography, there are also discussions of visual exegesis, the hermeneutics of Ulrich Luz, *Sachkritik*, and socio-rhetorical interpretation.

Rowland, Christopher. *Blake and the Bible*. New Haven, Conn.: Yale University Press, 2011. A major study of the biblical hermeneutics of William Blake, with particular attention to his visual interpretation.

Sawyer, John F. A. "The Role of Reception Theory, Reader-Response Criticism and/or Impact History in the Study of the Bible: Definition and Evaluation." 2004. http://bbibcomm.net/?page_id=183 [accessed November 30, 2011]. Paper given at the Society of Biblical Literature Annual Meeting, San Antonio. A wide-ranging discussion of interpretative approaches (from reader-response criticism through advocacy readings to *Wirkungsgeschichte*) that engage with the reception of biblical texts.

Sherwood, Yvonne. *A Biblical Text and its Afterlives: The Survival of Jonah in Western Culture*. Cambridge, UK: Cambridge University Press, 2001. An examination of the reception of the biblical Book of Jonah, attending particularly to "backwater" rather than mainstream readings, and engaging cultural studies, Jewish studies, literature, and art.

Christopher Rowland and Ian Boxall

Reconstructionist Interpretation

Reconstructionism is a contemporary Jewish movement founded in the United States in the 1930s by Rabbi Mordecai M. Kaplan (1881–1983). The central tenets of Kaplan's Reconstructionism include:

(a) the conviction that Judaism is an evolving civilization that encompasses all forms of cultural expression and develops positively over time;
(b) an embrace of rationalism and a consequent rejection of belief in a supernatural God;
(c) a vision of Jewish communities as voluntaristic and democratic collectives.

While Kaplan was not a primarily a biblical exegete, he did articulate a functionalist approach to traditionally authoritative material from the Jewish past. He asserted that his interpretive method would facilitate the creation of a modern, vibrant Jewish culture that was appropriate to the modern period and could flourish within it.

Kaplan was a Conservative rabbi, educated at Columbia University and the Jewish Theological Seminary of America, who set out to articulate a philosophy that would undergird a new form of Judaism that could survive and flourish in the twentieth century and beyond. Though Kaplan did not intend to create a new Jewish denomination, he did envision Reconstructionism as an ideology that would inform Judaism across non-Orthodox denominations. However, when the Conservative movement failed to adopt Kaplan's program, his followers, led by his protégée Ira Eisenstein, created the Reconstructionist movement as a distinct denomination within American liberal Judaism.

Reconstructionist Principles. In his 1934 book *Judaism as a Civilization*, Kaplan articulated the core principles of his ideology.

Judaism as an Evolving Civilization. By identifying Judaism as a civilization, Kaplan defined it as a phenomenon more comprehensive than race or religion. Like "Italian civilization" or "Western civilization," Judaism was a naturally occurring, self-perpetuating set of conditions, practices, and beliefs that its adherents developed and practiced over time. According to Kaplan, the practices and beliefs of a civilization serve two primary purposes. They impart a culturally distinctive flavor to the experience of its members. Some practices and beliefs, namely those that are commonly identified as religious, also function to facilitate the realization of the spiritual and ethical potential of both the individual and the collective. Because Judaism, like all civilizations, evolves over time, its constituent beliefs and practices change in accordance with wider historical, scientific, and philosophical developments. The goal of Kaplan's program was both to propagate this civilizational ideology and to contribute tools and material for the creation of a vibrant and appropriately modern Jewish civilization.

The Consistency of Human Nature over Time. While civilizations change over time, Kaplan believed that core elements of human nature remain consistent. Throughout his work, Kaplan asserted that all humans strive for ethical and spiritual betterment and the fulfillment of individual and collective needs and potential. In every era the individual strives to "find himself in a universe that is friendly to his highest purpose, to fulfill the most valued potentialities of his nature and to achieve a social order that is founded on justice and peace" (1934, p. 389). The religious practices and beliefs of each historical stage of a civilization represent specific expressions of these strivings and distinctive strategies for attaining them. These expressions will always reflect the character and limitations of their historical contexts. Nevertheless, it is possible to identify the common, timeless human aspirations encoded in any given practice.

Rejection of a Supernatural God. Like other theologians of his era, Kaplan strove to articulate a theology that would be compatible with modern rationalist perspectives and scientific convictions. Kaplan asserted that the belief in a supernatural God who possessed a personality and individual agency and was an independent agent in history was untenable in the modern period. He argued that the advances of modern science and philosophy have led to the necessity of asserting a non-supernatural theology. Informed by the work of contemporary process theologians, Kaplan (1962, p. 40) asserted that God was a real but abstract force in the cosmos: God is "the power that makes for salvation," where salvation is conceived as the realization of the highest ethical and spiritual potential of the individual and the collective.

Rejection of the Ideology of Jewish Chosenness. Kaplan rejected the traditional belief in chosenness on both theological and sociological grounds. On theological grounds, the idea of chosenness is incompatible with Kaplan's insistence on a non-supernatural God. Only a God with personality and will could establish a privileged relationship in history with a particular people. Since Kaplan rejected the notions of divine will, personality, and historical agency, such an ideology of chosenness became a logical impossibility. Kaplan's understanding of Judaism as a civilization also militated against the traditional ideology of Jewish chosenness or even of Jewish superiority grounded in non-theological terms. Kaplan's civilizational ideology affirmed the distinctiveness of all civilizations while also asserting their structural and moral equivalence. Each civilization is comprised of a distinctive set of practices and beliefs that, at their best, serve to express the common psychological experiences and aspirations of humanity. Because each civilization has the potential to perform the same function within human experience, one cannot be, in *de facto* terms, superior to another.

Vision of Judaism as a Voluntaristic Polity Governed by Democratic Processes. For Kaplan, one of the most significant changes in Jewish life in modernity was the fact that, after emancipation, Jews lived in two civilizations: the civilization of their home country and the civilization of their Jewish subgroup. Because he viewed Judaism first and foremost as a civilization, he argued that Jews living in conditions of freedom had a choice whether to participate in its cultural expressions, and they could therefore choose to what degree these cultural expressions would frame and inform their lives. This vision of a voluntaristic Judaism was both pragmatic and ideologically grounded. In 1930s America, affirmative Jewish practice was a matter of choice for individuals even as Jews faced many collective barriers to full participation in broader society. While many Jewish communal leaders saw this freedom as a threat to Jewish survival, Kaplan viewed it as an important and positive evolution in Jewish civilization that brought the reality of Jewish experience into conformity with the true nature of Judaism. Because, for Kaplan, the traditional texts of Judaism did not derive from a supernatural authority, and because each stage of Jewish civilization was distinct from the one that preceded it, the traditional claims to authority that were grounded in theories of revelation or precedent were philosophically untenable. Attempts to propagate these claims to authority were unethical, authoritarian, and inimical to the modern American values of autonomy, democracy, rationalism, and progress. While Kaplan acknowledged and celebrated the realization of a voluntaristic Judaism, he maintained a conviction that Judaism was a collective and communal enterprise. The combination of his voluntaristic and communal convictions led him to envision modern Judaism as a constellation of Jewish communities, organized on local, regional, national, and ultimately transnational levels, whose norms would be determined through democratic processes of debate, discussion, and communal consensus.

Functional Method of Interpretation. For Kaplan, the hermeneutical program of functional interpretation was a central strategy for the creation of a vibrant modern Jewish civilization. Informed by the American pragmatist philosophers William James and John Dewey, Kaplan believed that religious practices and beliefs express psychological realia and foster fulfillment of ethical and spiritual aspirations. Practices and beliefs from the Jewish past fulfill these functions in ways that are appropriate to the stage of societal evolution in which they arose. As such, ancient practices are often outmoded expressions of timeless human aspirations. Kaplan's program of functional interpretation was designed to identify and articulate the timeless referents of these practices and to reconstruct those practices in ways that were amenable to the modern world and productive in a modern context. In addition, functional interpretation was a strategy for transforming traditional practices that no longer felt compelling to many modern Jews into appealing and nourishing elements of a robust contemporary Judaism.

Kaplan described functional interpretation as a multistep process. First, the interpreter would apprehend ancient practices and beliefs as both historically-bounded artifacts and as potential expressions of timeless human experiences and aspirations. The interpreter would "regard the traditional religious teachings and institutions as a product of social life, reflecting the limitations of the various periods of their origin, [and] will yet discover to what extent those teachings and institutions made for faith, salvation and loyalty. By this means the pragmatic implications of the traditional teachings will be revealed and developed" (1934, p. 386). The interpreter would achieve this discernment by "disengaging from the mass of traditional lore and custom the psychological aspect which testifies to the presence of ethical and spiritual strivings" (1934, p. 390). Because these ethical and spiritual strivings were constant elements of human nature, the interpreter could then find "equivalents" for them in contemporary civilization. "Reinterpretation is the process of finding equivalents in the civilization to which we belong for values of a past stage of that or another civilization. While there is a qualitative difference between such values, yet in their relation to their respective civilizations, or considered morphologically, they possess equivalence" (1934, p. 389). The extraction of timeless psychological aspects and spiritual strivings, and the identification of their contemporary equivalents were the first stages in the process of functional reinterpretation. Next, the interpreter would, if possible, adapt the ancient practice or belief to modern sensibilities.

If the goal of functional interpretation is to identify those practices and beliefs from the past that are expressive of contemporary values, one might ask why it is important to engage with this material at all if it merely recapitulates convictions that moderns already hold. Kaplan's answer to this challenge was typically pragmatic. He argued that the "traditional concepts . . . carry with them the accumulated momentum and emotional drive of man's previous efforts to attain greater spiritual power" (1934, p. 386). By reevaluating and redeploying traditional concepts and practices, modern Jews are "conserving accumulated energy that would otherwise go to waste . . . it helps to conserve and foster all tendencies, individual and social, which make for the complete development of the individual and the progressive unification of mankind" (1934, p. 388). In addition, the retention of traditional material will also foster continuity within Jewish civilization, thereby maintaining its distinctiveness. For Kaplan, then, functional interpretation was a strategy for selectively drawing on material from the Jewish past to foster most efficiently spiritual and ethical progress. The functional interpreter would discern the function of a given tradition or practice and retain the aspects of that tradition or practice that could be redeployed effectively in the modern world. Those aspects that were deemed inconsistent with modern ethical, spiritual, and philosophical sensibilities would be jettisoned as historically obsolete and possibly destructive.

The Role of the Bible in the Program of Functional Interpretation. For Kaplan, both scripture as a category and the contents of the Hebrew Bible were necessary and fruitful subjects of functional interpretation. Through a functional reinterpretation of the category of *Torah*, Kaplan attempted to retain a sense of Torah's central value while divesting it of normative or doctrinal authority. As a rationalist, Kaplan rejected all assertions of Torah's supernatural origins or divinely grounded authority. In addition, his conviction regarding the evolving nature of civilizations rendered any claims of authority based on precedent or antiquity nonsensical: in Kaplan's evolutionary scheme societies get better, not worse. Thus, their later attempts at self-governance are bound to be superior to their earlier attempts. While rejecting its authority, Kaplan saw Torah, when defined as the Hebrew Bible, and later canonical Jewish works, as the prime repository of those practices and ideas that were historically limited attempts to foster the attainment of timeless spiritual and ethical aspirations. He argued that Torah was not a set of authoritative mandates for modern Jewish practice; rather, it served as an agenda enumerating those concerns whose contemplation would support the fulfillment of central human aspirations. Because the particular answers of the traditional material to questions of ultimate concern may well be outmoded, intensive study of the texts is not an efficient route toward the advancement of humanity toward its goals. Rather, what is necessary for the creation of a modern Jewish civilization is "the fostering of a mode of life that will be animated by whatever in the traditional attitude toward the Torah is of incontestable worth" (1934, p. 411). Kaplan also extended the definition of Torah further and argued that it should be equated with Jewish civilization as a whole and include all products of Jewish cultural creativity.

Kaplan's functional reinterpretation of the category of Torah differed significantly from traditional, Reform, and *Wissenschaft* understandings. In traditional Jewish thought, Torah is a category of revelation that is understood as a divinely inscribed or inspired road map to salvation within a covenantal system. It is imperative to study and analyze the text in all its minute details to arrive at a deeper understanding of the truths encoded within it and to achieve a deeper understanding of the mandates whose compliance will lead to national and personal salvation. By redefining Torah as the entirety of the Jewish civilization in all its expressions and Torah's function as a table of contents that delineates the set of concerns key to spiritual development, Kaplan not only denied the communal authority of Torah, but also challenged the fetishistic status of Torah as it was traditionally conceived, and Torah study as it was practiced in traditional Jewish culture. He argued that the topics of Torah are worthy of sustained and vigorous attention, but the ways in which those topics are addressed in the ancient texts are not. While Kaplan's conception of Torah was a clear departure from traditional views, it was also a rejection of the fully historicizing approach of the *Wissenschaft* school. According to Kaplan's evaluation, the *Wissenschaft* scholars laid the groundwork for functional interpretation by recognizing the historical nature of the biblical and rabbinic texts. However, they erred by severing the historical study of the Bible from consideration of the Bible's role in constructive theology. Because ancient texts addressed and fostered timeless psychological experiences and aspirations, a full appreciation of a text's historical specificity could coexist with an appreciation of its ongoing relevance.

His treatment of scripture's status also differed from that of traditional and Reform interpreters. Unlike both of these groups, Kaplan denied any special status to the biblical texts. In both traditional Judaism and the Reform Judaism of his day, biblical material occupied an ideologically privileged position over other Jewish texts. In traditional Jewish legal hermeneutics, biblical mandates were understood to be primary sources of law and, when interpreted correctly, to have a higher authority than those mandates that were of explicitly rabbinic origin. For the reformers, this privileged position was derived from an understanding of the Bible as a universalist text. Unlike rabbinic texts, which were seen as utterly parochial, the biblical texts, at their best, expressed values explicitly shared by Jews and Christians and relevant to all humanity. Kaplan's scheme denies scripture a privileged position. The Bible is integrated into the larger theological category of Torah and has no greater authority or value than any other spiritually or ethically useful text from the Jewish past.

Functionalist Interpretation of Theological Concepts. In his two most comprehensive works, *Judaism as a Civilization* (1934) and *The Meaning of God in Modern Jewish Religion* (1962), Kaplan subjected the central theological concepts of God, Torah, and Israel to functional interpretation. Kaplan treated these theological concepts as metonymic markers that pointed to still-relevant aspects of the human spiritual experience. In arguing for the ongoing relevance of the term "God," Kaplan wrote, "As long as we are struggling to express the same fundamental fact about the cosmos that our ancestors designated by the term, 'God,' the fact of its momentousness or holiness, and are endeavoring to achieve those ideals of human life that derive from its momentousness or holiness, we have a right to maintain their mode of expression" (1934, p. 398). After justifying ongoing use of traditional theological language, Kaplan focuses on reinterpreting the attributes traditionally ascribed to the deity. True to his method, he first identifies an equivalent contemporary value or force for progress that correlates to the ancient attribute. He then deploys traditional God language to name cosmic, social, and individual psychological manifestations of that value. In discussing the idea of God as helper and protector, Kaplan asserts:

> God . . . may be identified with the powers of nature which maintain life, and with the intelligence that transforms environment by subjugating and controlling the natural forces for the common good of humanity. In any act of social cooperation and good-will, in the striving for finer human relations, in man's courage and moral resistance, in his conquest of fear and death, we can discern the operation of the divine principle. (1934, p. 401)

In this interpretation, traditional descriptions of God as "helper" and "protector" are understood as metaphors that can be deployed to describe those constituent parts of the Godhead that are present in all manifestations of humans' desire for and progress toward the "common good of humanity."

Functional Reinterpretation of Jewish Practices. Kaplan's reinterpretation of traditional Jewish practices was grounded in his identification of these practices as "folkways." In traditional Jewish theology, practices such as prayer, *kashrut* (Jewish dietary practices), Sabbath, and festival observance, as well as a wide range of social practices, are identified as commandments (*mitzvot*) and are regarded as constituent parts of a larger system of Jewish law (*halakhah*). For Kaplan, this understanding of the status and function of traditional practices was untenable because he rejected the forms of religious authority on which their mandatory status was grounded. In addition, because Kaplan rejected a covenantal ideology in which compliance or noncompliance to a set of eternal mandates determined the fate of the individual or the nation, he could not accept an ideology of practice that saw compliance with Jewish "law" as the terms of a salvific contract. Rather, he argued that traditional Jewish practices were folkways—activities that gave a particularist Jewish flavor to the experience of individual Jews and Jewish communities. Those folkways that he characterized as religious functioned additionally to "express the feeling of life's significance in the individual manner of that people" (1934, p. 435). In each case of functional interpretation, he attempted to extract and identify both the insights imbedded in the practices and the positive behaviors that they fostered in order to argue for their ongoing inclusion, in some form, in modern Jewish practice.

His discussion of the dietary laws in Judaism as a civilization provides a typical example. Kaplan identifies the function of the dietary laws as the transformation of "the process of eating from a purely animal act to one in which spirituality plays a part. In so doing, the dietary laws have also served to give the Jewish civilization 'a high degree of distinction and dignity'" (1934, p. 440). These functions provide typical examples of the ways in which, for Kaplan, religious practices foster human spirituality and enhance Jewish civilization. After identifying these functions, Kaplan sketches out a modern version of dietary restrictions that would fulfill these functions while avoiding the ethical shortfalls of the traditional practices. Such a system would entail the maintenance of *kashrut* in the home but not outside of it, where the dietary laws create barriers between Jews and gentiles and significantly limit the practitioner's range of activities. If the practitioner of this modern form of *kashrut* were to understand the practice functionally, he would not suffer the negative psychological consequences that the traditional, normative view of the practice engendered. Such a practitioner would understand the function of the dietary practices, and he would not suffer from feelings of sin in cases of noncompliance or from "the self-complacency which results from scrupulous observance" (1934, p. 441). This example demonstrates Kaplan's attempt to articulate a method that would maintain basic structures of traditional Jewish life while stripping them of authority and granting practitioners license to revise them in accordance with their perceived function, rather than through exegetical processes of textual interpretation. In his treatment of *kashrut*, as well as other traditional practices, Kaplan attempted to demonstrate a method for the creation of modern Jewish civilization in which "[t]he ancient authorities are entitled to vote but not to veto" (1948).

Functional Interpretation in Historical Context. As Robert Seltzer and others have noted, Kaplan is the first Jewish interpreter to draw expressly on the work of American intellectuals. Kaplan's pragmatic and functional approach to Judaism was deeply influenced by the pragmatic philosophers John Dewey and William James, the process theologians of the Chicago School, and by contemporary American sociological discourse. His embrace of the autonomy of the individual, his insistence on the positive power of innovation, his enthusiasm for the creation of democratic and voluntaristic Jewish communities, as well as his confidence in the progressive evolution of human societies were reflective of a largely American ethos.

The immediate context of Kaplan's functional interpretation was a robust conversation that was taking place among American Jewish intellectuals of the period. Non-Orthodox Jewish intellectuals were working to articulate iterations of Judaism that would have integrity and be able to flourish in twentieth century America. Throughout his work, Kaplan identified his hermeneutical program as an alternative to the approaches being developed in the mainstream Conservative movement on the one hand, and the Reform movement on the other. Each of these groups was wrestling with the reality of a Jewish community that was increasingly integrated into the wider society, increasingly diverse in its degree of participation in Jewish practice and community, and increasingly inclined to prioritize the epistemological frameworks of modernity over those of Jewish tradition. The religious movements had a deep respect for the historical-scientific study of Judaism (although the Conservative movement was more resistant to the application of the *Wissenschaft* method to study the Bible), and they strove to articulate visions of modern Judaism that were informed by and compatible with the insights of that scholarly movement.

With regard to the Bible, the ideologues of the Reform and Conservative movements articulated hybrid visions of the text that were, in theoretical terms, similar to Kaplan's. Each movement described the biblical texts as having both timeless, and therefore contemporarily relevant, aspects, and timebound aspects that were outmoded in the modern era. However, several aspects of Kaplan's ideology of scripture differentiated him from ideologues to both his left and his right. Whereas both the Reform and Conservative ideologues identified the "timeless" aspects of the biblical texts as expressions of the divine will, Kaplan argued that the continual relevance of aspects of the biblical material emanated from essential and unchanging elements of human nature, experience, and aspiration. It was the Jewish people, as a transhistorical collective, that was abiding, not any Jewish belief or practice. In addition, Kaplan's insistence that ancient practices had spiritual and civilizational value but lacked normative authority also distinguished him from other liberal Jewish thinkers. While ideologues within the Conservative movement conceded that some biblical texts articulated imperfect human attempts to communicate divine truths, they maintained that biblical and rabbinic laws were binding, albeit in a modernized form, for the modern Jew. To his mainstream Conservative colleagues, Kaplan's denial of any normative status for Jewish law was untenable. In addition, his redefinition of commandments as folkways was seen as a radically voluntaristic move that would open the door to a radical reduction and/or revision of traditional practice akin to that advocated by his Reform contemporaries.

Reform ideologues concurred with Kaplan's identification of biblical and postbiblical mandates and practices as exclusively human creations. However, they did not accept his ascription of cultural or spiritual value to these practices. For the Reformers the litmus test of value was more narrowly ethical and theological. The only elements of biblical tradition that they wanted to maintain were those that transparently fostered universalist ethical practice. Any biblical text that fostered these ends was valid and binding. While the reform ideologues gave these "moral" mandates the force of law, they rejected all other traditional mandates entirely. All biblical and rabbinic mandates regulating diet, dress, and ritual behavior were deemed historical relics that were anathema to the more evolved spiritual state of modern Jews. Conformity to these laws was deemed an obstacle to spiritual development. Kaplan's willingness to consider traditional particularist practices both as potentially useful tools for the spiritual and moral development of contemporary Jews and as potentially useful material for the creation of a vibrant contemporary stage of Jewish civilization distinguished him from his Reform contemporaries.

Impact of Kaplan's Hermeneutical Program. In the second half of the twentieth century most explicitly Reconstructionist biblical interpretation appeared in the movement's publications and institutions. Reconstructionist rabbis, who were trained in a Kaplanian approach to Judaism and scripture, delivered sermons in their synagogues and published essays in *The Reconstructionist* journal that were explicitly informed by Kaplan's theory of Judaism as an evolving civilization and by his method of functional interpretation. In the more public arena in recent decades, Kaplan's approach has been echoed most strongly in the transvaluation of Jewish practices into contemporary social justice practices. The contemporary "eco-*kashrut*" movement provides an example. The term eco-*kashrut* was coined by Rabbi Zalman Schachter Shalomi and promulgated by Rabbi Arthur Waskow. Eco-*kashrut* activists argue that ancient Jewish practices regarding food, including the dietary laws and the laws of the sabbatical year, were ancient Israelite attempts to align farming and food practices with an awareness of humanity's place in the ecosystem and an awareness of the value and dignity of animals and plants as creations of God. The proponents of eco-*kashrut* argue that it is these principles, not the time-bound laws that express them, that should direct the food practice of contemporary Jews. As a result, the proponents of eco-*kashrut* argue for a new set of dietary principles that would address not only the way in which an animal is slaughtered but also the degree to which the entire food production process maintains the well-being and sustainability of all its participants. Although its advocates do not identify eco-*kashrut* as an explicitly Kaplanian or Reconstructionist concept, the assertion that ancient food and farming mandates express values equivalent to those of the contemporary environmental and food justice movements, the retention and reapplication of traditional language to contemporary practices, the assertion of eco-*kashrut* as spiritually and ethically beneficial, and its totally voluntary practice all bear witness to Kaplan's influence on the movement.

While not a Jewish movement, the worldwide Jubilee initiative that occurred in the year 2000 provides another contemporary example of functional interpretation. The proponents of this movement argued that the biblical principle of debt relief for Israelites in the fiftieth year encoded a trans-historical religious mandate to address the problem of crippling debt on the poor. The Jubilee 2000 activists urged the World Bank and lending countries to forgive the debts of developing countries as a contemporary enactment of the principle underlying the biblical command. It is important to note that these movements, and others like them, do not explicitly trace their heritage to Kaplan. In fact, the transvaluation of perceived ethical commandments, like the Jubilee, was also a central element of Reform biblical interpretation. However, these movements testify to the degree to which Kaplanian functional interpretation has become a common strategy for contemporary Jews and Christians who deploy biblical and other traditional texts and concepts in the service of contemporary social justice activism.

Contemporary Reconstructionist Biblical Interpretation. The civilizational approach to Judaism and the functional approach to biblical texts continue to inform the work of contemporary Reconstructionist biblical interpreters. However, whereas Kaplan engaged with the Bible primarily as a storehouse of potential material for the creation of a modern Jewish civilization, contemporary Reconstructionist biblical interpretation is far more concerned with exploring the function and meaning of biblical texts within their historical context. In addition, whereas Kaplan mined the biblical text for material that reflected humanity's highest aspirations and most admirable ethical qualities, contemporary Reconstructionist interpreters also see value in biblical texts that articulate resonant anxieties and spark reflection on less admirable, but equally human, tendencies. Reconstructionist interpreters are particularly interested in resurrecting elements of ancient texts that were marginalized by the biblical redactors and traditional Jewish commentators. As heirs to Kaplan's convictions regarding the essential heterogeneity of Jewish ideas and practices in every era, contemporary Reconstructionist interpreters often emphasize aspects of the biblical texts that gesture toward minority opinions, known but not advocated by the authors and redactors of the biblical texts. By drawing attention to these marginalized or submerged perspectives, contemporary Reconstructionist interpreters strive to reveal the heterogeneity of ancient Israelite civilization. These marginal or heterodox voices that bear witness to the heterogeneity of ancient Israelite belief and practice are also prime candidates for reconstruction and transvaluation. They are often identified as tools for voicing and including repressed or marginalized perspectives in contemporary Jewish culture.

Jacob Staub's commentary on the Torah pericope, *Hukat* (Num 19:1—22:1), provides an example. In his commentary (2000), Staub argues that the episode in which the Israelites look at the statue of the copper serpent and are healed of a plague can serve as a counter-text to centuries of Jewish exhortations regarding the strict control of heterosexual desire and the utter suppression of homosexual desire. He argues that this episode may gesture toward another ancient Israelite ethos or practice, largely suppressed by the biblical redactors, in which gazing at and reflection on sacred phallic symbols was considered legitimate and beneficial religious practice. Staub extends his discussion of the episode to the biblical and postbiblical rejection of physical representations of God and asks "whether at some earlier period, it was an embodied God at whom one cannot look—the one with an outstretched arm and flaring nostrils, the One who occupied a very definite physical space in the Temple's Holy of Holies . . . " (2009, 2010). He concludes his essay by arguing for reclamation of those ancient Israelite beliefs and practices, hinted at but ultimately rejected by the redactors of the biblical texts, that celebrate imaginative engagement and reflection on the body of God. He suggests that such reclamation would give Jews ancient material to use in the construction of contemporary Jewish practices that "affirm that materiality and physical pleasure are divine gifts rather than temptations" (Staub, p. 210).

Staub's commentary demonstrates how contemporary Reconstructionist biblical interpretation has changed since Kaplan. Whereas Kaplan would have rejected the reference to the veneration of the copper serpents as primitive, theurgic, and idolatrous, Staub embraces the episode as a corrective to centuries of hegemonic heterosexist, and anti-sensual discourse within Judaism. For Kaplan, the heterogeneity of contemporary Jewish practice and belief would arise from creative reflection by different Jews on the timeless elements of the ancient texts. For Staub, the texts themselves bear witness to the timeless heterogeneity of Jewish practice and to the impossibility of extracting universal principles from the diverse past. The diversity of perspectives within the biblical canon provides material for an alternative Jewish discourse on sexuality and also provides a polemical corrective to attempts to claim an essentially normative status for any single Jewish discourse.

[*See also* Conservative Jewish Interpretation; Historical Criticism, *subentry* Hebrew Bible; Midrash; Orthodox Jewish Interpretation; Rabbinic Exegesis; *and* Reform Jewish Interpretation.]

BIBLIOGRAPHY

Drinkwater, Gregg, Joshua Lesser, and David Shneer et al, eds. *Torah Queeries: Weekly Commentaries on the Hebrew Bible.* New York: NYU Press, 2009. A volume containing commentaries by many Reconstructionist interpreters. See especially the essays by Steve Gutow, Linda Holzman, Tamar Kamionkowski, Jason Gary Klein, Lori Hope Lefkovitz, Sarra Lev, Jane Rachel Litman, Amber Powers, and Toba Spitzer.

Goldsmith, Emanuel, Mel Scult, and Robert M. Seltzer, eds. *The American Judaism of Mordecai M. Kaplan.* New York: NYU Press, 1990. A volume of essays situating Kaplan in his twentieth century American context.

Jewish Social Studies 12:2 (2006). This special issue, entitled "Mordecai Kaplan's 'Judaism as a Civilization': The Legacy of an American Idea" was published on the occasion of the seventieth anniversary of Kaplan's seminal book. The volume contains articles by scholars from a range of disciplines reflecting on the nature and impact of Kaplan's work. The essay by Benjamin D. Sommer, titled "Functional Interpretation and Biblical Theology: Reflections on 'Judaism as a Civilization' in Relation to Biblical Hermeneutics" (143–157), deals directly with Kaplan's hermeneutical program.

Kaplan, Mordecai. *Judaism as a Civilization: Toward a Reconstruction of American-Jewish Life* (1934). Reprint, with an introduction by Mel Scult, Philadelphia: Jewish Publication Society, 2010. Kaplan's seminal work outlining his vision of Judaism as an evolving civilization. He describes and demonstrates his hermeneutical process in the chapters on Functional Interpretation (XXVI) and Jewish Folkways (XXIX).

Kaplan, Mordecai M. *The Meaning of God in Modern Jewish Religion* (1962). Reprint, with an introduction by Mel Scult Detroit, Mich.: Wayne State University Press, 1994. Kaplan's most sustained articulation of his theology. He employs his hermeneutical method on biblical and traditional Jewish material throughout.

Kaplan, Mordecai M. *Questions Jews Ask: Reconstructionist Answers* (1956). Reprint. New York: Reconstructionist Press, 1972.

Kaplan, Mordecai M. "Random Thoughts." *The Reconstructionist* 14:1 (1948).

Lefkovitz, Lori Hope. *In Scripture: The First Stories of Jewish Sexual Identities.* Lanham, Md.: Rowman and Littlefield, 2010. A book length example of contemporary Reconstructionist biblical interpretation that demonstrates contemporary practitioners' dual interest in ancient texts in their literary historical contexts as well as their role in constructing past and contemporary gender identities.

Scult, Mel Scult. *Judaism Faces the Twentieth Century: A Biography of Mordecai Kaplan.* Detroit Mich.: Wayne State University Press, 1993. The most comprehensive biography of Kaplan to date.

Staub, Jacob J. "The Healing Serpent: Re-covering Long Lost Jewish Fragments: *Parashat Bahar* (Num. 19:1—22:1)" In *Torah Queeries: Weekly Commentaries on the Hebrew Bible*, edited by Gregg Drinkwater, Joshua Lesser, David Shneer et al., 206–211. New York: NYU Press, 2009. An example of contemporary Reconstructionist biblical interpretation.

Elsie R. Stern

Redaction Criticism

[*This entry contains three subentries,* Hebrew Bible, Apocrypha and Deuterocanonical Books, *and* New Testament]

Hebrew Bible

Redactor and Redactions. The *Chambers Dictionary* defines the verb "to redact" by "to edit; to put (a text) into the appropriate literary form." Redactor and editor are synonyms. In the current meaning of the word, the idea of redaction is mostly related to the publication of a written medium (journal, book). The redactor is the one who prepares a book for publication by checking it for orthographical and other errors and who may also attempt to smooth the style of a work. The words "redactor" and "redaction" are thus mostly related to the very last phase in the publication of a book or a journal.

In Biblical research the term "redactor" can have a much broader meaning. Whereas some scholars (Knierim 1985; and Biddle 1999) want to restrict the term redaction to the last revision of a text, the one that leads to its "final" form, others use it to distinguish between the "original" work of an author and all subsequent versions (see Barton 1992). Others, especially German scholars, defend the view that "redaction" means the whole process of the literary formation of a text from its first written form to the last revisions that brought it into its definite shape (see Kratz 1977; and Schmitt 2004). These different usages of the concept reflect different theoretical models in regard to the formation of the books of the Hebrew Bible. Although the term "redaction criticism" arose only in the middle of the twentieth century the idea that biblical books underwent edition, revision, and additions can already be found in rabbinic discussion, especially in the Talmud.

Redaction Criticism from the Talmud to the Invention of the Deuteronomistic History.

The Beginnings. The idea that biblical books underwent "edition" or "redaction" can already be found in the famous passage Baba Bathra 14a—15b of the Babylonian Talmud, which discusses the order and the authorship of the books of the Hebrew Bible. In folio 15a the rabbis assert that Joshua, and not Moses, wrote the last eight verses of the Pentateuch: "Now is it possible that Moses being dead could have written the words, 'Moses died there?' The truth is, however, that up to this point Moses wrote, from this point Joshua wrote." According to this view, Joshua was the "editor" or "redactor." The same idea applies to the formation of the book of Joshua, which according to the rabbis was completed after Joshua's death first by Eleazar and then by Phineas. Of interest are also the considerations about the formation of the prophetic books. The book of Isaiah was written by King Hezekiah and his scribes, whereas the book of the prophet Ezekiel and of the Twelve Prophets is the work of the men of the "Great assembly." These attributions indicate that the rabbis had already some feeling that the prophetic books were so complex that one author (or the prophet himself) could not have written them; they are therefore considered to be the result of interventions of several hands, which edited the prophetic oracles and gathered them in a book.

Spinoza and Astruc. In the seventeenth century, Richard Simon advanced in his "Critical History of the Old Testament," that the original texts of the Bible were altered by "public scribes" who added some new ideas and also sometimes shortened the text that they were rewriting. For Spinoza, Ezra was the "final editor," not only of the Pentateuch, but of the whole Enneateuch (the books from Genesis to Kings). Although Moses, according to Spinoza, wrote the "book of the law," the kernel of Deuteronomy 12—26, Ezra when writing "the history of the Hebrew nation from the creation of the world to the entire destruction of the city," inserted Deuteronomy into this account (Spinoza 1951, pp. 131–132).

When Jean Astruc envisaged a Documentary Hypothesis in 1753, he did so in order to defend the idea that Moses was the author of the Pentateuch. He claimed that Moses had two parallel documents at his disposal, which he compiled, by cutting them into smaller pieces in order to create a new narrative without deleting anything. According to this view, Moses was a compiler (see Astruc 1999, p. 137). The inconsistencies and gaps in the present Pentateuch are due to later copyists and scribes who altered the original text.

The Idea of Redactors in Old Testament Scholarship of the Nineteenth Century. Before the "newer Documentary Hypothesis" of Kuenen and

Wellhausen triumphed at the end of the nineteenth century, other models—the Fragmentary hypothesis and the Supplementary hypothesis—were advanced to explain the formation of the Torah. These models also required the idea of a compiler or editor. Geddes and Vater advocated the idea that the Pentateuch was the result of the combination of hundreds of fragments compiled by several redactors. De Wette held a similar view in his *Beiträge*, considering the Pentateuch to be the result of the bringing together of formerly independent fragments. He argued, however, that the well-organized arrangement of the product necessitated the existence of a basic framework into which the different fragments were incorporated. This theocratic epic about Israel's origins was written in monarchic times and later complemented by fragments, which were combined in the books of Leviticus and Numbers. Leviticus was the work of later priests who added their ritual laws; the compilers of the book of Numbers imitated fragments of Exodus displaying a mixture of ceremonial laws and mythological accounts typical of a later composition. (*Beiträge*, II, p. 279). In the theocratic epic, later texts that imitated older ones were also incorporated, as, for instance, the account of God's covenant with Abraham in Genesis 15, which reinterprets Genesis 17.

The initiator of the so-called "newer Documentary Hypothesis" (in opposition to the "older" Documentary Hypothesis that postulated the existence of only two parallel documents) is probably Hermann Hupfeld. In his book *The Sources of Genesis and the Manner of Their Conflation* (1853), he tries to demonstrate that within the "Elohistic texts" (those that speak of God using the word *elohim*) one has to distinguish two documents: the older Elohistic source containing the narrative reaching from the origins of the world to the conquest of the land, and a second Elohistic source containing mainly the patriarchal narratives. The third and youngest document was the "Jhvistic" source (using the divine name Yahweh). These three sources were all originally independent and were brought together by a redactor who acted "in strict fidelity" and "inserted his sources verbatim and in full and brought them together retaining all of their peculiarities," but who also paid attention to the "overall structure of the narrative in order to avoid obvious repetitions or contradictions . . . reproducing on an expanded scale in the complete work the (epic) plan of the history inhering in the sources" (Hupfeld 1853, p. 196; English translation: Van Seters 2006, p. 222). Van Seters points out that Hupfeld based himself on the model of the "edited" Homeric epic and had in mind "a historian who is editing his sources in a diplomatic style. . . . It is this earliest description of the function of the Pentateuchal redactor that has persisted throughout its subsequent use" (p. 222). In the nineteenth century there was a close interaction between biblical and classical studies, and the idea of a redaction history may indeed stem from F. A. Wolf, a specialist in Homer, who asserted that the Homeric epics started as oral traditions that were collected and linked by a certain Peisistratus and an editorial committee in the middle of the sixth century B.C.E. Wolf's work was very influential and well known by the nineteenth century specialists of the Pentateuch (see Van Seters, pp. 133–163; Ska 2005, pp. 5–7).

Abraham Kuenen and Julius Wellhausen prepared the way for wide acceptance of the Documentary Hypothesis almost for a century. The four sources or documents of the Pentateuch on which they agreed: J (the Yahwist), E (the Elohist), D (the original core of Deuteronomy), and P (the Priestly Code) were originally four independent and coherent documents. Several redactors from the Assyrian to the Persian periods (eighth to fourth centuries B.C.E.) combined these documents in order to create a Pentateuch or a Hexateuch (at this time most scholars believed that the book of Joshua originally belonged to the first five books of the Bible). According to Kuenen: "We have to assume a redactor or harmonist for the union of J and E, and again for JE and D." There was a final redactor, who "had DJE and P before him, and he effected their union in the spirit and in the interest of P. We may therefore call him Rp in distinction of Rd (the Deuteronomistic redactor of D + JE) and Rj (the redactor of J + E, whom we have also indicated by JE)" (Kuenen 1886, p. 317, n. 5).

Although Wellhausen and Kuenen admitted that the redactors left out passages of the documents they brought together, they saw them mostly as compilers, editors, or harmonists, whose aim was the publication of the Hexateuch by a sort of a "Gospel harmony" comparable to Tatian's work in his Diatesseron. Wellhausen and others also identified Deuteronomistic redactors in the books of Joshua to Kings, but took not much interest in them.

At the same time redactors also appeared in historical-critical research on the Prophets. In his commentary on the book of Jeremiah, Duhm attributed no more than some sixty brief oracles to the historical Jeremiah. The main parts of the book (about 850 verses) were due to Deuteronomistic redactors, which could easily be recognized by their style, including repetitions and theological platitudes. Duhm asserted that "the book has slowly expanded, like a forest growing wildly," (p. xx) and that the Deuteronomistic scribes, (whom he sometimes referred to as "Pharisees"), edited the book from the Babylonian to the Maccabean period. Contrary to Mowinckel, who later adopted for the book of Jeremiah a documentary hypothesis that comes close to the Pentateuchal Documentary Hypothesis, Duhm's redactors had no clear concept. They worked without a clear agenda, even if the main part of the book was due to their work, which could be understood as the transformation of the message of the historical Jeremiah into a Deuteronomistic book. Duhm, like nineteenth-century biblical scholarship on the Prophets in general, was mainly interested in the search for the *ipsissima verba* (the authentic words) of the Prophets and not in the formation of the prophetic books.

Martin Noth and Redaction Criticism. The term *redaction criticism* was apparently coined only in 1956 in New Testament (NT) studies. In his book on "Mark, the Evangelist," W. Marxen tried to show (as H. Conzelmann already had for Luke) that Mark was not a compiler (*Sammler*), but a theologian with his own agenda. He edited and revised the traditional sayings and stories about Jesus in such a way that he provided his own interpretation and understanding of the life of Jesus. According to NT redaction criticism the Gospels are not merely a simple compilation of traditions about Jesus, but comprehensive theological narratives due to the Evangelists.

Although the term *Redaktionsgeschichte* or *Redaktionskritik* is missing, the same view appears in Old Testament scholarship already in Martin Noth's seminal work *Überlieferungsgeschichtliche Studien* of 1943 in which he invented the Deuteronomistic History. Although the title of his book refers to the "history of transmission" of the traditions contained in the books of Deuteronomy, Joshua, Judges, Samuel, and Kings (and also in the book of Chronicles which he analyzes in the second part of the book), Noth anticipates the redaction-critical approach. He presupposes with almost all of his colleagues that Deuteronomy and the Former Prophets contain older materials and narratives as well as Deuteronomistic passages and additions. They are so designated because of their literary and thematic relationship with the book of Deuteronomy. Noth was the first who was interested in knowing the aim of these Deuteronomistic texts. And he came to the conclusion that most of these texts are the work of one man, whom he called "the Deuteronomist." This man had experienced the destruction of Jerusalem and the fall of the kingdom of Judah in 587 B.C.E. and he edited the books of Deuteronomy to Kings as a comprehensive history or historiography (the German "Geschichtswerk" can have both meanings) in order to explain this catastrophe as a divine judgment. Yahweh had punished his people, who throughout their whole history from the conquest through the period of the two kingdoms had not obeyed the divine commandments transmitted by Moses in the book of Deuteronomy. Noth characterized the Deuteronomist as an "honest broker" (p. 128) because he integrated in his history older texts like the "story of David's ascension" without changing it, even if certain texts contradicted his own ideas. But the Deuteronomist was more than that: Noth compared him to Hellenistic and Roman historians "who use older accounts, mostly unacknowledged, to write a history not of their own time but of the more or less distant past" (p. 26). Therefore, for Noth, the Deuteronomist was a "redactor" who was at the same time an "author." In German, Noth's statement is somewhat ambiguous: the Deuteronomist "war nicht nur 'Redaktor,' sondern der Autor eines Geschichtswerkes" (German original, p. 11). This statement could be understood in the sense that he was "not merely an editor but the author of a history" (so the English translation, p. 26), but more probably Noth meant that the Deuteronomist was both: a redactor as well as an author. In any case, Noth's Deuteronomist appears to be a redactor who was an author in the same sense as the Evangelists according to redaction criticism: he respected his sources but also added new passages in order to construct a coherent history reflecting a specific theology.

The major modifications of Noth's theory, which cannot be dealt with in detail (see Römer, *Deuteronomistic History*, pp. 27–43), emphasize the fact that the Deuteronomistic History is the work of several Deuteronomistic editions or revisions. The model of F. M. Cross, which is mainly used in North American scholarship, distinguishes two editions of the Deuteronomistic History: a first Deuteronomist writing under King Josiah in the seventh century B.C.E., who edited older traditions (especially those about David) as a propaganda work for the political and religious innovations of Josiah; and a second Deuteronomist who updated this work after 587 B.C.E. by adding mainly the two last chapters of Kings as well as some other passages in order to take into account the new situation after the end of the kingdom of Judah. The so-called Göttingen-model, quite popular in European research, postulates three main editions of the Deuteronomistic History. The first, called DtrH (Deuteronomistic Historian), wrote shortly after the fall of Jerusalem. He was later revised by DtrP (the prophetic Deuteronomist), who inserted many prophetic narratives, and then by DtrN (the nomistic Deuteronomist), who added passages that emphasize the importance of the divine Law. In recent scholarship, Noth's theory as well as its modifications have been challenged and some scholars claim that a Deuteronomistic History never existed. They acknowledge the existence of Deuteronomistic "redactional" passages in the books of the Former Prophets but fail however to explain the origin and the intention of those Deuteronomistic texts.

Although Noth's theory may need modifications, it still remains a very good example of what redaction criticism is about: it tries to explain the several stages of the formation of biblical books or other major units by the idea that those texts were revised and rewritten by a number of redactors or editors, who added (and perhaps also eliminated) passages in order to actualize a text with regard to their own situation and their own theological agenda.

Redaction Criticism in Present Old Testament Scholarship. The brief history of the rise of the idea of redactors has shown a certain evolution. At the beginning of historical-critical scholarship, redactors or editors are mostly understood as editors or compilers who have no theological agenda and who mostly combine older sources. Starting in a certain way with Duhm and culminating with Noth the idea of a redactor changes: redactors add significant texts and passages in order to express their own concerns.

Pentateuch or Hexateuch. Since the 1970s European Pentateuchal research has tended more and more to give up the Wellhausen-Kuenen Documentary Hypothesis. Interestingly most of the new models that emerge to replace the "Newer Documentary Hypothesis" give a preponderant place to redaction criticism. Erhard Blum, followed by Thomas Dozeman and others, explains the Pentateuch as the result of a combination of a "D (Deuteronomistic)"—and a "P (Priestly)—Composition." Although he speaks of compositions, he considers the D and the P Compositions as two redactions of older texts and traditions that one cannot always reconstruct in their original form. E. Otto, R. Achenbach, and others understand the formation of the Hexateuch as the result of two competing redactions in the Persian period: a Hexateuch-redaction that wants to include the book of Joshua into Israel's Torah and a Pentateuch-redaction, which focused on the Mosaic Law. Before these two redactions there was no Pentateuch. There was only a priestly edition of Genesis-Leviticus (that had already integrated older traditions) and the book of Deuteronomy and maybe some traditions, which can now be detected in the book of Numbers. In this view, the narrative strand starting with the cycle of origins and ending with the death of Moses is exclusively the work of redactors, as are most parts of the book of Numbers.

This focus on redaction criticism can also be found in the very broad definition of the concept by R. Kratz: "redaction occurs as soon as a given text is reused and transformed" (p. 369). This emphasis on a redactional process in order to explain the formation of the Pentateuch is not so prominent in the North American context, where many scholars still stick to the Documentary Hypothesis. Some of them even radicalize this model and speak of a "Neo Documentary Hypothesis." J. Baden claims that there is no need for redactors, since the four documents of the Pentateuch can be entirely reconstructed (which he, however, does not successfully do). They existed as independent documents until a compiler combined them in order to create (for what reason?) the Pentateuch. The redactor added nothing except perhaps a few words. In this model there is no place for redaction criticism, only for traditional source criticism. It is doubtful that this model will succeed in convincing scholars to abandon redaction criticism, which appears as a major approach used in all parts of the Hebrew Bible.

Prophets and Psalms. Almost all prophetic books are understood today as the result of different redactions. In Jeremiah there are many passages that betray Deuteronomistic language and ideas, so that one speaks since Hyatt of one or more Deuteronomistic redactions that contributed to shaping the book in its two forms (the Greek and the Masoretic one). According to Pohlmann and others, the book of Ezekiel has been edited by redactors, who added passages in order to legitimate the Babylonian Diaspora as the true people of Yahweh. In a recent publication, Stromberg (2011) asserts that the so-called Trito-Isaiah is in fact the redactor of the whole book of Isaiah. The current debate about the formation of the Twelve Minor Prophets also emphasizes the fact that these scrolls underwent several redactions in order to create some theological coherence in the Book of the Twelve.

Recent research on the psalms also shows that the Psalter is not the result of a more or less mechanical compilation of independent poems. On the contrary, redactors apparently organized the Psalter through redactional interventions (catch words, inserts in order to strengthen the thematic unity of psalms that stand next to each other, etc.).

This short overview indicates the importance of the idea of redactional activity in the formation of the biblical texts. But did such redactors really exist?

Redactors or Authors? The focus on redaction criticism in recent biblical scholarship has been criticized by John Van Seters, who thinks that this theory emerged under the influence of ideas from the classics that are nowadays given up. He claims: "all talk of 'redactors' and 'redactions' should be scrupulously avoided in biblical studies" (p. 398). Van Seters wants to explain the formation of the Pentateuch and the Former Prophets as the work of three authors: two historians, the Deuteronomist and the Yahwist who wrote a "prologue" to the Deuteronomistic History, and the Priestly Writer who supplemented the Yahwist (but is he then not the "editor" of the Yahwistic history?).

There is some "empirical" evidence for the existence of redactors or editors not only in the Bible but also in the Ancient Near East. We have texts stemming from different versions of the Gilgamesh epic, the Egyptian Book of the Dead, and Assyrian Royal Inscriptions that indicate that the most recent version of these texts is the result of redactional reworking of the older texts, which were modified, augmented but sometimes also shortened or even ignored. The Book of Enoch is another example for the validity of redaction criticism: the different manuscripts attest that the book of Enoch in its present form is the result of redactional reworking and editing. Parts of the present book like the Book of the Watchers (1 Enoch 6–36) and the Astronomical Book (1 Enoch 72–82) existed as independent scrolls before they were revised and combined by redactors. A similar phenomenon can be observed in the Damascus Document from Qumran, of which we have several copies that can help to retrace the history of redaction of this book.

The last example also demonstrates that redaction criticism and textual criticism are closely related. In the book of Joshua, the Septuagint provides a somewhat shorter text than the Masoretic Text. The additions to the Masoretic Text look often very "Deuteronomistic." Apparently, late redactors could easily imitate the Deuteronomistic style. The same holds true for the book of Jeremiah, where the Septuagint attests a much shorter text (about 10 percent) and a quite different organization of the book. Apparently, the Greek and Masoretic versions of Jeremiah reflect two different stages of the book's redaction.

Contrary to Van Seters's assertion, the term "author" should rather be avoided when retracing the formation of the books of the Hebrew Bible. With the possible exception of some very late works (Qoheleth [Ecclesiastes], Ruth), all books of the Hebrew Bible are composite and anonymous as Knauf has rightly pointed out. The books of the Hebrew Bible are not "author literature" but "tradition literature," transmitted and revised by redactors.

How to Define "Redaction" and How to Do "Redaction Criticism." The preceding discussion leads to a rather broad understanding of redaction, in which the term applies to all stages during which an original *written* text receives the forms that are reflected in the different manuscripts available to us (there is no "final" text of the Bible, as shown by the variety of the manuscripts). Redaction criticism should therefore identify, on the basis of a supposed original narrative, legal, poetic, or wisdom text, the different redactions that edited the text in the several stages of its development. Like all exegetical methods, we can never obtain certainty about the existence of redactions, only plausibility.

The following criteria should be considered:

Repetitions. Redactors did not always want to hide their intervention. They quite commonly give some hints that they added something to an older text. In Genesis 16: 9–11, there are three speeches of Yahweh's angel to Hagar. Each verse is introduced by "Yahweh's angel said to her," without any reaction of Hagar. These threefold and unnecessary speech introductions most likely indicate three levels of growth of the narrative. Verse 11, the birth oracle, belongs to the original story. A first redactor added the promise of numerous offspring for Hagar in order to make her as important as Abraham. Another redactor added the order in verse 9 to return to her mistress so as prepare for the variant in Genesis 21 where Hagar is expelled by Sarah (in the original story of Genesis 16, Hagar's son Ishmael was born in the wilderness).

A similar phenomenon occurs in Exodus 3:14–15. Here we have two introductions of a divine speech to Moses. The second is unnecessary because there is no reaction of Moses after verse 14. So verse 15, which partly repeats verse 14, is probably due to a later redactor who wanted to add a liturgical emphasis on the divine name. Here the author even added the Hebrew word *'od* ("in addition"): "In addition, Yahweh said."

One must of course be aware that a repetition is not always an indication of redaction. Repetitions can also have poetic, stylistic, or other reasons.

"Wiederaufnahme" (Resumption). This scribal technique, which occurs also outside of the Bible too, can also indicate redactional activity. After adding a redactional insertion, the redactor repeats or imitates at the end of his insertion the verse or part of it, after which he had added his new text, so that the lemma that is repeated forms an *inclusio* around the insertion. A good example can be found in Exodus 6:10—7:6. In the priestly version of Moses's commitment, Moses objects in 6:12: "But Moses spoke to Yahweh, 'The Israelites have not listened to me; how then shall Pharaoh listen to me, poor speaker that I am?'" The divine answer to this speech only appears in 7:1–6. Interestingly just before 7:1, 6:28–30 offers a resumption of Exodus 7:10–12, ending with. "But Moses said in Yahweh's presence, 'Look, I am a poor speaker, why would Pharaoh listen to me?'" This resumption probably indicates that the long genealogy of Moses and

Aaron in Exodus 6:14–26 is an insertion of a redactor who wanted to add the name of their parents and stress their Levitical origins. Note however, that the *Wiederaufnahme* can also be a stylistic technique.

Grammatical Inconsistencies. In some cases, grammatical problems are triggered by insertions made by redactors. In the present text of Job 1, Job's misfortune results from a bet between God and the satan, according to which the satan receives the power to strike Job with all kinds of calamities. The first encounter between Yahweh and the satan ends in 1:12: "Yahweh said to the satan, 'Very well, all that he has is in your power; only do not stretch out your hand against him!' So the satan went out from the presence Yahweh." Verse 13 then continues: "One day *his* sons and daughters were eating and drinking wine in the eldest brother's house." According to grammatical rules the possessive pronoun in verse 13 should refer either to the satan or to Yahweh, which of course makes no sense. One can, however, very well read verse 13 as the direct continuation of verse 5: "And when the feast days had run their course, Job would send and sanctify them (= his children), and he would rise early in the morning and offer burnt offerings according to the number of them all; for Job said, 'It may be that my children have sinned, and cursed God in their hearts.' This is what *Job* always did. (13) One day *his* sons and daughters were eating and drinking wine in the eldest brother's house." Such a text runs smoothly. Apparently a redactor inserted the heavenly encounter between God and Satan in verses 9–12, and also the second scene in 2:1–7a. He had apparently theological concerns for his insertion. In the original story, there is no explanation for Yahweh's striking of Job. He acts unexpectedly, as in Exodus 4:24–26, or in the original text of Genesis 22. This incomprehensible God was a problem for the redactor, who tried to exculpate Yahweh by inserting the figure of the satan (see similarly the reinterpretation of 2 Sam 24:1 in 1 Chr 21:1).

Tensions, Contradictions. Tensions inside a narrative or a larger unit may also indicate redactional reworking. In Numbers 12:1 Miriam and Aaron criticize Moses's marriage with a Cushite woman, whereas in the following verses they complain that Yahweh apparently only speaks through Moses and not through them. There is no clear relationship between the two complaints. Verse 1 belongs together with verses 9–15 (Miriam who appears in v. 1 as leading the complaint is punished with leprosy). Verse 2 belongs together with verses 3–8, where Moses is presented as standing much closer to Yahweh than ordinary prophets. One may explain these observations as the combination of two independent narratives, or, and this seems more plausible, by as a redactional addition of the story of Moses's foreign wives (v. 1; 10–15) to the original story about Moses's superiority (Num 12:2–9) in order to legitimate mixed marriages which were a problem in the Persian period. The older story about Moses and the prophets may itself be a redactional addition to Numbers 11, where Moses appears as the father of charismatic prophecy (see Römer, "Israel's Sojourn," 2007, pp. 436–441). Again, one must be cautious when identifying "contradictions," because our modern criteria do not always fit the conceptions of the ancients.

Stylistic and Theological Differences. Stylistic changes in a text can sometimes be recognized even in English translations. This is especially the case for the Deuteronomistic style, which is easy to recognize. The book of Jeremiah contains several chapters written in prose, the style of which is very different from the style of the classical prophetic oracles. This is the case in chapters 7; 11; 25; and others, which belong to one or several Deuteronomistic redactions of the book. As we have seen, however, Deuteronomistic style can occur in very late layers, so that it is difficult to use it for dating redactions.

Quite difficult and subjective is the criterion of theological differences. One may however use it in addition to other observations. This is the case, for instance, in Genesis 22. In this chapter verses 15–18 are commonly considered to be an addition to the original narrative. One may first observe that this second speech is introduced by "Yahweh's angel called to Abraham a second time from heaven"

(v. 15), which is already a hint of a revision. The long and verbose speech also contrasts with the concise and ambiguous original narrative in verses 1–14 and 19. This narrative contains short sentences that often have double meanings. Verses 16–18, however, insist on the fact that Abraham receives a reward because he has obeyed God's strange order. This is apparently a theological rereading of the older narrative.

The Necessity and Limits of Redaction Criticism. None of the preceding criteria is always valid as a detector of redactional interventions. The best plausibility is reached when one can combine different observations. Tigay distinguishes two types of redactors: those "who showed great deference toward their sources" and those who "showed a greater willingness to revise the wording of their sources, and thereby produced smoother compositions." (1985, p. 172). He thinks that for the Bible the second type is more frequent, but the first type also exists. This means that we cannot in each case reconstruct *verbatim* the older text that the redactors revised. Redaction criticism must therefore always remain modest and conscious of its limits. Nevertheless it is probably one of the best methods for scholars interested in historical questions, wishing to retrace the formation of the Hebrew Bible from the beginnings to its canonization.

[*See also* Diachronic Interpretation; Exegesis; Form Criticism, *subentry* Hebrew Bible; Historical Criticism, *subentry* Hebrew Bible; Redaction Criticism, *subentry* Apocrypha and Deuterocanonical Books; Redaction Criticism, *subentry* New Testament; Source Criticism; *and* Tradition-Historical Criticism.]

BIBLIOGRAPHY

Achenbach, Reinhard. *Biblical Exegesis and the Formation of Christian Culture.* Beihefte der Zeitschrift für altorientalische und biblische Rechtsgeschichte 3. Wiesbaden, Germany: Harrassowitz, 2003.

Astruc, Jean. *Conjectures sur la Genèse. Introduction et notes de Pierre Gibert.* Paris: Noêsis, 1999.

Baden, Joel S. *The Composition of the Pentateuch: Renewing the Documentary Hypothesis.* Anchor Yale Bible Reference Library. New Haven, Conn.: Yale University Press, 2012.

Barton, John. "Redaction Criticism. Old Testament." In *Anchor Bible Dictionary* 5 (1992): 644–647.

Biddle, Mark E. "Redaction Criticism, Hebrew Bible." In *Dictionary of Biblical Interpretation*, edited by John H. Hayes, Vol. 2, 373–376. Nashville, Tenn.: Abingdon, 1999.

Blum, Erhard. *Studien zur Komposition des Pentateuch.* Beihefte zur Zeitschrift für die Alttestamentliche Wissenschaft 189. Berlin: de Gruyter, 1990.

Cross, Frank Moore, Jr. "The Themes of the Book of Kings and the Structure of the Deuteronomistic History." In *Canaanite Myth and Hebrew Epic: Essays in the History and Religion of Israel*, 274–289. Cambridge, Mass.: Harvard University Press, 1973.

Dozeman, Thomas B., Thomas Römer, and Konrad Schmid, eds. *Pentateuch, Hexateuch, or Enneateuch? Identifying Literary Works in Genesis through Kings.* Society of Biblical Literature: Ancient Israel and its Literature 8. Atlanta: Society of Biblical Literature, 2011.

Duhm, Bernhard. *Das Buch Jeremia.* Kurzer Hand-Commentar zum Alten Testament 11. Tübingen-Leipzig: Mohr, 1901.

Hupfeld, Hermann. *Die Quellen der Genesis und die Art ihrer Zusammensetzung von neuem untersucht.* Berlin: Wiegandt u. Grieben, 1853.

Hyatt, James P. "The Deuteronomic Edition of Jeremiah" (1951). In *A Prophet to the Nations. Essays in Jeremiah Studies*, edited by L. G. Perdue and B. W. Kovacs, 247–267. Winona Lake, Ind.: Eisenbrauns, 1984.

Knauf, Ernst Axel. "Der Text als Artefakt." In *Das Alte Testament und die Kunst*, edited by John Barton et al., 51–66. Altes Testament und Moderne 15. Münster: Lit, 2005.

Knierim, Rolf. "Criticism of Literary Features, Form, Tradition, and Redaction." In *The Hebrew Bible and its Modern Interpreters*, edited by Douglas A. Knight and Gene M. Tucker, 123–165. Philadelphia: Fortress, 1985.

Kratz, Reinhard G. "Redaktionsgeschichte I. Altes Testament." In *Theologische Realenzyklopädie*, Vol. 28, 367–378.

Kuenen, Abraham. *A Historical-Critical Inquiry into the Origin and Composition of the Hexateuch.* Translated by P. H. Wicksteed. London: Macmillan, 1886. English translation of *Historisch-critisch onderzoek naar het antstaan en de verzameling van de boeken des Ouden Verbonds*, first published 1861–1865.

Moore, George F. "Tatian's Diatessaron and the Analysis of the Pentateuch." *Journal of Biblical Literature* 9 (1890): 201–215

Mowinckel, Sigmund. *Zur Komposition des Buches Jeremia.* Kristiana, Norway: Jacob Dybwad, 1914.

Noth, Martin. *The Deuteronomistic History.* Journal for the Study of the Old Testament: Supplement Series 15. Sheffield, UK: Sheffield Academic, 1991 2d ed. (1981). English translation of the first part of *Überlieferungsgeschichtliche Studien* in the 2d ed. of 1957 (1943).

Otto, Eckart. "The Pentateuch in Synchronical and Diachronical Perspectives: Protorabbinical Scribal Erudition Mediating Between Deuteronomy and the Priestly Code." In *Das Deuteronomium zwischen Pentateuch und Deuteronomistischem Geschichtswerk*, edited by Eckart Otto and Reinhard Achenbach, 14–35. Forschungen zur Religion und Literatur des Alten und Neuen Testaments 206. Göttingen, Germany: Vandenhoeck & Ruprecht, 2004.

Pohlmann, Karl-Friedrich. *Ezechielstudien. Zur Redaktionsgeschichte des Buches und zur Frage nach den ältesten Texten.* Beihefte zur Zeitschrift für die Alttestamentliche Wissenschaft 202. Berlin: de Gruyter, 1992.

Römer, Thomas. "Israel's Sojourn in the Wilderness and the Construction of the Book of Numbers." In *Reflection and Refraction. Studies in Biblical Historiography in Honour of A. Graeme Auld*, edited by Robert Rezetko, Timothy H. Lim, and W. Brian Aucker, 419–445. Vetus Testamentum Supplements 113. Leiden, Netherlands: Brill, 2007.

Römer, Thomas. "Redaction Criticism: 1 Kings 8 and the Deuteronomists." In *Method Matters: Essays on the Interpretation of the Hebrew Bible in Honor of David L. Petersen*, edited by Joel M. LeMon and Kent Harold Richards, 63–76. Society of Biblical Literature Resources for Biblical Study 56. Atlanta: Society of Biblical Literature, 2009.

Römer, Thomas. *The So-Called Deuteronomistic History: A Sociological, Historical and Literary Introduction.* 2d ed. London: T&T Clark/Continuum, 2007 (2005).

Schmitt, Hans-Christoph. "Redaktionskritik der Bibel." In *Religion in Geschichte und Gegenwart*, Vol. 7 (2004): cols 139–141.

Ska, Jean-Louis. "A Plea on Behalf of the Biblical Redactors." *Studia Theologica* 59 (2005): 4–18.

Spinoza, Baruch, de. *A Theologico-Political Treatise and a Political Treatise.* Translated from the Latin with an Introduction by R. H. M. Elwes. New York: Dover Publications, 1951.

Stromberg, Jacob. *Isaiah after Exile: The Author of Third Isaiah as Reader and Redactor of the Book.* Oxford Theological Monographs. New York: Oxford University Press, 2011.

Tigay, Jeffrey H., ed. *Empirical Models for Biblical Criticism.* Philadelphia: University of Pennsylvania Press, 1985.

Van Seters, John. *The Edited Bible. The Curious History of the "Editor" in Biblical Criticism.* Winona Lake, Ind.: Eisenbrauns, 2006.

Wellhausen, Julius. *Die Composition des Hexateuchs und der historischen Bücher des Alten Testaments* (1899). Berlin: de Gruyter, 1963.

Wette, Wilhelm M. L. de. *Beiträge zur Einleitung in das Alte Testament.* 2 vols. Halle, Germany: Schimmelpfennig und Compagnie, 1806.

Thomas Römer

Apocrypha and Deuterocanonical Books

The term "Apocrypha" for a group of texts dating roughly between 300 B.C.E. and 70 C.E. was coined by Jerome (d. 420) when he was preparing the Vulgate from the Hebrew Bible. Jerome classified the Apocrypha separately because they were not available to him in Hebrew, but only in Greek. Following Jerome's lead, the Protestant reformers deemed the same group of books to be noncanonical, included them in their colloquial translations of the Old Testament as "Apocrypha," and refused to accord them canonical authority. At the Council of Trent (1546) Roman Catholicism declared (most of) the books in dispute to be "Deuterocanonical" and part of the Christian canon. Taking together those included in the Roman Catholic canon as Deuterocanonical works and those included in the Protestant canon as Apocrypha gives a list of fifteen works: 1 Esdras, 2 Esdras, Tobit, Judith, Additions to the Book of Esther, Wisdom of Solomon, Wisdom of Ben Sira, Baruch, Letter of Jeremiah, Prayer of Azariah and Song of the Three Young Men, Susanna, Bel and the Dragon (Serpent), Prayer of Manasseh, 1 Maccabees, and 2 Maccabees. None of these works are included in the Jewish Tanak.

Although the compositional histories of these books have received far less attention than the canonical books of the Jewish and Christian Bible, they have not gone unnoticed, and have been examined with the help of the full range of critical methodologies. This article surveys how one of those methodologies, redaction criticism, has been brought to bear in studying the Old Testament Apocrypha.

Redaction Criticism. Although redaction criticism is viewed as a separate method focused on the editorial activity of redactors who assembled existing source material of different forms or genres into a complete document, it often merges with the two methods alluded to in the preceding description, source and form criticism. Concomitantly, it is often thought that to perform redaction criticism reliably on a work requires access to the sources that its compiler-redactor used. If these two judgments are accepted without question in approaching the topic of "redaction criticism of the Apocrypha," treatment of it would be brief; indeed in only a handful of cases can one point with any confidence to sources that were integrated into the books of the Apocrypha as they have come down to us, and equally small is the number of books that have been treated *specifically* in redaction-critical analysis. Yet a look at the primary texts themselves and the secondary literature on them does in fact justify a standalone treatment. The average reader—and source and form critics—can and do discern the traces of sources within the existing texts of the books of the Apocrypha that have come down to us, and on the basis of those observations scholars have surmised in turn something of the editorial activity of the persons responsible for integrating them into the final forms of the books. The remainder of this article takes up each of the fifteen books in succession to report what redaction critics tell us about them, and concludes with reflections on the import of the survey for how we think about redaction criticism as a methodology for examining the Deuterocanonicals/Apocrypha.

1 Esdras. Apart from 3:1—5:6—an account of three young men flourishing in the court of Darius, with the result that one of them, Zerubbabel, is commissioned to return to Judah and rebuild the temple—1 Esdras looks to be a modestly free Greek translation of portions of texts we know of otherwise, all of them from the Hebrew Bible: 2 Chronicles (35:1—36:21 = 1 Esdras 1:1-55), Ezra (1:1–11; 4:7–24 = 1 Esdras 2:1–30; 2:1—4:5 = 1 Esdras 5:7–73; 4:24–10:44 = 1 Esdras 6:1–9:36), and Nehemiah (7:73—8:12 = 1 Esdras 9:37–55). Some who view this as a loose translation of the biblical books argue that the book is the fragmentary remains of a larger work that lost its beginning and conclusion, and holds greatest significance as the earliest translation into Greek of the canonical books (parts of which) the surviving form encompasses. On this theory the lack of an extant beginning and conclusion leaves fundamental uncertainty as to a redactor's purpose. Others argue that the book was nothing more or less than a rather perplexing compilation and modest reworking of the corresponding passages in the canonical books (which may have first been in Hebrew and Aramaic and then only later translated into Greek). The third view assigns to the redactor a much stronger authorial role, suggesting the work reflects an independent tradition that relied on Ezra, but also embraced entirely other additions. Views on the purpose someone might have had in reworking and redacting (and translating) the various elements of the canonical books into a single text vary, although the centrality of the temple in Jerusalem, the focus on the figure of Ezra, and intimations of an interest in the Davidic line have prompted various suggestions related to all three themes.

Recently some have argued a very different understanding of 1 Esdras—that it has priority over Ezra–Nehemiah. If this position has any merit it requires a complete rethinking of the questions concerning a redactor's intent, and in fact multiplies redactors we have to concern ourselves with: the one(s) responsible for gathering the various sources that make up 1 Esdras and the one(s) who re-used that assemblage to create Ezra–Nehemiah and Chronicles. It is well beyond the scope of this article to take up these questions; they remain very unsettled, although the weight of opinion rests for now with the traditional approach to the question of priority. (For a collection of various perspectives on the question, see Fried 2011).

2 Esdras. A work encompassing 4, 5, and 6 Ezra, 2 Esdras in the form it takes in the English Apocrypha is unequivocally a result of a compiler's activity. Chapters 3–14 make up 4 Ezra, a Jewish eschatological work (that is the principle focus of this discussion) framed as Ezra's struggle to accept the loss of the First Temple and Judah's defeat, but in fact reflects on the loss of the Second Temple and Rome's victory at the end of the first century C.E. Meanwhile, chapters 1–2 (5 Ezra) and chapters 15–16 (6 Ezra) are both later Christian additions to the early work. In this sense the present composition results from the work of a redactor or redactors. Redaction-critical explanations for why the three works were joined as one remain elusive, in part because critics have focused little sustained attention on the question, concentrating more heavily on the makeup of 4 Ezra alone.

With regard to 4 Ezra, the history of research is one of trying to explain the seemingly contradictory perspectives included in this apocalyptic work. It divides into seven sections that include visions, dialogues, and an epilogue, which feature (chiefly) Uriel and Ezra. The book traces Ezra's journey from Job-like dismay at the perceived injustice of God to general acceptance of God's just rule in spite of any evidence to the contrary. Hogan (2008) identifies three approaches to explaining the contradictions (especially between Uriel's vision of God's justice and Ezra's), only the first of which relies substantially on redaction-critical judgments: it is the view of late nineteenth and early twentieth century scholarship, which explained the contradictions as the result of a redactor's compilation of concomitantly conflicting source material. That view, however, has been almost entirely replaced by two alternatives. The first holds that the variance between Uriel and Ezra reflects a debate in Judaism of the first century C.E., with Uriel giving the author's view and Ezra that of his opponents. This approach does invite its proponents to treat the fifth and sixth episodes as secondary, and in that sense it falls back on redaction-critical analysis. The second alternative to the source- and redaction-critical hypothesis offers what is dubbed a "psychological" explanation for the contradictions in the book: it simply traces the pathos of Ezra's (the author's?) slow reconciliation to Uriel's view of God's justice, rendering the contradictions an integral part of the narrative's purpose.

Notably for our interest, the redaction-critical explanation of 4 Ezra's diverse perspectives was flawed from the beginning by its lack of respect for basic genre characteristics: apocalypses rarely go without conflicting and even contradictory elements; it is in the nature of the genre to contain such tensions. In that sense the case of 4 Ezra indicates something of the difficulty of performing redaction-critical analysis on apocalyptic texts.

Tobit. This Jewish novella from sometime in the third century B.C.E. is set in the "Assyrian exile." The book tells the tale of a faithful Jew, Tobit, who nonetheless experiences terrible misfortune, only to see those difficulties overcome by the faithful actions of his son, Tobias, who is assisted by God's angelic emissary, Raphael.

Redaction-critical theories are prominent in the study of Tobit because the tale seems to incorporate elements of several traditional folktales widely known in the ancient Mediterranean context (*The Story and Wisdom of Ahiqar, The Fable of the Grateful Dead,* and *The Monster in the Bridal Chamber*), the narration shifts from first-person to third-person at 3:7, and genres are quite mixed within the text. The various theories to explain these characteristics divide roughly into two camps. One posits a complex compositional history that began with an essentially secular tale or tales transitioning over time at the hands of several redactors to become the pious Jewish fable we have now; at the other extreme is the view that the text as it has come down to us is itself more or less the unitary composition of a single author (Fitzmyer 2003, pp. 36–45). In the middle are those who see only mild redactional activity, especially concentrated in chapters 4 and 13–14. The trend in scholarship, in any case, is toward the view that Tobit was more or less a unitary composition. Where one lands on the spectrum between the two poles described depends in large part on one's confidence in our capacity to make source-critical judgments and then build from those a theory of compositional development in ancient texts, as well as on one's assumptions about ancient compositional practices vis-à-vis our own contemporary predilections (and related general theories of literature and human discourse; see, e.g., Soll 1989). Taking a less sanguine view of our capacity to discern seams and sources and imposing no twenty-first-century theories or standards of literature on Tobit argues for the more modest end of the spectrum.

Judith. Probably composed in Palestine sometime under Hasmonean rule, Judith tells the story of the book's namesake, a woman from the tiny Israelite town Bethuliah, who was able to defeat the Assyrian army through a combination of faithfulness to her own traditions and deceit and treachery against her enemies. Thematically, the tale addresses challenges to the sovereignty of the God of Israel, in this case from a foreign king, Holofernes of Assyria (surely representative of the Hellenistic rulers of the author's time).

There has been little in the history of scholarship on Judith that seeks to ascribe to the final form traces of earlier redactional activity. To be sure, early critical studies implied that an (apparent) literary imbalance between chapters 1–7 and 8–16 might be attributable to the melding of sources, but that view is replaced now with a three-part division of a unitary narrative related to the theme named earlier: chapters 1–3, Nebuchadnezzar asserts divine status; chapters 4–7, the question is posed as to whether Yahweh is God instead; chapters 8–16 settle the argument in favor of Yahweh. True, the author does seem to have relied on material from Eupolemus, a second-century B.C.E. Jewish historian (preserved at *Praep. Ev.* 9.39), but this only argues that the writer knew this historian (and others) and relied on them in giving his historical fiction a degree of verisimilitude. Likewise, the poetic section in 16:1–17, which retells the prose account in chapters 1–15, could also be a source that was incorporated by a redactor, but even that amounts to very little in the way of redaction. Countering theories of substantial redactional activity, Craven (1983) has made a very convincing case for the unity of the work as a single, artistic composition of an individual author.

Additions to Esther. The Greek translation of the canonical book of Esther includes six additions. In revising the Old Latin version of the Bible on the basis of the Hebrew texts available to him, Jerome removed these and made them an appendix at the end of the book in his Vulgate. Thus, although their versification reflects that position, they are better understood in the narrative flow of the book as it comes down to us in Greek. Addition A (=Vulgate 11:2–12:6) introduces the book and reports a vision of Mordecai; Addition B (=Vulgate 13:1–7) gives Artaxerxes's command that the Jews be exterminated; Addition C (=Vulgate 13:8–14:19) records Esther's and Mordecai's prayers; Addition D (=Vulgate 15:1–16) narrates Esther's appearance before the king; Addition E (=Vulgate 16:1–24) is another decree of Artaxerxes; and Addition F (=Vulgate 10:1–11:1) gives an interpretation of Mordecai's dream, a conclusion, and a colophon.

The Additions to the Book of Esther are an unequivocal instance of redactional activity. It is generally agreed that the aim of the redaction was several fold: to fill in information missing in the canonical Hebrew version; to amplify the drama of the book by amending the character portraits (e.g., adding emotional tone to them); to introduce historical authenticity with the decree documents; and most of all, to make the book explicitly theological by introducing God as a key character in the narrative.

The question of interest regarding the redaction of Esther in its Greek form to include the Additions is whether they were all added at the point of translation or had been introduced before the book was translated. Additions B and E are generally considered to be Greek compositions, but the others may have already been part of a Hebrew edition of the book. There is no consensus on this question.

Wisdom of Solomon. The book is divided into three parts: an eschatological portion in 1:1—6:21; a "Book of Wisdom" in 6:22—9:18; and a "Book of History" focused on the Exodus narrative (and containing two diversions, one on God's mercy in 11:15–12:22 and another on idolatry in chapters 13–15). Wisdom of Solomon is usually assigned to the Egyptian diaspora, perhaps Alexandria, and dated to the first century B.C.E. It is, in some senses, a massive attempt to contend with the possibility of a "natural theology" competing with the Israelite tradition of revealed theology. In any case, it is also meant to encourage an audience to remain firm in their traditions in spite of challenges from their non-Jewish neighbors. The author employs a wide range of Greek conventions and philosophical notions, but mostly to affirm the abiding benefit of Jewish faith in the face of pressures to conform to other options.

While critics in the nineteenth century (and a handful in the twentieth century as well) were inclined to see evidence of a compositional history for Wisdom of Solomon that would entail moments of redactional activity—this on the basis of the perceived variation between chapters 1–10 and 11–19 or 1–5 and 6–19, or on the theory that there was a Hebrew original of part of the work (e.g., chapters 1–10)—the consensus since the late twentieth century has been that the existing work was composed in Greek as a unitary composition, and a carefully wrought one at that. Grabbe (1997, pp. 24–25) conveniently summarizes the evidence for that supposition: there is no reason to assume there was ever a Hebrew or Aramaic form of the text; a concentric structure that shapes much of the book argues strongly for a single author; vocabulary and linguistic style are consistent; the pervasiveness of the Golden Mean argues in favor of a single author; flashbacks likewise suggest a single, intentional author; and major themes are consistent across the book.

Wisdom of Ben Sira. A "book of wisdom" not unlike the canonical book of Proverbs (but different in the assembling of sayings in thematic groups), Wisdom of Ben Sira was composed by the title's namesake, probably a teacher-for-hire in Palestine in the early second century B.C.E. (ca. 195–180), and was translated into Greek by his grandson in the late second century B.C.E. (ca. 130) in Egypt. The author espouses a rather conventional wisdom that sees sensible action, guided by the Torah, as ensuring God's blessings. The concerns the author addresses along the way range widely: from practical advice on raising children, doing business, behaving well in the home of a rich man, and more, to scientific speculation on the nature of the cosmos, to reflections on human nature and being.

Because of its widely varying themes some have found reason to assume that a redactional history produced Wisdom of Ben Sira (although the majority view, if by a slim margin, is that it is a unitary composition). On this basis older scholarship posited the notion that the book is a collection of a student's notes on the teaching of Ben Sira. Recent scholarship has produced more sophisticated speculations about the book's redactional history, relying on the evidence of the author's self references, inclusios, etc. (see the summary of recent work in Corley [2008]). The latest contribution to the debate would posit five "editions" of the book: an original in 1:1—23:27; 51:13–30; the addition of 24:1—32:13 to make the second edition; the addition of 32:14—38:23; 51:1–12 to make a third; the addition of 38:24—43:33 to make a fourth; and the addition of 44:1—50:29 in three parts to make a fifth (Corley, pp. 41–44). Corley, however, acknowledges that these editions are to be assigned to the work's single author and that the redactional stages identified are "largely hypothetical" (p. 45). Corley's treatment demonstrates that while the contents of a work may provide fertile ground for positing a redaction history, without independent attestation of hypothetical source material, redaction criticism can seem a highly speculative enterprise.

Baruch. Baruch is best dated to the second century B.C.E. because of a few specific details, but it could be assigned to any time between the sixth century B.C.E. and the second century C.E. when its general focus on themes of exile, suffering, and loss, and its expression of hope for restoration might have found a welcoming Jewish audience. It consists of a narrative introduction (1:1–14), a prayer of confession and repentance (1:15—3:8), a wisdom speech and exhortation (3:9—4:4), and a poem of consolation and reassurance (4:5—5:9).

Seeing the diverse genres in the book, some have assigned the parts of Baruch listed in the preceding (or slightly different configurations of the book's contents) to widely different origins and authors and attributed the assemblage to a redactor. As is the case with some of the other texts, however, that sort of judgment about Baruch is based less on a reading of the book in its own context than on the application of modern literary conventions and biases about "good literature" to a work from an entirely different time and place. When read in its broader literary and historical context, Baruch can be seen as a carefully created work, to be sure by a redactor-author who gathers together disparate sources into a single work, but a coherent and meaningful work all the same. Saldarini (1999) makes the simplest and most powerful argument for this view: the first major section, 1:15—3:8, expresses the author's recognition of Israel's sin and expresses repentance; the second major section, 3:9—4:4, charts the way forward (wisdom) and exhorts the keeping of God's law; and the final section anticipates restoration and encourages perseverance in the meantime. Thus the work participates in the common Sin-Exile-Return and Redemption pattern seen elsewhere in much Jewish (and early Christian) literature of the long period to which we might assign Baruch (e.g., elements of Deuteronomy to *Testaments of the Twelve Patriarchs*). In this sense Baruch is a clear instance of a Jewish compiler-author who simply worked in a mode that was widely employed in Exilic and Second Temple Judaism.

Letter of Jeremiah. The Letter of Jeremiah is, as is commonly said, neither a letter nor authored by Jeremiah. Rather, it is a satirical polemic against idolatry, a Second Temple period genre. The Letter usually appears in the Apocrypha as chapter 6 of Baruch. After Jeremiah's warning that the people of Israel would see gentiles worshipping human-made idols (vv. 1–7), ten sections pile up largely unrelated arguments as to why the idols are not godlike (vv. 8–16, 17–23, 24–29, 30–40a, 40b–44, 45–52, 53–56, 57–65, 66–69, 70–73), with each one concluding with a refrain like the one in v. 69: "So we have no evidence whatsoever that they are gods; therefore do not fear them." Because it is referenced in 2 Macc 2:2 it has to date before 100 B.C.E., but when before that is difficult to tell.

In part because it is so brief, and in part because it is so transparently a single author's loosely constructed attack on idolatry, there is virtually no reason to consider this anything but a unitary work. Certainly the author borrowed on existing traditions and knew other works of this genre, but the polemic in the end seems the work of a single author. The only possibility for some sort of redactional activity would be at the stage of translation from a Hebrew original to the Greek form in the Septuagint (LXX); yet Wright (2010) has raised serious doubt about even that, arguing effectively for a Greek original and removing the last refuge for would-be redaction critics seeking to investigate the Letter.

Additions to Daniel. The three additions to Daniel, Susanna, Bel and the Dragon (Serpent), and Prayer of Azariah and Song of the Three Young Men, are all of interest from a redaction-critical perspective because they are explicitly *additions* to an existing text.

Inserted in the LXX between Daniel 3:23 and 24, the Prayer of Azariah and Song of the Three Young Men includes a prayer attributed to Azariah (= Abednego) as he strolled about in the fiery furnace (vv. 3–22), a narrative link that relates how the king's servants stoked the fire still more (vv. 23–28), and the hymn all three young men sang in praise of their God who delivered them from death (vv. 28–67). Impossible to date and just as difficult to locate (although some take v. 15's declaration that there was no place to worship to suggest a date around 170–168 B.C.E.), it *is* possible to suggest that the material was composed in Hebrew and translated before (or even for) inclusion in the Greek of Daniel. And inasmuch as most agree that the narrative transitions (vv. 1–2, 23–28) were composed by whoever included the material—perhaps the translator, but not necessarily—we can speak at least this much of a redactor's hand in making this addition to Daniel, but we can say little to nothing more than that. It is possible, however, to offer reflections on the redactional aims of the person who inserted the prayer and hymn into the LXX version of Daniel. The argument is made that the insertion turns the story of the young men in the furnace into something of a liturgical experience, even suggesting its use in such a context (see van der Horst and Newman 2008, pp. 186–191). One could even imagine this functioning as part of communal reading of Daniel as a liturgical-cathartic experience in times of perceived oppression and injustice.

The tale of Susanna is also very difficult to date and locate, so speaking of any redactional history of the text itself is nearly impossible. For our interest, the focus is more appropriately on how a redactor included it in the LXX version of Daniel. In fact, it appears in two places in two different Greek traditions. The Theodotionic version of the Greek Bible includes it at the beginning of Daniel, apparently to explain how the book's hero came to notice before turning to his story with full force. Yet this form of the tale also includes details that give it a stronger focus on Susanna's character. By contrast, in the Old Greek text the tale appears at the end of the book of Daniel (either before or after Bel and the Serpent) and draws to a close with words of special praise for Daniel and his confreres, and Susanna's character is less developed. In short, though nothing can be known of substance about the persons who made these arrangements, redaction-critical analysis allows us to imagine varying intentions in creating *different* Greek texts of the Book of Daniel.

Bel and the Serpent, appearing at the end of Daniel, is two interwoven satiric-polemical tales targeted at idolatry that pit Daniel against Cyrus and his priests, and against Cyrus and the Babylonians over the divine authenticity of an idol of Bel and a serpent identified with him. The tales conclude with Cyrus's complete conversion because of Daniel's miraculous survival in the lion's den. In this case the question of redactional activity in the composition of the account is complicated by its close affiliation with Daniel 6. Are these independent or codependent traditions? The question remains unresolved and intensified redaction-critical analysis could be of assistance in addressing it. As for the significance of the tale's placement at the end of the Greek Daniel, little of redaction-critical significance can be made of it.

Prayer of Manasseh. Assigned to the apostate seventh-century B.C.E. king of Judah, the prayer corresponds with the narrative in 2 Chron 33:10–13 that has Manasseh imprisoned in Babylon, from where he prayed in repentance and was returned to his lengthy rule over Judah (explaining in turn the puzzle of his reign's success in spite of the negative Deuteronomic review of it in 2 Kings 21 and the D author's judgment that his sins caused Judah's fall; cf. 2 Kgs 24:3–4). The earliest surviving form of the prayer appears in Syriac in the third-century C.E. Christian work *Didascalia Apostolorum*, and the second appearance is in the fifth-century Codex Alexandrinus as one of the Odes that follow that LXX manuscript's edition of the Psalms. That said, the prayer has at least one congener among earlier Jewish texts (e.g., 4Q381 33 8–11, a fragment of a "Prayer of King Manasseh"), suggesting that there was a tradition of composing prayers for the Manasseh of 2 Chronicles 33.

A redaction-critical perspective on this text comes into play when considering whether the prayer was composed precisely to reconcile a conflation of the Deuteronomic and Chronicles perspectives (Nickelsburg 2001, p. 701), or was merely an existing prayer adapted by a compiler (Van der Horst and Newman 2008, pp. 152–153). The latter view is that of the majority of commentators, and clearly offers less interest from a redaction-critical perspective. Nickelsburg's conjecture, though, raises the interesting possibility that an editor took a very active hand in weaving together the disparate traditions about Manasseh, going so far as to create a prayer to support the effort.

1 Maccabees. This late second-century B.C.E. apologetic history of Hasmonean rule is widely acknowledged to contain numerous source materials that a single author incorporated. Views on just what those sources were range widely; among the candidates there are Seleucid court documents, legends about key Hasmoneans (e.g., Mattathias, Jonathan), high priestly "yearbooks," and Judean state archives. In this instance, though, the integrative work of the compiler-author is so thorough as to make tracing the precise use of such sources—let alone establish with confidence their separate existence—more or less impossible. Williams (1999) provides superb evidence of the extent to which the author redacted his sources into a unitary work, creating two chiastic structures in 1:1—6:17 and 6:18—14:15 and a third, equally well-configured (but non-chiastic) structure in 14:45—16:24. With some irony one can say that in this instance we see redactional practice at its best, and can as a result say the least about the details of it.

2 Maccabees. Described by its "author" as an epitome of the five-volume history of Israel between 180–161 B.C.E. by Jason of Cyrene, most view 2 Maccabees as a unified work that bears few if any traces of the anonymous epitomizer's intervention, making redaction-critical analysis largely moot. However, in a recent work on the book, Daniel Schwartz argues that there is a discernible compositional history. First came Jason's five-volume work. Next, an anonymous redactor created a digest of the longer work, adding the Heliodorus story (chapter 3), martyrologies (6:18—7:42), a preface (2:19–32), an afterword (15:37–39), and "three sections of reflections" (4:16–17; 5:17–20; 6:12–17). Schwartz also believes that the redactor (he calls him an author) added 10:1—11:38 from a separate source and reordered parts of Jason's work on the mistaken impression that Antiochus IV died by 148 B.C.E. Schwartz further posits that 13:3–8 was added by the redactor as well, and that the Hasmonean authorities then sent the completed work to Jews in the diaspora, and in Egypt in particular, to encourage observance of Hanukkah (thus adding 10:1–8, as well as two letters at the outset of the book; Schwartz 2008, pp. 36–37; for a very different redaction history of 2 Maccabees, see Goldstein 1983).

Reflections on Redaction Criticism and the Apocrypha. A survey of the material covered in this article leads to what some might consider self-evident observations, but ones that are all the same often overlooked by many practitioners of redaction criticism. First, our survey shows that composing texts in antiquity was invariably a redactional activity in itself, and it was likewise an activity deeply shaped by normative patterns (genres) and practices. As a consequence, if one sets out to find sources in complete works, and discern their traces in the presence of known genres, one is certain to succeed. Likewise, one can discern from how those pieces are assembled something of the compiler's interests, and well one should, since communicating his views was the compiler-author's purpose in creating a new text. And, ironically, the compilers who created what we often deem to be the most elegant texts—they are at their best when they have so obscured their sources and adapted genres that one sees *only* them and their meaning. And at that moment we are most fond to call them *authors*, missing mostly, or even altogether, that they were, like their lesser literary colleagues, redactors first.

[*See also* Redaction Criticism, *subentry* Hebrew Bible; Redaction Criticism, *subentry* New Testament]

BIBLIOGRAPHY

Bartlett, John. *1 Maccabees.* Sheffield, UK: Sheffield Academic Press, 1998.

Corley, Jeremy. "Searching for Structure and Redaction in Ben Sira. An Investigation of Beginnings and Ending." In *Wisdom of Ben Sira: Studies on Tradition, Redaction, and Theology*, ed. Angelo Passaro, 21–47. DCLS 1. Berlin: Walter de Gruyter, 2008.

Craven, Toni. *Artistry and Faith in the Book of Judith.* SBLDS 70; Chico, Calif.: Scholars Press, 1983.

Crawford, Sidnie White. "The Additions to Esther: Introduction, Commentary and Reflections." In *The New Interpreter's Bible.* Vol. 3, 943–972. Nashville, Tenn.: Abingdon, 1999.

Fitzmyer, Joseph. *Tobit.* CEJL. Berlin: Walter de Gruyter, 2003.

Fried, Lisbeth, ed. *Was 1 Esdras First? An Investigation in the Priority and Nature of First Esdras.* Atlanta: Society of Biblical Literature, 2011.

Goldstein, Jonathan. *1 Maccabees.* AB 41. Garden City, N.Y.: Doubleday, 1977.

Goldstein, Jonathan. *2 Maccabees.* AB 41A. Garden City, N.Y.: Doubleday, 1983.

Grabbe, Lester. *Wisdom of Solomon.* Sheffield UK: Sheffield Academic Press, 1997.

Hogan, Karina Martin. *Theologies in Conflict in 4 Ezra: Wisdom Debate and Apocalyptic Solution.* SJSJ 130. Leiden, Netherlands: Brill, 2008.

Nickelsburg, G. W. E. *Jewish Literature Between the Bible and the Mishnah.* 2d ed. Minneapolis: Fortress Press, 2005.

Nickelsburg, G. W. E. "Prayer of Manasseh." In *Oxford Bible Commentary*, eds. J. Barton and J. Muddiman, 770–773. Oxford: Oxford University Press, 2001.

Saldarini, Anthony. "Book of Baruch." *NIB* 6:925–982.
Schwartz, Daniel. *2 Maccabees.* Berlin: Walter de Gruyter, 2008.
Soll, Will. "Misfortune and Exile in Tobit: The Juncture of a Fairy Tale Source and Deuteronomic Theology." *CBQ* 51 (1989): 209–231.
Van der Horst, Pieter, and Judith Newman. *Early Jewish Prayers in Greek.* Berlin: Walter de Gruyter, 2008.
Williams, David. *The Structure of 1 Maccabees.* CBQMS 31. Washington, D.C.: Catholic Biblical Association of America, 1999.
Wright, Benjamin. "The Epistle of Jeremiah: Translation or Composition?" In *Deuterocanonical Additions to the Old Testament Books: Selected Studies.* Edited by Géza Zeravits and József Zsengellér. DCLS 5. Berlin: Walter De Gruyter, 2010. 126–142.

Robert Kugler

New Testament

The English term "redaction criticism" freely translates *Redaktionsgeschichte*, "history of editing." As an exegetical technique redaction criticism may be practiced with any biblical book that bears discernible traces of its author's adaptation of antecedent oral or literary traditions. Thus, the redaction critic may attempt to identify later accretions or other modifications within a Pentateuchal book (e.g., Exod 20:1–21) or a Pauline letter (Phil 2:5–11). Within the New Testament (NT), redaction criticism has been most commonly applied to the Gospels' interpretation. This article considers six topics:

(1) a survey of redaction critics' assumptions and methods;
(2) an illustration of redaction-critical procedure;
(3) identification of pioneering redaction-critical studies;
(4) description of the method's subsequent development, including its influence on textbooks and commentaries on the Gospels;
(5) consideration of cognate exegetical approaches;
(6) an assessment of the method's contributions and limitations.

Assumptions and Methods. The Gospels originated in stories and sayings about Jesus that were orally transmitted throughout the first century after 30 C.E. form criticism is the attempt to identify discrete patterns in which the *kerygma* (the earliest proclamation of Jesus as Christ) circulated: e.g., miracle stories, parables, and the passion narrative (the story of Jesus's arrest, trial, and death). Source criticism postulates that these forms coalesced into larger clusters of material that may have been oral, literary, or some combination of both: Q (sayings found in both Matthew and Luke, though not in Mark: e.g., Matt 3:7–10 = Luke 3:7–9), M (material discernible only in Matthew: e.g., Matt 13:24–30, 36–43), L (traditions unique to Luke: e.g., 18:1–14), a special miracle tradition available to John (a "signs source": e.g., 2:1–11). Some scholars consider Mark to be an abridgement of Matthew (a position as old as Augustine of Hippo [354–430 C.E.]). The most widely accepted theory of the Gospels' interrelationships posits Mark as the earliest written and the template Matthew and Luke (perhaps also John) adopted while developing their own compositions (*see* SYNOPTIC PROBLEM).

The Gospels do not differ arbitrarily. Careful analysis of their contents reveals their authors' (or "the evangelists'") different emphases, particularly in those cases where they have used the same materials. Redaction critics concentrate on the distinctive ways in which traditional units have been assembled into coherent narratives, the formative role that each evangelist has played in composing his Gospel. Mark emphasizes Jesus's progression toward suffering and death. Into Mark's narrative, Matthew inserts five large discourses of Jesus, highlighting his disciples' radical obedience to the norms of the kingdom of God. Also adhering to Mark's narrative sequence, Luke inserts a long journey of Jesus to Jerusalem and unique material emphasizing reliable witness to Jesus as the herald of salvation for Israel and the nations. These qualities of the Synoptic Gospels—those that "see together" the ministry of Jesus—are evident in the following table.

John's narrative roughly corresponds to that of the Synoptics: a story of Jesus's mighty works and teaching, attracting disciples and repelling opponents,

TABLE 1. *Comparison of Synoptic Accounts*

Matthew	*Mark*	*Luke*
1:1—2:23 (Infancy Narratives)	– –	1:1—2:52 (Infancy Narratives)
3:1—4:25	1:1–39	3:1—4:44
– –	– –	5:1–11
5:1—7:29 (First Discourse: *The Sermon on the Mount*)	– –	– –
8:1–4	1:40–45	5:12–16
8:5–34	– –	– –
9:1–17	2:1–22	5:17–39
9:18—10:4	– –	– –
10:5–42 (Second Discourse: *Missionary Instructions*)	– –	– –
11:1–30	– –	– –
12:1–21	2:23—3:19	6:1–19
– –	– –	6:20—8:3 (The "Small Insertion," including *The Sermon on the Plain*, 6:20–49)
12:22–50	3:20–35	– –
13:1–52 (Third Discourse: *Parables of the Kingdom and the Church*)	4:1–34	8:4–21
– –	4:35—5:43	8:22–56
13:53—17:27	6:1—9:32	9:1–45 (excluding Mark 6:45—8:26: the "Great Omission")
18:1–35 (Fourth Discourse: *Instructions for Church Life and Discipline*)	9:33–50	9:46–50
– –	– –	9:51—18:14 (*Lukan Travel Narrative*: the "Great Insertion")
19:1—24:3	10:1—13:4	18:15—21:7
24:4—25:46 (Fifth Discourse: *Eschatology and the Church*)	13:5–37	21:8–38
26:1—28:10 (Passion Narrative)	14:1—16:8 (Passion Narrative)	22:1—24:12 (Passion Narrative)
28:11–20 (Resurrection Appearances)	– –	24:13–53 (Resurrection Appearances)

TABLE 2. *Comparison of the Four Gospels*

Matthew 26	*Mark 14*	*Luke 7*	*John 12*
[6]Now while Jesus was at Bethany in the house of Simon the Leper,	[3]While he was at Bethany in the house of Simon the Leper, as he sat at table,	[36]One of the Pharisees asked Jesus to eat with him, and he went into the Pharisees' house and took his place at the table.	[1]Six days before the Passover Jesus came to Bethany, the home of Lazarus, whom he had raised from the dead. [2]There they gave a dinner for him. Martha served, and Lazarus was one of those at the table with him.
[7]a woman came to him with an alabaster jar of very costly ointment, and she poured it on his head as he sat at the table.	a woman came with an alabaster jar of very costly ointment of nard, and she broke open the jar and poured the ointment on his head.	[37]And a woman in the city, who was a sinner, having learned that he was eating in the Pharisee's house, brought an alabaster jar of ointment. [38]She stood behind him at his feet, weeping, and began to bathe his feet with her tears and to dry them with her hair. Then she continued kissing his feet and anointing them with the ointment.	[3]Mary took a pound of costly perfume made of pure nard, anointed Jesus's feet, and wiped them with her hair.
			The house was filled with the fragrance of the perfume.
[8]But when the disciples saw it, they were angry and said, "Why this waste? [9]For this ointment could have been sold for a large sum, and the money given to the poor."	[4]But some were there who said to one another in anger, "Why was the ointment wasted in this way? [5]For this ointment could have been sold for more than three hundred denarii, and the money given to the poor." And they scolded her.	[39]Now when the Pharisee who had invited him saw it, he said to himself, "If this man were a prophet, he would have known who and what kind of woman this is who is touching him—that she is a sinner."	[4]But Judas Iscariot, one of his disciples (the one who was about to betray him), said, [5]"Why was this perfume not sold for three hundred denarii and the money given to the poor?"
			[6](He said this not because he cared about the poor, but because he was a thief; he kept the common purse and used to steal what was put into it.)
		[40]Jesus spoke up and said to him, "Simon, I have something to say to you." "Teacher," he replied, "Speak." [41]"A certain creditor had two debtors; one owed five hundred denarii, and the other fifty. [42]When they could not pay, he canceled the debts for both of them. Now which of them will love him more?" [43]Simon	

(*continued*)

[10]But Jesus, aware
of this, said to
them, "Who do
you trouble this
woman? She has
performed a good
service for me.
[11]For you always
have the poor
with you, but you
will not always
have me. [12]By
pouring this
ointment on my
body she has
prepared me for
my burial. [13]Truly
I tell you,
wherever this
good news is
proclaimed in the
whole world,
what she has
done will be told
in remembrance
of her."

[6]But Jesus said, "Let her
alone; why do you
trouble her? She has
performed a good
service for me. [7]For you
always have the poor
with you, and you can
show kindness to them
whenever you wish; but
you will not always have
me. [8]She has done what
she could; she anointed
my body beforehand for
its burial. [9]Truly I tell
you, wherever the good
news is proclaimed in
the whole world, what
she has done will be told
in remembrance of her."

answered, "I suppose the one for
whom he canceled the greater
debt." And Jesus said to him, "You
have judged rightly." [44]Then
turning toward the woman, he
said to Simon, "Do you see this
woman? I entered your house;
you gave me no water for my feet,
but she has bathed my feet with
her tears and dried them with her
hair. [45]You gave me no kiss, but
from the time I came in she has
not stopped kissing my feet. [46]You
did not anoint my head with oil,
but she has anointed my feet with
ointment. [47]Therefore, I tell you,
her sins, which were many, have
been forgiven; hence she has shown
me great love. But the one to whom
little is forgiven, loves little."

[48]Then he said to her, "Your sins are
forgiven." [49]But those who were at
the table with him began to say
among themselves, "Who is this
who even forgives sins?" [50]And he
said to the woman, "Your faith
has saved you; go in peace."

[7]Jesus said, "Leave her
alone. She bought it so
that she might keep it
for the day of my
burial.[8]You always have
the poor with you, but
you do not always have
me."

culminating in his death and resurrection. Yet most of the Fourth Gospel is substantively different from the other three. Scholars disagree whether John knew and used Mark or another Synoptic. John most closely resembles the Synoptics in the passion narrative (18:1—19:42; see Black 2011, pp. 277–281).

Beyond comparing narrative frameworks, redaction critics scrutinize terms and themes that appear especially important for each of the evangelists. For instance, Mark 8:22—10:52 repeatedly stresses Jesus's messiahship and his disciples' ministry as suffering for the gospel's sake. Matthew reiterates superlative righteousness as characteristic of Jesus, his precursors, and his disciples (1:18–19; 3:13–15; 5:17–20). Luke exhibits extraordinary concern for those on society's margins, especially women and the poor (1:24–56; 4:16–30; 10:29–37). From such emphases redaction critics infer historical circumstances out of which each Gospel may have emerged and to which each may have been addressed. Mark is often assumed to have been written for a persecuted church; Matthew, for a Jewish congregation distinguishing itself from first-century Pharisaism; Luke, for a gentile community defining itself *vis-à-vis* both Israel and the Roman Empire.

Redaction Criticism in Operation. A comparative analysis of the anointing of Jesus in the four Gospels illustrates the technique and deductions of redaction criticism.

Even a casual reader recognizes these as four versions of the same story. A form critic might type it as a "legend"—an anecdote about a religious figure—and concentrate on its common characters (Jesus, a benevolent woman, an accuser), similar settings and actions (the woman's anointing of Jesus at mealtime, which incurs scorn), and its memorable conclusion (Jesus's intervention for the woman and rebuttal of her accusers). A form critic might speculate that the early church remembered this legend of a woman who transgressed customary table manners to honor Jesus, who defends her discipleship and gives voice to the later church's perception of his significance.

Conceding the validity of such an assessment, a redaction critic attends to the differences among these four narrations, their locations in their respective Gospels, and their coherence with the evangelists' typical concerns. The Matthean and Markan versions exhibit the closest correspondence. Both set the story in Bethany at the home of Simon the leper, two days before Passover (Matt 26:2; Mark 14:1a) as the chief priests plot Jesus's arrest (Matt 26:3–5; Mark 14:1b–2). Both tell of the woman's anointing of Jesus's head: a tacit signification of messiahship. Both describe angry grumbling over her seeming waste of a lavish gift (in Mark 14:5, "more than three hundred denarii," almost a year's earnings for a day-laborer). In both of these accounts Jesus's reply is nearly identical.

(1) He defends an outsider against rebukes (cf. Mark 10:47–49 = Matt 20:30–32).
(2) Acknowledging the needs of the poor, Jesus upholds an appropriate season for recognition of his own significance (Mark 2:18–20 = Matt 9:14–15): in this case, his proleptic anointing for burial (Mark 16:1 = Matt 28:1).
(3) He weaves remembrance of this woman's "good service" to him (Mark 1:30–31 = Matt 8:14–15) into a reassertion of the gospel's future proclamation (Mark 13:10 = Matt 24:14).

The differences between Matt 26:6–13 and Mark 14:3–9 are minor. Mark's account is wordier, though not atypically so (cf. Mark 5:1–20 = Matt 8:28–34). Matthew's version identifies Jesus's disciples as the woman's critics (26:8; cf. Mark 14:4), though Mark implicates Judas in the material following this legend (14:10–11; cf. Matt 26:14–16).

As elsewhere in the passion narrative, here John is closely aligned with the Synoptics: "six days before the Passover in Bethany" (John 12:1; cf. Matt 26:2 = Mark 14:1 ["two days before"]). Jesus's defense of a woman's generosity in John 12:7–8 condenses longer explanations in Matt 26:10–12 = Mark 14:6–8, omitting assurance of the remembrance of her deed (Matt 12:13 = Mark 14:9). John specifies Judas as the woman's critic, describing at length his treachery and pilferage among the twelve (12:4–6; see 13:2, 11, 26–30; 17:12b). The most obvious difference in John's version is its identification of characters previously introduced in this Gospel (11:1–44) but absent from the others: Lazarus and his sisters, Martha and Mary (12:1–3). Only in John is the woman given a name: "Mary." None of the Gospels identifies the woman in this story as Mary Magdalene (cf. John 19:25; 20:1–18).

In general Luke's Gospel, like Matthew's, accords with Mark's. In this case, however, Luke diverges most conspicuously from the rest.

(1) The story no longer takes place before Passover. Luke transfers it from the passion narrative to a point much earlier in his narrative, while Jesus is in Galilee (7:1 [Capernaum], 11 [Nain]).
(2) The dispute is also relocated. In Luke the disciples do not lambaste the squandering of a precious commodity; instead, the challengers are Pharisees (7:36–37; see 5:17–32; 6:1–11; 7:29–30). The controversy turns on two intersecting points: the bathing of Jesus's feet (see John 12:3) by an anonymous "woman in the city who was a sinner" (7:37–39) and his acceptance of her affection (7:44–47).
(3) By including the parable in 7:40–43, Luke refocuses the legend on a subject dear to this evangelist's heart: repentance and release from sins within the economy of God's kingdom (3:1–14; 4:18–21; 5:18–32; 15:1–32; 18:9–14; 24:44–48).
(4) The woman's lavish expression of menial love toward Jesus resonates with Luke's depiction of other women, like Elizabeth and Mary (1:24–56) and the named females in Jesus's entourage (8:1–3; 23:10), who glorify God by honoring his messianic herald. Simon the Pharisee (not "the leper" [Matt 26:6 = Mark 14:3]) is "the rich sent away empty" of Jesus's commendation (Luke 1:53; 7:44–47). The penitent woman is one of "the lowly lifted up" (1:52; 7:50).

Pioneering Redaction-Critical Studies. During much of the history of interpretation, the Gospels' differentiating features have been harmonized. Emblematic of that procedure was Tatian's second-century *Diatessaron* ("through [the] four"), which integrated parallel passages, eliminated duplications, and reconciled contradictions. To the present day, Christian piety conflates "the seven last words of Christ" in observance of Good Friday (Matt 27:46; Luke 23:34, 43, 46; John 20:26–27, 28, 30).

Precursors. Like historical criticism generally, redaction criticism is a product of the Enlightenment. One may detect its earliest anticipation in the Wolfenbüttel *Fragments* (1774–1778) of Hermann Samuel Reimarus (1694–1768). Guided by a rationalism that deployed reason to falsify alleged revelation, Reimarus distinguished the evangelists' words from what Jesus himself taught (a "criterion of dissimilarity" still used in studying the Jesus of history; e.g., John P. Meier, *A Marginal Jew*, 1991). For Reimarus, the contradictions among the Gospels and their deviations from Jesus's own intent invalidated the essence of Christian revelation (1970). Sharing Reimarus's incipiently redaction-critical assumption that the Gospels express Christian concerns, Martin Kähler (1835–1912) drew an opposite, orthodox conclusion: the nineteenth-century "quest for the historical Jesus" was a blind alley. For Kähler, Christian faith depends not on the Gospels' historical authenticity but rather on their apostolic testimonies to the church's risen Lord (1964). Dedicated to historical criteria for the reconstruction of early Christian religion, William Wrede (1859–1906) encouraged source critics to attend more closely to the evangelists' theological biases. Reimarus had speculated on Jesus's messianic self-consciousness; Wrede attacked such psychological conjectures. For him the motif of "messianic secrecy" (Mark 3:11–12; 8:29–30) was an early church construct, projecting Easter faith onto a non-messianic tradition (1971). Though the arguments and conclusions of Reimarus, Kähler, and Wrede vary widely, all presuppose the Gospels' expression of Christian beliefs about Jesus.

The immediate impetus for twentieth-century redaction criticism was form critics' tendency to atomize the Gospels' traditional constituents, isolated from their narrative contexts. Correlatively, form criticism tended to denigrate the evangelists as mere carriers of tradition: incapable of mastering their inherited materials, they were hardly authors at all. Resisting this trend, B. W. Bacon (1860–1932) urged scholars to consider Matthew as more than an adept editor (1930). Important in bridging form and redaction criticism was R. H. Lightfoot (1883–1953), who wrote at a time when Mark was regarded in almost exclusively biographical terms. Acknowledging their historical value, Lightfoot emphasized that Mark and the other Gospels were not unvarnished records of historical fact but religiously edifying constructions. Their topographical details are theologically significant: Galilee typifies the sphere of salvation and Jesus's manifestation as Son of Man; Judea and Jerusalem represent the scene of Jesus's judgment and rejection (1938; so also Ernst Lohmeyer, *Galiläa und Jerusalem*, 1936). No less than the other evangelists, Mark was an author of individual genius, whose narrative interpreted Jesus's significance under sanction and on behalf of the primitive church (Lightfoot 1935).

The Method's Flowering. The earliest, most influential exercise in what would soon be styled as redaction criticism was Günther Bornkamm's (1905–1990) essay, "The Stilling of the Storm in Matthew" (1948). Building on the form-critical assumption that the Gospels should be understood first as Christian preaching, not as biographies, Bornkamm argued that Matthew 8:23–27 is the oldest exegesis of Mark 4:35–41. The distress and rescue of "the little ship of the Church" symbolize discipleship as the evangelist understands it. Attentive to Matthew's shifts in terminology and narrative context, Bornkamm assessed Matthew 8:23–27 as paradigmatic of discipleship's danger and glory. He extended this insight into an investigation of the Matthean church's uneasy relationship with both Pharisaic Judaism and an increasingly gentile Christianity. Bornkamm's students Gerhard Barth and Hans Joachim Held developed their teacher's sensitivity to the theological concerns of the Matthean community in analyses of (respectively) "Matthew's Understanding of the Law" (as a dispute against antinomianism) and "Matthew's Interpretation of the Miracle Stories" (which pare away miraculous details to concentrate on christology, faith, and discipleship). Collected in a single volume (1963), these studies laid the foundation for redaction-critical investigation of Matthew in the second half of the twentieth century.

The most influential redaction critic of Luke was Hans Conzelmann (1915–1989). By carefully distinguishing Luke's modifications of Mark's parallel text, Conzelmann traced a theological arc across the Third Gospel and the Acts of the Apostles. In place of the kingdom of God's imminent consummation, Luke's history of salvation unfolds in three stages: from the period of Israel until John the Baptist (Luke 16:16); through the period of Jesus's witness (3:21—9:50), journey (9:51—19:27), and vindicated suffering (19:28—24:51); to the period of the church's mission after Jesus's ascension (Acts 1:6–11). Jesus stands at "the center of time" (the German title of Conzelmann's book). For a church disappointed by the delay of Jesus's glorious return, Luke stretches out "the last days" (Acts 2:13) into an indefinite era. During that age the Holy Spirit strengthens the church, Israel's successor as the people of God, for ethical conduct, missionary proclamation, and endurance of persecutions by adversarial Pharisees or unknowledgeable agents of Caesar. Though many of his conclusions have been challenged, Conzelmann's study (1960) set the stage for subsequent research into Lukan eschatology, Luke's view of Israel, and the Lukan church's relationship to the Roman *imperium*.

Reviewing Conzelmann's monograph, Willi Marxsen (1919–1993) coined the term *Redaktionsgeschichte*; in his own book (1969) he developed the discipline's implications for Mark. Less systematically developed than Conzelmann's, Marxsen's work is a compilation of studies. The first, on John the Baptist, concluded that the evangelist composes backward: the Baptist appears in the narrative only to clarify claims about Jesus. Indebted to Lohmeyer and Lightfoot, Marxsen's second study interpreted Mark's geographical locations as theological concepts: the wilderness qualifies the Baptist as fulfilling Old Testament (OT) prophecy; Galilee is Jesus's "home," the locus of his ministry. In Marxsen's reading of Mark, "place" makes a theological statement, as "time" does in Conzelmann's interpretation of Luke. In his third study Marxsen argued that, for Mark, Jesus is both the herald of the gospel (*euangelion*) and its content. By comparison, Matthew is a collection of Jesus's sermons in a book and Luke writes a "life of Jesus." Mark 13, the subject of the fourth study, was, for Marxsen, a window onto the historical situation of Mark's community. Placed on Jesus's lips, the command in 13:14 is directed to Jerusalem's Christians, urging their flight to Galilee after the outbreak of the Jewish war against Rome in 66 C.E.

Subsequent scholarship regarded the conclusions of Marxsen's four studies with ambivalence: while perceptive in many respects, he tended to overstate his cases. The enduring significance of Marxsen's monograph lies in his clear assertions of the character and aims of redaction criticism, as the method was coalescing in the mid-twentieth century. Primarily the redaction critic is interested in the evangelist as an authorial personality who pursues a definite goal with a distinctive point of view. That goal is accomplished through a narrative with a carefully constructed theological framework, whose character may be discerned by comparison with those of the other Gospels. That narrative is addressed to a third "situation-in-life" (*Sitz im Leben*): the circumstances of the communities from which the Gospels emerged. (The first situation-in-life was that of Jesus's own activity; the second, that of the primitive church that mediated traditions to the evangelists.) Marxsen's monograph on Mark offers the clearest manifesto for redaction criticism: a reading of the Gospels that accents their character as theological creations by authors functioning as pastors for early Christian congregations.

Development and Influence. By 1965 redaction criticism had become the principal method for interpreting the Gospels. So it remained until near the end of the twentieth century, when it spawned a variety of cognate exegetical approaches.

Monographs. Rohde (1968) summarized and assessed twenty-nine major redaction-critical studies of the Synoptics, some of which still appear in standard bibliographies. During the following two decades British and American scholarship heightened the method's influence. It is difficult to name a significant monograph on any of the Gospels during 1965–1985 that was not redaction-critically informed. To identify a study of the evangelists' theologies not so engaged is impossible.

Mark and John present special problems for redaction critics: those Gospels' sources and modifications cannot be confidently identified. That, however, has not deterred scholars from identifying Mark's allegedly characteristic locutions (Pryke 1978) or John's putative signs-source (Fortna 1970). Lately some interpreters have presupposed John's use of one or more of the Synoptics (Van Belle 2007). Noncanonical gospels, such as that of *Thomas*, are subjected to redaction-critical analysis (Koester 1990). Kloppenborg Verbin (2000) has argued that Q, the hypothetical source underlying Matthew and Luke, is an edited document that drew from clustered wisdom and apocalyptic sayings.

Commentaries and Introductions. Once standardized in the guild, critical approaches to biblical interpretation shape the field's commentaries and introductions. Thus, until quite recently, most of the twentieth century's major commentaries on the Synoptics have been fundamentally redaction-critical (e.g., Ulrich Luz, *Matthew: A Commentary*, 3 vols., 1989, 2001, 2005; Joel Marcus, *Mark 1–8*, *9–16*, 2000, 2009; François Bovon, *Luke 1* [2002], *Luke 2* [2012]). The same applies to the Gospels' treatment in standard NT introductions (e.g., Raymond E. Brown, *An Introduction to the New Testament*, 1997; Robert A. Spivey, D. Moody Smith, and C. Clifton Black, *Anatomy of the New Testament*, 6th ed., 2010). The most influential of recent commentaries on Acts is redaction-critical (Ernst Haenchen, *The Acts of the Apostles*, 1971). The twentieth-century's most important commentary on any NT book may be Rudolf Bultmann's *The Gospel of John* (1971), even though many of his opinions about the Fourth Evangelist's sources and redaction have fallen from favor.

Cognate Approaches and Recent Trends. Redaction critics attempted to coordinate the Gospels' traditional, sociological, literary, and theological aspects. Recent scholarship has pursued each of those elements along different analytical lines.

Theological assessment of Matthew and Luke by comparison with Mark is now widely assumed, except among those who employ redaction criticism to argue that Mark used and abbreviated Matthew or both Matthew and Luke (Peabody, McNicol, Cope 2002). The majority, presupposing Mark's chronological priority, is less sanguine about the possibility of identifying traditions behind that Gospel: even the most disciplined attempts to separate Markan tradition and redaction have proved incoherent (Black 2012). Johannine redaction criticism continues unabated: though its underlying traditions are no easier to recover than Mark's, John's literary relationships with the Synoptics and the Johannine Letters are as fascinating as they are confounding (von Wahlde 2010).

For historical reconstruction of Jesus, the use of redaction criticism now appears somewhat equivocal. Since Wrede, it has well served historians as a tool for distinguishing probably authentic Jesus material from later interpretive accretions. On the other hand, the heavier the kerygmatic coating one presumes of the Gospels, the more impenetrable they become for historical excavation. (The concurrence of redaction criticism's heyday with a lull in historical reconstructions of Jesus is not purely coincidental.) Participants in the so-called "Third Quest" (1985 to the present) have not yet agreed on the best way to proceed: whether by chastened adoption of form and redaction criticism (E.P. Sanders, *Jesus and Judaism*, 1985), with a bias toward social anthropology (John Dominic Crossan, *The Historical Jesus*, 1992), or a critical acceptance of the Gospels as material against which large-scale historical hypotheses may be tested (N.T. Wright, *Jesus and the Victory of God*, 1996). Such variety is a good thing: what one can know of the Jesus of history may be more reliable if clear answers converge from questions posed by alternative approaches.

Redaction critics have attempted to identify the circumstances of early Christian churches for which the Gospels were first written. In theory that is a sensible question for historical criticism to raise; in practice it has proven impossible to answer with confidence. In itself redaction criticism cannot confirm the provenance of any of the Gospels, of which Mark is illustrative: though cases have been made for that Gospel's origin in Rome, Syria, or Palestine, none of these suggestions is entirely convincing (Black 2011, pp. 28–30). To this problem one may identify three scholarly responses.

(1) Some have redoubled efforts to identify with greater precision the Gospels' social and political contexts (Gerd Theissen, *The Gospels in Context*, 1991).
(2) Others have challenged redaction criticism's tenet that the Gospels were composed for particular congregations, instead arguing that they were intended for a general Christian readership (Richard Bauckham, ed., *The Gospel for All Christians*, 1998).
(3) Still others consider the evidence in the Gospels so ambiguous that attempts to locate them are futile and exegetically unnecessary (e.g., Dwight N. Peterson, *The Origins of Mark*, 2000).

Recently the most striking development of redaction criticism has been its proliferation into various literary interpretations. This is not surprising. Over time the method evolved from detailed differentiation of tradition and redaction to "composition criticism": the conveyance of an evangelist's theological point of view through narrative construction. The career of Norman Perrin (1920–1976) epitomizes this evolution. Perrin's earliest work surveyed *The Kingdom of God in the Teaching of Jesus* (1963). Within years he refined form-critical criteria for *Rediscovering the Teaching of Jesus* (1967). Soon he shifted, first, to redaction criticism of the Gospels (1969), then to the study of symbol and myth in *Jesus and the Language of the Kingdom* (1976). For Perrin, literary criticism was the necessary outcome of *Redaktionsgeschichte*. Necessary or not, this is indeed the turn that scholarship in the Gospels had taken by 1985. Many scholars adopted the techniques of the "New Criticism" of the 1940s, analyzing the plot, discourse, settings, and characters of the Gospels' narratives (David Rhoads and Donald Michie, *Mark as Story*, 1982; R. Alan Culpepper, *Anatomy of the Fourth Gospel*, 1983; Robert C. Tannehill, *The Narrative Unity of Luke–Acts*, 1986, 1990; Jack Dean Kingsbury, *Matthew as Story*, 1988). Consistent with redaction criticism, such readings located the interpretive center of gravity in the evangelists' designs (restyled as "the implied author"). The studies compiled by Janice Capel Anderson and Stephen D. Moore, *Mark and Method* (2008), tilted the emphasis away from history and narrative toward the experience of reading. Elizabeth Struthers Malbon's *Narrative Space and Mythic Meaning in Mark* (1991) exemplified both continuity with and deviation from redaction criticism. Like Lohmeyer and Lightfoot, Malbon noted patterns of opposition in pairs like Galilee and Judea. Unlike them, though, she concentrated not on authorial intent or historical reference, but rather on the ways in which Mark's narrative generates tensions for its reader.

Contributions and Limitations. A legatee of source and form criticism, redaction criticism evolved in a manner that set the agenda for the full range of critical inquiry into the Gospels during much of the twentieth century. Its premises and procedure have proved appropriable by the modern church across all major denominations and a broad theological range from conservative to liberal. In spirit if not by name, the papal encyclical *Divino Afflante Spiritu* (1943) espouses a redaction-critical perspective. So also do Demetrios Trakatellis's *Authority and Passion* (1987) and James A. Brooks's *Mark* (1991): two commentaries that operate, respectively, out of Greek Orthodoxy and American fundamentalism. Few historical-critical methods of biblical interpretation can claim such a degree of purchase on academic and ecclesiastical imaginations. Redaction criticism's emphasis on the Gospels' theological character resonates with the express intent of the evangelists (Luke 1:4; John 20:31) and of the patristic church in its identification of orthodoxy (Eusebius, *Hist. Eccl.* 3.39.3). The distance between Irenaeus's Rule of Faith (*Adv. Haer.* 3.18.6; 4.20.4) and Lukan salvation history (thus, Conzelmann) or John's *logos*-christology (*à la* Bultmann) is not as vast as one might suppose.

The limitations of redaction criticism have become evident across decades of its practice. Its classical exercise, separating an evangelist's adaptations of anterior sources, remains conjectural. Its focus on the evangelists as authors has sometimes warped the Gospels' interpretation, obscuring other salient aspects of the redaction-critical enterprise. The temptation to smuggle one's own theological biases into complex narratives is not easily resisted. Redaction critics have posed important questions about the Gospels' literary character and social settings that the method is ill equipped to answer. Other modes of analysis come into play; other questions are worth asking.

On balance, redaction criticism has proved to be an important resource for studying the Gospels, absorbing the insights of previous methods of inquiry while laying foundations for new interpretive ventures. It remains to be seen whether redaction criticism will retain its integrity as one exegetical technique among others, or whether it will gradually metamorphose into other strategies for understanding the Gospels.

[*See also* Form Criticism, *subentry* New Testament; Literary Criticism, Literary Theory, and the Bible; Redaction Criticism, *subentry* Hebrew Bible; Source Criticism; *and* Synoptic Problem.]

BIBLIOGRAPHY

Bacon, B. W. *Studies in Matthew*. New York: Henry Holt & Co., 1930. Devotes a chapter to the "Traits of the Redactor" of Matthew: diction, style, stereotyped phrases, and use of the Greek OT. Like Lightfoot, Bacon was a form critic whose work turned in a redaction-critical direction.

Black, C. Clifton. *The Disciples According to Mark: Markan Redaction in Current Debate*. 2d ed. Grand Rapids, Mich.: Eerdmans, 2012. A critical assessment of twentieth-century scholarship, which concludes that redaction criticism, when applied to Mark, is internally inconsistent, methodologically dubious, and impossible to execute satisfactorily.

Black, C. Clifton. *Mark*. Abingdon New Testament Commentaries. Nashville, Tenn: Abingdon Press, 2011. A close reading of Mark in its final form, indebted to redaction criticism's interest in theological influences on the Gospel's composition.

Bornkamm, Günther, Gerhard Barth, and Hans Joachim Held. *Tradition and Interpretation in Matthew*. Translated by Percy Scott. London: SCM, 1963. English translation of *Überlieferung und Auslegung im Matthäusevangelium*, first published in 1960. A collection of seminal redaction-critical studies, from which scholarship in Matthean theology evolved after World War II.

Conzelmann, Hans. *The Theology of St. Luke*. Translated by Geoffrey Buswell. London: Faber & Faber, 1960. English translation of *Die Mitte der Zeit: Studien zur Theologie des Lukas*, first published in 1953. The framework for all theological investigation of Luke-Acts in the second half of the twentieth century.

Fortna, Robert T. *The Gospel of Signs: A Reconstruction of the Narrative Source Underlying the Fourth Gospel*. Society of New Testament Studies Monograph Series 11. Cambridge, UK: Cambridge University Press, 1970. An influential extrapolation of Rudolf Bultmann's hypothesis of a signs-source edited by the fourth evangelist.

Kähler, Martin. *The So-Called Historical Jesus and the Historic Biblical Christ*. Translated and edited by Carl E. Braaten. Philadelphia: Fortress Press, 1964. English translation of *Der sogenannte historische Jesus und der geschichtliche, biblische Christus*, first published in 1896. Anticipating redaction-critical concentration on the evangelists as theologians, Kähler assailed the legitimacy of nineteenth-century "lives of Jesus."

Kloppenborg Verbin, John S. *Excavating Q: The History and Setting of the Sayings Gospel*. Minneapolis, Minn.: Fortress Press, 2000. To date, the most comprehensive account of scholarship on Q and its significance for understanding Christian origins, including the "lost document"'s redaction, composition, genre, and allegedly Galilean provenance.

Koester, Helmut. *Ancient Christian Gospels*. Philadelphia: Trinity Press International, 1990. A harvest of late-twentieth century form and redaction criticism, gleaning the historical development of ancient traditions and writings about Jesus.

Lightfoot, R. H. *History and Interpretation in the Gospels*. London: Hodder and Stoughton, 1935. Pivoting from form to redaction criticism, Lightfoot appreciated the Gospels as theological constructions by authors of "individual genius."

Lightfoot, R. H. *Locality and Doctrine in the Gospels*. London: Hodder and Stoughton, 1938. A consideration of the theological significance of places and place-names in the Gospels.

Marxsen, Willi. *Mark the Evangelist: Studies on the Redaction History of the Gospel*. Translated by Roy A. Harrisville, James Boyce, Donald Juel, and William Poehlmann. Nashville, Tenn. and New York: Abingdon Press, 1969. English translation of *Der Evangelist Markus: Studien zur Redaktionsgeschichte des Evangeliums*, first published in 1956. A collection of early redaction-critical essays that aimed to do for Markan interpretation what Bornkamm and Conzlemann had contributed to the study of Matthew and Luke.

Peabody, David B., with Allan J. McNicol and Lamar Cope, eds. *One Gospel from Two: Mark's Use of Matthew and Luke*. Harrisburg, Pa.: Trinity Press International, 2002. Challenges the current consensus that Mark was the earliest Gospel. Both this work and that of Kloppenborg Verbin proceed redaction-critically, though their assumptions and outcomes are diametrically opposed.

Perrin, Norman. *What Is Redaction Criticism?* Guides to Biblical Scholarship, New Testament Series. Philadelphia: Fortress Press, 1969. A concise yet thorough summary of the discipline's origins, development, and significance, from one of its ablest practitioners.

Pryke, E. J. *Redactional Style in the Marcan Gospel: A Study of Syntax and Vocabulary as Guides to Redaction in Mark*. Society of New Testament Studies Monograph Series 33. Cambridge, UK: Cambridge University Press, 1978. A meticulous attempt to reconstruct Mark's redactional layer, this study demonstrates the difficulty of distinguishing that Gospel's tradition and redaction.

Reimarus, Hermann Samuel. *Reimarus: Fragments*. Edited by Charles H. Talbert. Translated by Ralph S. Fraser. Lives of Jesus Series. Philadelphia: Fortress Press, 1970. Inaugurating modern critical investigation into the life of Jesus, this incipiently redaction-critical work was far ahead of its time.

Rohde, Joachim. *Rediscovering the Teaching of the Evangelists*. Translated by Dorothea M. Barton. New Testament Library. London: SCM Press, 1968. English translation of *Die redaktionsgeschichtliche Methode*, first published in 1966. Though long out of print, this volume, concentrated on the Synoptic Gospels, is worth retrieving for its balanced survey of important German redaction-critical monographs, few of which were ever translated into English.

Van Belle, Gilbert "Tradition, Exegetical Formation, and the Leuven Hypothesis." In *What We Have Heard from the Beginning: The Past, Present, and Future of Johannine Studies*, edited by Tom Thatcher, 325–337. Waco, Tex: Baylor University Press, 2007. Briefly presenting "the Leuven hypothesis" that John knew and adapted

Mark's Gospel, Van Belle's essay directs the reader to important studies in this vein.

Von Wahlde, Urban C. *The Gospel and Letters of John*. 3 vols. Eerdmans Critical Commentary. Grand Rapids, Mich.: Eerdmans, 2010. Through redactional analysis, von Wahlde posits three editions of John (c. 55–95), with the Johnannine letters having been completed prior to the third (c. 90). Most exegetes consider the Johannine epistles as subsequent to and based on the Fourth Gospel.

Wrede, William. *The Messianic Secret*. Translated by J. C. G. Greig. Cambridge and London: James Clarke & Co., 1971. English translation of *Das Messiasgeheimnis in den Evangelien: zugleich ein Beitrag zum Verständnis des Markusevangelium*, first published in 1901. A landmark study, which required scholars to acknowledge that Mark was driven by religious interests greater than historical reportage.

C. Clifton Black

REFORMED CHRISTIAN INTERPRETATION

The phrase "Reformed" is commonly used to designate those churches following the teachings and interpretive methods of Ulrich Zwingli, John Calvin, and John Knox. The term "Calvinist" is often used as a synonym for "Reformed" since, of these three reformers, Calvin's work had the greatest influence. What follows is a discussion of the interpretive work of these three. First, however, we must examine several factors preparing the way for these "Reformed" interpreters.

Background to the Rise of Reformed Biblical Interpretation. In 1517, when Martin Luther (1483–1546) nailed his ninety-five theses to the door of the Castle Church in Wittenberg, he inadvertently launched what has come to be called the Protestant Reformation. While the Roman Catholic Church had been ostensibly a single, homogenous entity, the forces Luther set in motion unleashed seismic tremors that quickly shattered the unified Church into a number of very different pieces. Each new piece developed perspectives and methodologies on biblical interpretation that, collectively, moved the overall discussion in significantly disparate directions. It was not that Luther single-handedly shattered the unity of Christendom. Rather, he ignited numerous forces already smoldering within the church and within the broader world. In order to understand the role that Reformed Christianity, one subset of the Protestant Reformation, played within this new, widely-diversified spectrum of Christianity after 1517, we must look at these rapidly growing forces that quickly transformed the nature of European Christianity after Luther's single act provided the catalyst.

One force was the return to the ancient roots of Christianity. For several decades, the phrase *ad fontes*, "back to the sources," became the rallying cry of the Renaissance Humanists, perhaps best exemplified in Erasmus of Rotterdam. To better study the Christian scriptures, these scholars sought first to correct obvious errors in the text of Jerome's Latin Vulgate, which over the centuries had suffered from numerous copying errors. In time, with the Westward movement of many ancient Greek texts after the fall of Constantinople in 1453 and with growing dialogue between Jews and Christians focused around the study of the Hebrew text of the Old Testament (OT), interest arose in studying the Christian Bible in its original languages, rather than in Jerome's Latin Vulgate. Since the Roman Church had long used Jerome's Vulgate as its official and authoritative version of scripture, studying the Bible in Hebrew and Greek had the potential, soon to be realized, to challenge seriously the Roman Church as the exclusive source for authoritative interpretation of scripture.

Gutenberg's introduction of the printing press into Western Europe in the mid-fifteenth century also dramatically challenged the power of the Roman Church to dictate truth in matters of theology and biblical interpretation. Although Gutenberg's first major publication, Jerome's Latin Vulgate (1454/55), was the translation endorsed by the Roman Church, it soon became obvious that the printing press could efficiently and widely disseminate throughout Western Europe numerous copies of *any* document, including those rapidly spreading rallying cries against Rome and its teachings. The broad distribution of printed copies also triggered significantly increased literacy rates throughout Europe, thereby enabling more people to interpret the Bible for themselves rather than being told by trained clergy what to believe. The Roman Church's control over the minds and religious beliefs of the common folk was thereby significantly reduced. Reformers, such as Luther, Zwingli, Calvin, and Knox, were able to quickly disseminate their teachings and biblical interpretations over considerable distances and among large populations eager to study their work.

As Europe enjoyed population growth and an increase of wealth from international trade, the guilds, and other economic endeavors, a national consciousness and a sense of ethnic cohesiveness led certain countries to become more assertive and independent-minded. In England, Henry VIII, himself quite religiously conservative, broke away from the Roman Church in his zeal to produce a male successor to his throne. The Germans, while a politically diverse group as late as the time of Bismarck in the late 1800s, nevertheless rallied around Luther as a fellow German and backed his reform measures directed against Rome. Clearly, the Roman Church's ability to navigate and dominate the political and religious affairs of Europe was in significant decline as the Protestant Reformation began to gain headway.

That reformation would not, however, present a united front against Rome. No sooner had the various reformers followed Luther's lead in breaking with Rome, than they took to squabbling among themselves. Having declared himself head of the Church of England, and while continuing to view Luther as a radical, Henry VIII endorsed few substantive religious changes beyond his lucrative seizing of the English monasteries, even though some of his clerics and people were of a mind to go further. Consequently, England's reformation was initially more political than it was religious, held in check by Henry and subsequently by his daughter Mary Tudor. The Lutheran Reformation moved further away from Rome than did the English, but still retained many features and teachings of the Roman Church after it had cleansed itself of perceived Roman errors of teaching, such as indulgences, purgatory, and the theology of the seven sacraments. Luther's use of Law and Gospel to understand and interpret scripture, however, introduced a dramatically new perspective into biblical interpretation. As we shall see shortly, so did Zwingli's emphasis on the importance of the Spirit in biblical interpretation. It was not long, however, before more radical reformers began to assert themselves, and the rifts within Christianity multiplied.

Ulrich Zwingli. Ulrich Zwingli was born 1 January 1484 into a family of farmers from the Canton of St. Gallen of the Swiss Federation. Early on, he was schooled in Scholastic thought, including that of John Duns Scotus, although Scholasticism's influence on him waned as he matured, no doubt due to his growing insistence on the importance of the rigorous study of the biblical text. Erasmus, the most famous and respected Christian humanist scholar of his time, exerted a strong influence on Zwingli's life and thought, perhaps most of all through the christocentric character of Erasmus's writings. In addition to being a classical scholar, Erasmus was a diligent student of the Church Fathers and a renowned biblical scholar. His publication of a Greek text of the New Testament (NT) in 1516, accompanied by his own Latin translation, had a major impact on contemporary scholars. Zwingli's biblical interpretation for the remainder of his life was modeled substantially upon the scholarly profile of Erasmus and other Renaissance Humanists, such as Johannes Reuchlin, whose recent publications on Hebrew syntax and grammar made advanced study of the Hebrew text of the OT more feasible for Renaissance scholars.

As one would expect, Zwingli, following in Erasmus's footsteps, diligently studied the NT in Greek. He was especially influenced by the Gospel of John and by Paul's writings. The early Church Fathers, rather than the medieval Scholastics he had studied as a youth, now engaged his interpretive interests. He was led to focus more on Christ as the center of biblical interpretation, guided by ancients such as Augustine (who also had a profound influence on Luther), Jerome, Origen, Ambrose, and Irenaeus, as well as by Erasmus. This focus on the text of the Bible itself led him to argue that all else beyond the Bible was the word and work of humans. In Zwingli's first major series of sermons, begun in Zurich in January 1519, he abandoned the practice of preaching on each Sunday's Gospel lesson, and decided instead to read through the Gospel of Matthew section by section on successive Sundays, giving his interpretation of the passage in his sermon to the congregation. He used this technique in preaching his way through Acts, various NT epistles, and eventually portions of the OT, such as Psalms.

Since Zwingli focused his scholarly work directly on the text of the Bible itself, rather than on the works of the Scholastics, the church councils, and the theologians, he employed the newly-available tools for intensive study of the text, such as the reconstructed Greek text of the NT published by Erasmus, and the Hebrew text of the OT recently published for the Jewish community by the Soncino brothers in 1488. Zwingli argued that Hebrew was important for understanding the text of both the OT and the NT, since all these writers were of a strongly Hebrew mindset. Following in the footsteps of the early fourteenth-century Franciscan scholar Nicholas de Lyra (1270–1349), Zwingli emphasized that setting passages of the OT and the NT in their scriptural context was crucial for uncovering the essence of their message. He pursued matters of etymology, geography, the nuances of words and their linguistic structure, and the ancient historical setting of particular passages. An example of this is Zwingli's desire to probe behind the parables of Christ in the Gospels to the original purpose behind their being told. Likewise, disagreeing strongly with Luther on the matter of the Eucharist, Zwingli argued that the words "This is my body" cannot mean literally that the bread and wine contain the body and blood of Christ, since they are followed by the words "Do this in remembrance of me," which, in Zwingli's opinion, clearly indicate a recollection, a spiritual eating, rather than a physical, bodily presence.

As much as Zwingli understood the importance of interpreting passages in their original biblical context, he did not see a cleft between the OT and the NT due to the considerable difference in their historical contexts and chronological settings. Rather, he saw them to be essentially one covenant, with deep and pervasive continuity between them. Zwingli based a good deal of his method for interpreting the OT on I Corinthians 10:11 (author's translation), "These things happened to them [OT figures and events] as a type of warning, but they were written down for our instruction." While affirming the historicity of these various events in the OT, he sees them also to be symbolic or typological in their pointing ahead to Christ. A good example, one in which Zwingli employs a motif from the Church Fathers, is Genesis 22, the story of Abraham's near sacrifice of his son Isaac. For Zwingli, Abraham the father is a type of God the Father, and Isaac is a type of Christ, who, unlike Isaac, truly becomes the sacrifice. The three days in this story are a type of Christ's resurrection on the third day, and the wood borne by Isaac is a type of Christ bearing his own cross. For Zwingli, all the Bible points clearly to Christ, and the search for him must lie at the center of all biblical interpretation. Significantly, in Zwingli's search of the OT, figures such as Noah, Melchizedek, Isaac, Jacob, Joseph, and Moses all serve as types of Christ. Zwingli also finds in the OT types of the church, evil powers, the end of time, the fatherhood of God, and so on.

In his discussions, Zwingli drew freely and favorably from the non-Christian writers of the ancient world, even while conscious of the necessity for Christocentric interpretation of the Bible. Given that caveat, he delighted in citing ancient classics. At times he employed elements of the multilayered system of interpretation practiced throughout the Middle Ages, which included the natural (straightforward) sense of scripture, the moral sense, and the mystical, which includes approaches such as the allegorical. Zwingli's use of the allegorical approach more closely resembles typology than allegory, and Zwingli asserts that allegory cannot be used to demonstrate doctrines or practices that cannot be established by the natural sense of scripture. Thus, the natural sense for Zwingli was the foundation on which all else must be built. This does not, however, mean that his interpretation was always "literal." Trained as a rhetorician, Zwingli believed that taking the text "literally" could easily lead the reader to miss the subtleties and nuances of the natural sense of the text, which uses figures of speech such as synesthesia, metaphor, catachresis, and synecdoche to convey meaning. For example, Zwingli understood some demands of the Sermon on the Mount to be figurative rather than literal. In the command to turn the other cheek after being struck on the first cheek, Zwingli considers Jesus to be employing hyperbole in order to make a point. The command in Matthew 5:34 to avoid all oath-taking Zwingli views as an exaggeration used by Jesus to encourage people to avoid using and, thereby, defaming God's name in oaths they could not keep.

Ultimately, understanding the meaning of the texts is heavily dependent on the infusion of God's Spirit, who alone provides the true insight into the Bible. All the available tools cannot begin to help an interpreter understand a passage if the power of the Spirit is not present, guiding the interpreter. However, Zwingli disagreed with others, such as the Anabaptists, who claimed that the Spirit plays a more active, energized role in the life of the church, independent of scriptural interpretation. Vital as the work of the Spirit is in the life of the church, Zwingli was firm in his conviction that the Spirit always guides the church *through* the process of interpreting scripture and not *apart* from that process. Here Zwingli closely parallels Calvin.

An interesting interpretive perspective of Zwingli is that, while Christ is the center and fulfillment of the OT, one must read back *from* him *to* the OT passages to find the meaning that he fulfils. If the interpreter begins with only the OT, the connection is not clear. Once Christ becomes the focus, what is in the OT is clarified; thus, without Christ to bring it to culmination, the OT is an obtuse book.

Zwingli's influence spread rapidly during and after his lifetime. Given the limited impact of the Swiss Confederation on the rest of Europe, the spread of Zwingli's influence was due to his personal contact with other reformers and to the ability of the printing press to disseminate his work quickly. Zwingli argued that the Roman Church was thoroughly corrupt and insisted that the church undergo a dramatic reorientation based on its biblical and, especially, its Pauline roots. This insistence led him to undertake serious work to reform his own church in Zurich. These factors, no doubt, explain his appeal well beyond Switzerland. Southern Germany was especially receptive to his teachings, although, following the Diet of Augsburg in 1530, this region moved toward Lutheranism. Zwingli had so much influence in France that six times between 1542 and 1546, the Sorbonne placed works by Zwingli on its index of forbidden literature. England, Eastern Europe, Italy, Spain, and the Netherlands were also impacted by Zwingli's thought. Refugees in Switzerland from England, France, and elsewhere also helped spread Zwingli's influence throughout Europe.

Zwingli died in battle at Kappel, Switzerland, 11 October 1531. His influence on the Reformed Churches was powerful, even though his work was gradually overshadowed by that of John Calvin.

John Calvin. John Calvin was born 10 July 1509 in Noyen, in the Picardy region of France. Being precocious, he attended various institutions, learning Latin and Greek, eventually studying law and the classics, becoming intrigued with Humanism, and going on to practice law. Around 1530, he experienced a religious conversion and broke away from the Roman Church. In Paris, Calvin became involved with Nicolas Cop, Rector of the College Royal, who advocated for reform within the Roman Church. First Cop, and then Calvin, fled to Basel, Switzerland, where, in 1536, Calvin published the first edition of his *Institutes of the Christian Religion*, which he continued to update for the rest of his life. After brief stops elsewhere, he found himself in Geneva in the fall of 1536, where he joined fellow Frenchman William Farel in efforts to reform the church in Geneva. That effort did not go well and he was ejected from the pastorate, settling in Strasbourg from 1538 to 1541. While there, he prepared the second edition of his *Institutes* and began writing his commentary on Romans. In the fall of 1540, the city council of Geneva changed its mind, asking Calvin to return, which he did in 1541. From then until his death on May 1564, Calvin was intensely involved in the reform movement in Geneva, which was highly interactive with the city council. Calvin frequently squabbled with the council, and opposition to his work was substantial until approximately 1553, the year Michael Servetus, an avowed anti-trinitarian, was put to death in Geneva as a heretic. From then until his own death, Calvin's authority in Geneva was essentially uncontested, and his reform effort had the strong endorsement of the council.

Most of Calvin's exegetical works were written during his years in Geneva and fall into several categories. He produced academic lectures in Latin for students and other interested parties; he provided sermons in French for the general population; he gave weekly Bible studies in French for ministers and laity; and he wrote formal commentaries for the clergy and laity in both Latin and French. In all these formats, Calvin typically approached interpretation of the text sequentially, book-by-book and chapter-by-chapter, rather than thematically. His commentaries are concise and focused, with brief discussions of philology, the meaning of the text, and an occasional application of the text. In them he avoided diversions into dogmatic discussions and philosophical analyses, and described his terse style of interpretive writing as *perspicua brevitas* (lucid brevity), which is frequently seen in humanist hermeneutics. His lectures on particular texts are more detailed and extensive. In sermons, Calvin focused particularly on the implications of the text for the belief and conduct of his contemporaries.

During his career, Calvin preached well over two thousand sermons. Almost all delivered prior to 1549 have perished, but a professional scribe helped preserve many of those delivered after 1549. Calvin did not use notes and was not enamored with having his sermons transcribed, feeling they were too prolix. His commentaries addressed all NT books, except 2 and 3 John, and Revelation. With respect to the OT, he wrote commentaries on Isaiah, the Pentateuch, the Psalms, and Joshua, typically using materials from his lectures to students and ministers. After 1557, Calvin gave permission for his lectures to be published from stenographers's notes. From this period, we have his commentaries on Jeremiah, Lamentations, portions of Ezekiel, Daniel, and the Minor Prophets.

Like Zwingli, Calvin was thoroughly trained as a humanist, and was committed to studying the Bible in its original languages. For example, in his commentary on Romans, Calvin provided his own translation of Romans from Greek into Latin, rather than using Jerome's Vulgate. In addition to his background in the classics, Calvin also depended heavily on the Church Fathers for suggestions and guidance in interpretation. John Chrysostom of Constantinople was one of Calvin's favorites, as may be seen in his unfulfilled intention to translate the homilies of Chrysostom into French. In the preface to the intended volume, Calvin provides a substantial argument for the benefits of reading the Church Fathers. Calvin argues here that the Fathers provide solid guidance in discerning the meaning of scripture and teach us about the life of the early church, which he perceived to be purer and in better order than the church of later times. The Fathers also exhorted their followers to moral uprightness and, thus, providentially provided resources relevant for the sixteenth century. Working in conjunction with the Holy Spirit, they provide later readers with the ability to discern the true meaning of scripture. Calvin, believing in an educated and perceptive laity, felt that the Fathers spoke plainly and, thus, could help laity in their reading of scripture.

Calvin's strong commitment to the literal, "historical" sense of the text was an earmark of his interpretation. Reacting, as did many of his contemporaries, to the church's so-called "spiritual" or allegorical exegesis, Calvin came down quite negatively on certain Church Fathers, especially Origen, whom he saw as obscuring scripture's plain meaning by repeated and excessive use of allegory. Calvin's definition of and attitude toward allegory will be discussed further in what follows, but suffice it for now to say that Calvin did not see most Church Fathers to have sinned as regularly and boldly in this regard as did Origen.

Calvin's fondness for Chrysostom's commitment to straightforwardness in interpretation does not mean, however, that he was convinced by all of Chrysostom's details of exegesis. Calvin regularly disagrees with Chrysostom on specific interpretive points. Nevertheless, it is to Chrysostom and his fellow Church Fathers that Calvin is likely to appeal first, before he will appeal to Scholastic and contemporary writers. Calvin had a special passion for debating exegetical details with the Church Fathers, frequently disagreeing with them, even though he typically cited them elsewhere as authorities in theological matters.

As a humanist, Calvin saw understanding the mind and intention of the biblical writer to be the central purpose of all interpretation. To that end, he worked to determine the background and historical context of a particular passage, which included studying matters such as geography and chronology. He sought to define the meaning of terms and phrases in the original Greek and Hebrew, and regularly used both languages in his interpretive work. He was well trained in, and often employed, the tools of rhetorical criticism. Determining the intent of the writer did not, however, mean that Calvin was denying the work of the Holy Spirit in guiding the meaning the writer embedded in the text. For Calvin, these two factors worked in tandem. Calvin gave priority to discerning the mind of the author who, under the guidance of the Holy Spirit, wrote each passage, rather than giving priority to finding a multiplicity of meanings in the text, as many medieval interpreters were wont to do. It is not unusual to find Calvin discussing the stylistic peculiarities of specific biblical writers and noting stylistic differences within individual books. Calvin also regarded as crucial the Holy Spirit's guidance of the later reader in discerning the true meaning of a scriptural passage. In this regard, his view was especially close to that of Zwingli.

An excellent example of Calvin's attention to the background and historical context of particular passages is his treatment of the book of Psalms. He avoids too quickly leaping to Christian interpretations when he addresses specific passages. The verses in Psalm 8:4–5 (author's translation), "Yet you have made him but a little lower than the angels," Calvin understands to be David's speaking about the nature of humans before the fall. Thus, while Calvin, like the NT, does read some psalms messianically, this messianic context does not override the original character of those psalms as relating to David and other OT figures. David's kingdom had its own cultural and historical integrity, even though it also foreshadowed the greater messianic kingdom subsequently established by Christ. In this regard, Calvin appears to follow the lead of Nicholas of Lyra, who, as noted earlier, also had an influence on Zwingli. Nicholas had spoken of a double literal sense in the psalms: the literal-historical, referring to the context of the OT figures such as David, and the literal-prophetic, referring to Christ. This duality of contextual referencing is, of course, quite different from the multiplicity of meanings uncovered through the traditional medieval three- or four-tiered approach practiced especially prior to the Renaissance, which prioritized not the context of the writer of the passage, but the spiritual, moral, and eschatological meanings that could be derived by getting beyond the simple, historical contextual meaning. Recognizing that the writer of Hebrews 2:6–7 views Psalm 8:4–5 as a reference to Christ, Calvin attributes this to the writer's enriching his own Christian interpretation by finding a new meaning in Psalm 8:4–5. This does complicate Calvin's insistence on discerning the writer's (in this case, the psalmist's) simple, original context and meaning, while nevertheless preserving the core of Calvin's understanding of each passage, both in Psalms and in Hebrews.

Calvin resolves another long-standing interpretive enigma, the difference between Paul (Rom 3:28) and James (2:26) on the relationship between faith and works, by arguing that Paul and James each configured their discussion to the specific problem they were addressing. Given Calvin's skill as a theologian, as evidenced in his *Institutes*, it is significant that he resolves this issue between Paul and James not by resorting to theological argumentation, but rather by referring to the context that each writer had to address, which led them to understand the terms "faith" and "justify" in different ways.

Another example of Calvin's contextually based interpretation is his understanding of Isaiah 7:14 (KJV), "Behold, a virgin shall conceive and bear a son." While Calvin does see this verse as pointing to Christ, he argues that it is not good for interpreters to move immediately to that point. Calvin focuses on the divine covenant God had made with Israel and how that covenant grants Ahaz assurance that Jerusalem will be delivered in Ahaz's time. Ultimately, that same covenant is also fulfilled in Christ. To put it differently, Calvin is careful to assert that the words of 7:14 do not simply point ahead to Christ, without also providing Ahaz a real hope of deliverance from the original situation. Again, we see Calvin's interest in the contextual understanding of a specific passage and the people to whom it relates.

It is evident, on the whole, that Calvin exercised restraint in his biblical exegesis. He was firmly committed to the continuity of salvation history throughout both testaments, and freely uses the term "church" in referring to the people of the OT. He also emphasized the OT's culmination in Christ's death and resurrection and the founding of the Christian church. Nevertheless, he was disciplined enough not to leap quickly to a christological understanding of a passage, event, or image from the OT. An interesting example is his treatment of the passage presenting Israel's crossing of the Red Sea (Exod 14–15) and of Paul's interpretation of that event in 1 Corinthians 10:1–5. In his commentary on 1 Corinthians, Calvin explores in detail Paul's typological reapplication of the motifs of the exodus story to the Christian practices of baptism and the Lord's Supper. In his commentary on Exodus, however, Calvin merely mentions in passing Paul's typological reapplications, while his primary focus is on the context of the exodus as a key component in ancient Israel's understanding of its history and its identity as the people of God. Again, Calvin's understanding of and confidence in the long-term development of salvation history allows him to focus closely on each stage as it develops, without moving directly to its culmination in Jesus's death and resurrection. However, while sensing the strong covenantal continuity of the OT and the NT, Calvin, unlike Knox, did not assume symmetry between the testaments: the OT, for Calvin, clearly awaits the NT.

This perspective of Calvin on the interwovenness and continuity of salvation history is crucial to understanding his strong commitment to a contextual, historical orientation in his exegesis, and his dislike, indeed disdain, for allegory. Calvin was so negative toward Origen's extensive dependence on allegory, as noted earlier, precisely because Origen had, in Calvin's opinion, thereby gutted the church's salvation history of its very core. Instead of prioritizing the historical and christological dimensions of salvation history narrated in scripture, Origen took many intricate allegorical detours that prevented the central message from being heard. Calvin does acknowledge the use of allegory in some parts of the OT, as in Ezekiel, but this does not change his overall negative attitude toward the use of allegory in interpretation.

Paul's use of the term "allegory" in Galatians 4:24, though, posed a problem for Calvin's opposition to allegory. Here Paul appears to endorse the use of allegory. Calvin counters by noting that Paul, despite using the term, is not really employing allegory, which customarily builds its interpretation on very loose associations between the core text and the wide-ranging interpretive understandings based upon it. In Galatians 4, Paul actually is using typology, which requires a much more closely related, historically based connection between the core text and its interpretation. Paul connects Hagar, the slave woman, to Israel's later slavery to the Torah and its requirements, and he associates the freewoman, Sarah, to the freedom of Christians from the Law. Hagar and Mt. Sinai are types of slavery, as is Ishmael, while, for Paul, Sarah, Jerusalem, and Isaac are types of the freedom brought by the gospel of Christ. While one might argue that Paul uses the types in a most creative way, the key for Calvin is that the historical base of the types makes them work within the broad perspective of

God's plan of salvation. The looseness of allegorical interpretation uncouples the text being analyzed from its link to God's plan of salvation.

This aversion to allegory does not mean that Calvin was a "strict constructionist," always adhering to a rigid, literal understanding of the wording of a particular text. As previously noted, he understood and appreciated the use of images, metaphors, analogies, and other figures of speech and linguistic devices. He was, like Zwingli, a humanist trained in the art of rhetoric, and these skills were sharp and deep. For example, he perceives as hyperbole the statement in Matthew 5:29 about tearing out one's right eye and throwing it away if it is the cause of sin. For Calvin, this saying makes the point that one must put aside whatever inhibits obedience to God. Likewise, Calvin registers the use of prosopopoeia (personification) in Matthew 2:18 (citing Jer 31:15), which describes Rachel weeping for her children. Matthew and Jeremiah, in these texts, rouse the feelings of the reader by conjuring up the dead mother of Benjamin from the grave in their depiction of her weeping inconsolably for her lost children. Calvin considers the effect of this rhetorical tool to be especially powerful. Thus, he used such rhetorical tools as a means of constructing a finely tuned understanding of the text within its own literary and historical context. Any tool, such as allegory, that required pulling a specific text away from its context was to be rejected. In short, all the linguistic tools available must point the interpreter back to the passage's own time and context. In their use of rhetorical tools for understanding the text, Calvin and Zwingli are quite similar.

Interestingly, there is a dark side to Calvin's historical, contextual understanding of biblical figures, as exemplified in his discussion of the patriarchs and other OT and NT figures, of whom Calvin frequently takes a dim view. In this regard, Calvin is more Augustinian in temper and parts ways with the more positive view of humanity held by most humanists of the time. Many biblical figures, such as Abraham, Jacob, Judah, Hagar and Ishmael, the Samaritan woman, Jephthah, Nicodemus, and even David lie, steal, commit adultery, practice polygamy, and murder, or in general act scandalously, with little or no criticism by the biblical narrator. Typically, interpreters ignored these behaviors or created excuses. Not so Calvin. He can be robust and stinging in his criticism of these figures, due to the poor moral example they would set, if uncensured, for Calvin's parishioners and readers. Calvin sees Hagar and Ishmael to be utterly reprobate, and he uses them as metaphors for the fallen Roman Church of Calvin's day, even consigning them to hell. Nicodemus is seen to be unwilling to commit himself to Christ, while Judah and Tamar, and the Samaritan woman are also viewed quite negatively. Calvin's harshness here perhaps reveals an excessively grim view of human nature, which prevented a more nuanced and balanced interpretation of the importance and meaning of these stories. In this regard, Calvin's sense of the fallenness of humans appears to have overpowered the sense of forgiveness so essential to the salvation history he values so highly. Perhaps Calvin expected too much of these ancient figures, whose essential human nature, warts and all, is laid bare to the reader.

Calvin's work had a widespread influence, in part because Geneva served as a haven for reformers from throughout Europe. Ultimately, Calvin's teachings and interpretations reached France, Spain, Italy, the Low Countries, parts of the Holy Roman Empire, England, Hungary, and Transylvania. Frequently, Zwingli's influence preceded Calvin's, but Calvin's came to dominate. Calvin also had a major influence on John Knox, the third Reformed biblical interpreter, to whom we now turn.

John Knox. John Knox, the famous Scottish reformer, was born in Haddington, Scotland around 1513 to a farming family. Having received his education at the University of St. Andrews (and/or the University of Glasgow), he was ordained a Catholic priest in 1536. Gradually becoming involved in the Protestant Reformation, he was captured by the French and spent nineteen months as a galley slave. In 1549, he escaped to England, where he served in a variety of church related roles until the death of Edward VI in July 1553. In January 1554, he fled from Mary Tudor's attempts to restore

Catholicism to England. He spent several years in Calvin's Geneva, which he called "the most perfect school of Christ that ever was in the earth since the days of the apostles" (Knox, Vol. 4, p. 240). In *The First Blast of the Trumpet against the Monstrous Regiment of Women* (1558), Knox staunchly asserted that governance by a woman is against the laws of nature, aiming this tract against Mary of Guise, Scotland's regent. Once back in Scotland, he continued a campaign for reform with tremendous zeal. When Mary Stuart returned to Scotland in 1561, he attacked Mary for having the Catholic Mass celebrated for her, and vigorously condemned the worldliness of her court. Unabashedly critical and straightforward, Knox easily made enemies but, nevertheless, wielded an enormous influence in his homeland. He died in 1572.

Knox saw himself not as a polished biblical scholar, but as a preacher sent to speak the Word of God to his contemporaries. He wrote no commentaries on biblical books; hence, his methods and perspectives in biblical interpretation must be gleaned from his pamphlets and letters and from his history of the Scottish Reformation, which covered events up to 1564. We possess no transcripts of his sermons, even though he was a powerful and moving preacher.

The OT played a central role in Knox's understanding of scripture. He took as his interpretive guide, as well as his foundation for reform, the words of Deuteronomy 12:32 (author's translation): "All that I am commanding you, you will keep; do not add to or take anything away from it." Taking these words as key for the church, Knox refused to allow into the worship service anything not explicitly endorsed by scripture. In this regard, Knox was very similar to Calvin. Using as a model the OT's condemnation of ancient Israel's idolatrous practices, Knox renounced as idolatrous many of the rituals and practices of the Roman Catholic liturgy.

It is not unusual to find Knox bridging the chronological gap between ancient Israel and sixteenth-century Scotland or England without any attempt to account for the major political, historical, and sociological gaps between the two eras, and without any attempt to mitigate the OT's severity with the NT's emphasis on forgiveness. In Knox's view, God and God's Word are immutable. Thus, the laws of Moses specifying the penalty of death for idolatry, adultery, and other offenses that disparage God's glory were still to be rigorously applied in Knox's own time, despite passages such as Christ's forgiving the adulterous woman in John 8. At times, Knox's endorsement of OT characters and events can be quite disconcerting, as when Knox looks with favor on Jehu's bloody annihilation of the house of Ahab (2 Kgs 9–10). Knox did not subordinate the OT to the NT, as reformers like Luther had done, and his interpretive methods lacked the christocentric focus of Calvin, Zwingli, and Luther.

In addition to his emphasis on the OT, Knox's interpretive approach leaned strongly toward a literal understanding of scripture. Other Reformation figures, such as Luther and Calvin, while typically taking a straightforward, historically and contextually oriented approach to scripture, also recognized the need to understand and at times reorient individual passages within the broader context of scripture as a whole. That is why Luther responded so negatively against the Epistle of James, feeling it ran counter to the overall message of scripture. Not so Knox. Focusing on scripture as, in the strictest sense, the "Word of God," Knox emphasized a quite literal approach to interpretation. Since reforming worship was his primary interest, Knox regarded the Bible as *the* source for precedents to be emulated in reforming the worship life of the church.

For Knox, the meaning of scripture is clear and understandable for all people. The occasional vague or obscure passages can be easily explained by clear passages found elsewhere. In Knox's view, the inspiration of each verse in scripture by the Holy Spirit ensured that the core meaning of God's message could be understood easily through the assistance provided by the selfsame Holy Spirit. In this regard, Knox's interpretive perspective closely parallels Zwingli's.

Placing the OT on an equal level with the NT, Knox certainly nuanced his understanding of scripture differently from other reformers. Calvin, while recognizing the unity of the two testaments, also recognized that the OT covenant is with Israel, while the NT covenant is with all people; the OT covenant is one of bondage, while the NT covenant is one of freedom; and the OT only foreshadowed the grace to come in the NT. This degree of discontinuity between the two testaments, as recognized by Calvin, was problematic for Knox. While appreciating the NT's reinterpretation of the doctrines of atonement and the covenant, Knox considered the OT *not* to have been superseded by the NT. Knox argued that the OT *must* have a high profile in the spectrum of revelation. For example, he proclaimed that the Word of God he was preaching in the sixteenth century was the same as that preached in the OT; that the Gospel was first preached in Genesis 3; and that the church had its beginnings in Genesis with Abraham.

Knox firmly believed that all interpretation must be done within the congregation, and the interpretation of the individual must agree with that of the congregation. Individuals studying the Bible were not free to promote their own interpretation apart from the church; rather, there must be consensus in order that the whole church may be edified. To this end, Knox placed great value in training individuals for the interpretation of scripture, so that they might guide the church in its interpretation.

If Knox had difficulty perceiving the discontinuity between the OT and the NT, he also was quick to bridge the gap between biblical times and his own. He presented stunning parallels between ancient Israel and sixteenth-century England. Knox saw the wicked court servants of David and Hezekiah as equivalent to the Catholic servants hidden within Edward VI's cabinet. The calm sea plied by Jesus's disciples paralleled the calm Reformation years under Edward VI, while the subsequent storm paralleled the violent years of Mary Tudor's rule. In fact, Mary Tudor is portrayed as the idolatrous Jezebel, the epitome of a cursed ruler. In another vein, the idolatrous practices of ancient Israel anticipate the idolatrous support of Roman Catholicism by rulers such as Mary Tudor. Just as Athaliah's vile actions (2 Kgs 11) spurred Jehoiada to depose and execute her, so Mary Tudor should be deposed by the nobility and people of England.

Knox's greatest impact fell within Scotland, where the Presbyterian Church originated. However, his emphasis on the deep continuity between the OT and the NT, his zeal for strongly literal interpretation and for finding parallels between the text and the early modern world, and his eagerness to use biblical passages and stories to encourage the overthrow of sitting kings and princes, have had a significant influence on the broad spectrum of subsequent Protestant interpretation.

Conclusion: The Praxis of Reformed Interpretation. It would be unreasonable to cluster together these three Reformed interpreters as if they were all cast from the same mold. Indeed, there are significant differences between them, both in emphasis and approach. Nevertheless, several central principles, with some nuances, are shared by all three:

1. They prioritized scripture above councils, the Church Fathers, interpretation as promulgated by the Roman Catholic Church, and the interpretation of the Scholastics. In this regard, they were very close to the Lutherans. This does not mean, however, that our three Reformed interpreters spurned the Church Fathers. Calvin in particular made great use of them, most especially Chrysostom, in his exegetical discussions, even though some Fathers, like Origen, he rated rather poorly. However, the Church Fathers, for these Reformed interpreters, were a garnishment to scripture, rather than the key to it. Councils, the Scholastics, the Fathers, and the teachings of the Roman Catholic Church all stood judged by what these Reformed interpreters saw to be the clear and simple meaning of scripture. Consequently, for all three reformers, allegory was not an appropriate part of the interpretive agenda, since it directed the reader away from the straightforward meaning of scripture. Typology, more closely tied to the scriptural sense, became a preferred alternative.

2. All were strongly influenced by Renaissance Humanism, which significantly reoriented their approach to scripture. The revival of interest in Hebrew and Greek, the ancient biblical languages, the recovery of many ancient biblical manuscripts, the publication of the Hebrew Bible by the Soncino brothers, the publication of the revised Greek text of the NT by Erasmus, and the revival of interest in ancient rhetoric all focused these Reformed interpreters' interests back onto the Bible. They used the many tools newly available to scrutinize the subtle details of the biblical text, profiting from recent improvements in grammars and lexicons. While all three Reformed interpreters were committed to this agenda of close study of the text, in its broader context, Zwingli and Calvin were more so than was Knox. Both Zwingli and Calvin wrote numerous studies and commentaries on biblical books. Knox, more outspoken and focused on his reform agenda, left behind no commentaries on biblical books.

3. These Reformed interpreters were strongly committed to using these new tools of interpretation as a means to better understand the mind of the writer. That is to say, they wanted to understand the background, circumstances, language, and historical context of each passage as a means of probing into the intention of the author. What was important was not what subsequent interpreters of the text, such as the Scholastics, saw, but rather what the biblical text itself engendered in the mind of the interpreter. The assumption, therefore, was that the gap between the mind of the biblical writer and the mind of the interpreter could be ably bridged by using the recently developed tools of interpretation to focus on the meaning of the text, rather than by studying the accumulated works of 1500 years of interpretation by the church.

4. Zwingli and Calvin were sensitive to the need to apply the plain, simple meaning of the text to their own time and circumstances, including the reform movements in which both were involved, although they both wrestled, on occasion, with the proper application of the text to these circumstances. Knox struggled less with this issue, and his tendency to leap from OT and NT texts directly into situations of his own age shows somewhat less interpretive sophistication than that demonstrated by Zwingli and Calvin. For Knox, there was little difference between the OT and the NT. Both presented essentially the same message. For Zwingli and Calvin, there was a more nuanced understanding of the progression from the OT to the NT, of the need, as Zwingli expressed it, to view the OT through the eyes of the NT.

5. Both Zwingli and Calvin were christocentric in orientation. Zwingli, while understanding the different historical contexts at work in the OT and the NT, viewed them ultimately to be one covenant, with OT figures and events often serving as types that point ahead to Christ. Viewed through Christ, the OT became an open book. Calvin strongly recognized the christological orientation of scripture, even while maintaining his commitment to the historical context of a passage, which subsequently can be understood to refer to Christ. Knox, being less inclined to see a difference in the focus and shape of the OT and the NT, was also less inclined to employ a christocentric focus in his understanding of scripture.

6. The role of the Spirit in interpretation is central for all three interpreters. For Zwingli, proper interpretation would be impossible without a heavy infusion of God's Spirit. No configuration of interpretive tools could replace the guidance of the Spirit. However, the Spirit was available to the church precisely through biblical interpretation, and not through means independent of biblical interpretation, as the Anabaptists claimed. Calvin emphasized the work of the Spirit both in guiding the meaning the writer inscribed in the biblical text, and in the work of the interpreter who was guided by the Spirit to discern the true significance of a biblical passage. Thus, the Spirit was key at both ends of the process. Knox concurred with Zwingli and Calvin in this regard. Knox also emphasized that the meaning of scripture is clear and understandable for all people. Zwingli and Calvin were more sensitive to the need to provide biblical interpreters with the tools and skills required to focus interpretation as the Spirit guided their work.

Zwingli, Calvin, and Knox had a profound impact on Reformed and, more broadly, Protestant biblical interpretation. Through their reorienting and refocusing of biblical interpretation, Zwingli, Calvin, and Knox helped lay the groundwork for the rise of modern biblical interpretation, and provided the interpretive soil in which would grow and flourish a number of major Protestant denominations.

[*See also* Allegory and Allegorical Interpretation; Catholic Biblical Interpretation; Exegesis; Historical Criticism, *subentry* Hebrew Bible; Historical Criticism, *subentry* New Testament; Lutheran Interpretation; Rhetorical Criticism; *and* Theological Interpretation.]

BIBLIOGRAPHY

Gordon, Bruce. *The Swiss Reformation.* Manchester, UK: Manchester University Press, 2002. A helpful guide to the historical, sociological, cultural, and religious context in which the Swiss Reformers did their work, focusing primarily on Zwingli, with an excellent bibliography.

Knox, John. *The Works of John Knox*, edited by David Laing. 6 vols. Edinburgh: Various publishers, 1846–1864. Vital to any study of Knox as an interpreter.

Kyle, Richard G. "The Hermeneutical Patterns in John Knox's Use of Scripture." *Pacific Theological Review* 17, no. 3 (1984): 19–32. Alternative, briefer sources presenting analyses of Knox's interpretation.

Kyle, Richard G. "John Knox's Methods of Biblical Interpretation: An Important Source of his Intellectual Radicalness." *Journal of Religious Studies* 12 (1985): 57–70. Alternative, briefer sources presenting analyses of Knox's interpretation.

Kyle, Richard G. *The Mind of John Knox.* Lawrence, Kansas: Coronado Press, 1984. A solid, comprehensive analysis of Knox's work, with an extensive bibliography on Knox.

McGrath, Alister. G. "Zwingli, Ulrich (1484–1531)." In *Dictionary of Biblical Interpretation*, edited by John H. Hayes, Vol. 2, 674–675. Nashville, Tenn.: Abingdon, 1999. A good starting point for an understanding of Zwingli's approach to interpretation, with a basic bibliography.

Olbricht, Thomas H. "Calvin, John (1509–1564)." In *Dictionary of Biblical Interpretation*, edited by John H. Hayes, Vol. 1, 159-160. Nashville, Tenn.: Abingdon, 1999. Good survey and analysis of Calvin's interpretive methods, with a basic bibliography.

Pitkin, Barbara. "John Calvin and the Interpretation of the Bible." In *A History of Biblical Interpretation*, edited by Alan J. Hauser and Duane F. Watson, Vol. 2, 341–371. Grand Rapids, Mich.: Eerdmans, 2009. Sound analysis of Calvin's approach to interpretation, with an extensive bibliography.

Reventlow, Henning Graf. *History of Biblical Interpretation.* Vol. 3: *Renaissance, Reformation, Humanism.* Translated by James O. Duke. Atlanta: Society of Biblical Literature, 2010. An excellent placement of Zwingli and Calvin within the interpretive environment of their age.

Stevens, W. P. *The Theology of Huldrych Zwingli.* Oxford: Clarendon Press, 1986. In depth analysis of the relationship between Zwingli's interpretive methods and his theology, with an extensive bibliography on Zwingli.

Stevens, W. P. *Zwingli: An Introduction to his Thought.* Oxford: Clarendon Press, 1992. Shows how Zwingli's basic methods of interpretation feed into his various theological teachings.

Thompson, John L. "Calvin as Biblical Interpreter." In *The Cambridge Companion to John Calvin*, edited by Donald K. McKim, 58-73. Cambridge, UK: Cambridge University Press, 2004. Provides a solid overview of the basics of Calvin's interpretive methods.

Alan J. Hauser

Reform Jewish Interpretation

Judaism's Reform movement originated in nineteenth century Germany, as Jews sought to adapt their religious practices in ways that would bring them into conformity with those of a then-welcoming European society. From there it moved to the United States, where Isaac Mayer Wise, the movement's most prominent leader, created three major institutions—a coalition of synagogues (Union of American Hebrew Congregations, 1873), a seminary (Hebrew Union College, 1875), and a rabbinical organization (Central Conference of American Rabbis, 1889). Although Wise had hoped that these would serve the entire American Jewish community, they soon became denominational centers. Each organization has only limited authority over its respective members; to this day, individual congregations are governed by autonomous boards of laypeople, just as members of the Central Conference of American Rabbis (CCAR) are not bound by its positions. This decentralization makes it difficult to define any specifically Reform modes of interpretation, much less ones that enjoy universal assent. Instead, individual constituencies can and have moved in very different and sometimes opposite directions. For example, in 1984 the CCAR published a translation of the Five Scrolls and ten years later the Union of American Hebrew Congregations (UAHC) produced a Haftarah commentary, both of which used the movement's own translations, even though members of the Hebrew Union College faculty had played a leadership role in producing a trans-denominational version that was published by the Jewish Publication Society of America and endorsed by the UAHC. More recently, the Women of Reform Judaism sponsored a women's commentary on the Torah in 2008, just three years after the Union of Reform Judaism published a revised version of its own Torah commentary. Moreover, both included voices from outside the Reform movement and even outside the Jewish community.

Because of this intentionally non-authoritarian approach, the Reform movement's treatment of the Bible must be gathered from several disparate sources, such as (1) doctrinal pronouncements, (2) publications, (3) seminary curriculum and faculty research, and (4) denominational stances. Viewed collectively, these show that the movement's positions have varied depending on circumstance, constituency, and the concerns of the time. This is most vividly evident in Reform Judaism's view of its relationship with the larger Jewish community and its treatment of nonbiblical Jewish tradition, especially those rabbinic teachings which are collectively called the "Oral Torah."

Biblicism. Following the model of their Protestant predecessors, the Jewish reformers justified their proposed changes by appealing to the Bible, which Central and East European Jewry had largely neglected in favor of rabbinic teachings. Thus, in 1842, Frankfort's *Jüdischen Reformfreunde* asserted that "the collection called the Talmud, as well as all the rabbinic writings and statutes which rest upon it, possess no binding force for us either in dogma or in practice." This attitude was expressed in ways that sometimes parallel earlier Christian critiques of Judaism. For example, the nineteenth century American rabbi David Einhorn argued that the Talmud's "morals are narrow; the exalted universal spirit of the Bible is strange to it; the letter into which [it] forces everything is its be-all and end-all."

The Reform rabbinate formalized this position when it resolved that "our relations in all religious matters are in no way authoritatively and finally determined by any portion of our Post-Biblical and Patristic literature." Instead, its 1885 Pittsburgh Platform characterized the Bible as "the record of the consecration of the Jewish people to its mission as the priest of the one God, and . . . the most potent instrument of religious and moral instruction." That stance provided the ideological justification for eliminating various traditional ideas, such as the belief in resurrection, and practices, like observing holidays for two days, on the basis that they are not found in the Bible. As a result, Reform Judaism has sometimes been equated with Karaism, a movement that originated in the Middle East during the eighth and ninth centuries and challenged the authority of rabbinic tradition. However, this approach created exegetical problems for deeply embedded practices, such as the holiday of Hanukkah, which commemorates events that took place after the time when Jewish tradition regards revelation as having come to an end. Several Reform communities addressed this by consolidating the blessings over the Hanukkah candles in a way that avoided attributing observance of this postbiblical holiday to a divine command.

Emphasizing that the Bible carried other risks, especially as nineteenth and early twentieth century scholarship raised ever more questions as to its accuracy and authenticity, many of these questions centered on the Pentateuch (Torah), which Judaism has traditionally regarded as the most important part of the Bible. Although Isaac Mayer Wise had defended the Mosaic authorship of the Pentateuch from what he called "Negative Criticism," insisting that "there is no Judaism without the Torah and Revelation," Reform leaders and institutions have typically been more open to both textual and historical criticism than their Conservative (Jewish Theological Seminary) and Orthodox (Rabbi Isaac Elhanan Theological Seminary) counterparts. The Pittsburgh Platform acknowledges that recognition in its assertion that the Bible reflects "the primitive ideas of its own age . . . at times clothing its conception of divine providence and justice dealing with man in miraculous narratives." Prominent synagogues in Chicago and Cleveland went so far as to remove the Torah scrolls from their sanctuaries, albeit in one case replacing them with an English Bible. More often, Reform thinkers adopted the Haskalah (Jewish Enlightenment) distinction between the Bible's ethical teachings and its ceremonial laws. Thus, the Pittsburgh Platform rejected "all such Mosaic and rabbinical laws as regulate diet, priestly purity, and dress," accepting "as binding only the moral laws, and . . . only such ceremonies as elevate and sanctify our lives."

Whereas Judaism had historically focused on the Pentateuch and especially its religious regulations, the reformers emphasized ethics, monotheism, and the biblical prophets, in accordance with the spirit of nineteenth century Protestant biblical scholarship. They linked these elements under the rubric "prophetic Judaism." Thus, Rabbi Stephen S. Wise, founder of New York's Jewish Institute of Religion, which merged with the Hebrew Union College in 1948, spoke of "the authority of the content of the Bible," specifying the Ten Commandments (Exod 20), the ethical precepts in Leviticus 19, prophetic passages which stress social justice (Mic 6 and Amos 5), and the theological themes found in Psalms 23 and 51. In accordance with this understanding, the UAHC's Commission on Jewish Education inaugurated a series of commentaries on biblical books in 1930. Over the next four decades, it published seven volumes, all of which dealt with poetic and prophetic books. Another series of commentaries was produced by the UAHC, now renamed the Union for Reform Judaism, from 2002–2010, with volumes on Proverbs, Jonah, and the Five Scrolls.

The movement's rabbinic curriculum has mirrored its religious pronouncements, with the Bible occupying a central place at the Hebrew Union College-Jewish Institute of Religion (HUC-JIR) in contrast to traditional Judaism's emphasis on talmudic law. Two of the College's first four presidents (Julian Morgenstern and Nelson Glueck) were Bible scholars, and a third (Kaufmann Kohler) wrote his PhD dissertation on the Bible (all three studied at German universities), as did Jacob Marcus, though he later became a specialist in American Jewish history.

The HUC-JIR faculty has included several prominent biblical scholars. Max Margolis, Sheldon Blank, Samuel Sandmel, and Harry Orlinsky all served as presidents of the Society of Biblical Literature (in 1923, 1952, 1961, and 1970 respectively). Margolis and Orlinsky, both of whom made major contributions to the study of the Septuagint, also played pivotal roles in the Jewish Publication Society's 1917 and 1985 Bible translations; Orlinsky, who was instrumental in securing the first of the Dead Sea Scrolls for Israel, also served on the committee that produced the (Protestant) Revised Standard Version. Others, such as Julius Lewy, Matitiahu Tsevat, and Stanley Gevirtz, specialized in the ancient Near East, a prominent focus of both American and Israeli biblical scholarship. In 1963, President Nelson Glueck, a renowned archaeologist, dedicated HUC-JIR's Biblical and Archaeological School in Jerusalem; it has supported important and productive excavations, most notably at ancient Gezer and Dan. The College-Institute also established a doctoral program, which has trained numerous Christian Bible scholars, and its *Hebrew Union College Annual* has published many important works of biblical scholarship. In keeping with broader academic trends, the focus has recently shifted to literary approaches as well as the homiletical interpretation of biblical texts.

Return to Tradition. As the movement became increasingly Americanized, it restored many elements that had earlier been rejected, most notably the rabbinic tradition that is embodied in the Talmud. Thus, the CCAR's 1937 Columbus Platform acknowledged that "the Torah, both written and oral, enshrines Israel's ever-growing consciousness of God and of the moral law [even though] certain of its laws have lost their binding force with the passing of the conditions that called them forth." By the end of the twentieth century, doctrinal statements no longer used the word "Bible" at all, or even "the Torah." Instead, the Conference's 1999 "Statement of Principles" spoke of "Torah" generically as "God's ongoing revelation to our people and the record of our people's ongoing relationship with God," thereby announcing Reform's embrace of the Oral Tradition it had once rejected. To be sure, the movement has continued its appeals to "prophetic Judaism," as when the CCAR devoted its 2011 convention to the theme "Prophetic Voice in the 21st Century"; however, these are accompanied by frequent references to "*tikkun olam*" (lit. "repair of the world"), a rabbinic phrase that played a major role in medieval Jewish mysticism.

Commentaries. This return to Jewish tradition is also evident in the movement's commentaries. Whereas the initial series focused on the Bible's poetic and prophetic books, in 1974 the UAHC produced a commentary on the Pentateuch that was designed for use during synagogue worship and not just classroom study. It presented traditional Jewish interpretations alongside those of modern scholarship, drawing on thinkers from the entire breadth of the Jewish world and even some non-Jews, though Reform leaders seldom cite Christian tradition when dealing with practical issues. Reflecting the movement's ambivalence toward traditional practice, the accent marks that indicate the melody by which the Torah is chanted during worship were left out, the text divided into logical units rather than according to the weekly portions (*parashot*) assigned by Jewish tradition, and the prophetic selections (*haftarot*) that accompany the reading during Sabbath worship relegated to the back of the book. However, the cantillation marks were inserted in a second printing seven years later; and the traditional divisions restored and each followed by its prophetic reading in a new edition that was produced in 2005, thereby bringing the commentary into alignment with those produced by the other, more traditional American Jewish movements as well as earlier Jewish commentaries. In addition, the UAHC website continues to provide discussions of the Pentateuch's weekly lections, some of which have been published in *Living Torah, Selections from Seven Years of Torat Chayim.* Movement leaders have also produced several other Torah commentaries, including a feminist commentary edited by a female Reform rabbi in 2000 and supplemented by a volume on the *haftarot* (2004), a commentary for Jewish men, edited by a male Reform rabbi in 2009, and another feminist commentary (2008), which was initiated by the Women of Reform Judaism under the editorship of a member of the seminary faculty. Tellingly, all three include contributions from authors who are not connected with the Reform movement, demonstrating its growing linkage to the larger Jewish community. That dynamic is also evident in the movement's seminary, which has long included biblical scholars with backgrounds outside the movement on its faculty.

Social Issues and Tradition. The movement's focus on social issues, coupled with Judaism's longstanding emphasis on behavioral norms rather than doctrine, led Solomon Schechter, a prominent Jewish scholar and chancellor of the Conservative movement's Jewish Theological Seminary at the turn of the twentieth century, to observe that the "Reform movement was not always a very trustworthy ally" of Jewish learning. Many of its commentaries have been written by practicing rabbis rather than academics, accounting for their pastoral, homiletical, and didactic elements. That orientation is also evident in the movement's treatment of social issues, where its commitment to liberal values can be at odds with its attachment to the Bible. Official stands are, therefore, frequently taken without reference to any Jewish source, even on issues that the Bible does address, such as abortion and economic justice. Appeals to tradition often take the form of citing biblical slogans, such as the book of Genesis's reference to humans as being in the image of God (Gen 1:27) or the prophetic call to be a light to the nations (Isa 42:6; 49:6; 51:4; cf. 60:3), an understanding of the prophet's message that was disputed by one of the movement's own Bible scholars. However, such phrases are drawn from rabbinic tradition as often as from the Bible. When traditional sources seem to diverge from the movement's liberal stance, they are sometimes contextualized, frequently on the basis of Reform's understanding of revelation, which the Columbus Platform described as "a continuous process, confined to no one group and to no one age." That approach allows for the citation of postbiblical sources, such as the Talmud or medieval philosophers. However, movement leaders occasionally reject biblical authority altogether. For example, some of those who found Lev 18:22 and 20:13 to be insurmountable obstacles to their inclusive position on issues relating to homosexuality justified their stance by comparing the Bible's statements on the subject to its inclusion of what they described as outdated ceremonial and even ethical provisions.

Similarly, the movement's recent efforts to encourage various traditional practices have been inconsistent as to whether the dietary laws (*kashrut*), for example, should be restored in their traditional form, reinterpreted as requiring healthy eating practices, applied to the treatment of farm animals and slaughterhouse employees, or rejected as outmoded ceremonial regulations. The persistence of these patterns of debate demonstrates the movement's diffuse authority structure, lack of an accepted hermeneutical process, and vacillation between its historical reliance on the Bible and its acceptance of the modernist understanding of the Bible's ancient and human origin.

[*See also* Conservative Jewish Interpretation; Diachronic Interpretation; Historical Criticism, *subentry* Hebrew Bible; Midrash; Orthodox Jewish Interpretation; Rabbinic Exegesis; Reconstructionist Interpretation; Source Criticism; *and* Tradition-Historical Criticism].

BIBLIOGRAPHY

Kaplan, Dana Evan. *American Reform Judaism, An Introduction.* New Brunswick, N.J.: Rutgers University Press, 2003.

Karff, Samuel E., ed. *Hebrew Union College – Jewish Institute of Religion at One Hundred Years.* Cincinnati, Ohio: Hebrew Union College Press, 1976.

Meyer, Michael A. *Response to Modernity, A History of the Reform Movement in Judaism.* New York: Oxford University Press, 1988.

Petuchowski, Jakob J. "Reform Judaism's Diminishing Boundaries: *The Grin That Remained,*" with responses by Leigh D. Lerner, Yoel H. Kahn, and Dow Marmur. *Journal of Reform Judaism* 33, no. 4 (Fall, 1986): 15–32.

Philipson, David. *The Reform Movement in Judaism.* Revised ed., New York: The Macmillan Co., 1931.

Plaut, W. Gunther. *The Growth of Reform Judaism.* New York: World Union for Progressive Judaism, 1965.

Plaut, W. Gunther. *The Rise of Reform Judaism: A Sourcebook of Its European Origins.* New York: World Union for Progressive Judaism, 1963.

Frederick E. Greenspahn

Relevance Theory and Biblical Interpretation

Relevance Theory (RT) is an inferential model of communication and interpretation that diverges significantly from the code model, which is the foundation for most contemporary approaches to biblical interpretation. RT provides a comprehensive theory of communication that shows how authors, readers, texts, and contexts interact in the communication of meaning and, as such, provides a rich model for understanding the interpretive task. Shifting from the code model of communication to an inferential model will naturally entail modifications in our understanding of hermeneutical theory as well as exegetical methodology. While those engaged in biblical translation have entered fully into discussions about the usefulness of RT as a theoretical foundation for their work, biblical scholars are only recently beginning to appreciate the descriptive value of RT.

Code and Inferential Models of Communication. According to the code model, a communicator pairs her message with a signal or a linguistic code, which is transmitted by gesture or through a verbal or written sign system. The role of the hearer or reader is then to decode the message. Misunderstanding comes when there is noise in the system (such as a distraction) or from a lack of understanding of the code. But if the code is mutually understood and the signal is not distorted through interference, the addressee will comprehend the message. The code model is inherently signal oriented rather than communicator or addressee oriented. This theory of communication accounts for the strong emphasis on lexical study, syntactical and discourse analysis, and intertextual study in contemporary exegetical methodology. Since words contain the meaning communicated, faithful decoding becomes the primary concern as readers seek to comprehend the canonical text.

An inferential model, however, views the sign system as a component in the communication of meaning but regards it as a piece of evidence that the communicator offers when she wishes to convey a message. The meaning of her utterance is not the same as the meaning of her sentence since part of the meaning she intends to communicate must be inferred from a combination of the sign system and context. The speaker or writer's meaning is a combination of encoded and inferred information. An inferential model of communication focuses on the intentions of the communicator and the inferences made by the addressee, not simply the linguistic code. There exists a gap between utterance meaning and sentence meaning which must be filled by an inferential process that accesses relevant contextual information. For example, in 1 Thessalonians 5:3, Paul says (1), "When they say, 'There is peace and security', then sudden destruction will come upon them, as labor pains come upon a pregnant woman, and there will be no escape!" Through an inferential process, the reader must assign reference to "they" and "them" in Paul's utterance. He must also disambiguate terms such as "peace and security," asking what kind of "peace and security" do "they" have in mind. The reader also must enrich the proposition that "there will be no escape" by asking, "From what will they not escape?" What Paul meant in his utterance consists of more than what he said in the lexical and semantic structures of the sentence. How, then, do we fill the gap between sentence and utterance meaning?

Relevance Theory and Ostensive-Inferential Communication. Relevance Theory, as developed by Dan Sperber and Deirdre Wilson, discusses the character of *ostensive-inferential communication*, which they define in the following way: "the communicator produces a stimulus which makes it mutually manifest to communicator and audience that the communicator intends, by means of this stimulus, to make manifest or more manifest to the audience a set of assumptions [**I**]" (1995, p. 63). Communication is *ostensive* in that the communicator wants her intention to communicate to be recognized. The communication is *inferential* from the perspective of the hearer or reader in that he must infer from the evidence provided what the speaker or author's intent was. Sperber and Wilson note that there are two kinds of intention at the heart of communication: the informative and the communicative. The *informative intention* is "to make manifest or more manifest to the audience a set of assumptions [**I**]" (1987, p. 58). On the one hand, the informative intention is the communicator's intention to inform the addressee about a set of assumptions, such as the fact that **(1)** "They will not escape" from some form of "sudden destruction." On the other hand, the *communicative intention* is the desire that the communicator has to make her informative intention known to the hearer or reader. According to Sperber and Wilson, the communicative intention "make(s) it mutually manifest to audience and communicator that the communicator has this informative intention" (1987, p. 61). Recognizing the speaker or writer's intent to communicate a set of assumptions moves us beyond the mere transfer of information to genuine human communication. According to RT, comprehending both the informative and communicative intention of the speaker or writer is the essence of communication. Humans possess the ability to represent their own thoughts through the linguistic sign system but also *metarepresent* the thoughts of others and ascribe intentions to them (Carston 2002, pp. 42–47; Green 2010). These abilities make ostensive-inferential communication possible.

Code and Context. Relevance Theorists recognize the role of the sign system in communication but argue that accessing the appropriate contextual information is essential in order to understand a speaker or writer's utterance. A word or sentence could mean a wide array of things by simply varying the contexts in which they are communicated. According to RT, the *context* of an utterance is not all the information available from the discourse in which a sentence is embedded (such as a paragraph, a section of a book, or a book as a whole), the wider literary corpus of a particular author (such as the writing of Paul), nor the wider cultural context shared by communicators and their addressees (such as the history and cultures of the Jewish and wider Greco-Roman worlds). Rather, context is a subset of all the salient or available information to the communicator and the addressee, which is accessed in the communication of an utterance. Context is not a preset and well-defined body of information but, rather, consists of all the information that is relevant for the interpretation of a particular utterance. As such, context is a psychological construct. As Gutt notes, context is only a select portion of the speaker/writer's and hearer/reader's "'assumptions about the world' or *cognitive environment*. The notion of 'cognitive environment' takes into account the various external factors but places emphasis on the information they provide and its mental availability for the interpretation process" (2000, p. 27).

Interpreters of biblical texts commonly invest a considerable amount of effort in understanding the cognitive environment of the biblical authors and their readers and selecting which aspects of that information are relevant for the interpretation of a particular utterance. Accessing the appropriate contextual information is essential for all communication since meaning is not entirely contained within the sign system. Supplying assumptions other than those that the communicator intended can change the meaning of an utterance significantly. When interpreting Genesis 4:1, **(2)** "Now the man knew his wife," the reader who understands "knew" (ידע) as a merely cognitive process has disambiguated the verb in a way that substantively alters the meaning of the utterance. The necessary contextual information needed to disambiguate "to know" appears in the following clause of the verse, "and she conceived and bore Cain."

The Principle of Relevance. The fundamental premises of RT are, first, that every utterance has a variety of possible interpretations, all of which are compatible with the information linguistically encoded. Second, not all of these interpretations are available to a hearer or reader at a particular moment. Third, readers and hearers are able to evaluate possible interpretations, either accepting or rejecting them, by the application of the general *principle of relevance* (discussed later). Supplying proper assumptions from context does not occur in a haphazard manner. And fourth, hearers or readers will invest processing effort to find the necessary contextual assumptions and, when found, will cease processing. Addressees do not explore all possible interpretations before coming to conclusions regarding the meaning of an utterance.

Within RT, *relevance* is not something that seems to be important or relevant, as in common usage. Rather, relevance is a technical term defined in relation to modifications of a hearer or reader's cognitive environment, called *cognitive effects*, and the processing effort invested to achieve cognitive effects. In other terms, for information to be relevant, it must produce some cognitive benefit in relation to the effort expended to achieve those cognitive effects. RT, therefore, asserts that (a) "The greater the cognitive effects, the greater the relevance" and (b) "The smaller the effort needed to achieve those effects, the greater the relevance" (Wilson and Matsui 1998, p. 16; and Sperber and Wilson 1995, pp. 118–171; 265–266). Wilson and Sperber ask, "When is an input relevant? Intuitively, an input (a sight, a sound, an utterance, a memory) is relevant to an individual when it connects with background information he has available to yield conclusions that matter to him: say, by answering a question he has in mind, improving his knowledge on a certain topic, settling a doubt, confirming a suspicion, or correcting a mistaken impression" (2004, p. 208). When someone communicates through an utterance, the information she presents will interact with assumptions that are manifest to both her and her addressee and will produce cognitive effects by strengthening existing assumptions, contradicting or eliminating existing assumptions, or combining with an existing assumption to yield some contextual implication (Wilson and Matsui 1998, p. 16; Sperber and Wilson 1995, pp. 263–266, 108-137). Information or input is relevant when it produces positive cognitive effects or pay-off for the processing effort invested.

In this search for a context within which to process an utterance, there is a fine balance between the processing effort expended and cognitive effects. If no cognitive effects are immediately available, the addressee will invest greater processing effort in a quest for cognitive effects. The addressee will expect that the speaker or writer is being optimally relevant in accordance with his or her preferences and abilities. This assumption of optimal relevance raises expectations and motivates the addressee to invest a sufficient amount of processing effort. If, in the end, the addressee finds no cognitive effects, then he may return for clarification or simply stop processing, assuming that the utterance was not relevant.

This search for relevance in relation to the assumption that the communicator is being optimally relevant both drives and constrains the interpretive process. Although any utterance could be interpreted in multiple ways, the hearer or reader is only justified in understanding the utterance in accordance with the principle of relevance. In secondary language situations, such as reading the biblical text, which comes from another time and culture, the reader may rightly expect to invest greater processing effort to achieve the kind of cognitive effects the first readers and hearers would have obtained. On the other hand, the principle of relevance predicts that when contemporary readers intuitively interpret a biblical text by drawing upon salient information from their own cognitive environment, they may skew the meaning of the biblical author's utterance. Those from a materialist culture may interpret John 10:10 as a promise of economic prosperity **(3)**: "I came that they might have life, and have it more abundantly." "Abundant life," in this case, has been disambiguated within the contextual frame of material and economic gain. Therefore, RT not only describes what occurs in successful, but also in unsuccessful communication.

The wedding feast at Cana in Galilee illustrates the processes that RT attempts to define. Jesus and his disciples attended this celebration, and John 2:3 states that **(4)** "When the wine gave out, the mother of Jesus said to him, 'They have no wine.'" The following verse implies that Jesus understood her statement as a petition to do something about the situation, even though his mother did not encode her utterance as a request or petition. The meaning of her utterance, which includes not only what she said but also what she implied, is linguistically underdetermined (although not indeterminate). Jesus understood both her informative and communicative intent. He also combined her statement, "They have no wine," with existing contextual assumptions about the necessity of having sufficient wine for the whole feast, likely to avoid dishonor, and an implied premise that Jesus is able to remedy the situation. Mary's statement combines with these existing assumptions and produces cognitive effects, thus achieving relevance for Jesus. There is an "ah-ha" moment and Jesus responds, albeit enigmatically, to her statement which he recognizes as a petition for him to act. The contemporary reader, as the first readers/hearers of this narrative, needs to supply the necessary assumptions as well in order to understand Mary's utterance as a request. He must supply these from his understanding of Jewish customs surrounding wedding ceremonies, the nature of honor and shame, and the story about the nature of Jesus unfolding in John's narrative.

The gap between sentence meaning and utterance meaning is filled via a rich inferential process constrained by the principle of relevance. Jesus, as Mary's first hearer, does not explore the multiple things the sentence, "They have no wine," could mean but combines it with contextual information manifest to him and Mary in the search for relevance—the greatest cognitive effects for the least processing effort. At this point, the interpretive process stops, and Jesus responds. No amount of lexical or syntactical analysis would have been sufficient for Jesus or any reader of this text to understand the meaning of Mary's utterance. The meaning communicated in her utterance is a combination of the semantic structures and inferred contextual information. The interpreter must attend to relevant contextual information, whether it is drawn from discourse, the wider corpus of literature, or a vast array of historical and cultural assumptions. The search for relevance constrains this inferential process as the hearer or reader seeks to work out the speaker or writer's informative and communicative intent.

Explicatures and Implicatures. According to RT, the speaker or writer's encoded sentence meaning must be sufficiently enriched with contextual information to yield the meaning of the communicator's utterance. The information communicated may be classified as either *explicatures* or *implicatures.* Indeed, the sum of the implicatures and explicatures constitutes the total of the communicator's utterance. These are technical terms in RT, as is the word *relevance*, and should not be confused with explicit and implicit information.

The *explicatures* of an utterance consist of the information encoded in the sign system and all the information inferentially connected to it through reference assignment, disambiguation, and enrichment. In example (4), Jesus and the reader/hearer of the gospel need to undertake reference assignment in order to understand who "they" are in the statement, "They have no wine." This information is not directly derived from the discourse but, rather, an understanding of the wedding customs of the time. Does Mary's utterance mean that the bride and groom have no wine, or are "they" the family hosting the feast? The explicature in this case is the encoded lexeme "they" and the inferred information about who "they" are. Also, as noted earlier in example (1), the reader must disambiguate the lexemes "peace and security" and "destruction." Is Paul talking about personal or political "peace and security"? And is the "destruction" he refers to something which will occur in the present time, or does it have to do with eternal judgment? Similarly in sentence (4), John comments that "the wine gave out" (ὑστερήσαντος). The lexeme in Greek could mean "to miss out on something," "to be in need," "to be lower in status," "to experience deficiency in something," or, as here, "to be in short supply" (BADG, p. 1043–1044). Even if the reader recognizes that in this context it means that there is some deficiency in the supply, the question remains whether the wine had run out completely or was in short supply.

The recovery of contextual information is necessary to disambiguate ὑστερήσαντος. The reader or hearer may also have to enrich a sentence to bring it up to its full propositional form. In example (1), the interpreter must supply contextual information to understand what people will not escape from in the clause: "and there will be no escape!" In this case, the preceding clause supplies the information needed to enrich the proposition: "there will be no escape *from sudden destruction*!" While this information is not encoded in the clause, it is an implied part of the writer's utterance meaning, or an explicature. The explicatures are developments of the linguistically encoded information. We could say that explicit communication necessarily entails implicit information. Translators of the biblical text often struggle with the question of whether or not to supply this implied information (Gutt 2000).

However, the implicit information of a communicator's utterance may not be tied to the sign system at all. RT calls such information the *implicatures*, that is, everything communicated in an utterance that is not an explicature. In example (4), the proposition, "They have no wine," must be combined with the implicated premises about the shame of running out of wine at a wedding feast and Jesus's ability to do something about the situation. The implicated conclusion is Mary's appeal to Jesus, "Get some wine!" or perhaps, "Make some wine!" In common discourse, I may say to a colleague (5), "It's 3:30" and, at that point, we both arise from our chairs and go to the department meeting. The implicated premise is that on this day at 3:30, there is a department meeting. That information, combined with sentence (5), yields the implicated conclusion, "Let's go to the meeting" or "We should go to the meeting." This implicature was strongly communicated in the utterance but was not in any way encoded in the linguistic sign system. The gap between the sentence meaning and utterance meaning is filled by an inferential process constrained by the principle of relevance. When relevance is achieved in both (4) and (5), understanding dawns, and a response follows. These inferential processes occur in all communication at a speed and with an ease that allows them to go largely unnoticed in common discourse. The communication of meaning is a highly inferential process.

Relevance Theory and Contextual Studies. Relevance Theory shapes the way we understand the process of biblical interpretation. In the first place, RT affirms the necessity of interpreting texts within the framework of the cognitive environments of their authors and first readers/hearers. Context is built into the biblical text's discourse as an author expects his readers to supply certain contextual information from both his discourse and the encyclopedic information he knows his readers/hearers share with him. RT does not ascribe any hierarchical order to the various aspects of their cognitive environment. The relevant information from their cognitive environment, which constitutes the context, may come from the discourse itself, or it may be derived from Jewish history and culture, or it could come from Greek or Roman history and culture. There is no predisposition toward any particular cultural context over the other.

We must simply inquire as to which aspects of their cognitive environment would allow a particular utterance to achieve relevance. On the one hand, knowledge of Jewish Passover customs would be important in supplying necessary contextual assumptions when interpreting **(6)**: "While they were eating, Jesus took a loaf of bread, and after blessing it he broke it, gave it to the disciples, and said, 'Take, eat; this is my body'" (Matt 26:26). On the other hand, understanding Greek and Roman banqueting customs is essential if the interpreter is to supply the appropriate contextual information to understand Paul's utterance regarding the Corinthian practice of eating the Lord's supper **(7)**: "For when the times comes to eat, each of you goes ahead with your own supper, and one goes hungry and another becomes drunk" (1 Cor 11:21). Interpreters who focus exclusively on discourse, or the Jewish world, or the Greco-Roman world may not be able to supply the essential inferred information to interpret an author's utterance. Since what is communicated by an author consists of both explicatures and implicatures, lexical and grammatical studies are inadequate in themselves for understanding the message communicated. While most contemporary interpreters acknowledge the importance of such contextual information for interpretation, RT offers a robust model of communication which sets parameters for interpretation within common cognitive processes and explains why such contextual study is a central and not secondary part of the interpretive task.

Relevance Theory and Lexical Studies. Relevance Theory also suggests that when interpreting the lexemes within an utterance, primary attention needs to be on the concepts the code suggests. Current studies in RT have moved from discussing *lexical semantics* to *lexical pragmatics*. Wilson (2003, pp. 273–274) comments that "The goal of lexical semantics is to investigate the relations between words and the concepts they encode and the goal of lexical pragmatics is to account for the fact that the concept communicated by use of a word often differs from the concept encoded." According to RT, the encyclopedic entry of a concept will vary between discourses and is, therefore, an *ad hoc* construction. The concept may broaden, such as the statement **(8)**: "His face is square." The face will not be perfectly SQUARE but only approximately to the eye, so the broadened concept here is SQUARE*. Concept narrowing also occurs, as in utterance **(9)**: "All doctors drink." The concept DRINK has been narrowed to drinking of a particular kind, that being alcohol consumption. This yields the *ad hoc* concept DRINK*.

The encyclopedic entry of the concept LORD (ὁ κύριος) must be disambiguated in every utterance where it occurs. In Matt 20:8 and 24:50, the ὁκύριος is the "owner" of the vineyard or slaves, while in Mark 12:29 it is a divine title. But even more dynamic contextual forces are in play. The concept LORD attached to ὁκύριος in the confession **(10)**: "Jesus Christ is Lord" (Phil 2:11) combines with an intertextual echo of Isa 45:23, which implies Jesus Christ's divine authority, yielding the *ad hoc* concept LORD*. Moreover, LORD* stands as a counterpoint to imperial claims regarding Caesar's lordship, a salient piece of contextual information available to those living in the Roman colony of Philippi. But the confession (10) is also an affirmation that Christ's lordship is that of one who humbled himself through incarnation and death (Phil 2:6–11). The concept LORD has become the *ad hoc* concept LORD* by this unique combination of contextual information drawn from the discourse, the canon (Isa 45:23), and the cultural understanding about imperial claims known to Paul and his readers in Philippi. Interpreting lexemes entails more than disambiguating various translation glosses for ὁκύριος found in a lexicon. The process includes paying attention to the pragmatic forces at play in the construction of these *ad hoc* concepts. In utterance interpretation, the meaning of words is not simply accessed and disambiguated but rather modified and constructed in discourse. For this reason, RT suggests that the emphasis in lexical studies should not be upon encoded concepts but, rather, on pragmatically inferred concepts. Contextual information, that which supplies the necessary assumptions in the process of interpretation, combines with the lexical information in the formation of *ad hoc* concepts. Available information is explored and received or rejected on the basis of the cognitive principle of relevance.

Relevance Theory and Discourse. Relevance Theory also has implications for the way we understand how speakers and authors construct coherent discourses (Blass 1990; Unger 2006). The grammatical structures of a sentence are not always an indication of how a sentence coheres together. For example, in 1 Thessalonians 4:9–12, Paul exhorts the Thessalonian believers to love one another and concludes with the exhortation (11): "But we urge you, beloved, to do so more and more, to aspire to live quietly, to mind your own affairs, and to work with your own hands, as we directed you." The command to love "more and more" does not seem to cohere with the following directive to live a quiet life, to mind one's own affairs, and to labor with one's hands. Contextual information is needed to understand the coherence in Paul's command, which we assume is optimally relevant. If interpreted within the conceptual frame of ancient practices and customs surrounding patron/client relationships, both the call to love and the need for labor and a quiet life, unlike that of dependent clients, cohere together (Green, *The Letters to the Thessalonians* [Grand Rapids Mich., 2002], pp. 202–213). Understanding grammatical structures is only one step in the process of utterance interpretation (see, for example, Mary's petition stated as a declaration in [4]). The same holds true for our comprehension of discourse and genre.

Relevance Theory provides a thick description of the inferential processes inherent in all communication. Exploration of RT for biblical interpretation will help explain many practices current among biblical interpreters and provides a framework to guide the interpretive task.

[*See also* Cognitive Linguistics and Biblical Interpretation; Exegesis; Genre Criticism; Reader-Response Criticism; Rhetorical Criticism; Semiotics; Socio-rhetorical Criticism; Speech-Act Theory, Textual Criticism, *subentry* Hebrew Bible; *and* Textual Criticism, *subentry* New Testament.]

Note from the Author: In conformity with general practice in literature on Relevance Theory (RT), this article uses "she" for communicators and "he" for addressees in general examples with the exception of instances where the male biblical author is the communicator. RT literature also tends to number examples—(1), (2), and so on—for sake of ease in referring to them, and this article has followed that practice as well.

BIBLIOGRAPHY

Blakemore, Diane. *Understanding Utterances. An Introduction to Pragmatics.* Oxford: Blackwell, 1992. An accessible introduction to RT written as a college text.

Blass, Regina. *Relevance Relations in Discourse. A Study with Special Reference to Sissala.* Cambridge, UK: Cambridge University Press, 1990. Using RT, Blass presents a cogent argument for understanding the construction of discourse from a cognitive rather than a strictly linguistic point of view.

Carston, Robyn. *Thoughts and Utterances: The Pragmatics of Explicit Communication.* Oxford: Blackwell, 2002. Explores the pragmatics/semantics distinction, with emphasis on the pragmatic dimension of explicit communication. An essential introduction to *ad hoc* concept formation as well.

Green, Gene L. "Lexical Pragmatics and Biblical Interpretation." *Journal of the Evangelical Theological Society* 50 (2007): 799–812. This essay introduces a Relevance Theory approach to lexical studies.

Green, Gene L. "Lexical Pragmatics and the Lexicon." *Bulletin for Biblical Research* (Submitted, forthcoming, 2012). This essay explores how RT informs lexical design as well as the use of lexicons. It compares RT perspectives with current studies in cognitive psychology and lexicography.

Green, Gene L. "Relevance Theory and Biblical Interpretation." In *The Linguist as Pedagogue. Trends in the Teaching and Linguistic Analysis of the New Testament,* edited by Stanley E. Porter and Matthew Brook O'Donnell, 217–240. New Testament Monographs. Sheffield, UK: Sheffield Phoenix Press, 2009. A short introduction to RT in relation to biblical interpretation.

Green, Gene L "Relevance Theory and Theological Interpretation: Thoughts on Metarepresentation." *Journal of Theological Interpretation.* 4 (2010): 75–90. An application of RT to the subject of theological interpretation, with special attention to the human faculty of metarepresentation.

Gutt, Ernst-August. *Translation and Relevance. Cognition and Context.* 2d ed. Manchester and Boston: St. Jerome, 2000. The first robust discussion of RT in relation to Bible translation. Not all who embrace RT as a theory to guide the translation process agree with Gutt's conclusions.

Hill, Harriet S. *The Bible at Cultural Crossroads: From Translation to Communication.* Manchester and Boston: St. Jerome Publishing, 2006. An application of RT to biblical studies and translation theory, with special attention to the role of contextual information in interpretation.

Hill, Harriet, Ernst-August Gutt, Margaret Hill, Christoph Unger, and Rick Floyd. *Bible Translation Basics: Communicating Scripture in a Relevant Way.* Dallas, Tex.: SIL International, 2011. A textbook for Bible translators based on RT.

Pattemore, Stephen W. S. *The People of God in the Apocalypse: Discourse, Structure, and Exegesis.* SNTSMS 128. Cambridge, UK: Cambridge University Press, 2004. An application of RT to the study of the book of Revelation.

Sperber, Dan, and Deirdre Wilson. *Relevance. Communication and Cognition.* 2d ed. Oxford and Cambridge, MA: Blackwell, 1995. The foundational work on RT by those who developed the theory from Gricean pragmatics.

Sperber, Dan, and Deirdre Wilson. "Précis of Relevance: Communication and Cognition." *Behavioral and Brain Sciences* 10 (1987): 697–754. A brief introduction to RT by the founders of the theory. See Wilson and Sperber (2004).

Unger, Christoph. *Genre, Relevance and Global Coherence. The Pragmatics of Discourse Type.* Basingstoke, UK: Palgrave, 2006. Using RT, Unger explores how genre considerations shape our understanding of coherence in discourse. http://www.ua.es/personal/francisco.yus/rt.html (accessed December 24, 2011) A comprehensive and up-to-date bibliography of literature on RT.

Wilson, Deirdre. "Relevance and Lexical Pragmatics." *UCL Working Papers in Linguistics* 16 (2004): 343–360. Wilson presents a new perspective on word meaning in this introduction to lexical pragmatics which moves beyond traditional studies in lexical semantics.

Wilson, Deirdre, and Dan Sperber. "Relevance theory." In *Handbook of Pragmatics,* edited by Laurence R. Horn and Gregory L. Ward, 607–632 Oxford: Blackwell, 2004. One of the basic introductions to RT by the founders of the theory.

Wilson, Deirdre, and Tomoko Matsui. "Recent approaches to bridging: Truth, coherence, relevance." *UCL Working Papers in Linguistics* 10 (1998): 173–200. An introduction to coherence in discourse from the perspective of RT.

Yus, Francisco. *Relevance Theory Online Bibliographic Service.*

Gene L. Green

Rhetorical Criticism

Rhetoric is essentially the deployment of available means of persuasion on the part of an author or speaker wishing to exercise influence upon the response of one or more readers or hearers to their situation. Rhetorical criticism, then, invites the analysis of how an author or group of authors mobilize particular means of persuasion in a given situation to advance a particular agenda for the people involved in that situation. Whereas the historical critic is interested in discovering the potential impact of a text in the historical setting of its first utterance (as is often the case in the study of the more clearly "occasional" texts in the Bible, such as the prophetic or epistolary corpus), rhetorical criticism works closely in tandem with contemporary–historical interpretation, immersing the interpreter in the situation and challenges of the first audiences so as to discover the author's rhetorical presentation of their situation and its challenges, and to examine the text as the means by which the author positions the hearers to identify the challenges and respond to them in a particular way.

New Testament scholars benefit greatly from the availability of a wealth of Greek and Latin handbooks on rhetoric at the elementary and advanced levels, particularly Aristotle's *Art of Rhetoric*, the near-contemporary *Rhetorica ad Alexandrum* (once attributed to Aristotle), Cicero's rhetorical treatises (particularly *On Invention*, *On the Orator*, *Partitions of Oratory*, *Brutus*, *The Orator*, and *Topics*), the *Rhetorica ad Herennium* (from the first century B.C.E., once attributed to Cicero), Quintilian's *Institutio Oratoria*, and the elementary exercises in rhetoric (the *Progymnasmata*) of Theon of Alexandria and Hermogenes of Tarsus.

The handbook tradition began as a more descriptive enterprise, a systematization of rhetorical practices that were observed to be effective in actual oratory. Even where they take on a prescriptive turn, their origin as snapshots of practice continues to make them valuable compendia of the rhetorical strategies to which early Christian (and Hellenistic Jewish) authors and audiences potentially would have been exposed. These, in turn, would also reflect the strategies that such authors might have been expected to engage when composing addresses, oral or written, intended to persuade. The handbooks also provide a language for speaking about a text's strategy and potential effects that derives from the same cultural and historical setting as the New Testament, making them a more fully *emic* guide to thinking about early Christian rhetoric. An inductive study of extant speeches-in-writing from both the Greco-Roman and Hellenistic Jewish backgrounds remains a desideratum, as this would greatly enhance our knowledge of the distance between the handbooks and actual practice and supplement our existing framework for discerning and analyzing appeals to the mind, the emotions, and the trust of the audience in ancient oratory.

Scholars of the Hebrew Bible have had to proceed far more inductively, since no comparable reflections on Semitic rhetoric have survived, if they were ever written. Rhetorical criticism of the Hebrew Bible entails discovering the rhetorical conventions from these writings and comparative literature afresh. The Greco-Roman and more modern traditions of rhetoric have at least helped to formulate questions to ask of a text: For example, how does a particular text construct authority and convey credibility? Or, how does a particular text appeal to what emotions, and to what end?

Rhetorical Criticism of the Hebrew Bible. James Muilenburg is almost universally acknowledged by practitioners of the discipline to have initiated rhetorical analysis of the Hebrew Bible. A practitioner and proponent of form criticism, Muilenburg urged that, alongside form criticism, scholars attend to a level of analysis that accepts the text in its present form as an object for study and interpretation as a coherent, literary work. "Beyond" form criticism lay an approach that *also* values the text as a literary creation and artifact in itself, and not merely a field for excavation for earlier strata of material.

The tasks of this new "rhetorical criticism" would include "understanding the nature of Hebrew literary composition . . . exhibiting the structural patterns that are employed for the fashioning of a literary unit," and "discerning the many and various devices by which the predications are formulated and ordered into a unified whole" (Muilenburg 1969, p. 8). This agenda distinguished rhetorical criticism from both form and source criticism. Source critics read a text looking for indications of the existence and contours of earlier texts and traditions that have been incorporated into it. A principal goal is to discover what can be learned about the history and culture of the community at the stage of those earlier texts and traditions. Rhetorical criticism, by contrast, reads a text in its present state as an intentional composition reflecting the interests and challenges facing the community at the time of composition (Watson and Hauser 1994, p. 5; Trible 1994, p. 93). Rhetorical critics tend to begin with the presupposition that "the Biblical texts are composed and well composed" (Meynet 1998, p. 169). Thus, a different view is taken of such features as repetition, changes in poetic meter, and the like, first exploring these as signs of intentional composition serving a communicative purpose before regarding them as signs of faulty editing (hence, literary seams and signs of older sources) or flawed composition (Watson and Hauser 1994, pp. 6–7, 12; Meynet 1998, pp. 177–180).

Form critics also study a text for what it can yield about the prehistory of the traditions that constitute a text, as well as the social settings in which those particular traditions (and, especially, forms) took shape. Form criticism is also more interested in the typical—the literary pattern of a given form, the typical circumstances under which the form becomes useful—rather than the unique features of a particular utterance. Rhetorical criticism, again, analyzes a particular text in its final form and in all its distinctiveness, with its variations on or departures from the typical receiving special attention (Watson and Hauser 1994, p. 8; Trible 1994, p. 93).

Rhetorical analysis of the Hebrew Bible generally begins with identifying the beginnings and endings of rhetorical units, a process that involves identifying the literary devices (e.g., acrostics, *inclusio*, repetitions) that create cohesion within a particular unit and that point to the unit's boundaries (Muilenburg 1969, p. 9). Once the "boundaries" are provisionally established, the rhetorical critic proceeds to identify internal structures (that is, the constituent units of the larger block of text), rhetorical devices (parallelism, chiasm, alliteration, and the like), and indications of the "movement" within the text (Muilenburg 1969, p. 10). Internal structures and correspondences are frequently discovered and displayed only through the painstaking process of re-writing and schematically organizing all the words of the unit being examined (Trible 1994, pp. 92, 104–106; Meynet 1998, pp. 309–314). The work of two of Muilenburg's students, Lundbom (1997) on Jeremiah and Trible (1994) on Jonah, exemplify very well the procedures and payoff of this approach.

Sometimes the scholar's focus remains at the level of style and literary composition; often it presses beyond this to the question of how, and in what direction, the composition moves the audience. Some definitions of the discipline suggest that an analysis must properly include an account of the latter, namely the dynamics of persuasion, if the study is to be differentiated from (or within) literary criticism. Thus Alan Hauser (Watson and Hauser 1994, p. 4) promotes the discovery and analysis of "the particular literary artistry found in a specific unit of Old Testament text" not as an end in itself, but as "the basis for discussing the message of the text and the impact it had on its audience." (See the positions reviewed in Trible 1994, pp. 48–49). An excellent study in line with these definitions is Yehoshua Gitay (1981). Gitay used classical (Greco-Roman) rhetoric as a framework for the study of Isaiah 40—48, not on the supposition that the author of Deutero-Isaiah used or had access to classical conventions, but on the supposition that knowledge of the latter can help the scholar interrogate the text to discover its own strategies of persuasion, for example, in the uncovering of the text's rational, emotional, and ethical appeals (1981, pp. 36, 62). Michael Fox's study of enthymemes in Proverbs (2004, pp. 165–177) also focuses on the persuasive force of the text, here specifically on how the audience itself participates in being persuaded as it supplies the necessary premises that complete the logic of the discrete proverbs and their interconnection.

Rhetorical criticism of the Hebrew Bible has born much exegetical fruit. It has brought scholarly attention back to the text and the setting of its decisive composition or shaping, rather than allowing attention to remain on the pre-history of the text. This, in turn, has meant new insights into the compositional "logic" of the text in its current form, the structure of units of the text, and the import of the same for discerning the logical, narrative, or poetic coherence of the text. Rhetorical criticism has provided a new set of lenses for the determination of literary units within a text, whether at the micro-level or at larger levels of paragraphs or extended passages, as well as the relationships between these units (Meynet 1998, pp. 317–336). It has called for attention to the internal correspondences and oppositions within a text, at its various levels of organization, which is important not only for exegesis but also for translators, so that their work can preserve key signals of literary connection and demarcation (e.g., through creating comparably parallel expressions or being careful to retain particular lexical equivalents at critical junctures; Meynet 1998, pp. 337–340). The burgeoning of the disciplines of literary criticism and rhetorical criticism in the last decades of the twentieth century and beyond has greatly multiplied rhetorical approaches to the Hebrew Bible that continue to draw on modern, "secular" theory (Trible 1994, pp. 55–87).

Rhetorical Criticism of the New Testament. The study of the rhetoric of the New Testament is by no means a novel phenomenon. Scholars trained in rhetoric themselves have been attentive to the rhetorical dimensions of early Christian discourse. Augustine addresses the topic directly in the fourth book of his *On Christian Doctrine*. Philip Melanchthon analyzes the rhetoric of Romans and Galatians in the course of his commentaries on the same, as does Erasmus in his work on 1 and 2 Corinthians. (On the history of rhetorical criticism, see Watson 1988, pp. 1–8; Mack 1990, pp. 9–17). The decline of classical rhetoric in the modern curriculum brought about a corresponding decline in rhetorical criticism of the New Testament until the later decades of the twentieth century, when Hans Dieter Betz brought it to the fore in his work on Galatians (see especially Betz 1979) and George Kennedy promoted a methodology for rhetorical analysis (Kennedy 1984; see Mack 1990; and, in a welcome update on the method and its fruitfulness, Witherington 2009).

Although many practitioners also draw upon the insights of modern theorists of argumentation and rhetoric (e.g., Perelman and Olbrechts-Tyteca 1991), the rhetorical criticism of the New Testament draws most heavily upon the classical Greco-Roman handbooks on rhetoric as heuristic tools to assist in discovering appeals to ethos, emotion, and rational argumentation and to help explain the rhetorical force and construction of the appeal. (For basic surveys of Greco-Roman rhetoric, see Kennedy 1984, pp. 12–33; Watson 1988, pp. 8–28; Mack 1990, pp. 25–48; deSilva 2000, pp. 39–46; 2009, pp. 18–27.) The importance of allowing the rhetoric of early Christian texts freely to overflow the bounds of that stream—even to the point of flooding the plain—is also becoming increasingly apparent within this discipline. The rhetorical critic is tasked with describing the topics and strategies invoked by the text and with extending the rhetorical theory, as it were, to include what the critic finds in the text, rather than to proceed as if the text conforms in every respect to the tradition reflected in the Greco-Roman handbooks. The text can still be understood to promote the credibility of the author's voice, move the hearers to feel emotions strategic to the author's accomplishing of his or her goals, and communicate a logical argument, but it may do so in ways never envisioned or experienced by Aristotle, Cicero, or Quintilian (see, for example, deSilva 2009 on Revelation). Early Christian discourse intersects significantly with the topics and strategies of Greco-Roman rhetoric, but does not by any means overlap completely. It would be a mistake to deny the importance either of the impact of Greco-Roman argumentative forms and strategies on early Christian rhetoric or to neglect the distinctive style and argumentative strategies of any particular New Testament author, which could very much reflect the rhetorical strategies of the Hebrew Bible. Either/or thinking in this regard does not suit the complexity of the first century, nor the evidence of the texts themselves.

The practice of rhetorical criticism is not bound to assumptions about the formal training of the authors of New Testament texts in this discipline, though a strong case can be made for at least an elementary level of formal training in regard to some of these authors (e.g., the author of Hebrews). It does presume, to some extent, at least some inductive appropriation of the practice of effective oratory through observation and interaction with the same in their culture. The place of oratory in Hellenistic culture—and the penetration of Hellenistic culture into Judea—makes repeated exposure to such oratory, and thus the possibility of at least the intuitive imitation of its strategies, a possibility for every New Testament author.

Questions have been raised concerning the suitability of classical rhetorical theory to written compositions. Some scholars would prefer to see analysis of Paul's letters, for example, draw not upon ancient rhetorical handbooks, but rather upon the epistolary handbooks of late antiquity (for example, those of Pseudo-Demetrius and Pseudo-Libanius from the third century CE or later). These handbooks provide catalogs of letter "types," brief statements of the goals that might lead a writer to choose the style of one type over others, and brief models of letters of each type. These cursory handbooks were not meant to be comprehensive treatments of how to write persuasively. Rather, they appear merely to seek to add the necessary information for users to learn to adapt their previous training in logic and rhetoric to communicating in the medium of the letter.

The objection that one should draw upon ancient epistolary handbooks to the exclusion of classical rhetorical theory overlooks the oral character of many New Testament writings. Several "letters" are not letters at all. First John has no epistolary opening or closing, and thus gives every indication of being a written sermon. The "Letter" to the Hebrews likewise opens with a stirring paragraph designed to impact the ears of the hearers rather than their eyes (deSilva 2000, 37–38), and with none of the typical letter-opening formulas. It, too, would be heard as a sermon—a "word of exhortation," the genre label given by its own author (Heb 13:22)—from its first words through the penultimate paragraph, where we encounter signs of an epistolary closing (Heb 13:18–19, 22–25; Witherington 2009, p. 20).

Moreover, even the true letters have a public character, being addressed not to a private reader but sent to be read aloud to the gathered community (see Col 4:16; 1 Thess 5:24; Rev 1:3; possibly 2 Cor 1:13)—the "assembly" of believers, who needed to be persuaded to respond to some circumstance in one way as opposed to another, or to be reminded of the fundamental values of the community they have joined. They represent the speech or sermon that the author would have delivered, had it been possible for him to be present. The "elder," in fact, defers as much material as possible to his next face-to-face visit to the congregations, writing only what he deems essential for pressing exigencies in the letters (2 and 3 John). Once again, an either/or approach to the use of epistolary versus rhetorical theory does not suit the complexities of the evidence.

One practical application of the method would be to work through the following steps, first proposed by George Kennedy (see Kennedy 1984, pp. 33–38; an alternative adaptation can be found in deSilva 2009, pp. 26–27).

1. Determine the boundaries of the rhetorical unit for analysis. A complete book might represent a single overarching unit (as would be the case with Galatians or Philippians) or a combination of units (as is arguably the case with 1 Corinthians, which takes up a number of disparate topics seriatim), with the result that the investigator should not make assumptions of the span of a rhetorical unit apart from some analysis of the matter. Even if one is committed to the analysis of an entire book, at some point it will be necessary to look for indications of the contours of constituent sections that make up the rhetorical steps in the argument and the path to persuasion. These constituent units might be marked by a combination of transitional words, *inclusio*, use of distinctive key words, change of mode, and many other such markers.

2. Describe the rhetorical situation and the exigency that calls forth the response found in the rhetorical unit. A rhetorical focus calls for attention to be given to the interaction between author, text, and an audience facing a situation, so it is critical to get as clear a picture of that interaction as possible, including what provokes the composition of the text in question. In some cases, the answer will be quite straightforward (see 1 Cor 7:1a; Gal 1:6–9); in others, the answer can only be elicited from the text itself and other evidence concerning the historical situation with some difficulty and tenuousness (as is especially the case with narratives like the Gospels).

It is important even in these early stages to be attentive to how the author's agenda is at work in how he speaks of the hearers' situation, to what features of the hearers' situation (among *many* such features) the author calls their attention, and how he might "problematize" features of the hearers' situation that might not otherwise be problematic or significant to his audience and "normalize" other features that his hearers might find problematic.

3. Determine the rhetorical problem or the point at issue, and determine the rhetorical genre of the unit (whether it presses a deliberative, judicial, or epideictic agenda). What is the sticking point at which the whole discourse, or at least the rhetorical unit, is driving? In Galatians, the point at issue seems rather straightforwardly to be whether or not the gentile converts in Galatia will submit to circumcision as a religious rite. In Philemon, the point at issue concerns whether Philemon will release Onesimus from the status of slave and allow him to return as Paul's assistant. In Jude, the point at issue concerns whether the recipients will allow certain teachers to continue to exercise influence upon the congregation, particularly in regard to their moral example. In many rhetorical situations, there are also other agendas at work, which contribute, in turn, to the rhetorical problem. The presence and potential credibility of the rival teachers, for example, is a major component of the rhetorical problem that Paul must address—and anything they might have said to compromise Paul's credibility adds layer upon layer to that rhetorical problem.

Determining the rhetorical problem is closely related to determining the "rhetorical genre" of the text. Rhetorical genre is directly related to the kind of goal toward which a text presses. If the sticking point has to do with a decision that the audience needs to make in regard to future action, the genre is "deliberative," and the text can be expected to use the kinds of strategies common and appropriate to deliberative oratory. If the sticking point has to do with a call to the audience to render judgment in favor of one party and/or against another party in regard to the party's past action, the genre is "judicial" or "forensic," and the text can be expected to use, with some measure of adaptation, the strategies found in courts of law. If the sticking point has to do with the audience's adherence to particular group values or acceptance of the correctness of a proposition, then the text will probably best be read in light of *epideictic* or "demonstrative" oratory, such as the orations that adorned public ceremonies by praising the fallen, hymning the gods or the virtues, or promoting a thesis.

4. Analyze the invention, arrangement, and style. This is the most detailed step, and perhaps the most exegetically rewarding. "Invention" refers to the first step in constructing an oration, the step in which the orator gathers together the possible arguments at his or her disposal to address the various facets of the rhetorical situation. When studying a finished work, the rhetorical critic looks primarily for those appeals that the author finally selected for inclusion, rather than the larger range of possibilities.

Classical rhetorical theory teaches us to be alert for three different kinds of appeal. The first, and arguably most critical, is the appeal to *ethos*, the attempt to win the audience's trust by displaying expertise, virtue, and concern for the audience's best interests, and to render the audience attentive, well-disposed, and receptive. How does the author establish credibility and authority for his message and, if relevant, diminish the credibility of voices that present an alternative view of the situation and promote alternative responses? What resources and strategies (like labeling) does he employ, and how do these resources advance his authority over rival speakers' authority? The second kind of appeal, the appeal to *pathos*, seeks to engage the hearers' emotions. Aristotle's *Rhetoric*, book 2, is particularly helpful here as an *emic* resource listing topics and situations likely to arouse eleven specific emotions, and hence helping the modern interpreter discern where a text, by evoking these topics, was likely to arouse a particular emotion. The rhetorical critic is interested not only in cataloging what emotions an author tries to elicit, but how these appeals to emotion potentially draw the hearers closer to the author's persuasive goal. The appeal to *logos*, or rational argumentation, is the third major kind. What instances and patterns of rational argumentation, whether deductive or inductive, can be detected in the text? What argumentative topics and strategies are employed? What premises would the hearers have to share in order to find the argumentation "persuasive"?

The second major heading of classical rhetoric involved "arrangement," the strategic lining up of one's arguments and appeals in a sequence that would produce the optimal effects. The speeches given in the settings envisioned by the writers of the classical handbooks tended to be rather uniform in this regard. A judicial speech would begin with an introduction largely devoted to dispelling or creating prejudice, launch into a narrative that interpreted the facts of the case in either the worst or the best possible light for the defendant, announce a proposition in regard to the interpretation of the evidence (whether for guilt or innocence), line out the proofs in support of the proposition, then close with a rousing peroration rife with emotional appeals. The deliberative speech proposing one course of action over another was outlined similarly, save for not needing the narration.

It is probably in regard to analyzing the arrangement of New Testament texts that scholars have drawn the most criticism. While a few texts may indeed be fitted to the basic pattern of the deliberative or judicial oration (Galatians, in fact, comes rather close), many cannot—despite the attempts of committed scholars to force them into this mold. This is a particularly important area in which to allow the text to display its own arrangement, and to take special care in the heuristic use of classical handbooks.

The third element of rhetoric was attention to style, to creating appropriate verbal ornamentation, thinking about use of figures of speech and thought, and attending to the proper emotional level or tone of the parts of the speech. As style was pursued not for its own sake, but as a tool enhancing persuasive impact, rhetorical critics ideally analyze it in terms of its contribution to persuasion and not in and of itself.

Classical rhetorical handbooks also covered two additional areas—"memory," as the speech would be communicated without manuscript or notes, and "delivery," reflecting on the effective use of voice, gesture, and the like. These areas are not as readily applicable to the analysis of an ancient text. While the smaller units of the Gospel tradition certainly enjoyed oral performance on the basis of memory, and the same might be true of the Gospels as wholes, this was not the case at least for the epistolary literature of the early church. Indeed, the only testimonies in regard to the oral performance of the latter indicate that memory was not involved, as the texts were to be "read out loud" to the church from the manuscript (see Col 4:16; 1 Thess 5:24; Rev 1:3; possibly 2 Cor 1:13). Similarly, Paul may make scattered comments about his delivery as opposed to that of his smoother rivals, but we have no access to the actual performance of any of his letters, however he might have coached his messengers in this regard.

5. Evaluate the rhetorical effectiveness of the rhetorical unit in its engagement of invention, arrangement, and style in meeting the rhetorical problem or exigency. At this step, the "analyst" truly becomes a "critic." Is the rhetoric of the text up to the challenge of persuading the audience in this situation? Generally, this step must content itself with answering questions like, "what would the audience have to believe to be true in order to accept and be persuaded by the rhetoric of this passage?" "Did the author adequately take into account and undermine opposing arguments and complications in the rhetorical situation?"

An Extended Example: Hebrews *5:11 6:12*. The so-called "Letter" to the Hebrews provides an excellent field for the practice of rhetorical criticism. The work opens not as a letter but as an oration, with a well-crafted sentence designed to capture the attention of auditors. The author's attention to rhetorical practice extends beyond invention to the principles of style and ornamentation.

1. Determine the boundaries of the rhetorical unit for analysis. This section explicitly interrupts the development of the topic of Jesus as the one "appointed by God to be a high priest after the order of Melchizedek" (5:10) to address the audience. The author brings this digression carefully back to the same place that he left his audience at 5:10, repeating the same language in 6:20 ("having become a high priest for ever after the order of Melchizedek"), so that he can resume the discourse in 7:1—10:18. An *inclusio* formed by the words "you have become sluggish" (5:11) and "in order that you not become sluggish" (6:12) also marks this segment as a rhetorical unit, highlighting the role of 6:13–20 as a transition back to the topic at hand.

2. Describe the rhetorical situation and the exigency that calls forth the response found in the rhetorical unit. The author responds to what he perceives to be a crisis of commitment on the part of some members, at least, of the congregation, in the face of society's ongoing disapproval and marginalization of members of the Christian group (10:32–34) and the failure of God's promised homeland to materialize (4:1–11; 10:13–16; 13:13–14). A number of converts have already withdrawn from open association with the group, perhaps in an attempt to rehabilitate their reputation in their neighbors' eyes and regain their place of belonging in their physical homeland (10:24–25). This impression is reinforced throughout the sermon wherever the author speaks of the danger facing the audience (2:1–4; 4:1, 11b; 6:6; 10:26–31, 39a; 12:15–17) or of the posture that he recommends adopting (3:6b, 13–14; 4:11a, 14, 16; 6:1, 12; 10:19–25, 35–36, 39b; 12:1–3, 12–13, 28; 13:12–14).

3. Determine the rhetorical problem or the point at issue, and determine the rhetorical genre of the unit (whether it presses a deliberative, judicial, or epideictic agenda). The audience faces a choice between continuing openly in their association with one another, and the name of Christ, and muting this commitment out of regard for their neighbors' disapproval. The situation calls for deliberation and a decision about how to proceed in the future. Hebrews represents primarily deliberative oratory, giving advice about which course to pursue. The author employs topics typical of deliberative rhetoric, promoting his preferred course of action as just (12:28), expedient (10:35–36; 13:12–14), feasible (4:14–16), and the alternative course as unjust (6:4–6; 10:29), inexpedient (2:1–2; 4:1; 6:8), and the like. Epideictic passages like 11:1–40 ultimately serve the larger deliberative goals (e.g., by demonstrating the nobility of manifesting "faith" by persevering as opposed to "shrinking back").

4. Analyze the invention, arrangement, and style. Hebrews 5:11–6:12 issues a second call for an attentive hearing, a facet of attending to ethos and appropriately presented in the middle of a speech (*Rhet. Her.* 3.14.9). The author dares to challenge and even reproach the hearers in 5:11–14, which could either enhance his credibility (he cares enough to speak to them frankly, showing his honesty and investment in them) or risk alienating the hearers. He guards against the latter by balancing reproach with assurance and expressions of confidence in the hearers in 6:9–12, using the technique of palliation following frank speech (*Rhet. Her.* 1.4.9).

The author engages the hearers' emotions throughout this unit, first appealing to feelings of shame (see Aristotle, *Rh.* 2.6) by suggesting that the hearers have failed to measure up to what might reasonably have been expected of them after so long a time in the Christian faith (5:11–14). He goads them to prove themselves "mature" by being more proactive in their profession of faith and reinforcement of one another's commitment. This strategically moves their focus away from the expectations of their non-Christian neighbors, who have used shaming to motivate the converts to be less actively and openly "Christian."

The author promotes aversion from the contrary course of action by arousing fear in connection thereto. Having developed the Son's honor and authority (Heb 1:1–14; 2:5–9), the author can now warn against affronting this Son (6:6) as a dangerous course of action, marking out the perpetrator as an object for divine vengeance ("fire," 6:8). Responding with ingratitude to God's favor shown the hearers in Christ would also justifiably arouse the benefactor's anger. The author thus portrays a scenario involving an "imminent evil that causes destruction or pain" (Aristotle, *Rh.* 2.5.1), an essential ingredient for stimulating fear. The impossibility of help (Aristotle, *Rh.* 2.5.12), here expressed as the impossibility of restoration (6:4), also enhances fear through the removal of its opposite, confidence.

The appeal to fear is balanced by an appeal to confidence, an emotion potentially aroused by the author's invocation of the topic of it being well between the hearers and God, with the latter favorably disposed to help them, and the topic of the expectation that theirs will be a favorable outcome (6:9–12; see Aristotle, *Rh.* 2.6). This, in turn, palliates the hearers and orients them yet once more toward the course of action to which they are being exhorted.

Appeals to rational argumentation are evident throughout this unit. The author invites the hearers to commit to a (general) course of action, "pressing on to completion," as the logical consequence ("Therefore," 6:1) of their failure to realize their full, expected potential to this point (5:11–14). He supports this with a rationale ("for," 6:4) framed as an argument concerning the consequences of the contrary course of action, namely "falling away" through re-assimilation into the larger society (Heb 6:4–6). A stylistic feature—the repetitive use of participial phrases in 6:4–5—creates an impression of having enjoyed a wide variety and rich supply of benefits, hence God's generosity toward them. This move amplifies the disgrace and injustice of shirking the obligations of the patron-client bond that generosity has created.

The author confirms this rationale with another rationale ("for," 6:7), an argument from analogy (6:7–8), drawn from familiar agricultural scenarios. The social knowledge of patronage and reciprocity shared by author and audience contributes to the latter's acceptance of the "impossibility" of restoring those who have made a noxious return for favors shown. Indeed, agricultural imagery was well suited to illustrating reciprocity scripts (see Seneca, *De beneficiis* 1.1.2; 2.11.4–5; 4.8.2; *Pseudo-Phocylides* 152; Isa 5:1–7). Ultimately, any course of action that alienated the divine benefactor must therefore be judged inexpedient (6:8), while the just course, namely that of continuing as a loyal, trusting client of God (6:1) and making a fair return for God's benefits (6:7, 9–10), results in the preservation of goods already enjoyed and the acquisition of greater goods in God's future (6:11–12). (For a detailed analysis, see deSilva 2000, pp. 209–248.)

5. Evaluate the rhetorical effectiveness of the rhetorical unit. The author shows considerable care in regard to maintaining *ethos* throughout this passage. He arouses emotions that strategically position his hearers to move in the direction of responding as he wishes. The logical development of the passage is clearly marked and strongly argued—and anchored in foundational social logic (e.g., reciprocity). To the extent that the audience reasons within the parameters of the Christian worldview (including the topics suggestively named by the author in 6:1–2, namely "resurrection of the dead" and "eternal judgment"), the author's rhetoric should be highly persuasive, since the hearers must consider advantage and disadvantage in terms of the circumstances they may find themselves in after death and for eternity.

Conclusion. Rhetorical criticism invites precise attention to the text in its essentially final form as a thoughtfully crafted composition. In particular, it invites attention to the text as a vehicle for exerting influence upon hearers or readers and upon their orientation and responses to their situation. Classical rhetorical theory provides a helpful heuristic framework especially for analyzing the persuasive impact of Jewish and Christian texts from the Hellenistic and Roman periods, though this framework may yet be helpfully expanded on the basis of close study of surviving specimens of Hellenistic and Roman speeches. The discipline would also be advanced by conducting an Aristotelian examination and classification of the rhetorical settings and strategies employed across Hellenistic Jewish and early Christian discourses in order to help bridge the gaps between the purposes and topics of classical oratory and the writings of the Bible.

[*See also* Form Criticism, *subentry* Hebrew Bible; Form Criticism, *subentry* Apocrypha and Deuterocanonical Books; Form Criticism, *subentry* New Testament; Genre Criticism; Literary Criticism, Literary Theory, and the Bible; Orality Studies and Oral Tradition, *subentry* Hebrew Bible; Orality Studies and Oral Tradition, *subentry* New Testament; Performance Criticism; Socio-rhetorical Criticism; Source Criticism; Speech-Act Theory; *and* Synchronic Interpretation.]

BIBLIOGRAPHY

Aune, David E. *The Westminster Dictionary of New Testament and Early Christian Literature and Rhetoric.* Louisville, Ky.: Westminster John Knox Press, 2003. A comprehensive reference work on the terminology, theory, and history of application of literary and rhetorical approaches to the New Testament. The vast majority of the entries were written by Aune himself, bringing a unity of perspective to the volume.

Betz, Hans Dieter. *Galatians.* Hermeneia. Philadelphia: Fortress Press, 1979. The first major critical commentary foregrounding classical rhetoric as an exegetical tool. Betz gives a great deal of attention to the arrangement of Galatians after the structural pattern of a judicial oration, as well as to the discovery and analysis of Paul's appeals to ethos, pathos, and logos.

deSilva, David A. *Perseverance in Gratitude: A Socio-rhetorical Commentary on the Epistle "to the Hebrews."* Grand Rapids, Mich.: William B. Eerdmans, 2000. A commentary oriented primarily around a rhetorical-critical approach to the Letter to the Hebrews, embedding the study of intertexture and socio-cultural scripts and topics into this framework.

deSilva, David A. *Seeing Things John's Way: Rhetoric and the Book of Revelation.* Louisville, Ky.: Westminster John Knox Press, 2009. An investigation of the persuasive strategies and effects of Revelation using questions generated from the standpoint of classical rhetorical theory, but answering these in terms of Revelation's very distinctive topics and strategies.

Jewett, Robert. *Romans: A Commentary.* Hermeneia. Minneapolis: Fortress Press, 2006. A critical commentary framed throughout with a view to rhetorical analysis of Romans. An appropriate counterpart to Betz, 1979, showing the maturation of the discipline.

Kennedy, George A. *New Testament Interpretation Through Rhetorical Criticism.* Chapel Hill, N. C.: University of North Carolina, 1984. The first, and still quite valuable, introduction to rhetorical criticism as a methodology.

Lundbom, Jack R. *Jeremiah: A Study in Ancient Hebrew Rhetoric.* 2d ed. Winona Lake, Ind.: Eisenbrauns, 1997. An excellent example of rhetorical criticism of the Hebrew Bible in terms of its interest in literary structure and composition.

Mack, Burton L. *Rhetoric and the New Testament.* Minneapolis, Minn.: Fortress, 1990. A helpful introduction to the history and method of rhetorical criticism, though some of the examples are rather flawed.

Mack, Burton L., and Vernon K. Robbins. *Patterns of Persuasion in the Gospels.* Sonoma, Calif.: Polebridge Press, 1989. An innovative approach to the Jesus traditions as examples of *chreiai* (brief narratives of a saying or action of a famous person, normally with an indication of the setting that called it forth or that it impacted) and passages from the Gospels as elaborations of *chreiai* (an exercise well-attested in the elementary exercises in rhetoric), contributing to understanding variations between traditions (restatement and paraphrase being basic exercises) and the logic behind the arrangement of sayings.

Meynet, Roland. *Rhetorical Analysis: An Introduction to Biblical Rhetoric.* JSOTS 256. Sheffield, UK: Sheffield Academic Press, 1998. A detailed and excellent introduction to rhetorical criticism as pursued mainly by scholars of the Hebrew Bible. This work is less useful for the study of New Testament and Hellenistic Jewish texts because of the author's dismissal of the relevance of classical rhetoric for any biblical text.

Mitchell, Margaret M. *Paul and the Rhetoric of Reconciliation: An Exegetical Investigation of the Language and Composition of 1 Corinthians.* Louisville, Ky.: Westminster John Knox Press, 1993. An important example of the application of classical rhetorical theory to the interpretation of 1 Corinthians as deliberative rhetoric aimed at overcoming factionalism within the Corinthian churches.

Muilenburg, James. "Form Criticism and Beyond." *JBL* 88 (1969): 1–18. The programmatic essay that helped push scholars of the Hebrew Bible toward analyzing the extant form of a text as a purposeful composition, and not as a field for excavating older traditions for their witness to the history and religion of ancient Israel.

Olbricht, Thomas H., and Jerry L. Sumney, eds. *Paul and Pathos*. SBL Symposium Series 16; Atlanta: SBL, 2001. A helpful collection of essays modeling judicious analysis of appeals to the emotions of the hearers, one of the more slippery facets of rhetorical criticism.

Perelman, Chaim, and Lucie Olbrechts-Tyteca. *The New Rhetoric: A Treatise on Argumentation*. Notre Dame, Ind.: University of Notre Dame Press, 1991. An important example of a modern theory of rhetoric to which biblical scholars often look for guidance in their investigation of the ancient texts.

Porter, Stanley E. *Handbook of Classical Rhetoric in the Hellenistic Period 330 B.C.—A.D. 400*. Leiden, Netherlands: Brill, 2001. An excellent resource on the practice of rhetoric in the Hellenistic and Roman periods, with attention to the contributions of individual theorists and the development of rhetorical theory.

Trible, Phyllis. *Rhetorical Criticism: Context, Method, and the Book of Jonah*. Minneapolis, Minn.: Fortress Press, 1994. The first portion of this book locates rhetorical criticism against the background of the many literary (and related) criticisms and approaches found in biblical scholarship and traces the history of its development. The second portion proposes a method for rhetorical criticism and displays the fruits of this method through a detailed analysis of the book of Jonah.

Watson, Duane F. *Invention, Arrangement, and Style: Rhetorical Criticism of Jude and 2 Peter*. SBLDS 104. Atlanta: Scholars Press, 1988. A thorough (and groundbreaking) analysis of Jude and 2 Peter consistently using the canons of rhetoric found in the classical handbooks. The dissertation is also valuable for the rich introduction it provides to Greco-Roman rhetorical theory.

Watson, Duane F. *The Rhetoric of the New Testament: A Bibliographic Survey*. Blandford Forum, UK: Deo Publishing, 2006. An updated edition of the New Testament portion of Watson and Hauser, 1994.

Watson, Duane F., and Alan J. Hauser. *Rhetorical Criticism of the Bible: A Comprehensive Bibliography with Notes on History and Method*. Leiden, Netherlands: Brill, 1994. An extensive bibliographic resource, listing articles and books written from a rhetorical-critical approach, either by the compilers' definition or the self-definition of a study given by the author. Each half is preceded most helpfully by an introduction to the history and approach of rhetorical criticism of the Hebrew Bible (Hauser) and the New Testament (Watson).

Witherington, Ben, III. *Grace in Galatia: A Commentary on Paul's Letter to the Galatians*. Grand Rapids, Mich.: William B. Eerdmans, 1998. Witherington foregrounds rhetorical analysis in all of his commentaries, but his treatment of rhetoric in Galatians is perhaps his most detailed and satisfying. This volume is also an important corrective to Betz's analysis of Galatians as forensic rather than deliberative rhetoric.

Witherington, Ben, III. *New Testament Rhetoric: An Introductory Guide to the Art of Persuasion in and of the New Testament*. Eugene, Ore.: Cascade Books, 2009. A survey of the rhetoric of Mark, Luke, the sermon summaries in Acts, and the epistolary literature of the New Testament by the most prolific author of studies conducted in a classical rhetorical mode.

David A. deSilva

S

Semiotics

Semiotics is a theory of meaning or a method for the analysis of signifying phenomena—that is, objects that are taken to be signs. A "sign" may include anything that someone finds significant, though most semiotic study is particularly focused on human language and other artifacts of human culture. However, semiotics is not to be confused with a method of interpretation; semiotics does not explain *what* the signs in question mean, but rather *how* they mean, or what mechanisms are involved in the production of meaning. As a result, there can be no such thing as a (pure, simple) "semiotic interpretation" of any text, including biblical texts.

Nevertheless, semiotic theory and analysis plays a crucial role in both structuralism and poststructuralism (which are sometimes called "structural semiotics" and "poststructural semiotics," respectively), and both of these theories do offer methods for the interpretation of texts, including biblical texts. Semiotics is also an important factor in other approaches to biblical texts, including narratology, reader-response criticism, and rhetorical criticism, and it is often (but not always) drawn upon in Marxist, feminist, queer, postcolonial, and other ways of reading the Bible. In principle there is no reason why semiotics could not be a significant component of "historical critical" approaches to the Bible as well, but that is not usually the case.

It is often said that the critical discipline of semiotics began in the nineteenth century with the independently developed theories of Ferdinand de Saussure (1857–1913), a Swiss linguist, and Charles Sanders Peirce (1839–1914), an American philosopher. In advance of presenting their theories, however, we briefly review earlier discussions concerning the use and function of signs in Western philosophy and Christian thought.

Ancient and Medieval Semiotics: Symptoms and Signs. The ancient Greek term *σημειον*—conveying a sense that something is known by means of a "mark," "trace," "track," "sign," "signal," "landmark," "boundary," "birthmark," or "limit"—is the etymological legacy of the modern term semiotics. The classical definition of sign, as summed up in Latin, is *aliquid stat pro aliquot*, or in other words, something stands for something (that is, for something else). What it meant for a sign to stand for another remained ambiguous or contested in early Greek thought. Ancient peoples generally took a "realist" view of language, for which there could only be one language (their own, of course, such as Greek or Hebrew) with an assessed direct connection to reality. Other languages appeared to be gibberish, like the sounds that animals make, and their speakers were therefore condemned (like animals) to ignorance.

Umberto Eco notes that *sēmeion* (sign) was a technical-philosophical term often employed by Parmenides and Hippocrates as early as the fifth century B.C.E. as a synonym of another term, *tekmērion,* which was itself taken to mean proof, clue, or symptom (1984, p. 26). In contrast, Aristotle tended to distinguish between *sēmeion* and *tekmērion. Sēmeion* indicated a sign in an argument that led to a probable conclusion—that is, an *inductive* argument, which cannot be judged either "valid" or "invalid," but can be judged "strong" or "weak." In ancient Greek medical contexts *sēmeion* named a "symptom" or "manifestation" from which one might infer the unseen goings on in the human body. On the other hand, *tekmērion* signaled an argument with a proof that supported a conclusion arrived at with certainty, or a valid *deductive* argument. Aristotle's discussion of signs appears in his treatise on inference, *Prior Analytics* (2012, 2.27.70a-b), where it provides a basis for differentiating between valid and invalid deductions—that is, correct and incorrect ways in which something may stand for or with something else.

These two terms for sign were further played upon by Stoic and Epicurean philosophers who conceived of a "sign" serving as an observable basis of inference to the unobserved or unobservable. According to Epicurus, "even the names of things were not originally due to convention, but in the several tribes under the impulse of special feelings and special presentations of sense, primitive man uttered special cries. The air thus emitted was molded by their individual feelings or sense-presentations and differently according to the difference of the regions which the tribes inhabited" (2009).

Eco argues that, with Plato and Aristotle, words are analyzed from a double point of view, which includes the differences between signifier and signified, and those between signification and reference. Signification or meaning says *what* a thing is and the function is performed by single terms, whereas in the act of reference one says *that* a thing is and this sense of reference is performed only by complete sentences. In other words, a single term rarely serves as an act of reference, and only reference involves what is now called "truth value." However, debate continues regarding the significance of Aristotle's solitary comment in *On Interpretation* where he called the word a "sign" (*sēmeion*) of the mental concept, which is not in keeping with his reluctance to use a single term as a reference in his works on logic and language. Nevertheless, the comment regarding the conjoining of word and sign in reference to some reality (that is, mental concept) was later valued in the development of the philosophy of signs in medieval thought, including Christian theology and the interpretation of scripture, and it persists in modern thought.

Influenced by Aristotle, Augustine maintained that "a sign is something that shows itself to the senses and something other than itself to the mind." Augustine assumed that the intrinsic relation of sensual sign and mental concept is shared by all humanity, and this provided a means for Augustine to frame Christian signs and by extension Christian convictions as "natural" (in a philosophical sense, following Aristotle). In other words, the "mental concepts" to which the signs referred were taken by Augustine to be metaphysically real and universally viable for all humanity. A true religion could not be restricted to a single people, language, or nation, and apart from this metaphysical and universal viability, the alternative within the limits of Augustine's philosophically-influenced theology would have been that Christian signs, symbols, and convictions could only be little more than "un-natural" provincial conventions (such as the gibberish of barbarians, or the "special cries" of Epicurus). For Augustine, what was at stake was whether Christian symbols and convictions were universally real (in terms of Aristotelian natural philosophy) and therefore true, or else limited by culture, society, and history.

Thus a sign might be a manifest indicator for inferring something latent, a trace or visible imprint of a previous contact, or "a peripheral manifestation of something which does not appear in its entirety" (Eco 1984, p. 15). Such concepts presuppose the service of signs in the making of inferences regarding some reality. For Christian realists, the signs and symbols of the faith were the visible imprints of contact with the hidden reality of the supernatural, ranging from the presence of the devil or the anti-Christ in the world, to foretelling the coming of the end of the world and the return of Christ. It is safe to say that as regards the interpretation of Christian scriptures, the texts were assumed to be, in whole or in part, the visible signs of reality for medieval Christendom, a reality that came to incorporate the natural and the supernatural in what appears to have been a dense Christian world of semiotic commerce.

Ferdinand de Saussure. The term "semiotic" was introduced into modern philosophical use by John Locke in the third book of his *Essay Concerning Human Understanding* (1690), in which he explored the science of signs and signification with respect to epistemological query. Locke's empiricist views differed significantly from the medieval "metaphysical realists" who drew upon Augustine and Aristotle in their discussions of the theory of signs, and who employed logic and grammar in the service of theological positions without consideration for the problem of empirical verifiability.

Ferdinand de Saussure preferred instead the term "semiology" (1959, p. 16). For him, the sign consists of two "primordial characteristics" (p. 67), which he called the *signified* and the *signifier*, and which he defined as "a concept and a sound-image" (p. 66). The signified, or conceptual content of the sign, is its meaning. The signifier is merely the physical medium through which a signified message is transmitted from a sender to a receiver. However, the signified and the signifier, as Saussure described them, should not be thought of as two separate things, but rather as two sides of one coin. They are partners in a single, complementary, but asymmetrical and intransitive system, like parent and child. Neither of them can exist as such without the other one, even though the signified is generally regarded as more important.

This understanding of the sign as composed of a signifier and a signified suggests the image of a channel, such as a pipe or wire through which something like water or electricity flows or passes, and this becomes a crucial concept in structural semiotics, or structuralism. At either end of the message channel stand, respectively, the sender and the receiver of the message. The sender and the receiver together make the message flow both possible and necessary. The message is fundamentally "dialogical" or "contractual"—the channel must have two ends, and transmission of the message requires two parties, each of which consists of one or more beings. Again, the signified meaning is privileged: the message that does not get through is not a message. The message transfers something from the sender to the receiver. Provided there is no interference (static or noise) on the channel—no break in the pipe or wire, no internal barricade or external force to distort or break the flow of meaning—the message gets through clearly. Misunderstanding or distortion of the language arises solely through such interference from "outside" of the dyadic system of signifier-signified.

This binary model is complicated by the fact that a signified can also serve as a signifier, and it is at this point that semiotic analysis gives way to interpretation. In connotative language, a second "level" of language is established (Barthes 1967, pp. 89–94). For example, on the denotative level of meaning, the statement "The Lord is my shepherd" suggests that I am a sheep who is herded by someone named "the Lord." Taken as a metaphor (as Psalm 23:1 usually is), this signified becomes the "vehicle" for a second, connoted meaning (the "tenor"), which may suggest something quite different, such as "God will always take care of me." Conversely, in metalanguage, words are used to describe other words, and the signifier itself is composed of another system of signifiers and signifieds. For example, "in the Bible, the words 'the Lord' describe God," explains one signifying system in terms of another, and a theological language replaces a biblical one. Nevertheless, even in these complications, the basic model of signifier and signified remains intact, and semiosis (the flow of meaning) is under control.

Charles S. Peirce. The term "semiotic" came to be once again more widely used as a result of the work of the mathematician and philosopher C. S. Peirce and later the linguist Charles Morris. Peirce is often regarded as the first American philosopher and is credited with setting in motion the intellectual legacy of American pragmatism, including influencing the development of the process school of thought commonly identified with its founder Alfred North Whitehead. Peirce distinguished three areas of semiotics: (1) pragmatics, the study of the way signs are used, (2) semantics, the study of the relations between signs and their meanings, and (3) syntax, the study of the relations among signs abstracted from their use and meaning.

Peirce conceived of the sign as a vehicle, and this may seem not unlike the Saussurean image of the channel, but in contrast to Saussure's binarism of signifier-signified, much of Peirce's thought is characterized by triadic patterns. This distinction makes a great deal of difference in the respective analyses of language. For Peirce, there are three general categories of signification for signs: qualisigns (qualities), sinsigns (existential facts, objects), and legisigns (conventions, habits, or laws). In other words, sign-vehicles signify by virtue of qualities, existential (physical) facts, or conventions (habit, or laws).

If successful signification of an object is restricted to representation of qualitative features of the object, the sign is an "icon." A simple example of an icon would be a photograph, which resembles the photographed person or event. Only a few words in any language are iconic: words such as "crunch" or "splash," which when spoken sound like the designated object. No written words in an alphabetic script are iconic, although hieroglyphs or ideograms may have iconic aspects. If the sign utilizes only some existential or physical connection between itself and its object, then the sign is an "index." An example of an index would be a cloud of smoke or the smell of smoke, which implies that something nearby is burning. Again, only a few words are indexes: words such as "I" or "that," which "point to" some specific object in the immediate context (spoken or written): for example, "the book that I want is that one." In language, indexes are far more important than icons are. Nevertheless, it would be impossible to have a complete human language that contained only icon- and index-words. Continued successful signification of the object requires signs that utilize some convention, habit, or social rule. This sort of sign is what Peirce called a "symbol," a successful signification that utilizes conventions, habits, or laws to connect sign and object. Nearly all the words in any human language are such symbols, which are entirely artificial and must be learned. There is no inherent relation, whether of quality or of existential connection, between the symbol and its meaning(s).

For Peirce, the process of signification is limited within this set of constraints between the sign and the object. Peirce describes this signifying process as composed (once again) of three interrelated parts: a representamen (which Peirce also, confusingly, called a "sign"), an object, and an interpretant. The relation between representamen and object is not a simple binary one, and without the third part, the interpretant, there can be no signification. The interpretant focuses understanding upon certain features of the signifying relation of representamen and object, and thus the interpretant in effect connects the representamen to the object, identifying some element of the sign (representamen) that serves as a vehicle for some but not all of the features of the object. Likewise, the object determines the sign in that it is necessary in order for successful signification to occur.

The interpretant is especially crucial in the case of the symbol because the interpretant is the learned part of the relation. Indeed, the interpretant may be minimal or even nonexistent in some icons or indexes, which is why photographs and smoke clouds do not usually present difficulties in understanding. However, there are no symbols without interpretants, and since the symbol is by far the most common linguistic sign, this means that the interpretant is particularly important in semiotic analysis. The interpretant is also the point at which differences of understanding appear, for different interpretants make it possible for different objects to be connected to the same representamen.

In this way Peirce's understanding of semiotics includes (and perhaps even requires) the possibility of differences or failures of understanding in the structure of the sign itself.

Peirce proposed early in his work that sign-chains are not finite, suggesting in strong contrast to Saussure that any sign-chain has no beginning and attains no final termination or end. In order to describe an interpretant, one must use words, that is, one or more signs. Just as every sign requires an interpretant, so the interpretants themselves may be signified by signs requiring further interpretants. Thus every sign depends upon other signs for its meaning (here is the beginning of the Poststructuralist concept of "intertextuality"). Furthermore, a representamen may also be the interpretant of yet another sign, and the designated object may itself serve as an interpretant for yet another object, or it may be the representamen of another symbol. Once again, this is connotation and metalanguage, but in this Peircean analysis the semiotic process has always already generated signs and will continue to do so *ad infinitum.*

However, in his later work, Peirce came to consider the connection between sign-chains and the process of inquiry, and accordingly he sought to account for the centrality of sign-chains in ends-directed scientific inquiry. He concluded that chains of signs might tend toward a definite idealized end in a process of inquiry where complete knowledge of an object could be obtained. Nevertheless, there are many sign-chain processes to which this concept of a limited set of sign-chains does not apply, and for many poststructural semioticians, the concept of "unlimited semiosis" is far more typical of language, especially the language of poetry, narrative, and literature in general, including the Bible.

Process Thought and Biblical Studies. The later works of Alfred North Whitehead in philosophy of science and religion, semiotics, metaphysics, and cosmology and their influence in the development of process/relational philosophy and theology are legendary. Peirce's influence mediated through Whitehead has come to be evident in process biblical interpretation in the late twentieth and early twenty-first centuries. However, process biblical interpretation is less dependent upon Whitehead's semiotics (evident in *Symbolism* and *Modes of Thought,* or his semiotically rich contributions to metaphysics) and more as a development from his cosmology (*Process and Reality*) and thematic works on religion. The influence of process thought in biblical interpretation led to the founding of a process biblical commentary series (Chalice Commentaries for Today) and the establishment of a biblical studies section in the International Whitehead Conferences.

Issues in the Semiotics of the Bible. A philosophical inquiry into semiotics may begin with a basic question that is indicative of metaphysical inquiry: "What is a sign?" And, while the question is indeed inviting, the answers to the query will be of the sort that already beg a question, maybe a previous question. For the answers to "what is a sign?" will inevitably be *some thing.* Various obvious signs (or sign types) can of course be identified that enjoy considerable commerce in the pedestrian uses of signage. But a previous question would be more along the lines of, how does a specific sign signify something else or more? What does it mean that there is signification? Or, what does it mean when signification fails, or is sporadic—as when a sign functions in one moment and not another, or for some but not others, or in the past but not in the present, or not in the past but in the present?

One of the debates in semiotics that bears on biblical interpretation has to do with a rather basic difference between Saussure and Peirce regarding the question of signification. For Saussure, the signifier and signified are inseparable in signification. In other words, a sign always bears a signifier and a signified. The status of any signification must be considered in regard to both the signified and the signifier, but in practice the signified is usually given priority and often is the predominant object of interest. Furthermore, although multiple levels of meaning in a text are quite possible, by way of connotation or metalanguage, for Saussure the Peircean prospect of "unlimited semiosis" is remote at best. The semiosis of most texts is generally treated as finite, and, in those cases, once the meaning of the text has been identified, the semiotic inquiry is ended.

In contrast, for Peirce, nearly every signification leads not to some final signified, but to a chain of signification opening up a process of semiosis without final resolution. In other words, any given text does not have just one correct or final meaning or reading. Instead, what brings the semiotic processes to a halt is the inevitability of practical limitations of the inquiry. The reader may settle upon a particular referent either due to external limitations (weariness, lack of interest or imagination, etc.), or because a prejudice for a predetermined specific terminus (such as a theological dogma) was satisfied, which presumably sanctions the chain of signification. In other words, the limitation of a specific disciplinary inquiry yields a conclusion that terminates the chain of semiosis and that is thereby itself "disciplined" or constrained. Indeed, if the terminus is predetermined—as is often the case with ecclesiastical or political interpretative endeavors—once the desired predetermined end is attained, the exploration of semiosis is concluded.

To the extent that our inquiry into semiotics is concerned with the study of biblical texts, we are limited in our thinking about how a text may or may not be said to be significant "to or for" a reader (with "to" and "for" conveying a rich diversity of approaches and presumptions regarding interpretation). At issue respecting academic disciplines in the field of biblical studies is the question of the epistemological status of such inquiry. Thus, according to Peirce's later views, a historical inquiry into a biblical text may proceed by means of a constrained endeavor limited by what is predetermined to count as evidence and sound argumentation. As such it is possible to attain disciplined historical knowledge respecting a biblical text within the (philosophical) limits of the theoretical enterprise.

In other words, the discipline of historical inquiry is constrained to raise the question of whether a specific sign is of "historical" signification. The discipline provides a means for assessing the historical veracity of a text. A text may be assessed employing the discipline(s) of historical inquiry regarding what is *historically* significant, and whether such content is historically true or false, or more finely whether a specific claim in a text that is historically significant (meaning that it is available for disciplined inquiry as historical) is probably *historically* true or false. But the truth value of such assessments will be restrained by the epistemological limitations of the historical academic enterprise (Kant) or the semiotic constraints of the historical disciplinary enterprise, which predetermine the acceptable ends or outcomes of the chain of semiosis.

The philosophically previous question to any historical endeavor of inquiry and assessment has to do with the philosophical assessment of the "discipline." Often the contest over the academic standing of approaches to the study and interpretation of biblical texts rests upon "disciplinary presumptions," often uncritically assumed. Semiotic analysis of interpretative methods employed in the study of biblical texts continues the critical philosophical endeavor of addressing the limitations (whether they be epistemic, ontological, or logical) of all methodologies.

An Example. As was noted earlier, semiotic analyses of biblical texts do not exist, except as they play roles in structuralist, poststructuralist, rhetorical, narratological, or other approaches that draw more or less heavily on semiotic theory (either that of Saussure or Peirce or their successors or critics). However, as an illustration of the relevance of semiotics to biblical studies, we describe in the following Eco's (poststructuralist) analysis of Genesis 2—3. Eco is himself a philosopher and popular writer and novelist, a leading semiotician in his own right, and one of the foremost contemporary interpreters of Peirce's views.

The Garden of Eden story provides Eco with a springboard from which he launches his study of an instance in which "aesthetic language" (Roman Jakobson) generates contradictory messages. Using basic semiotic concepts, Eco imagines the minimal language necessary for Adam and Eve to function in the Bible's Eden story. He lays out this language around two series of binary oppositions. The first pair of oppositions features the (simplified) conceptual signifieds that derive from possible experiences within the narrative world of the biblical story, such as "Good versus Bad." The second pair of oppositions features the physical signifiers used to refer to these signified contents. The signifiers also appear in their simplest form, namely, one consonant and one vowel, arranged according to a simple "combinatory rule." These two series of oppositions are correlated in the system of signs to form the Edenic language. For every difference of content (signified) there is a corresponding difference of expression (signifier). This double string of oppositions establishes a further series of "connotative chains" through which the language-user can move from one sign to another one.

However, a contradiction results from the double series of oppositions when they are placed into operation in the Eden narrative. The irregularity of the "Serpent" and "Apple" signs disrupts the connotative chains and introduces a semantic imbalance into the linguistic system, for the same signifier that designates forbidden, bad fruit also designates that which is good and beautiful. God's error in the creation of this language leads to the further creation by Adam and Eve of a metaphor that conceals linguistic contradiction without eliminating it. Adam and Eve's metaphor then produces a "language passion" that corresponds to their desire for the forbidden fruit. The metaphor opens up the "limitless possibilities of semiosis," which is both the power of signs to refer endlessly to other signs and the inability of any signifier to refer conclusively to any signified. The message undermines the oppositions that are essential to its own significance, and the story deconstructs itself. The Edenic language is inherently ambiguous because it permits and even requires this contradiction. In other words, the origin of sin is linguistic.

Although many of the messages in Eco's hypothetical Edenic language are nonambiguous, even these unambiguous messages are disturbed by the possibility of producing aesthetic messages in that same language. This is also true for many and perhaps all real languages. In aesthetic messages, alterations in the language produce an additional signifying level of the message—metaphors that do not merely enrich but disrupt the clear, Saussurean channel by interfering with the interpretant. What these metaphors signify is not some object in the extratextual world, but rather another message. This message, or further level of the aesthetic message, points self-referentially "back" to the physical stuff of the message itself, that is, the material aspect of the signifiers. This disruption of linguistic order is, as Eco notes, an effect of narrative and ideology.

As the creator of the Edenic language, God is responsible for subverting "the presumed natural order of things," but it may well be that this flaw is inherent in any language as such—that is, that even God could not have prevented it. Eco's argument suggests that it is in the very nature of any language to generate distortion of or disobedience to a message. The physical system of language itself invites and even demands distortion. Even the divine word, as represented in the Bible, brings with it *of necessity* its own misunderstanding and transgression. Furthermore, if humanity is created in the image of God, then the linguistic corruption that taints the human world already in the Garden of Eden itself arises in the supernatural realm. Even God is constrained by the inherent imperfections of language. God is either the one who creates this corruption, or else God is unable to prevent its occurrence.

[*See also* Deconstruction; Materialist Criticism; Narrative Criticism and Narrative Hermeneutics; Postcolonial Biblical Interpretation; Poststructuralist Interpretation; Queer Criticism and Queer Theory; Reader-Response Criticism; Rhetorical Criticism; Speech-Act Theory; *and* Structuralist Interpretation.]

BIBLIOGRAPHY

Aristotle. *Prior Analytics.* Translated by A. J. Jenkinson. Electronic book. Adelaide Australia: eBooks@Adelaide, 2012. The earliest known critical study concerned with logic.

Barthes, Roland. *Elements of Semiology.* Translated by Annette Lavers and Colin Smith. New York: Hill and Wang, 1967. English translation of *Éléments de sémiologie*, first published in 1964. A succinct survey of semiology, following Saussure and Louis Hjelmslev.

Eco, Umberto. "On the Possibility of Generating Aesthetic Messages in an Edenic Language." Translated by Bruce Merry. In *The Role of the Reader: Explorations in the Semiotics of Texts*, 90–140. Bloomington: Indiana University Press, 1979. An early poststructuralist reading of a biblical text, discussed earlier.

Eco, Umberto. *Semiotics and the Philosophy of Language.* Bloomington: Indiana University Press, 1984. Eco's analysis of semiotics in terms of the history of the philosophy of language.

Epicurus. "Letter to Herodotus." Available online at http://www.epicurus.net/en/herodotus.html, accessed 4 August 2009.

Kant, Immanuel. *The Conflict of the Faculties.* Translated by Mary J. Gregor. Lincoln: University of Nebraska Press, 1992. English translation of *Der Streit der Fakultäten*, first published in 1798. Kant's often neglected volume is a defense of the freedom of inquiry and the status of philosophers in the reasoned assessment of the study of religion, law, and medicine. Discussion is provided regarding the philosophical status of biblical exegetical endeavors.

Morris, Charles. *Foundations of a Theory of Signs.* Chicago: University of Chicago Press, 1938. Broadened the study of signs ranging from human language to animal communication by grounding semiosis in communication (any communication) without privileging either the kind of object interpreted or the biological standing of the interpreter.

Peirce, Charles Sanders. *Peirce on Signs: Writings on Semiotic By Charles Sanders Peirce.* Edited by James Hoopes. Chapel Hill: University of North Carolina Press, 1991. A useful introduction to the philosophy of Peirce through his writings on semiotics.

Saussure, Ferdinand de. *Course in General Linguistics.* Edited by Charles Bally et al. Translated by Wade Baskin. New York: McGraw-Hill, 1959. English translation of *Cours de linguistique générale*, first published in 1916. Perhaps the most important, and still very influential, discussion of modern semiotic theory.

Whitehead, Alfred North. *Modes of Thought.* New York: The Free Press, 1938. Whitehead's final major publication provides a clearly written introduction to his thought in general by means of thematic philosophical considerations that he contends seek to express the ultimate good sense that is civilization.

Whitehead, Alfred North. *Process and Reality: An Essay in Cosmology.* New York: The Free Press, 1929. Whitehead's *magnum opus*, the essay offers a coherent alternative process/relational "cosmology" to worldviews based on substance metaphysics.

Whitehead, Alfred North. *Symbolism: Its Meaning and Effect.* New York: Macmillan, 1927. A philosophical essay that offers a robust semiotic theory of perception that seeks to respond to epistemological challenges addressed by Hume and Kant. Offers a way of understanding symbolic activity at an elementary level of perception that is often prior to comprehension.

David Odell-Scott and George Aichele

SOCIAL SCIENCES

[*This entry contains two subentries,* Hebrew Bible *and* New Testament.]

Hebrew Bible

The social sciences are a constellation of several disciplines whose aim is to study society, both as a whole and in terms of its various dimensions. The social sciences pursue this aim by going beyond mere social description to develop social theories that can yield models or paradigms of use in analyzing particular societies and formulating hypotheses concerning social phenomena that can be tested for the probability of their accuracy. While there are a plethora of perspectives and methods in social inquiry, there is no firm agreement as to what constitutes an adequate "explanation" of society as a whole or in its varied aspects. Numerous social-scientific approaches have been used to identify the social information in the Hebrew Bible, to throw light on the social facets of specific biblical texts, and to explore the social and historical contexts in which particular texts were written.

What is Society? Society, as studied by the social sciences, is not simply an assemblage of individual persons. It is rather a group of people sharing a self-sufficient system of action that outlasts the lifespan of individuals within it. Society is composed of patterned relationships among human agents that are arbitrary in the sense that out of a great spectrum of possibilities different social groups often develop along strikingly different lines. A society is created by people, cumulatively over time, and it can and does change, but in such a way that the change may be either leisurely or catastrophic. The changes, being a result of collective social action, cannot simply be willed or contrived by single individuals, although they may supply forceful leadership for the larger forces of social change.

While there is general agreement among social scientists that society is not governed by "laws," it is also evident that social constructions are not random. The study of a large number of societies reveals significant similarities in structure and process, to the extent that one may speak of social "probabilities" that, given certain conditions, societies will tend to develop in more or less expected ways. This is an important point in the application of social sciences to the Hebrew Bible, because the biblical text lacks much social information that can only be hypothesized based on information from societies that demonstrate apparent similarities in certain regards. These hypotheses have to be tested by the degree of "fit" they show with what *is* actually known about biblical societies. A typical error in making comparisons between societies is to connect them on limited points that are torn out of their respective contexts without regard to how the compared features function in the two societies.

The History of Social-Scientific Biblical Criticism. The cardinal branches of the social sciences employed in biblical studies, both with respect to the Hebrew Bible and the New Testament, are sociology and anthropology, with political science and economics receiving increasing attention. Other disciplines often included in the social sciences are archaeology, demography, social psychology, culture studies, historiography, and law. Of these ancillary social sciences, archaeology plays a long-honored, though greatly recast, role in reconstructing Israelite society. Anthropology has contributed the difference between the way insiders understand their societies (the "emic" perspective) and the results of an analysis of the same societies by social-scientific observers (the "etic" perspective). Many new forms of biblical criticism share some of the premises and procedures of social-scientific criticism and have been both stimulated by the social sciences and in turn have contributed to a fuller comprehension of Israelite society. Some of these related disciplines are gender criticism, ideological criticism, postcolonial criticism, culture criticism, narrative criticism, reader-response criticism, new historical criticism, psychological criticism, and canonical criticism.

Among the various critical practices, social scientific criticism is one of the latecomers to biblical studies. The first critical practices applied to the Hebrew Bible in the late eighteenth century and early nineteenth century were drawn from the philological, literary, and historical sciences. This is understandable because the social sciences were not on the intellectual scene until the mid-nineteenth century. Nevertheless, to this day, even with a considerable body of sophisticated social-scientific criticism at hand, biblical interpreters have been slow, even hesitant, in appropriating the social sciences to study the undoubted social phenomena in the Hebrew Bible. This reluctance has been due in part to uncertainty that the social sciences can be fruitfully applied to the Bible, and in part to a decided tendency of biblical scholars to dismiss social factors in their analyses of the biblical text.

Among the first scholars to employ the social sciences in biblical studies were W. Robertson Smith, Antonin Causse, and Max Weber. As pathbreaking as their work proved to be, their pioneering contributions did not enter the mainstream of biblical studies. In the first third of the twentieth century, a more concerted effort at marshaling the social sciences to interpret the Bible was initiated by a group of biblical scholars teaching at or connected with the University of Chicago, namely, Graham Taylor, Louis Wallis, W. C. Graham, J. M. Powis Smith, Herbert May, and Chester McCown. The work of these scholars was fueled by the Social Gospel movement and profoundly shaped by social science premises and insights advanced by Albion Small, founder of the department of Sociology at the University of Chicago. Perceptive as their work was, in pursuit of what they called "Biblical Sociology," they did not develop theory and method in a way that could establish an ongoing tradition of social-scientific criticism of the Bible. Much of what they did would now be classified as cultural studies.

As late as the 1960s the social sciences were still enlisted sporadically and unsystematically in the research of biblical scholars. It was the work of George Mendenhall and Norman Gottwald that introduced social-scientific theory and method into Hebrew Bible studies as a recognized discipline. They did so by demonstrating how those resources, when used rigorously, could throw light on the murky topic of the origins of ancient Israel. Since then, the social sciences have been employed in exegeting biblical texts drawn from the whole range of the canon: Torah, Prophets, and Writings. Paralleling the exegetical work has been the application of social-science theory and methods to all periods of biblical history—premonarchic, monarchic, exilic, and postexilic eras—in such a way that the outlines of a coherent social history of ancient Israel are clearly discernible.

In Hebrew Bible studies the primary sources from sociology have been the foundational social theorists Emile Durkheim, Karl Marx, and Max Weber. Contemporary sociologists such as Gerhard Lenski, Eric Wolf, and John Kautsky have also contributed substantially to the work of biblical scholars. Primary sources from anthropology include Edward Evans-Pritchard, Mary Douglas, and Marshall Sahlins. Comparative sociology and anthropology have drawn attention to significant similarities between Israelite society and other societies on key points, such as Native Americans and Iceland on pre-state confederations and oral law; Saudi Arabia on the formation of a rudimentary state from a coalition of tribes; Africa on prophecy, millennialism, and religious conversion; and Korea on the struggle of peasants for economic livelihood and social autonomy. Used heuristically, these comparisons help corroborate or supplement our information about ancient Israel, and also raise new questions about Israelite society that have not emerged with the use of the historical-critical method.

The animus in some quarters toward the comparative method derives in part from instances of poor use of method, particularly the tendency, as noted, to make unfruitful or trivial comparisons by tearing the points of similarity out of their social context. This has resulted in what has been called "parallelomania," referring to an obsessive search for similarities between the Bible and other social phenomena, often on a global scale. This was evident in the case of James Frazier, who collected a large number of parallels without proper context, so it is not evident whether these are actually significant parallels in contrast to superficial associations. It is also true that some biblical scholars regard the principled use of the social sciences as an intrusion on the traditional domains of history and theology. Furthermore, to understand and employ the social sciences requires major professional "re-tooling" for scholars trained in traditional methods, a step which many biblical scholars understandably choose not to take.

Fresh Insights into Old Problems. It needs to be emphasized that the social sciences are a complement to, not a replacement, of other critical practices, be they the older historical-critical methods or the more recent forms of literary criticism. This is a very important point because practitioners of social-scientific criticism are repeatedly charged with trying to substitute the social sciences for the traditional critical disciplines. Far from being the truth, the disciplined study of societies is in fact an outgrowth of the historical method and has contributed important social information and perspectives on the history of ancient Israel. Nonetheless, the historical profile that social-scientific studies renders diverges in important respects from the historical reconstructions delivered by older critical methods. As a result, on a number of important points, Israel is socially viewable

- As a marginalized people emergent in the highlands of Canaan rather than escaped en masse from Egypt, a people who were in the main subsistence farmers, practiced decentralized self-rule and dispersed leadership roles, and resisted taxation and indebtedness. Their non-state society has been characterized insightfully by the anthropological terms "regulated anarchy" and "tribes without rulers." This decentralized society was celebrated and reinforced by its religious commitment to the cult of Yahweh.

- As a society brought under a loose form of state power that was more rudimentary in its structure and scope under Saul, David, and Solomon than normally supposed, and that broke apart, producing the larger, economically prosperous northern kingdom and the smaller, economically weaker southern kingdom. The northern kingdom under the ninth century B.C.E. Omri dynasty developed on a scale not matched in the southern kingdom until the mid-eighth century.
- As a largely peasant people who under the monarchy suffered a heavy tax and debt burden, made all the more crushing due to the intensification of agriculture for export rather than subsistence farming and by the tribute that foreign powers imposed on Israel and Judah.
- The tax and debt burden runs throughout monarchic and postexilic history, relieved only now and then by short-lived reforms such as those of Josiah and Nehemiah.
- As the subjects of prophecy, at first in the north and later in the south, severely criticizing their oppression, and often finding expression in use of the metaphor of "idolatry" to symbolize the single-minded pursuit of wealth and power by the elite social and political leaders. The dark future anticipated by these prophets was the overthrow of the unjust states of Israel and Judah by the foreign powers of Assyria and neo-Babylonia.
- As a people, bereft of state and temple after the collapse of the northern kingdom in the late eighth century B.C.E. and the southern kingdom in the early sixth century B.C.E. As the Judahite elite were deported to Babylon, the Bible focuses on the "exiled" leaders. In contrast, the populace remaining in the land had to improvise sociopolitical structures in the absence of their former rulers. Many folks voluntarily fled to other lands such as Egypt and Syria to escape the hardships of life in the land. It appears that all these population groups drew upon the longstanding traditions and practices of self-rule and determined survival that had characterized the first Israelites and fueled the prophetic movement.
- As a people reconstituted in their homeland amid conflict over who should be included within the boundaries of the community, how the recurrence of onerous tax and debt burdens might be curbed, and who should exercise the political and religious authority allowed them by the Persian empire, as embodied in the dual leadership and contested jurisdictions of governor and high priest.
- As a people subject to Persian, Hellenistic, and Roman empires, enjoying limited self-rule at best and vulnerable to the influences of outside cultures that had an impact on their religion, especially in its priestly and apocalyptic forms, and in the formation of the biblical canon in a climate where other peoples were developing bodies of literature, including written norms or laws.
- As a people whose religious beliefs and practices had been diverse, including non-Yahwistic cults that competed with Yahwism, not to mention various forms of Yahwistic worship, and who began to narrow down their religious choices to "mono-Yahwism" and "religion of the book" from the exile on. This trajectory of an increasing "standardization" of religious belief and behavior eventually issued, after socially and politically convulsive struggle, in the consensus of rabbinic Judaism.

Many of these features of Israel's social structures and social processes had been detected, at least partially, by traditional scholarship, but it remained for social-scientific criticism to flesh them out in greater detail by means of coherent research strategies, making use of theories and models that enriched an understanding of biblical texts anchored in a field of social action.

Other notions introduced by social-scientific criticism were new to the biblical field. This was the case with the account of the first Israelites as indigenous to Canaan, and the proposal of a radically scaled-back conception of the united monarchy. The hypothesis about early Israel as indigenous to Canaan has had the effect of helping to explain why it has been so difficult to locate Moses and the exodus historically. It also encourages literary readings of the Torah and speculation about why Israel developed such an extensive narrative about escape from Egypt if none, or few, of the first Israelites had been in Egypt. The hypothesis claiming that the so-called united monarchy may have been a weak effort at centralization of power, making David and Solomon far less epochal figures than the Bible makes them out to be, shakes up the conventional understanding of the origin of the state in Israel and certainly casts a curious eye on the Samuel—Kings texts that make so much of the two leaders. It turns out that archeology, with a new eye for evidence about social life, plays a reinforcing role in the discussion of both hypotheses. The flourishing of villages in the Canaanite highlands in the late thirteenth and twelfth centuries B.C.E., gives evidence of a people practicing subsistence agriculture after a long period when the highlands were sparsely populated. The striking absence of monumental architecture in the tenth and early ninth centuries seems to attest to a rudimentary state at best, certainly a far cry from the opulence and building program attributed to Solomon. As was the case with Moses, we face the challenge of trying to understand why the Bible attributes to David and, more oddly, to Solomon so much power and glory, and, more importantly, the significance of humble state beginnings for the course that the dual monarchies subsequently followed. In both instances involving the origins of tribal Israel and its transition to statehood, social-scientific criticism has been a stimulus to newer types of literary criticism and a tempering of over-confidence in historical criticism.

Class, Race and Gender. Three major ways of viewing social structure and process in ancient Israel are through the lenses of class, race, and gender. All three of these foci have been taken up in the social-scientific inquiry into the Hebrew Bible. Of the three, class has the longest history of serious study by social sciences.

Class. Class refers to divisions in a society based on indicators like wealth, power, and status. A Marxist understanding of class stresses that the class divisions are rooted in the means of production, depending on whether various social groups do or do not control the surplus that the economy produces. Class is seen to result not from disparities in natural ability as such, but from power relationships that perpetuate conditions of dominance and subservience from generation to generation. The study of the interlocking socioeconomic and political forces that produce class is called Political Economy, which addresses the complicated question, "Who gets what, and why?," to which may be added the question, "By what means do they get it?" Many biblical interpreters have objected that class, being a modern construct specific to capitalism, is an anachronism when applied to pre-capitalist societies. If, however, all theories and concepts developed in modern times were to be excluded from biblical studies, the possibility of any scientific approach to the Hebrew Bible, whether social, literary, or historical, would be categorically ruled out. Each modern social construct has to be tested for the insight it reveals or obscures when applied to the Hebrew Bible. When biblical societies are analyzed in terms of power and wealth hierarchies, the presence of class is readily apparent. For example, the widespread employment among biblical scholars of Gerhard Lenski's model of "the power pyramid" in horticultural societies depicts the social stratification apparent in Israel from monarchic times onward (1984).

Among practicing social-scientific biblical interpreters, several scholars stand out as having produced largely convincing studies of the workings of class in the Hebrew Bible. Norman Gottwald, employing a combination of Marxist social theory and cultural anthropology, has described the early Israelite tribal society as classless in the sense that everyone in principle was afforded access to the basic resources necessary for human livelihood. This is not to deny that there were differences in wealth and power among these tribalists. The relevant point is that those with greater goods were held in check by redistribution practices that socially sanctioned a leveling of wealth and power, while the power attached to social and religious offices was circumscribed and often granted only to particular leaders for specific tasks.

Roland Boer (2003) has undertaken a number of novel analyses of biblical texts making use of the theories and methods of several Marxist social and literary critics, showing how effectively they bring out features unseen by historical critical study. In exploring the subtle relationship between literature and social life, Boer has been able to illuminate the way class directly and indirectly shaped moral and religious values and behavior in ancient Israel, which in turn find their expression in biblical texts. His exemplary analysis of the social class factors operative in northern Israel's revolt led by Jeroboam against Jerusalem's monopoly of power, employs a nuanced use of Frederick Jameson's notion of "the political unconscious."

Marvin Chaney (1989), in a series of essays on prophetic texts, has exploited traditional methods of textual and historical-critical exegesis, coupled with analysis of socioeconomic systems, in order to bring to light the prophet's clear grasp of the social disruption and decay directly attributable to the greed and corruption of political and social leaders. Devadasan Premnath (2003) has extended Chaney's insights in an account of land accumulation and agricultural intensification in ancient Israel. Prophets such as Amos, Isaiah, and Jeremiah indicted the religious establishment for at worst sharing the same greed and corruption as the "civil" leaders, or at best "looking the other way" amid the impoverishment and victimization of the powerless. In particular, Chaney and Premnath have been able to show that features of prophetic texts often interpreted rather vapidly as socially neutral or irrelevant references to the religious breakdown of society are, in fact, metaphorical indictments of the way predatory upper class values and behavior severely damaged the fabric of society that religion depends on for its integrity and pertinence in sanctioning a system of social justice. It is not so much that religious breakdown created social and political breakdown but, virtually the opposite, that greed and corruption among the elite, unfettered by moral or religious constraints, shaped a decadent social situation in which religion was robbed of its power to inspire and sanction justice in the public realm.

David Jobling, conversant with postmodern and deconstructionist literary theories, has analyzed the unexpressed classism that lurks behind the assumptions and manner of representing social reality in narratives such as the account of Solomon's reign and the laudatory ideology embedded in the royal psalms such as Psalm 72 (1998). In this he has been informed by the work of the deconstructionist Jacques Derrida, by the Frankfurt School of Marxist criticism, and by the views of how ideology shapes literary discourse as "drama" in the theory of Terry Eagleton. Jobling's way of working with texts is typical of many scholars in its eclectic assemblage of theory and method drawn from varied social-scientific and literary strains of thought. Rather than working out of a predetermined monolithic theory, Jobling focuses on the social dimensions of texts and historical data by summoning whatever forms of theory and method will best lay bare those social dimensions. This point will be developed in the discussion of gender criticism.

Race. Race in the Hebrew Bible has been much less overtly studied than class. Nonetheless, rough-hewn notions, even prejudices, about race have played a confusing role in studies that address many aspects of Israelite literature, history, and religion that presumably have little, or nothing, to do with race. Sometimes this unexamined racialism elevates the biblical Israelites to the level of predestined superiority over other ancient Near Eastern peoples, and sometimes over societies in later times and places. At other times unexamined racialism plays into the notion of Israel's racial inferiority based on assumptions of some inborn defect that dooms them to a negative influence in human affairs. The legacy of the polarizing concepts of racial superiority and inferiority, coupled with confused notions of race among social scientists, sometimes treated in terms of simplistic biologism, has made it difficult to understand the topic, even when race is altered into social and cultural categories of ethnicity or nationhood. As a result, for the most part biblical interpreters have steered clear of a study of Israel as an embodied people. The tendency to prefer a more noncontroversial religious identity for Israel has the effect of ignoring Israel as a concrete cultural and social reality requiring a perspective that goes beyond merely religious descriptions.

The problematic concept of "race" has been largely replaced in biblical studies, as in the social sciences at large, with the notion of ethnicity. An ethnic group is characterized as a group of people, self-identified and usually recognized by others, who display common features such as language and a body of traditions that are a complex mixture of physical, historical, and cultural factors. In simplest terms, if a people identify themselves as distinct from other peoples, they are studied as such with a view to discovering how their ethnicity is understood by them (the insider or "emic" perspective) and how it is viewed from scientific study (the outsider or "etic" perspective). The consciousness of and claim to ethnic distinctiveness often arises, or is at least accentuated, in a group who suffer social marginalization, political disempowerment, and economic deprivation within a larger society.

In contrast, while most social-scientific study of race has been cautious, the notable exceptions are found in Afro-American interpretations that directly attack and undermine the racism buttressed by erroneous appeals to the Hebrew Bible, particularly in the work of Charles Copher (1993), Hope Felder (1989), and Randall Bailey (2003). In repudiating racism based on the curse of Ham (Gen 9:18–25) and on the conflation of race and slavery, these scholars have relied not only upon a scrupulous critical interpretation of biblical texts, but also on broader studies of race in antiquity indicating that race did not have the stigma and socially destructive effects that it has acquired since the era of western colonialism. This principled renunciation of racism in the Bible has had the effect of endorsing a shift in the study of "race" as popularly understood into the study of ethnicity.

Attempts to specify the ethnic character of ancient Israel have been diverse in their conclusions as to the point in time when Israel first experienced itself as an *ethnos*, why it did so, and the extent of change that its ethnic self-awareness and recognition by others underwent over the long course of its history. Clarification of ethnicity in the case of Israel is interwoven with issues of Israelite origins, demographic composition, political vs. sociocultural unity, and the fortunes of postexilic Israel among dominating empires, as well as debate over the degree of convergence or divergence in the use of the terms race, nation, and ethnicity. Max Weber already identified the puzzling problem in his famous query, "Hence we ask, how did Jewry develop into a pariah people with highly specific peculiarities?" (1952, 5). In using the term "pariah," Weber intended no negative judgment, but drew the word from Indian caste society to refer to "a distinctive hereditary social group lacking autonomous political organization and characterized by prohibitions against commensality (eating with nonmembers of the group) and intermarriage." (p. 13). In concluding that the answer to his question was self-chosen and externally reinforced "ritual segregation," he was alluding chiefly to postexilic Israel and not to its earlier history.

Present understanding of Israel's pre-exilic religion, endorsed by archaeological finds and studied in depth by scholars such as Mark Smith (2002) and Ziony Zevit (2001), recognizes that Israel had not reached a religious consensus until at least late monarchic times. There is ample evidence that the people known as Israel embraced a variety of religious beliefs and practices from earliest times without any official attempt at standardization before the reign of Josiah in the late seventh century. Thus, neither "ritual segregation" nor any purely religious explanations alone can account for preexilic Israelite ethnicity. In looking at the wider range of criteria of ethnicity, Gottwald has proposed that the struggle of emergent Israel as a peasant society engendered socioeconomic and cultural bonding that was facilitated but not wholly determined by religion. In citing the contributions of Smith and Zevit to an understanding of Israelite ethnicity, we note that they are not making use of social-scientific method in any strict sense but, nonetheless, their findings have enormous consequences for conceptualizing early Israelite society and religion as "a work in progress," not to be confused with the later stages of their growth and development.

Gender. Gender studies and their close affiliate feminist criticism have cut a wide swath through research on the Hebrew Bible, and have taken many forms dependent on, or closely related to, the social sciences. In many ways, the studies of race and gender have followed similar trajectories in rebutting erroneous views and in constructing fresh models. Phyllis Bird (1997) and Carol Meyers (1988) have employed anthropology, the former to plot distinctive forms of cultic practice among Israelite women that help to clarify why they are not described or developed with the same thoroughness as male-dominated worship, and the latter to argue that women in decentralized tribal Israel played major socioeconomic roles that were lost to male hierarchies in monarchic Israel. Mieke Bal's (1998) trenchant study of the shape of gender in Judges 4—5 is representative of a number of gender-oriented inquiries that have effectively joined literary criticism, feminist theory, and ideological criticism.

Of particular significance are studies influenced by the social sciences that address class, race, and gender integratively and systemically, attempting to show how they function respectively in distinct ways to reinforce one another in support of ruling classes. David Jobling, in writing a totally new kind of "commentary" on 1 Samuel (1998), has joined the three by showing the centrality of all three for the narrative: class for the emergence of the monarchy, race for the relations with Philistines, and gender for the subordinate roles of women who nonetheless facilitate the preeminence of men. A high-water mark in the insightful integration of class, race, and gender is Gale Yee's (2003) exposure of the way the Hebrew Bible repeatedly blames "evil" women as "symbolic alibis" for the conflicts and blunders of the male actors who hold socioeconomic, political, and religious power.

What Does Social-Scientific Criticism Accomplish? It is not excessive to say that social-scientific criticism, in concert with new forms of literary criticism, has contributed enormously to the exegesis of biblical texts and to an enriched understanding of the history of Israel. There is no book or stream of tradition or period of history in the Hebrew Bible that has escaped the attention of social-scientific theory and method. Even after one has set aside many studies that include "social" in the title but are merely descriptive or loosely cultural, the impact has been far-reaching. The fruit of this wave of social-critical study has been to bring the religion and theology of the Hebrew Bible into closer connection with how Israelites organized their lives in all other regards. Moreover, the social sciences have served to connect and relate a number of otherwise separate and distinct approaches to the Hebrew Bible, ranging from the realia of archaeology, demographics, geography, ecology, and agriculture, to the various subdisciplines that study the people who have been traditionally treated as instances of "the Other," such as feminist criticism, gay and lesbian studies, Afro American interpretation, Asian interpretation, Latino interpretation, culture studies, and postcolonial criticism. The social sciences have been equally important in meeting and at points overlapping with linguist studies such as rhetorical criticism, structuralism and deconstruction, and semiotics. A promising future for social-scientific criticism of the Hebrew Bible is assured for research programs willing to recognize that "only as the full *materiality* of ancient Israel is more securely grasped will we be able to make proper sense of is *spirituality*." (Gottwald 1999, p. 4). Finally, in appropriating biblical social ethics in contemporary moral debate, social ethicists such as Charles Cosgrove and Stephen Mott have gained precision and trenchancy from the cumulative results of social-scientific criticism of the Hebrew Bible.

[*See also* African American Interpretation; Asian American Biblical Interpretation; Canonical Criticism;

Cross-Cultural Exegesis; Economics and the Bible; Feminist Biblical Interpretation; Historical Criticism, *subentry* Hebrew Bible; Ideological Criticism; Lesbian, Gay, Bisexual, and Transgender Interpretation; Literary Criticism, Literary Theory, and the Bible; Narrative Criticism and Narrative Hermeneutics; New Historicism; Postcolonial Biblical Interpretation; Postmodern Interpretation; Poststructuralist Interpretation; Race, Ethnicity, and Biblical Criticism; Reader-Response Criticism; Rhetorical Criticism; *and* Structuralist Interpretation.]

Bibliography

Bailey, Randall. *Yet With a Steady Beat: Contemporary US Afrocentric Biblical Interpretation.* Atlanta: Society of Biblical Literature, 2003.

Bal, Mieke. *Murder and Difference: Genre, Gender and Scholarship on Sisera's Death.* Bloomington: University of Indiana Press, 1988.

Bird, Phyllis. *Missing Persons and Mistaken Identities. Women and Gender in Ancient Israel.* Minneapolis: Fortress Press, 1997.

Boer, Roland. *Marxist Criticism of the Bible.* London/New York: T&T Clark International, 2003.

Carney, T. F. *The Shape of the Past: Models in Antiquity.* Lawrence, Kans.: Coronado Press, 1975.

Carter, Charles E. and Carol L. Myers, eds. *Community, Identity, and Ideology: Social Science Approaches to the Hebrew Bible.* Winona Lake, Ind.: Eisenbrauns, 1996.

Chalcraft, David J., ed. *Social-Scientific Old Testament Criticism.* Sheffield: Sheffield Academic Press, 1997.

Chaney, Marvin L. "Bitter Bounty: The Dynamics of Political Economy Critiqued by the Eighth-Century Prophets." In *Reformed Faith and Economics,* edited by Robert L. Stivers, 15–30. New York: University Press of America, 1989.

Copher, Charles. *Black Biblical Studies: An Anthology of Charles B. Copher: Biblical and Theological Issues on the Black Presence in the Bible.* Chicago: Black Light Fellowship, 1993.

Cosgrove, Charles H. *Appealing to Scripture in Moral Debate. Five Hermeneutical Rules.* Grand Rapids, Mich./Cambridge, UK: Wm. B. Eerdmans, 2002.

Elliot, John H. *What is Social-Scientific Criticism?* Guides to Biblical Scholarship. Minneapolis.: Fortress Press, 1993.

Esler, Philip F., ed. *Ancient Israel. The Old Testament in its Social Context.* Minneapolis: Fortress Press, 2006.

Felder, Cain Hope. *Troubling Biblical Waters: Race, Class and Family.* Maryknoll, N.Y.: Orbis Books, 1989.

Gottwald, Norman K. *The Hebrew Bible in Its Social World and in Ours.* Atlanta: Scholars Press, 1993.

Gottwald, Norman K. *The Politics of Ancient Israel.* Louisville, Ky.: Westminster John Knox, 2000.

Gottwald, Norman K. *The Tribes of Yahweh: A Sociology of the Religion of Liberated Israel, 1250–1050 B.C.E.* Sheffield: Sheffield Academic Press, 1999.

Jobling, David. *1 Samuel [Berith Olam. Studies in Hebrew Narrative & Poetry].* Collegeville, Minn.: Liturgical Press, 1998.

Kessler, Rainer. *The Social History of Ancient Israel. An Introduction.* Minneapolis, Minn.: Fortress Press, 2008.

Lawrence, Louis J. and Mario I. Aguilar, eds. *Anthropology and Biblical Studies. Avenues of Approach.* Leiden, Netherlands: Deo Publishing, 2004.

Lenski, Gerhard. *Power and Privilege. A Theory of Social Stratification.* Chapel Hill, N.C./London: The University of North Carolina Press, 2d ed., 1984.

Matthews, Victor H. and Don C. Benjamin. *Social World of Ancient Israel 1250–587 B.C.E.* Peabody, MA: Hendrickson Publishers, 1993.

Mayes, Andrew. *The Old Testament in Sociological Perspective.* London: Marshall Pickering, 1989.

Meyers, Carol. *Discovering Eve: Ancient Israelite Women in Context.* New York: Oxford University Press, 1988.

Mott, Stephen. *Biblical Ethics of Social Change.* New York: Oxford University Press, 2011.

Pilch, John J., ed. *Social Scientific Models for Interpreting the Bible. Essays by the Context Group in Honor of Bruce J. Malina.* Leiden, Netherlands: Brill, 2001.

Premnath, Devadasan. *Eighth Century Prophets. A Social Analysis.* St. Louis, Mo.: Chalice Press, 2003.

Rogerson, John W. *Anthropology and the Old Testament.* Oxford: Basil Blackwell, 1978.

Smith, Mark S. *The Early History of God: Yahweh and the Other Deities in Ancient Israel.* Grand Rapids, Mich.: Wm. B. Eerdmans, 2002.

Weber, Max. *Ancient Judaism.* New York: The Free Press, 1952.

Yee, Gale. *Poor Banished Children of Eve. Woman as Evil in the Hebrew Bible.* Minneapolis: Fortress Press, 2003.

Zevit, Ziony. *The Religions of Ancient Israel. A Synthesis of Parallactic Approaches.* New York: Continuum, 2001.

Norman K. Gottwald

New Testament

At its simplest, social-scientific criticism pays careful attention to New Testament (NT) meanings and values understood in light of their ancient

Mediterranean cultural context—a process of discovery enriched with social-scientific models and perspectives. The approach developed alongside the established methods of historical criticism using the theoretical traditions of the social sciences (social anthropology, social psychology, sociology, ethnography). David Horrell (1999) observes that the development was part of a wider trend in biblical studies that began thirty years ago reflecting a desire for increased diversity within the discipline and greater interdisciplinarity within the humanities and the social sciences. John H. Elliott coined the label "social-scientific criticism" in 1986 and subsequently in 1997 gave the following definition:

> Social-Scientific Criticism of the Bible is that phase of the exegetical task which analyzes the social and cultural dimensions of the text and of its environmental context through the utilization of the perspectives, theory, models, and research of the social sciences. [It] investigates biblical texts as meaningful configurations of language intended to communicate between composers and audiences. In this process it studies not only (1) the social aspects of the form and content of texts but also the conditioning factors and intended consequences of the communication process; (2) the correlation of the text's linguistic, literary, theological (ideological), and social dimensions; and (3) the manner in which this textual communication was both a reflection of and response to a specific social and cultural context—that is, how it was designed to serve as an effective vehicle of social interaction and an instrument of social as well as literary and theological consequence.

Social-scientific criticism is a subdiscipline in NT interpretation that complements the many other methodological approaches to the NT. It focuses a spotlight on the geographic, economic, social, political, historical, domestic, and religious contexts in which the authors and audiences reflected in the NT wrote, heard, reacted, and interacted. Social-science criticism is a method that provides the appropriate cultural and social scenarios to read and interpret the ancient texts in their own terms and cultural nuances. With effort and perseverance it is possible for modern readers to bridge the cultural divide that separates them from the authors and audiences of antiquity.

Bridging Ancient and Modern Worlds. Understandably, we are tempted to take the easy road and think that the words and texts of the NT meant then what we mean by them now. The NT continues to be of profound significance personally for believers adhering to its religious demands; *politically* for preachers and politicians articulating domestic and international policies; *morally and ethically* for social activists espousing positions on social values such as euthanasia, alternate sexual orientations, gender, body, stem-cell research, and wealth and poverty; and *popularly* for disillusioned idealists promoting millenarian dreams and apocalyptic destruction. Yet the NT, made up of the Gospels, epistles, and apocalypses, was composed in Hellenistic Greek in Roman-occupied territory more than two thousand years ago where personal sensibilities and cognitive habits, political orientations, moral and ethical values and attitudes, and popular expectations and dreams differed sharply from those of our modern world. Modern translations of the Bible that render the ancient Greek into clear, colloquial languages of the world, while excellent, nevertheless mask the foreignness of these ancient texts. Richard Rohrbaugh (2008) points out that the NT is not a Western book even though it has generated ideas, images, music, theological treatises, movies, and popular narratives of Jesus, all of which are ubiquitous in Western cultural and religious history. Christopher Moore's national bestseller, *Lamb: The Gospel According to Biff, Christ's Childhood Pal* (2002), is but one of many examples that abound. Biff has been resurrected and finds himself in the modern world completing the story of Jesus—he recounts the decades of Jesus's life that are missing from the four NT Gospel accounts. Adele Reinhartz (*Jesus of Hollywood*, 1998) and Tatum W. Barnes (*Jesus at the Movies*, 2004) usefully chart the cinematic representations of Jesus via Hollywood noting that entertainment values and modern sensibilities often drive these silver-screen productions. Unfortunately, however, these representations of Jesus both mirror and have an effect on the modern cultural perceptions of Jesus and Judaism. Mel Gibson's 2004 well-publicized *The Passion of the Christ* depicts the danger of viewing the Gospels as transcending culture and speaking in universalizing and prescriptive ways about the teachings, life, and the execution of Jesus.

The Gospels, epistles, and apocalypses were written by authors who were thoroughly embedded in the language, social systems, cultural customs, economic realities, political ideologies, and religious practices of their day. In other words, the twenty-seven books of the NT were written in a social script that reflects their cultural contexts, not ours. Modern readers, who read these ancient texts with care and sensitivity, will notice the disparity between the ancient and modern, and are left perplexed about how best to make that transition without destroying the world of Jesus and Paul and their meaning systems. If modern readers do not make allowances for this disparity, they are in danger of the perils of ethnocentrism, namely, assuming that their contemporary values are superior to ancient values and anachronism, namely, that their cultural values and perspectives are the same as the ancient Roman society in which Jesus and Paul moved, lived, taught, and died.

A brief example will illustrate the point. Paul writes in Romans 1:26–27 that women gave up what was natural for the unnatural, and men gave up what was natural with women for each other—a more-or-less literal translation of the passages. The language is uncommon and cryptic to us—difficult for us to understand—so to bridge the gap we fill in the gaps in the translation and interpretative process. They are translated and interpreted to reflect modern sensibilities about homosexual, bisexual, or heterosexual behaviors—either to condone or condemn the behaviors. The word "homosexual," however, is an eighteenth-century C.E. coinage and labeled then as a psychopathology. Paul does not use that term nor does any other writer in the NT. Whatever Paul may have meant with exchanging the natural for the unnatural, it certainly would have meant something different for him from what we imagine that he may have meant. To discover his meaning requires asking what the terms "natural" and "unnatural" meant in the social world of Paul. Social-science readings alert us that Paul filled the words "natural" and "unnatural" with distinctive nuances drawn from his cultural system of meaning. If social context, language, texts, and meaning are inextricably intertwined in a communicational system in which ancient readers and hearers participated, how then do we best make sense of the NT by reflecting a cultural and social milieu frequently bewildering and alien to our own sensibilities and ways of seeing things?

What is required is an interpretative framework that helps modern readers make the transition from their world to the social systems of the ancient world. This essay puts forward a series of interpretative models from the social sciences to equip readers with the tools to mediate access and recover the social systems operative during the time of the authors and audiences reflected in the NT. Before setting out the essential features of social-scientific criticism, a brief history describing the rise of "social" considerations of the biblical text is useful.

A Brief History: Social History and Social-Scientific Criticism. Biblical interpreters have had a long-standing interest in elucidating a number of interrelated literary and historical features of the NT. Some of these literary and historical features were the historical circumstances that stimulated the composition of the books of the NT; the social forces that produced changes in oral and written communication; the social and literary settings of forms of traditions in the Gospels (e.g., parables, healing narratives, beatitudes, sayings of Jesus); the historical circumstances that triggered the production of differing literary genres (e.g., Q, gospels, epistles, apocalypses); the social dynamics that instigated the redactional activity in the Gospels; and the social factors that elicited certain rhetorical responses in the Pauline epistles. As useful and significant as these elucidations were for descriptively filling in the background for exegesis and textual analysis, they were not seen as adequately contributing to explaining the meaning of these texts in their broader social-cultural milieu. Generally, interests in the literary and historical features of early Christianity did not focus enough on the wider social context in which the NT found birth but focused in limited ways on the setting in the life of the early church—especially as seen in the Gospels and the form-critical approach promoted by Rudolf Bultmann. Indeed, form-critical approaches to the Gospels and the formation of early Christianity were thought to be curtailed by the prevailing interpretative interests of theology.

While the so-called Chicago school, which included Shirley Jackson Case, Shailer Mathews, Leander Keck, and Robert Funk, continued their explorations of the sociology of early Christianity, interest in the social aspects of early Christianity began to decline. Horrell (1999) documents that by the 1920s to the 1970s, concentration on the social dimensions of early Christianity declined for a variety of reasons. The ebbing tide of interest in the social milieu of the NT, however, created a resurgence of interest in the 1960s by the publication of E. A. Judges's book, *Social Distinctives of the Christians in the First Century*. The 1970s saw an explosion in the creative and varied uses of methods, models, and theories from the social sciences. By 1983 two approaches were born, with one committed to social history, the other to the social-science methodology.

Social History and Its Limitations. Questions of social history (*Sozialgeschichte*) have been extensively and fruitfully treated in the field of NT research. Interpreters of the NT pursuing social history are especially interested in knowledge of communities, institutions, and social structures of antiquity, along with the role of families and associations, the matter of honor and status, and the impact of social stratification and ancient economies. For example, an analysis and description of disparity in wealth distribution in antiquity helps explain the socioeconomic inequality reflected in the Letter of James. Noting the dominant persons and political events mentioned in Luke's Gospel gives important clues about Jesus's teaching, healing, and execution in the broader scheme of things. Practitioners of social-science criticism observed, however, that the descriptions offered by social historians on wealth and disparity in antiquity were generally based on modern perceptions of money and economic activity, and thus were not helpful to understanding James's letter—a latent anachronism hidden in the descriptive enterprise. Even the early representative works that described the radical teaching of Jesus on homelessness, separation from family, and renunciation of wealth (Theissen 1973) and the formation of early Christian groups (Gager 1975; Meeks 1983) could not escape this nagging apprehension. As Jerome Neyrey (2005) observes, these studies while influential were nevertheless plagued with persistent questions about methodology and the unacknowledged assumptions that drove the descriptive enterprise.

Without explicit admission of the conceptual apparatus that drove the conclusions reached, there was no way of replicating the results or of delimiting the imputation of cultural, historical, and theological biases on the initial authors of the NT texts. Knowledge, both ancient and modern, was socially conditioned and perspectival in character, thus identification of the social location of the ancient authors, readers, and hearers, as well as the social location of the modern interpreters, was a necessary part of the task. Both Elliott (1993) and Malina (1982) made calls for the systematic and explicit use of social-scientific models for analyzing the social realia and to make obvious the conceptual models that exegetes use to interrogate the texts of the NT.

Social-Scientific Criticism. With a social-scientific approach, dramatic efforts were made to treat social-cultural, economic, religious, and political matrices not simply as incidental background filler of the texts of the NT but as significant foreground material central to their meaning. Words took their meanings from a distinctive social context. Geography, genealogy, gender, economic conditions, political ideologies of Rome, agonism expressed in honor-shame challenges, lived expectations, and religious aspirations of the denizens of Rome profoundly shaped the outlook, form and content, rhetorical expressions, and narratives of the NT. These efforts were driven with the increasing consciousness that comprehension, imagination, perceptions, meaningful communication, and social engagement were socially and culturally conditioned. The authors of the Gospels, epistles, and apocalypses shared and exchanged meaning with their contemporaries that was deeply rooted in the social systems enveloping them. They wrote for and about cultural institutions and people, whose worldviews, cultural codes, social values, and lived experiences were radically different from ours. Indeed, having intimate knowledge of the social world of the NT was absolutely essential to appreciating the dynamic and meaning of these ancient texts (Neyrey and Stewart 2008). A method was needed that would identify and analyze the situations in the ancient world that impacted imagination, understanding, perception, behavior, and the cognitive habits of the NT authors and their audiences. Social-scientific critics argued for the use of explicit and appropriate cross-cultural models that were adapted culturally to suit the ancient world and its meaning systems. Models help identify places where a "common sense understanding or intuitive construal" of ancient texts might lead to anachronistic and ethnocentric readings. Periodic debate emerges about the utility of models—that they are an anachronistic imposition upon ancient texts at the proclivity of the interpreter. Osiek (1992) demurs, pointing to the utility of models to systematize and simplify social data for comparative purposes and to assist in the interpretation of the texts of the NT.

Social-scientific criticism thus entails a self-conscious use of the social sciences and the utilization of conceptual models for the assessment and interpretation of the social features of the biblical writings and their respective matrices. Both Horrell (1999) and Malina (2001) advocated the use of cross-cultural models, methods, and theories derived from cultural anthropology and ethnographical studies in which explicit interpretive frameworks are provided that enable readers to understand the world in which the texts of the NT were written. The goal is to offer models of social phenomena, which operate as interpretive frameworks that help modern readers become more knowledgeable about the ancient Mediterranean world.

Social-Scientific Models. Because the NT is anchored in the institutions and values of ancient Mediterranean society, an awareness of, and sensitivity to, those institutions and values is basic for our understanding of the texts. The following brief introduction to some of these ancient Mediterranean institutions and values will, of necessity, be selective but illustrative of the importance of these models in helping us to decipher the social world inhabited by Jesus and Paul. The selection discusses social institutions such as kinship and family, clientage, brokerage, and benefaction, and the core social values of honor and shame and the evil eye.

Kinship, Family, and Marriage.

> Teacher, Moses wrote for us that "if a man's brother dies, leaving a wife but no child, the man shall marry the widow and raise up children for his brother. There were seven brothers; the first married and, when he died, left no children; and the second married her and died, leaving no children; and the third likewise; none of the seven left children. Last of all the woman herself died. In the resurrection whose wife will she be? For the seven had married her." (Mark 12:19–23)

The question posed by the Sadducees of Jesus has no correlate with modern experience. The question assumed a type of marriage in which a brother was obligated to marry his brother's widow. Strong kinship structures and endogamous marriage (marriage between close kinship or clan members) rules determined the practice. Kinship was a prevailing type of social organization in ancient Mediterranean societies and an integral part of three other foundational social domains: politics, economics, and religion. Within the social organization of kinship, the family was an association of persons related by blood, marriage, patronage, and other contractual obligations. The family was structured for the purposes of enhancing the reputation of the family and the legitimate transfer of property. Property was kept in the family for generations. The primary means of accomplishing these goals were marriage and the raising of children. Boys and girls were socialized along specific gender expectations: boys were socialized to preserve family property, protect the women, and produce sons; girls, to contract good marriages to enhance the status of the family, maintain good alliances between two families, and produce sons. As such, social organization was patriarchal, organized according to the male line, and at marriage the couple took up residence either in the home of the husband's family (patrilocal) or in a newly established one (neolocal) while still retaining ties with the husband's family. Kinship groups tended to retain the custom of marrying, at least preferably and allowable by law, within the limits of a clan or tribe. Marriage was therefore a legal contract between two closely linked families for the production of legitimate offspring, for the preservation and transfer of family property, and for the protection and advancement publically of the reputation of each. In such a system, divorce was the dissolution of the relationship between the two families and the severance of property agreements.

Modern views of family, love, marriage, husband and wife, children, and a happy life-ever-after, therefore, do not accord well with ancient views of love, marriage, husband, wife, family, and children, Moreover, because Greek and Latin vocabulary concerning family, household, and kinship tend to overlap, they extend beyond common modern perceptions of family. While the Greek term *oikia/oikos* (house) and the Latin term *domus* (house) at times refer to a dwelling, residence, or house, most often they refer to a constellation of interrelated factors that make up a house, such as a household's property in which is included material goods, slaves, and extended kinship relationships. In some localities house, family, and fields are mentioned underlining the connection between the house and subsistence—families were both producing and consuming units. The stress on property possessions in this broader sense is often missed by modern readers when they conceptualize the constituent elements of the ancient family from a modern perspective. The house was also a place of privacy for women as well as a place of retreat for men. Protecting the private space and security of the house was important and related to the status of the family.

The notion of family is also closely tied to household management (*oikonomia*) so clearly expressed in Colossians 3:18—4:1. Here wives, husbands, parents, children, slaves, masters, and co-workers are addressed. These ancient household management codes reflect the traditional stance of the head of the house and of the slaveholder. The Latin term *familia* (family) refers to more than simply the basic family group consisting typically of father, mother, and their dependent children, and instead refers to the authority of the male head of the household (*paterfamilias*). All household possessions come under his jurisdiction and legal power (*patria potestas*). It is worth noting that the term is sometimes retained in legal discussions concerning household headship and control of property in cases where the property owner is a female. Even though there was considerable diversity of families in the Roman world that differed from one locality and city to another, the family had obligations to raise, feed, cloth, socialize, educate, marry, care for the ill, and bury the dead. The health-care system was limited so when illness struck, the family took care of its extended membership group.

Rhetorically, an established, well-run household signaled a unified and an efficiently run city. If these obligations were the glue that kept both family bonds and city organization cemented, how surprising it must have been for an audience to hear Mark record that Jesus's mother, brothers, and sisters were standing outside waiting and calling for him. Jesus, however, did not respond. A crowd informed him that "Your mother and your brothers and sisters are outside, asking for you." Jesus replies, "Who are my mother and my brothers?" (Mark 3:32–35). A fitting cultural model of family relationships in antiquity would help to make sense of this incident. It appears to fly in the face of Roman perspectives of the stable household as an indispensable unit of a stable society—good management within the household corresponded with good management of the city. The father's effective rule over the house was analogous to good leadership in society. Yet, in this incident, Mark records Jesus impudently dismissing a basic building block foundational to ancient cities.

Brokerage, Patronage, and Clientage.

According to the grace [favor/beneficence] of God given to me, like a skilled master builder I laid a foundation, and someone else is building on it. Each builder must choose with care how to build on it. (1 Cor 3:10)

For by the grace [favor/beneficence] given to me I say to everyone among you not to think of yourself more highly than you ought to think, but to think with sober judgment, each according to the measure of faith that God has assigned. (Rom 12:3)

Patronage at its heart worked within a stratified social system by providing goods, services, favors, land, food, and gifts between elites and persons of unequal social status in exchange for labor and honors. In this system of exchange, brokers occupied an important spot—a broker must possess the skills to bridge the different social levels, cultures, or localities, and thus must have significantly enough power to convince either patron or client to engage in a particular kind of exchange that might be of benefit to both of them—even when the benefits were dissimilar.

The system was pervasive and touched ancient religious structures and sensibilities. Gods and goddesses were perceived as patrons; followers, believers, and worshippers were their clients. Priests, priestesses, and other religious officials functioned as brokers. They mediated the favors of the deities in exchange for human acts of piety, praises, and prayers. The NT portrayed Jesus regarding his father in heaven as a patron and as his broker providing the good gifts of his father in exchange for the loyalty and honor of his followers. Moreover, Greco-Roman women, Jewish women, and early Christian women operated in this world as patrons and benefactors.

An interesting example of the difference an appropriate cultural model makes in the interpretive process is to look at Paul's conversion experience not from the psychologized, individualized perspectives of the Western, modern world but from the Mediterranean institutions of patronage and clientage. Crook (2004) has argued that Paul's conversion must be situated in the extensively diffused practice of patronage and benefaction (generous action or benefit) between humans that was in step with the equally pervasive awareness of patronage and benefactions between humans and their gods. Patronage defined a concrete relationship clearly marked by an exchange of goods and reciprocity between two, or more, unequal parties. Paul regarded his god as a patron who appeared to him and issued a call to him with the expectation that he respond appropriately and in kind—namely, that he refocus his energies on the mission to the gentiles. Paul's conversion in the context of a patron/client system did mean a turn in direction but generally not the type expected by modern readers. His was a reciprocal response to honor the appearance and call of his patron deity by taking up the mission to the gentiles. By locating patronage and clientage in the ancient model of exchange, Crook convincingly demonstrates that Paul, as a recipient of patronage from his deity, was under obligation to return loyalty and honor to the deity.

Honor and Shame.

Athenians excel all others not so much in singing or in stature or in strength, as in love of honor, which is the strongest incentive to deeds of honor and renown. (Xenophon, *Memorabilia* 3.3.13)

Blessed are you who are poor, for yours is the kingdom of God. Blessed are you who are hungry now, for you will be filled. Blessed are you who weep now, for you will laugh. Blessed are you when people hate you, and when they exclude you, revile you, and defame you on account of the Son of Man. (Luke 6:20–22)

Honor stood at the root of human motivation and human institutions. It was a value for which both men and women strove intensely whether aristocrat or slave or everyone else in between—even children. Cicero, noting children at play writes:

With what earnestness they pursue their rivalries. How fierce their contests. What exaltation they feel when they win, and what shame when they are beaten. How they dislike reproach. How they yearn

> for praise. What labours will they not undertake to stand first among their peers. How well they remember those who have shown them kindness and how eager to repay. (*De finibus* 5.22.61)

While honor and what counted for it varied in standards in different courts of reputation where honor was doled out, it all boiled down to garnering the recognition, fame, praise, respect, influence, and renown from those that counted. Women in their courts of prestige sought, gained, and lost it; men in their courts of reputation similarly gained or lost it on the judgment of their peers; slaves in their courts of slavedom were subjected to the relentless and ruthless weighing of honor. Indeed, slaves, tenant farmers, village artisans, the unclean and degraded, and expendables suffered the double disgrace of being the lowest of low in society in terms of honor status and the limited social interaction that it intimated. Pliny the Younger deems "that [the] man happiest of all [is] who enjoys the anticipation of a good and abiding fame, and who, assured of posterity's judgment, lives now in possession of the glory that he will then have (Pliny, *Ep.* 9.3, "*fama . . . gloria*"). Seneca noted that honor was based on the favorable opinion of respectable persons publically given. A person's honor was a public verdict of her good standing and personal qualities. Indeed, observed Dio Chrysostom (ca. 40–120 C.E.), scarcely a person could be found out of a multitude to do what was deemed noble for himself unless it were mediated through the public recognition and approval process of others. Weighing that honor was an unceasing process: generals and soldiers waged war for it; persons of influence schemed for it; philosophers argued philosophically for it; teachers sought for it; orators spoke for it; gospel writers presented Jesus in light of it; Paul grasped for it. Honor was never an assured attribute given that it could be gained or lost at moment's notice as courts of reputation passed out their judgments at their whim. It is clear from the experience of Paul in Corinth that the Corinthian congregation had passed along to him an unfavorable verdict of his honor standing in their community.

Honor was either ascribed or achieved. Ascribed honor included high birth, illustrious hometown, wealth (preferably not gained by an insatiable lust), grand house, legal status, and expensive clothes, proper education, accent, words, posture, and bearing. Those of ascribed honor never needed to ask about genealogies to realize their place on the honor map—all it took was a glance. Given that Jesus was an unknown with no honor credentials, it helps to explain why Matthew and Luke took extraordinary pains to locate Jesus on an honor map stemming from David, Abraham, and Adam. Achieved honor included prowess at athletic, military, and healing events. Jesus's reputation as a healer and exorcist climbed exponentially as rumors of his success spread. Acts of benefaction that brought with them acclaim were concretely signaled as deserving special recognition in the award of special seats at public events, construction of statues, contagious spread of successes in healings and exorcisms, and honorable placement at meals and assemblies. James appears to have in mind a system of favoritism where someone finely attired is given the best seat in the house and someone grubbily attired is offered no such honor.

> For if a person with gold rings and in fine clothes comes into your assembly, and if a poor person in dirty clothes also comes in, and if you take notice of the one wearing the fine clothes and say, "Have a seat here, please," while to the one who is poor you say, "Stand there," or, "Sit at my feet," have you not made distinctions among yourselves, and become judges with evil thoughts? (Jas 2:2–3)

Mark 6:1–6 records that Jesus's family background, education, and source of teachings are being questioned by a crowd. Notice that the evaluation is taking place in his hometown—a serious honor challenge coming from those who apparently knew him but were nevertheless suspicious of his credentials. Their gaze probed Jesus—whether anything great or unbelievable had occurred especially if he had divine origin; whether his family of origin was laudable (Mark 6:1–3); whether his birth circumstances matched the works he performed

(Mark 6:3); whether he had been educated, trained, and morally constituted to give legitimacy to his teaching (Mark 6: 2). Surely the estimation of a lowly occupation (Mark 6:3) and the questionable circumstances of Jesus's birth—that he was the son of Mary (Mark 6:3)—were intended to be malicious and offensive. The opinion community of those who interacted with Jesus were sceptical of his credentials and passed their verdict on him—acting as the public court of prestige in Jesus's hometown, they disbursed honor or shame as they saw fit. These examples are testament to the pervasive intensity of honor exchanges.

Evil-Eye Belief System.

> You foolish Galatians! Who has bewitched you? It was before your eyes that Jesus Christ was publicly exhibited as crucified! (Gal 3:1)

> But if your eye is unhealthy, your whole body will be full of darkness. If then the light in you is darkness, how great is the darkness! (Matt 6:23)

The eye was a powerful organ in the ancient world because from it emitted the most injurious of all evils—envy. Not surprisingly, therefore, evil-eye beliefs enter into the letters of Paul and the Gospels. References to the evil eye, however, are rarely understood and often mistranslated. The evil-eye belief system was an integral feature both of honor- and shame-based cultures and also of the competitive interactions of such cultures. Even to this day, the evil eye embodies an ancient and widespread belief throughout the circum-Mediterranean world. It is known by other names such as "the Salty," "the wounded eye," "the bad eye," "the look," "the glare," and the "murderous glance" (Nanos 2003). The evil eye was thought to threaten persons and things upon which it fell. It was a destructive gaze, intentional or unintentional, which was feared and from which one sought protection. Precautions included avoiding the direct gaze of others, hiding women, children, and prized possessions, denying recent good turns of fortune, spitting in the presence of those thought to have an evil eye, and wearing protective amulets. Why? The gaze of the evil eye harmed health, productivity, and fortune. Children, beautiful things, people, women who were pregnant, those engaged in rites of passage (birth, marriage, and transformation), and animals were especially vulnerable. Neighbors, relatives, those with ocular impairments, those with physical deformities, those who were socially displaced, and strangers and enemies were potentially possessors of the evil eye. John Elliott (1990) made the interesting observation that Paul in Galatians was countering a suspicion that he himself was an evil eye possessor.

The central emotion associated with the evil eye was that of envy. Plutarch remarks that

> Envy (*phthonos*), which naturally takes root more deeply in the mind than any other passion, also contaminates the body with evil. When those possessed by envy to this degree let their glance fall upon a person, their eyes (*opseis*), which are close to the mind and draw from it the evil influence of the passion, then assail that person as if with poisoned arrows; hence, I conclude, it is not paradoxical or incredible that they should have an effect on the persons who encounter their gaze. (*Table Talk* 681F-82)

The eye, therefore, was the portal through which envy was transferred, and the evil eye worked through envy to contaminate the whole body. The eye was the gateway to the inner state of a person and exposed a person's heart filled perhaps with envy, greed, stinginess, and malice toward another's sudden good fortune, health, and social standing. Envy was the grief and pain triggered at the sight of persons or groups enjoying valued goods and services regardless of one's own possession of the same goods and services. The envious gaze falling upon someone was rife with deadly consequences and was to be avoided at all cost. Strategies for deflecting a harmful gaze were many and varied. It might involve engaging in acts of generosity and of not begrudging the good fortune of another. Personal protective methods included concealing prized possessions, denying unexpected changes in fortune, avoiding eye contact, wearing amulets inscribed with anti–evil-eye symbols, and carrying small pouches of rue and garlic. Entrances to houses and public places were protected with plaques inscribed with anti–evil-eye incantations, mosaics, masks, and large statues of the phallus and testicles. It was thought that they would deflect or distract the eye before its evil intent landed on someone.

When Paul burst out in exasperation that the problems within the community had been precipitated by the malignant power of the evil eye, he was leveling a serious accusation against the community. Perhaps his accusation was to counter the community's expression of strong disapprobation, namely, that he himself possessed an evil eye. Although the evil eye was a significant, prevalent belief in Paul's world and in the wider Mediterranean, modern readers usually have no knowledge of the salient features of the evil-eye belief system and would, therefore, not understand Paul's outburst. Having the belief system in hand opens a new perspective for modern readers to reevaluate their comprehension of Paul's letter.

Relevance of a Social-Scientific Approach in the Modern World. The NT documents speak from particular social worlds. Knowledge of the social institutions and values and attitudes of the ancient Mediterranean world are essential to translating and interpreting the NT. The ability to penetrate the ordinary and everyday meaning systems of the original composers and their audiences requires an intimate awareness of the connection between language and the social values that made up their social worlds. Social-scientific approaches to the NT provide modern readers with the appropriate social and cultural lenses with which to interrogate its texts. The approach helps them to see the cultural gap and build a bridge to cross over it.

[*See also:* Cultural Anthropology, *subentry* New Testament; Form Criticism, *subentry* New Testament; Historical Criticism, *subentry* New Testament; *and* Social Sciences, *subentry* Hebrew Bible.]

BIBLIOGRAPHY

Barnes, Tatum W. *Jesus at the Movies: A Guide to the First One Hundred Years.* Santa Rosa, Calif.: Poleridge Press, 2004. A detailed and useful study of thirteen major Jesus films that exemplify the problems of not taking seriously enough the social milieu of Jesus.

Craffert, Pieter. *The Life of a Galilean Shaman: Jesus of Nazareth in Anthropological-Historical Perspective.* Eugene, Ore.: Cascade, 2008. Uses the model of "the shaman" as a cross-cultural social personage to try to account for the data we have about Jesus performing miracles, casting out demons, teaching, and experiencing altered states of consciousness.

Crook, Zeba. *Reconceptualising Conversion: Patronage, Loyalty, and Conversion in the Religions of the Ancient Mediterranean.* Berlin: Walter de Gruyter, 2004. A thoroughgoing reassessment of Paul's conversion experience from the perspective of patron/client relationships. Functions as an excellent corrective to cast Paul's conversion in the emotional terms of modern psychology.

Elliott, John H. "Paul, Galatians, and the Evil Eye." *Currents in Theology and Mission* 17 (1990): 262–273. Examines "envy." Ancients regarded envy as the most grievous of all evils especially when expressed in the evil-eye belief system.

Elliott, John H. *What is Social-Scientific Criticism?* Minneapolis: Fortress, 1993. An excellent foundational introduction to social-scientific criticism.

Esler, Philip Francis. *The First Christians in Their Social Worlds: Social-Scientific Approaches to New Testament Interpretation.* London: Routledge, 1994. Investigates the degree to which the NT documents are deeply lodged in particular social worlds and which must be investigated with the tools provided by the social sciences.

Gager, John. *Kingdom and Community: The Social World of Early Christianity.* Englewood Cliffs, N.J.: Prentice-Hall, 1975. An early interdisciplinary study of the religion and the social world of early Christians, drawing particularly on the works of the sociologists Peter L. Berger and Thomas Luckmann.

Horrell, David G. *Social-Scientific Approaches to New Testament Interpretation.* Edinburgh: T&T Clark, 1999. Gathers together a number of the classic, early essays in the field representing the variety of work created in the last twenty-five years in NT studies.

Judge, A. E. *Social Distinctive of the Christians in the First Century: Pivotal Essays.* Edited by D. W. Scholer. Peabody, Mass.: Hendrickson, 2008. Dr. Judge's essays stress the importance of social-science criticism of the Bible for reading early Jesus-group documents and reigniting interest in paying careful attention to the Ancient Mediterranean social and cultural values within which the NT was written.

Lawrence, Louise Joy. *Reading with Anthropology: Exhibiting Aspects of New Testament Religion.* Carlisle, UK: Paternoster, 2005. Brings to bear the social science of anthropology to cast new light on understanding the texts of the NT.

Malina, Bruce J. "The Social Sciences and Biblical Interpretation." *Interpretation* 36 (1982): 229–242. Noting the inadequacies of the social description approach, this article calls for social-scientific models that are area specific (e.g., honor/shame; healing) and capable of cross-cultural comparison and explanation.

Malina, Bruce J. *The New Testament: Insights from Cultural Anthropology.* Louisville, Ky.: Westminster/John Knox, 2001. Excellent study of the values of limited good, envy, honor, first-century personality, clean and unclean, fundamental to understanding the social world of the NT.

Meeks, Wayne. *The First Urban Christians: The Social World of Apostle Paul.* New Haven, Conn.: Yale University Press, 1983. A definitive work that explicates the social world of Paul and the ecology of his communities from the perspective of sociological analysis of the Roman urban environment.

Moore, Christopher. *Lamb: The Gospel According to Biff, Christ's Childhood Pal.* New York: HarperCollins, 2002. A novel that retells the story of Jesus's early childhood from the perspective of his best friend Biff.

Nanos, Mark D. "The Social Context and Message of Galatians in View of Paul's Evil Eye Warning (Gal 3:1)." Web-based article from 2003 at http://www.marknanos.com/EvilEyeWarning-6-20-03.pdf. A complete analysis of the evil-eye belief system in the ancient Mediterranean world.

Neufeld, Dietmar. *The Social Sciences and Biblical Translation.* Leiden, Netherlands: Brill, 2008. A series of essays designed to demonstrate the importance of a social-scientific approach to NT translation and interpretation.

Neufeld, Dietmar. *Understanding the Social World of the New Testament.* London: Routledge, 2010. Examines the cultural values of collectivism, kinship, gender, memory, ethnicity, healing, ancient economies, altered states of consciousness, purity, ritual, and social stratification with a view to grasping the meaning of the NT in which these cultural values are evident.

Neyrey, Jerome H. "God, Benefactor and Patron: The Major Cultural Model for Interpreting the Deity in Greco-Roman Antiquity." *Journal for the Study of the New Testament* 27/4 (2005): 465–492. Typical titles of God-as-benefactor are studied from the perspectives of exchange, power, knowledge, and material benefaction. It employs the cultural model of benefactor/client relations.

Neyrey, Jerome H., and Eric C. Stewart. *The Social World of the New Testament. Insights and Models.* Peabody, Mass.: Hendrickson, 2008. An overview of social-scientific models of greatest utility to elucidating the central aspects of the ancient cultural system and the NT.

Oakman, Douglas E. "The Ancient Economy in the Bible." *Biblical Theology Bulletin* 21 (1991): 34–39. Modern economic systems are radically different from ancient ones. Taxes, tolls, systems of exchange, social stratification, and the elements of a peasant economy are examined. Tax collectors are despised yet also pictured as part of the Jesus movement.

Osiek, Carolyn. *What Are They Saying about the Social Setting of the New Testament?* 2d. ed. New York: Paulist Press, 1992. A revised and expanded edition (1984) that summarizes the application of social-scientific theory to NT texts while also noting the grave problems that some have voiced of applying social-scientific models to the study of the NT.

Osiek, Carolyn, and M. Y. MacDonald, with J. H. Tulloch. *A Women's Place: House Churches in Earliest Christianity.* Minneapolis: Augsburg, 2006. A number of issues of women's daily lives are investigated, including the lives of wives, widows, women with children, female slaves, women as patrons, household leaders, and teachers. Moreover, central themes such as hospitality, dining practices, and female segregation also receive attention.

Reinhartz, Adele. *Jesus of Hollywood.* Oxford: Oxford University Press, 1998.

Rohrbaugh, Richard. "Foreignizing Translation." In *The Social Sciences and Biblical Translation,* edited by Dietmar Neufeld, 11–24. Leiden, the Netherlands: Brill, 2008. Entering the world of the NT is like entering a foreign country in which customs, cognitive habits, ways of speech, and attitudes and values are drastically different from the one familiar to readers.

Stewart, Eric C. "Social Stratification and Patronage in Ancient Mediterranean Societies." In *Understanding the Social World of the New Testament,* 156–166. edited by Dietmar Neufeld and Richard E. DeMaris. London: Routledge, 2010. Profitably analyzes a number of NT passages from the model of patronage and clientage.

Theissen, G. "Itinerant Radicalism: The Tradition of Jesus' Sayings from the Perspective of the Sociology of Literature." *Radical Religion* 2 (1975): 84–93. Originally published in German, *Zeitschrift für Theologie and Kirche* 70 (1973): 245–271. Taking the perspective of a social history approach, this informative essay proposes that the earliest Christian charismatics continued the preaching and wandering lifestyle of Jesus.

Dietmar Neufeld

Socio-rhetorical Criticism

Socio-rhetorical criticism is an interpretive analytic that uses rhetorical analysis and social and cognitive sciences to advance literary, historical, social, cultural, ideological, and religious interpretation in the twenty-first century. It began as a self-consciously constructed program of textual interpretation of the Bible during the 1970s and became established during the 1990s with specific relation to rhetorical and social-scientific criticism. During the first two decades of the twenty-first century it has used mental conceptions of space, called critical spatiality theory, and mind-brain theory about blending and integration of information, called conceptual integration/blending theory, to create a new mode of commentary. Socio-rhetorical commentary in this mode, which the proponents call a rhetoric of religious antiquity mode, begins with pictures that the text creates in the mind, which proponents call rhetography, continues with textural analysis focused on argumentation, which proponents call rhetology, and concludes with a description of the rhetorical force of emerging discourses that result from interaction between the rhetography and the rhetology (Robbins 2007, 2008, 2009b; Jeal 2008).

A Heuristic Interpretive Analytic. Socio-rhetorical criticism is a heuristic interpretive analytic. This means the interpreter creates taxonomies for the purpose of "finding" phenomena in contexts of ever newly emerging structures. These taxonomies are an intentional strategy for moving away from and beyond dualities, which regularly dominate literary-historical approaches and limit the ability of the interpreter to discern and interpret multiple nuances and meanings in texts. The strategy of finding new phenomena creates an interpretive environment where the taxonomies continually evolve and are reconfigured in relation to new phenomena that become present to the interpreters' perceptions. An overall goal and strategy, therefore, is to move beyond nineteenth and twentieth century "methods" where scientists purify their analysis by taking phenomena out of their living context into laboratories that recontextualize the data in a limited environment controlled by the scientific observer. Instead of a laboratory approach, socio-rhetorical interpretation strives to keep the data in the context of its home environment, where the data is related to an unlimited amount of other data in the world. Since this home environment is always in a status of moving and emerging, the interpreter seeks to interpret the emergent structures and processes at work among the data. This means that the strategies of analysis and interpretation themselves continually evolve in what proponents call an interpretive-analytic approach.

Using an interpretive-analytic approach, the socio-rhetorical interpreter continually seeks to find and understand emergent structures in contexts where phenomena functioned in the past and continue to function in the present in historical, social, cultural, ideological, and religious cognition. One of the special strategies that keeps the interpretive-analytic energy of the approach continually alive is the creation of new taxonomies that assure movement beyond binary modes of interpretation that instinctively create oppositional impulses that restrain the cognitive possibilities. A primary feature of this taxonomy construction lies in the inclusion of the body as fully as the mind in the conceptuality. Intentionally moving beyond a body-mind dualism, socio-rhetorical interpreters create taxonomies that introduce networks of embodied cognition, namely alternative modes of perception and conception based on interaction among various systems within the body and the mind including people's emotions, sensory-perceptions, instincts, and preferences. These taxonomies point an interpreter toward multiple, alternative emergent structures in literary, artifactual, historical, social, cultural, ideological, philosophical, political, religious, and theological phenomena.

Emergence in Biblical Interpretation. Vernon Robbins introduced the term "socio-rhetorical" into biblical interpretation in 1984 in *Jesus the Teacher* to describe a merger of insights from Kenneth Burke and Clifford Geertz to approach a text much like an anthropologist reads a village and its culture. The first sustained socio-rhetorical study appeared in 1975 showing the relation of the we-passages in Acts to ancient Mediterranean sea voyages (2010b). This study "revealed that traveling in a boat on the sea with other people created a social environment that made it natural for some authors in antiquity to use first-person plural "we" for literary accounts of sea voyages" (1992, p. xix). Subsequent study of social environments of teaching and learning in the Mediterranean world brought insights from the *Progymnasmata*, elementary Greek textbooks of prose composition and rhetoric, into socio-rhetorical interpretation (Robbins 1993). Instead of limiting itself to higher-level oratorical Greco-Roman rhetoric that emerged out of the Greek city-states, socio-rhetorical criticism uses lower-level progymnastic rhetoric as a beginning place for describing procedures of composition and argumentation in the religious literature of Mediterranean antiquity. This means that instead of limiting itself to the three primary locations of oratorical argumentation in the Greek city state—namely judicial rhetoric in the courtroom, deliberative rhetoric in the political assembly, and epideictic rhetoric in the civil ceremony—socio-rhetorical criticism uses all the strategies of expansion, abbreviation, elaboration, and enthymematic argumentation in thematic and narrative composition available in the *Progymnasmata* textbooks in addition to insights in the other well-known rhetorical handbooks available from Mediterranean antiquity. This broader rhetorical approach provides the interpreter with tools to describe the rhetorical nature and force not only of literary writings related to a wide variety of settings of human activity but also of material culture that includes artistic, architectural, and numismatic phenomena.

Tapestry and Textures. During the 1990s, social-scientific criticism became an internal part of socio-rhetorical interpretation with an initial focus on the social location of the implied author of Luke-Acts and the relation of social-scientific criticism to literary studies This led to a programmatic socio-rhetorical approach to texts guided by the metaphor of "tapestry" to describe the interwoven webs of signification in a text and the metaphor of "textures" to describe different literary, social, cultural, ideological, and religious dimensions of texts.

In this context Robbins created a heuristic taxonomy of five textures of a text (Robbins 1996a, 1996b): (1) inner; (2) inter-; (3) social-cultural; (4) ideological; and (5) sacred texture. In turn, each of these textures contains sub-textures:

1. Inner texture, which focuses on patterns of words in a text, contains six subtextures: repetitive; progressive; narrational; opening-middle-closing; argumentative; and sensory-aesthetic.
2. Intertexture, which refers to a text's representation of, reference to, and use of phenomena in the "world" outside the text being interpreted, contains four subtextures: oral-scribal; cultural; social; historical.
3. Social-cultural texture, which focuses on the social and cultural "location" of the language in the text and the social and cultural world the language evokes or creates, contains three subtextures: specific social topics; common social and cultural topics; and final cultural categories, which create dominant culture, subcultures, countercultures, contracultures, and liminal cultures.
4. Ideological texture, which focuses on the social, cultural, and individual location and perspective of writers and readers, contains four subtextures: individual locations; relation to groups; modes of intellectual discourse; spheres of ideology.
5. Sacred texture (1996b, pp. 120–131), which focuses on the relation between human life and the divine, contains eight subtextures: deity; holy person; spirit being; divine history; human redemption; human commitment; religious community; and ethics.

A *Topos* Approach. As a heuristic interpretive analytic, socio-rhetorical interpretation finds emergent structures through interpretation of "*topoi*" (sg. *topos*), which are locations of thought in historical, social, cultural, ideological, aesthetic, and religious networks of meanings and significations (Robbins 2009b, pp. 81–85). *Topoi* are embedded in all human cognition, in contrast to "themes," which are located in more restrained literary, musical, or artistic contexts. A *topos* has two dimensions: its rhetography, namely the descriptive, image, picturing, narrative-building dimension; and its rhetology, namely the enthymematic, argumentative, syllogistic dimension (Robbins 2008; 2009b, pp. 5–88). Robbins introduced an initial interpretation of the *topos* of forgiving in Luke—based on interaction among humans and between humans and God—and the *topos* of giving—which includes asking, friendship, hospitality, and receiving—in Jesus's elaboration of the Lord's Prayer in Luke 11:5–13 (Robbins 1998). The rhetography, which includes the picture of a man visiting a neighbor to ask for a loaf of bread during the night and a father giving his child a snake when he asks for a fish, interacts with syllogistic rhetology based on friendship, hospitality, and exceptionally generous patronage to explain the nature of petition and God's graciousness in the Lord's Prayer.

Rhetorolects. As socio-rhetorical analysis and interpretation was being applied to biblical and early Christian discourse, a taxonomy of argumentative modes began to appear which Robbins named "rhetorolects" (contraction for rhetorical dialect). By 2004, six rhetorolects emerged with the names of wisdom, prophetic, apocalyptic, precreation, priestly, and miracle. Guided by insights from critical spatiality theory and conceptual blending/integration theory, Robbins exhibited how each rhetorolect contains interaction among firstspace, secondspace, and thirdspace (Robbins 2009b, pp. 104–120). Firstspace is experienced social, cultural, and physical realia; secondspace is visualization, conceptualization, and imagination of God's world; and thirdspace is ongoing bodily effects and enactments in the lived space of religious life. Interaction and blending among these three create the ongoing context of alternatively perceived worlds in which people live on a daily basis.

Wisdom discourse emerged as the most commonly analyzed and interpreted rhetorical mode in the field of New Testament studies. Wisdom rhetorolect is a localization of Mediterranean moral philosophy. It interprets the visible world by blending human experiences of the household, one's intersubjective body, and the geophysical world (firstspace) with the cultural space of God's cosmos (secondspace). In the lived space of blending (thirdspace), people establish identities in relation to God, who functions as heavenly Father over God's children in the world. People perceive their bodies as able to produce goodness and righteousness in the world through the medium of God's wisdom. Metaphorically, this activity is understood as "fruitfulness" (productivity and reproductivity) in the realm of God's created world (Robbins 2009b, pp. xxix–xxx, 121–218).

Prophetic rhetorolect is a localization of Mediterranean oracular mantic (divine communication) discourse. First century Christian prophetic belief blends experiences in a kingdom that has political boundaries on earth (firstspace) with God's cosmos (secondspace), with the presupposition that God transmits God's will into the speech and action of a prophet through a divine message from God to the prophet. The prophet speaks and acts in contexts that envision righteous judgments and actions by kings, who should be God's leaders who establish justice on the earth. As a result of the nature of God's message, the prophet regularly experiences significant resistance, and often explicit rejection and persecution. In the space of blending (thirdspace), people who perceive themselves, or are perceived by others, to be sent as prophets confront religious and political leaders who act on the basis of human greed, pride, and power rather than God's justice, righteousness, and mercy for all people in God's kingdom on the earth (Robbins 2009b, pp. xxvii, 219–328).

Apocalyptic rhetorolect is a localization of Mediterranean visual mantic (divine communication) discourse. Apocalyptic rhetorolect blends human experiences of the emperor and his imperial army (firstspace) with God's heavenly temple city (secondspace), which can only be occupied by holy, undefiled people. In the space of blending, God functions like a heavenly emperor who gives commands to emissaries to destroy all evil in the universe and create a cosmic environment of peace and salvation. A primary goal of the blending is to call people into action and thought guided by perfect holiness (thirdspace). Apocalyptic redemption, therefore, means the presence of all of God's holy beings in a realm where God's holiness and righteousness are completely and eternally present (Robbins 2009b, pp. xxi, 329–482).

Precreation rhetorolect is a localization of Mediterranean speculative philosophy. Precreation rhetorolect interprets the invisible, while wisdom rhetorolect (a localization of moral philosophy) interprets the visible world. Precreation rhetorolect blends human experiences of divine emperors (like Roman emperors) and their households, which people hear about but often do not see (firstspace) with God's cosmos (secondspace). One manifestation of this is a biblical story line in which God has an eternal, primordial status as a loving heavenly emperor with a household and community populated by loving people. The result of the blending is the presence of the loving Emperor Father God in God's heavenly household before all time and continually throughout God's non-time. God's Son existed with God before time began with the creation of the world. This eternal Son does what His Father asks him to do, and heirs and friends of the eternal emperor and his eternal son receive eternal benefits from their relation to this eternal household and community. In the space of blending (thirdspace) that "runs" this story line, people establish relationships with the love of God the eternal heavenly Emperor Father by believing, honoring, and worshipping not only God but also his eternal Son. In this belief system, God's light is embodied love that provides the possibility for entering into eternal love, rather than being limited to light in the form of wisdom that is the basis for the production and reproduction of goodness and righteousness. The goal of the blending in precreation belief is to guide people toward community that is formed through God's love, which reflects the eternal intimacy present in God's precreation household and community (Robbins 2009b, pp. xxv–xxvi; 2012a).

Priestly rhetorolect is a localization of Mediterranean sacrificial and mystery ritual discourse. First century Christian priestly belief blends human experiences in sacrificial and mystery temples (firstspace) with a concept of God's cosmos and temple city (secondspace). In the space of blending (thirdspace), people enact rituals that are perceived to activate special benefits for humans from God. Things like food, possessions, and money but also things like comfort and honor may be given up to God in ritual actions. Much early Christian priestly belief somehow relates to Jesus's giving of his life on the cross, but other dimensions of it relate to entering into the mysteries of God through prayer, blessing, singing, and praise. The goal of the conceptual blending is to create people who are willing to engage in complex ritual actions to receive special divine benefits that come to them, because these ritual actions are perceived to benefit God as well as humans (Robbins 2009b, p. xxvi).

Miracle rhetorolect is a localization of Mediterranean healing ritual discourse. First century Christian miracle rhetorolect has a primary focus on human bodies afflicted with paralysis, malfunction, or disease. In this context, a malfunctioning body becomes a site of social geography. Miracle belief features a bodily agent of God's power who renews and restores life, producing forms of new creation that oppose powers of affliction, disruption, and death. The location of importance for early Christian miracle belief, therefore, is a space of relation between an afflicted body and a bodily agent of God's power (firstspace). In this belief system, social, cultural, political, or religious places on earth are simply places where bodies may be. A bodily agent of God's power, wherever it may be, is a location where God can function as a miraculous renewer of life (secondspace). A major goal of miracle belief (thirdspace) is to effect extraordinary renewal within people that moves them toward speech and action that produces communities that care for the well-being of one another (Robbins 2009b, pp. xxiv–xxv).

Critical Spatiality and Conceptual Blending/Integration Theory. By 2007, the use of critical spatiality theory clarified that a rhetorolect is a cultural activation of a conceptual blend of firstspace experiences with secondspace imagination that function in people's thirdspace "running" of blends through story lines populated with personages, places, and interactions (Robbins 2007, pp. 184–192). By 2008, the use of conceptual integration/blending theory in concert with critical spatiality theory created the context for introducing the concept of "rhetography," the rhetoric of a text that evokes image-pictures, frames, and story lines in the mind (Robbins 2008; Jeal). In the context of interpreting the interaction of rhetography with "rhetology," the argumentative-enthymematic rhetoric of a text, by 2009, it became clear that rhetorolects are Idealized Cognitive Models (ICMs), which contain image-picture frames, argumentative-enthymematic structuring, metaphoric mappings, and metonymic mappings (Robbins 2009b, p. 104).

The most recent example of socio-rhetorical interpretation using conceptual blending/integration theory exists in Robert H. von Thaden's book-length interpretation of 1 Corinthians 6:12—7:7 (2012). Viewing Paul's discussion as early Christian didactic wisdom, von Thaden argues that rhetography, namely vivid images and pictures Paul creates with his discourse, shows the Corinthians why *porneia* is the worst of all possible bodily sins (6:12–20). Then rhetology, namely strong argumentation by Paul, offers the Corinthians three modes for how to avoid *porneia* (7:1–7): (1) take one another as husband and wife; (2) engage regularly in sexual activity; (3) if agreeable to both, abstain from sex with one another for a limited time for prayer. Paul energizes this didactic wisdom both with apocalyptic rhetorolect focused on the end of time and with priestly rhetorolect concerned with purity, holiness, and sacred space, which includes people's bodies.

Another example focuses on the Colossians hymn, using critical spatiality and conceptual blending theory to exhibit dynamic interaction among precreation, apocalyptic, and priestly rhetorolect in emerging Christianity (Robbins 2007). Beginning with an inchoate, precreation image-picture of Christ as "the image of the invisible God," the hymn continues with an image of "firstborn" birth that energizes a process whereby all things are created, visible and invisible, until "all things hold together" in Christ (Col 1:15–17). This precreation rhetorolect blends with apocalyptic rhetorolect when imagery of thrones, dominions, principalities, and powers merge with imagery of resurrection in "firstborn from the dead" (Col 1:16, 18). In the midst of the blending of precreation and apocalyptic rhetorolect, priestly rhetorolect emerges through the rhetography of "making peace through the blood of his cross" (Col 1:20). The rhetorical force of this sequence of emergent structures in first century Christianity was to blend an inchoate, invisible image of Christ as a principle of creation-energy before the world came into being not only with a vivid image of Christ as the life-giving energy force among all kinds of powers at the end of all things, but also as the actor who unleashed the inner processes of sacrificial action that bring benefits from God to humans and from humans to God in the form of peace among all things in the cosmos. The rhetorical force of the blending of these rhetorolects had such a powerful effect during the last quarter of first century of emerging Christianity that some interpreters imagine that all of its effects were implicit within the historical death and resurrection itself. The ongoing force of its rhetoric is evident in the Nicene-Cosmopolitan Creed that emerges in the fourth century C.E. (Robbins 2012), which has dominated much of Western Christianity to the present day. Once the image-picture and inner reasoning of the Colossians hymn becomes present in the mind of interpreters, it is difficult for some interpreters to entertain the possibility that this cognitive frame was not present in the innermost beginnings of Christianity itself.

A New Form of Commentary. Currently the Rhetoric of Religious Antiquity research group, with its primary home in the Society of Biblical Literature, is producing programmatic commentary on religious texts in Mediterranean antiquity that begins with a presentation of rhetography in a section of text, continues with textural analysis and interpretation of that section, and concludes with a presentation of the rhetorical force of the section as emergent discourse in Mediterranean antiquity. A preview of this approach appears in Robbins's interpretation of

2 Peter 1–11 at the end of an essay on socio-rhetorical interpretation that appeared in 2010 (Robbins 2010a, pp. 203–207). Beginning with prophetic rhetography of Peter as a servant and apostle communicating with people who have attained a righteousness before God of equal standing with Peter himself (1:1), the discourse blends priestly, miracle, wisdom, and apocalyptic rhetorolect that evokes an image of the hearers as members of God's kingdom on earth as recipients of priestly holiness, possessors of wisdom from God, participants in God's miraculous powers, and visionaries of God's eternal kingdom (2010a, p. 205). After this introduction to the rhetography of the passage, the task of the interpreter is to analyze the rich textural nature of the discourse, namely its inner, inter-, social-cultural, and ideological texture. This sequence of commentary then moves to an interpretation of the rhetorical force of this argumentation, which is grounded in vivid rhetography, in emerging Christianity in its context in the Roman Empire.

[*See also* Cultural Anthropology, *subentry* New Testament; Greco-Roman Context; *and* Social Sciences, *subentry* New Testament.]

BIBLIOGRAPHY

Bruehler, Bart B. *A Public and Political Christ: The Social-Spatial Characteristics of Luke 18:35–19:43 and the Gospel as a Whole in Its Ancient Context.* Princeton Theological Monograph Series 157. Eugene, Ore.: Pickwick, 2011. This book presents the first full-scale social-spatial analysis and interpretation of public, political, and private spheres in a section of the New Testament with a focus on the socio-rhetorical force of place (nature), meaning (and religion), and social relations.

Gowler, David B., L. Gregory Bloomquist, and Duane F. Watson, eds. *Fabrics of Discourse: Essays in Honor of Vernon K. Robbins.* New York: Trinity Press International, 2003. This book advances Robbins's discussion of ideological texture with essays by John S. Kloppenborg, David B. Gowler, L. Gregory Bloomquist, Charles A. Wanamaker, Russell B. Sisson, Wesley H. Wachob, and Willi Braun. In addition it contains essays by H. J. Bernard Combrink on Matthew 23; John H. Elliott on Household/Family in Mark; Jerome H. Neyrey on the social location of Paul; Dennis C. Duling on ethnicity and self-identification in Philippians 3; Duane F. Watson on 1 John; David A. deSilva on Miracle Discourse in Revelation; and Gordon D. Newby on apocalyptic discourse in the Qur'an.

Jeal, Roy R. "Blending Two Arts: Rhetorical Words, Rhetorical Pictures and Social Formation in the Letter to Philemon." *Sino-Christian Studies* 5 (2008): 9–38. Exploring the intersecting of language art and pictorial art, this essay first explains and blends Ezra Pound's concept of *phanopoeia*, the casting of images upon the visual imagination; Robbins's concept of rhetography, the rhetorical effect of image-pictures on the mind; and Aristotle's description of metaphors, which "set things before the eyes." Then the essay explores especially the rhetorical force of the images of Philemon as "more than a slave," a "beloved brother" in the letter.

Robbins, Vernon K. "Bodies and Politics in Luke 1–2 and Sirach 44–50: Men, Women, and Boys," *Scriptura* 90 (2005): 724–838. With a special focus on the nature of people's bodies, the essay explores the prophetic wisdom discourse in Luke 1–2 that correlates Zechariah's priestly body offering the incense offering in the temple with Elizabeth's priestly blessing of Mary in their priestly home when Zechariah is mute. Then the essay explores the relation of the picturesque presentation of the high priest in the temple in Sirach 50 with the presentation of Jesus in the temple in Luke 2.

Robbins, Vernon K. "Conceptual Blending and Early Christian Imagination." In *Explaining Christian Origins and Early Judaism: Contributions from Cognitive and Social Science*, edited by Petri Luomanen, Ilkka Pyysiäinen, and Risto Uro, 161–195. Biblical Interpretation Series 89. Leiden, the Netherlands: Brill, 2007. Focusing on critical spatiality in early Christian rhetorical dialects (rhetorolects), this essay explains the nature of the conceptual blending of firstspace, secondspace, and thirdspace in early Christian wisdom, prophetic, apocalyptic, precreation, miracle, and priestly rhetorolect. Then the essay presents an interpretation of conceptual blending in 2 Peter 1:5–11 and Colossians 1:15–20, ending with a discussion of frames and characters in early Christian miracle discourse.

Robbins, Vernon K. *Exploring the Texture of Texts: A Guide to Socio-Rhetorical Interpretation.* Harrisburg, Pa.: Trinity Press International, 1996b. This book introduces socio-rhetorical criticism to the general reader, displaying analysis and interpretation in inner texture, intertexture, social-cultural texture, ideological texture, sacred texture and their subtextures. Throughout, the book applies socio-rhetorical analysis and interpretation of each texture and subtexture to Mark 15, and contains study guides for interpreting Mark 10:17–22; Acts 2; the woman who anointed Jesus; John 9; the conversion of the Ethiopian eunuch in Acts 8; and the injunction for women to keep silent in 1 Corinthians and 1 Timothy.

Robbins, Vernon K. "From Enthymeme to Theology in Luke 11:1–13." In *Literary Studies in Luke-Acts: A Collection of Essays in Honor of Joseph B. Tyson*, edited by Richard P. Thompson and Thomas E. Phillips, 191–214. Macon, Ga. Mercer University Press, 1998. This essay presents socio-rhetorical analysis and interpretation of enthymemes in argumentation, showing that reasoning in enthymemes is based on social and cultural logic, rather than formal logic. Focusing on the *topoi* of "forgiving" and "giving" in the Lord's Prayer, the essay presents rule/case/result analysis of deductive, inductive, and abductive reasoning to interpret the meaning of forgiveness in Luke and the meaning of giving, which includes, asking, friendship, hospitality, and receiving, in Jesus's elaboration of the Lord's Prayer in Luke 11:5–13.

Robbins, Vernon K. *The Invention of Christian Discourse. Vol. 1.* Rhetoric of Religious Antiquity Series 1. Blandford Forum, UK: Deo, 2009b. This lengthy volume begins with socio-rhetorical interpretation of the Apostles' Creed, the Nicene-Constantinopolitan Creed, the Sayings of the Fathers (*Pirke Aboth*), Cleanthes' *Hymn to Zeus,* and a *Hymn to Isis* by Isidorus followed by chapters on social location and conceptual blending in early Christian story. These opening chapters set the stage for six lengthy chapters that analyze and interpret early Christian wisdom, prophetic, and apocalyptic rhetorolect (rhetorical dialect).

Robbins, Vernon K. *Jesus the Teacher: A Socio-Rhetorical Interpretation of Mark.* Minneapolis: Fortress Press, c1984; ex libris 2009 (2009a). The 2009 edition of this book, which introduced the term socio-rhetorical into modern textual approaches in 1984, begins with the thirty-five page introduction to the 1992 paperback edition supplemented with a five-page 2009 preface. The body of the book presents Robbins's use of rhetorical forms from Kenneth Burke, anthropological insights from Clifford Geertz, rhetorical theory of folklore from Roger Abrahams, cultural anthropological role theory from Roger Keesing, and social psychological role theory from Theodore Sarbin and Vernon Allen to analyze and interpret the Gospel of Mark in the context of the Mediterranean biblical and Greco-Roman teacher-disciple cycle of calling, instructing, and learning.

Robbins, Vernon K. "Precreation Discourse and the Nicene Creed: Christianity Finds its Voice in the Roman Empire," *Religion & Theology* 18 (2012): 1–17. Exploring the emergence of creedal statements in Christianity about non-time before creation, this essay presents analysis and interpretation of the baptismal creed called the Roman Symbol, the Apostles' Creed, and the Nicene-Cosmopolitan Creed. Additions in the last creed create a precreation story line that became the basis for a lengthy chain of argumentation about belief in the divinity of Christ and the Trinity.

Robbins, Vernon K. "Progymnastic Rhetorical Composition and Pre-Gospel Traditions: A New Approach." In *The Synoptic Gospels: Source Criticism and the New Literary Criticism*, edited by F. Focant, 111–147. Bibliotheca Ephemeridum Theologicarum Lovaniensium 110. Leuven, the Netherlands: Leuven University Press, 1993. Setting the analysis and interpretation in the context of rhetorical culture and rhetorical composition as it was guided by the *Progymnasmata,* this essay describes the exercise of recitation and presents the major discussions of rhetorical elaboration in the *Rhetorica ad Herennium* and Hermogenes's *Progymnasmata* to introduce a context for rhetorical analysis and interpretation of Jesus's teaching about clean and unclean in Mark 7:14–34; Jesus's teaching in parables in Mark 4; and various other passages in the Synoptic Gospels.

Robbins, Vernon K. "Rhetography: A New Way of Seeing the Familiar Text." In *Words Well Spoken: George Kennedy's Rhetoric of the New Testament,* edited by C. Clifton Black and Duane F. Watson, 81–106. Waco, Tex.: Baylor University Press, 2008. This essay builds on Kennedy's insights into enthymeme and radical rhetoric in New Testament literature by distinguishing between rhetography (persuasive cognitive picturing) and rhetology (persuasive argumentation). The essay explains how rhetography helps a person identify implicit analysis and interpretation of early Christian prophetic discourse of God's earthly kingdom, apocalyptic discourse of the imperial divine courtroom, miracle discourse of the body, wisdom discourse of the family household, precreation discourse of the imperial household, and priestly discourse of the sacrificial temple in Kennedy's *New Testament Interpretation through Rhetorical Criticism.*

Robbins, Vernon K. *Sea Voyages and Beyond: Emerging Strategies in Socio-Rhetorical Interpretation.* Emory Studies in Early Christianity 14. Blandford Forum, UK: Deo, 2010b. This book contains a forty-five page essay by David Gowler on the continuing maturation of socio-rhetorical criticism; the originally expanded version of Robbins's sea voyages essay; a thirty-two page response by Robbins to his critics of the essay and to those who built on insights in it; ten key essays published from 1985 to 2001 that contributed to the development of socio-rhetorical criticism; and a bibliography of Robbins's publications to 2010.

Robbins, Vernon K. "Socio-Rhetorical Interpretation." In *The Blackwell Companion to the New Testament*, edited by David E. Aune, 192–219. Oxford: Wiley-Blackwell, 2010a. This essay presents a detailed account of the emergence of socio-rhetorical criticism, including references to the wide range of scholars who have applied the approach to fields including apocryphal Christian literature, rabbinic literature, the Qur'an, medieval writings, religious traditions in South Africa, the Book of Mormon, and African American slave songs. The essay ends with a display of the format for socio-rhetorical commentary being written by members of the Rhetoric of Religious Antiquity Research Group, which has its institutional home in the Society of Biblical Literature.

Robbins, Vernon K. *The Tapestry of Early Christian Discourse: Rhetoric, Society and Ideology.* London: Routledge, 1996a. Using the metaphor of tapestry to describe the "different configurations, patterns and images" that create "multiple textures of meanings, convictions, beliefs, values, emotions and actions" in texts (18), an opening chapter describes how socio-rhetorical criticism, described as an interpretative analytics (11–13), redraws the boundaries of interpretation through a socio-rhetorical model of textual interpretation built on a rhetorical axis of communication and a mimetic axis of representation. Then it presents a detailed discussion of inner texture, intertexture, social-cultural texture, ideological texture and their subtextures, ending each chapter with socio-rhetorical analysis and interpretation of each texture and subtexture in 1 Corinthians 9.

Von Thaden, Robert. *Sex, Christ, and Embodied Cognition: Paul's Wisdom for Corinth.* Emory Studies in Early Christianity 16. Blandford Forum, UK: Deo, 2012. This book presents the first full-scale socio-rhetorical conceptual integration/blending analysis and interpretation of a section of the New Testament: 1 Corinthians 6:12—7:7.

Vernon K. Robbins

Source Criticism

Source criticism involves the use of indicators in a biblical text to reconstruct probable written sources embedded within that text. Traditionally, many scholars associate the word "source criticism" with the Documentary Hypothesis, which postulates that the Pentateuch (or the Hexateuch) was created out of the combination of four main sources, J (the Yahwist), E (the Elohist), D (the Deuteronomist) and P (the Priestly source). This hypothesis will be discussed in more detail later in this article. At the same time, it is important to note that biblical scholars also have used source-critical methods to attempt to reconstruct other written sources in the Hebrew Bible. For example, a number of indicators suggest that the books of Ezra–Nehemiah may have been created through the combination of some kind of Nehemiah Memoir with traditions about Ezra and/or the rebuilding of the temple. Research in prophetic literature has developed hypotheses about an early Isaiah memoir and other collections standing behind the book of Isaiah, different sources behind Jeremiah, and so on. Moreover, over the last forty years a number of scholars of the Pentateuch have begun to doubt the existence of J and E sources and instead argue for other kinds of written sources embedded in the Pentateuch. For example, building on earlier tradition-historical studies of oral "cycles" of traditions beyond parts of the Pentateuch, many Pentateuchal scholars now think that the Pentateuch originated as a set of short compositions focusing on different eras, such as a primeval history of creation and flood and/or a Jacob-Esau-Laban composition and/or an early Moses story. Such studies fall under the general rubric of biblical source criticism.

In all these cases, biblical source criticism is distinguished from similar study of the prehistory of the biblical text by its focus on reconstructing potential independent *written* pre-stages of texts. Thus tradition history, though sometimes encompassing the reconstruction of written sources (and redactional layers), is distinguished from source criticism by its inclusion of reconstruction of possible oral traditions or motifs standing behind biblical texts. To be sure, we now believe that most ancient literary writings were memorized and/or performed orally, so that all such writings were *both* oral and written in a sense. Moreover, it is important to note that performers of exclusively oral (thus non-written) traditions in oral-primary societies have (and probably had) excellent memories. Nevertheless, anthropological studies of the development of oral traditions have documented considerable fluidity in their transmission. When writing is *not* part of the medium of memorization, such oral traditions more easily evolve. Biblical source criticism investigates features in texts that are best explained as the result of the embedding in those texts of more fixed, written traditions, often written traditions combined with other written traditions.

Such sources were expanded and/or harmonized through additional written material added by later authors. This additional material is often called "redactional" or (more recently) "compositional" by scholars. Though source criticism has focused to some extent on how authors added material in the process of combining sources, most study of later layers of authorial expansion fall under the rubric of "redaction criticism." Thus where redaction criticism generally has focused on scribal/authorial *expansion* of existing texts, source criticism has focused on reconstructing the contours of such independent texts in the first place. Despite this difference, source and redaction criticism share a focus on the development of *written* texts, and as such they both fall in the broader category of older-style "literary criticism" (*Literarkritik* in the original German).

The yet broader rubric of "transmission history" or "tradition history" (broadly conceived) encompasses all of these methods: tradition-critical study of the oral dimensions of the development of biblical texts, source-critical attempts to reconstruct possible independent written sources in biblical texts, and redaction-critical reconstruction of written extensions of earlier traditions. Such transmission history then represents the study of all potential dimensions of a text's process of formation—exclusively oral and oral-written texts as well as source and redactional/compositional elements. Within this broader complex, source criticism has some claim to be aimed at those dimensions of transmission history that often are more capable of reconstruction than those elements distinctive to tradition history and redaction criticism. Note was already made earlier of the more fluid nature of exclusively oral transmission, a fluidity which makes it particularly difficult to distinguish the dimensions and growth of oral traditions in a text dependent on them. In addition, study of documented cases of ancient scribal expansions of earlier texts—where we have both an earlier and a later expanded manuscript version of the same text—shows that it often would have been impossible for scholars to reliably reconstruct such redactional/compositional expansions if we did not have earlier manuscript documentation to help us do so. In contrast, analysis of those same sorts of documented cases where we can see a version of a text with and without a given source shows that—in many cases—scholars *could have* identified the source working exclusively on the basis of indicators left in the later text.

Ancient scribes seem to have felt a sense of loyalty to earlier, originally independent written sources that somewhat restricted their freedom to accommodate them to new literary contexts. For example, scribes seem to have been particularly inclined to add new material at the beginning or end of existing compositions. Moreover, even when they added material into the middle of a given composition or combined two independent sources, they often stayed so close to those sources that they left clues in the resulting text that contemporary source critics can use to identify such sources, at least in their broader contours.

Pentateuchal Source Criticism. The beginning of such source criticism can be traced back to the mid-eighteenth century (1753), when a doctor in Louis XIV's court, Jean Astruc, noted the presence of numerous doubled narratives across the Genesis creation, flood, and ancestral narratives. There were two narratives describing the creation of animals and humans (Gen 1:20–28; 2:7–24); two divine announcements of the flood to Noah and instructions to take animals into the ark with him (Gen 6:13–21; Gen 7:1–4); two statements that Noah complied with God's instructions (6:22; 7:5); two covenants with Abraham (Gen 15 and Gen 17); and many other doublets across this and other parts of Genesis. Moreover, Astruc noticed that these doublets were not random, but seemed to represent the combination of at least two parallel, relatively readable accounts of the time before Moses. Indeed, one of these accounts often used the divine name "Yahweh" to refer to God, while another seemed to avoid that divine designation and instead used other words, such as the Hebrew word for God ("Elohim"), to refer to the deity. These indicators led Astruc to propose that Moses, the traditional author of the Pentateuch, used multiple sources in writing about events before his own life. Since these sources used by Moses covered many of the same events in different ways (e.g. creation, flood, covenant with Abraham), the Pentateuch that resulted from their combination contains many doubled narratives and other contradictions.

Over the next century, scholars gradually dropped the idea of Mosaic authorship of the Pentateuch and extended Astruc's preliminary source-critical insights into the books of Exodus through Joshua. In addition, scholars such as Hermann Hupfeld (1853) and A. Knobel (1857, 1861) began to distinguish two layers within the "Elohim" materials initially identified by Astruc: an early "Elohist" and a later "Elohist." Building on this, in 1869 the great Semitist, Theodore Nöldeke, identified what he thought was an early "Elohist" source extending across Genesis—Joshua that is remarkably close to the Pentateuchal "P" source identified by most academic scholars today. For Nöldeke and most of his colleagues, this early Elohist (//P) source represented the starting point of Pentateuchal tradition, with the other Pentateuchal materials constituting later versions of the same events. In this sense, his and other early source-critical studies of "P" represented a search for the earliest written origins of the Pentateuch.

Already, however, serious questions were being raised by E. G. Reuss (lectures from 1834 onward) and K. H. Graf (1865) about the entire chronology presupposed by Theodor Nöldeke and others, and works by Abraham Kuenen (1869) and Julius Wellhausen (1876–1877, 1883) convinced the bulk of the scholarly world that the Elohist/P-layer identified by Nöldeke was not the earliest source of the Pentateuch, but its last. Instead, Pentateuchal materials that used the divine designation Yahweh, a hypothesized "Yahwist" source, were taken to belong to the earliest of the Pentateuchal sources. Since many of the scholars leading this discussion were German, and Germans spelled Yahwist with a J (Jahwist), this source came to be known more generally (also in English) by the siglum "J." Finally, most scholars came to believe that the other hypothesized "Elohist" source (initially identified by Hupfeld) was to be dated later than "J" but before "P." It was designated "E" for "Elohist" (to be sure, a somewhat confusing term since P is also frequently characterized by use of the divine designation "Elohim" as well). This whole theory came to be known as the "Documentary Hypothesis" for the formation of the Pentateuch. Though crucial parts of it were critiqued by some scholars, notably within Jewish academic circles opposed to the anti-Jewish tenor of much Christian source-critical scholarship, the identification of hypothesized, early "J" and (somewhat later) "E" sources alongside the book of Deuteronomy ("D") and the later "P" source came to dominate most academic research on the Pentateuch up into the late 1970s. Indeed, the Documentary Hypothesis remains the most prominent view of the growth of the Pentateuch in many universities, especially in North America, Britain, and Israel.

Nevertheless, already in the 1960s through 1980s, several scholars raised serious questions about parts of the documentary hypothesis. By the 1990s these questions had taken hold in Continental Europe, the birthplace of source-criticism. An increasing number of major works discarded the idea of early "Yahwist" and "Elohist" sources, or identified "Yahwist" or "Elohist" sources that were significantly different in contents from the "Yahwist" and "Elohist" sources that were part of the documentary hypothesis. Though a few still defended the idea of an "Elohist" source, most Pentateuchal specialists in Europe (and some in North America) completely rejected the idea that any "E" source like the "E" source of the documentarians could be found in the Pentateuch. Moreover, by the 2000s two major multiauthor works chronicled the doubt by many scholars, especially in Continental Europe, that one could reconstruct any pre-Priestly "Yahwist" source spanning the Genesis and Moses stories (Gertz, Schmid, and Witte 2002; Dozeman and Schmid 2006). Even parts of the "P" source hypothesis came into question. An increasing number of scholars, again in Continental Europe, came to believe that the portions of "P" once identified in Numbers, Deuteronomy, Joshua, and even much of Leviticus, were *not* part of an early separate "P" source. Instead, the "P" portions of Numbers—Joshua (and much or all of Leviticus) were various layers of authorial/redactional expansions on combined "P" and non-P material.

This ferment has led some to defend the documentary hypothesis, others to propose alternative pictures of the growth of the Pentateuch, and yet others to despair of ever finding assured results in Pentateuchal source criticism. On the one hand, several scholars (especially in the US and Israel) have mounted a vigorous defense of the documentary hypothesis, whether in traditional or revised forms. On the other hand, an increasing number of scholars in Europe and elsewhere are more inclined to find different sorts of probable written "sources" in the Pentateuch—often a Priestly source that originally extended only to the Exodus tabernacle narrative or a bit beyond, an early form of Deuteronomy, some kind of (non-Priestly) Moses story, and some non-priestly compositions standing behind different parts of Genesis (e.g. the primeval history, Jacob story, and/or a Joseph novella).

Meanwhile, many who are not specialists in Pentateuchal source criticism find it difficult to know how to orient themselves to this fractured field. Source-critical studies have established the high probability *that* the present Pentateuch/Hexateuch contains multiple sources, but clarity on *what* those sources are has not been achieved. Beyond isolation of Deuteronomy as a distinctive block and shared broad distinctions between Priestly and non-Priestly portions of other books in the Hexateuch, there seems to be little overall consensus.

An Example of Source-Criticism in Action—Genesis 1—9 The Genesis primeval history, especially Genesis 1—9, is an example of a place where source criticism has achieved repeatable results, using indicators within the text to reconstruct intertwined sources on which there is relatively widespread agreement. Here, already three hundred years ago (1711), a German pastor, Hennig Bernhard Witter, used doublets and contradictions between Genesis 1:1—2:3 and 2:4—3:24 to argue that Moses used a prior poetic source to write Genesis 1:1—2:4 before composing his own account in Genesis 2:4 and following. For example, in Genesis 1 God creates the animals first (1:24–25) before creating both male and female humans (1:26–27), whereas in Genesis 2 God creates the male human first (2:7), then animals (2:18–20), then the first woman (2:21–24). These and other stylistic differences, among them the fact that God is referred to as "Elohim" ("God") in Genesis 1:1—2:3 and as "Yahweh Elohim" ("Lord God" in many English translations) in Genesis 2:4—3:24, led subsequent authors to see different sources in the 7-day creation account of Genesis 1:1—2:4a and the garden of Eden story in Genesis 2:4b—3:24.

These sources then both appear to continue in Genesis 4 and 5. On the one hand, Genesis 4:1–16 appears to replay, now with the children of the couple featured in Genesis 2—3, many of the same dynamics of disobedience, divine interrogation, and punishment found in Genesis 2—3. This story, along with the following genealogy from Adam to Noah's father, Lamech (Gen 4:17–24) seems to be a continuation of Genesis 2:4b—3:24. Yet Astruc and others following him astutely noted that the next chapter, Genesis 5, continues themes characteristic of Genesis 1, such as humans being made in the divine image (5:1, 3). Moreover, Genesis 5 gives a *duplicate* genealogy leading from Adam to Lamech that features a virtually identical list of names to that seen in the Adam-Lamech genealogy found in 4:17–24 (see 25–26), albeit in occasionally different order (see Figure 1).

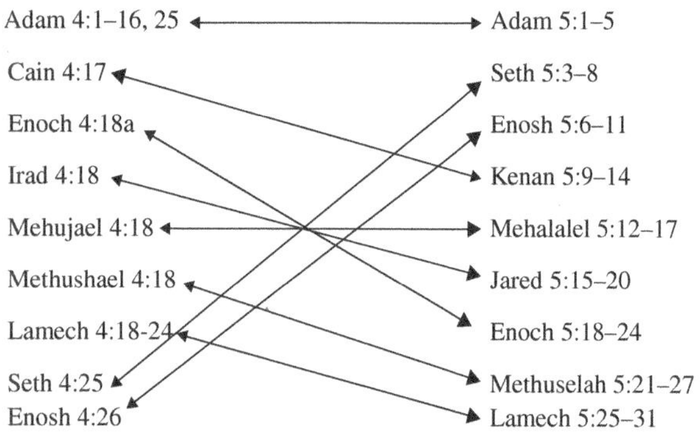

Figure 1.

These duplications and disagreements have suggested to most source-critics that Genesis 4 is from one source and Genesis 5 from another. Furthermore, the multiple links of Genesis 4 to the garden of Eden story, including but not at all confined to ongoing references to God as "Yahweh" ["Lord" in many English translations] have led most scholars to see Genesis 4 as a continuation of the Yahweh/"J" source seen in Genesis 2:4b—3:24. And Genesis 5, with its continuation of motifs from Genesis 1, such as humanity's resemblance to God and references to God as "Elohim" ["God"] is seen as a continuation of the Elohim/"P" source seen in Genesis 1.

Finally, the flood narrative across much of Genesis 6—9 offers an especially compelling example of how a biblical text appears to betray the presence in it of intertwined sources. As previously mentioned, almost all of the narrative elements of the flood are narrated twice: description of evil that helped prompt the flood (Gen 6:1–4 and 6:11); narration of God perceiving the problem (Gen 6:5 and 6:12); assertion that Noah was an exception to the problem (Gen 6:8 and 6:9); divine announcement of the flood to Noah and instruction to bring animals into the ark (Gen 6:13–21 and 7:1–4); general statement that Noah complied with God's instructions (Gen 6:22 and 7:5); specific description of Noah, his family, and animals entering the ark (Gen 7:7–9 and 7:13–16a); paired descriptions of all life dying (7:21 and 7:22); interwoven descriptions of the end of the flood (8:2b–3a and 8:1–2a, 3b, 5); and concluding divine promises not to bring another flood (8:20–22 and 9:8–17).

Furthermore, a closer examination of these pairs shows that they contain different concepts of the chronology of the flood and the types of animals brought onto the ark. For example, one strand, referring to God as Yahweh ["Lord"], asserts that Noah was instructed by Yahweh to bring extra pairs of clean animals onto the ark (7:2), and having these extra pairs of sacrificial animals then allows him to sacrifice a few such animals after the flood (8:20), an action that prompts Yahweh to promise not to bring another flood (8:21–22). The other strand, which refers to God with the Hebrew word Elohim ["God"], features no such sacrifice before God's promise not to bring a flood (cf. 9:8–17). Therefore, in this strand Noah is instructed to bring only one pair of each kind of animal onto the ark (6:19–20; see 7:15–16). To be sure, these strands seem to have been harmonized with each other by later authors (e.g. through the insertion of 7:8–9 into the J report of Noah's entry into the ark), and whoever combined these strands did not attempt to preserve absolutely every element of both narratives.

Nevertheless, the vast extent of duplication that is evident in Genesis 6—9 is poorly explained by any other model than the combination of written sources. A redactor who was just expanding on a given source would have had no need to add so many duplicate episodes, and an author working with competing oral traditions would have been able to exercise more freedom in accommodating such oral traditions to each other. In contrast, Genesis 1—9 in general, and 6—9 in particular, preserve numerous detailed duplications and conceptual contradictions that seem best explained by a theory that an author combined and only partially harmonized originally independent written narratives about creation, the genealogy from Adam to Noah, and the flood.

Insofar as this theory of combined sources in Genesis 1—9 is correct, and it stands as one of the more assured results of historical biblical scholarship, it can greatly inform interpretation of these chapters. To start, scholars can investigate each strand of Genesis 1—9 separately, attempting to identify the background and unique perspective of each strand. For example, the Yahweh/"J" strand of Genesis 1—9 shows some striking links to Mesopotamian traditions of creation and flood, and it may even have originated as a separate Judean composition about creation and flood that was partially modeled on the early Mesopotamian epic of Atrahasis, which likewise focuses on creation and flood. In turn, the distinctive theological accents of the Elohim/"P" strand of Genesis 1—9, such as the emphasis on Sabbath and blessing, are picked up in specific ways by other Priestly texts across the rest of the Pentateuch. Yet source-criticism need not just lead to isolation and separate interpretation of hypothesized "sources." Greater sensitivity to the distinctive perspectives of the source strands in Genesis can lead to an enhanced reading *of the present, combined text.* Rather than attempting to harmonize their different chronological and theological systems, source critically informed readers can appreciate the artistry of the narrative "duet" created by their combination in Genesis 1—9. For example, the author did not just tell how God made humans in God's image ("P" in Gen 1:26–27) or of the troubles that came from human attempts to be godlike ("J" in Gen 3:5–24), but wove the two together in one narrative tapestry to play off each other. In this sense, Genesis and other books of the Bible begin to emerge as finely-crafted, multivoiced compositions, and as such can be appreciated more like "choral" rather than "solo" works.

Source Criticism of Other Parts of the Hebrew Bible. Moving beyond the Pentateuch, scholars have used a variety of indicators to identify probable written sources embedded in other books of the Hebrew Bible. In the case of Chronicles, scholars have the advantage of having at their disposal one of its main sources, the books of Samuel—Kings. To be sure, we likely do not have access to the particular version of Samuel—Kings used by the author of Chronicles. Nevertheless, the extensive verbatim agreement across much of Samuel—Kings and Chronicles suggests some kind of source relationship between the two. Furthermore, most scholars agree that this relationship is likely that of the author of Chronicles drawing—sometimes quite creatively and/or selectively—on some form of the narratives now found in Samuel—Kings. In this sense, a form of Samuel—Kings was a source for Chronicles and is now embedded in it.

In addition, scholars have used source-critical indicators to identify potential sources in Joshua, Judges, 1–2 Samuel, and 1–2 Kings. For example, a 1963 study by Wolfgang Richter identified a possible "book of deliverers" in Judges 3:12—9:55 focusing on several Northern figures, and later reshaped through several layers of Deuteronomistic additions. Whether or not one follows the details of Richter's analysis, it seems clear that Judges contains a core of Northern "judge" traditions that had enough fixity, perhaps as a result of being written, that they can be distinguished from later Deuteronomistic materials added to them. The same may also be true of the core of Joshua, particularly traditions in Joshua 2—9 that are associated with the central hill country of Benjamin. Nevertheless, scholars have been more inclined in this case to see these materials as part of an exclusively oral cycle of traditions, and any written source is so thoroughly adapted to later Deuteronomistic theology that precise source identification would be difficult in any case. Finally, following on the work of Leonard Rost in 1926, many have identified an early "Succession Narrative" embedded in most of 2 Samuel 9—20; 1 Kings 1—2. Nowadays this hypothesis of a "Succession Narrative," along with the idea of other early sources in Samuel—Kings (e.g. an "ark narrative" in 1 Sam 4:1—7:1; 2 Sam 6:2–23; or "history of David's ascent" in 1 Sam 16—2 Sam 5, 7–8) are subject to some of the same kinds of controversy as that summarized earlier regarding the documentary hypothesis.

The books of Ezra-Nehemiah may contain the closest biblical analogy to the sorts of intertwined sources postulated for the Pentateuch. In 1783, just 30 years after Astruc's early work on the Pentateuch, Johann David Michaelis concluded on the basis of overlap and parallels between the stories of Ezra and Nehemiah that two histories—one about Ezra and one about Nehemiah—had been combined to form the present Ezra-Nehemiah story. In this case, the book of 3 Esdras (found in the Septuagint) may be a Greek translation of the Ezra story that lacks the Nehemiah materials. To be sure, some have explained the lack of Nehemiah materials in 3 Esdras as the result of subtraction. Nevertheless, as demonstrated in particular detail by a study by Böhler (1997), there are signs that 3 Esdras preserves a form of the Ezra tradition *before* it was combined with the story of Nehemiah's rebuilding of Jerusalem. As Böhler points out, 3 Esdras is distinguished from parallel material in the Hebrew version of Ezra–Nehemiah by numerous references *already in the story of Ezra* to the rebuilt walls of the city, marketplace, and Jerusalem in general, well before the time of Nehemiah. Böhler argues persuasively that such references to a rebuilt Jerusalem already during Ezra's time were eliminated when this story was combined with a Nehemiah story that attributed such rebuilding of Jerusalem to Nehemiah. Yet the creation of this combined Ezra–Nehemiah book does not seem to have led to immediate elimination of the sources that constitute it. Not only was a revised and expanded version of the Rebuilding–Ezra story translated in 3 Esdras, but the Jewish historian, Josephus, knew of the Ezra and Nehemiah stories in separate form as late as the first century C.E. (Ant. XI: pp. 159–183). In this case, which continues to be disputed, source critics can work with both internal evidence of multiple manuscript traditions and potential external testimony to identify potential sources of Ezra–Nehemiah.

Written sources are not as easy to identify in poetic books, largely because one cannot rely on indicators specific to narratives, such as doubled episodes, temporal conflicts, and other logical contradictions. Nevertheless, scholars have achieved varying levels of consensus on the identification of some blocks of earlier, probable written sources in some prophetic and other poetic books. For example, Isaiah 6—8 contains a block of largely first-person texts about Isaiah's prophecies during the Syro-Ephraimite war that begins with an account of his commissioning in Isaiah 6 and concludes with an apparent account of God's command to Isaiah to respond to the people's rejection of his message by binding up his message and sealing it among his disciples (Isa 8:11–18). Though some dispute whether these materials ever were some kind of "Isaiah memoir," this hypothesis of an embedded memoir would explain the distinctive first person language across much of this material and the curious placement of a prophetic commissioning, which usually occurs at the outset of other prophetic collections (e.g. Jer 1 and Ezek 1—3), here in Isaiah 6 (well into the book of Isaiah, but at the outset of the "Isaiah memoir"). Other probable written "sources" embedded in the book of Isaiah include material adapted from 2 Kings 18—20 now in Isaiah 36—39, a block of probable exilic (or partly post-exilic) oracles by another prophet (Second Isaiah) in much of Isaiah 40—55, and a probable exilic communal lament in Isaiah 63:7—64:11.

So also, many have sought sources in the book of Jeremiah, especially since the book itself contains a tantalizing account in Jeremiah 36 of the initial production and performance before King Jehoiakim of a "scroll" of Jeremiah's sayings, a scroll which the king is said to have destroyed, but was then re-dictated to Baruch by Jeremiah ("along with many more similar words," 36:32). Especially since Duhm (1901) and Mowinckel (1914), many have distinguished between an early poetic scroll of Jeremiah embedded in Jeremiah 1—25 (source A; perhaps somehow related to the scroll of Jeremiah 36), prose biographical material found especially in parts of Jeremiah 26—29, 36—44 (source B), various Deuteronomistic prose speeches of Jeremiah (source C), and a collection of words of salvation in Jeremiah 30—31 (source D). Nevertheless, the Deuteronomistic portions of Jeremiah are increasingly seen as redactional, not part of a separate source. Moreover, scholars are ever more skeptical about our ability to reconstruct any original scroll of Jeremiah, especially insofar as such scholarly efforts at reconstruction have been motivated by the highly ideological account of textual production and performance in Jeremiah 36.

Whatever the plausibility (or not) of written sources in Isaiah and Jeremiah, it is yet more difficult to find consensus on sources in other books comprised primarily of poetic material. Perhaps the best potential locus for additional source reconstruction is Daniel, a book comprised of a mix of poetry and narrative. First, the book contains a set of legends about Daniel and other figures in Daniel

1—6 that are distinguished by both content and language (Aramaic) from (most of) the materials following them (Dan 7 briefly continues the Aramaic; Dan 1:1—2:4a is probably a translation of original Aramaic into Hebrew). Second, the prayer in Daniel 9:4–19 shows linguistic signs of late origins and may be attested as a separate composition on one of the Dead Sea Scrolls (4QDan^{e}). In cases like this, we may have the benefit of independent manuscript attestation of a biblical source, much as seems to be the case with the Ezra and Nehemiah materials. Some additional cases of such independent attestation of a possible source of poetic parts of the Bible include the oracle in Psalm 89:20–38 (ET 89:19–37), which is also attested on a separate scroll at Qumran (4QPs^{x}) and Psalm 20, which is attested in an alternate edition in the Amherst Papyrus 63 12, 11–19. Nevertheless, in these and similar cases, we have come a good distance from the hypothesized interwoven Pentateuchal sources reconstructed by Astruc and his successors.

Prospect. After over two centuries of work, source criticism has brought mixed results. Some distinctions, such as of Priestly and non-Priestly Pentateuchal materials, are relatively secure, while other hypotheses have risen and fallen, or at least become subject to intense dispute. Recent debates about the formation of the Pentateuch and other books have shown room for further reflection on documentary models once thought to be firmly established. In addition, the focus of interest has shifted somewhat in biblical studies as a whole. Where early source critics were preoccupied with identifying the Bible's earliest sources, and sometimes focused on them to the exclusion of the present form(s) of the biblical text, contemporary exegetes are more interested in how source-critical results might inform exegesis of the complex biblical text before us.

Finally, an increasing wealth of documented examples of source appropriation and combination can inform further study of biblical sources and their combination and/or redaction. Such examples show *that* ancient scribes appropriated prior written sources. They also show *how* scribes appropriated such sources, often selectively and creatively. Finally, such documented examples illustrate how hard it would be, in many cases, to have reconstructed such source appropriation purely on the basis of the latest versions of texts, without having had manuscript documentation of different stages. Informed by such documented examples of source appropriation and hundreds of years of prior source-critical scholarship, today's source critics can approach the data of the biblical text with better models for scribal work, and yet a healthy dose of humility about the prospects for achieving lasting and/or precise reconstructions of written sources standing behind the present Bible.

[*See also* Dead Sea Scrolls; Form Criticism, *subentry* Hebrew Bible; Historical Criticism, *subentry* Hebrew Bible; Orality Studies and Oral Tradition, *subentry* Hebrew Bible; Redaction Criticism, *subentry* Hebrew Bible; *and* Tradition-Historical Criticism.]

BIBLIOGRAPHY

Baden, Joel. *The Composition of the Pentateuch: Renewing the Documentary Hypothesis.* Anchor Bible Reference Library. New Haven, Conn.: Yale, 2012. This is a well-written introduction to a new form of the documentary hypothesis for the formation of the Pentateuch. It well exemplifies the previously mentioned vigorous defense of the hypothesis mounted by some North American scholars.

Bailey, Lloyd. *The Pentateuch.* Interpreting Biblical Texts. Nashville, Tenn.: Abingdon, 1981. The first chapter of this book (13–59) provides a good introduction to problems surrounding Mosaic authorship, source-critical criteria, and the documentary hypothesis along with a brief summary of Rolf Rendtorff's alternative approach to the formation of the Pentateuch (See the following).

Carr, David. "Changes in Pentateuchal Criticism." To be published in Magne Saebø (ed.), *The History of Old Testament Interpretation,* Vol. 3.1, *The Twentieth Century.* Göttingen, Germany: Vandenhoeck & Ruprecht. Provides a chronicle of the development of the debate about Pentateuchal sources.

Carr, David. *The Formation of the Hebrew Bible: A New Reconstruction.* New York: Oxford University Press, 2011. The first part of this book gives an overview of some documented cases of scribal revision and considers what one can learn from them. The latter two parts attempt to reconstruct major stages in the growth of the Hebrew Bible, including its earliest sources.

Dozeman, Thomas B., and Schmid, Konrad. *Farewell to the Yahwist? The Composition of the Pentateuch in Recent European Interpretation.* SBL Symposium Series 34. Atlanta: SBL, 2006. The essays in this volume provide an introduction for English-language readers of recent European Pentateuchal scholarship on the origins of the non-Priestly portions of the Pentateuch.

Gertz, Jan Christian, with Angelika Berlejung, Konrad Schmid, and Markus Witte. *The T&T Clark Handbook of the Old Testament: An Introduction to the Literature, Religion, and History of the Old Testament.* London: T&T Clark, 2012 (German original 2010). A judicious synthesis of recent research on the Old Testament from a European perspective, including various forms of redaction and source criticism of individual books.

Gertz, Jan Christian, Konrad Schmid, and Markus Witte. *Abschied vom Jahwisten: Die Komposition des Hexateuch in der jüngsten Diskussion.* BZAW 315. Berlin: De Gruyter, 2002. This international collection of essays documents the widespread dissolution of the documentary hypothesis among many Pentateuchal specialists across the world working from different perspectives.

Habel, Norman. *Literary Criticism of the Old Testament.* Guides to Biblical Scholarship. Philadelphia: Fortress, 1971. Though now forty years old, this book provides a solid introduction to the types of source-critical reasoning used in analysis of Genesis 1–9 and summarized more briefly in this article.

Rendtorff, Rolf. *The Problem of the Process of the Transmission of the Pentateuch.* Translated by John Scullion. JSOT Sup 89. Sheffield, UK: JSOT Press, 1990 [German original 1976]. Because it was brief and translated into English, this book has served as the main entry-point for most English-language readers to alternative thinking about the sources of the Pentateuch. Much has happened in Pentateuchal studies in the thirty plus years since it was published.

Ska, Jean-Louis. *Introduction to Reading the Pentateuch.* Translated by Pascale Dominique. Winona Lake, Ind.: Eisenbrauns, 2006 (Italian original 1998). This book is a good introduction both to the modes of reasoning of source critics and some recent developments in Pentateuchal source criticism.

David M. Carr

Speech-Act Theory

It is well known that speech-act theory (SAT) developed from the work of Oxford philosopher J. L. Austin, whose 1955 William James lectures at Harvard were published as *How To Do Things with Words* in 1962. The most obvious insight promulgated by Austin was that language does things as well as says them, and he claimed initially that his own work was "neither difficult nor contentious," something that was challenged by a number of later writers (Austin 1962, p. 1). Since this early stage, SAT has developed and been applied in a number of directions and in a great many discourses. Its use in biblical interpretation has been varied, depending on a range of philosophical insights, from Austin himself, his student John Searle, and other scholars such as Stanley Fish, H. P. Grice, Mary Louise Pratt, and Sandy Petrey, all of whom engaged in argument about the direction and usefulness of Austin's ideas. This article will outline some of the major insights (and conflicts) within the field of SAT and show how they have been applied within the biblical studies field.

Founders of Speech-Act Theory.

J. L. Austin, "How To Do Things with Words." In his admirable introduction to SAT, Richard S. Briggs notes that SAT is not a comprehensive philosophy of language, and he criticises John Searle for trying to make it such (2001, pp. 9–10). This is a useful observation as it leaves scope to understand SAT as a polyvalent approach based on the Austinian basic claim: that language is performative in nature. Even this claim, though, went through a number of developmental stages in Austin's own work. His fundamental project concerned describing and evaluating the two functions he detected in spoken language, those of saying and doing. Austin was primarily interested in ordinary or oral language rather than written language, and thus his theory is not axiomatically suitable for a text-based discourse such as biblical studies, but his view that "utterances made in a specific context have a specific 'force,' not necessarily related to the form of the utterance but certainly distinguishable from it" (Botha 1991, p. 64) has potential for rhetorically attuned scriptural texts.

To begin with, Austin used the term "performative" for language that did something, that performed an act, while "constative" was reserved for language that said something, or made a statement. His initial formulations concerned these two groups, although the terms became somewhat conflated as Austin's thinking developed during his lectures. While constative allowed for judgements of true or false, the performative could only be evaluated in terms of its success or the lack of it. Austin used terms such as felicitous/infelicitous, happy/unhappy, effective/ineffective, or appropriate/inappropriate to mark and maintain this distinction. Further, he analyzed the performative function of natural language as encompassing three possible acts: locution, illocution, and perlocution. The *locutionary* act produces a coherent and acceptable grammatical utterance. It will be noted that speech-act theory deals in utterances rather than sentences, which are understood as relating to the study of grammar and semantics rather than as contextualized in particular situations and thus performing an act. The *illocutionary* act produces an utterance with "illocutionary force," a combination of language and social practice as the speaker utters a particular locution in a certain context. Austin writes:

> For there are very numerous functions of or ways in which we use speech, and it makes a great difference to our act in some sense . . . in which way and in what *sense* we were on this occasion 'using' it. It makes a great difference whether we were advising, or merely suggesting, or actually ordering, whether we were strictly promising or only announcing a vague intention, and so forth. (1975, p. 99)

Austin goes on to distinguish a third category of performative function, that of the *perlocutionary* act, one which concentrates on the "consequential effects upon the feelings, thoughts, or actions of the audience, or of the speaker, or of other persons: and it may be done with the design, intention, or purpose of producing them" (1975, p. 99). The issue here is that the speaker has performed an act that has only an oblique, if any, reference to the performance of the locutionary or illocutionary act. The locutionary act, argued Austin in summary, has a meaning, the illocutionary act has a certain force in saying something, and the perlocutionary act is the achieving of certain effects by saying something (1975, p. 121). This last act may be of particular interest in biblical studies, to those who would interpret texts that have been accorded some level of authority by generations of communities who come from quite different interpretive contexts.

These definitions, which are by no means absolute, form a basis for an understanding of Austin's SAT, which, it should be remembered, applies to ordinary or spoken language. Austin went so far as to schematize some of the necessary conditions for the happy or felicitous function of a performative act, and he argued that a similar set of rules exists for nonverbal conventional acts, but he continued to claim that this scheme was tentative, a work by no means complete (1975, 14–15).

Briggs usefully sees Austin's work as laying down a foundation that invited further development (2001, p. 43). It was thus left to Austin's student John R. Searle to develop and spread these ideas in ways that partly helped and partly hindered their application to literary texts in ways that could be creative for biblical interpretation. Searle's work provides, without doubt, the most comprehensive account of SAT.

John R Searle. No one who engages with SAT can ignore the work of John R. Searle, who, it can be argued, is the major theorist in the development of SAT. Searle's two major contributions to SAT are *Speech Acts: An Essay in the Philosophy of Language* (1969) and *Expression and Meaning: Studies in the Theory of Speech Acts* (1979), in both of which Searle forms something approaching a developed philosophy of mind. A major modification, which would become a standard feature of later SAT, was to distinguish the illocutionary act from the propositional act—that is, the act of expressing the proposition (a phrase that is neutral as to illocutionary force) (Briggs 2001, p. 46). Further, Searle challenges several elements of Austin's taxonomy, developing it further in ways that have rendered his theories on the whole less attractive to biblical scholars than those developed from Austin's work by a number of scholars. There is no doubt, though, that Searle's categorizations have been as influential in understanding SAT as a philosophical idea as those of any other scholar. He summarizes his fundamental hypothesis thus:

> I have said that the hypothesis of this book is that speaking a language is performing acts according to rules. The form this hypothesis will take is that the semantic structure of a language may be regarded as a conventional realization of a series of sets of underlying constitutive rules, and that speech acts are acts characteristically performed by uttering expressions in accordance with these sets of constituent rules. (1969, pp. 36–37)

It can clearly be seen that Searle's interest remains firmly in the area of spoken language and he proceeds to categorize speech acts in careful and distinctive ways, refining the rather over-complex categorizations Austin suggested toward the end of his work. Searle's taxonomy has become standard, even canonical, for speech-act theorists, attempting to show that there are five (or perhaps six) types of speech act, arranged around categories of direction of fit between word and world (see Briggs 2001, pp. 50–56). These types of act include assertives or representatives, directives, commissives, expressives, declarations (and possibly assertive declarations). As Sandy Petrey points out, "For students of literature, the thorniest aspect of *Speech Acts* is its proclivity for the abstract notation of logical analysis—Searle represents the general form of illocution not by discussing society and conventions, but by writing 'F(p),' for example—and for positing the simplified context on which this notation depends" (1990, p. 60). This tendency to abstract has certainly formed a barrier for those who wish to use the very real insights of SAT in the understanding of real, conventionally contextualized language, as many studying literary, let alone biblical texts, which deal with situations not covered by logical theory, would want to do. Searle also complicates matters by introducing an idea of fiction as pretence, which makes things difficult for those who want to apply these theories to literary texts. This insistence that fiction operates with distinct and different sets of conventions from those operating in the real world is unattractive to critics seeking to develop the theory in just these areas and raises questions associated with genre, particularly with texts of mixed provenance and complex manuscript traditions. His emphasis on the tenet that "speaking a language is a rule-governed form of behavior" has been influential for critics who would use SAT in a variety of ways (1969, p. 22).

Further treatments of SAT as linguistic philosophy can be found in the various debates between and among Austin, Searle, Jacques Derrida, and Stanley Fish. These very important conversations should be acknowledged, but they have only been tangentially used in biblical interpretation.

SAT and Literary Theory. There have been a number of attempts to bring SAT as linguistic philosophy into dialogue with theories of reading literary texts. This section introduces and evaluates the work of the major contributors to this field, noting that there are a variety of approaches to the task, not all of which are equally successful.

Mary Louise Pratt. Perhaps the most influential application of SAT to literary, and therefore biblical, texts has been based on the work of Mary Louise Pratt, especially *Toward a Speech Act Theory of Literary Discourse*, in which she argues robustly against making a firm, or any, distinction between literature and ordinary or spoken language. Indeed, Pratt challenges the whole formalist school of structuralist linguistics for making such a distinction, which she sees as both unnecessary and destructive (1977, p. xii).

In a trenchant argument, she claims that all language can be considered under the general umbrella of communication theory, arguing that "[u]nless we are foolish enough to claim that people organize their anecdotes around patterns they learn from reading literature, we are obliged to draw the more obvious conclusion that the formal similarities between natural narrative and literary narrative derive from the fact that at some level of analysis they are utterances of the same type" (1977, p. 69). She uses this insight as a point of departure for the development of a "context-dependent theory of literature," which allows her to describe literary utterances in the same terms as other types of utterance and provides a platform for a speech-act theory and practice for written texts (1977, p. 89; Gilfillan Upton 2006, pp. 96–102).

This context-dependence has proved informative for biblical interpretation in its emphasis on the "intentions, attitudes and expectations of the participants, the relationships existing between the participants, and, generally, the unspoken rules and conventions that are understood to be in play when an utterance is made and received" (Pratt 1977, p. 86). Pratt incorporates into her theoretical framework the work of the pragmatist H. P. Grice, who introduced his idea of the Cooperative Principle in a series of lectures given in 1967 (but not published until 1975). Grice, like Austin, concentrates on conversational language, and insists that the most important element of language use is the success of an utterance. In his view, communication is governed by

> A rough general principle which participants will be expected to observe, viz.,"Make your conversational contribution such as is required, at the stage at which it occurs, by the accepted purpose or direction of the talk-exchange in which you are engaged". (1975, p. 45)

Grice enlarges this Cooperative Principle by proposing four maxims or overall appropriateness conditions that he assumes to be in force when any conversation takes place. They are:

1. The maxim of Quantity, which dictates that a contribution to an exchange should be as informative as required, not more, not less. It can be summarized as "Be economical."
2. The maxim of Quality, which states that a contribution should be true, summarised as "Be sincere."
3. The maxim of Relation. "Be relevant."
4. The maxim of Manner. "Be perspicuous or clear." (Summary in Gilfillan Upton 2006, p. 98)

Other maxims have been suggested, including those of politeness or morality, and Kent Bach and Robert Harness made the helpful underpinning suggestion of "Other things being equal, construe the speakers' remarks so as to violate as few maxims as possible" (1979, p. 68).

In neither the spoken nor the written word are all the maxims or appropriateness conditions held at the same time. A helpful notion is that of implicature, which is a method of reconstructing meaning when one or more of the maxims has been flouted. This aspect, of the flouting or nonfulfilment of an appropriateness condition, is particularly helpful when dealing with literary texts rather than the spoken word. Botha points out, indeed, that it is the only possible kind of nonfulfilment in a literary speech situation (1991, p. 68). He and Pratt both agree that "in literature it is always the flouting of a maxim that is relevant when there is a failure to fulfil a maxim; i.e. whenever flouting has taken place in literature, it is the intention, at the level of the communication between the implied author and the readers or hearers, that the situation should be resolved by implicature" (Gilfillan Upton 2006, p. 99). Interestingly, this reintroduces to SAT the concept of intentionality, which is central to Searle's understanding but is often rather overlooked in treatments that arise from narratology rather than the philosophy of language. I argued then that the concept of implicature justifies the inclusion of Gricean pragmatics into a basically Austinian model, and it still seems to be the case.

Pratt's development of Grice's model includes the introduction of a "display text" with its associated principles of "assertibility" and "tellability," referring to new and interesting information respectively. She argues that display-producing relevance is characteristic of an important subclass of assertive or representative speech acts that includes natural narrative, much conversation, and nearly all literary works. Tellable assertions represent unusual states of affairs that are problematic in some way. The speaker who makes such an assertion is both reporting and displaying a certain state of affairs, "inviting his addressee(s) to join him in contemplating it, evaluating it, and responding to it" (Pratt 1977, p. 136). In this way the hearer is invited into an imaginative and affective involvement in this state of affairs to evaluate it in some way, that is, to enter into an interpretive dialogue with the speaker or text. The point of the display text, then, is to offer the recipient a text to observe, experience, or contemplate. Botha observes that Pratt's idea can be used to refer to narrative texts that are thought to be problematic in some way (Botha 1991, p. 73; see further in what follows).

In *The Narrative Act*, Susan Lanser suggested the addition of a sixth (or perhaps seventh) category to Searle's taxonomy to account for the nature of fictional texts, which are typically a mixture of fictional and nonfictional discourse. Her view is that a writer brings a consistent hypothetical world into being and commits herself to representing that world with some consistency, bringing to bear the same conventions that would apply to nonfictional texts (1981, p. 290).

As evident from the work of Austin, an illocutionary act cannot be evaluated as true or false, but for effective communication to take place, the rules or conditions that apply to the exchange need to be identified and adhered to. Some of these rules are general and others particular to a specific situation. Different illocutionary acts, then, have different appropriateness or felicity conditions for communication to be achieved. What is important here is the relationship between the speaker/writer and addressee. Pratt uses an account of the appropriateness conditions for the illocutionary act of asking a question, part of the category of directives, as an example:

1. The speaker does not know the answer.
2. The speaker believes it is possible that the hearer knows the answer.
3. It is not obvious that the hearer will provide the answer at the time without being asked.
4. The speaker wants to know the answer (Pratt 1977, p. 81–82).

If these conditions have not been met, the act of communication has not been felicitous or appropriate.

Similar conditions can be suggested for other illocutionary acts. Such rule-bound behavior can be of great value when assessing effective communication in speech or text and acts as a point of departure for a number of biblical speech act analyses.

Sandy Petrey. In *Speech Acts and Literary Theory* (1990), Petrey further examines the implications of Austin's theory, noting that its importance lies in shifting "attention from what language *is* to what it *does* and sees a *social process* where other linguistic philosophies see a *formal structure*" (1990, 3). The value of his book lies both in his introduction of SAT itself and in the value of the survey he provides of applications of the theory to literary texts. His evaluation of the work of Pratt and other literary figures such as Paul de Man, Jacques Derrida, and Stanley Fish has provided a useful point of departure for many later studies.

Some Counter-Arguments. Before considering some examples of the application of SAT to biblical texts, it is worth looking at some of the arguments of those who would challenge the very thought of such an enterprise. In a 1979 article, Joseph Margolis challenged the whole project of applying a speech-act theory to literature, claiming both that "Grice's maxims are extraordinarily vacant or unqualified," and that the absence of a settled scheme of speech acts renders the attempts of Grice as well as Austin and Searle largely invalid. He also thinks that Pratt "conflates the matter of the difference between fiction and non-fiction with the fact that the narrative may be either fictional or non-fictional" (1979, pp. 43, 49). Margolis contends that fiction and non-fiction are logically quite different, but that the difference cannot be marked by speech act models. He concludes that "the speech act theory appears to yield no special advantage to the theory of literature or to the analysis of particular literary passages" (1979, p. 50). This seems an unnecessarily negative assessment since Pratt draws a distinction between fictional text and fictional discourse, the imaginatively constructed component of that text, thus allowing for the treatment of texts of mixed genre or provenance.

A more trenchant critique is offered by David Gorman (1999), who challenges the whole basis of applying SAT to literary texts. He argues that most practitioners who attempt to do this pick and choose from aspects of theory without a clear understanding of the analytical philosophical foundations of the theory. To be fair, he brackets the work and influence of H. P. Grice and thus cannot assess the work of Mary Louise Pratt, but he is keen to engage Sandy Petrey, whose work has been used to a significant extent in biblical interpretation. Gorman's main critique of Petrey resides in his understanding that "acceptance of current buzzwords and preoccupations replace critical thought in much of Petrey's book" (1999, p. 116), something that indicates that his project is much wider than a particular attack on literary SAT. He culminates his argument with the view that "[i]n effect, literary theorists have yet to discover speech-act theory—although some of them have discussed it a great deal" (1999, p. 117). Such criticisms should not be ignored; neither, though, should those who seek to apply SAT to literary texts be blamed for not being analytical philosophers in a manner that Gorman would approve.

Applications of Speech-Act Theory to Biblical Texts. This section will include a selection of studies that engage with the application of SAT to biblical texts. It is neither detailed nor exhaustive, but should provide a number of jumping off points for those who would take this aspect of hermeneutics further. Book-length studies are the focus here, but it should also be remembered that a number of articles on specific texts have also used these methodologies. A useful summary of many aspects of SAT and implications for biblical scholarship can be found in Anthony Thiselton's *New Horizons in Hermeneutics: The Theory and Practice of Transforming Biblical Reading* (1992).

Hugh C. White. A foundational collection for the application of SAT to biblical texts is that edited by Hugh C. White and published as *Speech Act Theory and Biblical Criticism* (1988). This volume contains an extensive introduction to SAT along with an outline of various possibilities of its application and a number of essays in which different aspects of SAT are explored. In the introduction, White summarizes the basic features of SAT, based on Austin's philosophy, that he sees as being most relevant to biblical studies. Usefully, he suggests a number of approaches that might be open to such interpretation: studies of texts that can themselves be understood as speech acts; studies that view literature itself as a type of speech act; and studies that concentrate on the performative aspects of literature itself. His own essay, "The Value of Speech Act Theory for Old Testament Hermeneutics" (1988, pp. 41–63) explores the third aspect, suggesting that SAT might form a mediating discourse between the work of Jacques Derrida and that of Roland Barthes. Other essays include a study of Genesis 2–3 by Susan Lanser that uses SAT to engage with feminist readings of this controversial text by Phyllis Trible and Mieke Bal (1988, pp. 67–84). Lanser is interested in the way in which Gricean implicature might be used to acknowledge the dissonance between this material and that in Genesis 1, thus suggesting that the tradition of Genesis might already represent a situation of tension within the canonical text. A contribution by Daniel Patte (1988, pp. 85–101), well known for his structuralist readings of biblical texts, seeks to develop a "speech act exegesis" concerned with "religious intentionality" in an attempt to take the discourse further (1988, p. 100). These essays, among others, form a basis for many later studies and are still of great value to those who would work with SAT and to those who are interested in this aspect of the history of interpretation.

J. Eugene Botha. An early full-length treatment of SAT as an approach to New Testament texts is *Jesus and the Samaritan Woman: A Speech Act Reading of* John 4:1–42 by J. Eugene Botha (1991). Botha sets out to use SAT for a very specific purpose, that of discovering something of the style of the Fourth Gospel, and this combination of intentions becomes characteristic of a number of speech act readings of biblical texts. It is Botha's contention that stylistics had not, at the time of writing, been attended to satisfactorily in Johannine studies and that aspects of speech-act theory are ideally placed in combination with concepts of narratology, reception theory, and literary and linguistic analysis, to provide a fresh insight into the style of the Fourth Gospel. Such combinations of methodologies have also become rather typical of studies that utilize the insights of speech-act theory. Interestingly, and in contradiction to the comments of David Gorman (earlier) in relation to a lack of understanding of analytical philosophy by those who choose to use SAT, Botha suggests that "New Testament scholars need not be trained linguists in order to utilize this tool to supplement their study of the New Testament" (1991, p. 63). Botha's chosen path through SAT relies on the work of Pratt, and therefore of Grice, for literary texts, and he comes to the conclusion that the theory has much to offer in describing "the vitality and dynamics" of the text (1991, p. 199). This concept of textual dynamics is important as it opens the way to perceive the reading of texts as a form of communication.

Dietmar Neufeld. Dietmar Neufeld's *Reconceiving Texts as Speech Acts: An Analysis of 1 John* appeared in 1994. In this work Neufeld engages with SAT with particular reference to the writing of Austin, Donald Evans, who treats biblical language on creation by such means, and Derrida, developing a new methodological approach that he applies to the Christological confessions and ethical exhortations of 1 John. Neufeld is interested in the work of Evans for his project at least partly because of Evans's development of a new logic of self-involvement, especially as it applies to religious discourse. If religious language is self-involving rather than propositional, such an approach is attractive to those who are engaged in a study of the confessional and exhortative language of scripture. Neufeld's book provides an approach to speech-act theory that is more nuanced in the direction of theological hermeneutics than the work of Botha, partly because of Neufeld's chosen conversation partners, and partly because of the texts he chooses to work with.

Richard S. Briggs. Richard S. Briggs's *Words in Action: Speech Act Theory and Biblical Interpretation* (2001) is arguably the most comprehensive introduction to SAT in terms of its philosophical background and its application to texts of theological significance, including the confession of sin, forgiveness, and teaching. Briggs's work is notable for significant engagement with all the main theorists of SAT, explicating and evaluating the various aspects in some detail before moving on to examine the work of Donald Evans on a hermeneutic of self-involvement. He offers a critique of Neufeld's work, among others, arguing that a flaw in his work can be found in trying to set up SAT as a way of getting around the problems caused by the uncertainty of historical elements. Briggs suggests that these should not be seen as in opposition to each other, but should suggest that the function of a particular passage can be viewed in its historical context to good effect. This critique is worth mentioning as it shows an early example of speech-act theorists in dialogue with each other within the literature. Briggs's contention is that "the point of New Testament language as confessing, forgiving or teaching may only be understood with reference to its self-involving nature" (2001, p. 181) and he tries to follow Austin's self-designation as a "linguistic phenomenologist" as he proceeds to explore biblical texts of self-involvement, demonstrating a pastoral as well as a linguistic concern. This is a valuable work that builds on the insights of Briggs's own teacher and supervisor, Anthony Thiselton.

Bridget Gilfillan Upton and Derek Tovey. Gilfillan Upton's *Hearing Mark's Endings: Listening to Ancient Popular Texts through Speech Act Theory* (2006) is a less specifically theological work, drawing on the insights of Pratt and Grice to offer SAT as a method of reading texts that are written on the cusp of orality and writtenness. Building on an analysis of some aspects of ancient rhetoric in an attempt to show that Mark's Gospel was designed to be read aloud, and using Xenophon of Ephesus's *An Ephesian Tale* as a control text, speech act readings of various endings of the Gospel are offered. These readings discover the material to be new and interesting, assertible and tellable, in a way that is generated by the dynamics of engagement with the performative nature of the texts. Perhaps the most significant contribution of this study lies in the attempt to bring some elements of ancient rhetoric into conversation with SAT, both approaches dealing with aurally attuned texts, despite their different historical contexts. Derek Tovey's *Narrative Art and*

Act in the Fourth Gospel (1997), as its title suggests, uses SAT as one method in a narratological toolbox to illuminate his chosen texts, interestingly once again from the Fourth Gospel. Overall his book centers on the concept of point of view, but he uses SAT to some effect in making his case, especially perhaps in his consideration of authorial intention and its relation to point of view. Tovey's principal conversation partners in his project are Austin, Searle, Grice, and Lanser.

Evaluation and Overview. This article has outlined some of the basic tenets of speech-act theory as initiated by Austin and also indicated some of the range of theories and applications that can be found hidden inside a term that has become something of an umbrella for a number of methodological approaches, ranging from analytical philosophical analyses, through the work of Searle, through pragmatic insights using the work of Grice and Pratt, to deconstructive readings suggested by Fish and Derrida and interpretations within the range of reader response criticisms, which in biblical hermeneutics typically draw on the work of Wolfgang Iser (1974, 1978). Such a broad array of approaches is part of the attraction of this type of reading strategy or application of communication theory; it also contains the seeds of disillusion for some, as is evidenced by the critiques of, among others, Margolis and Gorman. Perhaps there are two major contributions and possibilities of further insight in these applications: (1) applying these methodologies to texts that are evidently performative in nature is one way forward (Neufeld; Briggs), concentrating on material that is liturgical, prophetic, ritual, or rhetorical in genre; (2) applying SAT as part of an interdisciplinary toolbox, including narratology, reception theory, film and performance studies (Botha; Tovey; Gilfillan Upton) is another possibility that could bear much fruit.

[*See also* Cognitive Linguistics and Biblical Interpretation; Deconstruction; Performance Criticism; Poststructuralist Interpretation; Reader-Response Criticism; Rhetorical Criticism; Semiotics; *and* Structuralist Interpretation.]

BIBLIOGRAPHY

Austin, J. L. *How To Do Things with Words.* Oxford: Oxford University Press, 1962; Cambridge, Mass.: Harvard University Press, 1975. This short philosophical work lies at the heart of all speech act applications, and most books and articles start with an exposition of it. It is, however, worth reading in its own right as it is foundational for all that follows.

Bach, Kent, and Robert Harnish. *Linguistic Communications and Speech Acts.* Cambridge, Mass.: MIT Press, 1979. A useful linguistic volume that adds to Grice's maxims.

Botha, J. Eugene. *Jesus and the Samaritan Woman: A Speech Act Reading of John 4:1–42.* Leiden, Netherlands: Brill, 1991. One of the earliest full-length treatments of SAT as applied to New Testament texts. Botha uses SAT to illuminate a study of the style of the Fourth Gospel, mainly via the insights of Pratt and Grice.

Briggs, Richard S. *Words in Action: Speech Act Theory and Biblical Interpretation.* Edinburgh and New York: T&T Clark, 2001. This book provides probably the most comprehensive introduction to the philosophical aspects of SAT and proceeds to apply the theory to theological hermeneutics via the concept of self-involvement posited by Evans.

Cole, Peter and Jerry L. Morgan, eds. *Syntax and Semantics, Vol. 3: Speech Acts.* New York, San Francisco, London: Academic Press, 1975. A component of a major multivolume work. Introduces the work of H. P. Grice in published form.

Evans, Donald D. *The Logic of Self-involvement: A Philosophical Study of Everyday Language with Special Reference to the Christian Use of Language about God as Creator.* London: SCM Press, 1963. An early application of SAT by a student of Austin, in which the author attempts to show that the use of biblical language has the effect of drawing the speaker into a particular kind of relationship with God and other human beings.

Fish, Stanley. "How To Do things with Austin and Searle: Speech Act Theory and Literary Criticism." In Fish, 1980, 197–245. An entertaining reading of *Coriolanus*, in which the author argues that a distinction between serious and fictional discourse cannot be maintained if the implications of SAT are clearly seen.

Fish, Stanley. *Is there a Text in this Class? The Authority of Interpretive Communities.* Cambridge Mass., London: Harvard University Press, 1980. A selection of sometimes provocative essays that engage with SAT among other forms of linguistics.

Gilfillan Upton, Bridget. *Hearing Mark's Endings: Listening to Ancient Popular Texts through Speech Act Theory*. Leiden, Netherlands: Brill, 2006. An attempt to engage with SAT as an appropriate theory for texts received at the interface of orality and written works and usually written to be read aloud. Also engages with aspects of ancient rhetoric.

Gorman, David. "The Use and Abuse of Speech-Act Theory in Criticism." *Poetics Today* 20 (1999): 93–119. A trenchant argument against some of the ways in which SAT has been applied to literary texts.

Grice, H. P. "Logic and Conversation." In *Syntax and Semantics*, edited by Peter Cole and Jerry L. Morgan, 3:41–58. The publication is, in great part, from a 1967 lecture series, in which Grice sets out the Cooperative Principle and associated maxims.

Iser, Wolfgang. *The Act of Reading: A Theory of Aesthetic Response*. Baltimore: Johns Hopkins University Press, 1978.

Iser, Wolfgang. *The Implied Reader: Patterns of Communication in Prose Fiction from Bunyan to Beckett*. Baltimore: Johns Hopkins University Press, 1974. Reader-response theories that interact with SAT at certain points and have been widely used in biblical interpretation.

Lanser, Susan Sniader. "(Feminist) Criticism in the Garden: Inferring Genesis 2–3." In White, ed., 1988, 67–84. Lanser uses SAT to engage with the readings of this foundational text given by Phyllis Trible and Mieke Bal to challenge what she considers to be their revisionist attempts to see gender equalities in these passages.

Lanser, Susan Sniader. *The Narrative Act: Point of View in Prose Fiction*. Princeton, N.J.: Princeton University Press, 1981. Uses SAT to link the novel with its context.

Margolis, Joseph. "Literature and Speech Acts." *Philosophy and Literature* 3 (1979): 39–52. A critique of those who apply ordinary language philosophy to written texts.

Neufeld, Dietmar. *Reconceiving Texts as Speech Acts: An Analysis of 1 John*. Leiden, Netherlands: Brill, 1994. Like Briggs, Neufeld engages with the work of Evans because of his interest in the logic of self-involvement in his selected texts. Rather unusual in biblical interpretation for sustained employment of the insights of Derrida.

Patte, Daniel. "Speech Act Theory and Biblical Exegesis." In White, ed., 1988, 85–102. This essay explores the interface of speech-act theory and biblical exegesis and ends up calling for the development of a "speech act exegesis."

Petrey, Sandy. *Speech Acts and Literary Theory*. New York and London: Routledge, 1990. A work that explores the implication of the work of Austin and other speech-act theorists in the work of later writers, including Derrida and Fish as well as Pratt and Grice. A useful introduction to SAT and literary texts.

Pratt, Mary Louise. *Towards a Speech Act Theory of Literary Discourse*. Bloomington: Indiana University Press, 1977. One of the most widely used books by biblical scholars in this field. Pratt introduces into SAT the work of the pragmatist H. P. Grice, integrating it into the philosophy of J. L. Austin, and makes a sustained argument for the validity of using SAT for literary texts.

Searle, John R. *Expression and Meaning: Studies in the Theory of Speech Acts*. Cambridge, UK: Cambridge University Press, 1979.

Searle, John R. *Speech Acts: An Essay in the Philosophy of Language*. Cambridge, UK: Cambridge University Press, 1969. Two books by Austin's student and the scholar who takes SAT into the realm of a developed philosophy of mind. A major player in the field who cannot and should not be ignored, notably for his development of a classification of speech acts that has attained something approaching canonical status in the field.

Thiselton, Anthony C. *New Horizons in Hermeneutics: The Theory and Practice of Transforming Biblical Reading*. London: HarperCollins, 1992. A comprehensive volume summarizing biblical and theological hermeneutic methodology. Valuable for its clarity and scope.

Tovey, Derek. *Narrative Art and Act in the Fourth Gospel*. Sheffield, UK: Sheffield Academic Press, 1997. A reading of the Fourth Gospel that uses SAT as a tool among more classically narratological methods to illuminate the Fourth Gospel.

White, Hugh C., ed. "Introduction: Speech Act Theory and Literary Criticism." In White, ed., 1988, 1–24. A useful and thorough introduction to the volume of essays in which White summarizes the work of Austin and traces its implications through to a consideration of deconstruction.

White, Hugh C, ed. *Speech Act Theory and Biblical Criticism*. Semeia 41. Atlanta: Society of Biblical Literature, 1988. An early volume that contains a comprehensive introduction to SAT and a series of essays in which various aspects are tested on biblical texts. Retains its value for all who would come to grips with SAT as used in biblical interpretation.

White, Hugh C, ed. "The Value of Speech Act Theory for Old Testament Hermeneutics." In White, ed., 1988, 41–63. An attempt to create a method to serve as the basis for a type of narrative hermeneutics in which literary and historical criticism could be more satisfactorily integrated than was current at the time of writing.

Bridget Gilfillan Upton

Structuralist Interpretation

"Structuralist interpretation" includes a multiplicity of interpretive approaches for analyzing texts (or any kind of discourses and cultural artifacts) and/or for assessing their previous interpretations. These approaches are based upon *structural* semiotic theories—that is, theories concerning how meaning is produced when a reader/interpreter "makes sense out of a text" by choosing as most significant in a discourse a particular textual dimension and constructing out of it a "meaningful discourse." This role of the reader in the production of meaning out of texts is possible (1) because meaning is not contained in texts; and (2) because any given text has a multiplicity of meaning-producing dimensions, each characterized by particular *structures* that have the potential to generate particular meaning effects.

Structuralist interpretation can be used to study existing interpretations in order to elucidate the textual dimension(s) that each given interpretation chose as most significant in a text and how it constructed meaning out of this dimension. Investigating the process of "textualization" (Greimas's terminology) as reflected in existing interpretations of the Bible opens the possibility to raise issues of ethics in biblical interpretation: since each interpretation involves a *choice* of textualization (choosing to view certain features of a text as more significant than others), interpreters can be—indeed, should be—held accountable for their interpretive choices.

"Structural Exegesis" is the kind of structuralist interpretation that is used for the study of the biblical texts themselves. It takes the form of a set of literary methods for the study of particular dimensions of these texts. Structural exegeses usually begin by focusing on readily accessible narrative structures of biblical texts (narrative syntax). While this can be an end in itself, the study of narrative structures is often the first step toward another end: the elucidation of the ideology (fundamental syntax) posited by the text, and primarily the elucidation of the system of convictions embedded in the text under study and expressed by particular mythical structures (the text's fundamental and narrative semantics) and by the thematic and figurative features of this text in dialogic relations with other texts (discursive semantics).

Beginnings: Seeking to Address Two Sources of a Hermeneutical Problem. The turn toward structural exegesis came about in an effort to address the strange failure of historical critical exegesis to account for the religious character of biblical texts—which, after all, are religious texts! This failure was promoted by (1) too narrow an understanding of the religious character of biblical texts (reduced to the content of faith, with the blessing of the Enlightenment) and (2) too narrow an understanding of language, of semiotics, and thus of texts (still reflecting the reductionist view of the signified as the "universalist content" of signifiers, posited in the West since Aristotle). Structural exegesis was largely developed in an effort to retrieve broader understandings of these essential dimensions of biblical texts. This process was brought to fruition in the mid-1970s but began long before, in the nineteenth century, through the pioneering work of certain biblical scholars and, independently, in the no-less pioneering work of linguists and semioticians. In order to understand present-day structural exegesis we need to review briefly this twofold history.

The Quest for the Religious Dimensions of Biblical Texts. The statement that historical critical exegesis fails to account for the religious character of biblical texts might sound strange. Did not historical critical exegesis produce many studies concerning the theological and ethical teaching of the Bible? It did. But in the process it reduced the religious character of biblical texts to a religious content, and faith to the cognitive appropriation of this content. Religious experiences, including mysticism and apophatic encounters with mystery, and their expressions in mythical, figurative, poetic language (which in turn need to be experienced) were excluded.

As is well known, historical critical exegesis was developed in the eighteenth and nineteenth centuries to seek to correct the misguided religious interpretations that believers and theologians gave of biblical texts that they read as scripture. For proponents of higher biblical criticism in that time (and still for many today), believers and theologians misread biblical texts by reading into them their own religious convictions—their preunderstandings about what these texts are saying. Consequently, much attention has been devoted to find out how to overcome such pre-understandings—indeed, to eradicate them from the process of interpreting. Yet, Bultmann (1884–1976), in his 1957 essay "Is Exegesis without Presuppositions Possible?" (in *Existence and Faith: Shorter Writings of Rudolf Bultmann*, translated by Schubert M. Ogden [New York: Meridian, 1960], pp. 289–295), and many of his followers, conceded that no interpretation is possible without pre-understandings. Thus, conceiving of the task of critical biblical studies as the overcoming of believers' convictions brought to the text is a misguided endeavor. Scholars have their own pre-understandings/convictions!

Before considering the role of the readers' convictions, biblical studies needs to begin by an investigation of the religious character of biblical texts, as Bultmann already emphasized in his project of "demythologization." Yet, how are biblical texts related to faith? How does one elucidate their religious character? These are the questions that structural exegesis seeks to address. But these are not new questions.

The traditional answer has been (and still is, for many) that biblical texts provide the content of faith. Faith is the cognitive appropriation either of dogmas or (most importantly for our topic) of the content of scripture. From this perspective, it is essential that the contents of scripture be preserved from any corruptions brought about by (wrong) pre-understandings. But, by pointing out that pre-understandings are not the problem, Bultmann presupposed a different view of faith. As Carl Braaten lamented in a polemical article against the "new hermeneutics," for Bultmann (and his followers) "everything in the Bible is divided up between presuppositions of faith or expressions of faith, with nothing left for the ground and content of faith apart from the bare assertion that faith has an objective, though not objectifiable, point of support outside of itself in the kerygmatic Christ" ("How New Is The New Hermeneutic?" *Theology Today*, 22/2 [1965], p. 227). What Braaten forgot is that all this was not new with Bultmann. Actually, the very possibility of proceeding with critical biblical studies had been opened by Friedrich Schleiermacher (1768–1834) and his different understanding of faith and of the Bible as scripture.

For Jacqueline Mariña, Schleiermacher's "Copernican revolution in theology" was his affirmation that (contrary to the view still presupposed much later by Braaten), faith is *not* the cognitive appropriation of either dogmas or the content of scripture. Scriptural texts are second-order statements reflecting the religious experiences of their authors. When this is acknowledged, critical biblical studies become possible. Since biblical texts do not provide the content of faith, they can be studied as any other texts. For Schleiermacher (see especially *On Religion* [1799, 1831] and *The Christian Faith* [1821–1822, 1830–1831]), Christian theology is grounded in the religious experience that precedes the subject/object dichotomy: the feeling of absolute dependence awakened in and through believers' relation to God or Christ—what contemporary theologians Daphne Hampson and Sarah Coakley (in *Swallowing a Fishbone? Feminist Theologians Debate Christianity*, edited by Daphne Hampson, pp. 1–16 and 82–111 respectively [London: SPCK, 1996]) and Cristina Grenholm (*Motherhood and Love* [Grand Rapids, Mich.: Eerdmans, 2010]) call "heteronomy," and what Greimas (in *Semiotics and Language*) calls the "proprioceptive" or "thymic" experiences re-presented in the fundamental semantics of a discourse. Thus, for Schleiermacher (*Hermeneutics and Criticism*, 1830), hermeneutics—

"the art of understanding . . . the discourse of another correctly"—is a process that includes (a) "grammatical" interpretation that concerns the meaning of utterances in relation to a preexisting language and its vocabulary, syntax, morphology, and phonetics and (b) the "psychological" interpretation concerning how the author employs this language for his or her own purposes. In the case of biblical texts, the "psychological" interpretation should acknowledge that biblical texts express the religious experiences of their authors (i.e., heteronomous experiences) and should elucidate the particular ways in which these texts do so.

This being acknowledged, it remained for Schleiermacher to envision how to make a clear distinction between the "grammatical" and the "psychological" aspects of the way authors represent their relation to historical situations and religious experiences. For David Strauss, Schleiermacher did not succeed in applying his own theory. Strauss (in his *The Christ of Faith and the Jesus of History*, 1865) critiqued Schleiermacher's *Life of Jesus* (1832) for not taking enough into account the religious, indeed "mythical," character of Gospel texts. Yet, what is the relationship between the historical and the mythical (heteronomous) components of religious texts? This was an issue that remained to be resolved.

Beyond Strauss, the so-called "history of religion" school (e.g., in New Testament, William Wrede, 1859–1906; Wilhelm Bousset, 1865–1920; Johannes Weiss, 1863–1914; with whom I associate Albert Schweitzer, 1875–1965; and the "theologian" Ernst Troeltsch, 1865–1923) kept in mind that biblical texts reflect the religious experiences of their authors. Thus these scholars investigated, for instance, Jesus "in the faith of early Christians" (Weiss; Bousset; Wrede) or the apocalyptic character of New Testament texts (Weiss; Schweitzer). Since, following Schleiermacher, Troeltsch affirmed that the faith of early Christians was not dependent upon "dogmatics," an alternative "historical" method was needed—namely a comparative method. In *The Absoluteness of Christianity* (1902), Troeltsch argued that the characteristics of Christianity should be apprehended by comparing Christian texts with texts of other religions, as his colleagues in the history of religion school were doing.

This comparative approach has the effect of emphasizing the "figures" (for Greimas's structural semiotic theory these are central features of "discursive semantics") of biblical texts. Thus historians of religion studied apocalyptic figures, and especially the figures of the kingdom and of Christ in the New Testament, by comparing them with similar figures in early Jewish texts. In brief, the authors' religious experiences (or heteronomous convictions) can be indirectly apprehended through an analysis of the figurative dimensions of biblical texts that express how they compare and differ from other religious texts, since, by definition, a figure brings together features from two distinct semantic worlds (as is easily recognized when one remembers that a metaphor is a figure). Yet, should the "religious" in biblical texts be once again reduced to one of its dimensions—this time, the set of mythical and figurative re-presentations of religious experiences? Beyond his work with the history of religion school, Troeltsch was also engaged in sociological studies in dialogue with Max Weber (*The Social Teaching of the Christian Churches*, 1912). For him biblical texts reflect religious views through their re-presentations of the social world, as well as through their figures.

These insights from the history of religion school parallel the work of the Roman Catholic Modernist movement (led by Friedrich von Hügel, 1852–1925, and including Alfred Loisy, 1857–1940), which sought to account for the religious dimensions of religious texts by theorizing that the author's religious experience was not only expressed by the figurative dimensions of the text, but also by its presentation of the institutional, social relations, as well as by rational (theological or philosophical) arguments. As Ellen Leonard shows (in *Creative Tension: The Spiritual Legacy of Friedrich von Hügel* [Scranton: University of Scranton Press, 1997]), for Catholic Modernists, religion involves three types of elements or features—"the authoritative, historical, institutional" (that we can call the "social" or "relational"); "the critical, speculative, philosophical" (the assertion "I believe," the assertion or argument of the "autonomous" believer); and "the intuitive, vocational, mystical" (the "heteronomous" religious experience, expressed through figures and in other indirect ways, since it is apophatic). For the Modernists, these three religious elements are kept in creative tension, as von Hügel exemplified in *The Mystical Element of Religion as Studied in St. Catherine of Genoa and Her Friends* (1908) and Loisy implemented in his study of early Christianity, *The Gospel and the Church* (1902).

This acknowledgment of the multidimensional "religious" elements in biblical texts was short lived. Despite the rejection of positivism, biblical studies continued to develop historical critical studies as a scientific endeavor, limited to the grammatical aspect of Schleiermacher's view of hermeneutics, and bracketed out its "psychological" aspect, and thus the religious experience that the biblical authors represented in their works. Thus Wilhelm Dilthey (1833–1911) extended Schleiermacher's approach by placing hermeneutics within the broad context of the human sciences, while "form criticism," followed by historical criticism, strove to domesticate ("formalize!") the feeling of absolute dependence that religious experience is according to Schleiermacher.

Beyond his formalist work, Bultmann, from an existentialist perspective, strove to come back to the work of the history of religion school by viewing the task of biblical studies as a demythologization of the ancient cultural assumptions of the Bible that was ultimately aimed at expressing the biblical message in the idiom of modern thought. Yet, together with other biblical critics, Bultmann failed because he ignored Schleiermacher's fundamental insight that faith is not to be limited to the cognitive appropriation of the content of scripture (even if this content is an existential experience); faith is also a religious experience, a heteronomous feeling of absolute dependence that is beyond what language "refers to"—beyond words, apophatic—conveyed through figures, poetry, arts. Thus, the primary message of biblical texts—the religious experiences of biblical authors—cannot be accessed as long as one has a traditional view of language as a container of meaning, the "content" (including an existential content). Actually, this view makes it impossible to study the symbolic dimensions of religious texts.

The Linguistic and Semiotic Quest for a View of Language Free From Universalist Blinders. While biblical scholars were struggling with these issues, linguists and semioticians challenged similar presuppositions regarding the nature of language. The semiotician Charles Sanders Peirce (1839–1914) explored the implications of Augustine's triadic definition of sign: "A sign is *something* that shows itself to the *senses* and something other than itself to the *mind*" (emphases added). A sign is (1) a "signifier," *something*, for example, the uttered word "tree," (2) which shows itself to the *senses* (the ear), points to a "signified," namely what the sound "tree" refers to—for Augustine, an intrinsic, universal reality; (3) the *mind* of the "interpretant" envisions the signifier as related to her/him—in our example, by envisioning a particular kind of tree known to the particular "interpretant" (Pierce's term). Augustine had pondered consistent symbol systems (which presume connections between individual, community, and ultimate reality), such as sacraments ("sacred signs") as acts in which material signs (e.g. water, bread, wine, oil) are bearers of grace and divine presence. Augustine, following Aristotle, maintained the intrinsic relation between the signifier and the signified. He regarded the signifier as a symptom, and, as a symptom is an intrinsic part of a disease, so a signifier and its signified are intrinsically related. Although the material signifiers (words of different languages) vary, they "refer to" the same concept for all humans. Thus, faith can be understood as the appropriation of the universal meaning content to which religious signs "refer."

This understanding of sign as the relation of a signifier and a signified is most helpful for theology as a discourse about a mystery: God who transcends human language. Consequently sign theory was also the concern of Boethius (fifth–sixth c.), of Anselm of Canterbury and Abelard (eleventh c.), of later Scholastics, as well as of Roger Bacon and John Duns Scotus (thirteenth c.). But for Charles Sanders Pierce

(1839–1914), Augustine's proposal does not truly account for the triadic understanding of sign: the "interpretant" (reader, hearer, viewer) plays a central role, acknowledged but not explored by Augustine. Pierce explored the implications of this triadic definition of sign for logic, pragmatism, and communication—leading to linguistic and semiotic theories (such as Umberto Eco's *A Theory of Semiotics* [Bloomington: Indiana University Press, 1976]) concerned with communication through different types of signs. But the work of the linguist Ferdinand de Saussure (1857–1913) provided the theoretical grounding for a different kind of semiotic, "*structural* semiotics"—primarily concerned with how meaning is produced (constructed, structured) through language in discourse.

For Saussure, a sign is the *arbitrary* (not intrinsic) relation of a "signifier" (e.g. the four letters and uttered sounds in "tree" or five letters and sounds in "*arbre*") and a "signified" (the similar but not identical mental concept of the reality "tree"). Through this view of language, Saussure and his many followers, including the Danish linguist Louis Hjelmslev (1899–1965) and the French linguist Émile Benveniste (1902–1976), radically challenged the universalist view of the signified (all humans have the same signified concept) posited from Aristotle and Augustine to the Enlightenment (when cultural diversity was viewed as transcended in an intelligible realm). Rather, in itself a sign is a *constructed, structured* linguistic entity that sets in relation a signifier and signified.

In addition, Saussure made a significant distinction between "*parole*" (the use of language in discourse) and "language" as a system of signs. Accordingly one can make a distinction between diachronic linguistics (how a given language and its signs change with time by being used in "*parole*"—the primary concern of philological exegesis) and synchronic linguistics (the study of language as a system of signs). In this latter case, linguistics includes a study both of the *structured* relations between signifiers and signifieds and of the *structured* interrelations of signs in a system. A sign *refers* to or *denotes* something; its arbitrary signifier points to a signified. A sign also acquires *connotations* through its interrelations with other signs in language as a (constructed) system of signs.

Louis Hjelmslev refined Saussure's theory by underscoring the complexity of the interrelations of signs in a system. A system of signs must be viewed as structured in a twofold way—through the interrelations of its signifiers (or "expressions" for Hjelmslev) and also through the interrelations of its signifieds (or "contents"). This complexification is not futile. It opened the possibility of acknowledging that the system of connotations (or convictions) of a semiotic system includes both broader cultural connotations (related to the structure [or "form" for Hjelmslev] of the system of signifiers, e.g., a phonetic system) and communal connotations (related to the structure of the system of signifieds, e.g., the semantic universe shared by one of the communities using this phonetic system). A discourse (the use of language in "*parole*") both *refers* to (*denotes*) what the speaker/writer consciously wants to communicate through a particular use of language and conveys (most often subconsciously) *connotations* (*convictions*) embedded in the twofold structure of the language (as a system of signs) he/she uses.

Transitions and Developments: Hermeneutics, Theory, Exegesis, Ethics. This development of linguistic and semiotic theories made it possible to bring together biblical studies and the quest for the "religious" in biblical interpretations by making room for hermeneutical questions, which, in turn, led to the development of structural semiotic theories and their applications in biblical studies.

When Semiotics and Biblical Studies Are Brought Together by Hermeneutics. Despite the efforts of the "new hermeneutic" school (led by James M. Robinson and John B. Cobb, Jr., which was calling biblical scholars to read Hans-Georg Gadamer's *Truth and Method*, 1960), in the mid-1960s (as is still the case for many today) exegesis remained aimed at establishing "the" true meaning of the text—a meaning-content in the text-container, what the author meant. Yes, the role of the scholar's pre-understandings was acknowledged (no exegesis is free from pre-understandings, as Bultmann acknowledged), but the task of historical biblical exegetes is to minimize the role of these pre-understandings. The role of exegesis is to establish the true meaning of the text, which, accordingly, is to be prolonged by hermeneutics. Exegesis was first (e.g., for Bultmann exegesis was aimed at demythologizing the biblical text to uncover its true existential meaning), followed by the hermeneutical task, in order to re-mythologize this meaning in another cultural and religious context.

But a number of biblical scholars (such as Franz J. Leenhardt) were in dialogue with Gadamer and Paul Ricoeur (already preparing *The Conflict of Interpretations*). Consequently they were struggling with the perplexing possibility that any interpretation, including the most rigorous historical exegesis, might be the result of a hermeneutical process necessarily shaped by the interpreters' cultures, their concrete life-contexts, and their religious experiences—and that this is as it should be! Paraphrasing Leenhardt (who had recently published both his commentary on Romans and *La parole et le buisson de feu*), one should respect the differences among interpretations (a) by believers of a scriptural text as Word-to-live-by ("*parole*" in a life-context); (b) by believers as Sacrament (part of the reader's "*feu*" [fire] of religious experience); and (c) by critical exegetes. This is a matter of ecumenical spirit and also of humility and probity; critical exegetes should acknowledge that their interpretations are, as any other interpretations, shaped not only by many analytical/textual choices among plausible alternatives, but also by contextual and theological interests. In *The Conflict of Interpretations* (1974; French 1965), Ricoeur made two complementary points that opened the possibility to develop structural semiotics and structural exegesis:

(1) For Ricoeur, any interpretation leaves out a "surplus of meaning" because it chooses to focus on one aspect of the text viewed as "most significant" and excludes others; consequently there is a plurality of legitimate interpretations. The role of the reader becomes primordial; as Greimas said, in any interpretation the reader "textualizes"—that is creates a text—out of one meaning-producing dimension, while bracketing out other dimensions (the surplus of meaning). Hermeneutics and semiotics begin to come together.

(2) For Ricoeur, one meaning-producing dimension of the text (commonly ignored in biblical exegesis) is its mythical structure studied by the anthropologist Claude Lévi-Strauss. The mythical vision of life and of the world—the religious feeling of absolute dependence (Schleiermacher), "the intuitive, mystical" dimension of human experience (Catholic Modernists), heteronomy as the deepest religious experience (Coakley, Grenholm), the "proprioceptive" or "thymic" experiences of fundamental semantics and the "semantic universe" (Greimas)—is not expressed by what a myth *refers to* (e.g. to humans and animals and what happened to them) but by the *structure* that holds together "mythemes" (bundles of narrative elements). Without proceeding to a comparative study (as the history of religion school was doing), one can analyze a religious text (a myth, a biblical text) to elucidate the characteristics of a mythical system—or a "system of convictions"—by showing how it is structured.

From Structural Semiotic Theories To Structural Exegesis. Structural exegesis could then be envisioned. The difficulty was that, unlike Lévi-Strauss who could analyze many myths from the same indigenous groups (as he did in his four volume series *Mythologiques*, 1964–1971), in biblical studies we are usually limited to very few texts from a given historical person or group. Lévi-Strauss's famous "formula" (see *Structural Anthropology* [New York: Basic Books, 1963], ch. 11; English translation of *Anthropologie structurale*, first published in 1958) proved to be impossible to use by itself; yet his general structural model of subsequent mediations of oppositions proved helpful, e.g., for the study of Galatians (Patte 1976), and of the Gospel of Mark (Elizabeth Struthers Malbon 1986). But even in these studies, Lévi-Strauss's approach and its universalist claims were complemented by the analysis of other structures of the biblical texts—

"structural" exegesis was already becoming "post-structural."

During that time, Roland Barthes was analyzing myths of popular culture (*Mythologies*, 1957) and fashion as a semiotic system, while studying Hjelmslev's linguistic theory and developing on this basis what he called "semiology" (French 1964; English 1968). Following Hjelmslev, Barthes emphasized the multiplicity of structures. This led him to develop the analysis of thematic or semiotic "codes," which reflect through their interwoven structures the plurality of meaning-producing dimensions of the text in literature (analyzing Balzac's short story "Sarrasine" in *S/Z*; French 1970; English 1975). Each code offers the possibility to develop one kind of reading of a text; the plurality of codes in each text calls for a plurality of legitimate readings. Now, at last, this was a practical model that biblical scholars could use.

So in July 1969 a group of biblical scholars led by Xavier Léon-Dufour gathered together with Barthes, reflecting on how structural semiotics transformed the relationship between exegesis and hermeneutics (Léon-Dufour, ed., *Exégèse et herméneutique* [Paris: Seuil, 1971]). This group included Jean Delorme, Jean Calloud, Jean Panier, and many others who became regular participants in the semiotic seminar of A. J. Greimas at L'École des Hautes Études (Paris). Greimas had recently published *Structural Semantics* (French 1966, which proposed a fundamental model for the most basic production of meaning, "the semiotic square," to hold together Lévi-Strauss's studies of myths, Vladimir Propp's studies of Russian folktales, and Hjelmslev's linguistics) and *On Meaning* (French 1970, which refined this model by relating it to other meaning-producing dimensions, including narrative and syntax). Barthes's "codes" were cataloged according to specific structures to which they belong, such as "narrative syntax codes," "discursive codes," and "thematic (or figurative) codes" (also called "isotopies").

Greimas and his collaborators (including biblical scholars) often chose biblical texts in their quest for a semiotic theory. This observation is significant. Semioticians were exclusively preoccupied with the development of a semiotic "theory"—through the structural modeling of the processes of meaning production. By contrast, biblical scholars wanted to develop new exegetical approaches that would account for those meaning-producing dimensions ignored in traditional studies of biblical texts. At first these divergent goals led to much confusion. Semioticians were much puzzled by biblical scholars who got hold of a structural model regarding one of the many meaning-producing dimensions and who strove to apply it for some exegetical purpose. Conversely, biblical scholars were disappointed as they read for their exegetical payoffs the analyses of biblical texts by semioticians who were trying to clarify one or another aspect of semiotic theory. Such were the cases of Edmund Leach's structural analysis of *Genesis as Myth* (London: Cape, 1969), aimed at demonstrating that Lévi-Strauss's model could be verified through its application to myths from a very different cultural milieu; and of Louis Marin's *The Semiotics of the Passion Narrative* (1980; English translation of *Sémiotique de la Passion, topiques et figures*, first published in 1971), aimed at testing how to interrelate models proposed by Lévi-Strauss, Barthes, and Greimas, as well as the linguistic theories of Saussure, Jakobson, Hjelmslev, and Pierce.

For several years, in their quest for a method of structural exegesis, biblical scholars had to become semioticians, i.e., through their analysis of biblical texts, they had to participate in the development of semiotic theories regarding the identification of the various meaning-producing dimensions in text/discourse (of any kind) and demonstrate how the meaning-producing process of each could be modeled. This is what the Groupe d'Entrevernes (including Delorme, Calloud, and Panier, as well as George Combet, Corina Galland-Combet, François Génuyt, Jean-Claude Giroud, and Annie Perrin) did in their journal (*Sémiotique et Bible*, since 1975) and in their first collective volume (French 1977), while attempting to move "from theory to practice" in their second volume (1979)—as each of the members of the group did in their individual publications. This is what Olivette Genest (and her colleagues in Québec) did as she moved from a verification of semiotic models in a study of the Passion according to Mark (1978) to a harvesting of exegetical results on the basis of her analysis of the New Testament texts about Jesus's death (1995). Similarly, following *Biblical Structuralism* (Semeia Studies; Philadelphia: Fortress Press, 1977), a theoretical-methodological book, Robert Polzin developed (beginning in 1980) a series of studies on the Deuteronomist (*Moses and the Deuteronomist: Deuteronomy, Joshua, Judges* [New York: Seabury Press, 1980]; *Samuel and the Deuteronomist: 1 Samuel* [San Francisco: Harper & Row, 1989]; *David and the Deuteronomist: 2 Samuel* [Bloomington: Indiana University Press, 1993]).

Nevertheless, some biblical scholars remained semiotic theorists, such as Ellen van Wolde who, after a theoretical and methodological analysis of Genesis 2—3 (*A Semiotic Analysis of* Genesis 2–3: *A Semiotic Theory and Method of Analysis Applied to the Story of the Garden of Eden* [Assen, Netherlands: Van Gorcum, 1989]) and exegetical works on Genesis, Ruth, and Job, still pursues theoretical/methodological research as she brings together biblical studies and linguistics, semiotics, cultural, and cognitive studies (*Reframing Biblical Studies: When Language and Text Meet Culture, Cognition, and Context* [Winona Lake, Ind.: Eisenbrauns, 2009]). Similarly, Daniel Patte moved back and forth between methodological works (e.g. *Structural Exegesis for New Testament Critics* [Minneapolis: Fortress, 1990]), to pure semiotic research (translation of the first volume of Greimas's semiotic dictionary, 1982; contributions to the second volume, 1986; his own theoretical book, 1990), and structural exegeses of Paul (*Paul's Faith and the Power of the Gospel: A Structural Introduction to the Pauline Letters* [Philadelphia: Fortress Press, 1982]) and Matthew (*The Gospel According to Matthew: A Structural Commentary on Matthew's Faith* [Philadelphia: Fortress Press, 1987]) aimed at elucidating their respective systems of convictions. Also several scholars have used a plurality of structural approaches with one exegetical goal: Timothy Cargal analyzed discursive and semantic structures to elucidate the system of convictions of James (1993); and Yung Suk Kim analyzed discursive and semantic structures to elucidate a key figure, *Christ's Body in Corinth: The Politics of a Metaphor* (Minneapolis: Fortress, 2008).

Structural Exegesis Complementing the Quest of the History of Religion: Mythical and Semantic Structures. What was gained through these and many other theoretical, methodological, and then exegetical works in structural semiotics? The person of Pierre Geoltrain (1929–2004) symbolizes the advance in part. Without abandoning the editing of apocryphal texts, Geoltrain was a fervent semiotician (and colleague of Greimas), who strove to develop in his teaching the practice of structural semiotic analysis of biblical texts. Nevertheless, his primary research project remained the development of critical approaches in "history of religion" (the program he led at L'École des Hautes Études, Paris). Through the use of Lévi-Strauss's structural model for the study of myths, Barthes's exemplary studies of codes, and especially Greimas's structural semiotic models for "fundamental semantics" (the traces of fundamental religious experiences), "narrative semantics" (the semantic universe as a more concrete representation of these religious experiences, yet still prior to the subject/object dichotomy), and "discursive semantics" (the thematic and figurative intertextual presentation of this semantic universe in terms of the enunciatee's own semantic universe), one can lay the groundwork for history of religion comparative studies. Indeed, by identifying how the religious dimensions of a biblical text are constructed prior to the subject/object dichotomy (as Schleiermacher wanted), one can proceed to a more rigorous comparison with religious texts from other traditions or from other cultural and historical contexts (as the history of religion school—as well as the Catholic Modernists—strove to do, with only partial success). Whether or not such comparative approaches—including the history of the receptions of biblical texts (as in Panier, *Récit et commentaires de la tentation de Jésus* [Paris: Cerf, 1984])—make it explicit, they are often framed by structural categories that reflect structural theories; one commonly studies how the "view" or "conception" of a feature of human existence is "constructed," that is, "structured."

From Multiple Types of Structural Exegeses to Structural Interpretation and Ethics of Biblical Interpretation. The development of more mature structural semiotic theories—marked by Greimas's publication, with the contributions of many collaborators, of his two-volume semiotic dictionary (French 1979–1986; English 1982) and the publications by other scholars on "narratology"—made it possible to envision other types of structural exegeses. For instance, the "actantial model," together with the models of other features of "narrative syntax," as well as the models for "temporalization," "spatialization," and "characterization" of "discursive syntax" prompted the development of narrative analyses of biblical texts (see, e.g., Malbon, *In the Company of Jesus: Characters in Mark's Gospel* [Louisville: Westminster John Knox, 2000]). The model for the "fundamental syntax" opened the possibility of analyses of the ideology that frames a discourse (see Carlos Reis 1993). And the discursive components ("discursive syntax" and "discursive semantics"), because they reflect the interactions between enunciator and enunciatee, open the possibility to relate certain types of structural exegeses to traditional exegeses. Yet the main payoff of using structural semiotics in biblical studies is not in these discrete exegetical methods, but in the fact that it opens the possibility of assuming ethical responsibility for our choices of interpretation.

As noted, structural semiotic theories distinguish among six meaning-producing dimensions—indeed, many more since their subcomponents are also meaning-producing. First, this means that each meaningful component—e.g., a (discursive semantic) figure, a (discursive semantic) theme, a (semantic) value, a (syntactic) concept, a (discursive syntactic) character—in a biblical text can be "deconstructed" to show its distinctive formulation. Deconstruction is what structural exegesis is all about.

Second, and most importantly, Greimas's semiotic theory underscores that, in the process of reading/interpreting, the reader creates a text ("textualizes") by focusing upon a single *one* of these many meaning-producing dimensions as "the most significant one." The reader makes meaning out of it by complementing it and framing it with features from her/his context (and its economic, social, political features) and her/his hermeneutical perspective (and its cultural, philosophical, theological, religious views). Mieke Bal demonstrates this process through a remarkable analysis of the "codes" (Barthes's concept refined in such a way that these codes are equivalent to Greimas's structured meaning-producing dimensions) used in scholarly interpretations of Judges 4 and 5 (the two stories of the death of Sisera). She finds that the scholars she consulted constructed their interpretations by using either historical codes (focusing on discursive syntax), theological codes (focusing on a part of fundamental syntax), anthropological codes (focusing on aspects of narrative semantics), or literary codes (focusing on figurativization, an aspect of discursive semantics). Then Bal shows that one can also read these chapters by using thematic codes (focusing on thematization, another aspect of discursive semantics) or gender codes (focusing on the combination of discursive syntax [characterization] and discursive semantics [thematization]). Thus, it becomes clear why there is a multiplicity of legitimate and plausible interpretations of the same text and a conflict of interpretations (Ricoeur).

As we acknowledge the role of the reader—a threefold role, including a textual/analytical choice (of the most significant features of the text), a contextual choice, and a hermeneutical choice—in the production of meaning with a text, we also have to acknowledge our ethical responsibility. Our interpretation is never the mere presentation of "what the text says" but our construction of a meaning on the basis of one of the many structured dimensions of the text. Therefore, we have to be accountable for the ways in which our choice of an interpretation affects, positively or negatively, other people around us. Thus, the ultimate payoff of structural exegesis is the possibility to envision an ethics of interpretation.

[*See also* Deconstruction; Formalist Interpretation; Literary Criticism, Literary Theory, and the Bible; Narrative Criticism and Narrative Hermeneutics; Poststructuralist Interpretation; Reader-Response Criticism; Reception Criticism and Theory; Rhetorical Criticism; Semiotics; Speech-Act Theory; *and* Synchronic Interpretation.]

BIBLIOGRAPHY

Barthes, Roland. *Mythologies.* Paris: Seuil, 1957. English translation under the same title, *Mythologies,* by Annette Lavers. London: Paladin, 1972; New York: Hill and Wang, 1972. Analyses of myths of popular culture serve as concrete examples as Barthes develops "semiology" and other elements of semiotic theory.

Barthes, Roland. *S/Z: An Essay.* Translated by Richard Miller. New York: Hill and Wang, 1975. English translation of *S/Z,* first published in 1970. Barthes's analysis of Balzac's short story "Sarrasine" emphasizes the multiplicity of structures through the analysis of thematic or semiotic "codes," which shows how their interwoven structures explain the plurality of meaning-producing dimensions of the text in literature. Each code offers the possibility to develop one kind of reading of a text; the plurality of codes in each text calls for a plurality of legitimate readings.

Barthes, Roland. *Writing Degree Zero* and *Elements of Semiology.* New York: Hill and Wang, 1968. English translation of *Le degré zéro de l'écriture. Suivi de: Eléments de sémiologie,* first published in 1964. *Elements of Semiology* provides a good introduction to Hjelmslev's linguistic theory, showing how its major features provide a framework for "semiology," or structural semiotics.

Cargal, Timothy Boyd. *Restoring the Diaspora: Discursive Structure and Purpose in the Epistle of James.* Atlanta: Scholars Press, 1993. A study of the epistle of James using structural exegesis aimed at elucidating characteristic features of James's religious teaching.

Delorme, Jean. *Au risque de la parole: lire les évangiles.* Paris: Seuil, 1991. A study of the Gospels using structural semiotics in order to elucidate their figurative and religious features.

Eco, Umberto. *A Theory of Semiotics.* Bloomington: Indiana University Press, 1976. A "sign centered" semiotic theory, by contrast with structural semiotics, which is semiotic theory concerned with the process of the "production of meaning."

Entrevernes Group (Groupe d'Entrevernes). *Analyse sémiotique des textes: introduction, théorie, pratique.* Lyon: Presses Universitaires de Lyon, 1979. A methodological book showing how to analyze—and thus deconstruct—texts (especially biblical texts), in order to elucidate their different meaning-producing dimensions.

Entrevernes Group (Groupe d'Entrevernes). *Signs and Parables: Semiotics and Gospel Texts.* With a study by Jacques Geninasca; postface by A. J. Greimas; translated by Gary Phillips. Pittsburgh, Pa.: Pickwick Press, 1978. English translation of *Signes et paraboles,* first published in 1977. A study of parables and other Gospel texts primarily aimed at confirming or developing aspects of semiotic theory.

Genest, Olivette. *Le Christ de la passion: perspective structurale: analyse de Marc 14,53–15,47, des parallèles bibliques et extra-bibliques.* Montréal: Bellarmin; Tournai: Desclée, 1978. An analysis of the passion narratives using structural semiotics aimed at elucidating characteristic features of the religious/theological teaching of these texts.

Genest, Olivette. *Le discours du Nouveau Testament sur la mort de Jésus: Épîtres et Apocalypse.* Sainte-Foy, Québec: Presses de l'Université Laval, 1995. An analysis of the presentation of the death of Jesus in the New Testament letters and the Apocalypse using structural semiotics aimed at elucidating characteristic features of the religious/theological teaching of these texts.

Greimas, Algirdas Julien. *Du sens; essais sémiotiques.* Vol. 1 & Vol. 2. Paris: Seuil, 1970–1983. Partly translated by Paul J. Perron and Frank H. Collins; foreword by Frederic Jameson; introduced by Paul J. Perron in *On Meaning: Selected Writings in Semiotic Theory.* London: F. Pinter, 1987. The volumes that have defined "semiotics" as a theory concerning the structured production of meaning, rather than a theory regarding signs.

Greimas, Algirdas Julien. *Sémantique structurale, recherche de méthode.* Paris: Larousse, 1966. Translated by Daniele McDowell, Ronald Schleifer, and Alan Velie; with an introduction by Ronald Schleifer in *Structural Semantics: An Attempt at a Method.* Lincoln: University of Nebraska Press, 1983. Foundational methodological research aimed at showing that the semantic dimensions of discourses are structured, including at the deepest level by the "semiotic square."

Greimas, Algirdas Julien and Joseph Courtés. *Sémiotique: dictionnaire raisonné de la théorie du langage.* Vol. 1 & 2. Paris: Hachette, 1979–1986. *Semiotics and Language: An Analytical Dictionary.* Translation of Vol. 1 of *Sémiotique* by Larry Crist, Daniel Patte, et al. Bloomington: Indiana University Press, 1982. The volumes presenting a mature structural semiotic theory developed by Greimas's seminar and showing that any meaningful reading of a discourse/text is constructed on the basis of one among many structured meaning-producing dimensions of the given discourse/text.

Hjelmslev, Louis. *Prolegomena to a Theory of Language.* Translated from the Danish (1943) by Francis J. Whitfield. Madison: University of Wisconsin Press, 1961 (a revised translation; original translation 1953). The linguistic theory that, together with that of de Saussure, is foundational for structural semiotics, and thus for structuralist interpretation/structural exegesis.

Leenhardt, Franz J. *La parole et le buisson de feu: les deux sources de la spiritualité chrétienne et l'unité de l'Église.* Neuchâtel, Paris: Delachaux et Niestlé, 1962. An early study showing the tension between and complementarity of exegesis (*la parole*) and liturgical/religious readings (*le buisson de feu*).

Malbon, Elizabeth Struthers. *Narrative Space and Mythic Meaning in Mark.* San Francisco: Harper & Row, 1986; Sheffield, UK.: Sheffield Academic Press, 1991. While demonstrating the usefulness of a Lévi-Straussian structuralist methodology for the study of the Gospel of Mark, Malbon does not allow the methodology to obscure Mark's narrative itself as she clarifies its mythic meaning.

Patte, Daniel. *The Religious Dimensions of Biblical Texts: Greimas's Structural Semiotics.* Semeia Studies. Atlanta: Scholars Press, 1990. A comprehensive presentation of Greimas's mature structural semiotic theory and its implications for the study of four religious dimensions of biblical texts.

Patte, Daniel. *What is Structural Exegesis?* Guides to Biblical Scholarship. Philadelphia: Fortress Press, 1976. Reprinted in 1978, 1981, and 1983. A methodological book seeking to show the need to complement historical critical studies with structural exegesis and illustrating Greimas's semiotic model for structural semantics and Lévi-Strauss's model for the structuralist study of myth for the study of New Testament texts.

Reis, Carlos. *Towards a Semiotics of Ideology.* Berlin and New York: Mouton de Gruyter, 1993. An illustration of the way semiotics provides tools to deconstruct ideologies—by contrast with the fundamental semantics and semantic universes, which are mythical religious dimensions of discourses/texts.

Ricoeur, Paul. *The Conflict of Interpretations: Essays in Hermeneutics.* Edited and translated by Don Ihde. Evanston, Ill.: Northwestern University Press, 1974. English translation of *Le conflit des interprétations: Essais d'herméneutique*, first published in 1969. Essays emphasizing that any interpretation or reading leaves out a "surplus of meaning" and that the "mythical structure" studied by Claude Lévi-Strauss should not be neglected.

Saussure, Ferdinand de. *Course in General Linguistics.* Edited by Charles Bally and Albert Sechehaye, with Albert Riedlinger. Translated by Roy Harris. English translation of *Cours de linguistique générale*, first published in 1916. London: Duckworth, 1983. One among several translations of the notes of de Saussure's students taken during his teaching at the University of Geneva between 1906 and 1911. The linguistic theory that, together with that of his follower, Louis Hjelmslev, is foundational for structural semiotics, and thus for structuralist interpretation/structural exegesis.

Daniel Patte

SYNCHRONIC INTERPRETATION

Synchronic interpretation of biblical texts emerged across the turn of the second and third millennia C.E. In synchronic interpretation, an interpreter approaches a text as a unified, literary whole. This development in biblical studies was accompanied by a number of significant literary scholars who turned their attention to the Bible as literature (e.g. Northrop Frye 1982; Stephen Prickett 1986). Their focus was upon the many narratives found in both the Hebrew Bible and the New Testament, some of them extremely formative of the different expressions of Jewish, Christian, and Islamic culture. For the Hebrew Bible, this is especially, but not only, true of the impressive narratives from Genesis (e.g., the story of Adam and Eve, the experiences of Abraham and the successive Patriarchs, the Joseph story), Exodus (dominated by Moses and the formation of a People of God through the gift of the Law, accompanied by numerous experiences of failure and subsequent divine punishment, especially the long wandering in the desert, and the prohibition of Moses's entry into the Promised Land), and the Historical Books (e.g., the dramatic cycles of Elijah and Elisha, the ambiguous leadership of King David). In the New Testament, the Gospels and the Acts of the Apostles are obviously stories, however distant they may be from contemporary narratives, that have formed Judaism, Christianity, Western culture, and other cultures that have developed from the biblical tradition, especially Islam.

A literary reading of biblical texts questioned contemporary scholarship, which, since the nineteenth century, was dominated by a historical, rather than literary, approach. In the eighteenth century, European Christianity was threatened by the emergence of a rational mindset, initiated by what is broadly called the Enlightenment. Affirmations about a God who intervenes in human history and speaks to patriarchs and prophets, a Chosen People, virgin birth, miracles, especially those that change the normal course of nature, the saving power of a man's death and resurrection from the dead were all questioned. All truth had to be judged by the criteria of rational proof. The many contradictions, repetitions, and biblical affirmations that could not be proven but had to be accepted in faith were attacked by the English Deists and others who sought to understand God and the human story on the basis of a more rational reading of the past and present.

The Diachronic Approach to Texts. The response of Christian (although not Jewish) scholarship to these questions was to adopt many of the critical methods that came from the Enlightenment. Historical questions asked of the text assumed that it did not come from heaven as an inviolable word of God. Each story had its own historical development, its own cultural setting, and was the work of human minds and hands, using the traditions and materials available to them. This explained many of the tensions highlighted by a more skeptical readership. Modern biblical scholarship, since the nineteenth century, employed a method known as diachronic. The expression "diachronic" derives from the meaning of the Greek preposition *dia*, which means "through," and *chronos*, which refers to "time." A diachronic interpretation looks "through" the text to the many backgrounds behind the text, especially the text in its originating time period/s. Two brief examples demonstrate how this works.

The Old Testament. The tensions and literary complexities of the first five books of the Bible—Genesis, Exodus, Leviticus, Numbers, and Deuteronomy—widely known by the Hebrew word Torah, could be explained by a theory of sources. Diachronic studies showed that, although the texts were unified in the fifth century B.C.E., some of the traditions reached back to a period close to 1000 B.C.E. Although not the first to develop a theory of traditions, Julius Wellhausen's *Prolegomena zur Geschichte Israels* (1883; Eng. trans., 1957) greatly influenced most Old Testament scholars.

Such scholars accepted at least four traditions: the so-called Jahwist, Elohist, Deuteronomistic, and Priestly (identified as J, E, D, and P, respectively). Each strand had its own long history and literary and theological characteristics. The Jahwist and the Elohist were both ancient storytellers, most likely recalling and recording folk stories, originally composed between 1000–900 B.C.E. The two traditions used different names to refer to the one God of Israel (Jahweh [J] and Elohim [E]). The Deuteronomist is most powerfully represented in the book of Deuteronomy but had a profound impact upon much of the Hebrew Bible beyond the Torah, especially the historical books and some prophetic traditions. There is a tradition that the book of Deuteronomy was found in the Temple at the time of King Josiah (621 B.C.E.), though its history is certainly more complex than this and may have originated in the Northern Kingdom. About 510 B.C.E. the Deuteronomist was responsible for combining J, E, and D as Israel pondered its failure and its experience of Exile (circa 587–537 B.C.E.). The Deuteronomist is highly exhortative, reflecting upon the never-failing love of God and the fragility of Israel. Already at this stage, the unification of much of the Torah as we know it was under way (a unified JED probably existed). Finally, perhaps four hundred years before the Common Era, the Priestly tradition introduced its own unique contribution. It had a long history and was highly ordered, as can be seen in the systematic presentation of the creation in Genesis. 1:1—2:4a (so different from the Adam and

Eve story and its aftermath, the product of a combination of the J and E traditions). P is responsible for the careful articulation of long lists of the minutiae of Israel's legal traditions and the many genealogies that join one part of the narrative to another. It was the work of the Priestly authors and redactors that gave us the Torah as we now have it (JEDP). Most likely the Torah that Ezra brought back to Israel from Babylon in 400–420 B.C.E. was this fully combined Torah.

Thus, although there are epic stories, patriarchal family narratives, poetry, legal texts, genealogies, exhortations, and much else in the Torah, they are juxtaposed traditions that cross a span of almost a thousand years. The use of source criticism to explain the tensions in the Torah, once extremely fashionable, is now out of favor. Even the brief description offered earlier is hotly debated by those who still defend a theory of sources. It serves, however, as a good example of how diachronic scholarship approached major Hebrew Bible passages until recent times.

The New Testament. As with Hebrew Bible scholarship, critical Christian scholars also looked to the sources that might lie behind the documents we now have in the New Testament. Even the earliest Christian documents, the letters of Paul (circa 50–65 C.E.), were subjected to intense analysis in an attempt to find pre-Pauline, Christian traditions that Paul picked up from very early tradition and incorporated into his letters. Identification of what was pre-Pauline enabled the interpreter to follow the Pauline redaction that produced the letter as we have it. The Gospel of Mark was deemed to be the earliest of the Four Gospels (circa 70 C.E.), and Matthew and Luke, in their own ways, depended upon Mark, another early tradition that they shared (called Q, an abbreviation for the German word *Quelle* = source), and their own unique sources (circa 85–90 C.E.). Source criticism began the diachronic study of the New Testament (e.g., Heinrich J. Holtzmann, *Die synoptische Evangelien: Ihr Ursprung und geschichtlicher Character*, 1863). It was followed by what is known as form criticism. Literary forms present in non-Christian literature were traced in the Gospels. Passages were broken down into their different "forms," as transmitted through the Gospel texts, and their origin and meaning determined (e.g., Martin Dibelius, *Die Formgeschichte des Evangeliums*, 1919; Eng. trans., 1971).

The Gospel of John, so different from Mark, Matthew, and Luke, was seen as the result of several editions, reaching its final form about 100 C.E. The most systematic analysis of the sources that formed the Gospel of John was published by Rudolf Bultmann (*Das Evangelium des Johannes* [Göttingen: Vandenhoeck & Ruprecht 1941]; Eng. trans., 1971). Although Bultmann's work was not without its predecessors, many have followed his method, if not his conclusions, since then. The Fourth Gospel began with a source similar to that of Mark, Matthew, and Luke, but eventually developed in a more Greco-Roman (and even gnostic) setting, before its final shape was produced by an evangelist and a final redactor who sought to bring this story of Jesus more into conformity with an emerging mainstream Christian Church.

Increasing dissatisfaction with these diachronic readings of the biblical texts led to attempts to see the documents of the New Testament not only as a collection of pearls, but also as a necklace, in which a unified theological perspective strung those pearls together. This approach is nowadays known as redaction criticism. All diachronic readings ask historical questions. What is the historical background that produced these sources? How did they emerge in their present form? What was the historical situation in the early Church that generated the theological perspective represented in a finished narrative? In a diachronic interpretation, the text is not read and interpreted at face value; the interpreter gazes "through" the text to discover, for example, the many possible elements that indicate the hand of J, E, D, and P in the Torah, or the sources, the literary forms, and the theological persuasion that generated a Gospel text. The interpretation of the text depends upon the responses given to diachronic questions. It could be said that background determines meaning.

The Turn to Synchrony. Biblical scholarship became dissatisfied with the arid search for possible historical and literary forerunners to the text as we now have it. Diachronic scholarship devoted almost 200 years to the rediscovery of the world behind the text to interpret the world in the text. Synchronic interpretation devotes increased attention to the world in the text, not to look through it to the world that formed it, but to appreciate the text in its final form, and to look beyond it, to trace how any particular text might address the world in front of the text. Influenced by the growing interest in the Bible as literature rather than adopting the critical tools that emerged from the Enlightenment, a synchronic interpretation approaches each document, however limited and flawed it might be, as a work of art. A synchronic interpretation takes it for granted that, whatever its history, each biblical document found its way into the Bible because it was regarded as a single utterance, a document that made sense from beginning to end. The expression "synchronic" depends upon the Greek proposition *syn*, "with, side by side." It questions the primacy of a method that looks "through" (*dia*) the text, in an attempt to interpret how the document as a whole (*syn*) addresses those who read it, hear it, or see it performed at a point in time (*chronos*).

The text is read from verse to verse, from chapter to chapter, allowing the text as it now stands to force the interpreter to understand it in its own right. In synchronic interpretation, the text determines meaning. An initial warning must be issued, though. Critical synchronic readings do not ignore difficulties that arise from textual uncertainty. One must determine, in each case, what the original text might have been. Similarly, while one can speak of reading steadily from verse to verse and chapter to chapter, such divisions can only be used as helpful guides. They were not part of the original Greek manuscripts, which are, in their own turn, not originals. It is irresponsible to interpret texts that may be up to three thousand years old, written in Hebrew, Aramaic, and Greek, without asking historical questions. Diachronic questions must not be ignored.

Synchronic Interpretation. Contemporary biblical studies have developed synchronic approaches to the text known as narrative criticism or reader-response criticism. These are not identical but can be presented side by side. In brief, narrative criticism traces the dynamics of a narrative as such. Reader-response criticism focuses upon the impact the narrative may or may not have upon a reader. Adapting and applying theories of narrative developed by literary theorists, Old Testament scholars were the first to seize upon this possible approach, given the large amount of narrative text found within the pages of the Hebrew Bible. Whatever the diachronic analysis of the Torah may have said about the sources that produced the Torah, the patriarchal narratives, including the Joseph story, can be analyzed as narratives, irrespective of their sources. Many critics adopt the approaches described in what follows for Hebrew Bible narratives (Robert Alter, *The Art of Biblical Narrative* [New York: Basic Books, 1981]; Adele Berlin, *Poetics and Interpretation of Biblical Narrative* [Sheffield, UK: Almond, 1983]; Meier Sternberg, *The Poetics of Biblical Narrative: Ideological Literature and the Drama of Reading* [Bloomington: Indiana University Press, 1985]; Robert Alter and Frank Kermode, eds., *The Literary Guide to the Bible* [London: Collins, 1987]), while others insist that the biblical canon must determine interpretation and not the processes that formed it (Brevard S. Childs, *Introduction to the Old Testament as Scripture* [London: SCM, 1979]). New Testament critics have not been slow to follow.

Narrative Theory. The literary theory that has been adopted by most narrative and reader-response critics claims that behind each story there is a real author who has a definite person or group of people in mind as she or he tells the story, the intended real reader. In narrative theory, neither of these figures can be found in the story itself. An author constructs a narrative as a means to communicate a message to an audience. The real author, whoever he or she might have been, is long since dead, as are the original recipients of the book. But we still have the story, the words on a page. The biblical narratives have widespread readership and have been formative of culture, politics, mores, art, music, architecture, and much else. The biblical narratives have generated interested readers, hearers, and viewers for three thousand years.

Although the real author and the real reader(s) do not play an active role in the events of the narrative, they leave their traces. Narratives have deliberately contrived plots and characters that interact throughout the story along a certain time line, through a sequence of events, displaying certain emotions and various levels of character development. An author devises a use of time and space, and rhetorical features, to hold plot and character together so that the reader will not miss the author's point of view. These rhetorical features are in the narrative. Although narrative theoreticians dispute the exactness of the scheme, one can broadly claim that the communication between a real author and a real reader who are outside the text takes place through an implied author, a narrator, a narratee, and an implied reader who are inside the text. However obscure the details of the concrete situations of the original real author and the original real reader(s) may be, we still have the text, and much can be gleaned from it.

This may sound overly complex, but it reflects everyone's reading experience. Whether or not one knows whom the historical author was, and whether or not a story was directed specifically to the reader who has it in hand, any reader senses the presence of a storyteller, generally called "the narrator." Behind the narrator hides an author who is directing affairs. This author is called the implied author. She may not reveal herself but she determines the communication process in the narrative. Although not narrative, an example might serve as a guide to the complexities of the literary theory described earlier. A lost letter picked up by a disinterested third party quickly tells the reader something of the person writing the letter. The rhetoric of the letter also reveals something of the implied author's understanding of and approach to the implied reader. The person who has found the letter knows neither the real author nor the original intended reader, but the real reader—the person who picked up the letter from the pavement—is able to identify the communication attempted by the letter. The person who found the letter traces an author and a reader "implied" by the letter. Indeed, a very beautiful letter may even move the "eavesdropper." When that happens, mutuality is established between the reader "implied" by the letter and the real reader of the letter (the "eavesdropper"). One does not have to be part of the original communication process between the original writer of the letter and its original reader to be moved and inspired by the power of the emotions expressed by the letter. The literary form of a letter is very different from the sometimes complex literary shape of a narrative, especially those written up to three thousand years ago. However, the process of communication between an author and a reader takes place in both. Contemporary narrative approaches to the Gospels attempt to enter into the process of communication between an author and a reader whom we do not know, and who are long since dead, so that the contemporary reader might be moved and inspired by the passionate convictions of the author.

Although not ignoring historical questions that inevitably lie "behind" the text of a biblical narrative, synchronic interpretation focuses on the literary features found in the details of the narrative. Attention is given to the literary shape of each section of the story; the way each section follows logically from what went before and leads directly into what follows; the roles of the various characters in the story, their development (or lack of it) and their interaction; the passing of time; the identification of locations that may have a symbolic or historical importance; unresolved puzzles that emerge as the narrative unfolds, forcing the reader to look further into the narrative to tie these puzzles together; the consistency of the underlying point of view of an author who has shaped and told the story producing a satisfying and convincing complete utterance that is unified from beginning to end. Like the reader who "eavesdropped" on the letter found on the pavement and was moved by the sincerity and power of the emotions communicated by the letter, we "eavesdrop" on an ancient biblical story.

"Eavesdropping" on biblical stories, however, has been going on for some time, and it has served as an inspiration for Jews and Christians from all walks of life for almost three thousand years. The communication process that is established between the implied author and the implied reader necessarily elicits a number of responses in a contemporary real reader. They may be ethical, emotional, intellectual, or ideological, to mention only some of the major identifiable responses. This element in the reading process has determined the lasting value of biblical narratives.

The historical author of the book, long since dead and beyond our knowledge and scientific control, as well as the flesh-and-blood historical first real readers, are outside our control. We cannot be sure of the reception biblical stories received. The ongoing existence of the Bible demonstrates that they were received, treasured, and passed on. However, there is evidence in the Bible itself that reception was not always uniform. For example, the evidence of the Johannine Letters indicates that the readers did not always agree on what the author of the Gospel of John wanted to communicate. Indeed, they quickly broke into argument, and even division, over the christological and Christian significance of the Gospel. This is understandable. How one might respond to a biblical narrative may vary from day to day, depending on any number of circumstances. We are well aware of the numerous circumstances that affect, for better or worse, the reading process. Yet, within the narrative there is a reader addressed by the implied author, as there was an identifiable reader implied by the letter described previously. As the narrative unfolds, the reader is gradually provided with information and experiences that such a reader cannot avoid. This reader is shaped by the desires of the author and emerges as the text unfolds.

Synchronic Readings of Nonnarrative Texts. Although different in genre, the Pauline and other nonnarrative literature has been subjected to serious synchronic analysis in recent times. As with the interpretation of narratives, focus is given to the impact that the rhetoric of the such documents makes upon a reader, but more attention is necessarily devoted, for example, to the real Paul and an identifiable real readership in Thessalonica, Corinth, Galatia, Philippi, Rome, and the church in Philemon's house. The search for tiny fragments of pre-Pauline material, and the identification of the Pauline redaction of that material, is less important in contemporary readings. As with narrative critical and reader-response interpretations, the document is read as a unified document, a literary and artistic whole, determined by a rhetoric of persuasion. This has been strongly argued for the Letter to the Romans (Brendan Byrne, *Romans* [Collegeville, Minn.: Liturgical Press, 1996]) and 1 and 2 Corinthians (Charles H. Talbert, *Reading Corinthians: A Literary and Theological Commentary on 1 and 2 Corinthians* [New York: Crossroad, 1987]; Frank J. Matera, *2 Corinthians: A Commentary* [Louisville, Ky.: Westminster John Knox, 2003]). Such readings, however, continue to be strongly contested, for equally rhetorical reasons (Margaret Mitchell, *Paul, the Corinthians and the Birth of Christian Hermeneutics* [Cambridge: Cambridge University Press, 2010]). In these studies, the world that generated the text retains its central importance. What were the situations in Rome and Corinth (or Thessalonica, Galatia, and Philippi) that determined Paul's persuasive intervention? What must be known about master-slave relationships in the culture of the Roman Empire in the first century (Philemon)? Synchronic interpretations of narrative biblical texts must ask similar questions.

The Importance of History (Diachrony). What has been indicated about the emerging implied reader, based in contemporary literary theory, does not fully exhaust the task faced by a synchronic reading of biblical texts. As with synchronic interpretation of nonnarrative material (e.g. the Pauline Letters), so also the world that produced the narrative must be considered. For example, it is impossible that the reader of a Christian Gospel has no knowledge or experience of the story of Jesus of Nazareth and Christian life and its practices. The direct importation of contemporary literary scholarship into biblical studies would presuppose a "virginal" reader. This is unrealistic in reading ancient narratives, and even more so of ancient biblical narratives. The authors of biblical texts take it for granted that the reader knows many things. The implied reader knows Hebrew or Aramaic or Greek, depending on the text under scrutiny. To take one example, the reader in the Fourth Gospel is able to understand double meanings behind Greek words (e.g. John 3:3–5, 14; 8:28; 12:32), subtle ironies (e.g. 9:28–29; 19:14–15), and language that was used in the sacramental life of the community (6:51–58; 19:35). References to Jesus's resurrection are taken as understood from quite early in the story (cf. 2:22). More than knowledge of the syntactically correct and simple Greek of the Fourth Gospel is presupposed of its reader. The unexplained use of certain Jewish messianic categories (e.g. 1:19–51), religious customs (e.g. 2:6; 5:9; 6:4; 7:2; 10:22), and the geography of Palestine (e.g. 5:2; 18:1; 19:17) indicates that such things are taken as known.

The reader knows everything that the author presumes but does not explain. The reader in any Gospel story must be credited with some knowledge of the Jesus story, but the Markan, Matthean, Lukan, and Johannine shape of that story is presented to bring readers (or listeners or viewers) to accept a particular point of view. The same must be said for those who read and heard the Pauline letters. They are credited with a knowledge of major figures from Israel's history (especially Abraham), and take the life and teaching, especially the death and resurrection, of Jesus as unique moments in God's dealings with humankind. They are equally credited with an awareness of subtleties of Hellenistic rhetoric (Mitchell 2010). Paul builds his particular rhetoric of persuasion upon foundations that he can take for granted as known by his readers and hearers. The reader knows that Jesus died on a cross, but the author of the Gospel of Mark insinuates that Jesus is only the Christ and Son of God when he is crucified, in an agonizing and abandoned death (see the Markan use of the so-called "messianic secret" and MK 14:60–62; 15:21–39), while the author of the Gospel of John insists that Jesus's death is both a "lifting up" (cf. 3:14; 8:28; 12:32) and a glorification (11:4; 12:23). On two rare occasions the implied author of the Fourth Gospel does not hesitate to tell this implied reader why the story is being written in this particular way (19:35; 20:30–31). The same must be said of the presupposed knowledge of major Jewish traditions and Israelite religious practices for readers of the Hebrew Bible. Knowledge of the pre-history of Genesis. 1–11, the Mosaic tradition, the centrality of Torah, and the patriarchal history, to mention only the major elements, are presupposed of all readers of Old Testament texts.

It is dishonest in synchronic readings of ancient biblical texts not to recognize that every word is historically and culturally conditioned. The fact that it is written in Hebrew or Koine Greek is *prima facie* evidence of this truth. There is inevitably something "strange" and "foreign" about the biblical text that demands we wrestle with it. The ancient Near East and first-century Jewish, Christian, and Greco-Roman history and culture must play a part in interpretation. Synchronic interpretations of biblical texts must wrestle with their strangeness when read in our present cultural context. Many of the questions asked by diachronic interpreters must still be asked. Biblical texts were not passed down in miniscule pieces of text provided by ancient literary forms. The redaction critics exaggerated their attempt to identify verses and sections of verses that came from a prior tradition, so that they could identify an overall theological agenda that brought the various parts together. Nevertheless, we must devote serious attention to the original historical context of the text, and it is impossible properly to appreciate the place of any given text within that context without making judgment about its source(s). Contemporary literary studies insist that all meaning is context bound. If that is the case, the original context and meaning of biblical texts retains its importance. "Whatever tension there may be between literary- and historical-critical methods, the two approaches are complementary" (Adela Yarbro Collins, "Narrative, History and Gospel," *Semeia* 43 [1988]: p. 153).

The Contemporary Reader. Every text generates a reader as it unfolds, but the task of interpretation is not concluded by tracing the point of view of a narrative through the experience of an emerging reader. The world behind the text must be respected and studied in order to understand its strange distance from our world and our concerns. What must be asked in responsible synchronic readings is this: How does the reader in the text, who emerges as an ancient story unfolds, speak to the knowledge and experience of the twenty-first-century reader of the text?

There is, of course, a context that unites the original and subsequent readers of the Bible: a context generated by communities of believing Jewish and Christian readers. The secret of the lasting value of a narrative lies in the mutuality that is created between the implied reader in the text and the real reader of the text, and the contexts of Jewish and Christian belief help this mutuality. But there are libraries of Jewish and Christian books that have not created such mutuality. There must be an understanding and respect for the world behind the text, which shaped the reader in the text, but there is more. When one reads a good novel for the first time, she becomes the implied reader. She becomes part of the story, caught up with its characters, events, time, and places as the pages turn. This is the case with any good book, but in a classic there is an even deeper relationship between the reader in the text and the reader of the text. A mutuality is generated between the implied reader in the text and the real reader of the text that makes any given text a classic. The practice of reading and the community of readers that produced the Bible is an example of that truth.

As the Bible continues to be read, there has long been mutuality between its implied and real readers. Synchronic interpretations must recognize an inevitable response that is independent of the implied reader, and thus outside the control of the author. It is unavoidable that Jewish and Christian responses to the Bible will be the result of our privileged position as the recipients of three thousand years of the Jewish and Christian practice of reading, listening, and even viewing. There is a theoretical distinction between various elements that combine to form a satisfactory reading experience, but a synchronic interpretation attempts to create a meeting of horizons between the worlds behind the text, in the text, and in front of the text. Traditional historical-critical scholarship and a contemporary literary approach should be combined to create a space where a satisfied reader is born.

Assessment. Synchronic reading pays less attention to the real author and the real reader and instead traces a communication between an implied author and an implied reader that can be found in the text. The search for what is being communicated leads to a focus on the narrative's impact (emotional, intellectual, ethical, etc.), generated through the implied author's uses of characters, spatial and temporal settings, and the like on the implied reader within the narrative. In addition, the theoretical claim was made here that a good reading experience takes place when the impact made upon the implied reader in the text and the real reader of the text are at one. Yet behind this apparently logical and scientific identification of different readers, different literary techniques, and different levels and qualities of impact (emotional, intellectual, ethical, etc.) lies the danger that the interpreter becomes the implied reader. An attempt to avoid this could be made by locating the narrative within its original historical and literary setting. The implied reader must have the characteristics, the experiences, and the knowledge of a reader of that time and in that setting. But the danger still lurks, especially when Jewish and Christian scholars are reading and explaining texts that have nourished and inspired faith and practice for three thousand years. The shadow of the real reader (the interpreter) always lurks behind the implied reader (the heuristic device).

The withering attack on the first quest for the historical Jesus by Albert Schweizer in *Vom Reimarus zu Wrede: Eine Geschichte der Leben-Jesu-Forschung* (1906; Eng. trans., 2001) laid bare the fact that each scholar created a Jesus in his own image, and this attack brought the first quest to an end. Exactly the same critique was made of the form critics, whose identification of literary forms outside the biblical literature and the subsequent use of those forms to locate pericopes *im Leben Jesu* (in the life of Jesus) or *im Leben der Kirche* (in the life of the Church) eventually fell under the critique that other agendas were running underneath. The world of the interpreter was too much of a determining factor in the interpretation of the text. The same had to be said of redaction criticism. The theology of the Evangelist identified by the redaction critics was all too often determined by the theological perspective of the interpreter. This danger remains in synchronic interpretations: the critic finds herself or himself in the implied reader.

What has been described represents mainstream synchronic interpretation, but more radical synchronic interpretations and newer methods have emerged and are emerging. Many postmodern readings of biblical texts question the ethnic, theological, anthropological, literary, social, and religious premises (to name just a few) taken for granted by biblical interpreters. Deconstruction and poststructuralist approaches question the unity and wholeness of literary texts presumed by synchronic interpretation, pointing to inconsistencies, disjunctions, and gaps within the texts themselves but interpreting these in synchronic not diachronic ways. Performance criticism recognizes that very few people in the original audience "read" a biblical text; they heard it read or saw it performed, thus the "literariness" of biblical texts needs to be interpreted in an oral/aural framework. Of course, the problem inherent in synchronic interpretation mentioned earlier also applies to performance criticism: To what degree does the interpreter in performance criticism play to the audience? Does the contemporary performer or performance critic find himself in the implied audience? As with all methodological approaches to ancient texts, especially religious texts, synchronic interpretations have their limitations.

Synchronic interpretation, in its various forms (narrative, reader-response, and performance criticism), exists side by side with more traditional historical approaches (source, form, and redaction criticism). All approaches are further questioned by deconstructive readings. Different biblical interpretations can mutually enrich one another. Synchronic interpretations need to be situated in history, historical interpretations should be aware of the text as a whole, and internal tensions, inconsistencies, and disjunctions must not be ignored. They too can play into interpretation. However, each methodological approach has its own internal logic, structure, and processes that are to be respected as they contribute something unique to the interpretative process. Synchronic interpretations seek to recapture the text as a whole utterance and to engage the form and rhetoric in which it was originally recited or written. For this reason alone, synchronic interpretations have brought rich new insights, especially in the interpretation of narratives, and they will continue to do so. They have an ongoing role to play in contemporary biblical scholarship.

[*See also* Deconstruction; Diachronic Interpretation; Form Criticism, *subentry* Hebrew Bible; Form Criticism, *subentry* Apocrypha and Deuterocanonical Books; Form Criticism, *subentry* New Testament; Narrative Criticism and Narrative Hermeneutics; Performance Criticism; Poststructuralist Interpretation; Reader-Response Criticism; Redaction Criticism, *subentry* Hebrew Bible; Redaction Criticism, *subentry* Apocrypha and Deuterocanonical Books; Redaction Criticism, *subentry* New Testament; *and* Source Criticism.]

BIBLIOGRAPHY

The Bible and Culture Collective. *The Postmodern Bible.* New Haven, Conn.: Yale University Press, 1995. A significant collection of essays, attending to reader-response, structuralist, narratological, poststructuralist, rhetorical, psychoanalytic, feminist, womanist, and ideological criticisms.

Booth, Wayne C. *The Rhetoric of Fiction.* 2d ed. Chicago: University of Chicago Press, 1983. An important study of the implied author and reader in narratives in general.

Chatman, Seymour. *Story and Discourse: Narrative Structure in Fiction and Film.* Ithaca, N.Y.: Cornell University Press, 1978. The fundamental study of the communication between author and reader within a narrative and the relationship with the real reader of the narrative. Most biblical narrative critics depend upon Chatman's theory of communication.

Culpepper, R. Alan. *Anatomy of the Fourth Gospel: A Study in Literary Design.* Foundations and Facets.

Philadelphia: Fortress, 1983. Foundational presentation of a synchronic reading of the Gospel of John.

Fowler, Robert M. *Let the Reader Understand: Reader-Response Criticism and the Gospel of Mark.* Minneapolis: Fortress, 1991. Using Mark as a focus, a wide-ranging application of literary theory to a Gospel narrative is explored, assessing its strengths and weaknesses.

Frye, Northrop. *The Great Code: The Bible and Literature.* New York: Harcourt Brace Javanovich, 1982. Major study of the literary impact of the Bible upon literature and culture.

Genette, Gerard. *Narrative Discourse: An Essay in Method.* Translated by Jane E. Lewin. Ithaca, N.Y.: Cornell University Press, 1980. English translation of a portion of *Figures III*, first published in 1972. Especially important for its study of many elements within the narrative (e.g. events, time, characters, focalization, voices) that generate its impact.

Iverson, Kelly R. "Orality and the Gospels: A Survey of Recent Research." *Currents in Biblical Research* 8 (2009): 71–106. Well-documented survey of emerging appreciation of the role of orality in both the generation and the reception of the Gospels.

Kelber, Werner H. *The Oral and Written Gospel: The Hermeneutics of Speaking and Writing in the Synoptic Tradition, Mark, Paul, and Q.* Philadelphia: Fortress, 1983. Groundbreaking study of the role of orality, betrayed by the fixing of that tradition in writing.

Malbon, Elizabeth Struthers. *Mark's Jesus: Characterization as Narrative Christology.* Waco, Tex.: Baylor University Press, 2009. Significant study of the character of Jesus that emerges from a synchronic reading of the Gospel of Mark.

Moloney, Francis J. *The Gospel of John.* Sacra Pagina 4. Collegeville, Minn.: Liturgical Press, 1998. Synchronic reading of the Gospel of John, devoting due attention to diachronic issues.

Moloney, Francis J. *The Gospel of Mark: A Commentary.* Grand Rapids, Mich.; Baker Academic, 2012. Synchronic reading of the Gospel of Mark, devoting due attention to diachronic issues.

Moore, Stephen D. *Literary Criticism and the Gospels: The Theoretical Challenge.* New Haven, Conn.: Yale University Press, 1989. Critical study of the application of literary criticism to the Gospels, with openness to more radical postmodern readings.

Prickett, Stephen. *Words and the Word: Language, Poetics and Biblical Interpretation.* Cambridge, UK: Cambridge University Press, 1986. Impressive study of the Bible as literature.

Rhoads, David. "Performance Criticism: An Emerging Methodology in Second Testament Studies—Parts 1 and 2." *Biblical Theology Bulletin* 36 (2006): 118–33; 164–84. Clear and well-documented survey of the emerging use of performance criticism.

Rhoads, David, Joanna Dewey, and Donald Michie. *Mark as Story: An Introduction to the Narrative of a Gospel,* 2d ed. Philadelphia: Fortress, 1999. Foundational presentation (original 1982) of a synchronic interpretation of the Gospel of Mark.

Ricoeur, Paul. *Time and Narrative.* Translated by Kathleen McLaughlin and David Pellauer. 3 vols. Chicago: Chicago University Press, 1984–1988. English translation of *Temps et Récit,* first published in 1983–1985. Work of an outstanding European philosopher who has greatly influenced synchronic readings of narrative, symbol, metaphoric and poetic language.

Rimmon-Kenan, Shlomith. *Narrative Fiction: Contemporary Poetics.* New Accents. London: Methuen, 1983. A lucid presentation of narrative theory, dependent upon Genette (see earlier).

Stibbe, Mark W. G. *John.* Readings: A New Bible Commentary. Sheffield, UK: JSOT Press, 1993. The first synchronic reading of the entire Gospel of John.

Francis J. Moloney

SYNOPTIC PROBLEM

The Synoptic Problem is the study of the similarities and differences among the Synoptic Gospels (Matthew, Mark and Luke) in an attempt to explain their literary relationship: The problem arises from the observation that the first three of the four canonical Gospels can be viewed together (*syn-optic*) in a synopsis, a book that sets them out in parallel columns (see the table that follows).

In contrast with John's Gospel, the synoptics often have similar wording, and they often show a parallel order of events. These similarities are so great that they demand some kind of literary explanation. One or more of the evangelists has been copying from one or more of the others, or from their source material. The synoptic problem is therefore a subset of source criticism of the New Testament. As well as a fascinating literary puzzle, it asks key historical questions for the study of Christian origins, and is foundational for related tasks including the dating of the Gospels, redaction criticism, and historical Jesus research.

Matthew 9:9	*Mark 2:14*	*Luke 5:27*
And having passed on	And having passed on	And
from there, Jesus saw	he saw	he saw
a man	Levi son of Alphaeus	a tax-collector named Levi
seated in the tax-office, named Matthew,	seated in the tax-office,	seated in the tax-office,
and he says to him, 'Follow me.' And	and he says to him, 'Follow me.' And	and he said to him, 'Follow me.' And having left
having arisen,	having arisen,	everything and having arisen,
he followed him.	he followed him.	he followed him.

History and Hypotheses. The father of the study of the synoptic problem is Johann Jakob Griesbach who produced the first Synopsis of the Gospels in 1776. Griesbach followed his construction of this synopsis with a critical theory on the composition of the Synoptics in 1789. Griesbach's theory was that Mark was the third Gospel to have been written and that its author used both Matthew and Luke in his composition. The theory was popular for much of the nineteenth century, and it had the advantage of cohering with the patristic view that Matthew's Gospel was the first to have been written.

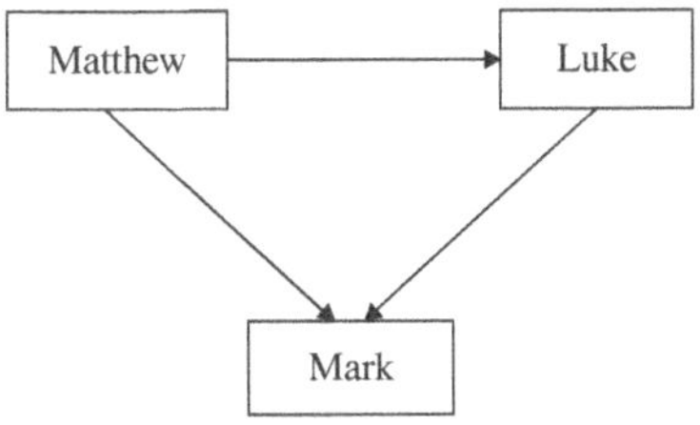

Figure 1. Griesbach Theory.

By the end of the nineteenth century, however, another theory was ascendant. The Two-Source Theory is founded on the idea that Mark was the first Gospel to have been written and that Matthew and Luke used it independently. This theory also appeals to a hypothetical document known as "Q," derived from the German word *Quelle*, "source."

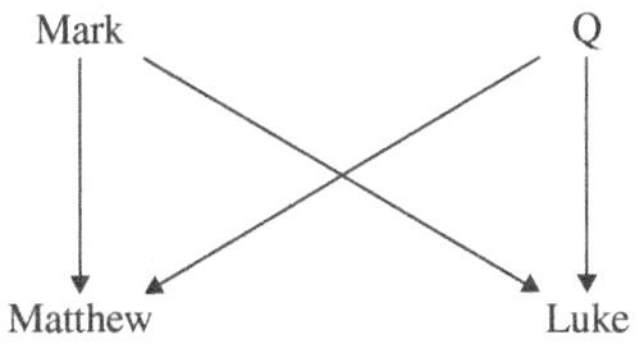

Figure 2. The Two-Source Theory.

This theory, according to which Matthew and Luke independently draw on the "two sources" Mark and Q, was so popular in the twentieth century that many scholars regarded the synoptic problem as having been solved. The Two Source Theory (also known as the Two Document Hypothesis) is still sometimes used as the sole means by which synoptic source issues are discussed.

One of the key contributions on the synoptic problem in the twentieth century was made by B. H. Streeter, whose *Four Gospels* (Streeter 1924) argued not only for Matthew's and Luke's use of Mark and Q but also for Matthew's use of a source called "M" and Luke's use of a source called "L." This modification of the Two-Source Theory is known as the Four-Source Theory (or Four Document Hypothesis).

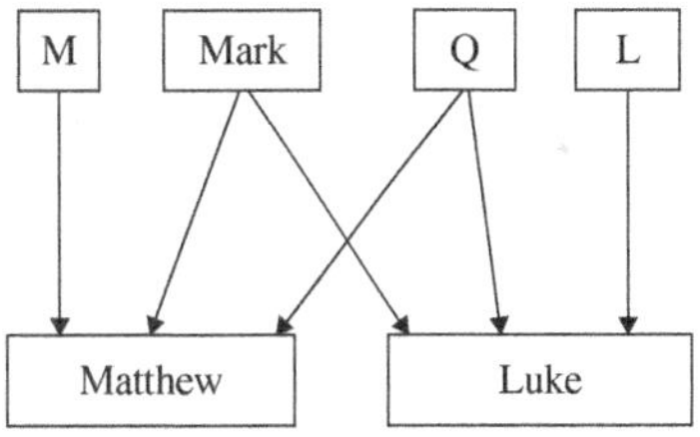

Figure 3. The Four-Source Theory.

While still popular, recent scholarship has become more sceptical about the existence of "M" and "L" as discrete documents. For Streeter and others, they were the sources for Matthew's "special" (unique) material and for Luke's "special" (unique) material respectively. However, contemporary scholars are more inclined to see Matthew's and Luke's special material as deriving from a range of sources, perhaps largely oral. Many also see this material as being particularly prone to influence from

Matthew's and Luke's creative minds, not least given the presence of apparently legendary materials in Matthew's special material (e.g. Pilate's wife's dream [Matt 27:19] and the saints rising from their tombs [Matt 27:51–53]) and distinctively Lucan themes in his special material (e.g. Luke 24:13–32, Road to Emmaus).

In spite of the popularity of the Two-Source Theory, there have always been vocal minorities championing other theories. Between the 1960s and the end of the twentieth century, a revival of the Griesbach theory, now renamed "The Two Gospel Hypothesis," posed a significant challenge to the Two-Source Theory, especially in North American scholarship. The revival was associated especially with William R. Farmer who published his major book *The Synoptic Problem* in 1964. Although it kept the discussion of the synoptic problem open, it remained a minority view. Another popular alternative, especially in the United Kingdom, was the Farrer Theory, named after Oxford theologian Austin Farrer's essay, "On Dispensing with Q" (Farrer 1955).

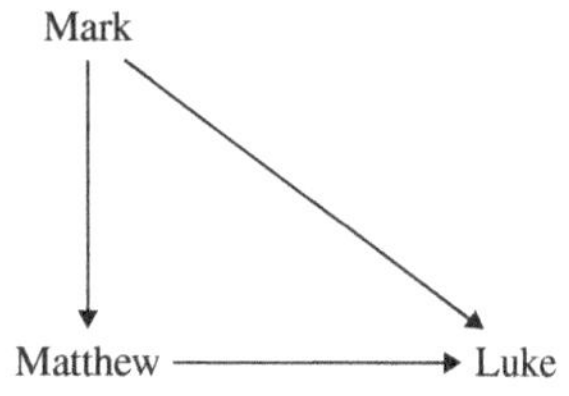

Figure 4. The Farrer Theory

In this theory, Matthew and Luke are dependent on Mark, as in the Two-Source Theory, but a direct line is drawn from Matthew to Luke. The suggestion is that if Luke also knew Matthew, then there is no need for the hypothetical Q. The exposition of this theory in the late twentieth and early twenty-first century is particularly associated with Michael Goulder and Mark Goodacre (Goulder 1989; Goodacre 2001; 2002).

A Literary Problem. The synoptic problem emerges from the observation that the Synoptic Gospels have some kind of literary relationship. The order and wording of the synoptic passages is often so close that it is impossible that there is not some kind of literary link. In some passages there is almost one hundred percent verbatim agreement, as in this example from Matthew and Luke:

Here, John the Baptist's preaching is identical in the Greek of Matthew and Luke with only the words for "presume" and "begin" differing. This kind of literary agreement requires some kind of literary explanation; one evangelist is dependent on the other or both are dependent on a hypothetical source. They are not independently recounting words from the oral tradition.

It is telling that agreement between the synoptics also occurs in peculiar literary constructions, an example of which occurs in the healing of the Paralytic:

The Greek here is bizarre, almost clumsy. The sentence "In order that you may know that the Son of Man has authority on the earth to forgive sins . . ." is unfinished. The narrator intervenes before Jesus's speech continues. This points to some kind of literary borrowing among the evangelists. Similarly telling are places where the evangelists agree on the same narrator's comment, as when Matthew and Mark feature the identical narrator's

Matthew 3:7–10	*Luke 3:7–9*
Offspring of vipers! Who warned you to flee from the coming wrath? Bear fruit therefore worthy of repentance and do not presume to say in yourselves, "We have Abraham as father;" for I say to you that God is able from these stones to raise up children to Abraham. Already the axe is laid at the root of the trees; for every tree not producing good fruit is cut down and cast into the fire.	Offspring of vipers! Who warned you to flee from the coming wrath? Bear fruit therefore worthy of repentance and do not begin to say in yourselves, "We have Abraham as father;" for I say to you that God is able from these stones to raise up children to Abraham. Already the axe is laid at the root of the trees; for every tree not producing good fruit is cut down and cast into the fire.

Matthew 9:6	*Mark 2:10–11*	*Luke 5:24*
"But in order that you may know that the Son of Man has authority on the earth to forgive sins," then he says to the paralytic, "Arise, take up your bed and go to your house."	"But in order that you may know that the Son of Man has authority on the earth to forgive sins," he says to the paralytic, "I say to you, Arise, take up your pallet and go to your house."	"But in order that you may know that the Son of Man has authority on the earth to forgive sins," he said to the paralytic, "I say to you, Arise and take up your bed and return to your house."

aside, "Let the reader understand" (Matt 24:15 // Mark 13:14), in their version of Jesus's Apocalyptic Discourse, an aside that also draws attention to the literary nature of the speech. Further, the agreements in order between different synoptic passages often clearly point to a literary relationship.

The emphasis on the literary links between the synoptics might seem to contradict studies that recognize the importance of orality and memory in antiquity but a balanced understanding of the composition of the Gospels requires attention to both orality and literacy. In his preface, Luke appears to mention both those who have composed narratives and those who have communicated with him orally (Luke 1:1–4). Similarly, early patristic writers like Papias stress their knowledge of both the written text and the spoken word.

The Contours of the Problem. Any attempt to solve the synoptic problem begins by analyzing the different sets of data that make up the Synoptic Gospels. Broadly speaking, there are four types of material: triple tradition, double tradition, special Matthew, and special Luke. The triple tradition is a large body of material consisting of passages found in all three synoptics. Examples include the Parable of the Sower (Mark 4:1–9 and parallels); the Feeding of the Five Thousand (Mark 6:30–44 and parallels); and much of the Passion Narrative (Mark 14—15). It features more narrative than sayings material and most of Mark's Gospel is made up of triple tradition material.

The double tradition material is made up of passages found in both Matthew and Luke but not in Mark. It is rich in sayings material and includes the Lord's Prayer (Matt 6:9–13 // Luke 11:2–4), the Beatitudes (Matt 5:3–10 // Luke 6:20–23) and the Parable of the Talents / Pounds (Matt 25:14–30 // Luke 19:12–27).

Special Matthew is made up of passages unique to Matthew like the Parable of the Ten Virgins (Matt 25:1–13) and the Sheep and the Goats (Matt 25:31–46). Although it features a lot of sayings material, there are also narratives like the Coin in the Fish's Mouth (Matt 17:24–27). Special Luke is made up of passages unique to Luke and it is rich in the kind of material that marks out Luke as the great storyteller of the New Testament such as the parables of the Good Samaritan (Luke 10:25–37) and Prodigal Son (Luke 15:11–32).

Although these categories are helpful ways to subdivide the data and to analyze the problem, it is important to note that there are also passages that blur these neat categories. Some material, like the Temptation of Jesus (Matt 4:1–11 // Mark 1:12–13 // Luke 4:1–13), might be described as halfway between double tradition and triple tradition in that the passage is present in all three Synoptics but the most extensive and substantial agreement occurs between Matthew and Luke.

In analyzing the data, one key factor emerges, that Mark is usually the "middle term." Mark plays some kind of mediating role. We can see this in three ways. First, while Matthew and Luke have a lot of their own unique material, Mark has very little. Nearly everything in Mark's Gospel is also found in Matthew, or Luke, or both. Second, in the material that they share, the triple tradition material, there are substantial agreements in wording and order between Matthew, Mark and Luke, between Mark and Luke, and between Mark and Matthew. There

Matthew 8:16	*Mark 1:32*	*Luke 4:40*
That evening,	That evening,	
	at sundown,	As the sun was setting,
they brought to him	they brought to him	
many who were	all who	all those who had any who
	were sick or	were sick with various
possessed with demons;	possessed with demons.	kinds of diseases brought
and he cast out the spirits		them to him; and he laid his
with a word, and cured all		hands on each of them and
who were sick.		cured them.

are only minor agreements between Matthew and Luke against Mark. In other words, where all three synoptics are present in a given periscope, Mark is usually the common denominator. Third, the order of the passages that make up the triple tradition is generally the same as the order of Mark's Gospel. Where Matthew does diverge from Mark's order, Luke generally follows it. Where Luke does diverge from Mark's order, Matthew generally follows it.

Weighing the Solutions to the Problem. Each of the major solutions to the synoptic problem attempts to explain the composition of the Synoptic Gospels on the basis of their readings of this data. The major strength of the Griesbach (Two Gospel) theory is that it provides a robust account of how Mark became the middle term. Advocates argue that it is no coincidence that Mark appears to mediate between Matthew and Luke—it is the product of Mark's own conflation of the two Gospels he was working with. Thus he retains the order of Matthew and Luke where their order is the same but chooses one or the other of them when they diverge from one another. And his conflation is not only on the level of entire passages but also on the level of precise wording as in this example:

Here, Matthew parallels the first half of Mark's setting, "That evening," and Luke parallels the second half, "at sundown." The Griesbach Theory suggests that this arises because Mark is conflating the two sources he has in front of him.

Advocates of the Griesbach Theory have struggled, however, to overturn the consensus viewpoint of Markan Priority (an element in both the Two-Source and Farrer Theories), according to which both Matthew and Luke used Mark. Several arguments have been put forward for Markan Priority, the strongest of which relate to additions and omissions of material, harder readings and editorial fatigue.

Omissions and Additions. If Mark used Matthew and Luke, then he often omits material we might expect him to include, e.g. the Lord's Prayer (Matt 6:9–13 // Luke 11:1–4), which appears congenial and would have found an ideal context at Mark 11:20–25. If, however, Mark was written first, it is much easier to imagine why Matthew and Luke omit the handful of verses that are unique to Mark. This unique Markan material includes the Healing of a Deaf Mute (Mark 7:33–36) and the Blind Man of Bethsaida (Mark 8:22–26). These difficult stories are much more likely to have been omitted by Matthew and Luke than added specially by Mark. Both healings have Jesus using spit, and the healing of the blind man is not instantaneous but takes time.

The difficulty relates to the confusing picture of Mark that emerges if he was the third evangelist rather than the first. He omits all of the double tradition material in spite of the fact that some of it seems congenial, and he goes out of his way to add one or two odd, primitive-looking passages.

Harder Readings. Mark often has readings that would be difficult to explain as secondary to Matthew and Luke, but which are more straightforward to explain as Matthew's and Luke's modifications of Mark. In the story of the Rich Young Ruler, for example, Matthew appears to modify the potentially embarrassing implication in Mark that Jesus was not good:

Matthew 19:16–17	*Mark 10:17–18*
	As he was setting out on a journey,
Then someone came to him and	a man ran up and knelt before him, and
said, "Teacher, what good deed must I	asked him, "Good Teacher, what must I
do to have eternal life?" And he said to him,	do to inherit eternal life?" Jesus said to him,
"Why do you ask me about what is	"Why do you call me
good? There is only one who is good."	good? No one is good but God alone."

An apparently minor redactional adjustment in Matthew reduces the potentially troubling Christological impact made by Mark.

Editorial Fatigue. There are several examples of Matthew and Luke making characteristic changes to Mark in the earlier part of a passage, but failing to sustain these changes throughout, gradually lapsing into the wording of their source. The lapse creates a minor contradiction, and this phenomenon, labelled "editorial fatigue," is a telltale sign of Markan Priority. In the Death of John the Baptist (Matt 14:1–12 // Mark 6:14–29), for example, Matthew begins by correctly calling Herod a "tetrarch" (14:1), only to lapse into calling him the less correct "king" (14:9), apparently reproducing Mark (6:26) who calls him "king" throughout. Similarly, Luke re-sets the scene for the Feeding of the Five Thousand (Mark 6:32–44 // Luke 9:10–17) in "a city called Bethsaida" (Luke 9:10) only to lapse into the Markan wording later, "We are here in a deserted place" (Luke 9:12, cf, Mark 6:35), which contradicts his new setting earlier in the passage. Examples like these only seem to occur in the one direction, in Matthew's editing of Mark and Luke's editing of Mark. It is very difficult to find possible examples that would make sense in the other direction.

If Markan Priority successfully explains the existence of the triple tradition material, the double material still requires explanation. According to the Two-Source Theory, Matthew and Luke used Mark independently of one another, so the high levels of agreement in the double tradition material necessitate the existence of the hypothetical source Q. The independence of Luke from Matthew is postulated on several grounds. The two most important arguments are those from order and from alternating primitivity.

Order. Matthew's Gospel is structured around five great discourses (Matt 5–7; 10; 13; 18; and 24–25). If Luke used Matthew, it is thought inexplicable that he would have ruined Matthew's fine order, instead relocating the discourse material to different parts of his Gospel, much of it to his own large Central Section. Luke's treatment of the Sermon on the Mount (Matt 5–7) is thought especially unlikely; if he knew Matthew, he has abbreviated it drastically (Luke 6:20–49), omitting some and redistributing the remainder. It is thought much more likely that Matthew and Luke are both working from Q, with Matthew doing a lot of relocating and reordering.

Alternating Primitivity. It is argued that sometimes Matthew, and sometimes Luke has the more original form of the sayings that appear in the double tradition. This phenomenon only makes sense if Matthew and Luke are dependent on Q, and not if Luke is dependent on Matthew. The key example usually given of Luke's greater primitivity is the first beatitude:

Matthew 5:3	*Luke 6:20*
Blessed are the poor in spirit	Blessed are the poor
for theirs is the kingdom	for yours is the kingdom
of the heavens.	of God.

The Q beatitude must have read "Blessed are the poor," which is more primitive than Matthew's "spiritualized" version.

Advocates of the Farrer Theory suggest that these arguments have been overplayed. The question of Luke's reordering of Matthew's discourses makes sense in the light of the way that he treats Mark's discourses too. Just as Luke abbreviates, omits, and redistributes elements from Mark 4 (the Parables

Matthew 26:67–68	*Mark 14:65*	*Luke 22:64*
Then they spat into his face, and struck him; and some slapped him, saying, "Prophesy to us, you Christ! Who is it that struck you?"	And some began to spit on him, and to cover his face, and to strike him, saying to him, "Prophesy!"	Now the men who were holding Jesus mocked him and beat him; they also blindfolded him and asked him, "Prophesy! Who is it that struck you?"

chapter), so too he abbreviates, omits, and redistributes elements from Matthew's discourses, which are sometimes very long. With respect to passages like the Beatitudes, it is just as straightforward to see Luke as secondary, not least given his well-known preference for the poor (cf. Luke 4:18) in eschatological reversal scenarios (cf. Luke 16:19–31).

One of the biggest difficulties for the Two-Source Theory, however, is the existence of many agreements between Matthew and Luke against Mark. If Matthew and Luke are independent of one another, there ought not to be so many non-Markan agreements in the triple tradition. Sometimes these are "minor agreements," like the addition of five words in Matthew's and Luke's Passion narrative:

At other times, these are more major agreements, like the material about John the Baptist and Jesus in Matthew 3, Mark 1, and Luke 3. Q theorists explain the major agreements as examples of "overlap" between Mark and Q. The minor agreements are explained in a variety of ways, including coincidental redaction and textual assimilation.

Importance for Biblical Interpretation. Study of the synoptic problem sheds light on the composition of the Gospels and is a key component in the discussion of the dates of the synoptics. A date for Mark's Gospel during or after the Jewish War of 66–70, for example, necessitates dates also for Matthew and Luke in the post–70 period. Many feel that Mark's Apocalyptic Discourse (Mark 13) shows signs of composition during or even after the Jewish War, especially given its focus on the destruction of the Temple (Mark 13:1–2), a theme that is repeated in Mark's Passion Narrative (Mark 14:58 and 15:30). Matthew's and Luke's familiarity with Mark's Gospel coheres with a post–70 date. Jesus's lament over Jerusalem (Matt 23:37–39 // Luke 13:34–35) prophesies that the Temple will be forsaken, echoing similar themes in Josephus' *Jewish War*. If Luke's Gospel is the third of the three to have been written, his

Matthew 27:50–54	*Mark 15:37–39*
And Jesus cried again with a loud voice and yielded up his spirit. And behold, the curtain of the temple was torn in two, from top to bottom; and the earth shook, and the rocks were split; the tombs also were opened, and many bodies of the saints who had fallen asleep were raised, and coming out of the tombs after his resurrection they went into the holy city and appeared to many. When the centurion and those who were with him, keeping watch over Jesus, saw the earthquake and what took place, they were filled with awe, and said, "Truly this was the Son of God!"	And Jesus uttered a loud cry, and breathed his last. And the curtain of the temple was torn in two, from top to bottom. And when the centurion, who stood facing him, saw that he thus breathed his last, he said, "Truly this man was the Son of God!"

claim of "many" prior narratives (Luke 1:1) may also prove noteworthy here.

The synoptic problem has an especially close relationship with redaction criticism of the Gospels. Markan Priority has been foundational in the attempt to explicate Matthew and Luke's distinctive perspectives. When redaction critics compare Matthew with Mark, they are able to point to modifications that Matthew has made which may illustrate a particular theological stance, as when he adds apparently legendary, apocalyptic imagery to Mark's account of the death of Jesus:

If Matthew is using Mark, he has transformed the latter's darkly mysterious scene with its solitary centurion so that it becomes a magnificent apocalyptic scenario with multiple witnesses of earth-shattering events.

Similarly, redaction critics draw attention to Luke's modification of his Markan source material with a view to illustrating Luke's special emphases. In the account of Jesus's death, for example, Luke also has similarities and differences from Mark:

In contrast with Mark, Luke's centurion, after having praised God (cf. 19:37; 24:53), declares Jesus "innocent" or "righteous" in line with a major theme in Luke's Passion Narrative, in which Pilate (23:4, 14-15, 22) and even one of the thieves crucified with Jesus (23:41) similarly declare Jesus innocent of any crime.

The synoptic problem is also of major importance in the quest of the historical Jesus. Differing solutions to the problem have a major effect on scholarly judgments about the authenticity of different materials. Most historical Jesus scholars accept the theory of Markan Priority and show a general historical preference for his versions of triple tradition passages. The popular view that Jesus was an apocalyptic prophet expecting the imminent restoration of the world and transformation of Israel rests in part on Mark's presentation, which includes lines like "Some of those standing here will not taste death before they see the kingdom of God coming with power" (Mark 9:1), a line modified in both Matthew (16:28) and Luke (9.27).

Q has also played a major role in Jesus research. The hypothetical document is often thought to have been one of the earliest Christian works and so a valuable witness to the earliest stage of the tradition, and a potentially useful source for the sayings of the historical Jesus. For scholars who emphasize the criterion of multiple attestation, traditions like the baptism of Jesus, which are alleged to have appeared in both Mark and Q (Matt 3:13–17, Mark 1:9–11, Luke 3:21), have particularly good claims to historicity. For some scholars, traditions witnessed in both Q and the *Gospel of Thomas* are especially valuable in life of Jesus research. Several of the beatitudes and the parables that are witnessed in both Q and *Thomas* take on a decisive importance. This kind of appeal, however, relies not only on the existence of Q but also on the theory of an early, independent *Thomas*, which is by no means the universal view of Jesus scholars.

Some historical Jesus scholars, recognizing the precarious nature of judgments on the synoptic problem, prefer to avoid engaging with it extensively while others underline the danger of applying synoptic models in too wooden a way. The same caution can be expressed more generally in relation to other areas where the synoptic problem interacts with scholarship on Christian origins. Understanding

Mark 15:39	*Luke 23:48*
And when the centurion, who stood	Now when the centurion
facing him, saw that he thus breathed his last,	saw what had taken place,
he said, "Truly this	he praised God, and said, "Certainly this
man was the Son of God!"	man was innocent!" And all the
	multitudes who assembled to see the
	sight, when they saw what had taken
	place, returned home beating their
	breasts.

the contours of the problem sheds light on the questions that Biblical scholars ask in a range of areas, and dogmatic positions are best avoided.

[*See also* Diachronic Interpretation; Historical Criticism, *subentry* New Testament; Historical Jesus, Quest for the; *and* Redaction Criticism, *subentry* New Testament]

BIBLIOGRAPHY

Aland, Kurt, *Synopsis Quattuor Evangeliorum*. Editio quindecima revisa; Deutsche Bibelgesellschaft, 1996, 1997.

Farmer, William R. *The Synoptic Problem: A Critical Review of the Problem of Literary Relationships Between Matthew, Mark and Luke*. New York: Macmillan, 1964; 2d ed, Dillsboro, N.C.: Western North Carolina Press, 1976.

Farrer, Austin, "On Dispensing with Q." In *Studies in the Gospels: Essays in Memory of R. H. Lightfoot*, D. E. Nineham (ed.), 55–88. Oxford: Blackwell, 1955.

Foster, Paul Andrew Gregory, John S. Kloppenborg, and Jozef Verheyden (eds.). *New Studies in the Synoptic Problem: Oxford Conference, April 2008: Essays in Honour of Christopher M. Tuckett*. BETL 239; Leuven, Belgium: Peeters, 2011.

Goodacre, Mark. *The Synoptic Problem: A Way Through the Maze*. London & New York: T&T Clark, 2001.

Goodacre, Mark. *The Case Against Q: Studies in Marcan Priority and the Synoptic Problem*. Harrisburg, Pa.: Trinity Press International, 2002.

Goulder, Michael. *Luke: A New Paradigm*. JSNTSup, 20; Sheffield, UK: Sheffield Academic Press, 1989.

Griesbach, J. J. *Synopsis Evangeliorum Matthaei, Marci et Lucae*. Halle, Germany: Curtius, 1776.

Griesbach, J. J. *Commentatio qua Marci Evangeliorum totum e Mathaei et Lucae commentariis decerptum esse monstratur* (Jenna, 1789–1790). In *J. J. Griesbach: Synoptic and Text-Critical Studies, 1776–1976*, edited by Bernard Orchard and Thomas Longstaff, 103–135. Cambridge, UK: Cambridge University Press, 1978.

Kloppenborg, John S. Excavating Q: The History and Setting of the Sayings Gospel. Minneapolis, Minn.: Fortress; Edinburgh: T&T Clark, 2000.

Kloppenborg, John S. *Q, the Earliest Gospel: An Introduction to the Original Stories and Sayings of Jesus*. Louisville, Ky.: Westminster John Knox Press, 2008.

McNicol, Allan J., with David L. Dungan and David B. Peabody, eds. *Beyond the Q Impasse–Luke's Use of Matthew: A Demonstration by the Research Team of the International Institute for Gospel Studies*. Valley Forge Pa.: Trinity Press International, 1996.

Peabody, David Barrett, Allan James McNicol, and Lamar Cope, *One Gospel from Two: Mark's Use of Matthew and Luke*. Harrisburg, Pa.: Continuum International Publishing Group, 2002.

Sanders, E. P. and M. Davies. *Studying the Synoptic Gospels*. Philadelphia: Trinity Press International; London: SCM, 1989.

Stein, Robert. *The Synoptic Problem: An Introduction*. Grand Rapids, Mich.: Baker Book House, 1987.

Streeter, B. H. *The Four Gospels: A Study of Origins, Treating of the Manuscript Tradition, Sources, Authorship and Dates*. London: Macmillan, 1924.

Throckmorton, Jr., Burton H. *Gospel Parallels: A Comparison of the Synoptic Gospels*. 5th ed, Nasville, Tenn.: Thomas Nelson, 1993.

Tuckett, Christopher M. *Q and the History of Early Christianity: Studies on Q*. Edinburgh: T&T Clark, 1996.

Tuckett, Christopher M. *The Revival of the Griesbach Hypothesis: An Analysis and Appraisal*. SNTSMS 44. Cambridge, UK: Cambridge University Press, 1983.

Mark Goodacre

T

Textual Criticism

[*This entry contains three subentries,* Hebrew Bible, Apocrypha and Deuterocanonical Books, *and* New Testament.]

Hebrew Bible

The Hebrew text of the biblical books underwent a process of manuscript transmission for more than a millennium and a half until the first printed editions. Textual criticism intends to restore the text to its original state, as purified as possible from every element alien to the archetype, the first edition, or the successive editions if such existed. To do so, it accumulates the whole of the preserved manuscripts and proceeds to their documental and historical analysis. Afterwards, it examines the variants of each manuscript and selects those that either fit better with the archetype or are nearer to the original form of the text.

Witnesses of the Biblical Hebrew Text. Prior to the discovery of the Dead Sea Scrolls in 1947 the known witnesses of the Hebrew text were the Masoretic, the Samaritan Pentateuch, and the Hebrew original, or *Vorlage*, of the Greek version known as the Septuagint.

The Masoretic Text (MT). This is the traditional form of the text of the Hebrew Bible in vocalized, accented, and annotated manuscripts.

The consonantal text. The term Masoretic is applied also to the type of consonantal text of such manuscripts, characterized by an exceptional homogeneity and fidelity in the copy, which means an almost total absence of consonantal variants. This is due to the fact that it remained stable after the Jewish wars of 70 and 135 C.E. That is proved by the manuscripts found in the non-Qumranic Dead Sea caves: Wadi Murabba'at, Wadi Sdeir, Naḥal Ḥever, Naḥal Se´elim, and Massada. For example, the text of Psalms 18:17–43 in the manuscript 5/6ḤevPs (ca. 115 C.E.) is identical to the Masoretic Text of the Middle Ages. The consonantal variants of the medieval manuscripts collated in the eighteenth century by Kennicott and De Rossi usually respond to "the law of scribes," namely, to changes that are spontaneously generated in every period and cannot be used as indicative errors.

The vocalized text. Since the fifth century C.E. three main systems of textual vocalization began to be developed, namely, the Tiberian, the Palestinian, and the Babylonian. They reflected slightly different pronunciations but the same tradition of reading aloud, the origins of which go back to the Second

Temple period. Only in this way can many phonological and grammatical details that predate the medieval period, such as the distinction between the sound *śin* and *shin* of the letter ש, be explained. Of those vocalization systems, only the Tiberian, which blossomed in the tenth and eleventh centuries, has survived. Its main representatives are the Codex Leningradensis (1008–1009), the Aleppo Codex (ca. 980), and the Cairo Codex (895).

Accentuation and text division. The Masoretic Text is endowed also with accentuation signs—over the syllable that receives the accent on each word or in two words linked by *maqqeph*—as well as with signs of division of verses in meaningful units. The medieval manuscripts did not know the division into chapters and verses that was first introduced in the Vulgate Bibles and that, since the sixteenth century, was applied also to the printed rabbinic Bibles.

The Masora. The indications of the *Masora parva* reproduced on the right and left margins of the manuscripts mark, among other things, whether a word must be read as it is written (*Kĕtîb*) or according to the pronunciation transmitted by oral tradition (*Qĕrê*). For instance, in Judges 20:13 the *Kĕtîb* is *binyāmim* (Benjamin), and the *Qĕrê* is *benê binjāmin* (sons of Benjamin, or Benjaminites). In this case the *Qĕrê* reading in plural is to be preferred, since it corresponds to the plural verb of the clause. In some cases, the *Kĕtîb* should be preferred, but in others the *Qĕrê,* although the values of both readings are equivalent in many cases. Other marginal notes look after the careful and exact transcription of the text as the ones that mark the number of times in which the precise form of a word is found in other places, or the ones that draw the reader's attention to parallel passages. The *Masora magna* written in the superior and inferior margins offer several levels of information; thus they deal with words or verses which show some kind of unusual form. The work of the Masoretes continued that of the old *soferim* that counted (*spr* in Hebrew) the words and that, besides other annotations, pointed out the omissions and corrections of the scribes.

The Samaritan Pentateuch (SP). This text was known in the West from 1516 and reproduced in the polyglots of Paris and London. It contains approximately 6000 variants with respect to the Masoretic Text, most of them of small importance. It agrees with the LXX against the MT in 1900 cases. Some readings reflect the Samaritan point of view instead of the Jewish. Thus it makes Mount Gerizim the place chosen by God instead of Mount Zion in Jerusalem. To do so, as part of the tenth commandment, it introduces after Exodus 20:17 a gloss taken from Deuteronomy 17:28 and 11:29–30. Other variants are the usual ones in the "vulgar" text, such as orthographical regularization, the substitution of archaic terms by modern ones, and the harmonization of passages.

The Hebrew Original of the Greek Version (LXX). The translation of the Pentateuch known as the LXX (the Seventy) was carried out in Alexandria ca. 280 B.C.E. Its antiquity and the quality of the translation make it an extremely important witness of a Hebrew text that circulated at the beginning of the Hellenistic period. The historical and prophetic books, as well as the Writings, were translated progressively afterwards. The translation of Qohelet, Song of Songs, and Ezra–Nehemiah could be as late as the second century B.C.E. In some books, the translation is quite literal, so that each Greek word corresponds to a Hebrew one, imitating Hebrew expressions, which are always translated by the same Greek term(s), and following the Hebrew word order. The versions of other books are freer as in the cases of Isaiah, Job, Proverbs, Daniel, and Esther.

The divergences between the LXX and the proto-Masoretic Hebrew motivated a process of revision of the Greek text to adapt it to the proto-Masoretic Hebrew, which was acquiring authoritative status in rabbinic circles around the turn of the era. This work of revision was carried out by Jewish translators in the second century C.E.—Theodotion, Aquila, and Symmachus—and by Christian revisers in the fourth century, especially Origen and Lucian. Readings of these three Jewish translators were incorporated in the hexaplaric revision of Origen. The revision of Theodotion shows characteristics of translation that are found in the Minor Prophets scroll of Naḥal Ḥever. This fact means that a school of translators was active in Palestine at the beginning of the first century B.C.E. or perhaps earlier. It represented the first attempt to bring the Old Greek text in line with the form of the Hebrew text that was in use by that time in rabbinic circles, an early form of the Hebrew Masoretic tradition.

The LXX version was the basis for new translations into Latin, Coptic, Armenian, Georgian, Syriac, Ethiopic, and Arabic. The Old Latin version attests a Greek text that preceded the Hexaplaric revision. It has then a high critical value, although this is blurred by the deficient state of its textual preservation in several books. On occasion, the combined evidence of some of these versions can represent Greek readings for which the Hebrew original differs from the MT.

The critical use of the LXX as witness of a Hebrew text different from the Masoretic depends on the previous establishment of a critical text of the Greek version, such as the one carried out in the Göttingen edition. On this basis, it is possible to reconstruct its Hebrew *Vorlage* and to compare the different Hebrew readings that have been preserved in order to establish which one is the oldest or the nearest to the original form of the text.

Secondary Versions. The Vulgate, Syriac, and Aramaic versions were made after the Hebrew text was fixed in the second century C.E. They reflect a text almost without consonantal variants.

The old Syriac version or Peshitta. It was produced in the second half of the second century C.E. on the basis of a Hebrew text, although some books show influences from the LXX. Some of its readings suppose a Hebrew original different from the MT but they do not have enough critical value to support textual changes with respect to the Masoretic Hebrew text.

The Aramaic versions or Targumim. These show characteristics of oral translation with the specific purpose of interpreting the Hebrew text. They combine the aim of a faithful translation with an effort to explain the text and comment on it. In this way they contribute more to the history of Jewish exegesis than to the critical reconstruction of the Hebrew text.

The Latin translations. The Old Latin was progressively replaced by the version produced by Jerome at the end of the fourth century C.E. Jerome based his translation on the Hebrew text, although respectful to the church tradition of the Greek version. Only on a few occasions does Jerome's translation reflect Hebrew variants that differ from the MT. This translation became the *Vulgata* or common Latin version.

The Qumran Biblical Manuscripts: Textual Plurality. Textual criticism of the Hebrew Bible received a major boost thanks to the contribution of the biblical scrolls found in the Qumran caves, almost a quarter of the 800 manuscripts preserved there. According to the paleographical dating confirmed by carbon-14, they go back to a period between 250 B.C.E. and 68 C.E. The Isaiah scrolls from the first Cave of Qumran (1QIsa^{ab}) showed a striking coincidence with the medieval manuscripts, thus reaffirming the faithfulness of the biblical textual transmission during a millennium from which no manuscript evidence was known. Manuscripts published later revealed progressively the existence of texts that diverged more and more from the MT.

Proto-Masoretic Texts. Despite its coincidence with the MT, 1QIsa^{b} presents nevertheless a hundred textual variants. 1QIsa^{a} makes evident a process of textual growth from this text to that of the LXX and, finally, to the MT. Besides 1QIsa^{ab}, a significant portion of the Qumranic manuscripts represent a proto-Masoretic text. Thus 4QGen^{b} agrees exactly with Leningradensis and 4QGen^{g} or 4QProv^{b} attest almost no differences with it. 4QpaleoGen-Exod^{l}, 4QExod^{c}, 4QSam^{b}, 4QJer^{ac} can be added to this proto-Masoretic group as well.

Protosamaritan Texts. Some "proto-Samaritan" manuscripts transmit a text very near to the Samaritan Pentateuch. 4QpaleoEx^{m} offers additions from Exodus or Deuteronomy typical of this group. 4QNum^{b} offers a quite developed text, akin to the Samaritan Pentateuch, although still nearer to the LXX text. 4QExod-Lev^{f}, a copy from around 250 B.C.E., could be the oldest biblical text of Qumran.

Texts Related with LXX. A group of Qumran manuscripts transmits a text related to the Hebrew *Vorlage* of the LXX. 4QJer^{b,d} are similar to the LXX against the order and longer readings of the MT. In the same way, 4QDeut^{q}, 4QSam^{a,c}, and also

4QNum[b] are close to the LXX although with a greater degree of divergence. At the end of the "Song of Moses" (Deut 32:43) 4QDeut[q] agrees with the LXX in a portion of text omitted by the MT due to its polytheistic connotations.

Texts of Unknown Affiliation or of Mixed Affiliation. A very significant group of manuscripts "unaligned" or "independent" do not follow the MT, PS, or LXX. 4QJosh[a] presents a different order of pericopes: Josh 8:30–35 appears before 5:2–7. Thus, the first altar in the newly entered land was built by Joshua at Gilgal immediately after the crossing of the Jordan (after Josh 4), not later on Mount Ebal (cf. 8:30–35 MT and 9:3–8 LXX). 4QJudg[a] omits the whole pericope of Judges 6:7–10. Even more significant is the case of 4QReworked Pentateuch (4QRP), a composition published as nonbiblical and later reclassified as a biblical text. It rearranges some Torah pericopes and shows a significant number of extensive exegetical additions. Other manuscripts of this group are 4QDeut[b.c.h.k], 4QSam[a], 4QIs[c], 4QXII[c], 4QDan[a], and 11QpaleoLev[a].

Texts in Paleo-Hebrew Script. Around 11 or 12 manuscripts written in paleo-Hebrew script represent rather heterogenous texts: 4QpaleoGen-Exod[l] and 4QpaleoDeut[r] are proto-Masoretic; 4QpaleoExod[m] is proto-Samaritan, and 11QpaleoLev[a] is independent.

Texts of the Qumran Scriptorium. E. Tov attributes a fifth of the fragments to scrolls written according to the "Qumran practice," characterized by a modernized vocabulary, a simplified syntax, and a long orthography (with extensive use of *matres lectionis*). However, these characteristics could also correspond to manuscripts copied in Palestine and not specifically in the Qumran community. Important examples are 4QIsa[a,c] and 4QSam[c].

The classification of other manuscripts is still a source of debate. Such is the case of 4QCant[a], which can be an excerpted text to be disregarded in text-critical analysis (Tov) or a biblical text analogous to the rearranged book of Jeremiah or to the shorter form of the book of Daniel (Ulrich). Similarly the Psalms scrolls from Caves 4 and 11 have been considered as liturgical anthologies or as biblical texts parallel to the MT.

History of the Biblical Text. Prior to the discovery of the Dead Sea Scrolls there were two opposed theories regarding the history of the biblical text, whose essential approaches keep acting upon today's research.

Lagarde-Kahle. According to the theory of the archetype, or *Urtext*, of Paul de Lagarde the whole of the Hebrew manuscript tradition derives from an archetype. Similarly the Greek textual tradition comes from the first original version whose text branched out in the recensions of Origen, Lucian, and Hesiquius. According to Paul Kahle, on the other hand, at the outset of the biblical tradition a plurality of "vulgar texts" continued to be unified until eventuating in the proto-Masoretic text, the Samaritan version of the Pentateuch, and the Hebrew original of the LXX. This Greek translation was merely the end result of a selection process from an assortment of previous Greek versions made from "vulgar" Hebrew texts. The nature of these translations would be similar to that of the Aramaic *targumim*.

Cross-Talmon. The theory of the local texts proposed by F. M. Cross reduces the textual plurality shown by the Qumran manuscripts to a limited number of textual families developed independently in the main centers of Second Temple Judaism: Egypt (a proto-LXX text), Babylon (proto-MT), and Palestine (an expansionistic and harmonistic proto-Samaritan text). According to S. Talmon a greater number of textual families was finally reduced to those preserved in three socio-religious contexts: the proto-MT preserved in post-70 Jewish communities, the SP in the Samaritan community, and the LXX in Christian communities.

Tov-Ulrich. In the last decades Tov has focused on the complexity of the textual witnesses in the Qumran manuscripts. The previous description of the Qumranic textual plurality is mainly Tov's proposal. On the other hand, E. Ulrich has focused on the deliberate activity of creative scribes who produced multiple literary editions of the biblical book. Revised literary editions thus caused variant text types.

These explanations tend either to underline or to reduce the textual plurality, placing it at the beginning or at the last stage of the process of textual growth. Qumran has modified our vision of the history of the text, which is not, as could have been thought before, that of a manuscript transmitted along a straight line until it reached its canonical form. Today we know that the biblical books had a complex history of composition, redaction, edition, and textual transmission.

Multiple Literary Editions of Biblical Books. Successive editions of a book differ mainly by the addition of prologues and epilogues and by a divergent order of pericopes. The Qumran manuscripts as well as the LXX and its secondary versions contribute to identifying two or more editions in some biblical books.

Genesis: MT, SP, and OG show variant schemata in the chronological sections of chapters 5 and 11.

Exodus: LXX, MT, 4QpaleoExod[m], and the Samaritan Pentateuch respectively attest four successive stages in the edition of this book. The OL (*Monacensis*) knew a different version of chapters 36—40, where the LXX lacks some sections of the MT, and in a few places it also adds details.

Numbers: MT and 4QNum[b] also indicate two successive editions.

Joshua: 4QJos[a] (together with Josephus), LXX, and MT represent three different editions.

Judges: 4QJudg[a] omits 6:7–10. A comparison of the MT and the LXX helps to recognize the addition of successive prologues and appendices.

Samuel: The story of David and Goliath (1 Sam 17–18) has been transmitted in two editions, a short one, known from the LXX, and a longer one, preserved in the MT.

Kings: MT and LXX represent two different arrangements of the text in 1 Kings 2—12 and also along 1–2 Kings in connection with two diverging chronological systems.

Jeremiah: LXX and 4QJer[b,d] transmit a first edition of this book, and the MT, together with 4QJer[a,c], that of a second augmented edition. The OG was revised from 29:1 onwards (following the LXX order) on the basis of the MT. The OL (codex *Wirceburgensis*) omits MT 39:1–2.

Ezekiel: The long MT edition depends on the short one represented by the LXX. The considerable differences between both texts in chapter 7 reflect two different Hebrew forms. The LXX went through a revision that affected chapters 28–39 (36:23c–38 was missing in the first version). The OL (*Wirceburgensis*) and Greek manuscript 967 are the only witnesses preserved which show that the oldest text followed the sequence 38–39–37 and omitted 36:23c–28.

Minor Prophets: The LXX order seems to have been modified to the proto-MT order.

Psalms: MT and 11QPs[a] represent two different editions. Several authors consider 11QPs[a] a liturgical scroll.

Proverbs: LXX and MT represent different editions, neither of which is clearly prior to the other.

Song of Songs: In 4QCant[a] 6:11 follows 4:7. Also 4QCant[b] goes from 4:3 to 4:8, and in the previous column it might go from 3:5 to 3:9 (at least there is text missing between 3:2 and 3:10). The OL presents the same verse order in chapter 5 as Greek Papyrus R 952 (5:12, 14b, 13, 14a, 15).

Daniel: MT, together with 1QDan[a.b], 4QDan[a-e], 6QDan, and, on the other side, the LXX, represent two editions, the former shorter and the latter characterized saliently by the Greek additions to this book. The LXX represents a form of tradition that is earlier than the Aramaic of Dan 2—7. It goes back to Hebrew and Aramaic originals of the fourth/third centuries B.C.E. Papyrus 967 represents the more original form of the Greek text, showing the order of chapters 1—4; 7—8; 5—6; and 9—12, followed by the stories of *Bel and the Dragon* and *Susanna*. This arrangement is found in the Latin writer Quodvultdeus.

Job: The Hebrew *Vorlage* of the LXX differed from the preserved Hebrew text. To the shorter text, closer to the Greek original (attested by OL and the Sahidic Coptic version), were added a series of passages taken from Theodotion's version, aimed at bringing the Greek version closer to the MT.

Esther: The first Greek translation, whose text is attested exclusively in OL, was revised on the basis of the MT, producing the traditional Greek text. Some of the six major additions to the Greek version appear to have been done in Hebrew or Aramaic.

Ezra: Ezra–Nehemiah and 1 Esdras (LXX) represent two editions, each with its own distinct literary shape.

The plurality of editions spreads to the apocrypha and pseudepigrapha as well as to Qumran writings such as 4QReworked Pentateuch, the Temple Scroll, the Community Rule, the Damascus Document, and the Hodayyot hymns. The study of the composition techniques in these writings, especially those of the transposition of pericopes and ring composition (*Wiederaufnahme*), contribute greatly to the study of the formation and growth of the biblical books.

Editions of the Hebrew Bible. The modern editions of the Hebrew text are diplomatic editions that reproduce the Codex Leningradensis or the Aleppo Codex.

Biblia Hebraica Stuttgartensia (BHS). The standard edition of the Hebrew Bible reproduces a virtually unchanged copy of the Codex Leningradensis. The critical notes recommend reading an alternate version of a text or adding or deleting a certain reading on the basis of the evidence offered in the apparatus. Otherwise they simply list variants and expect readers to make their own judgments.

Biblia Hebraica Quinta (BHQ). This new edition makes full use of all the extant Dead Sea Scrolls manuscripts. It includes the Masorah and a neutral critical apparatus with extensive introductions to the text history of each individual book, commentaries on the Masorah, and on data offered in the textual apparatus. The edition has the particularity of marking with the abbreviation *lit.* those readings that according to the editor's judgment go back to a literary development of the text, suggesting in this way that the book or a section of it has been transmitted in two or more different literary forms. The following volumes have appeared thus far: The Five Megilloth (2004), Ezra and Nehemiah (2006), Deuteronomy (2007), Proverbs (2009), The Twelve Minor Prophets (2010), and Judges (2012).

The Hebrew University Bible (HUB). Based on the Aleppo codex, this is an *editio critica maior* that documents every textual datum, consonants, vowels, accents, and divisions of the text in *seṭumot y peṭuhot*, besides the witness of the Dead Sea Scrolls, the early versions, rabbinic quotations, and medieval manuscripts. It is a descriptive edition that neither establishes relationships of dependence or priority between the different textual witnesses nor sets out to establish a critical text. The following volumes have appeared thus far: Isaiah (1995), Jeremiah (1997), and Ezekiel (2004).

The Hebrew Old Testament Project (HOTTP). This project gives special attention to the history of research of the difficulties of the text from the point of view of early and medieval Jewish and Christian sources and modern textual criticism. The edition was trusted to D. Barthélemy (*Critique textuelle de l'Ancien Testament*).

The Oxford Hebrew Bible (OHB). The new materials furnished by the Dead Sea Scrolls and the recent studies on the history of the biblical text and its versions pose today the convenience and necessity of undertaking an eclectic edition as proposed in the OHB that sets out to reconstruct the textual form(s) nearest to the original(s), which is the aim of modern textual criticism.

The Biblica Qumranica Project. intends to produce a synoptic edition of the biblical materials from the Judean desert alongside the LXX and MT.

The textual plurality and the existence of multiple editions together with a better assessment of the witness of the versions may make a polyglot model of an edition advisable, much in the way of the sixteenth and seventeenth century polyglots; it would profit from the new techniques of electronic edition in the same way as those used at the invention of the press. A digital synoptic edition is the best basis for the study of each textual tradition by itself—in Hebrew and in the languages of each version—and for specific text-critical analysis.

The Practice of Textual Criticism. Textual criticism establishes the rules and principles that make it possible to identify and correct accidental or deliberate changes introduced during the copying of the manuscript tradition.

Accidental Changes in the Copy of Manuscripts. Among these, the critic has to take into account the ones produced by:

Confusion between similar letters in the square script such as *d/r* (ד/ר), *b/k* (ב/כ), and *h/ḥ* (ה/ח), or in the paleo-Hebrew script as *'/t, k/n, b/r,* and *m/n.*

Confusion between homophonous words or words of similar pronunciation as in *lô* ("his") / *lō'* ("not") in Psalms 100:3.

Alternate vocalization as in Isa 9:7 MT *dābār* ("Word") / LXX *thanaton* = *deber* (pestilence or death).

Transposition of adjacent letters or metathesis as in Psalms 49:12 *qibrām* ("their tomb") / *qirbām* ("their inner [thought]").

Omission by homoioarcton or homoioteleuton. This occurs when the copyist jumps unintentionally from one word or expression to another that has the same beginning (*-arcton*) or the same ending (*-teleuton*). In Isa 5:8, where the MT is "house against house" (*bayit bĕbayit*), 1QIsa[a] omits the preposition *b-* through *homoioarcton*, which results in the meaningless "house house." Isaiah 4:5–6 suffered in 1QIsa[a] the loss of a clause because the copyist's eye skipped from *yômām* to *yômām* (*homoioteleuton*).

Dittography. This occurs when a letter, word, or sentence is written twice successively. In 1QIsa[a] *wĕhišmîa* is repeated twice in Isa 30:30.

Incorrect word division. This was common in the continuous consonantal script, which left no space between words. In Psalms 42:6 the sentence "(He) is the salvation of my face and my God" (*yšw't pny w'lhy*) is cut off so that the last word, "my God" (*'lhy*), forms part of the following verse.

Incorrect join of words. In Amos 6:12 the translation "to plough with cows" corresponds to the Hebrew word *bbqrym* (MT), whereas "to plough with cattle in the sea" translates two Hebrew words, *bbqr yam* (BHS). The context speaks of impossible or difficult things such as ploughing the sea or galloping on rocks.

Conflate or double readings. Such readings combine variants from two or more sources. In Isa 37:9 1QIsa[a] *wyšm' wyšwb* and LXX *kai akousas apestrepse* combine MT *wyšm'* ("he heard it") and 2 Kings 19:9 *wyšwb* ("again").

Deliberate Changes. These can be of different types:

Substitution because of modernization as in Isa 39:1, where 1QIsa[a] changed the verb *ḥzq,* which had the archaic meaning of "to heal," with the verb *ḥyh,* the usual one in the Qumran period for that meaning.

Harmonization. In Genesis 2:2 SP, the Peshitta and Jubilees (2:16) have the variant "the sixth day" instead of "the seventh day" in order to harmonize the sentence: "(Elohim) finished the work on the seventh day . . . he rested on the seventh day."

Assimilation to parallel passages. In Leviticus 5:25 the MT adds the reading "to the priest," taking it from v. 18 by assimilation to this verse. This reading is absent from the SP and LXX.

Corrections for moral or theological reasons. Due to euphemism, the expression "to curse Yahweh" (Job 1:5.11; 2:5.9) is replaced by "to bless Yahweh" even though the first expression fits the context better.

Glosses. In Josh 1:15 "then you will return to your land [and you will take possession of it], which Moses gave you," the clause "and you will take possession of it" is an added gloss missing from the LXX. It interrupts the syntactic sequence between the foregoing clause and the following relative.

Addition of epithets. In Jeremiah the MT adds "(Yahweh) of hosts, the God of Israel" (39 times), frequently missing from the LXX.

Addition of the names of the subject. In Jeremiah the MT adds the name "Nebuchadnezzar" on eight occasions, while the LXX ignores this addition or even the expressions of MT referring to Nebuchadnezzar.

Conflate readings. The readings of 1 Samuel 18:6 *bbw'm*, "When they came," and *bšwb dwd*, "When David returned," are editorial insertions ignored in the LXX. Their purpose is to connect the following section with two preceding episodes (17:54 and 17:55–18, omitted in the OG).

Besides the variations that are explained as the result of either error or specific sorts of exegetical or theological modification, it is also necessary to take into account variations that result from the transmission of texts by way of memory, like the exchange of synonymous words, word order variation, the presence and absence of conjunctions, and minor modifiers, and the like. In texts transmitted through memory, such as sayings in Proverbs, "the search for an Ur-text and clear lines of dependence and revision often will be fruitless" (Carr 2011, p. 33).

Rules of Textual Criticism. With the aim of selecting the variants that better fit with the archetype or that are nearer to the first form of the text, textual criticism has developed some basic rules that should not be applied with rigidity but with an acute critical sense. The main rules are the following:

- *Lectio difficilior.* Between two or more variants, the "more difficult" has a greater probability of being the original. This is due to the tendency of the scribes to make the reading of a text easier.
- *Lectio brevior.* In principle, the shorter reading is also the oldest one, since the copying of manuscripts tends toward the amplification of the text by inserting glosses or by repeating parallel passages.
- The reading that explains the origin of other variants is, in principle, preferable to these.
- The reading that differs from its parallels is preferable to the one that shows hints of assimilation or harmonization with them.

Textual Criticism and Literary Formation of the Biblical Books. Qumran has not changed the principles and methods of textual criticism, but it offers new knowledge that opens up new perspectives for their application. Textual criticism aims at recovering the text of a biblical book as it came from the last redactor's or editor's hands. Literary criticism tries to reconstruct the process of literary formation of the book to the moment of its final redaction. These two disciplines converge and even overlap in the study of those variants generated in the editorial process, particularly in the case of books transmitted in two or more textual forms or editions that circulated in parallel and influenced each other thus creating new variants. A joint analysis of textual and literary criticism is therefore particularly necessary in those books transmitted in two or more editions or textual forms.

The reconstruction of the "original" or Ur-Text still remains the theoretical object of textual criticism. Nevertheless, the oldest text that can be reconstructed is no longer that of an autograph or of a first or last edition, but that of the closest to a given textual form or edition, behind which lies at times, as a conjecture, an archetypal form from which it is derived. Beyond the correction of typos and deliberate changes introduced in the copying of manuscripts, textual criticism has to describe the larger-scope changes introduced by editors, such as the rearrangement of paragraphs and the inclusion of comments, prologues, or epilogues that left traces in the textual transmission. Editors' activities can be distinguished from those of redactors through the textual traces left by the former that are most easily discernible by a joint analysis of textual and literary criticism.

The history of the Hebrew text is not that of a progressive homogenization of a previous plurality according to Kahle's perspective nor that of a progressive diversification from a single text according to Lagarde's vision. From beginning to end a limited textual plurality was present. Thus the *veritas hebraica* entailed since its inception a *varietas* within itself, which in good measure could be also qualified as *trifaria* in a gradation of brief (LXX), large (MT), and expansive (proto-SP and other rewritten texts) and reflected in the Greek textual tradition: the Alexandrine (close to LXX), the Palestinian or Hexaplaric (close to MT), and the Antiochene (eclectic when compared to the former). As a consequence, the histories of the Hebrew and the Greek text (with their versions) cannot be taken apart from each other today. Biblical textual criticism distances itself from textual criticism of classical texts whose manuscript tradition starts with an autograph or author's original work, and in the same measure it gets closer to criticism of texts transmitted in a plurality of textual forms, like those of apocryphal and pseudoepigraphic writings, and of Qumran, New Testament, and Rabbinic works. In this sense the history of the text is connected to the history of its exegesis.

[*See also* Dead Sea Scrolls; Exegesis; Masora and Masoretic Interpretation; Rabbinic Exegesis; Redaction Criticism, *subentry* Hebrew Bible; Textual Criticism, *subentry* Apocrypha and Deuterocanonical Books; Textual Criticism, *subentry* New Testament; *and* Translation Techniques, *subentry* Ancient Versions.]

BIBLIOGRAPHY

Abegg, Martin, Jr., Peter Flint, and Eugene Ulrich. *The Dead Sea Scrolls Bible.* San Francisco: HarperSan Francisco, 1999.

Carr, David M. *The Formation of the Hebrew Bible. A New Reconstruction.* Oxford: Oxford University Press, 2011.

Cross, Frank M., and S. Talmon (eds.). *Qumran and the History of the Biblical Text.* Cambridge, Mass./London: Harvard University Press, 1975.

Barthélemy, Dominique. *Critique textuelle de l'Ancien Testament.* 4 vols. Fribourg/Suisse: Éditions Universitaires—Göttingen: Vandenhoeck & Ruprecht, 1982, 1986, 1992, 2005.

De Troyer, Kristin. *Rewriting the Sacred Text. What the Old Greek Tells Us about the Literary Growth of the Bible.* Atlanta: Society of Biblical Literature, 2003.

Hugo, Philippe, and Adrian Schenker (eds.). *Archaeolgy of the Books of Samuel. The Entangling of the Textual and Literary History.* Leiden, Netherlands: Brill, 2010.

Hendel, Ronald S. *The Text of Genesis 1—11. Textual Studies and Critical Edition.* New York, Oxford: Oxford University Press, 1998.

Lange, Armin. *Handbuch der Textfunde vom Toten Meer.* Vol. 1., *Die Handschriften biblischer Bücher von Qumran und den anderen Fundorten.* Tübingen: Mohr Siebeck, 2009.

Martin, Gary D. *Multiple Originals. New Approaches to Hebrew Bible Textual Criticism.* Atlanta: Society of Biblical Literature, 2010.

McCarter, P. Kyle. *Textual Criticism: Recovering the Text of the Hebrew Bible.* Philadelphia: Fortress, 1986.

Orion Center: http://orion.mscc.huji.ac.il/

Preliminary and Interim Report on the Hebrew Old Testament Text Project. 5 vols. New York: United Bible Societies, 1973, 1976, 1977, 1979, 1980.

Schenker, Adrian. *The Earliest Text of the Hebrew Bible. The Relationship between the Masoretic Text and the Hebrew Base of the Septuagint Reconsidered.* Atlanta: Society of Biblical Literature, 2003.

TC: A Journal of Biblical Textual Criticism: http://purl.org/TC

Tov, Emanuel. *Textual Criticism of the Hebrew Bible.* 3d ed., revised and expanded. Minneapolis: Fortress, 2012.

Ulrich, Eugene. *The Dead Sea Scrolls and the Origins of the Bible.* Grand Rapids, Mich.: Eerdmans; Leiden, Nethlands: Brill, 1999.

Ulrich, Eugene. "The Text of the Hebrew Scriptures at the Time of Hillel and Jesus." In *Congress Volume—Basel 2001*, edited by A. Lemaire, 85–108. Leiden, Netherlands—Boston: Brill, 2002.

Waard, J. de, P.B. Dirksen, and Y.A.P. Goldman, eds. *General Introduction and Megilloth*, BHQ 18. Stuttgart: Deutsche Bibelgesellschaft, 2004.

Julio Trebolle Barrera

Translated from Spanish by Pablo Torijano Morales

Apocrypha and Deuterocanonical Books

The books of the Apocrypha, or deuterocanonical books, are commonly thought to be products of Jewish communities between the third century B.C.E. and first century C.E. The writings, composed in Hebrew, Aramaic, and Greek, may stem from Palestine, Egypt, Syria, or other parts of the Eastern Diaspora. Many of these reflect the challenges of Jewish communities living in a predominantly Hellenized world (DeSilva 2004, p. 16). These writings would not become authoritative for Jews but instead were preserved in Greek (along with other writings shared with the Hebrew Bible (HB) that were translated to Greek) and included in Greek Bibles used by Christians. As part of the Greek translation of the Hebrew Scriptures, also referred to as the Septuagint (LXX), many of the writings have been included finally in the Christian

Bible's Old Testament (OT) but were not included in the HB when its collection of writings became fixed, likely late in the first century C.E.

For Roman Catholic and Orthodox communities these writings are authoritative or canonical, a status that can be understood, though, in different ways. Roman Catholics refer to seven books—Tobit, Judith, 1 and 2 Maccabees, the Wisdom of Solomon, Sirach, Baruch (with the Letter of Jeremiah)—and additions to Esther and Daniel (designated often as the "Prayer of Azariah and the Song of the Three Jews," "The Story of Susanna," and "The Story of Bel and the Dragon") as deuterocanonical ("second canon"); the designation acknowledges the production of these works in a period later than many of the writings of the HB, and also their formalization as canonical writings at the Council of Trent (1545–1563). These writings are, however, no less canonical than other writings in the Old and New Testaments of the Roman Catholic Bible. Orthodox Christians recognize an even greater number of writings within the OT; in addition to those already named, the Greek and Slavonic Bibles include 1 Esdras, the Prayer of Manasseh, Psalm 151, and 3 Maccabees. The Greek Orthodox Church considers these writings suitable and understands them to have biblical status, though the view on their canonical status has varied. The Slavonic Bible includes also 2 Esdras, but in the Russian Orthodox Church there is some ambivalence about the status, place, and function of the deuterocanonical books in the canon. The Ethiopian Orthodox Church, which understands "canon" in a manner that is not as fixed as other communities, may also include the book of Enoch (also referred to as 1 Enoch) and Jubilees in its OT (Stuckenbruck 2010, p. 145).

The differing contents of Greek Bibles from late antiquity vis-à-vis so-called deuterocanonical texts demonstrate that people then also entertained a plurality of views about which of these texts to include among collections of authoritative writings (Harrington 1999, p. 4). Protestant Bibles, for which these works are not authoritative or canonical (though these may be understood as beneficial for reading), often feature many of these writings in a special section outside of the OT and New Testament (NT) designated as the "Apocrypha." The Greek term "Apocrypha," which means hidden (here with the sense of "hidden" or "secret" writings), appears to have been used in reference to the deuterocanonical writings first by Jerome (cf. *Prologus in libro regum*, p. 365 as cited by Hengel 2004, p. 50).

While the Pseudepigrapha (writings traditionally associated with false attributions of authorship) and NT Apocrypha are broad, artificial categories and suggest contemporary collections or anthologies of various texts (not ancient collections), the texts we consider in this article (books of the Apocrypha for Protestants; deuterocanonical books for Roman Catholics; additional books of the Orthodox OT) have tended to circulate within certain collections at least from the fourth and fifth centuries (deSilva 2004, 17). Still, designations like Apocrypha that are used today do not describe these writings or communicate the way they were perceived or used in antiquity (Stuckenbruck p. 143, p. 151).

The Aim and Method of Textual Criticism. Textual criticism concerns recovering or reconstructing the original wording of a text, in light of perceived difficulties with a particular reading or in light of other readings preserved in manuscripts (van der Kooij 2006, p. 582). Though it may not be possible to arrive at the *Urtext*, the textual critic, when faced with variants, can make the case for a preferred reading from among the different witnesses (van der Kooij 2006, pp. 583–584).

While textual criticism attempts to adjudicate among different readings often with the purpose of discerning or offering conjecture for an *Urtext*, a dividend is what the methodology can communicate about the history of the transmission of a text and also about the relationships among manuscripts. Textual criticism can illumine also how texts were read and interpreted. Through comparison of manuscripts, scholars can create critical texts for readers that provide variants in the apparatus (Soulen and Soulen 2001, p. 189). In terms of works in the Apocrypha or deuterocanonical books, critical texts are available, for example, in the Göttingen editions that are also part of the Göttingen Septuagint.

Textual criticism is necessitated by differences in texts or by difficult readings. Divergent or uncertain readings may concern a word, a sentence, a pericope, or a larger unit of text (for example, different editions). In the case of two or more distinct readings, the contrast might concern variants (dissimilar text), plusses (additional text that is missing in another manuscript), or minuses (text lacking that is present in another manuscript).

How does one approach different or difficult readings and attempt respectively to adjudicate among these or assess the challenging texts? The classical scholar and poet A. E. Housman (1921, p. 68) describes textual criticism as both a science—though not an exact science—that relies on reason and common sense and as an art, in as much as the approach involves emendations and recensions. In the gathering and weighing of evidence, textual criticism also involves linguistic, philological, exegetical, literary, and cultural considerations (van der Kooij 2006, p. 585).

One aspect of textual criticism involves study of how manuscripts are related to one another and awareness of the quality of manuscripts (as superior or inferior vis-à-vis transmission of content), a characteristic that is not necessarily bound to the age of a manuscript. When examining a particular reading, textual criticism has tended to favor the following principles: (1) the more difficult reading is to be preferred (*lectio difficilior*) because of the assumption that subsequent editing would have moved in the direction of being more comprehensible, not less; (2) textual critics also ask and attempt to discern which reading would give rise to the other, in explaining how a variant could arise; and (3) textual critics tend to prefer the shorter reading, later augmented, as the earlier or original reading and to look for readings that are characteristic in some manner of the biblical author in question (Soulen and Soulen 2001, p. 190). These principles are not absolute, however, and scholars have called attention to how these rules may not in every instance lead back to an original or earlier reading (van der Kooij 2006, p. 585).

Textual criticism also considers how scribes and translators might have erred in their work, and it attempts to identify such missteps. For example, in the process of translation, it is possible that the translators misread or misunderstood the Hebrew or Aramaic in front of them, leading to unintended variants (Ulrich 2010, p. 103). As manuscripts are products of copyists, common scribal mistakes include accidental omission; dittography (erroneous repetition where a letter, word, or line is repeated by mistake); haplography (omission of a syllable, word, or line due to confusion with comparable material at hand); homoioteleuton (a "similar ending" in a text that results in the copyist mistakenly omitting a portion of the text); and homoioarchton (a "similar beginning" of a text that leads the copyist to overlook a portion of text in making a copy). In addition to variants caused by errors, different or challenging readings can result from scribes intentionally modifying texts for clarification, correction, or for theological or ideological reasons (Soulen and Soulen 2001, p. 189).

Sources for the Study of the Apocrypha and Deuterocanonical Books. The books explored here have been preserved in Greek and in languages that primarily are translations made from Greek versions; on occasion, selections of books considered part of the Apocrypha or as deuterocanonical are extant in Hebrew and Aramaic also.

The most complete forms of these books are from Greek translations of the books we have come to associate with the Hebrew scriptures; we refer to these Greek translations as the Septuagint (LXX), though, in contrast to the idealized account of the *Letter of Aristeas* (a Jewish Hellenistic work, ca. second century B.C.E.), we know little of the circumstances for these works' translation or composition (Greenspoon 2010, p. 1218). The translations of these works indicate a range of approaches from very literal to free translations, and Greenspoon (2010, p. 1218) concludes that there was not an overarching philosophy that governed the translations in the LXX.

Further, text critical work on the LXX is rendered more complex by the pluriform nature of the Hebrew and Aramaic "biblical" texts. Some of translations in the Septuagint suggest *Vorlagen* or previous texts close to the Masoretic Text (MT; known today for its authoritative description of Hebrew consonants, vowel and accent markings in the text of the HB, dating from ca. 900–1000 C.E.), but other books suggest variant readings and even different editions in Hebrew and Aramaic originals. Some ancient readers noting differences between later Hebrew and Aramaic biblical texts and those in the LXX were motivated to make the latter conform to the MT; later Jewish translators of the LXX include Theodotion, Aquila, and Symmachus. In addition to revisions made to translations and retranslations, sometimes translators also made changes in the texts at hand to reflect the historical or cultural contexts of their times, environments heavily influenced by Hellenism (Greenspoon 2010, p. 1218).

The Dead Sea Scrolls (ca. second century B.C.E.–68 C.E.) proved important as well in helping scholars understand better the *Vorlagen* available to Greek translators of the Septuagint. Hebrew texts preserved at Qumran resemble in many instances the text of the Septuagint and suggest use of a common type of text (Ulrich 2010, p. 103). The Dead Sea Scrolls not only assist one in evaluating the Hebrew or Aramaic on which the Greek text was based, but in the case of some books of the Apocrypha they demonstrate that Semitic *Vorlagen* did, in fact, exist. Among the Dead Sea Scrolls are fragments of Sira, Tobit, Letter of Jeremiah, and Psalm 151.

The great codices Vaticanus, Alexandrinus, and Sinaiticus from the fourth and fifth centuries C.E. are primary witnesses for the LXX (Knibb 2006, p. 161). The fourth-century Codex Vaticanus includes the books Wisdom of Solomon, Sirach, Judith, Tobit, Baruch, and the Letter of Jeremiah. Codex Sinaiticus of the fourth century includes Tobit, Judith, 1 and 2 Maccabees, Wisdom, and Sirach. Dated to the fifth century, Codex Alexandrinus has Baruch, Letter of Jeremiah, Tobit, Judith, 1 and 2 Maccabees, 3 and 4 Maccabees, Wisdom, Sirach, and Psalms of Solomon among the writings of the OT. Text critics should keep in mind the observation of Ulrich that the time from these important witnesses to the original translations is more than six centuries allowing a lengthy span for copyists' transmission and the potential for introducing inadvertent errors, corrections, and supplements (Ulrich 2010, p. 104).

There are additional uncials (early medieval Greek manuscripts copied in capital letters) and miniscules (medieval Greek manuscripts copied in a script, rounded and often connected, and smaller than uncials). Many of the miniscules support readings found in the Codex Sinaiticus, Codex Vaticanus, and Codex Alexandrinus. The Greek texts of the Apocrypha/deuterocanonical books served as the basis for later translations into Old Latin, Syriac, Coptic, Armenian, Ge'ez, and Arabic. Challenging to the task at hand is that each translated version has its own history and development that pertain also to text critical matters. Another important source for the study of Apocrypha/deuterocanonical books includes the quotations of these works in early Christian literature (Knibb 2006, pp. 161–164). Finally, manuscripts from much later periods—the Middle Ages—are also sources for textual criticism. Even if these texts do not assist us in establishing earlier or better readings, these later texts can still "widen the text-critical horizon" by showing the variety of styles and translations, as well as by providing contemporaries with the history of how a text of the Apocrypha or a deuterocanonical text has been read and interpreted (van der Kooij 2006, pp. 581–582).

Text Critical Issues in the Apocrypha/Deuterocanonical Books. A discussion of how text criticism relates to the Apocrypha/deuterocanonical books is complicated because the texts under consideration have such diverse backgrounds—some are available in their language of composition, others are extant only or primarily in translations—and histories of transmission. Although the writings of the Apocrypha have been included in manuscripts of the Greek Bible and excluded from the HB, in fact, many of the books were composed in Hebrew or Aramaic and translated to Greek "as part of the wider process by which the books of the HB were translated into Greek, and for similar reasons" (Knibb 2006, p. 160). Tobit, Sira, Psalm 151, writings attributed to Enoch that are now in the collection 1 Enoch, and Jubilees have been discovered in Hebrew and Aramaic, which are thought also to be the language of composition. At the same time, there are writings whose Greek style suggests composition in Greek. Those writings of the Apocrypha/deuterocanonical books thought to have been composed in Greek include additions B and E to the book of Esther, Wisdom of Solomon, 2 Maccabees, 3 Maccabees, 2 Esdras 1—2, 15—16, 4 Maccabees, and likely the Prayer of Manasseh (Knibb 2006, p. 160).

Further, there are writings of the Apocrypha/deuterocanonical books that would seem to have been written in Hebrew or Aramaic but for which proof is lacking. Such writings include Judith, additions to the book of Esther (A, C, D), Baruch, the Letter of Jeremiah, additions to the Greek book of Daniel, 1 Maccabees, and 1 Esdras (Knibb 2006, p. 160). Such speculation extends back to Jerome, who suggested that Sira and 1 Maccabees had been composed in Hebrew; in terms of potential Semitic *Vorlagen*, Jerome indicated that he translated Tobit and Judith from Aramaic. Still, on the matter of language of composition, there are notable challenges to the idea that all of the aforementioned texts were composed in Semitic languages. Authors could, for example, mimic the style of translation one finds in the LXX, one that seems to effect a type of equivalence to Hebrew and to adhere to Hebrew idiom, but in Greek. In the case of Judith, Jeremy Corley, along with Toni Craven (1983, p. 5) and Erich Zenger (1988, pp. 404–407), argues that the book need not have been composed in Hebrew and that composition in Greek is very possible, even though Judith exhibits Hebraicisms. Corley's study demonstrates how the book of Judith frequently alludes to the LXX with quotations and echoes of Septuagintal phrases (Corley 2008, pp. 68–80); additionally, Corley explains the Hebraicisms through mimetic appreciation of the Septuagintal style or through Semitic interference by using Greek as a second language and employing non-Greek idioms that follow Semitic patterns (Corley 2008, pp. 67; 80–96).

Issues of translation and the unavailability of some texts in their languages of composition impact text critical work on the Apocrypha/deuterocanonical books. Though it is not possible to offer a summary for all text critical issues given the disparate nature of the writings in question, a few key examples are provided to illustrate various text critical matters as they relate specifically to the books of the Apocrypha or deuterocanonical books. These also serve to call attention to the role of recensions and important ancient witnesses that text critics consider in their study of a particular writing of the Apocrypha.

Assessing Recensions. Although one of the principles frequently invoked in textual criticism is the rule that the shorter text is to be preferred, study of recensions has shown this not to be true for Tobit (Ego 2006, p. 372). Some initially held the shorter Greek version, GrI, to be earlier than the longer version, GrII, as represented in Sinaiticus, but the latter proved to be the earlier. Qumran manuscripts seem to attest this as well, agreeing with Sinaiticus (Milik 1966, pp. 522–530; Spencer 1999, pp. 147–180). In this instance, GrII appears to have been reworked and shortened to avoid redundancies (Ego 2006, p. 372).

The Wisdom of Joshua (Jesus) Ben Sira, as it is known in Hebrew, or Sirach, according to the Greek Bible, expresses well some of the complications involved in the study of the Apocrypha/deuterocanonical books. Study of Ben Sira involves numerous translations and different recensions. Initially, text critics had no version of Ben Sira in the language of composition, Hebrew, but then new discoveries of Hebrew manuscripts of Ben Sira from Qumran and Masada called for reassessment of text critical work on the book.

Ben Sira has been known especially from its Greek translation, which, as its prologue indicates, was made from the Hebrew by the author's grandson. There are two extant forms of the Greek text. The first, GrI, is found in codices Sinaiticus, Alexandrinus, and Vaticanus, as well as in many miniscules. The second, GrII, is an expanded form with 160 additional cola, thought by some to be a revision of GrI on the basis of Hebrew. GrII is not represented by a single manuscript (Knibb 2006, p. 169). In addition to the Greek, Syriac, and Old Latin versions, rabbinic literature also expresses knowledge of Ben Sira in the form of quotations that read like paraphrases of the text. Rabbinic references to proverbs associated with Ben Sira, which are not derived from versions of the book as we have it, suggest that the book was being gradually expanded (Wright 2010, p. 437). In the late nineteenth century and first half of the twentieth century, scholars identified Hebrew manuscripts from the Cairo Genizah as selections of Sira, which are typically dated to the eleventh or twelfth century.

The Cairo Genizah manuscripts revealed two Hebrew versions of Ben Sira that have been designated HI (the original Hebrew text) and HII (a second recension with numerous additions to the original text). Some of the additions of HII were comparable to the additions in GrII. The similarities were explained by the idea that additions to GrII resulted from revisions to GrI on the basis of Hebrew manuscripts like HII (Ziegler 1965, pp. 83–84; Skehan and Di Lella 1987, pp. 57–59). However, some scholars challenge the idea that there is textual evidence that additions to Ben Sira in ancient versions like GrII and the Syriac are "the result of a systematic Hebrew recension" (Gile 2011, p. 256). Instead, they posit gradual accretion of the book and multiform expansions of Ben Sira (Gile 2011, p. 256; Gilbert 1991, p. 77).

Significant text critical work on Ben Sira has been made possible also by the discovery of manuscripts of the book in Hebrew among the Dead Sea Scrolls and at Masada. Initially, many were dubious as to the antiquity of the Cairo Genizah texts of Ben Sira, thinking them to be a later retranslation from the Greek (Di Lella 1966, pp. 27–46). The discoveries from Qumran and Masada, and the text critical work of scholars like Di Lella, have demonstrated that the version of Ben Sira preserved in the Cairo Genizah is not a retranslation of the Greek but an authentic Hebrew version of the text.

Another important witness for Ben Sira is the Old Latin version, which drew on GrII as a source and contains some additions from recensions of Origen and Lucian (Knibb 2006, p. 170), as well as additions from a Greek text no longer extant. The Syriac apparently drew on both HI and HII (or a combination of the two) and includes additions of the type found in HII and GrII. This translation was based on a Hebrew version, which was revised by Christians by the end of the third century (Owens 2011, p. 196).

Friedrich Reiterer (1997, p. 27) summarizes the state (and challenges) of text critical work on Ben Sira: "When research in this field started, there was some hope of reconstructing the 'Urtext,' or at least a text near it;" yet research has demonstrated that "in each version one must assume revisions." Moreover, Reiterer observes that "it seems that even the 'oldest' text is already an interpretation, so that every scholar is in fact interpreting interpretations." Even so, Reiterer (1997, pp. 27–30) allows that if criteria for interpretation can be identified, perhaps one can make comparisons and look for a common base. Examining doublets of Ben Sira 42:14–15 and 20:30–31 in the Greek, in the Hebrew Ben Sira manuscripts A and B, and also the marginal readings of B, Masada, Reiterer (1997, p. 30) demonstrates that all versions must be examined on their own merits when one investigates coincidences and differences.

Textual Criticism and the Study of the Greek Translations. Among the writings of the Apocrypha/deuterocanonical books are the additions to Esther. In addition to six passages not found in the Hebrew, the Greek translation differs from the Hebrew in many respects (Knibb 2006, p. 175). These additional passages in Esther, as in the case of other books of the Apocrypha or deuterocanonical books, provoke discussion about the language of composition and *Urtexten*. Because of the presence of Semitisms in the additional Greek passages labeled A, C, D, and F, some scholars have argued that these selections were composed in Hebrew or Aramaic (Moore 1977, p. 155). Passages B and E, from among the additions to Esther, were assumed to have been composed in Greek on the basis of style. Because there is no manuscript evidence of the six additional passages in a Semitic language, and since the style and syntax seem to betray a Greek base text, other scholars (e.g., Jobes 2007, p. 424) are skeptical about a Hebrew or Aramaic original for the majority of the extra passages.

In the case of the Greek text, Esther is extant in two distinct versions: the LXX (Old Greek) and the Alpha Text (AT). In the absence of a clear consensus as to whether one should be regarded as older or as dependent on the other (Jobes 2007, p. 424), variant readings of the two versions necessitate textual criticism to sort through the relationship of the versions to each other and to craft an argument for superior readings. Because the six additional chapters in Old Greek and AT are very close, some have argued that these came after an initial Greek text and were later inserted into both versions or were copied from one to the other. Some have argued that AT preserves older forms of some of the additional passages (A, B, C, E, F); this view does not necessarily establish the priority of AT, but instead can communicate that AT's additional passages were not subject to as much revision as the Old Greek (Jobes 2007, p. 425). The AT has been thought to be a revision of the LXX; others suggest that it derives from an earlier form of Esther in Hebrew, with the additions later incorporated into the AT.

Toward assessing the AT and its variants, Kristin De Troyer (2003, pp. 59–89) examines the text at 7:33b–38, which concerns the letter sent by Mordecai. This selection is absent from all other traditions concerning Esther. De Troyer argues that these verses are not only typical for the AT, but are based on the LXX version of Esther and exemplify how the AT has rewritten LXX. For example, additions and omissions in AT accord with the LXX Esther in different respects. De Troyer calls attention to commonalities in language found in 7:33b–38 and Esther 8, which she explains came about as a result of AT drawing on the Old Greek. Further, she notes that the AT attempts to copy the style of the LXX.

Textual Criticism and the Reading Horizon for the Apocrypha/Deuterocanonical Books. Even when recovery of the *Urtext* is unattainable, text critical work can reveal how deuterocanonical books were transmitted and received by various communities. For example, Beate Ego (2006) demonstrates in her study of Tobit how variants in Sinaiticus, Alexandrinus, and Vaticanus resulted from influences of redactors' cultural and religious settings. The subject of Ego's study is Tobit 3:17, where Greek recensions differ in reporting what Raphael does to the demon Asmodeus. In Tobit 3:17 of Sinaiticus, Raphael frees (λυ=σαι) Sarah from the wicked demon Asmodeus. In Tobit 3:17 of the Alexandrinus and Vaticanus codices, Raphael is sent to bind (δη=σαι) the demon Asmodeus.

The Greek λυ/ω is thought to be the equivalent for the Aramaic word רטופמ (dismissed). The latter was used in Babylonian Judaism as a *terminus technicus* for "divorce" (cf. Matt 5:31–32 and 1 Cor 7:10–11 for comparable use of the Greek) and in Aramaic and Mandaic magical texts for expulsion of demons. Since a demon was understood to be married to its victim, a human wishing to be free of a demon sought a divorce (Ego 2006, pp. 374–375). Ego argues that the original Greek translation did suggest that the demon loved Sarah, which is preserved still in Tobit 6:15 of MS 319, Alexandrinus, and Vaticanus; in Sinaiticus also, Raphael pursues Asmodeus to Upper Egypt and binds him hand and foot (see Tob 8:3). The idea of demonic love eradicated through divorce and then binding was well known in the Eastern world. The reference in the shorter recension (GrI) of Alexandrinus and Vaticanus to "binding" Asmodeus in Tobit 3:17 reflects a different concept. Ego speculates that the copyists and redactors of the Greek original did not know the association of λυ/ω to divorce from demons and instead reflect in their texts the motif common in Greek literature of binding a demon. The original form of Tobit, probably a product of the Eastern Diaspora, was affected at the level of copying and redaction in its later context in the West (Ego 2006, pp. 376–378). This example serves to demonstrate how textual criticism can profitably examine recensions of books in the Apocrypha and deuterocanonical books illumining the reception of these writings for various communities.

[*See also* Diachronic Interpretation; Exegesis; Form Criticism, *subentry* Hebrew Bible; Historical Criticism, *subentry* Hebrew Bible; Redaction Criticism, *subentry* Apocrypha and Deuterocanonical Books; Redaction

Criticism, *subentry* New Testament; Source Criticism; *and* Tradition–Historical Criticism.]

BIBLIOGRAPHY

Beentjes, Pancratius C. "Reading the Hebrew Ben Sira Manuscripts Synoptically: A New Hypothesis." In *The Book of Ben Sira in Modern Research: Proceedings of the First International Ben Sira Conference, 28–31 July 1996, Soesterberg, Netherlands*, edited by Pancratius C. Beentjes, 23–60. Berlin: Walter de Gruyter, 1997.

Corley, Jeremy. "Septuagintalisms, Semitic Interference, and the Original Language of the Book of Judith." In *Studies in the Greek Bible: Essays in Honor of Francis T. Gignac, S.J.*, edited by Jeremy Corley and Vincent Skemp, 65–96. Washington D.C.: Catholic Biblical Association of America, 2008.

Craven, Toni. *Artistry and Faith in the Book of Judith.* Chico, Calif: Scholars Press, 1983.

DeSilva, David A. *Introducing the Apocrypha: Message, Context, and Significance.* Grand Rapids, Mich.: Baker, 2004.

De Troyer, Kristin. *Rewriting the Sacred Text.* Atlanta: Society of Biblical Literature, 2003.

Di Lella, Alexander A. *The Hebrew Text of Sirach: A Text-Critical and Historical Study.* The Hague: Mouton, 1966.

Dines, J. *The Septuagint. Understanding the Bible and its World.* London: T&T Clark/Continuum, 2004.

Ego, Beate. "Textual Variants as a Result of Enculturation: The Banishment of the Demon in Tobit." In *Septuagint Research: Issues and Challenges in the Study of the Greek Jewish Scriptures*, edited by Wolfgang Kraus and R. Glenn Wooden, 371–378. Atlanta: Society of Biblical Literature, 2006.

Gilbert, Maurice. "The Book of Ben Sira: Implications for Jewish and Christian Traditions." In *Jewish Civilizations in the Hellenistic-Roman Period*, edited by S. Talmon, 81–91. Philadelphia: Trinity Press International, 1991.

Gile, Jason. "The Additions to Ben Sira and the Book's Multiform Textual Witness." In *The Texts and Versions of the Book of Ben Sira: Transmission and Interpretation*, edited by Jean-Sébastien Rey and Jan Joosten, 237–256. Leiden, the Netherlands: Brill, 2011.

Greenspoon, Leonard J. "Septuagint." In *Eerdmans Dictionary of Early Judaism*, edited by John J. Collins and Daniel C. Harlow, 1217–1220. Grand Rapids, Mich.: Eerdmans, 2010.

Hanhart, Robert. *Text und Textgeschichte des Buches Tobit.* Göttingen: Vandenhoeck and Ruprecht, 1984.

Harrington, Daniel J., S.J. *Invitation to the Apocrypha.* Grand Rapids, Mich.: Eerdmans, 1999.

Hengel, Martin. *Septuagint as Christian Scripture: Its Prehistory and the Problem of its Canon.* Translated by Mark E. Biddle. Grand Rapids, Mich.: Baker, 2004.

Housman, A. E. "The Application of Thought to Textual Criticism." *Proceedings of the Classical Association* 18 (1921): 67–84.

Jobes, Karen H. "Esther: To the Reader." In *A New English Translation of the Septuagint*, edited by Albert Pietersma and Benjamin G. Wright, 424–425. Oxford: Oxford University Press, 2007.

Knibb, Michael A. "Language, Translation, Versions, and Text of the Apocrypha." In *The Oxford Handbook of Biblical Studies*, edited by J. W. Rogerson and Judith M. Lieu, 159–183. Oxford: Oxford University Press, 2006.

Milik, J. T. "Le Patrie De Tobie." *Revue biblique* 73 (1966): 522–530.

Moore, C. A. *Daniel, Esther and Jeremiah: The Additions.* New York: Doubleday, 1977.

Owens, Robert J. "Christian Features in the Peshitta Text of Ben Sira: The Question of Dependency on the Syriac New Testament." In *The Texts and Versions of the Book of Ben Sira: Transmission and Interpretation*, edited by Jean-Sébastien Rey and Jan Joosten, 177–196. Leiden, the Netherlands: Brill 2011.

Reiterer, Friedrich V. "Review of Recent Research on the Book of Ben Sira (1980–1996)." In Beentjes, *Book of Ben Sira in Modern Research*, 23–60. Berlin: Walter de Gruyter, 1997.

Skehan, P. W., and A. A. Di Lella. *The Wisdom of Ben Sira.* New York: Doubleday, 1987.

Spencer, R. A. "The Book of Tobit in Recent Research." *Currents in Research: Biblical Studies* 7 (1999): 147–180.

Soulen Richard N., and R. Kendall Soulen. *Handbook of Biblical Criticism.* 3d ed. Louisville, Ky.: Westminster/John Knox, 2001.

Stuckenbruck, Loren. "The Jewish Scriptures: Texts, Versions, Canons." In *Eerdmans Dictionary of Early Judaism*, edited by John J. Collins and Daniel C. Harlow, 143–162. Grand Rapids, Mich.: Eerdmans, 2010.

Ulrich, Eugene. *The Dead Sea Scrolls and the Origins of the Bible.* Grand Rapids, Mich.: Eerdmans, 1999.

Ulrich, Eugene. "The Jewish Scriptures: Texts, Versions, Canons." In Collins and Harlow, *Eerdmans Dictionary of Early Judaism*, 97–119. Grand Rapids: Eerdmans, 2010.

van der Kooij, Arie. "Textual Criticism." In Rogerson and Lieu, *Oxford Handbook of Biblical Studies*, 579–590. Oxford: Oxford University Press, 2006.

Weeks, Stuart, Simon Gathercole, and Loren Stuckenbruck. *The Book of Tobit: Texts from the Principal Ancient and Medieval Traditions with Synopsis,*

Concordances, and Annotated Texts in Aramaic, Hebrew, Greek, Latin, and Syriac. Berlin: Walter de Gruyter, 2004.

Wright, Benjamin G., III, "Ben Sira, Book of." In Collins and Harlow, *Eerdmans Dictionary of Early Judaism*, 436–438. Grand Rapids, Mich.: Eerdmans, 2010.

Zenger, Erich. "Judith/Judithbuch." In *TRE* 17 (1988): 404–408.

Ziegler, J. *Sapientia Jesu Filii Sirach*. Göttingen, Germany: Vandenhoeck and Ruprecht, 1965.

Kelley Coblentz Bautch

New Testament

New Testament textual criticism is the analysis of the transmission of the text of the New Testament with a view to identifying variations from the original text. Textual criticism is required by two facts. (1) We do not possess any of the original manuscripts (autographs); we have only copies, usually copies of copies several times removed from the originals. (2) Since these copies were produced entirely by hand, both accidental and intentional changes were introduced into the text. As a result, the extant copies present an enormous number of variations, even though they have a great deal in common. The task of textual criticism is to determine, as far as possible, the original wording of the text by comparing and evaluating the readings in the extant manuscripts.

No other ancient document is as richly preserved or as diversely represented as the New Testament. Any corpus of writings copied by hand over a millennium and a half will necessarily display considerable variation. The eventual sacred status of the New Testament, combined with the numerical and geographical growth of the early church, insured that these documents would be copied and translated countless times. New Testament textual criticism is, therefore, both extremely well-resourced and extremely complex. It is also the most technical aspect of biblical interpretation. Basic text critical work requires, at a minimum, a working knowledge of both Greek and the critical apparatus of the Greek New Testament. Advanced expertise in textual criticism requires knowledge of several other languages of the early Church: Latin, Syriac, Coptic, Gothic, Armenian, Ethiopic, and Georgian. In addition, textual critics must have knowledge of paleography, ancient scribal practices, and early Christian controversies. Persons who lack the linguistic expertise to do independent text critical analysis will find the textual commentaries by Metzger (1994) and Comfort (2008) especially helpful.

The relationship between textual criticism and interpretation might seem to be straightforwardly sequential: one must first establish the text and then interpret it. While this is generally true, there is also a feedback loop from the interpretive process. The meaning that emerges may assist the textual critic in deciding that one variant is more likely than the other(s), based on congruence with the author's theology, the literary context, or a subtlety that was not initially evident.

The importance of textual criticism varies greatly from one passage to the next. Nearly every verse of the New Testament would present multiple variants if one scoured the entire textual tradition. Nevertheless, many verses have no significant text critical issues, i.e., none in which the best reading is seriously in question and the choice among the variants is exegetically significant. On the other hand, the interpretation of some passages may be profoundly affected by a text critical decision. In such cases, a text critical judgment may be one of the most decisive steps in interpretation.

The Materials of Textual Criticism. As previously indicated, the New Testament textual critic has an abundance of material with which to work. Many writings from classical antiquity are known to us by manuscripts numbering in the dozens; a few works survive in a single manuscript or merely a handful. These documents are often centuries or even a millennium or more removed from the originals. The epics of Homer, the *Iliad* and the *Odyssey*, probably the most revered classical writings, are represented by a total of about one thousand manuscripts for the two works combined. In contrast, the textual remains of the New Testament are an embarrassment of riches: more than 5800 Greek manuscripts, about three times that number in other ancient languages, and countless quotations in writers of the early church. Many of these manuscripts do not contain the entire New Testament, however, and some are fragments containing only a portion of a single book. The three major categories of ancient witnesses to the New Testament text deserve fuller discussion.

Greek Manuscripts. Greek manuscripts of the New Testament have the highest priority. The oldest of these are papyri, some of them as old as the second or third century. They are designated by the Gothic letter "p" followed by a superscript number. Currently about 130 papyri have been cataloged. Of special interest is p^{52}, the oldest extant copy of any portion of the New Testament. About the size of a credit card, p^{52} contains only a few verses of John 18 and was originally part of a codex, given that writing appears on both of its sides. Most papyri of the New Testament are fragmentary, containing small portions of a single book. Their value lies in their relatively early date (most of them third to sixth century C.E.) since, other things being equal, an earlier witness is generally more likely to preserve the original reading.

Also very important are the majuscule (written in capital letters, sometimes called "uncial") manuscripts written on parchment or vellum (animal skins). More than 320 of these have been cataloged. Originally they were designated by a capital letter of the Latin, Greek, or Hebrew alphabet, but when their number exceeded the number of available letters, they were reassigned an Arabic numeral preceded by a zero, and subsequently cataloged majuscules continue to use this system. The earliest known majuscules therefore have both a letter and a number designation. Among the most valuable majuscule manuscripts are Codex Sinaiticus (א or 01) and Codex Vaticanus (B or 03). These manuscripts are distinguished by their early date (mid-fourth century) and their extensive contents (Sinaiticus containing a complete New Testament and much of the Old; Vaticanus lacking two portions of the Old Testament and a few Pauline letters and Revelation from the New Testament). Some scholars have hypothesized that Sinaiticus and Vaticanus were among the fifty copies of the Bible that the Emperor Constantine commissioned Eusebius to produce in the fourth century. Most other majuscule manuscripts date from the fifth through the tenth centuries and contain anywhere from a single chapter of scripture to a large portion of the New Testament.

Minuscules constitute a third group of Greek manuscripts. In the early ninth century a new style of script was developed using smaller letters and a cursive style. The compactness and ease of the minuscule script enabled texts to be transcribed faster and in less space. These advantages led to the swift replacement of the majuscule style such that the two scripts represent two eras in paleography with a slight overlap. Majuscules largely disappear by the end of the tenth century; minuscules span a period from the ninth century to the invention of the printing press (mid-fifteenth century) and about two centuries beyond. Because of their relatively late date, the value of minuscules as witnesses to the New Testament text is generally less than that of majuscules, but occasionally a late minuscule will contain a text copied from a much earlier manuscript and thus be closer to the original than it first appears. This is the case for minuscules 33, 81, and 1739. More than 2900 minuscules have been cataloged to date.

Lectionaries make up the final group of Greek manuscripts. A lectionary is a system of scriptural readings, modeled on the synagogal custom of readings from the Law and the Prophets. Selections from the Gospels and the Epistles were designated for reading on particular Sundays and other holy days. The beginning and ending of a selection were marked, and other notes to aid the lector might be written in the margins. The oldest lectionaries date to the seventh or eighth century and used a majuscule script, but the great majority are later, minuscule manuscripts. More than 2450 lectionaries have been cataloged.

Ancient Versions. Ancient versions are the second major category of witnesses to the New

Testament text. As Christianity spread, it became necessary to translate its sacred writings into the languages of people whose native tongue was not Greek. The earliest versions were Syriac, Coptic, and Latin, corresponding to missionary efforts in the northeast, southeast, and western regions of the Mediterranean world. The great advantage of the earliest versions is their origin in the second and third centuries and the likelihood that a very early Greek text may lie behind them. The disadvantage of all versions, however, is the frequent disparity between languages and the resultant inability to move behind the translation with precision and certainty to the original Greek. For example, Coptic has no passive voice, Latin has no definite article, and Syriac verb tenses lack certain nuances of Greek. Such variations between languages remind us that, while versions may be very early witnesses, they are always indirect witnesses. Later versions, such as the Gothic, Armenian, Georgian, Ethiopic, and Old Slavonic, suffer from both the indirectness of all translations and their distance from the Greek autographs.

Patristic Quotations. Patristic quotations comprise the final category of witnesses. In sermons, commentaries, and essays written from the second century on, early church leaders pervasively cited the writings that came to constitute the New Testament. Indeed, if all other witnesses to the New Testament were destroyed, nearly the entire canon could be reconstructed from these quotations. The advantages and deficits of patristic quotations are similar to those of the early versions. Quotations can be dated with some precision and often located geographically by our knowledge about the author. Thus, scholars may conjecture that a certain textual reading was current in early fourth century Caesarea because it is found in the writings of Eusebius. On the other hand, quotations always remain secondary witnesses because they are not found in New Testament manuscripts per se. A factor that complicates the use of patristic quotations is our uncertainty about whether the writer is carefully consulting the text, quoting from memory, or paraphrasing.

Generally, the earlier the writer, the weightier the witness to the biblical text. Thus, readings attested by Irenaeus and Clement of Alexandria (second century) are more important than readings in Theophylact (eleventh and twelfth centuries). The Greek and Latin church Fathers have been studied far more than the Syrian and Coptic Fathers, and accordingly New Testament quotations in the former more often enter into text-critical decisions.

Sources of Textual Variants. Variations enter the textual tradition for a variety of reasons and can be broadly divided into two groups: unintentional changes and deliberate changes.

Unintentional Changes. These involve various errors of perception or cognition.

1. Errors of sight occurred when a scribe mistook one letter for a similar one. Since the earliest manuscripts were written in block capital letters in a continuous series without spaces between words (*scriptio continua*), confusion of letters or skipping of letters was a common error. Errors of sight were sometimes occasioned by similar strings of letters at the end of a word or a line (*homoioteleuton*) in which the scribe's eye would jump from one occurrence to the next, omitting the letters in between. In this way several manuscripts of Luke 14:26–27 omit verse 27 entirely since these two verses end with the same sequence of five Greek words. This same phenomenon could lead to writing a letter or a string of letters once that actually occurred twice (*haplography*). If, after writing a few letters on the new copy, the scribe's eyes returned to the very same place in the exemplar (the older manuscript from which the new copy is being made) without advancing, an error known as *dittography* could arise, the writing of a letter or a string twice that should have been written once. In Acts 19:34 a riotous mob chants "Great is Artemis of the Ephesians!" Codex Vaticanus gives the chant twice, a likely instance of dittography, but one that produced a rhetorical effect rather than nonsense. Errors of sight typically occurred when a scribe was working individually, producing a single new manuscript.

2. Errors of hearing arose when manuscripts were produced by dictation. A lector in a scriptorium would slowly read aloud from an exemplar, and a room full of scribes would simultaneously produce multiple copies. This method had certain advantages, especially when exemplars were scarce, but it was susceptible to auditory errors. In the early Christian centuries a phenomenon called *itacism* (or *iotacism*) arose, by which the sounds of several Greek vowels and diphthongs converged and were virtually indistinguishable from one another in spoken Greek. This confusion could easily produce minor variations in manuscripts produced in a scriptorium. A ubiquitous problem in New Testament manuscripts is the confusion of the pronouns "we" and "you." In Greek, these words differ only in the initial vowel, vowels whose sounds *itacism* would have blurred. Thus in 1 John 1:4, does the author claim that the epistle was written "so that our joy may be complete" or "so that your joy may be complete"?

3. Errors of the mind include memory lapses by which words disappeared, or by which inadvertent substitutions were made. If the lector in a scriptorium dictated too long a clause, a scribe might forget one or more words, perhaps omitting them if they were inessential, or changing them to whatever occurred to the scribe in the interval between hearing and writing. In a similar fashion scribes might rearrange the order of words, since word order in ancient Greek was quite flexible. Finally, scribes might inadvertently change a passage to harmonize it with a parallel text or a more familiar wording. This type of error verges on deliberate change, and there are times when the textual critic is hard-pressed to say whether a harmonized reading was intentional or not.

Unintentional changes, by their very nature, usually introduce nonsensical readings whose causes are readily recognized. Such accidents reveal more about scribal shortcomings than about scribal ingenuity. Somewhat more interesting and revealing, therefore, are the changes that scribes made deliberately.

Deliberate Changes. These are of several types. They include:

1. Improvements in vocabulary, grammar, or style might be introduced by a scribe who thought the exemplar to be deficient or obscure. A familiar word might be substituted for a rare one; awkward syntax cleaned up; harsh expressions might be softened. Thus in John 2:15, where Jesus fashions a whip of cords, several manuscripts read "something like a whip of cords," perhaps a scribal effort to alleviate the portrait of a seemingly violent Jesus.

2. Pious or liturgical expansions were common, especially as the devotional and liturgical traditions of the church grew. It was hard for a scribe to copy a prayer or an epistle without adding a concluding "Amen" or some other doxological flourish. (See the various expansions to the Lord's Prayer in Matt 6:13.) Divine names and titles were frequently expanded. In Galatians 6:17 the bare name of Jesus is elaborated with "Christ," "Lord," and "our Lord" in various manuscripts.

3. Correction of historical, geographical, and intertextual errors would be made by scribes trying to improve the clarity and accuracy of the text. Mark 2:26 speaks of David entering the house of God when Abiathar was high priest. In fact, this occurred during the priesthood of Ahimelech (1 Sam 21:1–6), and so a number of scribes removed the temporal reference from the verse. In Mark 7:31 Jesus takes a bizarre route, passing from Tyre to Galilee by way of Sidon, which was twenty miles out of the way. Several scribes modified the text to read "going forth from the region of Tyre and Sidon, he went to the Sea of Galilee." Finally, Mark 1:2 attributes to Isaiah an Old Testament quotation that actually conflates Malachi and Isaiah. Some scribes corrected the text to read "Just as it is written in the prophets."

4. Harmonizations occurred when a scribe changed a reading to make it conform to a parallel passage. This was a natural reaction for scribes, who often knew large portions of scripture by heart. A text from one Gospel might be assimilated to that of another Gospel that was more detailed, more elegant, or was simply the scribe's favorite. Thus the

order of Jesus's temptations in Luke 4 was changed by some scribes to harmonize with that of Matthew 4.

5. Theologically motivated changes probably hold the greatest interest for students of early Christianity. Here we see scribes removing offensive words or adding clarifying comments to align the text with emerging Christian orthodoxy. In Mark 13:32 Jesus declares that no one knows the day or hour of his return, "neither the angels in heaven, nor the Son, but only the Father." Scribes who felt that a divine Jesus would certainly not be ignorant of the time of his return deleted the words "nor the Son." Similarly, Luke 2:33 speaks of the father and the mother of the infant Jesus. As the doctrine of the virgin birth became widespread Christian belief, some scribes felt obliged to replace "his father" with the name "Joseph." Although theologically motivated changes to the text of the New Testament account for less than 1 percent of the total number of variants, their existence shows that Christian doctrine exerted at least some influence on textual transmission, and that the sacred text was not so sacrosanct as to preclude modifications in accord with the emerging rule of faith. Although the textual critic is primarily concerned with the determination of the original text and will usually lay aside those readings determined to be secondary, the rejected readings are sometimes revealing of theological and social phenomena in early Christianity. (See Metzger and Ehrman 2005, pp. 280–99; Ehrman, 1993.)

A Brief History of New Testament Textual Criticism. The history of New Testament textual criticism began with the first scribe who deliberated over the wording of a text, based on discrepancies in the manuscripts available to the scribe or the scribe's sense of what the text ought to say. Scholars as early as Origen (185–254 C.E.) began to reckon with variants, and Jerome (345–420 C.E.) and Augustine (354–430 C.E.) already formulated principles by which to evaluate them. Although critical literary study waned during the Middle Ages, beginning in the fourteenth century, the Renaissance led to renewed interest in ancient Greek and the study of biblical manuscripts.

The writings of the Greek New Testament were copied by hand for about 1350 years before Gutenberg invented moveable type in the mid-fifteenth century and made printed books possible. Even then, the privileged status enjoyed by the Latin Vulgate delayed the production of a printed Greek New Testament for about 60 years. In 1514 a polyglot edition of the Bible (Hebrew, Aramaic, Greek, and Latin) was printed in Alcalá, Spain. It became known as the Complutensian Polyglot, derived from the Latin name of the city, *Complutum*. The Greek manuscript base for the Complutensian Polyglot is uncertain; its claim to fame lay in its primacy and its elegance. In 1516, Erasmus (1469–1536), the Dutch humanist, produced a Greek New Testament (the first actually published, i.e., marketed), which was based on a handful of inferior manuscripts and, due to a lacuna at the end of Revelation, famously required Erasmus to back-translate the final six verses from the Latin Vulgate.

Over the next century several more editions of the Greek New Testament were published, for the most part based on Erasmus's text with minor modifications. Robert Estienne, a.k.a. Stephanus (1503–1559), published several editions in the mid-sixteenth century and was responsible for the division of the text into numbered verses. In the first half of the seventeenth century the Elzevir brothers, a Dutch family of printers, published two editions of the Greek New Testament, the second of which (1633) included a preface with the immortal line: "Hence, you have the text that is now accepted by all, in which we give nothing changed or corrupted." From this incidental remark came the designation *Textus Receptus*, or the standard, accepted text. This version of the Greek New Testament lies behind the King James Version and several other European translations. It acquired a near sacred status that held sway for about 200 years, a status that was undeserved in view of its meager manuscript base.

The establishment of the *Textus Receptus* was the first phase in the history of the printed Greek New Testament. The second phase spanned the next two centuries from 1633 to 1831, during which time a mass of textual data was collected. Manuscripts were found in libraries throughout Europe and the Middle East, and their texts were collated against the *Textus Receptus*. Thousands of variants were identified, but the evidence for these (often superior) readings was relegated to the apparatus. They did not, in other words, directly challenge and displace the time-honored but inferior readings of the *Textus Receptus*. It was inevitable, however, that such a mass of textual evidence would eventually call into question the validity of the printed text.

This era involved more than just the amassing of data; there was also further development of text critical principles. J. A. Bengel (1687–1752) formulated criteria that are still in use today, such as preferring the more difficult reading. (See "Principles of Textual Decisions" later). Bengel also pioneered the concept of text types, i.e., families of manuscripts with a distinctive character. He identified an Asiatic family and an African family, groupings that would be much refined in the years to come but not entirely abandoned. J. S. Semler (1725–1792) revised Bengel's text types into a threefold system: Alexandrian, Eastern, and Western. J. J. Griesbach (1745–1812), a student of Semler's, furthered the analysis of text types, renaming the Eastern type "Byzantine" and describing it as late and conflationary. Griesbach also elaborated fifteen canons of textual criticism by which to evaluate variants. His work was of paramount importance to the discipline, and he paved the way for the overthrow of the *Textus Receptus*.

The first scholar who broke decisively with the *Textus Receptus* and printed a truly critical text of the Greek New Testament was the classical philologist Karl Lachmann (1793–1851). His text, published in 1831, was based on several early majuscule manuscripts, the Old Latin, the Vulgate, and a few early patristic writers. Lachmann did not claim to have restored the original text of the New Testament, a goal he considered impossible, but rather the text current in the fourth century. His execution of that task has been criticized, but his work was a watershed in that it employed critical methodology rather than deferring to traditional readings.

Lachmann's edition marks the beginning of the third phase in the history of the printed Greek New Testament: the overthrow of the *Textus Receptus* and the struggle toward a modern critical text. Contributors to the third phase are many, but three in particular must be named. Constantin von Tischendorf (1815–1874) was a tireless traveler throughout Europe and the Middle East in pursuit of biblical manuscripts. He published more manuscripts than any other scholar and produced a total of eight editions of the Greek New Testament, the last of which is still consulted for its massive apparatus. The most famous episode of his career was his discovery of Codex Sinaiticus at the monastery of St. Catherine on Mount Sinai. Finally, two towering figures in the history of textual criticism were the Cambridge scholars, B. F. Westcott and F. J. A. Hort. In 1881 they published a two-volume edition of the Greek New Testament, the second volume of which articulates the critical principles that they used. Their contribution had little to do with the collection of variants, for which they relied on previous work, and more to do with the refinement and judicious application of their critical methodology. They distinguished four text types—the Syrian, Western, Alexandrian, and Neutral—and described them in some detail. The work of Westcott and Hort has been foundational to all subsequent text critical scholarship.

Modern Critical Editions of the Greek New Testament. Two critical editions of the Greek New Testament are currently available. The twenty-seventh edition of the Nestle-Aland text (1993) is the culmination of a series begun in 1898 under the editorship of Eberhard Nestle. Editorial leadership passed to his son, Erwin Nestle, and eventually to Kurt and Barbara Aland. The twenty-seventh edition is now the standard text for scholarly study. The textual apparatus of the Nestle-Aland text uses a compact system of symbols and abbreviations that enabled the editors to pack much information into a small space. The introduction to the Nestle-Aland 27th, provided in both German and English, is essential reading for users of that edition.

The first edition of the United Bible Societies' Greek New Testament appeared in 1966. The editorial committee included Kurt Aland, and for some years work on the two editions continued in parallel. The cooperative effort led to the adoption of the same Greek text for both the twenty-sixth edition of the Nestle-Aland and the third edition of the UBS text. This text remains unchanged in the NA^{27} and the UBS^4 (1998). The most important difference between the two editions is their intended readership. The UBS text is designed especially for Bible translators. Because of its readership the UBS apparatus is limited to variants that give rise to significant differences in translation. Although fewer passages are treated, the citation of witnesses is more complete for those passages. Textual variants are cited in full—that is without employing the symbols and abbreviations used in the Nestle-Aland edition. This makes the UBS apparatus more user-friendly, although somewhat less informative.

Principles of Textual Decisions. The most basic rule for the evaluation of variant readings is to choose the reading that best explains how the others came about. This rule has been elaborated by textual critics into a series of criteria, traditionally grouped under two headings: external evidence and internal evidence. The former has to do with the quality of the manuscript evidence; the latter with the habits of scribes and the tendencies of the author.

External evidence includes: (1) the date of the manuscripts supporting each variant. An earlier manuscript is generally less likely to have been substantially altered than a later one. But one must consider not only the date of the manuscript itself, but the date of the text it contains. In other words, a ninth century manuscript may have been carefully copied from a third century exemplar and, therefore, effectively be a witness to the text of that century. (2) The geographical distribution of the manuscripts supporting a variant is also important. A reading that stems from a single locale is more likely to be idiosyncratic than a reading found in a variety of places. Use of this criterion obviously requires knowledge of the provenance of the manuscripts as well as the reasonable certainty that geographically diverse texts are independent of one another. (3) Finally, the genealogical relationship of manuscripts is pertinent. A thousand manuscripts that depend on a late, unreliable source may have less weight than a handful of early, more reliable manuscripts. Thus the maxim: manuscripts must be weighed, not counted.

Internal evidence includes transcriptional probability—the changes that a scribe is more likely to have made—and intrinsic probability—what the biblical author is more likely to have written. Transcriptional criteria include the following principles: (1) The harder reading is more likely to be original. This assumes that a scribe will usually improve or smooth out a text rather than make it worse. (2) Similarly, the shorter reading is more likely to be original since scribes were more likely to add material than to delete. But a shorter text might be secondary, as when a scribe accidentally omits something or intentionally censors an offensive text. (3) Harmonizations are likely to be secondary. Scribes were known to harmonize parallel texts, such as passages in the Synoptic Gospels, and to smooth out New Testament quotations of the Old Testament. Variants that are at odds with parallel texts or misquote the Old Testament are more likely to be original.

Intrinsic criteria pertain to the author's vocabulary, style, and theology. Departures from the author's usual mode, as evidenced elsewhere in the writing, are usually the work of the copyist. This principle cannot be applied rigidly, however, since authors sometimes vary their vocabulary and style, and a scribe who is well acquainted with the author's work may emend the text to conform to the author's style.

No single criterion, external or internal, can be made the supreme principle. The textual critic's criteria will sometimes contradict one another, such that priority will have to be given to one consideration over another. Two primary methods for integrating the external and internal criteria emerged in the twentieth century: thoroughgoing eclecticism and reasoned eclecticism. Both methods obviously are eclectic, drawing from a variety of materials and not giving priority to a single manuscript or text type. Thoroughgoing eclecticism gives primary consideration to authorial style and literary context, i.e., internal evidence. Reasoned eclecticism, the method employed by most textual critics, combines internal and external criteria and seeks the balance of probabilities in textual decisions. Neither method provides a foolproof system by which the original text can be mechanically determined. It has been said aptly that textual criticism is as much an art as a science.

Textual Criticism and the Theological Interpretation of Scripture. Textual criticism has traditionally been called "lower criticism," allegedly having its sole focus on establishing the wording of the text, in contrast with "higher criticism" that was focused on the content and context of scripture's message. That distinction is not absolute, however, since internal criteria of textual criticism routinely take into account authorial style and theology as well as scribal habits. Textual criticism has, without question, been regarded as a sacred task by many of its practitioners over the centuries. While it is largely preparatory to theological interpretation, textual criticism is not unrelated to it.

Textual criticism impinges upon theological interpretation of scripture in at least the following two ways: (1) It raises questions of canon. The two largest portions of the New Testament that are textually suspect are the long ending of Mark (16:9–20) and the so-called Pericope of the Adulteress (John 7:53—8:11). Scholars are nearly unanimous in identifying these passages as secondary. Are they then to be regarded as part of the canon? Should they inform faith and practice? Should they be texts for Christian proclamation? (2) Textual criticism has some bearing on scripture's authority. Those who affirm the inerrancy of scripture must reckon with the fact that the biblical manuscripts we possess do, in fact, contain errors. Most of these errors can be identified and corrected by other manuscripts, but thoroughgoing inerrancy can only be affirmed of documents that we no longer possess. The inspiration of scripture, a more modest and defensible thesis, can be seen as dependent on the truth of scripture rather than the exactitude and absolute preservation of the text. Needless to say, the truth of scripture is hardly separable from the text of scripture, but unqualified inerrancy seems to depend on the certain recovery of the latter. Inspiration depends on the substantial recovery of scripture.

[*See also* Translation Techniques, *subentry* Ancient Versions; *and* Translation Techniques, *subentry* Modern Versions.]

BIBLIOGRAPHY

Aland, Kurt and Barbara Aland. *The Text of the New Testament*. 2d ed. Grand Rapids, Mich.: Eerdmans, 1995. An authoritative introduction with major sections on the history, materials, and praxis of textual criticism.

Black, David Alan, ed. *Rethinking New Testament Textual Criticism*. Grand Rapids, Mich.: Baker Academic, 2002. Contains essays making the case for reasoned eclecticism, thoroughgoing eclecticism, and Byzantine priority.

Center for the Study of New Testament Manuscripts: http://www.csntm.org. An organization whose mission is make digital photographs of extant manuscripts of the Greek New Testament, to develop technological tools for their analysis, and publish the results. (Accessed 26 September 2011)

Comfort, Philip Wesley. *Encountering the Manuscripts: An Introduction to New Testament Paleography & Textual Criticism*. Nashville, Tenn.: B & H Academic, 2005. A thorough introduction with an emphasis on the characteristics of the ancient manuscripts.

Comfort, Philip Wesley. *New Testament Text and Translation Commentary*. Carol Stream, Ill.: Tyndale House, 2008. An extremely useful tool that offers brief discussions of every significant text critical problem in the New Testament and the arguments relevant to them.

Comfort, Philip W., and David P. Barrett, eds. *The Text of the Earliest New Testament Greek Manuscripts*. Carol Stream, Ill.: Tyndale House, 2001. Contains transcriptions of 68 early manuscripts along with descriptions and several photographs.

Croy, N. Clayton. *The Mutilation of Mark's Gospel*. Nashville, Tenn.: Abingdon, 2003. A study of the most famous text critical problem in the New Testament; argues for a lost ending to Mark's Gospel.

Ehrman, Bart D. *The Orthodox Corruption of Scripture: The Effect of Early Christological Controversies on the Text of the New Testament.* New York: Oxford University Press, 1993. Demonstrates how the theological struggles of early Christianity left their mark on the textual tradition of the New Testament writings.

Ehrman, Bart C., and Michael W. Holmes, eds. *The Text of the New Testament in Contemporary Research: Essays on the Status Quaestionis.* Grand Rapids, Mich.: Eerdmans, 1995. A collection of essays that survey major issues in textual criticism over the last 50 years.

Elliott, J. K. *A Bibliography of Greek New Testament Manuscripts.* 2d ed. Cambridge, UK: Cambridge University Press, 2005. A full list of Greek manuscripts and where one can obtain facsimiles, photo reproductions, collations, and studies.

Epp, Eldon Jay. "Textual Criticism (NT)." In *The Anchor Bible Dictionary*, edited by David Noel Freedman, Vol. 6, 412–435. New York: Doubleday, 1992. A concise introduction with a focus on textual materials, history, and contemporary praxis.

Epp, Eldon J., and Gordon D. Fee. *Studies in the Theory and Method of New Testament Textual Criticism.* Grand Rapids, Mich.: Eerdmans, 1993. Seventeen essays by two leading practitioners on key terms, current theories, papyri, patristic evidence, and textual relationships.

Hull, Robert F., Jr. *The Story of the New Testament Text: Movers, Materials, Motives, Methods, and Models.* Williston, Vt.: Society of Biblical Literature, 2010. A concise introduction to the discipline using a narrative, chronological approach.

The Institute for New Testament Textual Research: http://www.egora.uni-muenster.de/intf. Devoted to textual research on the New Testament and the publication of the *Editio Critica Maior* as well as other editions and scholarly tools. Maintains up-to-date lists of manuscripts. (Accessed 26 September 2011).

Metzger, Bruce M. *The Early Versions of the New Testament: Their Origin, Transmission, and Limitations.* New York: Oxford University Press, 1977. Describes all versions of the New Testament up to the year 1000; an authoritative treatment of the topic.

Metzger, Bruce M. *A Textual Commentary on the Greek New Testament.* 2d ed. Stuttgart, Germany: Deutsche Bibelgesellschaft, 1994. Contains concise discussions of the textual decisions made by the committee who produced the Nestle-Aland 27th and UBS 4th editions.

Metzger, Bruce M., and Bart D. Ehrman. *The Text of the New Testament: Its Transmission, Corruption, and Restoration.* 4th ed. New York: Oxford University Press, 2005. The most readable, authoritative, and up-to-date survey of the topic.

Parker, D. C. *An Introduction to the New Testament Manuscripts and their Texts.* Cambridge, UK: Cambridge University Press, 2008. Discusses all the categories of witnesses as well as modern editions and text critical issues relevant to particular writings in the New Testament.

Rodgers, Peter R. "Textual Criticism." In *Dictionary for Theological Interpretation of the Bible*, edited by Kevin J. Vanhoozer, 784–787. Grand Rapids, Mich.: Baker Academic, 2005. A short entry arguing that textual critics and exegetes are necessarily partners in the task of interpretation.

N. Clayton Croy

Theological Interpretation

Paradoxically, theological interpretation is one of the newest approaches to the Bible and yet the most ancient one. If we think of modern biblical interpretation as a series of *turns*, then the historical turn that dominated the twentieth century was followed in the 1970s by a literary turn; this was followed by the postmodern turn, which is now being followed by a theological turn. The turns do not replace the previous ones but significantly alter the landscape of biblical interpretation and raise important questions about the relationship between these different emphases. With the emergence of theological interpretation, it is as though interpretive approaches have come full circle, but a renewed theological interpretation cannot turn the clock back; it has to take account of the history of interpretation and orient itself amidst the current situation. As a relative newcomer, theological interpretation is still in its early stages, and the term covers a diversity of approaches.

In essence, theological interpretation is the attempt to recover a reading of the Bible as Christian scripture for today. Until the Enlightenment, the Bible was read almost universally as scripture. In the modern period, this approach to reading changed, and under the aegis of the historical-critical method, biblical scholars began to seek scientific, objective ways of reading scripture apart from theological presuppositions. The recovery of the Bible as literature challenged the hegemony of historical criticism in major ways; but before it could be fully appropriated, postmodernism shattered any idea of objective interpretation as it penetrated every aspect of biblical interpretation and generated a plethora of methods for reading the Bible. Amid that pluralism, theological interpretation has found a seat at the table of biblical interpretation.

The Background to Theological Interpretation. The major source for the contemporary renaissance in theological interpretation is undoubtedly the rich, creative, theological work of Karl Barth. Almost single-handedly Barth took on the liberal theology of his day. What is often less known is the amount of exegesis contained in his multivolume *Church Dogmatics*. As Barth's theological framework takes hold, he practices more and not less theological interpretation, with large swaths of the *Church Dogmatics* devoted to detailed exegesis. For example, in *CD* III/1 (2004, pp. 98–228), he devotes some 150 pages to a rich, rigorous exegesis of Genesis 1—2 full of theological insights. In biblical studies, Barth has largely been ignored as an exegete, but his work is the primary source for the current renewal of theological interpretation. As a Fulbright scholar, Brevard Childs, the other major father of current theological interpretation, was deeply influenced by his time studying with Barth and went on to devote his life to recovering a theological reading of scripture along the lines of his well-known canonical approach. Indeed, the Yale school of Hans Frei, George Lindbeck, Christopher Seitz, and so on, all of whom have contributed in different ways to the renaissance of theological interpretation, is influenced by Barth.

Theological interpretation is also *a reaction* to the perceived aridity of historical criticism. Rigorous, critical work was done on the Bible, not least by German scholars, but without leading to a consensus and without producing much help in terms of attending to scripture as God's address. Still, there remain important differences among theological interpreters as to how to relate to historical criticism. A further contributing factor is that amid the pluralism of postmodern approaches and the growing awareness that we all bring our presuppositions to interpretation and that historical criticism too has its own prejudices, space and awareness have been created for overtly theological work in biblical interpretation. What had become a chasm between theology and biblical studies is being breached in all sorts of ways.

The Primary Context for the Reception of the Bible. Theological interpretation has manifested itself as an academic phenomenon largely independent of official church bodies, which raises the question of the primary context for the reception of the Bible as scripture. In line with Magrassi (1998) and most scholars who work within the theological interpretive context, the predominant view is that the ecclesial context is the primary one for attending to the Bible as scripture. As scripture the Bible is God's Word to God's people, and, thus, the liturgical context should be privileged as *the* context for listening to scripture. Closely connected with such a listening to and for God's Word is the ancient practice of *lectio divina* (spiritual reading) which extends the ecclesial reception to the personal level. Not least is the form of *lectio divina* developed by Ignatius Loyola, author of the *Spiritual Exercises*, which encourages the use of the imagination to enter into the stories of the Bible and is experiencing something of a renewal today. An exceptional example of such a reading of the Bible is Jean Vanier's *Drawn into the Mystery of Jesus through the Gospel of John*.

From this perspective, academic theological interpretation is secondary to such primary reception and should work out of such an ecclesial reception and feed back into it to deepen it. Naturally, theological interpretation should be free to raise critical questions about ecclesial reception, but both approaches should work from faith, and ecclesial reception should also be in critical dialogue with academic theological interpretation.

Theological Interpretation and Historical Criticism. The historical criticism that emerged in the late nineteenth century and came to dominate biblical studies in the twentieth century remains the basic paradigm for biblical studies today. Although historical criticism is diverse, it is rooted in Enlightenment presuppositions that preclude a theological starting point. In some way, all theological interpretation affirms the triune God as the primary author of scripture and scripture as the primary means through which we hear his unified address. Many think that historical criticism has shattered any apparent unity of the Bible, and, thus, the relationship between historical criticism and theological interpretation has to be attended to.

Theological interpreters differ in how they negotiate this relationship. Brevard Childs's (1979) canonical approach, in line with Barth, tended to accept the role of objective, historical criticism while limiting its role and finding ways to combine a theological reading with the insights of historical criticism. The problem with this approach is the uneasy and potentially contradictory relationship between the results of historical criticism and canonical readings of biblical texts. An alternative approach is to see theological interpretation as simply another dish on the smorgasbord of methods. Childs rejected such an approach.

The view of the majority of theological critics is that the historical dimension of biblical interpretation cannot be ignored. Since scripture emerged in the life of an ancient Near Eastern nation and through the Christ event and his followers in the first century, theological interpretation has to take this incarnate aspect of scripture seriously. Much depends, however, on *how* it is taken seriously. Historical criticism has made genuine progress in attending to the data of the biblical texts and to the historical backgrounds of the Bible but too often in the grip of philosophies of history that are foundationally anti-theological. As Stephen Neill (1988) perceptively noted in relation to New Testament (NT) studies, we urgently need a theology of history, not because it will automatically solve the problems of NT studies, but because it would provide the space where solutions may be found.

The historical dimension of the Bible has to be rethought in the light of the literary turn and within the context of a theological paradigm with a robust theology of history. In Old Testament (OT) studies, Iain Provan (2003) has done important work in this direction, and in NT studies, N.T. Wright's (1992) critical realist approach to history, as evidenced in his multivolume, *Christian Origins and the Question of God,* blazes a fresh trail. The complexity of such work should not be underestimated; theological interpretation cannot afford a naïve affirmation of scripture as inspired without attending closely to the tough questions of its historicity.

Hermeneutics and Philosophy. A significant difference among theological interpreters is the question of whether the discipline of biblical studies requires a regional or a general hermeneutic. The regional approach argues that we require a theological hermeneutic for biblical interpretation and that attention to philosophical hermeneutics is too often a detour that precludes a reading of the Bible for the church. By comparison, a general hermeneutical approach argues that Christian faith shapes our approach to reading and textuality in the broadest sense—indeed our philosophy—and that we need a theological hermeneutic for all reading including how we read the Bible. Bearing in mind, as Meir Sternberg (1985) has noted, that biblical interpretation functions at the intersection of the humanities, there is a considerable amount at stake in this debate.

The challenges of historical criticism and postmodernism compel theological scholars to attend to all the dimensions of interpretation from a theological perspective, not in order to avoid the mainstream of biblical studies, but to orient interpretation within the diversity and work out how best to despoil the Egyptians (Augustine) for theological interpretation today. For example, the philosophy of language is at the heart of most postmodern readings, and critical engagement with it will require a sense of a Christian perspective on language and how it works. In *Real Presences,*

George Steiner argues, for example, that Jacques Derrida's work confronts us with the choice of either nihilism or "In the beginning was the Word." Clearly theological interpretation will side with the latter if this is the choice and will need to work out what John 1:1 means for a view of language today.

The larger philosophical questions of epistemology, ontology, and anthropology inevitably shape biblical interpretation, and theological interpretation will need to draw on the now substantial work of Christian philosophers such as Nicholas Wolterstorff, Alvin Plantinga, and Eleonore Stump, all of whom have engaged with biblical interpretation. Within biblical studies, Anthony Thiselton (1992) stands out as the scholar who has done substantial work on the relationship between philosophy and exegesis.

The Canon. The focus of theological interpretation is the canon of scripture. Its affirmation of the unity of the two Testaments goes back, as de Lubac (1958, p. 88) notes, to Christ himself, who saw himself as fulfilling the Hebrew Bible (HB). In Jesus the kingdom has come and is still to be consummated so that eschatology is at the heart of theological interpretation and its view of the canon. Christ affirms the HB as authoritative, and the NT stems in one way or another from the eyewitness apostolic testimony. Theological interpretation's focus on the canon as the Word of God bearing witness to Christ is, thus, theologically *and* historically grounded.

It must be noted that while the Protestant canon is contained within the Catholic and Orthodox canons, the Greek Orthodox affirm 76 and Catholics affirm 73 rather than just the 66 books that Protestants alone regard as canonical. On this issue, the debate goes back at least as far as the dialogue between Jerome, who followed the Hebrew canon, and Augustine, who followed the Septuagint, and we cannot solve it here! The immense common ground should be noted, as well as the fact that when Luther published his German Bible and when the King James Version was first published, the apocryphal books were included albeit as earmarked for edification rather than as inspired.

The issue of canon also alerts us to the relationship of the Old Testament to the *Tanak* (the Jewish Bible). This is a much discussed topic in biblical studies today (Levenson 1993; Brueggemann 1997, pp. 107–112). Undoubtedly some of the most creative theological interpretation has been done by Jewish scholars (see, for example, Kass's 2003, unique commentary on Genesis) but much of this is not done from an overtly Jewish perspective. Furthermore, as Levenson (1993, pp. 33–61) argues, for a variety of reasons Jewish scholars have not been interested in biblical theology, a discipline central to theological interpretation. Within Judaism there is clearly a major interest in reading the HB as scripture and such reading should form an important dialogue partner with Christian theological interpretation.

Biblical Theology. Theological interpretation raises the question of how, or even whether, we can take hold of scripture in its totality. David Kelsey has addressed this issue in his *The Uses of Scripture in Recent Theology* in which he identifies a series of models and argues that the *discrimen* for such a move should come from outside of the Bible. In the early church, a rule of faith was variously articulated as the framework within which to interpret the "Bible." However, this was a short description of the essence of the faith/scripture, and as F. F. Bruce notes, "when once the limits of holy scripture came to be generally agreed upon, holy scripture itself came to be regarded as the rule of faith" (1988, p. 18).

The major answer to this question is to be found within the parameters of biblical theology. A central concern of theological interpretation is to listen to the unified voice of God in scripture, and, not surprisingly, the renewal in theological interpretation has been closely connected with a renewed interest in biblical theology. Biblical theology is that theological discipline which seeks to discern the inner unity of scripture according to scripture's own categories, by comparison with systematic theology, which generally uses systematic categories not necessarily derived from scripture.

Brevard Childs, whom we identified earlier as a father of theological interpretation, addressed the issue of biblical theology early in his career. In his *Biblical Theology in Crisis,* Childs assessed and sought to diagnose the demise of the Biblical Theology Movement that had flourished during the middle of the twentieth century. In 1992, Childs published his *Biblical Theology of the Old and New Testaments,* one of the first comprehensive biblical theologies to appear in many years. The only other major biblical theology to appear in English since then is Scobie's *The Ways of Our God: An Approach to Biblical Theology.* Several OT theologies and NT theologies have appeared but few biblical theologies.

Reventlow (1986) identifies the HB-NT relationship as *the* central problem of biblical theology. Theological interpreters continue to debate the status of the "OT" with some proposing a change in the terminology to First Testament and Second Testament, not least in order to do justice to the HB as the Hebrew / Jewish Bible. Brueggemann (1997) and Rendtorff (1993, pp. 31–45) argue that we should attend to the voice of the Hebrew Bible largely on its own terms independent of the NT witness. Brueggemann reads the Old Testament as a Christian, but, he asserts that "It is clear on my reading that the Old Testament is not a witness to Jesus Christ, in any primary or direct sense, as Childs proposes, unless one is prepared to sacrifice more of the text than is credible" (1997, p. 107).

The Christian tradition has always maintained that we have two Testaments and one Bible, both understood in the context of the Trinitarian God's economy of salvation and whose unified testimony to Jesus Christ is authoritative. Irenaeus's great contribution was to discern the Bible as a unified telling of the one story of salvation through Jesus Christ. The eschatology that is central to such an approach goes back to the Christ event, so that biblical theology must do justice to several elements: the radical newness of the Christ event, the Christ event as the fulfillment of the HB in a diversity of ways, and thus the overarching narrative unity of scripture as identified by Irenaeus., In the writer's view, much is to be gained from a narrative, dramatic approach to the Bible. In this respect, Wright's (1992, pp. 139–143) creative account of the Bible as a drama in five acts has gained considerable traction.

Undoubtedly, such an approach will and should influence a theological reading of the HB, but as Childs points out, in the context of such a view, theological interpretation should attend to the discrete witness of the HB and beware of forcing it into NT categories. Biblical theology should do justice to the progressive unfolding of the drama of redemption while also taking the radical newness of the Christ event into account and allowing it to illuminate the earlier parts of the drama. Barth once noted that the best apologetics is a good systematic, and a challenge of theological interpretation will be to produce a series of major biblical theologies using the diversity of possible approaches to demonstrate the inner coherence of scripture.

Mission. Mission is a major theme in the Bible, centripetal in the HB and centrifugal in the New. The canon begins with the creation of the whole world, narrows down after the fall to God's election of Abraham, but always with a view to recovering his purposes for all the nations: through Abraham, God will bring blessing (the reversal of curse) to the nations (Gen 12:1–3). At Sinai the Israelites formally entered into a covenant relationship with God as a royal priesthood, designed from the beginning to be a window for the nations to see how life was to be lived under the reign of the creator/redeemer God. David Bosch notes that "The entire history of Israel unveils the continuation of God's involvement with the nations. The God of Israel is the Creator and Lord of the whole world. For this reason, Israel can comprehend its own history only in continuity with the history of the nations, not as a separate history" (1991, p. 18). Israel, of course, did not actively engage in mission but for the NT, as Paul says in Galatians, the Gospel *is* the blessing of the nations through Christ's redemptive work (Gal 3:8). The whole impetus of the NT is centrifugal, spreading the news of Christ throughout the world.

Karl Barth articulated the notion of *missio dei*, of mission as primarily *God's* activity in which we at best can be partners. Since then, missiology has emerged as a highly creative field of theological reflection including the advocacy of a missional hermeneutic. Just as the church has come to be seen as inherently missional, so too theological interpreters argue for a missional hermeneutic for the Bible. Lesslie Newbigin, another major missiologist, argued that we should read scripture as the true story of the whole world and indwell it as such. If we take Wright's dramatic analogy seriously, then scripture itself provides us with a hermeneutic; it tells us which act of the drama we are currently in, and that act is quintessentially the era of mission. Furthermore, it is not an era alien to the story of scripture but an indispensable act in its fulfillment. As theological interpretation develops, close dialogue with missiologists will be essential.

Telos (Goal). The question of the goal of theological interpretation relates back to the primary context for the reception of the Bible; if the context is the church, then one answer will be given; if the academy, then another. Since the renewal of theological interpretation has largely remained an academic exercise thus far, much theological interpretation is oriented toward theology or toward opening up a dialogue between exegesis and theology. While helpful and valid, these foci will not successfully overcome the chasm between biblical studies and theology unless the deeper levels are attended to. Academic work inevitably concentrates on *analysis*, whereas the sort of ecclesial reception we previously referred to privileges *listening* over analysis. Listening makes attending to the *kerygma* (message) of a text primary rather than the theology of the text. Such an approach fits with the concept of scripture as God's Word, which is to be received through prayerful, attentive listening. From this perspective, analysis follows on from such listening, and the test of analysis is whether it deepens our listening to the Bible for God's address.

A gap in much theological interpretation is that it neither begins with spiritual reading nor orients its rigorous scholarship toward the goal of listening for God's address (Bartholomew and Beldman 2012). Calvin is instructive in this respect. He wrote his *Institutes* to help Christians read the Bible better, whereas too often today the Bible becomes the stepping stone toward theology, which then takes on a life of its own without reengaging the biblical text. Theological interpretation may have multiple legitimate goals, but all should function within such a paradigm of listening and make its goal the deepening of such practice.

The History of Theological Interpretation. Theological interpretation is inevitably a process of retrieval from the long history of Christian interpretation. The twentieth century witnessed an astonishing effort in translation and publication of new editions of the church fathers and medieval interpreters. Not least among these was the Catholic *ressourcement* movement and in particular the massive work of Henri de Lubac, exemplified in his four-volume work, *Medieval Exegesis*. De Lubac argued for the rehabilitation of the fourfold method of interpretation known as the *quadregia*—literal, allegorical, moral, and anagogical—as a viable way forward for the recovery of spiritual interpretation. In this call, he has been followed by a growing number of Protestants.

This takes us back to the debate between the Alexandrian and Antiochene fathers. The former favored allegorical exegesis as the key to the spiritual sense, whereas the Antiochene fathers like Diodore and Theodore of Mopsuestia were strongly opposed to allegorization, while affirming typological reading. Daniélou (1951), *contra* de Lubac, argued for typology but against allegory. The Reformers similarly argued against allegory unless clearly warranted by scripture and insisted that the plain sense of the text be the focus of interpretation. For the Reformers, the plain sense *was* the spiritual sense, and they developed a concept of the literal meaning with ample room for typology.

The Reformers and their seventeenth and eighteenth century followers privileged the plain sense of scripture, probably in reaction to the practice of allegory among the church fathers whose interpretations the reformers felt often obscured the meaning of the text and its place in the historical development of God's people in the quest to get at a deeper spiritual meaning. The plain sense should not be confused with a literalism, which does allow for the literary and metaphorical dimensions of the biblical texts while insisting that these are part of the plain sense.

Thus far, theological interpretation has sought its resources largely in the early church where indeed, especially among the Antiochene tradition, major resources can be found.; Less work has been done on the rich vein of theological interpretation in the Reformers and their followers. The Protestant orthodoxy that followed the period of the Reformation has often been marginalized as a time of sterile, Protestant scholasticism. Although the major work of Richard Muller and others has gone a long way toward rectifying this underrepresentation, the extensive works of this period remain an important source waiting to be mined.

Amid the understandable reaction of theological interpretation to historical criticism, critics should not lose sight of the significant resources of the past. Gerhard von Rad stands out as a historical-critical scholar who did remarkable theological work on the HB. His *Wisdom in Israel*, for example, remains a classic. There is also a significant history of Jewish interpretation of the HB. A study of the history of biblical interpretation reveals that at many points, Christian scholars were in dialogue with and drew upon Jewish exegesis. Such a practice needs to be continued today.

The literary turn contains major resources for theological interpretation as has been demonstrated by the best work done in this tradition. Literary and rhetorical readings of biblical texts have been refreshing in their focus on the literary texture of the Bible and in their attention to the poetics of the text, through which we hear the message. But the temptation to study the Bible solely as literature is a danger of the literary approach to interpretation. This is highlighted unequivocally by George Steiner (1988) in his review of *The Literary Guide to the Bible*. For these interpreters, however, the Bible is far more than literature and, consequently, requires a hermeneutic that integrates the literary, historical, and theological dimensions of the biblical texts. Meir Sternberg and N.T. Wright have made major efforts in this direction.

Some theological interpreters have found in postmodernism the means to rehabilitate a faithful reading of the Bible due to postmodernism's foregrounding and critiquing of the presuppositions of historical criticism, but the weakness with much of postmodernism has been its limited constructive agenda. In terms of hermeneutics, Paul Ricoeur's *constructive* postmodernism has proved a more fertile source for biblical interpretation.

Theological Frameworks. The history of theological interpretation alerts us to the variety of theological frameworks that have shaped interpretation. Not surprisingly, the renewal of theological interpretation today is diverse in this respect. A helpful way to get at the most foundational dimension of theological interpretation is to recognize that, from a Christian perspective, a religious starting point is unavoidable, the question being which starting point. From this perspective, a Marxist or history of religions approach is as religious as a theological one. The most fundamental questions informing a worldview are never finally decided rationally but involve faith.

Much of the radically secular readings of scripture today involve *unbelief seeking understanding*. They presuppose the impossibility of there being a God and of God speaking and acting in history. Dale Allison (2009, p. 5) describes his approach to Jesus studies as *doubt seeking understanding*. The more common approach among Christians historically is *faith seeking understanding* (Augustine, Anselm, etc.). In his magisterial *At the Roots of Modern Atheism*, Buckley points out the danger of conceding the epistemological starting point in the quest for knowledge, but his perspective alerts us to a significant divide among theological interpreters.

For some—not least those in the Thomist tradition—*theology* may start with faith but not other disciplines, which should operate neutrally and objectively, and if they do so correctly, there will be no clash ultimately with Christian faith. The question then becomes whether biblical studies is a *theological* discipline or not. By contrast, reformed epistemologists Alvin Plantinga, Nicholas Wolterstorff, and a growing number of scholars argue that Christians are rationally justified in adopting a Christian starting point epistemologically in all disciplines. In *Warranted Christian Belief*, Plantinga examines (different types of) Historical Biblical Criticism and compares the approach to Traditional Biblical Commentary. He argues that epistemologically, Christians are warranted in starting with a belief and trust in the Bible as God's Word.

It is at these deep levels that all theological interpretation will be decisively shaped, especially by the question of theological frameworks. Luther's law–gospel dialectic, for example, shapes exegesis in a significantly different way than does Calvin's more covenantal approach. Seeking to read through the lens of the poor and oppressed, a liberation hermeneutic will interpret differently with different results. Although these approaches are not necessarily antithetical, theological interpreters should look for a theological framework that arises from scripture and yields more and richer exegesis as it takes hold. Unlike many of his followers, Barth's work is exemplary in this respect, and a more recent example is that of Oliver O'Donovan's (1996) works on ethics.

Theological Commentary. As the theological turn has gained traction, a spate of theological commentary series have appeared. Not surprisingly, these commentaries vary in quality even within a series and espouse diverse methodologies. Our aim in this section is to inquire as to what shape a theological commentary should take. At the very least, theological commentary should restructure the traditional modern commentary while retaining the strengths of the latter. Rigorous linguistic and historical works should be retained, but now clearly in the service of elucidating the message of the book in the context of scripture as a whole for today.

Such an approach would reconfigure the use of traditional methods of interpretation. The book would be treated as a whole with literary analysis utilized to explore the structure internal to the text. Synchronic and diachronic analysis would be in close dialogue but with synchronic privileged for the purpose of interpreting the message of the text as a whole. Reception history would play an important role with attention given to insights from the reception of the book in and outside of the history of the church. Thiselton's *1 Corinthians* is exemplary in this respect, as is Childs's *The Struggle to Understand Isaiah as Christian Scripture*. Comparative methods would be used but critically and in a manner designed to allow the distinctive message of the text to appear.

Theologically, a book is authoritative in the context of *tota Scriptura*, and thus, biblical theology and intertextuality would play a significant role in discerning the interplay between *this* book and the rest of the canon and how it contributes to the overarching theology of the Bible. Theological commentary would be upfront about the theological framework it brings to the text and would bring the text into dialogue with contemporary theology. However, theological interpretation would be incomplete if all its work does not have as its *telos* the explicating of the *kerygma* of the text for today.

For theological interpreters who agree that ecclesial reception is primary, the preaching of the book investigated and the fruits of a *lectio divina* approach to it may also find a place in such a commentary. The result should be a rich commentary that relinquishes not an iota of critical rigor but is in dialogue with the Christian tradition and opens out into powerful contemporary application of the message. Landmark commentaries in this respect have been Barth's *Romans*, Childs's *Exodus* and Bruner's (2004) work on Matthew. While none of these fulfills all the criteria mentioned in the preceding, they are major works in this direction.

For All of Life. Acts describes Jesus as the "author of life," and theological interpretation will work to relate the *kerygma* of the Bible to all of life and not just church life. Childs (1974) identifies failure in this regard as one of the reasons for the downfall of the Biblical Theology Movement, but it is a critique that could be leveled against much interpretation, scripture deals with universal history and views Israel, Jesus, and the church in this light, and theological interpretation must do no less. There are few major examples of such work today. Brueggemann stands out as one who has tirelessly and creatively sought to navigate the distance between the Bible and contemporary culture. In a similar way, O'Donovan's work repeatedly seeks to make this journey. An older example is the work of Jacques Ellul who, alongside his sociological studies, published a series of important expositions of scripture. Ellul's work reminds us that to do such work, sophisticated cultural analysis will be required. John Stott's concept of double listening is helpful in this respect: the exegete needs one ear to scripture and one to contemporary culture in order to connect the two.

Quo Vadis? The renaissance of theological interpretation presents exegetes with a major opportunity. Different schools will undoubtedly appear as the movement matures, but theological interpretation should resist becoming just another method on the smorgasbord of methods. As with Childs' canonical hermeneutic, theological interpretation should aim to be comprehensive and allow its work to come to full fruition so that real dialogue with other traditions of exegesis may take place. A feast awaits but one that will require the hard work of dusting off old recipes, updating them for today, and developing new ones, all with a view to serving up a great feast.

[*See also* Allegory and Allegorical Interpretation; Canonical Criticism; Cultural-Historical Criticism; Diachronic Interpretation; Evangelical Interpretation; Exegesis; Historical Criticism, *subentry* Hebrew Bible; Historical Criticism, *subentry* New Testament; Homiletics; Inner-biblical Interpretation; Liberation Hermeneutics; Literary Criticism, Literary Theory, and the Bible; Narrative Criticism and Narrative Hermeneutics; Pentecostal Interpretation; Postmodern Interpretation; Reception Criticism and Theory; Rhetorical Criticism; Synchronic Interpretation; *and* Tradition-Historical Criticism.]

BIBLIOGRAPHY

Allison, Dale C. Jr. *The Historical Christ and the Theological Jesus.* Grand Rapids, Mich.: Eerdmans, 2009.

Barth, Karl. *Church Dogmatics.* Edited by G. W. Bromiley and T. F. Torrance. Translated by G. W. Bromiley et al. 4 vols. in 14. Repr., Edinburgh: T &T Clark, 2004. Barth's *Dogmatics* is a mine of theological interpretation when doing exegesis. It is much under utilized in this respect by biblical scholars but rewards careful attention.

Bartholomew, Craig G. and David Beldman, eds. *Hearing the Old Testament: Listening for God's Address.* Grand Rapids, Mich.: Eerdmans, 2012. An attempt to rethink OT studies making the goal of exegesis listening for God's address.

Bosch, David J. *Transforming Mission: Paradigm Shifts in Theology of Mission.* Maryknoll, N.Y.: Orbis, 1991.

Bruce, F. F. *The Canon of Scripture.* Downers Grove, Ill.: IVP, 1988.

Brueggemann, Walter. *Theology of the Old Testament: Testimony, Dispute, Advocacy.* Minneapolis: Augsburg Fortress, 1997.

Bruner, Frederick D. *Matthew: A Commentary.* Vol. 1, 2d ed. Grand Rapids, Mich.: Eerdmans, 2004.

Bruner, Frederick D *Matthew: A Commentary.* Vol. 2, 2d ed. Grand Rapids, Mich.: Eerdmans, 2004. Bruner's work is a great example of theological interpretation.

Buckley, Michael J. *At the Origins of Modern Atheism.* New Haven; London: Yale University Press, 1987.

Childs, Brevard S. *Biblical Theology in Crisis.* Philadelphia: Westminster Press, 1970.

Childs, Brevard S. *Exodus* (OTL). London: SCM, 1974.

Childs, Brevard S. *Introduction to the Old Testament as Scripture.* Philadelphia: Fortress, 1979.

Childs, Brevard S. *Biblical Theology of the Old and New Testaments.* Minneapolis, Minn.: Fortress, 1992.

Childs, Brevard S. *The Struggle to Understand Isaiah as Scripture.* Grand Rapids, Mich.: Eerdmans, 2004. Childs was a student of Barth's and devoted his life to redirecting biblical studies in the service of the church. His entire corpus is worth attending to.

Daniélou, Jean. *Qu'est-ce que la typologie?* In *L'Ancien Testament et les chrétiens,* edited by P. Auvray et al. Paris: Éditions du Cerf, 1951.

Kass, Leon. *The Beginning of Wisdom: Reading Genesis.* Chicago and London: University of Chicago Press, 2003. A wonderful and unique commentary which opens out the multiple issues Genesis addresses when read seeking wisdom for today.

Kelsey, David H. *The Uses of Scripture in Recent Theology.* Philadelphia: Fortress, 1975.

Levenson, Jon D. *The Hebrew Bible, the Old Testament, and Historical Criticism: Jews and Christians in Biblical Studies.* Louisville, Ky.: Westminster John Knox, 1993.

Lubac, Henri de. *Catholicism: A Study of the Corporate Destiny of Mankind.* New York: Sheed and Ward, 1958.

Magrassi, Mariano. *Praying the Bible: An Introduction to Lectio Divina.* Collegeville, Minn.: Liturgical Press, 1998. Translated by E. Hagman. English translation of *Bibbia e preghiera: La lectio divina*, first published in 1990. A profound book which is indispensable reading for those interested in the the Bible and lectio divina.

Neill, Stephen and N.T. Wright. *The Interpretation of the New Testament. 1861–1986.* Oxford: Oxford University Press, 1988.

O'Donovan, Oliver. *The Desire of the Nations: Rediscovering the Roots of Political Theology.* Cambridge, UK: Cambridge University Press, 1996. O'Donovan is a rare example of a theologian who does a great deal of exegesis as his theological concepts take hold.

Plantinga, Alvin. *Warranted Christian Belief.* New York and Oxford: Oxford University Press, 2000. This book by one of the great philosophers of our day contains a perceptive examination of historical biblical criticism and what Plantinga calls traditional biblical commentary.

Provan, Iain, V. Philips Long, and Tremper Longman III. *A Biblical History of Israel.* Louisville, Ky.: Westminster John Knox, 2003.

Rendtorff, Rolf. *Canon and Theology.* Philadelphia: Fortress, 1993.

Reventlow, H. Graf. *Problems of Biblical Theology in the Twentieth Century.* London: SCM, 1986.

Scobie, Charles H.H.. *The Ways of Our God: An Approach to Biblical Theology.* Grand Rapids, Mich.: Eerdmans, 2003.

Steiner, George. "Books. The Good Books." *The New Yorker*, 11 January 1988, 94–98.

Steiner, George. *Real Presences.* London: Faber and Faber, 1989.

Sternberg, Meir. *The Poetics of Biblical Narrative. Ideological Literature and the Drama of Reading.* Bloomington: Indiana University Press, 1985. *The* book on the poetics of the HB.

Thiselton, Anthony C. *New Horizons in Hermeneutics.* Grand Rapids, Mich.: Zondervan, 1992.

Thiselton, Anthony C. *The First Epistle to the Corinthians: A Commentary on the Greek Text.* Grand Rapids, Mich.: Eerdmans, 2000. Thiselton has done more than anyone to alert us to the importance of hermeneutics for interpretation. His commentary on 1 Corinthians is renowned for its attention to reception history.

Vanier, Jean. *Drawn into the Mystery of Jesus through the Gospel of John.* Ottawa, Canada: Novalis, 2004. One of the best examples today of a lectio divina reading.

Wright, N.T. *The New Testament and the People of God.* Minneapolis: Fortress, 1992. Wright's work is highly creative and while advertised as historical is remarkably rich in its theological yield.

Craig Bartholomew

TRADITION-HISTORICAL CRITICISM

Tradition-historical criticism takes as its starting point the notion that the biblical text is not merely a concatenation of various literary works, but that each of those works is itself the product of a long process of development. This process entails the accumulation, combination, change, and transmission of originally independent and usually oral traditions: sayings, stories, liturgical pieces, and other artifacts of cultural memory. The task of the tradition historian is to identify those earliest traditional units and explain how they were brought together, altered, and transmitted such that they resulted in the canonical text. Given the scope of the tradition historian's task, in that it examines the entire history of the development of the biblical text, it is no surprise that tradition-historical criticism brings under its methodological umbrella a number of other critical methods and theories, including most prominently source criticism and form criticism, from which it emerged.

History of Scholarship. Tradition-historical criticism began as an offshoot of form criticism. In the early twentieth century, Hermann Gunkel (1862–1932) recognized that the purely literary analysis of the biblical text as practiced most prominently by Julius Wellhausen (1844–1918) and his contemporaries did not provide a complete picture of the textual history. In particular, Wellhausen's view that the Pentateuchal sources are able to inform us only about the state of Israelite thought at the time of their composition, rather than preserving any genuine historical information about the times they describe, was considered by Gunkel to be faulty. Gunkel recognized that each of the sources must have had its own pre-literary history, that each author was as much a collector and editor as he was an original contributor. The search for the individual elements that the authors collected, therefore, needed to be undertaken, and the method that Gunkel used to do this was that of form criticism: the attempt to isolate individual oral genres underlying the text and to set each genre in its particular communal context (*Sitz im Leben*), such as the cult, prophetic circles, the village campfire, and so on. By getting back to the original cultural settings, it would be possible to reconstruct something of the Israelite society out of which the literary text eventually emerged.

Form criticism proper dealt only, however, with genre; to identify a cultural context for a genre did not, in theory, provide any information about a given specific representation of that genre. Thus, for example, the recognition that the various narratives in Genesis in which the patriarch builds an altar have their generic origins in the local cult etiology reveals only that in ancient Israel there were such etiologies; while this is no small historical matter, it does not speak to any of the specific episodes in Genesis in an independent fashion. Form criticism abstracts the biblical materials, thereby opening to view the broader culture in which they were created, but the process by which the actual text itself came into being, not in the abstract but in the very particular, is not part of form criticism's purview.

This latter task falls under the heading of tradition-historical criticism (often simply called "tradition criticism"), which can be described as a move from genre to content. From the tradition-historical perspective, rather than examining the local cult etiology as a generic phenomenon, it is required to examine what a given manifestation of an etiology says and how it is to be understood as a tradition stemming from a particular place and time. Thus, for example, there are three narratives in Genesis about a patriarch at Bethel: one in which Abraham builds an altar (Gen 12:8), one in which Jacob builds an altar (Gen 28:18–22; 35:1–7), and one in which God appears to Jacob (Gen 35:9–13). Form-critically, these all exemplify the genre of the local cult etiology; tradition-critically, they all stem from a local tradition in Bethel that an ancestor founded the sanctuary there. Having established this, the tradition historian can then consider which elements of the three stories are held in common, and may therefore be understood as the earliest and most basic tradition out of which all three emerged, which aspects can be attributed to secondary growths of the tradition, and whether it is possible to put these secondary changes into chronological order. Tradition-historical criticism thus builds on the insights of form criticism by specifying and historicizing them.

Such tradition-historical investigations were already beginning to be incorporated in Gunkel's own work (as with the earlier example, for instance); they were developed further by Gunkel's close form-critical associate, Hugo Gressmann (1977–1927), in his study of the development of the Moses traditions. Gressmann systematically stripped away the layers of the Moses story in Exodus—Numbers, identifying the individual traditions at the base of the overarching narrative, though he refrained from any attempt to reconstruct the development of the text. Gunkel and Gressmann, in their concentration on the pre-literary history of the biblical text, prepared the way for the two giants of tradition-historical criticism, Gerhard von Rad (1901–1971) and Martin Noth (1902–1968).

Von Rad and Noth. The fundamental flaw that von Rad identified in Gunkel's work was that while it highlighted the diversity of materials evident in the biblical text it did not sufficiently explain how it was that these materials had come together to form narratively and theologically sophisticated overarching compositions. Von Rad therefore suggested that through a lengthy process of accretion of traditions the basic outline of Israel's early history, from the patriarchs through the conquest of Canaan, had already taken shape by the time the Pentateuchal authors began writing. The evidence for this, according to von Rad, was the existence of the "historical credo" in Deuteronomy 26:5–9 and

Joshua 24:2–13, which recounts in brief and stereotypical form the outline of the traditional narrative. Following this basic pattern, and incorporating numerous other secondary traditions, the Pentateuchal authors created their major literary works, beginning most importantly for von Rad with the Yahwist (J), who was the first to incorporate the Sinai event into the traditional outline.

Although von Rad suggested quite specific cultic backgrounds for both the "historical credo" and the Sinai event, for the most part he left the details of the formative process that led to the traditional outline unexamined, noting only that there must have been such a process, and that it was entirely an oral one. He did, however, formulate what may be the guiding dictum for all subsequent tradition-historical investigations: "None of the stages in the age-long development of this work has been wholly superseded; something has been preserved of each phase, and its influence has persisted right down to the final form of the Hexateuch" (Rad 1966, p. 78).

It is the challenge to scholarship implicit in von Rad's classic dictum that was taken up by Noth. In his book on the tradition history of the Pentateuch, Noth attempted to provide a nearly complete picture of the growth of the Pentateuchal traditions. He began by isolating the "major themes" present in the text, taking his cue from von Rad's study of the historical credo: guidance out of Egypt, guidance into the arable land, promise to the patriarchs, guidance in the wilderness, and revelation at Sinai. It will be noted that these are set not in the order in which they appear in the canonical text, but in what Noth perceived to be their tradition-historical chronology, from earliest to latest. To these basic themes were added numerous additional traditions, often independent and with their own lengthy prehistories; these elements served to elaborate on the major themes, to give them particular shape and invest them with detailed specificity. For example, the major theme of the patriarchs, according to Noth, originally centered on the figure of Jacob (Israel), which was filled out with the various traditions about Abraham and Isaac. The Jacob tradition, for its part, was not of a single piece, but was rather the combination of several independent Jacob stories (and so, *mutatis mutandis*, for the Abraham and Isaac traditions).

These sundry traditional materials, both major and minor, were joined together by a variety of mechanisms. Episodes that once described anonymous groups or individuals were secondarily associated with specific figures who operated across traditional boundaries; perhaps Noth's most striking contention in this regard was that the protagonists of the Exodus story were originally the unnamed elders, and that the thorough introduction and integration of Moses is a later tradition-historical development. Entire episodes could be adopted or even newly fashioned so as to link major complexes; here the Joseph story, which links the patriarchal traditions to those of the Exodus, is an easy example. Genealogical relationships were created to connect traditionally independent figures; thus Abraham, Isaac, and Jacob were construed as related so as to bring together local ancestral traditions. Travel itineraries were inserted to bridge once-independent episodes into a geographical and chronological continuum; for example, the Korah story of Numbers 16–17, originally construed, according to Noth, without any specific location, was set in the wilderness of Sin to bring it into line with the overarching narrative.

Noth's isolation of the earliest independent traditional units depended upon a set of methodological assumptions: that the smaller and more abbreviated elements in the canonical text are usually earlier, while longer and more coherent elements are later; that earlier traditions dealt with types more often than with specific figures; and that the earliest traditions emerge from specific localities (and are often etiological) and have a cultic background. To return as an example to the Jacob tradition: Noth separated the Jacob stories into two main units, those dealing with Jacob's experiences in Shechem and Bethel and those dealing with Jacob's interactions with Esau and Laban. The first of these, insofar as it describes the cultic activities of establishing sanctuaries, is deemed to be earlier, and even within this early unit the Shechem tradition, which can be reduced essentially to the notice that Jacob bought a piece of land in Shechem, is considered prior to the Bethel tradition. The second unit, later because of its secular nature, is itself composite, bringing together an early tradition of Jacob in East Jordan with a typological tradition equating Esau with the hunter and Jacob with the shepherd. It is clear how Noth's analysis, both in identification of traditions and in their chronology, is dependent on his fundamental assumptions. It is not surprising that these assumptions are largely in line with those Gunkel used to identify the earliest form-critical units, since both approaches seek to isolate the earliest units.

Noth, however, was interested less in recapturing the cultural spirit of early Israel, as Gunkel was, and more with actually reconstructing the early history of Israel. To that end, the earliest traditions were associated with actual places and events experienced by Israel's ancestors, and the combination of traditions spoke to the historical assimilation of various Israelite tribes and other social groups, especially in the centuries preceding the establishment of the monarchy. So the tradition of Isaac at Gerar in Genesis 26 can be understood as recording the historical experience of a group of people who identified themselves as descendants of someone called Isaac, and who would go to Gerar in the summer to use the well in the area known as Rehoboth but were forbidden to use the other wells. And the Abraham traditions, insofar as, according to Noth, they secondarily adopted many traditions originally associated with Isaac, provide evidence that those early people who worshipped the God of Abraham expanded into the territory of the Isaac-followers and thus appropriated their traditions. The combination of traditions equals the combination of peoples. In this way, Noth's program was not unlike that of Wellhausen: while Wellhausen used the source-critical separation of the Pentateuchal documents as evidence for the development of Israelite religion, Noth used the tradition-critical analysis of the text to reveal the growth of Israel as a people and a nation. The literal historicity of the Israelite traditions is not of central importance, but the history of their conception and transmission is; for Noth, Israel's history is essentially equivalent to its tradition history.

In the years since Noth's work was published, however, a number of critiques have been leveled against his tradition-historical reconstruction of Israel's past. Most prominently, Noth argued extensively for the existence of a twelve-tribe league (*amphictyony*) in Israel, with regular cultic celebrations at a central sanctuary; the bringing together of the tribes into this league and their mutual worship of Yahweh were, for Noth, fundamental to the process of the combination of the early independent traditions, for it was at these public events that the fictive kinships between the previously independent groups were created, their stories linked and assimilated. Yet the *amphictyony* theory has been almost universally discarded in scholarship, thereby undermining many of Noth's most basic claims. In fact, the entire notion that the creation and recitation of traditional narratives can be linked to various pan-Israelite festival celebrations, central to both von Rad and Noth, has come under heavy criticism. The current intellectual climate is one of great doubt regarding the ability to reconstruct positively almost anything of Israel's past on the basis of the biblical material. Although it may be that much of Noth's work in uncovering the traditional elements underlying the biblical text is unaffected by this scholarly turn, his attempt to write a history of Israel on the basis of those traditions cannot be judged a success.

Like Gunkel, Gressmann, and von Rad, Noth accepted the basic source-critical conclusions of Wellhausen and understood that the tradition complexes at the base of the Pentateuchal narrative were essentially compiled before any of the Pentateuchal authors began putting them into a fixed written form. Unlike von Rad, however, Noth did not attribute the inclusion of the Sinai event to the Yahwist, but proposed instead that the first complete overarching narrative existed before either J or E. He called this rather shadowy narrative the *Grundlage*, or G, and allowed that it could have been either oral or written. Importantly, however, Noth also recognized that the date of the source in which the manifestation of a tradition is found has no bearing on the date of the underlying tradition itself. Thus, for example, Noth saw in the Bethel stories an earlier tradition, in which it was Jacob who founded the cultic site there, and a younger development of that tradition, in which the story originally associated with Jacob was transferred to Abraham. Yet the younger tradition of Abraham at Bethel appears in J, the earliest source according to Noth, while the older tradition of Jacob at Bethel appears in E, a later source. It is important to note that, in Noth's estimation, the division between the oral and the written is not of particular relevance to the tradition history. Traditions could be and were created, adopted, and transmitted equally in both forms. Because of this view, Noth was able to trace the tradition history of the text from its earliest preliterary origins all the way through the written biblical sources. Yet Noth's treatment of both the oral and the written, and particularly his continued adherence to the classical Documentary Hypothesis, lies at the basis of the two significant schools that have challenged the tradition-historical program, that which arose contemporaneously in Scandinavia, and that which developed as an explicit reaction to Noth in Germany.

Scandinavian Scholarship. A line of tradition-historical criticism arose in Scandinavia in the 1930s–1950s that pushed the notion of oral tradition to its limits. Beginning with the work of H. S. Nyberg (1889–1974) and reaching its most prominent expression in that of Ivan Engnell (1906–1964), this school of thought held that the shape of the biblical text is almost entirely dependent on oral transmission, rather than on written expression. It was argued that the main mechanism for the transmission of almost all of the biblical materials, law, narrative, and prophecy, were oral for much longer than had previously been thought—all the way through the exile—and that it was only in the post-exilic period that anything was written down. The various contradictions, duplications, and other disjunctures in the biblical material are not, according to this theory, the result of the interweaving of multiple written works (in the case of the Pentateuch) or of the successive layering of a single piece (in the case of the prophetic literature), but are rather the natural accumulation of oral tradition, the retelling and reinterpretation of stories and sayings within various circles.

Two significant claims were made along these lines. First, it was held that those traditions transmitted orally are fundamentally trustworthy, that those who passed on the traditions did so in a remarkably accurate fashion (frequently this claim was made on the basis of the Islamic transmission of the Qur'an). This is not to deny that traditions were transformed over time, but rather that accretions to the traditions occurred organically over time, and are not part of a written process. The written text is little more than the transcription of the oral tradition as it had developed to that point. Second, and as a natural corollary to the first, it was claimed that it is not possible to distinguish between earlier and later traditions with any accuracy, since all of them were worked together naturally by those who possessed the traditions. The final tradition—that represented in the written text—despite the recognition that it is composed of various distinctive elements, is to be taken as a single tradition unit. This final form is the only tradition that can be considered; it is this tradition that needs to be interpreted and explained, because it is the authentic representation of Israel's self-image. The Scandinavian school paid great attention to the prophetic corpus, where these claims may be exemplified by the notion that it is not only impossible but methodologically unsound to attempt to reconstruct the *ipsissima verba* of the prophet; the prophetic tradition contains words that are traditionally ascribed to the prophet, plus various other elements (narrative, other prophetic sayings, and the like), all of which were transmitted orally and all of which must be taken together. Because, it was claimed, the oral process of transmission was so definitive for the shaping of the prophetic corpus—with adherents selecting, reformulating, rearranging, and updating the prophet's original words—there could be no hope of reaching back through the tradition to any firm authentic origin.

It is not the case that every major Scandinavian scholar adhered to this basic approach. Most notably, Sigmund Mowinckel (1884–1965) protested strongly against the complete abnegation of literary-critical methods in favor of purely tradition-critical ones, against the abandonment of the written in favor of the oral. He argued that each has its place, and that in fact it is necessary to bring some of the literary-critical techniques, especially of discerning layers, to bear on the pre-literary traditions. Otherwise, what we are left with is not tradition history, but merely tradition; without at least the attempt to stratify the traditions, to see how they grew, the historical aspect of the process is entirely lacking. It was also pointed out in response to the Scandinavian position that its first premise—that the predominant mode of transmission in ancient Israel was oral—has no evidentiary basis, but is rather an assumption made on the grounds of far more recent comparative studies. Indeed, it may be noted that the evidence from Ugarit and Mesopotamia, which had written texts (in some cases with a clear history of textual transmission) many hundreds of years before the composition of Israel's own literature, stands in sharp counterpoint to the basic claims of the Scandinavian school.

The Scandinavian position was very important in its time, but lost much of its influence, in part because of the direct challenges to it, and in part because Noth's work was so widely accepted. Yet already in the first generation after Noth, his theories were being challenged from the completely opposite direction.

Recent Trends in Pentateuchal Criticism. In the late 1970s, Noth's student Rolf Rendtorff (1925–) published a book in which he argued that Noth's adherence to the Documentary Hypothesis had significant negative consequences for the logic of the tradition-critical method. He claimed that if the method is taken to its logical conclusion, then there is no reason to believe that there were sources as Wellhausen and others had argued; instead, it was necessary to begin with the smallest tradition-critical units and see how they have been brought together, without any *a priori* literary-critical assumptions. The Pentateuch, Rendtorff argued, was not primarily a literary product—that is, the compilation of multiple literary documents—but rather the result of successive layers, each building on and reinterpreting that which came before it. Continuous documents were no longer to be found; rather, we have to deal with original independent units and layers of redaction.

The major methodological distinction between Rendtorff and Noth can be identified in their conceptions of orality: for Noth, the traditions were brought together at the pre-literary stage, the evidence for which was to be found in the many traditions present in more than one of the Pentateuchal sources; for Rendtorff, the traditions were brought together entirely at the literary stage. The significant interpretive move made implicitly by Rendtorff, but explicitly by many of those who have followed him, is that the traditional units identified by Noth are no longer represented by the text; they are the text. For Noth, the earliest Jacob-at-Bethel tradition was oral, and it found a variety of expressions both orally and subsequently in the Bible. For those scholars who follow Rendtorff, especially his student Erhard Blum (1950–), the earliest Jacob-at-Bethel tradition is to be found in the actual words of the Bible; the narrative of Gen 28:10–22 can be stripped of its secondary layers until the original words of the tradition are isolated, and those secondary layers can then stand as evidence of multiple stages of reinterpretation and redaction. Noth's oral traditions are transmuted into written texts. This obviously has a significant impact on the evaluation of the composition of the Pentateuch.

It also, however, has a significant impact on the nature of tradition-historical criticism. Even while accepting Noth's basic divisions of the Pentateuch into various traditional units, from small to large, these recent Pentateuchal scholars have jettisoned the central theory on which Noth's analysis was based: that there were recoverable oral traditions underlying the text. Tradition-historical criticism is, in this view, an entirely literary investigation. Because every layer is present in the text, it is therefore possible, according to this theory, to reconstruct in almost complete detail the history of the growth of the text.

Prospectus. Classical tradition-historical criticism, as exemplified by Noth, is no longer a productive part of current scholarship. The two sides of tradition-historical work—the exploration of the relationship between the oral and written aspects of ancient Israelite tradition and the historical analysis of the creation, transformation, and transmission of the individual pieces that came together to form the canonical text—have not been employed together in the way that they previously were. Instead, these two areas of research have developed their own scholarly trajectories, sometimes directly at odds with each other.

In recent scholarship the oral-written binary has been the topic of much discussion. Advancements in our understanding of oral literature, especially in light of the seminal Lord-Parry studies in the mid-twentieth century, have led some to detect in the written texts of the Bible a strong oral component. This view, associated largely with the work of Susan Niditch, argues for the mutual influence of oral performance and written text, and challenges the usual assumptions regarding the exclusively literary origins of biblical materials. It is argued that oral recitation remained a productive mechanism for transmission of traditional materials even after texts began to be written. Along these lines, scholars such as James Crenshaw and David Carr have begun to consider the ways in which written texts were used for pedagogical purposes in ancient Israel, as texts for memorization, or to instill certain viewpoints and values. Hand in hand with the recognition of a continuing oral tradition, recent scholarship has seen a rise in the consideration of the role that scribes played in the transmission and canonization of traditions and texts, with the result that much attention is now paid to the mechanics of writing in the ancient world (especially in the works of William Schniedewind and Karel van der Toorn). While this avenue of research has contributed greatly to our understanding of the cultural modes of oral and written expression in ancient Israel, it also suggests that it may be far more difficult than was previously thought to pin down the precise development of the biblical text in any comprehensive way.

On the other hand, the trend particularly in Pentateuchal research has been to continue down the road laid out by Rendtorff and Blum, and to reconstruct in painstaking detail the exact words of the text that can be attributed to the earliest isolated traditions and the subsequent layers of reworking that led to the final form of the Bible. In the work of Christoph Levin, for instance, we can see something of a return to Gunkel's position regarding the Yahwist as a collector: Levin pulls from the canonical text those words that belonged to each of the individual written sources with which the Yahwist worked, those added by the Yahwist in bringing those sources together, and the layers of rewriting that accreted to the Yahwist. Similar attempts at isolating the earliest individual texts and the manner of their combination and redaction have been made by Reinhard Kratz. Scholars have also tried to work out Noth's conclusions regarding the larger tradition complexes on a purely textual level. Thus Konrad Schmid has argued at length for the separation of the patriarchal and exodus traditions, taking each as an independent corpus until their late combination in the priestly work; Frank Crüsemann has claimed that the primeval history of Genesis 1–11 was originally a separate unit; and Jan Christian Gertz has examined the independent Exodus narrative. As noted in the preceding, the tradition-historical work of Noth has been transformed into purely literary criticism, as traditions have become identified with actual biblical texts.

There is some irony in the fact that these Pentateuchal scholars, who have most closely appropriated Noth's conclusions, have done so at the cost of the tradition-historical program itself. For there are no longer any oral traditions to be investigated in recent Pentateuchal criticism; everything is entirely textual. Thus it is possible for some current scholarship to hold that there were in fact no oral traditions whatsoever in ancient Israel; that if it were possible to ask an ancient Israelite who Moses was, for example, he would have no idea at all. There is a logical basis for such a claim, and it is not to be treated lightly. The theories of Noth and other classical tradition historians depended on the reconstruction of oral traditions, frequently very detailed, but for which there is no hard evidence. We have no real access to the oral traditions; all we have is the biblical text, and it is sensible to pursue analyses that take only the written material into consideration, as anything beyond that is purely speculative. At the same time, however, such logical arguments run up against the question of how likely it is that ancient Israelite culture had no oral traditions at all, or that, if it did, none of them are represented in the biblical text. The fact that our knowledge of Israel's traditions is based solely on a literary work does not ipso facto mean that there were no oral traditions. Absence of evidence is not evidence of absence; but we are right to be cautious about just how much dependence is placed on the reconstructed oral traditions presumed to stand behind the written text.

Where classical tradition-historical criticism still seems to have some importance, somewhat ironically, is in the work of modern adherents to the Documentary Hypothesis. In the most current form of this theory, it is held that the three documents represented in Genesis–Numbers, J, E, and P, were composed independently of one another, without any mutual knowledge or influence. Yet it is abundantly clear that the three sources shared in common both the overarching framework of the narrative, from the patriarchs (or even creation) through the death of Moses, as well as many individual episodes, from the flood to Jacob at Bethel to the plagues. If the literary analysis suggests that these authors were not familiar with each others' work—that one did not receive these stories from another—then the most likely explanation for these similarities is that each wrote on the basis of a common stock of Israelite traditions. This also explains the differences between the individual renderings of the common stories: the traditions developed differently in different times, places, and social settings. In short, the logical consequence of current documentary scholarship is not so very different from the conclusions of classical tradition-historical criticism.

At the same time, it seems that there can hardly be any going back to the positivistic historical reconstructions of von Rad and especially Noth. Where early traditions can be identified underlying the biblical text, there is little possibility of convincingly reconstructing any authentic historical event at its basis, nor is it likely that we can justifiably argue that the combination of traditions is the result of the combination of peoples. There is a far stronger sense now that what is lost to us in the mists of pre-literary transmission is, indeed, lost. Yet the fundamental notion of tradition history—that there were pre-literary traditions that became and shaped the written text we have today—is a valuable one. As Gunkel recognized in his form-critical work, tradition-historical criticism reveals aspects of ancient Israelite culture, in its various constituent parts and in its whole, that purely literary investigation cannot. Our sense of the environment from which the Bible emerged is expanded and deepened when we come to appreciate, even in a relatively vague way, the traditional background of the biblical materials.

[*See also* Folklore and Biblical Interpretation; Form Criticism, *subentry* Hebrew Bible; Orality Studies and Oral Tradition, *subentry* Hebrew Bible; Redaction Criticism, *subentry* Hebrew Bible; *and* Source Criticism.]

BIBLIOGRAPHY

Baden, Joel S. *The Composition of the Pentateuch: Renewing the Documentary Hypothesis.* Anchor Yale Reference Library. New Haven, Conn.: Yale University Press, 2012.

Blum, Erhard. *Die Komposition der Vätergeschichte.* Wissenschaftliche Monographien zum Alten und Neuen Testament 57. Neukirchen-Vluyn: Neukirchener Verlag, 1984.

Carr, David. *The Formation of the Hebrew Bible: A New Reconstruction.* New York: Oxford University Press, 2011.

Carr, David. *Writing on the Tablet of the Heart: Origins of Scripture and Literature.* New York: Oxford University Press, 2005.

Crenshaw, James. *Education in Ancient Israel.* New York: Doubleday, 1998.

Crüsemann, Frank. "Die Eigenständigkeit der Urgeschichte: Ein Beitrag zur Diskussion um den 'Jahwisten.'" In *Die Botschaft und die Boten,* 11–29. Edited by J. Jeremias and L. Perlitt. Neukirchen-Vluyn: Neukirchener Verlag, 1981.

Engnell, Ivan S. *A Rigid Scrutiny: Critical Essays on the Old Testament.* Translated by John T. Willis. Nashville, Tenn.: Vanderbilt University Press, 1969.

Gertz, Jan Christian. *Tradition und Redaktion in der Exoduserzählung: Untersuchungen zur Endredaktion.* Forschungen zur Religion und Literatur des Alten und Neuen Testaments 186. Göttingen, Germany: Vandenhoeck und Ruprecht, 2000.

Gressmann, Hugo. *Mose und seine Zeit: Ein Kommentar zu den Mose-Sagen.* Forschungen zur Religion und Literatur des Alten und Neuen Testaments 1. Göttingen, Germany: Vandenhoeck & Ruprecht, 1913.

Gunkel, Hermann. *Genesis.* Translated by Mark E. Biddle. Macon, Ga.: Mercer University Press, 1977.

Knight, Douglas A. *Rediscovering the Traditions of Israel: The Development of the Traditio-Historical Research of the Old Testament, with Special Consideration of Scandinavian Contributions.* Rev. ed. Society for Biblical Literature Dissertation Series 9. Missoula, Mont.: Scholars Press, 1975. The seminal survey of Scandinavian research.

Kratz, Reinhard. *The Composition of the Narrative Books of the Old Testament.* London: T&T Clark, 2005.

Levin, Christoph. *Der Jahwist.* Forschungen zur Religion und Literatur des Alten und Neuen Testaments 157. Göttingen: Vandenhoeck und Ruprecht, 1993.

Niditch, Susan. *Oral World and Written Word.* Library of Ancient Israel. Louisville, Ky.: Westminster John Knox, 1996.

Nyberg, H. S. *Studien zum Hoseabuche: Zugleich ein Beitrag zur Klärung des Problems der alttestamentlichen Textkritik.* Uppsala: Lundequistska Bokhandeln, 1935.

Rad, Gerhard von. "The Form Critical Problem of the Hexateuch." In *The Problem of the Hexateuch and Other Essays,* 1–78. Translated by E. W. Trueman Dicken. New York: McGraw-Hill, 1966.

Rendtorff, Rolf. *The Problem of the Process of Transmission in the Pentateuch.* Translated by John J. Scullion. Journal for the Study of the Old Testament Supplement Series 89. Sheffield, UK: Sheffield Academic, 1977.

Schmid, Konrad. *Genesis and the Moses Story: Israel's Dual Origins.* Siphrut 3. Winona Lake, Ind.: Eisenbrauns, 2010.

Schniedewind, William. *How the Bible Became a Book.* Cambridge: Cambridge University Press, 2004.

Toorn, Karel van der. *Scribal Culture and the Making of the Hebrew Bible.* Cambridge, Mass.: Harvard University Press, 2007.

Wellhausen, Julius. *Prolegomena to the History of Israel.* Translated by J. Sutherland Black and Allan Enzies. Reprint: Atlanta: Scholars Press, 1994.

Joel S. Baden

TRANSLATION TECHNIQUES

[*This entry contains two subentries,* Ancient Versions *and* Modern Versions]

Ancient Versions

In the mid-first century B.C.E (c. 46 B.C.E), the Roman orator and politician Cicero introduced his Latin translation of the speeches of the Attic orators Aeschines and Demonsthenes in this way (*De optimo genere oratorum*):

> And I did not translate them as an interpreter, but as an orator, keeping the same ideas and forms, or as one might say, the 'figures' of thought, but in language that conforms to our usage. And in so doing, I did not hold it necessary to render word for word, but I preserved the general style and force of the language. (H. M. Hubbell, *Cicero: On Invention. The Best Kind of Orator*, Cambridge, 1949, p. 365)

Four centuries later (c. 395 C.E), the church father Jerome describes his translation strategy in this way (*De optimo genre interpretandi*): "Now I not only admit but freely announce that in translating from the Greek . . . I render not word for word, but sense-for-sense." And then: The translator "did not bind himself to the drowsiness of literal translation, or allow himself to be chained to the literalism of an inadequate culture, but, like some conqueror, he marched the original text, a captive, into his native language" (Paul Carroll, *The Satirical Letters of St.*

Jerome, Washington, D.C., 1956, pp. 136–137 and 140, respectively).

But when it came to Sacred Scripture—Jerome is, after all, most famous for his rendering of the Bible into Latin—he advised a very different approach: "—except of course in the case of the Holy Scripture, where even the syntax contains a mystery. . . . " (Carroll, pp. 136–137).

Thus it was that at least a few ancient translators publicly acknowledge that there were competing approaches—what we might broadly speak of as literal and free—when it came to crafting a text from one language to another. In addition, these translators express a decided preference in favor of sense-for-sense or figure-for-figure, unless (in the case of the Christian, Jerome) the text being translated was the Bible.

In these statements, neither Cicero nor Jerome expresses any doubt about the value or validity of the process of translating or the text that results. Did they, in fact, have any doubts about the entire enterprise of translating? If not, was their confidence shared by others who undertook similar projects? Although we may not be certain about the answer to the former query, the following admission, from the prologue to the Wisdom of Ben Sira (Sirach), dated to c. 132 B.C.E., shows quite clearly that some individuals in the ancient world recognized what they viewed as possibly insurmountable difficulties in translating, in this case from Hebrew to Greek:

> You are urged therefore to read with good will and attention, and to be indulgent in cases where, despite our diligent labor in translating, we may seem to have rendered some phrases imperfectly. For what was originally expressed in Hebrew does not have exactly the same sense when translated into another language. Not only this work, but even the law itself, the prophecies, and the rest of the books differ not a little as originally expressed. (0:15–26)

Because translation, in one form or another, is as old as language itself, we can easily imagine that the specific examples cited here could be multiplied many times if we had access to the writings, to say nothing of the thoughts, of all those who were engaged in translating during the period of antiquity. From such an expanded database, as it were, it would be immediately apparent that all translation is not of the same sort and that the translations that Cicero, Jerome, and Ben Sira had in mind—namely, literary translations—were only a minority, and a small minority at that, of translated texts, being far outnumbered by diplomatic correspondence, bureaucratic notations, and economic records.

But it is this minority, literary translations, that will be the subject of this article, and then only the genre or sub-genre of biblical versions—that is, versions of the Old and/or New Testaments. Of necessity, this focus is limited further to material translated by Jews and Christians primarily for other Jews and Christians. As will be seen, even within this "limited" compass, there was amazing, richly textured variety fully deserving of the attention of modern readers.

Jewish Translations: The Septuagint. The Septuagint or LXX, a version of the Bible in Greek, is the earliest known biblical translation. Its origins can be traced geographically to the city of Alexandria, Egypt, chronologically to the early third century B.C.E. On what basis can we make such determinations?

From antiquity, the *Letter of Aristeas* is the oldest and fullest ancient account of the LXX, even though it speaks only of the Greek translation of the Pentateuch and devotes only about 15 percent of its 322 verses to this topic. The *Letter* purports to be a contemporary account from the reign of Ptolemy II (Philadelphus), who ruled from 285–247 B.C.E. As related by Aristeas, the impetus for the translation came from the royal librarian Demetrius, who wished to add "the lawbooks of the Jews" in Greek to a collection numbering over 200,000 volumes (Shutt 1985 pp. 9–11). Ptolemy agreed and sent a letter to Eleazar, high priest in Jerusalem, requesting 72 elders (six from each tribe) "of exemplary lives, with the experience of the Law and ability to translate it" (Shutt 1985, p. 39).

The high priest acceded to this request and also sent "fine skins on which the Law had been written in letters of gold in Jewish characters" (Shutt 1985,

p. 176). The central part of the *Letter* describes the gifts, banqueting, and conversation between the Egyptian monarch and his Jewish guests. At the end of a week (and with only twenty-two verses left in the document), Demetrius led the seventy-two translators across a jetty to an island identified as Pharos, where after exactly seventy-two days, they completed their task. The resulting document was read to the Jewish community, which received it with great acclaim and rejoicing, as did Ptolemy, who suitably rewarded each of the seventy-two for his labors.

The procedures adopted by the translators, as outlined in the *Letter*, accord well with translation-by-committee to this very day: "They set to completing their several tasks, reaching agreement among themselves on each by comparing versions. . . . The business of their meeting occupied them until the ninth hour [3:00 p.m.] of each day" (Shutt 1985, pp. 302–303). Only the luxury of their surroundings and their freedom from other commitments—"a magnificent building in a very quiet situation" (Shutt 1985, p. 301)—separate them from modern Bible translators. With the possible exception of the fact that 72 happened to be the number both of the translators and of the days of translation, a phenomenon very briefly noted by Aristeas, there is nothing of the "miraculous" about the entire process that produced the Greek Pentateuch.

Through the Middle Ages, the *Letter of Aristeas* was understood as an essentially historical account of how the first five books of the Septuagint came about. The Jewish historian Josephus (late first century C.E.) knew it; the Jewish philosopher Philo (early first century C.E.), himself a native of Alexandria, even adds some details. Christian writers also knew the *Letter* and considerably embellished it. Thus, although the earliest copies of the *Letter* itself date from the eleventh century C.E., there is no doubt that the *Letter* itself is of ancient date.

But what of its historical accuracy? Because of certain discrepancies—for example, Demetrius was not the librarian at the time of Ptolemy II, and the Septuagint of the Five Books of Moses does not represent the work of one group or individual—there is uniform agreement today that the *Letter* cannot be the eyewitness account it claims to be. In all likelihood, it dates to the mid-second century B.C.E., that is, a century later than the events it appears to reflect. On the other hand, there is good linguistic evidence from the Septuagint of the Pentateuch itself that the Greek version of these books does indeed date to the first half of the third century B.C.E., and the Jewish names mentioned in the *Letter* are compatible with this era.

Considerable scholarly attention has been paid to the assertion by the *Letter*'s author that the Septuagint owes it origins to royal decree as opposed to the internal needs of the Alexandrian Jewish community, where knowledge of the Hebrew language was quickly receding. A strong case can be made, both from the historical record and historical parallels, that in this instance internal and external exigencies coalesced, with the result that the Jews of Alexandria and their royal patron could well have worked together to produce this earliest written translation of the Hebrew Bible.

The translation of a sacred text from a "barbarian" language like Hebrew into Greek was an unprecedented enterprise. Thus, it is appropriate to consider what specific needs, internal to Alexandria's Jewish community, would be met by this version. Contemporary scholars have identified four areas of communal life that might have formed a nexus or environment in which to situate LXX translators.

Among LXX specialists, the interlinear paradigm is well known, in and of itself and as one of the major underpinnings of the New English Translation of the Septuagint (NETS). According to this paradigm, one is to imagine that initially the Greek text circulated primarily among those who also had access to the Hebrew. Thus, the Greek version was dependent on the Hebrew for a full and cohesive explication of its form and meaning. LXX specialist Albert Pietersma ("A New Paradigm for Addressing Old Questions: The Relevance of the Interlinear Model for the Study of the Septuagint." In *Bible and Computer: The Stellenbosch AIBI-6 Conference, Leiden*, the Netherlands, *2002*, edited by Johann Cook, pp. 337–364) locates the institutional support for this undertaking—which aims (among other things) to bring the reader to the text by privileging Hebrew as the source language—within the context of a system of Jewish schools in Ptolemaic Egypt.

Another view has been expressed by the scholar Mêlée Modrzejewski (*The Jews of Egypt*, Philadelphia, 1995). He discerns the origins of the LXX Pentateuch in the needs of the Jewish community to provide a Greek version of their Law that could be included in the judicial system of Ptolemy II, under whose royal administration certain groups (including the Jews) would be allowed a considerable degree of internal legal autonomy.

More recently, Sylvie Honigman (*The Septuagint and Homeric Scholarship in Alexandria: A Study of the Narrative of the Letter of Aristeas*, London, 2003) has found cultural prestige more than piety as the key motivating factor in the production of the LXX Pentateuch. By contrast, the oldest interpretation is that of H. St. John Thackery (*The Septuagint and Jewish Worship: A Study in Origins*, London, 1923), who argues in favor of a liturgical setting for the Old Greek of the Pentateuch.

It may well be that the Greek Bible originated in several contexts (school/court of legal/royal province/court of popular opinion/synagogue), answering to different needs of the community. Moreover, these needs in all likelihood defy neat categorization as either internal or external. An explanation that broadly incorporates both/and rather than the narrower either/or is more likely to be true to the complex factors responsible for the LXX.

The Septuagint as Immutable. Near the end of the *Letter of Aristeas*, after the Greek text is proclaimed, the leaders of the Jewish community "commanded that a curse should be laid . . . on anyone who should alter the version by any addition or change to any part of the written text, or any deletion either" (Shutt 1985, p. 311). This episode brings to mind the ratification of the Torah by the Israelites at Mt. Sinai (as recounted in Exodus 19 and 24) and strongly suggests that, at least as described by Aristeas, the Greek Pentateuch was held to have authority equal to that of the Hebrew Torah. It is likely that this view reflects the author's perception of events of his own day (that is, mid-second century B.C.E.), when rival Greek versions, in the form of revisions and fresh translations, began to challenge the unique place held until then by the Greek Pentateuch of the third century.

The first century C.E. Alexandrian Jewish philosopher Philo, who apparently knew no Hebrew, saw the translators in a rather different light: they were "prophets and priests of the mysteries," who, "under inspiration, wrote . . . the same word for word, as though dictated to each by an invisible prompter" (*De Vita Mosis* 2, 7:37–40). In Epiphanius (*De Mens. et Pond.*), a Christian writer of the fourth century C.E., the level of embellishment reached its peak, with a narrative that places thirty-six pairs of translators in individual cells. Working in isolation, each pair completed its work in the same amount of time and with exactly the same results, such that comparison of the thirty-six texts found no discrepancy at all. Only divine oversight or intervention could produce such unanimity, it was asserted; this was in accord with the elevated status that the Septuagint enjoyed among early Christians.

The Translators of the Greek Pentateuch. Given their role as pioneers, the earliest LXX translators might be thought to have hit upon an essentially literal approach as the safest way to render their Hebrew. And indeed essentially, or responsibly, literal might be an apt description of the approach taken, overall, by these translators. This would not be in keeping with Cicero's dictum nor with Jerome's practice with respect to nonbiblical material. But it does accord well with Jerome's approach to the biblical text—and these translators were working more than 600 years before him.

But there are other portions of the Greek biblical text that reflect a heightened interest in literary and other stylistic features of the Hebrew. Moreover, it is clear that many passages of the Greek Pentateuch are very difficult to fathom without access to the underlying Hebrew. It is this very real amalgam of literalism and literary, of clarity and obscurity—in the Pentateuch and elsewhere in the LXX—that confounds simplistic descriptions of the LXX.

LXX Translators and Their* Vorlage: *Translation Technique. What was the nature of the Hebrew text(s) underlying the Greek translation of the LXX? Was it the traditional or Masoretic Text (MT)? Was it another Hebrew version? If it was a combination of two or more textual traditions, were they in some way intertwined or were there stretches of one followed by another? And was there consistency in this regard throughout the Hebrew text, or did circumstances differ book-by-book, section-by-section, or even within a given book?

These very issues continue to divide LXX specialists. Prior to the Second World War, it was widely asserted that the MT, at least its consonants, represented throughout antiquity (as it does today) the standard against which all transcribers and translators would regularly check their work. It was this text that, by and large, the LXX translators had before them. Thus, deviations from the MT were seen as the result of deficiencies on the part of scribes, whose minds were muddled or distracted. The "original" LXX, in this reconstruction, can be located in those manuscripts that are closest to the MT.

Not all scholars, even during the first half of the twentieth century, were comfortable with this formulation. Surely, it can be agreed, a consonantal text very much like, if not in all particulars identical to, our MT was available to some LXX translators. Nonetheless, is it not also possible that the Hebrew that lay before LXX translators sometimes differed extensively from the MT? If this is the case, then MT–LXX differences should be sought in the Hebrew that lay before the translator (that is, his *Vorlage* [exemplar text]), rather than linked to any initiative on the part of the translator.

Intriguingly, the discovery and publication of biblical scrolls from Qumran provided primary data to support both of these views. Some of the biblical scrolls present a consonantal text that is indeed, to all extent and purposes, identical to our MT. At the same time, there are Qumran scrolls that bear witness to a Hebrew text that is close to what the LXX translators may have had in front of them. This is true for portions of the books of Samuel and Jeremiah in particular.

In other words, these Qumran manuscripts provide firsthand evidence for what is often spoken of as textual fluidity in the period prior to the destruction of the Jerusalem Temple by the Romans in 70 C.E. It becomes apparent that even where there was a consensus as to what constituted Sacred or Holy Writ, this applied only to books as a whole and not to the particulars or details of wording. Thus, there is no good reason to assert that the LXX, where it follows its Hebrew *Vorlage* away from the MT, presents an aberrant or secondary tradition.

No matter what the Hebrew wording, is it not also possible that ancient translators, much like their modern counterparts, might stray from that Hebrew for any number of reasons? The evidence, including Greek scrolls from Qumran and nearby sites, reveals a varied and variegated history that is as old as the oldest Greek Bible.

What of changes made by translators themselves? In such cases, it is helpful to distinguish between those the translators subconsciously or accidentally made and those that were made as a result of conscious efforts on the translators' part. As for the former, they consist primarily of omissions—caused by similar wording at the beginning or end of words or phrases or by other easily confused graphic elements. Thus, the net result of such "accidents" is to shorten the text in comparison with the Hebrew that is being rendered.

Conscious or deliberate intervention by translators tends to lengthen the text, as the translators seek to clarify, smooth out, explain, update, or otherwise "improve upon" the Hebrew that lay before them: these alterations may be referred to as quantitative changes. On occasion, substituted wording does not result in any substantive change in the text's length; these are referred to as qualitative changes.

However, scholars must resist the temptation to apply globally what is the case for a given book. In the past, lack of such restraint has led to the positing of a strongly anti-anthropomorphic tendency throughout the LXX or an equally widespread promotion of certain messianic ideas. Neither of these assertions has stood the careful scrutiny of later researchers.

The LXX beyond the Pentateuch. Were the translators of the non-Pentateuchal books aware of what their "predecessors" had accomplished, and did this form something of a paradigm for their efforts? This was certainly the case in some books, such as Joshua. On the other hand, a book like Proverbs is widely understood to contain a number of passages reflective of the translators themselves rather than their Hebrew text—and thus to be essentially independent from earlier Greek translations, such as that of the Pentateuch.

The Septuagint "Canon." Which books or parts of books did the Greek translators render—or in some cases (where original Greek composition is involved), transmit? In other words, what counted as "canon" for these translators and for the Jewish communities in which they resided? For the B.C.E. period and for the first centuries C.E., we simply do not know. Only with the great codices of the third and fourth century C.E. do we have individual books or sections of the Septuagint collected into anything approaching a Bible. And here the evidence is mixed: Codex Vaticanus (B) contains all of the books of the Hebrew Bible, and the following material that is today classified as deuterocanonical: 1 Esdras, 2 Esdras, Psalm 151, the Wisdom of Solomon, Ecclesiasticus or Ben Sirach, the additions to Esther (several of which were originally composed in a Semitic language, others of which are original Greek compositions), Judith, Tobit, Baruch, the Letter of Jeremiah, and the additions to Daniel (Azariah and the Three Jews, Susanna, and Bel and the Dragon). Codex Alexandrinus (A) contains all of this and, in addition, 1—4 Maccabees and the *Odes of Solomon*. Although there is some uncertainty as to the contents of Codex Sinaiticus, it is reliably viewed as encompassing the Old Testament according to the canon of the Septuagint, including the Apocrypha, but without 2 and 3 Maccabees. Other manuscripts and traditions include further works or omit material contained in these uncial codices.

Jewish Translations: The Targums. The other major Jewish translation of antiquity was the Targum (plural: Targumim or Targums), from Hebrew to Aramaic. In this regard, it is worth remembering that portions of the biblical books of Ezra and Daniel, along with a few expressions elsewhere, are also in Aramaic (rather than Hebrew).

According to traditional Jewish sources, the origins of the practice of translating from Hebrew to Aramaic can be detected in Nehemiah 8, which is dated to the mid-fifth century B.C.E. As Ezra the scribe read from the Scroll of the Teaching or Law to the assembled crowd at Jerusalem's Water Gate, a group of individuals provided a "translation" (so the JPS Tanakh at Neh 8:8), so that the crowd would understand the reading. According to this interpretation, which received its classical formulation from the third century C.E. Jewish exegete Rav, Ezra was reading in Hebrew; the translation was in Aramaic (*Meg.* 3a). The relevant term used in Nehemiah 8 is not related to the word "Targum"; that root, t-r-g-m (a rare quadriliteral root) does appear in Ezra 4, in a context where it describes something that was undoubtedly a translation.

Whatever Aramaic renderings did occur in the pre-Christian period were, on the basis of extant evidence, orally composed and transmitted until the first century B.C.E. From the end of that period come two small fragments of an Aramaic version of Leviticus 16 and two from the early chapters of the book of Job; all of these were found in Cave 4 at Qumran. In Cave 11, extensive portions of Job, from the middle of chapter 17 until the end of the book, were discovered.

If the term "targum" is used broadly to refer to any biblical version in Aramaic, then it would perhaps be appropriate to refer to these Dead Sea Scrolls as exhibiting a "targumic" text. However, the classical Targums, which are from the slightly later rabbinic period, exhibit a set of interrelated characteristics that identify them as a particular breed of Aramaic translation, which will be discussed next.

Targums to the Torah. The most important and best-preserved Targumim were composed in Palestine. There are several Targumim for the Torah, the Former Prophets, the Latter Prophets, and the Writings. At least initially, these Targumim functioned as supplements to the Hebrew in liturgical settings.

Targum Onkelos is the best-known Aramaic rendering of the Torah or Pentateuch. So far as we know, it was the only Targum to have undergone a thorough process of redaction. The attribution of a targum to Onkelos is made in the Babylonian Talmud.

Linguistically, *Targum Onkelos* combines elements of Western (that is, Palestinian) and Eastern (that is, Babylonian) Aramaic, giving rise to several theories on its origins. The most likely explanation is that the Targum originated in Palestine and was later redacted in Babylon. The Aramaic of this Targum, while necessarily exhibiting diversity, does display prominent features that allow for a dating of its earliest portions to first century C.E.

Of the Targums to the Pentateuch, *Onkelos* is the most literal—that is, it contains the least number of interpretive additions. It is clear that those responsible for this Aramaic rendering worked with a Hebrew text that was, for all intents and purposes, equivalent to the consonants and wording preserved in the Masoretic Text. For the most part, this is true for the other Targums as well.

As is also the case, to distinctly varying degrees, with all other Targums, those responsible for *Targum Onkelos* parted company with their Hebrew *Vorlage* (that is, underlying text) on a number of occasions. This can lead to the assertion that the Targumim are for the most part periphrastic. Although such a characterization overstates the percentage of targumic text given over to such explanatory material and understates the amount of literal rendition, the inclusion of paraphrase is a characteristic feature of the Targumim.

For the most part, the nonliteral sections were designed to provide their intended audience with a means of understanding the Hebrew in an accessible manner that was at the same time consistent with the theological views being promoted by those responsible for the Targumim. Thus, language that is figurative is typically rendered according to sense, rather than literally; in general, difficult words, phrases, or ideas are simplified.

Of special notice are the many efforts to guard against what the translators would have argued was a misunderstanding of the nature of God. Thus, for the most part, anthropomorphisms and anthropopathisms related to God are restyled. Even the suggestion that other beings could be categorized (however mistakenly) as "gods" was to be avoided. Alongside these efforts, the translators apparently had no difficulty in supplementing or even contradicting biblical law, no matter that it was understood to be of divine origin, when such legal passages failed to give support to communal practice contemporary with the translators.

Of the other Targums to the Pentateuch, two are fairly well known. The first is *Targum Pseudo-Jonathan*, which may have been composed as early as the second half of the fourth century C.E. It contains all but fifteen verses from the Pentateuch. The second is *Codex Neofiti I*, which was discovered in the mid 1950s in the Vatican Library. It covers every verse in the Pentateuch.

As codified in the Mishnah and later rabbinic writings, an oral translation, or Targum, in Aramaic was provided after every verse of Torah read in the Hebrew during synagogue services. Interestingly, the Talmud places a certain emphasis on the oral nature of these explanations, on occasion forbidding the use of a written Aramaic text in the synagogue. Written texts could be used for classroom purposes or for private study. Thus, it can be hypothesized that both of these environments, the synagogue and the school, played some role in the development of the Pentateuchal Targums that have been discussed here.

Targums to the Prophets. Generally, much of the preceding is also true for Targums to the Prophets (Former and Latter). A prophetic portion, linked by rabbinic exegesis to the Torah reading, was also part of the synagogue service. In this case, the Aramaic explanation was also orally rendered, but (only) after every third verse. The primary Targum to the Prophets is *Targum Jonathan*, attributed to

Hillel's student Jonathan b. Uzziel. This is considerably earlier than the generally accepted date for the final redaction of this Targum, which is usually set in the seventh century C.E.

The Talmudic text also holds that Jonathan b. Uzziel produced this Targum "at the dictation of Haggai, Zechariah, and Malachi," who were the last three prophets in Jewish tradition. Their linkage with the Targum and its human "author" is intended to provide something of a direct link from the Hebrew Bible to its Aramaic rendering.

Targum Jonathan holds together as a unified composition based on similar stylistic features throughout. This Targum also exhibits noteworthy linguistic and stylistic points of affinity with *Targum Onkelos.* It can also be observed that the translator appears to be working with a Hebrew at variance (if only slightly) from the MT.

Targums to the Writings. In the Jewish tradition, the third part of the Hebrew Bible is known as the Writings or Ketuvim. Although the contents of this rather miscellaneous collection of books were established at a fairly early date, the "biblical" order of these books fluctuated considerably. Moreover, with few exceptions (see the following), they did not play a role in the liturgy of the synagogue.

Therefore, it is not surprising that the Targums to this portion of the Bible were composed book-by-book, by different authors. Thus, a single Targum covering all of the Writings is lacking. The Targums that do exist are in general comparatively late compositions. Nor is it entirely surprising that we lack a Targum for both Daniel and Ezra–Nehemiah. It may be coincidental, but again worthy of note, that these two books (with Ezra and Nehemiah constituting a single composition) each have extensive sections in Aramaic within the Hebrew Bible.

In an early period the reading of the book of Esther arose as a primary constituent of the public celebration of the holiday of Purim. For Esther, there are two fully preserved Targums. They both include numerous additions, somewhat more in the second than in the first. At later dates, four other books from the Ketuvim found their way into public worship: the Song of Songs, Ruth, Lamentations, and Ecclesiastes. For the most part, the Targums to these books, collectively spoken of as the Five Scrolls, are filled with midrashic additions, with paraphrase predominating and literal renderings rare.

As a whole, the Targums are a rich source of evidence for midrashic development and, in any case, are difficult to ignore. At the same time, we should keep in mind that the individual (or individuals) responsible for the literal approach to the Hebrew is most likely the same person (or persons) responsible for the additions. For these translators/interpreters, the goals for all sections of their Aramaic version were the same: to provide an easy-to-understand and updated version of the Bible for their audience and to insure that this version was consistent with the Jewish practice and belief of their community.

Earliest Christian Versions. The earliest followers of Jesus, who were themselves Jewish, presumably used Aramaic for their daily transactions. From the evidence of the New Testament, however, it is apparent that many of them drew upon the Septuagint for their knowledge of scripture. Although not all "scriptural" quotations or citations in the New Testament are attested elsewhere in Greek-language manuscripts, a large number of these references do show familiarity with wording and imagery that are distinctive to the LXX vis-à-vis the MT. Thus it was that the Septuagint, in origins a Jewish document, came to be part of the Christian "Bible" from a fairly early period.

Most likely, the first translation under Christian auspices of all or part of what came to be known as the Bible took place in the second half of the second century C.E. in northwest Mesopotamia. This is the Syriac version; Syriac itself is an Aramaic dialect. Over the next few centuries, a half-dozen or so competing Syriac texts appeared, of which one, the Peshitta (meaning "simple" or "clear"), ultimately achieved predominant status in the Syriac churches. Those responsible for the Old Testament of the Peshitta apparently worked with a Hebrew text;

although many of the translators were Christian, it cannot be ruled out that some were Jewish or at least had access to Jewish exegetical traditions.

The Vulgate. Syriac remained an important language, liturgically and otherwise, for many in sections of the Near/Middle East. Meanwhile, the Christian church was enjoying considerable growth in Europe and North Africa. In these lands, Latin was most commonly spoken. It is then not surprising that Latin versions of the Bible sprang up from an early period. As such versions proliferated in number, so did their textual disagreements. For the Roman (Catholic) Church, such textual variation presented all sorts of unwanted—and, from its perspective, unwarranted—possibilities for exegetical and liturgical squabbles. It was to Eusebius Hieronymous, better known as Jerome, that the church, through Pope Damasus, turned to remedy this situation.

Jerome was born in northeastern Italy around 350 C.E. As a youth, he was sent to Rome, where he gained mastery of Latin. Through his travels to the Near East, including Palestine, he gained thorough grounding in Greek and even studied Hebrew—which was very rare for Christians of his day. The Pope's first commission, in 382 C.E., was for Jerome to prepare a revised version of the text of the Four Gospels. During this period he also worked extensively on a Latin rendering of the Psalms, later known as the Roman Psalter, the first of three Jerome produced. He may have also begun revising other parts of the New Testament while still in Rome, where he remained until the Pope's death in 384 C.E.

Jerome then traveled for two years, finally settling in Bethlehem, where he continued his work of Bible revision for three decades. Along with his translations, Jerome also produced commentaries. As he delved more deeply into his work on the Old Testament, he realized that the old(er) Latin manuscripts he was revising, based as they were on the Septuagint, varied, at some points considerably, from the Hebrew, which his earlier exposure to that language allowed him to consult directly. With these observations in mind, he abandoned his project of revision and instead undertook a fresh Latin rendering of the Hebrew itself. This move, which was very unpopular with many of his contemporaries, including Augustine, led him to produce two further editions of the Psalms (the Gallican Psalter, actually based on the LXX, was the second; the third, and last, was the Hebrew Psalter).

Moreover, as Jerome came to recognize, some books in the Septuagint were not part of the Jewish canon of the Hebrew Bible. Although he had rendered into Latin some of these books, as well as passages from other books that were not found in the Hebrew, he argued against their inclusion in the Latin text he was preparing. Succeeding generations of scribes and theologians rejected this decision by Jerome. Thus it was that editions of the Vulgate, as the work came to be called, included the very books of the Apocrypha that Jerome had excluded. It is also likely that some parts of the Vulgate, as it was transmitted over the centuries, were initially prepared or supplemented by individuals other than Jerome. Nonetheless, the Vulgate, attributed entirely to Jerome, eventually won its unique status as the Bible of the Roman Catholic Church.

Other Christian Versions. Although Greek, Syriac, and Latin were important languages for early Christians, the spread of Christianity not unexpectedly led to the production of biblical versions in a number of other languages as well. In some cases, the Bible was the first written text in a given language or dialect, thus proving foundational in more than one sense.

According to the traditions of the Copts, Christianity reached their native land of Egypt by the mid-first century C.E. (see Acts 18:25 in some manuscripts). While the upper classes of Egypt wrote and spoke in Greek, the urban masses and those in rural areas used Coptic. Spoken well before it was written, this language was the culmination of ancient Egyptian. Its alphabet made use of letters in Greek script, mostly in uncial form.

Old Testament manuscripts in Coptic perhaps go back to the fourth century C.E. The translators made use exclusively of Septuagint manuscripts; thus, we speak of the Coptic versions, among others, as "daughter versions" of the LXX. New Testament manuscripts appeared perhaps a century earlier. Complete texts of the Coptic Bible from the ninth and tenth centuries have also survived.

Of the seven known dialects of Coptic, two are especially relevant for translations of the Bible: Sahidic and Bohairic. The Sahidic dialect originated in Upper (or Southern) Egypt; Bohairic, in Northern (or Lower) Egypt. Most of the earliest biblical manuscripts in Coptic are in Sahidic, although Bohairic became dominant among later Christians in Egypt.

Further south on the continent of Africa, Christianity gained a foothold in Ethiopia; the first missionaries may have arrived in the fourth century C.E. or perhaps even earlier. There are few, if any extant biblical manuscripts in the Ethiopic language that date from antiquity. Most are considerably later, from the sixteenth century on.

Nonetheless, there is no doubt that medieval and later Ethiopic manuscripts do display texts that do, to a greater or lesser degree, go back far earlier. Although the Old Testament in Ethiopic has been subjected to considerable research, there is no consensus as to whether it was based primarily on the Greek or the Syriac; some scholars have also detected traces of Hebrew influence. As preserved, the New Testament in Ethiopic combines both literal and free approaches. It is also relevant to observe that the biblical canon of the Ethiopic Church contains some books not found in any other Christian Bibles.

Early Christians were also on the move in other directions. As reported in some sources, the church was established by the mid-third century C.E. in Armenia. Unlike the circumstances in which most ancient translations were produced, where (even if we have some details about time and place) we lack knowledge of specific individuals involved, two names stand out in connection with the earliest Armenian versions: Sahug and Mesropius. Sahug was a patriarch, who, along with Mesropius, provided the first Armenian Bible along with the liturgy in Armenian. These efforts, which also involved the creation of the Armenian script and alphabet, took place during the first decade of the fifth century C.E. Thus, their translations were part of efforts to establish the Armenian language in general and, with specific reference to the liturgy, its use over against Syriac.

As it happens, Sahug and Mesropius made primary use of a biblical text in Syriac, along with recourse to the Greek, for their Armenian Old Testament. After first rendering the book of Proverbs, they tackled the Gospels, returning then to the Old Testament, which they completed by 415 C.E. The Armenian Bible, sometimes called the "Queen of the Versions," is widely represented in extant manuscripts; only manuscripts of the Vulgate outnumber them.

Coming some four centuries later, the Slavonic (generally called the Old Church Slavonic) version has, in its origins, some similarities with the Armenian version. For this version also, two individuals are known by name; in this case, two apostles to the Slavs, Cyril and Methodius. To achieve their goal, Cyril devised an alphabet, as had been done for the Armenian language as well.

Unlike their Armenian predecessors, however, Cyril and Methodius began with the Gospels. Their work was completed near the end of the ninth century C.E. One edition of the Old Church Slavonic has become the standard text for many Eastern Orthodox Churches.

Assessment. From the examples cited and discussed in this article, it becomes clear that serious efforts were undertaken by both Jews and Christians to make scripture available to their respective communities in an accessible and comprehensible manner. Various approaches to translation, from literal to free, were used, presumably reflecting the translators' best judgment as to what type of text would be most easily and widely accepted by members of their target audience.

Jews made use of a Hebrew text; for the most part, Christians, lacking knowledge of Hebrew and suspicious of Jews from whom they could learn it, used a form of the Septuagint as their base text. They were typically unaware, of course, of the Jewish origins of the LXX.

In addition to the central task of rendering scripture in the language of their day, many translators had subsidiary goals in mind as well. For some, this meant creating a written language, along with an alphabet. For others, it entailed reliance on new technologies, such as the use of the codex (or book) rather than the scroll.

In all cases, a full appreciation of a given version is not possible without the knowledge requisite for placing a translation, and its translators, into proper historical, religious, political, and cultural context. Where such information is available, it enriches our understanding; even where the available information is rather incomplete, we gain perspective from seeking out as much detail as possible. After all, these translations, as is true for those from later periods, are the product of real people, grappling with real difficulties (and possibilities), in real circumstances. Through study of them, we can come closer to appreciating the lives of those from whom we can continue to advance our own lives—spiritually and otherwise.

[*See also* Dead Sea Scrolls; Masora and Masoretic Interpretation; *and* Textual Criticism, *subentry* Hebrew Bible.]

BIBLIOGRAPHY

De Hamel, Christopher. *The Book: A History of the Bible.* London: Phaidon, 2001. A profusely illustrated, well-written account of the transmission and translation of the Bible that is especially strong on the history of the Latin Bible. It offers many beautifully reproduced, full-cover pages from biblical manuscripts.

Dines, Jennifer. *The Septuagint.* London: T&T Clark, 2004. This is among the most recent introductions to the LXX. Its compact length and lucid style recommend it as a starting point for advanced undergraduate or graduate students.

Flesher, Paul V. M., and Bruce Chilton. *The Targums: A Critical Introduction.* Waco, Tex.: Baker University Press, 2011. An up-to-date analysis of all aspects of the Targums by two experienced specialists in the field.

Gamble, H. Y. *Books and Readers in the Early Church: A History of Early Christian Texts.* New Haven, Conn.: Yale University Press, 1995. A lucid and accessible introduction to the production and spread of books in the first centuries of Christianity. Among other topics covered are the rise of the codex and the degree of literacy among early Christians.

Gilmore, Alec. *A Concise Dictionary of Bible Origins and Interpretation.* London: T&T Clark, 2006. This handy reference tool contains concise discussions of almost every topic related to biblical translation, transmission, and interpretation. It is an ideal first stop for all sorts of research into these topics.

Greenspoon, Leonard. "Septuagint." In *The New Interpreter's Dictionary of the Bible*, Vol. 5, 170–177. Nashville, Tenn.: Abingdon, 2009. This is among the most recent extended encyclopedia entries on the LXX. It contains up-to-date discussions, including the application of Translation Studies to the explication of the LXX and current theories of Septuagint origins.

The International Organization for Septuagint and Cognate Studies (IOSCS). http://ccat.sas.upenn.edu/ioscs. In addition to information about the IOSCS, this website includes authoritative discussions of topics such as modern editions of the LXX and links to other resources, many of which contain bibliographies.

Metzger, Bruce M. *The Bible in Translation: Ancient and English Versions.* Grand Rapids, Mich.: Baker, 2001. The first half of this book contains succinct and authoritative discussions of the ancient versions mentioned in this article, among others. Metzger's breadth and depth of knowledge were unsurpassed.

Muraoka, Takamitsu. *A Greek-English Lexicon of the Septuagint.* Leuven, Netherlands: Peeters, 2009. This lexicon has received very favorable reviews. In addition to translating the Greek, Muraoka also provides examples and contexts for words with several connotations. Meanings are derived from contemporary and earlier Greek usage without recourse to the underlying Hebrew.

Shutt, R. J. H. "Letter of Aristeas, A New Translation and Introduction." In *The Old Testament Pseudepigrapha*, Vol. 2, edited by James H. Charlesworth, 7–34. Garden City, N.J.: Doubleday, 1985. This constitutes the most recent English-language translation of, and commentary on, the *Letter of Aristeas.*

Leonard Greenspoon

Modern Versions

Translating the Bible is as old as the Bible itself, or one might argue even older, if we consider the process of writing down the oral traditions as "translation." This article addresses modern Bible translations and translation techniques, and discusses three clusters of translations: the translations that are connected to the missions and colonizations of non-Western countries; contemporary translations and secularism; and translations into non-written media. While the first cluster engages translations into several non-Western languages, the second cluster focuses precisely on translations into Western languages. The third cluster is what George Aichele calls an "intermedial translation," that is, translations from one medium (writing) into another (images) (2001, p. 63). What is important is to remember that translating the Bible is *never* only about representing a text in a different language. Missionary activity has made that abundantly clear. Bible translations are a powerful tool and function on the surface to make the biblical message accessible in a given language at a given time, but also to write that time and place *into* the Bible. These aspects are two sides of the same coin, and both will be given attention in the following article. But first some comments on translation techniques.

Translation Techniques: "Dynamic Equivalence" and "Literal Translation." Which is the more important: the source language or the target language? Should translators focus on following the source language and make the reader work hard to understand the text, or should the translator present a smooth text, which does not look like a translation? Should the translation be visible or invisible? These questions have framed the debates over Bible translations for centuries, beginning with Martin Luther and his translation of the Bible into German, creating, as it were, a new Bible and a new national language. Luther's objective was, on the one hand, to undermine the Catholic Church's scriptural authority and practice, which had been closely tied to the Vulgate and its interpretive tradition. At the same time, he also attempted to minimize the role of the Jewish and rabbinical traditions, which had influenced translations of the Hebrew Bible for centuries (Seidman 2006, p. 119). In her study on the politics of translation, Naomi Seidman emphasizes how Luther produced "a Bible in which God speaks, without impediment, not only to the German folk but even, as it were, as a German" (p. 129). According to Seidman, this endeavour places Luther and his orientation toward the reader in a straight line with Eugene Nida, the man behind the translation technique called "dynamic equivalence," or "meaning-based translation," which aims to reproduce the content of the biblical text rather than "merely" its linguistic form. Dynamic equivalence has become the translation technique of various Bible societies in both missionary and domestic settings, and is connected not only with the Summer Institute of Linguistics, but also the American Bible Society and its Nida Institute for Biblical Scholarship. The focus on content with the dynamic equivalent approach brings out the meaning of the text. This is presented as different from previous approaches, which sought to reproduce "stylistic specialities," taking delight in reproducing "rhythms, rhymes, plays on words, chiasmus, parallelism, and unusual grammatical structures" (Nida and Taber 1969, p. 1). For Nida and Taber, style should take second place to meaning (p. 12), a notion that positions them as the true harbingers of evangelization since they, contrary to earlier translators, focus on the receptor or target of the message and allow for changing the form if this is necessary to convey the content "properly." Seidman and Boer both emphasize the evangelical aims that are grounded in a scientific apparatus, namely linguistic theory. For Seidman, this is precisely what connects Nida and Luther, in that both regard the transparency of the word as the prerequisite for the dissemination of the Word, while presenting themselves as culturally and linguistically neutral (Seidman, p. 129). But this connection between Luther and Nida also points to the fact that Nida's approach is not new, but rather is a rehashing of an old debate (Boer, forthcoming). As Boer notes in his analysis of translation theory, not only does Nida's approach generate an opposition between dynamic equivalence and formal correspondence, it also quickly achieved hegemonic status within translation studies by firmly "othering" formal correspondence and presenting itself as something completely new (Boer, forthcoming). By lumping together anything that is not dynamic equivalence under the label "formal correspondence," Nida thus obliterates important differences between various methods and presents a caricature of translation approaches, ignoring theological, philosophical, and cultural differences in these approaches.

As Luther's goal of translating for the mother in her house, the children in the street, and the ordinary man in the market makes clear, the framing of the debate as between an inadequate formalistic approach and a fresh appreciation of the Bible's content is not new. A couple of centuries later, Schleiermacher noted that "Either the translator leaves the writer alone as much as possible and moves the reader towards the writer, or he leaves the reader alone as much as possible and moves the writer towards the reader" (quoted in Seidman, p. 118). Here too we see a polarization, which frames the debate in a similar way with a stark either-or position.

If we turn to the Jewish tradition, from Moses Mendelsohn in the eighteenth century to Walter Benjamin, Franz Rosenzweig, and Martin Buber in the early twentieth century, we find them advocating for a position in between the bifurcation of form and content. This was a way of addressing the German-Jewish identity issues of the time by negotiating cultural hybridity through theories of translation. Thus Rosenzweig, writing in 1926, argues that "it is impossible to transmit the content without at the same time transmitting the form. How something is said is not peripheral to what is said" (quoted in Hughes, p. 24). Importantly, this particular strain of translation theory and its equal emphasis on form and content is tied to Hebrew, the language of the Hebrew Bible, from which Jewish thought cannot be separated. For Luther, however, the Old Testament was dependent on the New Testament for its true meaning, and he took decisive steps to separate Hebrew studies from Jewish tradition, steps that in time led to the source criticism of the Enlightenment (Seidman, pp. 121, 160). Such an approach places an emphasis on language as an instrument or a vehicle for the message, which would become important for translations of the Bible, in particular the Old Testament, since Hebrew was the language whose alterity needed to be domesticated and christianized. Framing the discussion as a primary focus on *either* form *or* content, such as Luther, Schleiermacher, and Nida do, is to frame the discussion on Protestant-Evangelical terms so as to exclude any "middle ground," which the Jewish translators actually sought to occupy.

The relations between power, scripture, translation, and exegesis are also significant components in Jonathan Sheehan's analysis of the Bible's transition from being a theological document of the Reformation to becoming a cultural phenomenon in the Enlightenment. Sheehan highlights the proliferation of Bible translations in the sixteenth century and the stagnation of translations in the following century. He explains this circumstance through a two-stage model in which the first stage was the wresting of the Bible from the Catholic scriptural tradition, and then the consolidation of a new tradition that was, according to its advocates, in complete accordance with the original text (Sheehan 2005, p. 17). Thus the many translations produced in the century after the Reformation served to reveal how the Bible had been used to undergird human interests and how, by destabilizing Catholic scriptural tradition, the Catholic Church could be attacked. This process was set in motion by a mixture of exegesis, princely power, and the invocation of a divine authority, but it also needed closure as well as consolidation through sanctification by the Protestant churches. This was achieved in the second stage by a separation of exegetical research and Bible translations and a growth in biblical research, which glorified the text in its original languages of Greek, Hebrew, and Aramaic.

Missions and Translations. The various Bible translations produced in the century after the Reformation had a profound influence on the various languages of the Protestant countries, such as the King James Version (KJV) for English and Luther's Bible for German. Once these Bibles were firmly in place they functioned as originals after which other translations would be carried out, thus creating a hierarchy of translations in varying distance from the "original" version. For instance, Luther's German translation was the basis for the Danish translation of 1550; the Danish Bible, in turn, became the basis for the translation of the Greenlandic Bible, from its first translation of the New Testament in 1766 to the most recent translation of the whole Bible in 2000.

The role of translations in indigenous societies under colonialism is complex and multifaceted. In Greenland, for example, the transformation of Greenlandic into a written language meant that for indigenous writers the written language could function as a mode of expression, resistance, and community beyond the initial intentions of the colonizers. This has resulted in an exquisite and extensive literary tradition in Greenlandic, a language that is still way beyond the grasp of most Danes, and thus it also functions as resistance against Danish linguistic hegemony. The ongoing argument between Chinua Achebe and Ngugi Wa Thiong'o over whether to write in English or Kikuyu would also be inconceivable without the missionary activity in colonial Kenya, where Kikuyu became a written language in the early twentieth century. Thus Thiong'o's decision to write only in Kikuyu and Kiswahili in the statement that prefaces *Decolonising the Mind* is possible because the English missionaries created Kikuyu and Kiswahili as written languages in the first place. In Australia, the indigenous language Awabakal, one of the 600 languages that have died out since the conquest in the eighteenth century, is now in the process of being resurrected on the basis of the Congregational missionary Lancelot Threlkeld's translation of a couple of New Testament texts and the grammatical studies he produced (see Boer 2008, pp. 151–156). As studies by Vicente Rafael and Roland Boer show, the translations of religious texts carried out by the missionaries into various vernaculars, as well as their reception in the local cultures, are crucial for assessing ambivalence, domination, and subversive practice in a colonial context (Boer 2008; Rafael 1993).

However, other studies emphasizing the darker side of translation and colonialism argue that the practice of translating into vernaculars also provides the missionaries with valuable and powerful tools of denigration and subjugation of the indigenous culture and elevation of the colonizer's culture (Dube 1999; Rafael 1993). A feature of earlier Bible translations was a reluctance to use an indigenous word to refer to God since this would question the radical alterity of Christianity. As Assmann notes in a different context, "If one religion is wrong and the other is right, there can be no question of translating the gods of one into those of the other. Obviously they are about different gods" (Assmann 1996, p. 31). In Greenland, the Danish word for God, *Gud*, was inserted into the text as a self-evident signifier for God, as was the case in the Philippines, where the Castillian term *Dios* was used instead of a Tagalog term.

God's untranslatability is thus fixed within a presupposition that Danish (and Castillian) culture is different, superior, and closer to "the truth" than Greenlandic (and Tagalog) culture. The terms in which Greenlandic shamanic practice and its spiritual world were expressed could not, and more importantly *should not*, in any way articulate the Christian or Danish God, and so Danish words must be imported to designate this. This importation of central concepts into Greenlandic in turn conferred an authoritative status to the Danish language and, by extension, Danish theology and their ability to express truth.

There was a way, however, that the Greenlandic religious words could signify theological terms within this hierarchy of language and culture. From the very beginning the relationship between the missionaries and the local religious elite was at best antagonistic. The missionaries immediately attacked the practices of the shamans, who played a significant role in the societal structure. Hans Egede aggressively incorporated the world of the shamans into the Christian worldview by using the term for the central guiding spirit of the shaman, the *Toornarsuuk*, to translate the devil (Kleivan 1979, p. 176). The shamans themselves were known as witch masters (*hexe-mestre*) within Egede's terminology. In the preface to his New Testament translation, Paul Egede mentions that if Christ had been born in Greenland, his opponents would not have been Pharisees and Sadducees, but *hexe-mestre*. Thus the

Egede missionaries recast the struggles between themselves and the shamans into a cosmic tale of good and evil, with the Greenlandic cosmology placed on line with the devil and printed in the Bible. Within colonial contexts, this is not an unknown procedure. Turning to the African continent, biblical scholar Musa Dube and anthropologists John and Jean Comaroff have shown that the same practice occurred in the Moffat translation of the Bible into Setswana in 1857, some 89 years after Paul Egede's translation. Moffat translated the demons from Matthew into *Badimo*, which means ancestors but, as the Comaroffs note, signifies "an entire cultural order in which the dead had and still have, a hallowed place" (Comaroff and Comaroff 1991, p. 218,).

In her study on translation, history, and colonialism, Tejaswini Niranjana bemoans the lack of awareness of "the constructed nature of cultural translations" in that "translation is always *producing* rather than merely reflecting or imitating an 'original'" (Niranjana 1992, p. 81; emphasis in original). Niranjana's discussions pertain primarily to translations into English, but her point is worth exploring in the present context.

On the one hand we have the text itself, in this case the Bible, which is produced in a different context far away from its point of origin. It is produced through the Greenlandic language, with Greenlandic culturally specific terms employed to convey its message. On the other hand we have the Greenlandic language, which not only is written down and shaped to conform to the message it is intended to convey, but also new words and concepts are introduced into it that initially would present themselves as "opaque signifiers with no prior signifieds" (Rafael 1993, p. 117).

The first transformation—that of the Bible—is largely the focus of studies that seek to emphasize the indigenous appropriation of the Bible and Christianity, as well as the subversive potential of such an appropriation. The second transformation—that of the language—is, conversely, an indication of the extent of colonial violence and intrusion into the very means of communication and social coherence. As mentioned earlier, Greenlanders made good use of the written language and the new means of communication and abstraction this offered. Yet, the translations and their grasp (in every sense of the word) of the language provided means of reaching into the everyday lives of indigenous people. Luther's aim with vernacular Bible translations was precisely to use the language of everyday people, or, as he put it, the language spoken by the man on the field and the woman in the kitchen(!), and thus to penetrate all levels of society. Thus the *means* of communication are reconstructed according to European standards so that a process that generates a social disruption resets the parameters of Greenlandic social action. This then also provides a role for a translator into which indigenous people with double language skills could step. Venuti, while interested in the operation of translation and the invisibility of the translator, nevertheless follows this logic in that he is uninterested in the concrete figure of the translator (Seidman, p. 127). This is an important matter in the colonial context, since the indigenous people helping the missionaries would either come from or achieve a privileged position within the colonial hierarchies, thus causing yet another disruption to indigenous societies and their internal dynamics.

Herein lies the complexity of translation and colonialism. A final point concerns the relationship between scientific study of language and missionary activity. The various missionaries from different colonial settings were, as indicated earlier with Threlkeld, also precursors to linguistics and anthropology. Most missionaries compiled dictionaries or lexica and grammars in the service of translating the Bible. These linguistic tools were of great use in serving colonial centers such as churches, schools, and businesses, which were in competition with local institutions (Dube 1999, p. 45).

Modern Translations and Secularism. In 2007 the Danish Bible Society published a new translation of the New Testament into contemporary Danish. The translation was named "The New Deal" and had as its inspiration The Good News Bible from 1966 and the German version *Gute Nachtricht Bibel* of 1982.

Not only are these translations ecumenical, with translators from various denominations, but they also use inclusive language and, needless to say, dynamic equivalence techniques. Furthermore they use language that addresses people who are not used to "church language." The target group was that segment of the population not familiar with the Bible and church as common points of reference. The basic idea was to give them a Bible they could read on the train, and the aim was to use the language of everyday people. This marketing strategy of focusing on the language encourages people to see the Bible as everyday literature, distinguished from the incomprehensible and lofty church Bible, which is a way of compartmentalizing and setting at a distance institutional Christianity while drawing out and focusing on the cultural influence of the Bible.

These Bibles, to which we may add the *New Living Translation*, are targeted at "ordinary" people and are thus attempts to reach groups who would normally not pick up a Bible. But they also seem to aim at dominating the public sphere, which in most cases in today's globalized world also includes non-Christian populations. While this aggressive evangelization may be a way of selling more Bibles, it could also be a way of resurrecting a dormant Christian cultural consciousness within secular and multireligious societies. This could also be seen as a feature of the intermedial translations to which we now turn.

Intermedial Translations. One of the most significant modes of intermedial translation is, without doubt, the cinematic. Since the beginning of the twentieth century various stories from the Bible have been interpreted on the screen. While Jesus films are the most popular, some of the narratives from the Hebrew Bible have also been reproduced a number of times, especially Samson and Delilah, Moses and the Ten Commandments, and King David. These translations stretch back into the late nineteenth century, beginning with Léar's (alias Albert Kirchner) *La Passion*, from 1987 (Campbell 1981, p. 73).

In recent years translations have extended into other media. Most well-known is probably the Manga Bible series published by Next from 2007–2011 (http://nextmanga.com/). The five volumes are (in order of publication) *Manga Messiah* and *Manga Metamorphosis*, both told by Kozumi Shinozawa, and *Manga Mutiny*, *Manga Melech*, and *Manga Messengers*, told by Ryo Azumi. All five volumes translate parts of the Bible into the characteristic Japanese cartoon, manga. While *Mutiny* covers the creation narrative, *Melech* retells the story from the desert wanderings to the time of Saul, and *Messengers* describes the period of the kings and prophets of Israel. *Messiah* tells the story of the unknown king Yeshua, and *Metamorphosis* recounts that of Yeshua's followers and their challenges. Criticisms of the series include allegations of anti-Semitism in the portrayal of the Jews, especially in the *Manga Messiah.* In spite of this, the books have become a huge commercial success, and they have been distributed by Bible societies from Finland to the Philippines, using where possible the colloquial translations mentioned earlier.

Another example of intermedial translation is a work titled *Bible Illuminated: The Book*, a project originating in Sweden that was taken up by the American Bible Society. It is comprised of two volumes, one for each Testament. The New Testament volume of *Bible Illuminated*, like its Old Testament counterpart, is presented in a glossy magazine format. The Bible message is accompanied by a host of images and photographs from popular culture (e.g., the Dalai Lama, Princess Diana, and Bono), as well as pictures related to various political and social issues (the Middle East, abortion, the suffragette movement, responsible consumption, and the environment). The explicit motivation is to reach people who normally would not pick up a Bible by combining a more contemporary format with the New Living Translation. The strategy appears to be working—the publisher's home page mentions that Bible sales in Sweden have increased by 50 percent since the *Bible Illuminated* project was launched (http://bibleilluminated.com/aboutwithimage.aspx?page=199).

What these intermedial translations demonstrate is how culturally contingent the biblical text is, especially when it is communicated in a different medium. Western print culture domesticated the Bible a long time ago, and people have become accustomed to reading and hearing the text in their own languages, many of which the early modern Bible translations helped to shape (see Sheehan). But these new ways of presenting the Bible raise some important and provocative questions. While intermedial translations continue to make the Bible accessible in the vernacular, the way they do so can have significant social and political implications. In the case of the *Bible Illuminated* project, it could be argued that the Bible has been co-opted as a tool in capitalist liberal discourse by highlighting issues like environmentalism, poverty, fair trade, and human rights that are directed at a predominantly white middle class.

The Socioeconomic Context of Translation. In the afterword to his *The Bible and Empire: Postcolonial Explorations*, Sugirtharajah notes a host of other translations of the Bible: *The Green Bible, The Gay and Lesbian Bible, The Amplified Bible, New American Bible, Youth Bible, The Bible in Cockney*, and a *People's Bible*. He also points to niche Bibles, namely the *Canongate Bible, The Scroll: The Tabloid Bible, The Street Bible*, and *Revolve: the Teenage Bible* (also a magazine format) (Sugirtharajah 2005, pp. 229–230). To this might be added the *Princess Bible*, a pink devotional Bible aimed at pre-teen girls. This is, according to Sugirtharajah, a lamentable situation, a marketization of the Bible that commodifies the "Holy Writ" (p. 230).

In the current phase of capitalism, with its fragmenting of identities, this should hardly come as a surprise. As history demonstrates, the Bible can and will support the worldview into which it is translated. If the emphasis is on the meaning of the text, then that meaning will inevitably be shaped by the present economic and social context. This becomes clear if one considers the translation of certain texts, like 1 Kings 10:28–29. In the meaning-based translation of the New International Version (2005), the passage reads: "Solomon's horses were *imported from* Egypt and from Kue—the royal merchants purchased them from Kue *at the current price*. They *imported* a chariot from Egypt for six hundred shekels of silver, and a horse for a hundred and fifty. They also *exported* them to all the kings of the Hittites and of the Arameans."

Such a translation introduces into the text explicit capitalist terminology even though it was written within a different economic system. Not only does this mean that the text is domesticated, but also that capitalism is read into an ancient Near Eastern setting. In this way, meaning-based translations can sometimes erase the distance between then and now, the ancient cultural context and a later one, thereby enculturating the Bible to a particular context, and neutralizing its challenges to contemporary society.

Lawrence Venuti addresses this issue with the distinction he draws between a *domesticating method and* a *foreignizing method* of translating. A domesticating method, which he considers to be ethnocentric in nature, reduces the foreign text to the target language and its cultural context. A foreignizing method, on the other hand, acknowledges the linguistic uniqueness and cultural difference of the foreign text. Venuti is an advocate of the foreignizing method, and he accuses Nida's approach of ethnocentric violence because it creates the illusion of transparency by masquerading as "true semantic equivalence when it in fact inscribes the foreign text with a partial interpretation, partial to English-language values, reducing if not simply excluding the very difference that translation is called on to convey" (Venuti 2008, p. 20).

A similar thing can be seen in translations that adopt inclusive language, which veils the gender bias of the New Testament. For example, the Greek word "brothers" in Paul's letters is sometimes translated either "brothers and sisters" (NIV) or "friends" (Good News). If the text is translated in all its bias, then gender-conscious scholars can problematize it and address the issue in relation to contemporary power structures. However, if the bias of the text is concealed, then the means for addressing the power structures in faith-based settings are diminished while the power structures remain in place.

Bible translations should always be sensitive to their historical and political contexts. If difference remains present in translations, as Venuti proposes, readers are better equipped to confront the ideologies of biblical texts and to recognize the agendas of their translations, social, theological and political.

[*See also* Postcolonial Biblical Interpretation.]

BIBLIOGRAPHY

Aichele, George. *The Control of Biblical Meaning: Canon as Semiotic Mechanism.* Harrisburg, Pa.: Trinity Press International, 2001.

Assmann, Jan. "Translating Gods: Religion as a Factor of Cultural (Un)translatability." In *The Translatability of Cultures: Figurations of the Space Between,* edited by S. Budick and W. Iser, 25–36. Stanford, Calif.: Stanford University Press, 1996.

Boer, Roland. "The Dynamic Equivalence Caper." In *Translation, Ideology & Culture, Semeia Studies,* edited by Scott Elliott and Roland Boer. Atlanta: Society of Biblical Literature, forthcoming.

Boer, Roland. *Last Stop before Antarctica. The Bible and Postcolonialism in Australia.* Semeia Studies 64, 2d ed. Atlanta: Society of Biblical Literature, 2008.

Campbell, Richard H., and Michael R. Pitts, *The Bible on Film: A Checklist 1897–1986,* Landham, Md.: Scarecrow Press, 1981.

Comaroff, Jean, and John Comaroff. *Of Revelation and Revolution.* Vol. 1, *Christianity, Colonialism and Consciousness in South Africa.* Chicago and London: University of Chicago Press, 1991.

Dube, Musa W. "Consuming a Colonial Cultural Bomb: Translating Badimo into 'Demons' in the Setswana Bible (Matthew 8.28–34; 15.22; 10.8)." *Journal for the Study of the New Testament* 21 (1999): 33–58.

Egede, Paul. *Testamente Nutak eller Det Nye Testamente oversat i det Grønlandske sprog, med Forklaringer, Paralleler og udförlige Summarier.* Kiøbenhavn: Trykt paa Missionens bekostning af Gerhard Giese Salikath, 1766.

Hughes, Aaron W. *The Invention of Jewish Identity: Bible, Philosophy, and the Art of Translation.* Bloomington: Indiana University Press, 2010.

Kleivan, Inge., 1979 Studier af ordforrådet i grønlandske bibeloversættelser. In *Eskimosprogenes vilkår i dag. Majoritetssprogs indvirkning på eskimoiske minoritetssprog.* Edited by B. Basse and K. Jensen, 173–186. Århus, Denmark: Arkona.

Manga Bible, http://www.bible.or.jp/e/manga.html

Metzger, Bruce. *The Bible in Translation. Ancient and English Versions.* Grand Rapids, Mich.: Baker Academic Press, 2001.

Nida, E. A., and C. R. Taber. *The Theory and Practice of Translation.* Leiden, Netherlands: Brill, 1969.

Niranjana, Tejaswini. *Siting Translation. History, Post-Structuralism, and the Colonial Context.* Berkeley: University of California Press, 1992.

Petterson, Christina. "Configuring the Language to Convert the People. Translating the Bible in Greenland." In *Translation, Ideology & Culture, Semeia Studies,* edited by Scott Elliott and Roland Boer. Atlanta: Society of Biblical Literature, forthcoming.

Rafael, Vicente L. *Contracting Colonialism. Translation and Christian Conversion in Tagalog Society under Early Spanish Rule.* Durham, N.C. and London: Duke University Press, 1988.

Seidman, Naomi. *Faithful Renderings: Jewish-Christian Difference and the Politics of Translation.* Afterlives of the Bible Series. Chicago: University of Chicago Press, 2006.

Sheehan, Jonathan. *The Enlightenment Bible. Translation, Scholarship, Culture.* Princeton, N.J. and Oxford: Princeton University Press, 2005.

Simon, Sherry. *Gender in Translation: Cultural Identity and the Politics of Transmission.* London: Routledge, 1996.

Sugirtharajah, R. S. *The Bible and Empire: Postcolonial Explorations.* Cambridge, UK: Cambridge University Press, 2005.

Venuti, Lawrence, *The Translator's Invisibility: A History of Translation.* London: Routledge, 2008.

Walsh, Richard. *Reading the Gospels in the Dark: Portrayals of Jesus in Film.* London: Continuum, 2003.

Christina Petterson

Trauma Theory

In the late 1990s and the early 2000s, Hebrew Bible scholarship refocused on the experience of exile, its effects on the community of Judeans who experienced it (538–332 B.C.E.), and the literature that the exilic community produced. Influenced by insights of psychological biblical criticism, poststructuralist and postmodern biblical interpretation, ideological criticism, and postcolonial theory, scholars began to look at products of the exilic period as survival or trauma literature. In the early twenty-first century, attention has moved beyond the obvious connections between trauma and survival in literature of the exile into other areas of the canon that either were produced in the aftermath of a traumatic event or include traumatic content. The use of trauma theory in the study of biblical texts does not constitute a method of interpretation but a perspective, which can be intertwined with other forms of biblical criticism, including historical, psychological, literary, postcolonial, and theological approaches, to name a few.

Trauma Theory's Roots in Psychology and Poststructuralist Theory. The study of trauma literature naturally begins with a basic knowledge of psychological trauma, posttraumatic stress disorder (PTSD), and the rifts that the traumatic experiences produce in the victim's psyche. Cathy Caruth defines trauma as "an overwhelming experience of sudden catastrophic events in which the response to the event occurs in the often delayed, uncontrolled repetitive appearance of hallucinations and other intrusive phenomena" (Caruth 1996, *Unclaimed Experience,* p. 11). Among the characteristics of trauma, Caruth registers often delayed responses to overwhelming events that can manifest in hallucinations, dreams, thoughts, or behaviors. There can also be a numbing of the victim's psyche that may begin either during or after the experience, or, conversely, an increased arousal to stimuli that recall the event (Caruth *Trauma*, 1995, p. 4). The external event so shapes the inner psyche of individuals and communities that the trauma begins to define the very nature and preoccupations of its victims. While many associate trauma with particular and limited moments in history, the effects of trauma can last for years and have far-reaching implications.

The occurrence of trauma places the victim into the precarious position of needing to testify to his own experience while never possessing adequate language for the task of such testimony. Shoshana Felman and Dori Laub lament the predicament that trauma survivors face when seeking to articulate their experience: "This imperative to tell and be heard can become itself an all-consuming life task. Yet no amount of telling seems ever to do justice to this inner compulsion" (Felman and Laub 1991, p. 78). This conundrum leads to a central concept in trauma theory—the question of how traumatic literature functions as *testimony* that bears witness to a crisis. Felman suggests that "texts that testify do not simply *report facts* but, in different ways, encounter—and make us encounter—*strangeness*" (Felman and Laub 1991, p. 7). Because the initial experience is missed, Felman proposes that texts that testify to trauma comprise fragments of memory that the victim cannot integrate into an existing frame of reference (Felman and Laub 1991, p. 5). Texts that testify to trauma perform the action of witnessing, which leads them to share certain characteristics. The encounter in some ways helps the community re-experience the event of their catastrophe (Felman and Laub 1991, p. 68), but, because the "missed" nature of the encounter, any representation of the event in art and literature exists in a world beyond analogy (Langer 1982, p. 25).

Terrence des Pres similarly suggests that language of survival cannot be embodied in the more currently acceptable "objective language" because recourse to this language would lead to "cynicism or despair." Nor can survivor language be characterized by a sense of linguistic play—such language would border on the hysterical. Des Pres articulates this problem of language in his research of Nazi concentration camps and ultimately decides that only one type of language suffices: "a kind of archaic, quasi-religious vocabulary . . . only language of ultimate concern can be adequate to facts such as these (des Pres 1980, p. vi). Characteristically, trauma literature includes heightened fissures in language, puns, wordplay, and multiple levels of meaning.

Because of the "missed" nature of the event and the iterative qualities of the memory, texts of trauma are typically repetitive. Moreover, the "missed" nature of the experience coupled with its overwhelming force propels the survivor of trauma into a tension between the imperative to tell and the impossibility of the telling. According to Dori Laub:

> There are never enough words or the right words, there is never enough time or the right time, and there is never enough listening or the right listening to articulate the story that cannot be fully captured in *thought, memory* and *speech.* (Felman and Laub 1991, p. 78)

Despite the impossibility of telling, Laub insists on the need to bear witness to and transmit even these narratives that defy articulation (Felman and Laub 1991, p. 85). In this way, the transmission of traumatic texts is "no longer straightforwardly referential." According to Caruth, this lack of referentiality does not eliminate history, but that those attending to trauma literature must permit "*history* to arise where *immediate understanding* may not" (Caruth 1996, p. 11). The history of trauma, in other words, does not deny access to history, but it prevents history from being lost in abstraction. Appealing to Paul de Man's essay, "The Resistance to Theory," Caruth suggests that the refusal to contain events in a straightforward system of reference "precisely registers, in language, the impact of an event" (Felman and Laub 1991, p. 74).

Kai Erikson widens the perspective on trauma by shifting the emphasis from individual to collective trauma. Traumatized communities are more than the sum of their parts; they are not merely a collection of traumatized individuals. Erikson applies the metaphor of the body to the community, suggesting that the "tissues of community" are equally vulnerable to traumatic rupture. Moreover, multiple occurrences of individual trauma can create a communal trauma "that is different from (and more than) the sum of the private wounds that make it up" (Erikson 1995, p. 185). This collective trauma constitutes "a blow to the basic tissues of social life that damages the bonds attaching people together and impairs the prevailing sense of communality." The community offers a cushion for the pain and serves as a repository for building traditions (Erikson 1995, pp. 187–188).

Just as the nature of traumatic testimony defies the systematization of straightforward reference, trauma literature itself seems to defy definition or categorization. The testimony in trauma literature transcends *genre* as different survivors of trauma bear witness to their particular experiences through various media, such as autobiography, novelized fiction, and poetry. One way of defining trauma literature derives from the language of trauma itself. A direct transliteration of the Greek word, "trauma" means a "wound" or a "hurt." In trauma theory, the initial trauma is the historical experience of the wound. While the initial experience is "missed," not fully integrated into the psyche of the victim, the experience perpetuates itself through recurrent manifestations of memory of the initial event. One way the survivor can testify to the experience is through literature—attempting to bear witness to the event through various literary forms. If trauma is the initial wounding experience, trauma literature could be considered the scar—the visible trace offered by the survivor that points in the direction of the initial experience.

Roots of Trauma Theory Interpretation in Psychological Biblical Criticism. With the advent and establishment of modern psychology in the late nineteenth and early twentieth centuries, biblical scholars increasingly experimented with psychoanalytic and diagnostic approaches to the biblical literature (Kille 2001), often beginning with the obviously strange activities of the Hebrew prophets. For example, Ezekiel's abnormalities in particular have long perplexed exegetes, and as far back as 1877 August Klostermann (1877) suggested that Ezekiel's oddities exhibited symptoms of catalepsy, a disorder characterized by muscular rigidity and a lack of response to external stimuli. Hermann Gunkel sought to understand the ecstatic experiences of the Hebrew prophets by their "external actions and *symptoms*" (Gunkel 1924, p. 356). Regarding the case of Ezekiel, Gunkel describes the exilic prophet's actions such as laying siege to a stone with the pot (Ezek 4:1) or baking a "nauseous cake" over human excrement (Ezek 4:9) as "purely convulsive" (Gunkel 1924). Edwin C. Broome suggested that Ezekiel's oddities were caused by acute paranoid schizophrenia and that, "like the writings of schizophrenics, the writings of Ezekiel are difficult to follow: rules of ordinary logic simply do not apply" (Broome 1946).

David Halperin revived interest in Ezekiel's supposed pathology in order to explain the book's harsh treatment of women. Halperin claims that Ezekiel suffered from a "dread and loathing of female sexuality" and that Ezekiel's "radical misogyny" harkens to devastating childhood experiences perpetrated by his parents (Halperin 1993). He also suggests that his psychoanalytic reading of Ezekiel provides a solution for the plethora of problematic and grotesque images in the book. David Jobling, however, questions Halperin's ability to provide a solution, suggesting that biblical scholars were so busy trying to diagnose a historical figure that they forgot to attend to the literary nature of the biblical texts. According to Jobling, biblical interpreters diagnose texts, they do not psychoanalyze persons (1995). Jobling's sentiments reflect an increasing influence of postmodern and poststructuralist literary theory on biblical studies. Almost simultaneously, poststructuralist thought was also influencing the developing field of trauma theory, and it would not be long before several scholars began looking to trauma theory as a perspectival aid in studying the same biblical texts that earlier forms of psychological biblical interpretation addressed.

Trauma and the Study of Exile.

Lamentations. A few scholars have worked on various exilic texts, most prominently on Lamentations, Jeremiah, and Ezekiel. In his study of Lamentations as survival literature, Tod Linafelt defines survival literature as "literature produced in the aftermath of a major catastrophe and its accompanying atrocities by survivors of that catastrophe" (Linafelt 2000, p. 18). While not relying on trauma theory per se, Linafelt's work on Lamentations as survival literature suggests a reading strategy for such works in light of survival literature from twentieth century C.E. atrocities, especially the Holocaust. Linafelt suggests that many Christian readers "survive" the book by overemphasizing the brief words of hope (Lam 3:21–22). Conversely, several Jewish interpreters have survived the book by valuing the lament language and squarely facing the questions of theodicy that the book poses. By focusing on the suffering Zion figure from chapters 1 and 2, Linafelt concludes that Lamentations is more concerned with the expression of suffering than it is about suffering's "meaning" (Linafelt 2000, p. 18). Linafelt's conclusion reflects a trauma theory perspective that sees the pursuit after meaning within acute suffering as absurd. Rather, a trauma theory reading fulfills an ethical imperative to allow for the expression of suffering when meaning is fleeting.

Jeremiah. Similarly, Kathleen O'Connor combines theological interpretation, biblical studies, and pastoral sensibilities, suggesting that trauma theory and disaster studies can open one's eyes to the "physical, spiritual, and psychological collapse that underlies the book of Jeremiah in the most visceral ways" (O'Connor 2011, p. 19). O'Connor addresses the varied genres of texts within Jeremiah from the perspective of testimony and healing. First, she reads the texts that describe "God's broken family" as a metaphorical account of the disaster of exile. Second, she analyzes the war poems in Jeremiah as testimony to the invasions and horrors of military assault. Third, she considers Jeremiah's lament poems as "instruments that encourage the expression of grief" (O'Connor 2011, p. 34). She then turns her attention to the character of Jeremiah as an exemplar for how to survive catastrophe, suggesting for example, that Jeremiah's captivity stories mirror the captivity of the community itself. Likewise, his escapes from captivity provide hope for the people's future liberation. Finally, she investigates Jeremiah's Deuteronomistic sermons and messages of comfort. O'Connor concludes by acknowledging the haphazard structure and mysteries of Jeremiah's composition. In her understanding of trauma and disaster studies, the shape (or lack thereof) of Jeremiah "reflects the massive disorder that produced the book in the first place. . . . [The book's] bewildering array of voices, themes, metaphors, genres, and its lack of narrative order suggest to me that similar interpretive dilemmas plagued the lives of its audience." (O'Connor 2011, pp. 126, 127)

Ezekiel. Ezekiel's abnormalities have led to a great number of psychological theories, some of which focus on the traumatic nature of the prophet's experience of exile. Derek M. Daschke attributed Ezekiel's strangeness to a form of posttraumatic stress disorder (PTSD). Daschke addresses the problems of Ezekiel's imagination in terms of Freud's work on melancholia (Daschke 1999, pp. 119–120). Although still attempting to diagnose the historical prophet, he moves in a more fruitful direction than

Halperin, focusing on the immediate events that gave rise to the written text—military and cultural defeat, the loss of the temple, and the displacement of exile—instead of reconstructed childhood trauma. Daniel L. Smith-Christopher has also read Ezekiel in light of PTSD and comparative refugee studies. Rather than search for childhood experience as the answer to Ezekiel's abnormalities, Smith-Christopher suggests that one examine the book in the context of sociopolitical events and consider the prophet's behavior in the light of the "actual traumatic circumstances" of the exile (Smith-Christopher, *Biblical Theology*, 2002, pp. 88–89). Gale Yee combines postcolonial thought and trauma theory in her analysis of Ezekiel's use of extremely graphic and sexual imagery in Ezekiel 23. The colonized community testifies to its traumatic experience by composing a text of emasculation or symbolic castration. For Yee, this interpretation contextualizes, while not condoning, the priestly elite male experience of colonization (Yee 2003, p. 133). In my work on Ezekiel, I suggest that the writer of the first twenty-four chapters of Ezekiel employed various forms of prophetic speech in attempts to testify to the overwhelming and inarticulable trauma of the destruction of Jerusalem, and especially the Temple (see Garber 2004; 2005). Brad Kelle identifies three major streams of inquiry into the book of Ezekiel: (1) the book's priestly theology, (2) trauma studies, and (3) ecological hermeneutics. Kelle concludes that Ezekiel uses the trope of Yahweh's destruction and rejuvenation of nature to testify to the experience of war as well as a priestly understanding of Yahweh's sovereignty. "By bringing the language of the devastation and rejuvenation of nature into line with the categories of the priestly tradition, Ezekiel offers a way to deal with the trauma of defeat and destruction experienced by the Judean community" (Kelle 2009, p. 490). Moreover, the same Yahweh who has the power to destroy creation can also re-create, opening up the narrative possibility of hope to the book's audience.

Other Hebrew Prophets. David Carr has posited a major gap in the biblical literature that purports to be from the exilic period. With the notable exceptions of Jeremiah and Ezekiel, Carr points out that no other biblical prophets confess to be active during the exilic period, the majority of scholars identifying large portions of Isaiah as exilic notwithstanding. This mirrors the lack of narrative material in the so-called historical books during the years from 586 B.C.E. to Cyrus's decree in 538 B.C.E. Carr reads this absence of material produced during the Exile as a hint toward the traumatic nature of the Exile itself, the in-between time of Judah's national story. Appealing to Caruth's (1995) understanding of trauma as a "speechless terror," Carr argues that these absences or gaps in the biblical record testify to the "incomprehensibility of pain—the difficulty or unwillingness of the exiles to speak and think directly about their experience of living in diaspora" (Carr 2011, p. 297). He suggests, instead, that the displacement of the Exile forced the Judeans to form a nationalistic identity that allowed them to process their past while looking forward to an eventual restoration. For example, while many hold that Deutero-Isaiah was composed during the Exile, the book never explicitly refers to the history of exile itself. Rather, it expounds on the national narratives of the distant past or the possibility of restoration in the future.

Trauma Beyond Exilic Literature. While literature written in direct response to the destruction of Jerusalem in 586 B.C.E. and the experience of exile that followed is an obvious starting point for the use of trauma theory for interpreting biblical texts, there are several other places in biblical literature where scholars and theologians are exploring its use.

Job. Samuel Balentine applies the study of trauma to the book of Job, a text that is notoriously difficult to date due to its lack of concrete historical references (Balentine 2008). Although the text itself never mentions the catastrophe of 586 B.C.E., Balentine suggests that Job's author(s) "engages with the same or at least a very similar set of issues" as the other poetic witnesses to the fall of Jerusalem (Jeremiah, Lamentations, Deutero-Isaiah, Ezekiel, and the Lament Psalms). Indeed, Balentine suggests that the poetic dialogues within the book of Job provide a microcosm of the conflicting testimonies to trauma found in Lamentations, Deutero-Isaiah,

Jeremiah, and Ezekiel, each of which provides a different answer to the "why" question of the exilic experience. For Balentine, though, Job presents the question of the theological meaning of trauma more acutely: "When texts lacquered with authority affirm that God executes and/or sanctions the loss of life, possessions, and property *both with and without cause*, what does this mean for those who must respond with real-time commitments?" (Balentine 2008, p. 217). In his reading of Job 2:3, Balentine emphasizes that God has afflicted Job "for no reason." In comparing the rationale for the suffering of Job in Job 2:3 ("for no reason") to the rationale for the suffering of the exilic community in Ezekiel 6:10 ("not for no reason"—Balentine's translation), Balentine suggests Job's "for no reason" could be a "traumatized concession" to the reality of unwarranted suffering. But, true to the contradictory nature of traumatic witness, Balentine also suggests that Job's "for no reason" clause is a "traumatizing assertion" that could be positive because it acknowledges the "'why me?' question that typically dogs the victim" of trauma (Balentine 2008, p. 223). Rather than search in vain for a perpetrator of the traumatic experience, this traumatizing assertion can free victims to jettison such a search in favor of treating the wound. While Balentine acknowledges the inadequacy of these two explanations to the "for no reason" clause in Job 2:3, he remains true to the paradox of trauma theory, ending his treatment of Job with an ellipsis that does not bring a satisfying closure to Job's woundedness, yet it opens up the interpretation of Job's conundrum to the process of further testimony and interpretation.

The Gospel of John. Shelley Rambo uses the insights from trauma theory in her theological reading of the Gospel of John's presentation of the middle day, the day between Christ's death and resurrection (John 19). Appealing to John's use of water throughout as a symbol of the Spirit—for example with Jesus's baptism (John 1) and Jesus's conversation with Nicodemus about birth (John 3:5)—Rambo suggests that Jesus's wound in John 19:33–34 contains the fluids of both death (blood) and life (water). Reading John in light of trauma theory, Rambo suggests that this "living wound" and the testimony to it in John 19:35 "provide a guiding image for exploring what it means to witness between passion and resurrection, death and life" (Rambo 2010, p. 82). John thus provides a testimonial backdrop against which witnesses wrestle with the meaning of life in the aftermath of death. Rambo focuses on two primary witnesses to Jesus's death, Mary Magdalene and the Beloved Disciple. Reading through the lens of trauma theory, Rambo suggests that the stories of Mary and the Beloved testify to the messiness and impossibility of envisioning life beyond the death of Christ. Rather than suggesting the traditional interpretation of the resurrection as life's victory over death, Rambo suggests that Mary's and the Beloved's testimony to the death event give a "persistent witness to love's survival," which finds its expression in John's theology of the Spirit (2010).

Paul. Sandra Hack Polaski (2008) explores the use of trauma theory in interpreting Paul's "thorn in the flesh" attested in 2 Corinthians 12:1–10. Polaski draws upon the notion of the impossibility of articulating a traumatic event to suggest that any narrative description or testimony to trauma would be imprecise and possibly even illogical. Instead of trying to discover the referent of Paul's "thorn," which has been the goal of many interpreters, Polaski suggests that understanding the thorn as a witness to Paul's unidentified and unidentifiable trauma may lead interpreters to consider the oft-neglected narrative context of this testimony. She suggests that Paul's combination of a physical description of his trauma—the thorn—with a spiritual one—the messenger of Satan—reflects the traumatic nature of his experience in two ways. First, Paul cannot definitively locate or describe the source of his trauma, and, second, the trauma permeates his entire being, both physical and spiritual. Moreover, reading the "thorn in the flesh" as testimony to trauma manifesting or recurring during a time in which Paul's authority is also being questioned (2 Cor 10–13) suggests that the experience of trauma never leaves the victim, but becomes a facet of the victim's personality in perpetuity, often manifesting due to other stressors. In Paul's witness to the thorn in his flesh, then, the apostle becomes an exemplar for others who must continue to live in the aftermath of traumatic experience.

Future Directions for Trauma Theory and Biblical Interpretation. As the preceding survey of uses of trauma theory attests, most explorations of trauma have centered on the experiences of exile or the events that led to the Exile. Relatively little work has been done to date on the impact of trauma beyond the first and second generation of exiles. What does it mean for the community of canonizers who lived in Judea after the Exile to continue to bear the mark of the traumatic memory of Jerusalem's destruction and their ancestral experience of exile? What does it mean for them that the restoration envisioned in some of the exilic and early postexilic prophetic work did not come to fruition in the magnificent manner that their forebears had suggested? How does the memory of their displacement, accompanied by their national narrative of monarchy before the Exile, impact the understandings of the majority of Jews in the Second Temple era who continued to pay subservience to Persian, Greek, and Roman authorities? Questions in this avenue could complement postcolonial readings and diaspora studies to explore postexilic and early New Testament texts. What traumas or traumatic memories might give rise to the literature shaped in this period leading up to the Maccabean revolt, the emergence of Christianity, or the destruction of the Second Temple in 70 C.E.? Such attention, for example, could shed light on how a trauma theory approach might benefit readings of apocalyptic works such as Daniel or postexilic nationalistic texts such as Esther (see, e.g., Smith-Christopher, "Reading War," 2011). How might one see the trend toward apocalyptic dualism, messianism, and eschatology in these later writings as a response to the trauma of the failure of nationalistic dreams of restoration in light of the continued colonization of Judea and its inhabitants? Certainly, much of the continued application of trauma theory in HB studies will also depend heavily on the interpreter's evaluation of when certain texts were produced and/or preserved and must be done in tandem with historical approaches in order to best reconstruct the possible events behind traumatic testimony.

From a purely literary perspective, however, there are clearly many texts within the Hebrew Bible (HB) that relay traumatic experiences: the cosmic flood of Genesis and the confusion of language at the tower of Babel; the near sacrifice of Isaac and the expulsion of Hagar and Ishmael; the rapes of Dinah, the Levite's Concubine, and Tamar; the genocide of Canaanites in the book of Joshua; the infanticide in the opening scenes of the Exodus material and Yahweh's final plague; the lament traditions in the Psalms as well as the many war narratives throughout Joshua, Judges, Samuel, and Kings, to name just a few. Likewise, the NT passion narratives, the tales of diseased persons seeking Christ's healing, stories of the struggles of early Christians in the book of Acts, and the persecution that lies behind the apocalyptic literature in Revelation could be explored as traumatic testimony.

Finally, the field of trauma studies is a rather new and constantly evolving field itself. Trauma studies in the academy at large have focused on modern experiences of individual or collective trauma such as Vietnam War memoirs, the experiences of survivors of Hiroshima and Nagasaki, the testimonies of Holocaust survivors, and other modern atrocities. While some trauma readings have delved into classical literature, the primary focus of trauma studies remains on these more modern events. Biblical scholars have an opportunity, then, to contribute greatly to understanding both how ancient victims testified to their traumatic experiences and how the texts that they produced have continued to be a resource for people throughout the ages who turn to these ancient texts in an effort to process their own experiences.

[*See also* Diaspora Studies; Literary Criticism, Literary Theory and the Bible; Postcolonial Biblical Interpretation; Poststructuralist Interpretation; Psychological Biblical Interpretation; *and* Theological Interpretation]

BIBLIOGRAPHY

Balentine, Samuel E. "Traumatizing Job." *Review and Expositor* 105, no. 5 (Spring 2008): 213–228.

Broome, E. "Ezekiel's Abnormal Personality." *Journal of Biblical Literature* 65 (1946): 277–292.

Carr, David M. "Reading into the Gap: Refractions of Trauma in Israelite Prophecy." In *Interpreting Exile: Displacement and Deportation in Biblical and Modern Contexts,* edited by Brad E. Kelle, Frank Ritchel Ames, and Jacob L. Wright, 309–322. Atlanta: Society of Biblical Literature, 2011.

Caruth, Cathy. *Unclaimed Experience: Trauma, Narrative, and History.* Baltimore: Johns Hopkins University Press, 1996.

Caruth, Cathy, ed. *Trauma: Explorations in Memory.* Baltimore: Johns Hopkins University Press, 1995.

Daschke, Dereck M. "Desolate Among Them: Loss, Fantasy, and Recovery in the Book of Ezekiel." *American Imago* 56 (1999): 119–120.

Des Pres, Terrence. *The Survivor: An Anatomy of Life in the Death Camps.* Oxford: Oxford University Press, 1980.

Erikson, Kai. "Notes on Trauma and Community." In *Trauma: Explorations in Memory,* edited by Cathy Caruth, 183–199. Baltimore: Johns Hopkins University Press, 1995.

Felman, Shoshana, and Dori Laub. *Testimony: Crises of Witnessing in Literature, Psychoanalysis, and History.* New York: Routledge, 1991.

Garber, David G., Jr. "Traumatizing Ezekiel: Psychoanalytic Approaches to the Biblical Prophet." In *Psychology and the Bible: A New Way to Read the Scriptures,* edited by J. Harold Ellens and Wayne G. Rollins, 215–235. Westport, Conn.: Praeger, 2004.

Garber, David G., Jr. "Trauma, History, and Survival in Ezekiel 1–24." PhD diss., Emory University, 2005.

Garber, David G., Jr. "A Vocabulary of Trauma in the Exilic Writings." In Kelle, Ames, and Wright, *Interpreting Exile,* 309–322. Atlanta: Society of Biblical Literature, 2011.

Gunkel, Hermann. "The Secret Experiences of the Prophets." *Expositor* 9, no. 1 (1924): 356–366, 427–433.

Gunkel, Hermann. "The Secret Experiences of the Prophets." *Expositor* 9, no. 2 (1924): 23–32.

Halperin, David J. *Seeking Ezekiel: Text and Psychology.* University Park: Pennsylvania State University Press, 1993.

Jobling, David. "Review of David J. Halperin, *Seeking Ezekiel: Text and Psychology.*" *Religion* 25 (1995): 392–394.

Kelle, Brad E. "Dealing with the Trauma of Defeat: The Rhetoric of the Devastation and Rejuvenation of Nature in Ezekiel." *Journal of Biblical Literature* 128 (2009): 469–490.

Kille, D. Andrew. *Psychological Biblical Criticism.* Guides to Biblical Scholarship. Minneapolis: Fortress, 2001.

Klostermann, August. "Ezechiel: Ein Beitrag zu besserer Würdigung seiner Person und seiner Schrift." *Theologische Studien und Kritiken* 50 (1877): 391–439.

Langer, Lawrence L. *Versions of Survival: The Holocaust and the Human Spirit.* SUNY Series in Modern Jewish Literature and Culture. Albany: State University of New York Press, 1982.

Linafelt, Tod. *Surviving Lamentations: Catastrophe, Lament, and Protest in the Afterlife of a Biblical Book.* Chicago: University of Chicago Press, 2000.

O'Connor, Kathleen. *Jeremiah: Pain and Promise.* Minneapolis: Fortress, 2011.

Polaski, Sandra Hack. "2 Corinthians 12:1–10: Paul's Trauma." *Review and Expositor* 105, no. 5 (Spring 2008): 279–285.

Rambo, Shelly. *Spirit and Trauma: A Theology of Remaining.* Louisville, Ky.: Westminster/John Knox Press, 2010.

Smith-Christopher, Daniel L. *A Biblical Theology of Exile.* Overtures to Biblical Theology. Minneapolis: Fortress, 2002.

Smith-Christopher, Daniel L. "Reading War and Trauma: Suggestions Toward a Social-Psychological Exegesis of Exile and War in Biblical Texts." In Kelle, Ames, and Wright, *Interpreting Exile,* 309–322. Atlanta: Society of Biblical Literature, 2011.

Yee, Gale A. *Poor Banished Children of Eve: Woman as Evil in the Hebrew Bible.* Minneapolis: Fortress, 2003.

David G. Garber, Jr.

U

Ugaritology and Biblical Interpretation

Right from its discovery in 1928, Ugarit (modern Ras Shamra, Syrian northern coast 35°35′ N, 35°45′ E) became an important context for the understanding of ancient Israel and the Hebrew Bible. Ugaritology itself is also an established research area in archeology, philology, linguistics, history, and religious studies in its broadest sense.

Ugarit and the Bible. The Ugaritic civilization reached its peak in the beginning of second half of the second millennium B.C.E. and became extinct following the city's destruction by the "people from the sea" by the end of the thirteenth century. Though it goes back several centuries before the beginning of Israel, Ugaritic civilization has a significant bearing on biblical interpretation. The richly documented entry on Ras Shamra in the *DBS* IX (1979: 1123–1446) gives a comprehensive picture of the diverse areas of Ugaritic studies such as archeology, history, the Sumero-Akkadian culture, the Hurrian milieu, and Ugaritic literature. Very useful is the synthesis on Ras Shamra and Old Testament by E. Jacob and H. Cazelles (pp. 1426–1439). Along these lines, the study by Loretz (1990) is also valuable for its accurate information and insights. The massive handbook of Ugaritic studies edited by Watson and Wyatt (1999) contains readable contributions covering various important sectors of this large field.

For biblical interpretation the epigraphic finds are the more relevant materials. The most important texts were discovered during the first couple of decades following the discovery of the site. They are written in cuneiform, both syllabic and alphabetic. The alphabetic cuneiform writing was used to write the local language, that is, Ugaritic, which is the oldest directly attested Northwest Semitic language. The content of the texts varies: literary (myth and legends), religious (rituals, lists of sacrifice, omina, curses), epistolary (letters), administrative (deeds), pedagogical (school exercises, abecedaries), and medical (texts to cure sick horses). The convenient edition of these texts is KTU/CAT. The texts written in syllabic cuneiform are mostly in Akkadian, the common language of the Ancient Near East of the period. These texts are letters, administrative documents, and a few literary compositions in the Mesopotamian literary tradition. There are also lexical texts with Sumerian, Akkadian, Hurrian, and their Ugaritic equivalent. On the special importance of these texts for the understanding of Ugaritic, see Huehnergard (2008).

Four periods of Bible and Ugaritic studies can be distinguished according to the scholarly achievements in both fields (Smith 2001a). In the first period, that is, 1928–1945, scholars concentrated on decipherment, textual editions, and the possible significance of Ugaritic for biblical studies. It was in the second period, that is, 1945–1970, that the real impact of Ugaritic on biblical studies first began to be felt, especially in the United States, with William Foxwell Albright at the Johns Hopkins University as one of its most important figures. Ugaritic started to be taken into account in Hebrew grammars such as Meyer (1969, 1996). Gordon's classic grammar of Ugaritic (1965) reached its definitive shape in this period, after going through different forms since 1940.

The influence of Ugaritic studies on biblical studies became solidly established in the third period, that is, 1970–1985. The multi-authored three-volume work edited by Fisher (Vol. 1: 1971; Vol. 2: 1975; Vol. 3, by Rummel 1981) gathered parallels from Ras Shamra with the Hebrew Bible. Work on Ugaritic lexicography is reflected in the standard Hebrew dictionary *HALAT/HALOT*. Many of the Old Testament commentaries in the Anchor Bible series also made extensive use of Ugaritic, especially Dahood's three-volume treatment of the Psalms (Vol. 1: 1965; Vol. 2: 1968; Vol. 3: 1970; the final volume includes a grammar of the Psalter from the Ugaritic-Hebrew perspective, pp. 361–456). Dahood frequently offered fresh readings of the Hebrew consonantal text, re-dividing words and re-vocalizing them on the basis of his understanding of Ugaritic. A brief but representative sample of his approach can be seen in his treatment of Job 3 (1974); Barr's response to it (1974) is equally representative of the scholarly critical reaction.

During this third period, with the discoveries of new texts, Ugaritological studies proper also made progress. Materials other than myths and legends were studied in more depth, bringing new understanding of Ugaritic civilization itself. This development ushered in a cautious and sometimes critical attitude toward comparison between Ugaritic studies and biblical scholarship.

In the fourth period, that is, 1985–1999, scholars became more interested in refining the tools and theory for the study of Ugaritic itself. There was a growing tendency to revisit studies by the earlier generation. A generally positive and sobering assessment of Dahood's contributions in Hebrew studies was published by Althann (1997). During this period the first complete dictionary of the Ugaritic language was published (Olmo Lete—Sanmartín, 1996–2000; Eng. trans., 2003). Knowledge of the language has also been refined and reflected in new grammars such as Segert (1984), Sivan (1997), and Tropper (2000). Progress along these lines continues to improve and advance.

Further development in the first decade of the twenty-first century still awaits assessment. There is already a tendency to study social institutions and economic life at Ugarit itself, as illustrated in the well-documented works by Zamora (2000) on socio-economic aspects of viticulture and wine making, and Marsman (2003) on the role of women at Ugarit. Advanced knowledge of the Ugaritic language has also become more widespread thanks to new teaching grammars, especially those of Tropper (2002) and Bordreuil and Pardee (2009); the latter makes available texts in excellent copies and photographs. Smith (2004, with ongoing updates) is an online bibliography on Ugaritic and Hebrew grammar.

What follows is an outline of the bearing of Ugarit studies for biblical interpretation under the headings of language and literary texts.

Language. Ugaritic belongs to the second millennium B.C.E. Northwest Semitic languages together with the indirectly documented languages in Syria-Palestine of the same period. Gianto (2012) provides a sketch of Ugaritic, demonstrating its interrelationship with the other regional languages. For study of Ugaritic, the exhaustive reference grammar is Tropper (2000); see its review by Pardee 2003/2004. The Northwestern Semitic language group eventually split into the Aramaic and the Canaanite languages during the first millennium B.C.E. Belonging to the latter are Phoenician, Hebrew, and some lesser-attested Transjordanian dialects like Moabite, Edomite, and the dialect found in the Deir Alla inscription. This situation represents a dialect continuum from the earlier period down to the latter period and gives ground for the use of Ugaritic in Hebrew studies.

Linguistic Affinity. The affinity among the languages varies. Some verbs of movement indicate that Ugaritic is closer to Phoenician and Hebrew than Aramaic. Thus while the first three all have *hlk* ("to go"), *yrd* ("to do down"), *ʿly* ("to go up"), *yṣʾ* ("to go out"), and *ṯwb* (or *šwb*) ("to go back"), Aramaic uses other roots for the same movements, namely *ʾzl, nḥt, slq, npq, hpk*. There is also a graded affinity between Ugaritic-Phoenician-Hebrew: in the first two "to give" and "to be" are expressed by *ytn* and *kwn*, in contrast to Hebrew *ntn* and *hyy*. The most common word for "to do" in Ugaritic is *ʿdb*, while Phoenician prefers *pʿl* and Hebrew *ʿśy*. Many words are etymologically the same in these languages, but their value is not always the same. Grammatical features shared in Northwest Semitic languages also exhibit such graded affinities. It is true that grammatically Ugaritic and Hebrew are generally closer to each other than each is to other Northwest Semitic languages. Therefore, on the basis of these shared features and genetic similarities, there is some justification in using Ugaritic to elucidate Hebrew.

Several linguistic features of Ugaritic help to clarify certain problems in Hebrew grammar. The traditional "*he*-locale" in Hebrew can no longer be considered as a remnant of the accusative case ending since the ending is the same as the Ugaritic directional *-h*.

The narrative use of *yqtl* in Ugaritic, referring to past events, corresponds to the use of the Hebrew *yiqtol* with past reference in archaic poetry and in the Hebrew narrative (*way*)*yiqtol*.

It is in the realm of particles that comparison with Ugaritic has stimulated new proposals for the understanding of Hebrew. A number of instances of the Hebrew prepositions *k-* and *l-* have been understood as the vocative "O!" following Ugaritic usage, though this is somewhat controversial; for a discussion on this topic, see Althann (1997, p. 93–120). Various Ugaritic enclitic particles *-m*; *-y*; *-k*; *-t*, which are found with any word, have been used to explain problematic constructions in Hebrew, especially where these consonants occur with a construct noun before its genitive. By rule, nothing other than these particles can stand between the nouns. In Hebrew these have been interpreted as other elements like the masculine plural ending, first/second person singular possessive suffix, or even preposition *k*, feminine ending.

Stylistic Affinity. The largest corpus of Ugaritic texts with continuous content consists of poetry. The basic unit of Ugaritic poetry is a two-line poetic structure, the "bicolon"; each is said to be in parallelism with the other. This is applicable to Hebrew poetry. A bicolon can be expanded with a third colon, resulting in a tricolon. These units can combine among themselves to build larger structures analogous to strophes or stanzas. In Ugaritic the bicolon or tricolon are generally of equal length, which is reflected in earlier Hebrew poetry; later Hebrew poetry also exhibits unequal length. The poetic structure lies not so much in the meter or rhythm, but in the semantic parallelism of the lexical and syntactical expressions within the bi- or tricolon. For a still useful outline, see Gordon (1965, par 13.108–170); for the features found in Hebrew, see Watson (1986: 114–200).

An example of a bicolon is KTU 1.14 I:26–27, *yʿrb . bḥdrh . ybky* || *bṯn . ʿgmm . wydmʿ* ["He (Kirta) went into his chamber crying, into the inner room and weeping"]. The parallelism can be described as a b c || b′ c′. The parallelism is incomplete since there is no parallel to *ʿrb* ["he went into"]. Yet the absent parallel expression is syntactically significant and can be described as an ellipsis or gap that creates a special effect. Thus, while the event narrated in the first part, that is, Kirta's entering his chamber, continues to be true in the second part, attention now shifts to the inner part of the room (*ṯn . ʿgmm*), and is no longer on Kirta's movement as such. The more specific word or expression in the second part is sometimes longer than its parallel, e.g., *bṯn . ʿgmm* vs. *bḥdrh*. The longer expressions often occur when there is gapping and serve as "ballast variants" to compensate for the omitted expression.

There is a bicolon in 1 Samuel 18:7b (*ḥikkâ šāʾûl baʾălāpāw* || *wədāwid bəribəbōtāw* ["Saul killed by the thousand || but David by the myriad"]) that also exhibits the a b c || b′ c′ structure. Like the Ugaritic example, there is no parallel to the verb *ḥikkâ* in the second part of the bicolon. This gapping draws the attention to the change of actor, that is, from Saul to David. The use of the word-pair "thousand"—"myriad" also enhances the contrast.

A bicolon, as noted above, can be expanded with a third colon, resulting in a tricolon, as in KTU 1.14 I:28–30: *tnkn . udmʿth* || *km . ṯqlm . arṣh* || *km ḫmšt mṯth* ["His tears were pouring || like shekels to the ground, like five weights onto the couch"]. The parallelism can be described as exhibiting the structure a b || c d || c′ d′, where the first is completed by the second, which is then expanded with a third line that intensifies the second. Compare this with the similar structure in Songs 1:16–17: *ʾap-ʿaršēnu raʿănānâ* || *qōrōt battênû ʾărāzîm* || *raḥîṭēnû bərôtîm* ["Our couch is luxuriant || the beams of our house are cedars || our rafters are cypresses"]. Note also that the third line in both examples contains words that are more specific than their pair in the second line.

Literary Texts. These texts contain passages that reveal the world of Ugaritic deities and their dealings with humankind, just like in the sacred literature of Ancient Israel. A closer look at the divine epithets and the literary traditions suggests that the two literatures share the same background.

Divine Epithets. The idea that Ugaritic religious thought provides a matrix to the sacred literature of Ancient Israel has become established since the publication of Cross's collection of essays, *Canaanite Myth and Hebrew Epic* (1973). His insights are echoed in Smith (2001b, 2002; for more recent trends, see Smith 2007).

The comparative discussions generally concentrate on the deities and their roles. Many of the deities at Ugarit are, in fact, found in the Bible under quite different forms. This is evident from the Biblical imagery of Yahweh "the LORD," which in a number of ways shares the metaphors and symbols of El, the supreme god of the Ugaritic religion. At a very early stage in the development of Israelite religion, El was assimilated to Yahweh. The God of the Patriarchs is basically El, as evident from the names such as El-Elyon (Gen 14:18), El-Olam (Gen 21:33), and El-Bethel (Gen 31:13). Exodus 6:2–3 states that Yahweh is the same as the El known to the patriarchs with the name of El-Shaddai ("The Most High"). Some epithets of El as found in Ugaritic texts are also applied to Yahweh. Thus El is said to be "eternal king" (KTU 1.108), just like Yahweh who lives forever (Ps 102:27; Job 36:26; Isa 40:28; Hab 3:6; Dan 6:27). El presides over the assembly of gods (KTU 1.2.1), as does Yahweh (Isa 6:1–8; 1 Kgs 22:9; Ps 29:1–2; 82:1; 89:5–8; Isa 14:13; Jer 23:18, 22; Dan 3:25). El is often mentioned as being gracious and the father of humanity, and these traits correspond to Yahweh being merciful and gracious (Exod 34:6; Ps 86:15), the Father (Deut 32:6: Isa 63:16; 64:17; Jer 3:4.9; 31:9; Mal 1:6; 2:10; also Exod 4:22; Hos 11:1). The Ugaritic El is often imagined as residing in a pavilion (KTU 1.2 III:5; 1.3 V:8; 1.4 IV:24; 1.17 V:49), just like Yahweh who dwells in a tent (Ps 15:1; 27:6; 91:10; 132:23; those who seek Him can come to the tent of meeting (Exod 33:7–11; Num 12:5.10; Deut 31:14–15).

That Baal was known in Israel from early times is clear from place names like Baal- Peor, Baal-Hazor, Baal-Hermon, Baal-Perazim, and Baal-Zaphon, that are associated with the sanctuary of a fertility god. In the Ugaritic mythological texts, there is a scene where Baal invites Anat, his consort, to come to his divine mountain, Zaphon, his inherited mountain, the mountain where his glory is manifested (KTU 1.3 III:28–31). In the ninth century B.C.E. there was a growing hostility in Israel to the Baal cult, presumably because of the association with foreign power (Jezebel of Tyre), which reappeared in the polemical passages of the prophets. Nonetheless, Baal's character as divine warrior who fought against the forces of chaos and evil is very much alive in the imagery of the God of Exodus.

The goddess Asherah has an important role in Ugaritic religion. She is the consort of El, and together with him she is said to be the procreatrix of gods. In some Hebrew inscriptions of Kuntillet Ajrud, the goddess Asherah is paired with Yahweh. In the Bible, Asherah is depicted as a foreign goddess (1 Kgs 18:19; 2 Kgs 23:27), her statue considered as an idol (1 Kgs 15:13; 2 Kgs 21:27). In other passages the word refers to a sacred pole in high-places. For further studies, see Binger (2011).

Anat, Baal's sister and consort, is the goddess of war known for her violent and vengeful character. In the Bible, however, this goddess is only vestigially reflected in a few place names: Beth-anath (Judg 1:33; Josh 19:38); Beth-anoth (Josh 15:59); Anathoth (Josh 21:18; Jer 11:1), and in the personal name Shamgar son of Anath (Judg 3:31; 5:6). The spectacular military prowess of this judge might have been associated with this goddess of war.

In sum, some important traits of El, Baal, Anat, and Asherah are also found in the figure of Yahweh within the Hebrew Bible. This explains the multifaceted religious experience of the people of Israel with their God: benevolent and life-giving as a father (Patriarchal narratives and Exodus), yet sometime jealous as a spouse (Deuteronomistic History; Prophetic literature, esp. Hosea), but on other occasions compassionate and protective as a mother (e.g. Psalms of Lament).

Literary Traditions. Of special importance for biblical interpretation are the literary traditions of Ugarit, namely, stories about the god Baal, stories of the ancient heroes Kirta and Aqhat, the birth of the twin gods Shahar and Shallim, and the marriage of the lunar divinities. The tablets containing these stories were discovered at the acropolis, in the house or library of the high priest. These texts are conveniently presented, translated, and annotated by a group of scholars working under the editorship of Parker (1997). There are similar works by single authors, such as Olmo Lete (1981), Wyatt (1998; 2d ed., 2002).

The Stories of Baal. The stories of Baal are preserved mainly in six tablets (KTU 1.1–6), each originally having six columns, but the order of the stories is not clear due to the fragmentary and broken parts of the tablets. Taken together these tablets give an account of the rise of Baal to power, his glory, and his descent into the underworld, presumably his resurrection from the realm of the dead too. Other deities enter into the stories in connection with this dramatic movement. At the beginning El, the highest god, bequeathed his dominion to the younger god Yamm, that is, Sea, also called Judge or River. Yamm's rule caused disorder and strife among the gods. They chose their champion, the god Baal, to take the divine kingship from Yamm. Equipped with powerful weapons by Kothar-wa-Hasis, Baal conquered Yamm in a combat. Order was restored. In order to manifest his divine kingship, Baal needed a palace. Anat, Baal's sister and consort, asked Asherah, the mother of all gods, to intercede with El to give Baal the permission to build his palace.

The building of the palace has been compared to the building of the temple in Jerusalem, considered also the dwelling place of Yahweh. At this point the traditions diverge. The Ugaritic cycle continues with the events that led to the descent of Baal to the underworld to meet Mot, the god of death; in Israel Yahweh maintained the supremacy as the eternal king.

The combat between Yamm and Baal—disorder against order—has been compared to the clash between the hostile attitudes of the Egyptian king against Yahweh's claim to the enslaved Israelites in Egypt as narrated in the book of Exodus, especially in the crossing of the Sea. The victory of Yahweh is fundamental to the faith of Israel just like the victory of Baal over Yamm was decisive for the worship of Baal at Ugarit. In Ancient Israel, Yahweh not only acts like Baal, but also has the traits of El as the supreme god, wise and benevolent. Israel has also preserved a tradition of the holy mountain where Moses saw and received the laws from Yahweh. This strand is closer to the role of El in Ugaritic texts, who was known to dwell in a mountain, imparting his wisdom from there.

It is not without significance that the tablets containing the stories of Baal were found in the library of the high priest's house, not in the royal palace. It seems that the high priest of Ugarit had a function of keeping the sacral traditions and ethos that the king of Ugarit had to observe. The stories of Baal are meant to explain the origin of the power of Baal, the divine protector of the Ugaritic kingship: Baal's kingship comes from his ability to subdue the unruly forces of Yamm. The king's authority should be measured by his ability to maintain order. There is also a clear statement that despite his victory over Yamm, Baal's power still faces threats. There are thus also constant destabilizing forces against the king's rule. The Davidic kingship also seems to follow this kind of ethos. For the interpretation of the Baal cycle, see Smith (1994–2009).

The Stories of Kirta. The stories of Kirta are recorded in three tablets (KTU 1.14–16). Deprived of all of his offspring and wives, Kirta's kingship will not continue. But his protector god, El, comes in a dream and gives him instructions to take Lady Huriya, the daughter of Pabil, the king of Udum, as wife and through her he will beget sons and daughters. He is also told to offer sacrifice before embarking on this expedition, which he does. On his way to take his wife, Kirta makes a vow to Asherah of Sidon that he would make a special present to the goddess if he succeeds in bringing back Huriya to Hubur, his capital, to be his wife. His marriage to Huriya is blessed by El, who promises many children. Kirta prospers, but at a later period he falls incurably ill. Social and natural disorder follow. This is probably a punishment for Kirta's failure to fulfill his vows to Asherah. One of his sons wants to take Kirta's throne, but the old king resists. He is cured by Shataqat, who is sent by El to help him.

El's role as protector to Kirta is very clear. He arranges for Kirta to find a new wife who, in turn, gives him a progeny. When Kirta falls sick, El sends a healer. This narrative is meant as praise for El's role as the divine protector of the king. The story also contains an ethos: a king should be good to his people just like El is good to the king.

The stories of Kirta emphasize the necessity of the king's religious integrity in order to stay under divine protection. Throughout the story the importance of the rightful progeny is also stressed. The motive of preserving kingship, an offense committed to a deity, and the subsequent punishment by sickness are also familiar biblical motifs.

The Stories of Aqhat. The stories of Aqhat, preserved in three tablets (KTU 1.17–19), start with an account of Danel's childlessness. He performs a sacrifice to ask for a progeny. At the end of the seventh day Baal, Danel's protector, intercedes with El to give Danel a son, detailing the duties of the progeny. El agrees. He also gives a list of duties that a son should perform, the main one being to take care of his father's afterlife through various rituals. In the end a son is born, who is named Aqhat. When he grows up he receives a bow and arrow from Kothar-wa-Hasis. This is the beginning of his troubles. The goddess Anat is attracted by the weapons and tries to lure him to give them up in exchange for immortality. Convinced that Anat is only trying to deceive him, Aqhat refuses her offer. Anat is offended and vows vengeance. She goes up to El and forces him to deliver Aqhat's life into her hand. She orders Yatpan to kill Aqhat. Yatpan transforms himself into an eagle and kills Aqhat. His body is eaten up by other birds of prey. Following his death, drought comes to the land. When Danel discovers his son's fate, he collects his remains and brings them home for seven years of mourning. At the end of the period, Pughat, Aqhat's sister, vows to revenge her brother's death. She disguises herself as Anat and meets Yatpan who tells her what he did. The tablet breaks off at this point so that the conclusion is not certain. Presumably the story must have ended with Pughat's killing of Yatpan.

Throughout this story El's role is not as active as in Kirta's legends. Though El remains the highest god, he lets the younger gods take the lead in the action: in the first part, Baal intercedes with El for Danel; at a later point, Anat forces El to give up Aqhat to her.

The importance of having a son whose main duty is to continue Danel's life and take care of his afterlife is reminiscent of Abraham's childlessness, hence his having nobody to take care of his household (e.g., Gen 15:32). In both stories, progeny is secured but the characters go through some crisis. The Aqhat stories include greater focus on ritual ceremonies than other narrative texts, and this has been the subject of Wright's monograph (2001). This interweaving of ritual and stories is also found in the stories of the biblical patriarchs.

The Rapiuma. The Rapiuma tablets (KTU 1.20–22) represent scenes from a ritual banquet. The mention of Danel suggests a connection with the Aqhat story. Pardee (2011) re-examines the tablets and puts together solid epigraphic and literary evidence demonstrating that these texts indeed belong together. The text starts with the mention of the spirits of the dead, presumably the Rapiuma themselves, who make a three-day journey on chariots to El's shrine to join his banquet. The Rapiuma seem to be ancestors who now take part in El's entourage and enjoy eternal life as divine beings.

Shorter Texts. There are several other shorter texts representing mythological traditions, the most important are: KTU 1.23 (Smith 2006), the birth of the twin gods Shahar and Shallim fathered by El, interspersed with ritual instructions, and KTU 1.24, a hymn celebrating the marriage of the West Semitic moon God Yarih with the Mesopotamian moon goddess Nikkal. They provide a different imagery of the world of the gods than do the stories of Baal and the ancient heroes like Kirta and Aqhat. These texts also contain accounts of rituals, a field that is increasingly studied, making them extremely valuable alongside about a hundred cultic texts such as various ritual manuals, divinatory texts, and lists of gods who are to receive offerings (Pardee 2002).

Mesopotamian Wisdom Texts at Ugarit. There are two important wisdom texts in the Mesopotamian tradition adapted to the Western Semitic/Syrian-Palestinian setting. One is a seventeen-line, bilingual Sumero-Akkadian composition on human destinies; the text is also preserved in Emar with seven more lines in the middle (Dietrich 1992). It contains a challenge to the traditional sapiential view that human destinies are unequal and at the same time immutable. The text instead asserts that human beings are destined to be happy, and therefore they should strive for this rather than accepting the traditional ideals that lead to futility. This composition has a special bearing on the interpretation of the Book of Qohelet, which affirms joy as a gift from God despite all sorts of predicaments of human condition (Gianto 1998). The other text is a longer collection of sayings, set in a kind of dispute between a son by the name of Shupe-ameli and his father. The text is preserved in four columns, each originally having 33 or 34 lines. The text is preserved also in Emar (Dietrich 1991); a Hittite version was also found at Bogazköy. This composition, like the previous, represents a critical attitude toward traditional wisdom represented by the father. These two texts seem to be preserved by scribes who were familiar with Mesopotamian literature.

[*See also* Assyriology and Biblical Interpretation; *and* Mythology and Biblical Interpretation.]

BIBLIOGRAPHY

Althann, Robert. *Studies in Northwest Semitic.* Biblica et Orientalia 45. Rome: Pontificio Istituto Biblico, 1997.

Barr, James. "Philology and Exegesis. Some General Remarks, with Illustrations from Job 3." In *Questions disputées d'Ancien Testament. Méthode et théologie. XXIIe session des Journées Bibliques de Louvain*, edited by C. Brekelmans, 39–61. Leuven, Belgium: Leuven University Press, 1974.

Binger, Tilde. *Asherah: Godesses in Ugarit, Israel and the Old Testament.* Journal for the Study of the Old Testament, Supplement series 232. Sheffield, UK: Academic Press, 1997.

Bordreuil, Pierre and Dennis G. Pardee. *A Manual of Ugaritic.* Winona Lake, Ind.: Eisenbrauns, 2009.

Cross, Frank Moore. *Canaanite Myth and Hebrew Epic.* Cambridge, Mass.: Harvard University Press, 1973.

Dahood, Mitchell. "Northwest Semitic Texts and Textual Criticism of the Hebrew Bible." In *Questions disputées d'Ancien Testament. Méthode et théologie. XXIIe session des Journées Bibliques de Louvain*, edited by C. Brekelmans, 11–37. Leuven, Belgium: Leuven University Press, 1974.

Dahood, Mitchell. *Psalms.* 3 vols. Anchor Bible Commentary. Garden City, NY: Anchor 1966, 1968, 1970.

Dictionnaire de la Bible. Supplément IX. Edited by H. Cazelles and A. Feuillet., Paris: Letouzay et Ané, 1928-. [=*DBS*]

Dietrich, Manfried. "Der Dialog zwischen Šūpē-amēli und seinem 'Vater.' Die Tradition babylonischer Weisheitssprüche im Westen." *Ugarit-Forschungen* 23 (1991): 33–74.

Dietrich, Manfried. "'Ein Leben ohne Freude . . .'" Studie über eine Weisheitskomposition aus den Gelehrtenbibliotheken von Emar und Ugarit. *Ugarit-Forschungen* 24 (1992): 9–29.

Dietrich, Manfred, Oswald Loretz, and Joaquín Sanmartín. *Cuneiform Alphabetic Texts from Ugarit, Ras Ibn Hani and Other Places* (Translation of *Die keilalphabetischen*

Texte aus Ugarit [1976]; second, enlarged edition). Münster: Ugarit-Verlag, 1995. [=KTU/CAT]

Fischer, Loren R. (ed.). *Ras Shamra Parallels: Texts from Ugarit and the Hebrew Bible.* 2 vols. [Vol 3, edited by Stanley Rummel]. Analecta Orientalia. Rome: Pontificio Istituto Biblico, 1972, 1975, (vol 3) 1981.

Gianto, Agustinus. "Human Destiny in Emar and Qohelet." In *Qohelet in the Context of Wisdom*, edited by Antoon Schoors, 473–479. Leuven, Belgium: Leuven University Press 1988.

Gianto, Agustinus. "Ugaritic." In *Languages from the World of the Bible*, edited by Holger Gzella. Boston/Berlin: De Gruyter, 2011.

Gordon, Cyrus H. *Ugaritic Textbook.* 3 parts. Analecta Orientalia 38. Rome: Pontificio Istituto Biblico, 1965. [Revised reprint 1998].

Huehnergard, John. *Ugaritic Vocabulary in Syllabic Transcription.* Harvard Semitic Studies 32. Rev. ed. Winona Lake, Ind.: Eisenbrauns, 2008.

Koehler, Ludwig and Walter Baumgartner. *The Hebrew and Aramaic Lexicon of the Old Testament.* 5 vols. Leiden: Netherlands, 1994, 1995, 1996, 1999, 2000. [=HALOT]

Loretz. Oswald. *Ugarit und die Bibel. Kanaanäische Götter und Religion im Alten Testament* Darmstadt: Wissenschaftlicher Buchgesellschaft, 1990.

Marsman, Hennie J. *Women in Ugarit & Israel. Their Social & Religious Position in the Context of the Ancient Near East.* Leiden, the Netherlands: Brill, 2003.

Meyer, Rudolf. *Hebräische Grammatik.* 4 vols. Berlin: De Gruyter, 1969, 1972, 1972, 1996.

Olmo Lete, Gregorio del. *Mitos y leyendas de Canaan segun la tradición de Ugarit.* Madrid: Ediciones Cristiandad, 1981.

Olmo Lete, Gregorio del and Joaquín Sanmartín. *A Dictionary of the Ugaritic Language in the Alphabetic Tradition.* Translated by Wilfred G.E. Watson. 2 vols. Leiden, Netherlands: Brill, 2003. English translation of *Diccionario de la lengua ugarítica.* 2 vols. Sabadell-Bercelona: Editorial Ausa, 1996–2000.

Pardee, Dennis. "Nouvelle étude épigraphique et littéraire des textes fragmentaires en langue ougaritique dits Les Rephaïm (*CTA* 20–22)." *Orientalia* 80, no. 1 (2011): 1–65.

Pardee, Dennis G. Review of *Ugaritische Grammatik*, by Josef Tropper. *Archiv für Orientforschung* 50 (2003–4) 1–404.

Pardee, Dennis. *Ritual and Cult at Ugarit.* Society of Biblical Literature Writings from the Ancient World 10. Atlanta: Society of Biblical Literature, 2002.

Parker, Simon B., ed. *Ugaritic Narrative Poetry.* Society of Biblical Literature Writings from the Ancient World 9. Atlanta: Scholars, 1997.

Segert, Stanislav. *A Basic Grammar of the Ugaritic Language with Selected Texts and Glossary.* Berkeley: University of California Press, 1984.

Sivan, Daniel. *A Grammar of the Ugaritic Language.* Leiden, the Netherlands: Brill 1997.

Smith, Mark. "A Bibliography of Ugaritic Grammar and Biblical Hebrew Grammar in the Twentieth Century." 2004 http://oi.uchicago.edu/OI/DEPT/RA/bibs/BH-Ugaritic.html

Smith, Mark S. *The Early History of God: Yahweh and the Other Deities in Ancient Israel.* 2d ed. Grand Rapids, Mich./Cambridge, UK: Eerdmans, 2002.

Smith, Mark S. *The Origins of Biblical Monotheism: Israel's Polytheistic Background and the Ugaritic Texts.* Oxford: Oxford University Press, 2001.

Smith, Mark S. "Recent Study of Israelite Religion in Light of the Ugaritic Texts." In *Ugarit at Seventy-Five*, edited by K. Lawson Younger, 1–25. Winona Lake, Ind.: Eisenbrauns, 2007.

Smith, Mark S. *The Rituals and Myths of the Feast of the Goodly Gods of* KTU/*CAT 1.23*. Atlanta: Society of Biblical Literature, 2006.

Smith, Mark S. *The Ugaritic Baal Cycle.* 2 vols. Leiden, Netherlands: 1994–2009.

Smith, Mark S. *Untold Stories: The Bible and Ugaritic Studies in the Twentieth Century.* Peabody, Mass.: Hendrickson, 2001.

Tropper, Josef. *Ugaritisch: Kurzgefasste Grammatik mit Übungen und Glossar.* Münster: Ugarit-Verlag, 2002.

Tropper, Josef. *Ugaritische Grammatik.* Münster: Ugarit-Verlag, 2000.

Wright, David. P. *Ritual in Narrative. The Dynamics of Feasting, Mourning, and Retaliation Rites in the Ugaritic Tale of Aqhat.* Winona Lake, Ind.: Eisenbrauns, 2001.

Wyatt, Nicholas, *Religious Texts from Ugarit.* Sheffield, UK: Academic Press, 1998, 2d ed. 2002.

Wyatt, Nicholas, and Wilfred G.E. Watson (eds.). *Handbook of Ugaritic Studies.* Leiden, the Netherlands: Brill, 1999.

Yon, Marguerite. *The City of Ugarit at Tell Ras Shamra.* Winona Lake, Ind.: Eisenbrauns, 2006 (French original, 1997).

Young, Gordon D. *Ugarit in Retrospect: 50 Years of Ugarit and Ugaritic.* Winona Lake, Ind.: Eisenbrauns, 1981.

Younger, K. Lawson. *Ugarit at Seventy-Five: Its Environs and the Bible.* Winona Lake, Ind.: Eisenbraun, 2007.

Zamora, José-Ángel. *La vid y el vino en Ugarit.* Madrid: Consejo Superior de Investigaciones Científicas, 2000.

Agustinus Gianto

W

Wesleyan Biblical Interpretation

John Wesley (1703–1791) and his brother, Charles (1707–1788), were early leaders of the Evangelical Revival and founders of an arm of the pietistic religious movement within the Church of England, which took root in the late 1730s and became known as Methodism. The design of the early Methodists was to preach the "Scripture Way of Salvation" and to "reform the nation, and in particular the Church, to spread scriptural holiness over the land" (*Works*, 10:845). Scripture was central to the thought and practices of the early Methodists, and methods of interpretation are no less significant for present church communities who see themselves as the Wesleys' ecclesial descendants. However, the eponymy of the topic of "Wesleyan interpretation" has typically been associated solely with John Wesley, and thus the significance of the influence of Charles—whose hymnic expositions of scripture formed the core of what John Wesley himself claimed superseded all other hymn collections in providing "so distinct and full an account of scriptural Christianity" (*Works*, 7:75)—has often been overlooked. Ironically, it might be observed that Charles's hymns, more than the "doctrinal standards" of John's *Sermons* (rarely read in the congregational setting today) and *Explanatory Notes* on the Bible (now out-of-print), have preserved a popular congregational identification with the Wesleyan scriptural emphases through repeated liturgical use. Charles's approach to scripture, much as John's, is central to the study of Wesleyan hermeneutics. While the Wesleys' individual methods were at times in disagreement and resist conflation, there remain many points of commonality, and the present article offers a survey which incorporates scholarship concerning the significance of both.

John became the presumptive leader of Methodism as a Connection of societies and preachers, but he and Charles shared much in common with regard to their context. They were sons of Susanna (née Annesley) and the Rev. Samuel Wesley, who were of dissenting backgrounds, but had returned to the Church of England. Samuel was the Rector of Epworth in Lincolnshire, though often absent from his parish for various reasons, and all of the Wesley children could credit their early education to Susanna who methodically developed a regimen of teaching, prayer, study of scripture, and reading. Samuel's influence was also formative, particularly his involvement with the early Anglican religious societies and his participation in a stream of Anglican churchmanship which sought to revive the ideals and practices of the "primitive Church." Both brothers matriculated at Oxford University (John in 1720; Charles in 1726), and John eventually became a fellow of Lincoln College. They were members of the Holy Club at Oxford where they were first called "Methodists." Both were ordained priests in the Church of England, and both experienced Evangelical conversion in the spring of 1738. As committed churchmen, they highly valued the *Articles*, *Homilies*, and liturgy of the Church of England, the influence of which was prominent in their biblical interpretation. Despite the tensions that sometimes arose between John and Charles, their views were similarly formed and mutually informing.

John was an incessant itinerant preacher, and his *Sermons* provide a large portion of the evidence for his hermeneutics. These, together with his *Explanatory Notes Upon the New Testament* and the Methodist Conference *Minutes*, came to form the doctrinal standards of the Methodist societies, providing an implicit model for biblical exposition. Charles was also a preeminent leader of the Methodists, and a powerful preacher in his own right, though he is generally remembered for his composition of more than 9,000 early Methodist hymns. His poetic enterprise was not an alternative to engagement in biblical interpretation, but rather was the product of it, covering the themes of nearly every book of the Bible. Taken together, the interpretation of scripture by John and Charles forms the starting point for understanding a distinctively Wesleyan hermeneutics.

Interpretive Presuppositions. The Wesleys stood in the mainstream of orthodox hermeneutics, and the basic emphases of the early church fathers and the reformers are reflected in their presuppositions regarding the concept of biblical authority, inspiration, and illumination.

Authority of Scripture. A dual basis of authority developed in the first few centuries of Christianity: the written deposit of the scriptures and apostolic writings, and the traditions of the church's teachings as maintained by the bishops in the rule of faith. These two streams worked together, although varying hermeneutics developed. Throughout the Middle Ages, the grammatical/historical meaning of the text of scripture was subordinate to the innovative allegorical method of Origen and the Alexandrian school. In the later Middle Ages, scholars such as Thomas Aquinas and Hugh and Andrew of St. Victor began to question the use of allegorical interpretation and renewed an interest in the literal sense of scripture and the role of the mind of the human author in the process of inspiration by the Holy Spirit. Others, like Nicholas of Lyra pressed further, emphasizing the literal message of scripture as the basis for all other meanings.

With the dawning of the Protestant Reformation, a new and fresh role developed for scripture in the church. Luther's emphasis on *sola scriptura* (scripture alone), became the watchword of the Reformation. Not only did he assert that scripture was authoritative, but he denied the authority of the pope and the traditions and interpretations of the church. In contrast to the Roman Catholic view that the authority of scripture rested on that of the church, Luther pointed out that the Bible derives its authority from itself as inspired by the Holy Spirit. For Luther, the authority of scripture rested on several issues: its inspired character, its reliability for salvation, and the internal testimony of the Holy Spirit. It is the subject matter of scripture—Christ the Word—to which the Spirit witnesses, and scripture mediates the living Word by the operation of the Spirit, thus becoming the medium of salvation.

The inspiration of the scriptures lies, then, in their ability, through the Spirit, to produce in the believer all that is needed for salvation, and it is because the Spirit makes Christ present through the scriptures that they have redemptive effectiveness. The scriptures are reliable because they produce in the reader the conviction that they proclaim God's power to save. Finally, Luther held, as did Calvin and Zwingli, that the internal testimony of the Holy Spirit (*testimonium Spiritus Sancti internum)* affirms the Bible's inspiration and thus its authority. This internal witness to the church of the reality of Christ crucified attests the scripture as the genuine Word of God. It is Jesus Christ working in and through scripture who is the infallible Word of God. The scripture is authoritative because it faithfully reveals Christ through the human instrumentality of the biblical writers, whose inspiration comes from the Spirit. Ultimately, then, it is the inspired content of scripture, not its form or written style, that is authoritative.

The Wesleys held this Reformation view of scriptural authority. The purpose of scripture for them was to communicate the way of salvation. John Wesley's famous statement that he wanted to be *homo unius libri* (a man of one book) was directly tied to his functional view of scripture. "I want to know one thing," he wrote, "the way to heaven... God Himself has condescended to teach the way... hath written it down in a book [i.e., the Bible]" (*Works*, 1:104–105). Charles also saw Christ and his redemptive work as the theological center of scripture and with the reformers, believed that this soteriological content that pointed always to Christ was the foundation of biblical authority. This view liberated him from purely dogmatic approaches to scripture allowing him imaginatively to paraphrase the biblical content in verse. As Wall states, for the Wesleyan interpreter, "The Bible has authority to mediate God's grace to and delineate the theological boundaries of the one holy catholic and apostolic church; that is, the terms of Scripture's authority... are understood in functional and formative rather than in epistemic and dogmatic terms" (Wall 2000, p. 166). In this way, scripture is (in the *Book of Common Prayer* [1662] phrase), a "means of grace," one of the "ordinary channels whereby [God] might convey... preventing, justifying, or sanctifying grace" (*Works*, 1:381).

John Wesley did not accept that saving faith was mere mental assent to a set of propositions about God in the creeds nor even to "all that God hath revealed in Scripture," but the "revelation of Christ in our hearts... a sure confidence in his pardoning mercy, wrought in us by the Holy Ghost" (*Works*, 1:405). Thus, Wesley based his view of authority upon the historical canons concerning the reliability of scripture for communicating salvation and upon the internal witness of the Holy Spirit to the body of Christ. The work of grace in convicting one of sin and leading that person to repentance and justifying faith was solely the province of the Holy Spirit, although the searching of the scriptures was the great and fullest means of this divine providence (cf. Shelton 1992).

Inspiration, Revelation, and Illumination. The inspiration of scripture is axiomatic for a Wesleyan hermeneutic. Commenting upon 2 Timothy 3:16, John Wesley wrote, "The Spirit of God not only once inspired those who wrote [the Bible], but continually inspires, supernaturally assists those that read it... Hence it is so profitable for doctrine, for reproof or conviction of them that are in error or sin, for the correction... and for instructing or training up" (*ENNT*, p. 794). The Spirit operates not only in the production, but in the preservation and interpretation of scripture. The Holy Spirit interacts with the personalities and natural abilities of human agents. Inspiring involves more than just speaking or performing other isolated functions related to the transmission of information.

Although John Wesley appears at times to endorse a dictation theory of inspiration, he also saw the concursive action of the Spirit with the biblical authors in both writing and compiling the Old and New Testaments—a cooperative, redemptive, interpersonal process, validated by an existential encounter with the Holy Spirit. Because its inspired-ness originates with God, Wesley wrote of the Bible as "a most solid and precious system of divine truth... wherein is no defect, no excess." And, the experiential and observable redemptive effects of the scripture attest to the reality of the spiritual encounter.

John Wesley spoke of revelation as the "revelation of Jesus Christ," seeing Christ as the ultimate communication and act of revealing of God to the world. God communicated through divine speech and acts, and the Holy Spirit inspired the writers to record in words that "accurately answered the impression made upon their minds" (*ENNT*, p. 9). As Charles expressed it, "And Christ his pard'ning grace reveals / And whispers I am his / Till God his Spirit pours / His fulness from above/ In streams of righteousness, and showers / Of everlasting love" (*SHHS*, 1:112). It is only by the work of the Spirit illuminating the meaning of scriptures and applying it to one's heart that anyone can understand the salvific message and respond. Charles's Scripture Hymn on Isaiah 29:11 is illustrative of the Wesleyan view of illumination, which insists that although diligent and careful study of the scriptures is necessary, it is the Holy Spirit who opens the soteriological implications of the text: "Proud learning boasts its skill in vain / The sacred oracles t' explain / It may the literal surface show / But not the precious mine below / The saving sense remains concealed / 'Till by the Spirit of faith revealed" (*SHHS*, 1:324). Or, more prosaic and reminiscent of a phrase from Augustine, John Wesley explained that "we need the same Spirit to *understand* the Scripture which enabled the holy men of old to *write* it" (*Works*, 11:509). Charles's hymns served as a way of disseminating such an understanding of the inspiration and illumination of scripture amongst the Methodists who were encouraged "Before Reading the Scriptures," to invite, "Holy Ghost, our hearts inspire . . . Source of the old prophetic fire . . . Come, Holy Ghost . . . Unlock the truth, thyself the key . . . Unseal the sacred book" (*Works*, 7:185).

Consequently, for a Wesleyan hermeneutics, scripture is the final authority in faith and practice, concordant with classical Reformed positions that the scriptures are self-authenticating, and it is the Holy Spirit in the experience of the entire Body of Christ which witnesses to the authority of scripture as the Spirit reliably shows the way of salvation to successive generations (Shelton 1992).

Reason, Tradition, and Experience. The Wesley's sought the best resources available to aid in their exposition. They did not assume that the text was self-interpreting, and reason, tradition, and experience functioned as important means for authenticating one's interpretation.

Wesleyans have never been as negative toward reason, nor as exclusively dependent upon it, as some segments of the Lutheran and Reformed traditions, due to the differing views of depravity and grace. John Wesley believed reason was a gift from God, a part of the divine image. When confronting the mystics, he stressed the importance of reason for understanding the Word of God, while in confronting the rationalists of his day, he stressed that reason did not produce revelation. Contrary to those who rejected reason, he warned that "irrational reason is a false religion." He urged clergy to study other disciplines in their approach to scripture, including knowledge of profane history, ancient customs, chronology, geography, and the sciences, and he explicitly implored them to make use of logic (defined by him as "the art of good sense") in order to clear apprehension, good judgment, and conclusive reasoning. This approach reveals his appraisal of the appropriateness of reason in theological reflection.

For the Wesleys, experience was a means of actualizing one's relationship with God. It is a context for interpreting the Word of God, while always being guided by the Spirit. Experience is never an end in itself. John Wesley disapproved of the Quaker reliance on experience, even though it was understood as the perception of the Spirit, because it tended to place the authority of the scripture in a subordinate role. He also criticized some of Charles's hymns for savoring too much mysticism. Yet, some of Charles's mysticism was a confession that understanding and internalizing the sometimes "mystic words" of scripture required complete dependence upon the Holy Spirit (*SHHS*, 2:412). Experience was not intended to replace the authority of scripture, but to confirm and explicate it. When John was challenged that he leaned too heavily on experience toward enthusiasm, he agreed with his accuser that "Experience is not sufficient to prove a doctrine which is not founded on Scripture," but defended his method, showing that if a doctrine had already been founded upon scripture, then "experience is properly alleged to confirm it" (*Works*, 1:293).

Tradition was important for the Wesleys, who had imbibed its significance from their parents, and from their Oxford education an emphasis on the primitive Church and a devotion to the expressions of faith in the formularies of the Church of England. Foremost among the latter was the *Book of Homilies*, which their Holy Club at Oxford often set next to scripture "in settling their judgment as to the grand point of justification by faith" (*Works*, 3:505). Diligent study of the scriptures, John averred, should be aided by a knowledge of the church fathers, whom he referred to as "the most authentic commentators on Scripture, as being both nearest the fountain, and eminently endued with that Spirit by whom all Scripture was given" (*Works* [J], 10:484).

Thus, reason, experience, and tradition offered an interpretive matrix that, in submission to the Holy Spirit, supplied a means of interpreting the theological content of scripture within the context of the total heritage of the Christian Church. Functionally, this model was framed and developed for the contemporary setting as the "Wesleyan Quadrilateral" by Albert C. Outler and other Methodist scholars in the second half of the twentieth century. The Quadrilateral as a paradigm of religious authority has been challenged on numerous fronts, not least for its indeterminate epistemological assumptions. However, despite its epistemological liabilities and its tendency to be read anachronistically into interpretations of the Wesleys' respective views of authority, the Quadrilateral has provided fertile ground for discussing the issue of authority and interpretation by its advocates and its critics alike.

Canon and Community. The Wesleys understood the main purpose of biblical interpretation soteriologically, which implied not only a proclamation and a community of hearers, but also a community of those who were seeking to understand God's purposes and to grow in lives of holiness. The societies, bands, and classes were set up with this in mind, encouraging what Maddox (2011) has called reading the Bible "in Conference." John Wesley wrote that when in doubt of an interpretation, he consulted with more experienced Christians. While the Methodist meetings were not Bible studies in the contemporary sense, scripture reading and expounding was a central part of those times of fellowship, aided by the evidence from the Wesleys' correspondence as well from those who led the bands and classes; such makes it clear that there was significant interplay between the reading of scripture and the testifying to God's work of grace in the lives of converts. Wesley even collected and published hundreds of conversion narratives and experiences of individual Methodists as a means of assessing the validity of his interpretations as tested against common experience of all believers in redemption and sanctification. Such an emphasis is a reminder that a Wesleyan interpretation must be "in relation to its functions within the community" (McCown 1982, p. 10). John entreated clergy to improve upon their cultural competency, to gain knowledge of the world and of people, "of their maxims, tempers, and manners, such as they occur in real life. Without this [a biblical expositor] will be liable to receive much hurt, and capable of doing little good; as he will not know . . . how to deal with [people] according to the vast variety of their characters" (*Works* [J], 10:483–484).

Interpretive Principles. The following list summarizes one or both of the Wesleys' own (explicit or inferential) principles of biblical interpretation and exposits implications for a contemporary Wesleyan hermeneutics under three headings: the interpreter, the text, and the interpretive task.

The Interpreter. The Wesleys insisted that personal spiritual preparation was essential to the proper understanding of scripture, amongst which the most important were humility, prayer, and a deep personal familiarity with the whole Bible.

Humility. The Wesleys' belief that reliance upon the Holy Spirit was required for a proper understanding of scripture meant that the text must be approached with a humble attitude rooted in gratefulness for God's condescension in providing the scripture as the most explicit means of knowing the way of salvation. As Susanna Wesley once reminded John, "we can't contemplate . . . or conceive [God] present, without the most exquisite diminution of ourselves before him!" (*Works*, 25:178). Or, as Charles expressed it, "With deepest shame, / with humblest fear, / I to thine oracle draw near" (*SHHS*, p. 292).

Prayer. One must also approach the Bible prayerfully. As Charles expressed in a reflection on Isaiah 66: "Draw out the milk by faith and prayer, / The sweetness of the word" (1762). John, in the preface to his Old Testament *Notes*, exhorted students to use prayer before, during, and after consulting the "oracles of God." The principle, as John made explicit, was to be found in the Anglican formularies, recommending in the 1790 publication of his translation of the NT that readers of the Bible use the Collect for the Second Sunday in Advent from the *Book of Common Prayer*.

Familiarity with the Text. Biblical language permeated the Wesleys' speech, aiming "always to express Scripture sense in Scripture phrase" (*Works* [J], 12:58). The reason for prioritizing biblical language was that they were wary of the various schisms that had been caused by importing non-scriptural language into exegesis. The Wesleys' writings appear as sequences of biblical quotations and allusions, and they expected their followers to internalize the scriptures to the degree that even their conversational speaking would be conformed to biblical idiom, borne of meditation on the text. The earliest Methodists were even called, "Bible Bigots" or "Bible Moths," who feed "upon the Bible as Moths do upon cloth" (*Works*, 3:504). Charles's poetry, with rhyme, meter, and sometimes tune serving as mnemonic aids, was a key to bolstering this agenda of internalization, although once put into verse, a second hermeneutical step had, of course, been taken. Such a step, however, as Kimbrough (1988, p. 153) has noted, is consonant with the practical purpose of Wesleyan interpretation, for as texts are sung, a move is made from merely studying the text to praying it.

The Text and Tools. The Wesleys were well-trained and preferred to study scripture in the original languages and in the most accurate editions modern textual criticism up to that time could provide. Indeed, when John was writing *ENNT*, he made thousands of alterations in his translation into English, seeking to improve upon the Authorized Version. He aimed to provide the best English translation in order that "plain, unlettered [people], who understand only their mother-tongue" could read it meaningfully, and excluded the use of Greek or Hebrew in his *Notes* for this reason. This was in no way inconsistent with his regard for the original languages. As Maddox (2011) has observed, Wesley recommended preaching in the plainest language possible while attempting to increase the level of education in the original languages, making Greek and Hebrew part of the course of study at his school at Kingswood. In all, he desired to remove any hindrance to reading, and to provide what he referred to as the "naked Bible," a text which best represented the original languages in the vernacular. Thoroughgoing knowledge of the original languages provides the exegete with freedom to translate the text within the parameters of the other principles of interpretation, a liberty exercised extensively by Charles Wesley in his scripture hymns to offer a better sense than he found in the Authorized Version.

John's insistence that he aimed to be a "man of one book" in no way precluded his use of other scholarly works for the purpose of interpretation. Indeed, the majority of his own literary output served to provide tools, consisting in expositions of scripture (i.e., sermons), applications of scripture doctrine (e.g., the numerous religious works he edited for his *Christian Library*), and critical commentaries upon every biblical book, giving "the direct, literal meaning, of every verse, of every sentence, and as far as I am able, of every word in the oracles of God" (*Works* [J], 14:252). Such critical tools were meant "barely to assist those who fear God, in hearing and reading the bible itself" (*Works* [J], 14:252). He recognized that even the act of translation required interpretation, and that brief notes which helped the reader to understand the "natural sense" of the text could serve to clarify what might otherwise be unclear in a direct translation.

Whether John Wesley was a "critical" or "pre-critical" interpreter of the Bible has been debated without producing any general consensus, although recent scholarship has articulated a more nuanced view giving more recognition to Wesley's use of some critical methodology. Wesley, by his own testimony, appreciated the text-critical methods of the Pietist exegete, Johann Bengel (1687–1752), whose *Gnomon Novi Testamenti* (1742) formed the basis of *ENNT*. Though several scholars have noted that the Wesleys would probably have been aware of the developing source criticism of Richard Simon (1638–1712) and Jean Astruc (1684–1766) and others, it appears that the Wesleys both rejected or ignored the new theories of biblical authorship, holding instead to the traditional Mosaic authorship of the Pentateuch. Both John and Charles used the best Greek and Hebrew lexicons and grammars of their day. John recognized the usefulness of commentaries other than his own, though he favored those that offered translations with expositions over those that paraphrased the text.

The Interpretive Task. The works of the Wesleys reveal several observable (often overlapping) principles of interpretation. Some examinations of Wesleyan interpretation tend to atomize John Wesley's approach into a series of between four and ten hermeneutical principles, which has merit for presenting a clear typology. The present article, however, aims to amplify the areas of overlap in order to show how the principles operated in the Wesleys' practice. Three broad categories are outlined here. The Wesley's sought to interpret scripture according to: the rule of faith; the priority of the literal sense; and the simultaneity of scripture.

The rule of faith. The Bible functions as the guide to Christian belief, spiritual formation, and ecclesial practice. But how is one to extract from the scriptures the core message of faith and practice? How is an initiate into the Christian faith to come to know how to read and understand the Gospel message in the scriptures? The Wesleys were not innovators in their answer but, instead, borrowed from the orthodox tradition of the early church and the Reformers.

Resistant to any Marcionite tendencies toward prioritizing the NT to the exclusion of the OT, John and Charles studied and preached from the whole Protestant canon. Immersion in the entire Bible gives the expositor a sense of those themes, commands, promises, and doctrines that are concordant with what John called the "whole scope and tenor of Scripture." When faced with an apparently anomalous reading, he could assess its validity by the degree to which it resonated with the "oracles of God" (one of John Wesley's favorite terms for scripture). Likewise, the concept of the "whole tenor" could be applied to smaller units within the canon. Thus, John could speak of "the grammatical construction of the four Gospels; of the Acts; of the Epistles" (*Works* [J], 10:490), and could test the interpretation of a part of St. John's Gospel against the "whole tenor of his discourse" (*Works*, 1:421). Because God's revelation was made available through the inspiration of the written Word, the whole could be considered to have integrity in bearing faithful witness to Christ and his salvation. John Wesley frequently pointed out that in like fashion the lives of those who were justified and growing in holiness should have the same integrity, holding the whole tenor of their conversation and behavior in agreement with scripture (*Works*, 3:127–128).

As was true in the first centuries of the Christian Church, even a commitment to reading the whole of scripture could not guarantee a reading that preserved even the most basic tenets of the Christian message. The Gnostics themselves had access to the same body of scripture as the early Christians, yet came up with a heterodox reading. It was in response to this obvious problem that Irenaeus, Augustine, and others developed the "rule of faith." It was the theological center (in the words of Ignatius), of Christ's "cross and death and resurrection, and the faith that comes through him," which testifies that the scriptures are connected to God. The "rule of faith," developed by the fathers, consisting in the creeds and other means of grace, guided a faithful reading of the scriptures. Taking his phrasing from the Greek text of Romans 12:6, where the phrase "analogy of faith" is found (*let us* prophesy according to the proportion [Gr. *analogian*] of faith), John Wesley insisted on a reading of scripture consistent with the teachings of the Creeds and with the liturgy of the Church of England. He used "love" as a synecdoche for the "religion of the Bible . . . which runs through both the Old and New Testament [s] . . . The inward and outward fruits of this love are . . . described by the inspired writers. So that whoever allows this to be the Word of God must allow this to be true religion" (*Works*, 3:586). Such was the religion, he explained, of the primitive church.

The analogy of faith was not external to scripture, but the marrow of the life-changing message it proclaimed. John Wesley offered several summaries of the analogy of faith. In *ENOT*, he exhorted readers, "Have a constant eye to the *analogy of faith*; the connection and harmony there is between those grand, fundamental doctrines, Original Sin, Justification by Faith, the New Birth, Inward and Outward Holiness" (p. ix). This soteriological emphasis, manifested in God's love toward humankind, and the offering of salvation that results in a life devoted to loving God and loving one's neighbor, "runs through the Bible from the beginning to the end" (*Works*, 2:483). This was in no way inconsistent with his claim, "The written Word is the whole and sole rule of [the Methodists] faith, as well as practice" (*Works*, 3:496).

The Wesleys' emphasis on reading the whole of the Bible has led scholars to agree generally that they (particularly John) did not have a functional "canon within the canon." Yet there is evidence from John Wesley's writings that he did rely on what he saw as concise, plain, and clear summations of the whole tenor of scripture. His study of the scriptures in the context of the traditions of both Christian antiquity and the Church of England led him to what he believed was a true summary in form of "all the commands of God." "Love is all," he wrote, "all the commands beside are only means of love" (*Works*, 18:212–213). While at one point he stated that "faith and salvation . . . include the substance of all the Bible, the marrow, as it were, of the whole Scripture" (*Works*, 2:156), John Wesley's view of salvation was teleological, seeing salvation in terms of its goal, perfection in Christ, summed up by the theological prism of love of God and love of neighbor (*Works*, 3:74). Robert Wall (2010) recently posited that 1 John was for Wesley a canon within the canon, offering both the most exemplary biblical text on which preachers should base their homiletical style, and the hermeneutical center for understanding the whole tenor of scripture.

Literal sense. Concordant with the reformers, the Wesleys emphasized the "literal sense" of the scriptures. John Wesley wrote, "it is a stated rule in interpreting Scripture never to depart from the plain, literal sense, unless it implies an absurdity" (*Works*, 3:50). The use of the term "literal" in early modern biblical interpretation, however, is somewhat perplexing, for it included interpretation according to the historical, grammatical, and literary context of the original author. Thus, if the original context suggested a figurative reading such as in the cases of metonymy, synecdoche, or metaphor, then such readings were considered to be the plainest sense. There are numerous examples of this in both *ENNT* and in Charles's hymns on scripture.

In order to understand the literal sense, John insisted that one must be thoroughly acquainted with all of scripture such that upon the mention of any text the interpreter would immediately know the grammar, context, and the parallel places in scripture. Like the reformers before him, John Wesley challenged the Roman Catholic doctrine of transubstantiation on the grounds that, for Christ, when he said of the bread, "This is my body," that it would be absurd to think that Christ was speaking of "his real, natural body" (*Works* [J], 9:278). In order to interpret this text nonfiguratively, Wesley explained, there would need to be "like forms" elsewhere in scripture that demonstrate that the literal sense is plainer than the figurative. Furthermore, the literal sense cannot stand in contradiction to the whole tenor of scripture or to the analogy of faith. For example, because the "whole tenor" demonstrates that God's very nature is love, John Wesley argued (in a polemic sermon against Calvinist predestination), the claim that God literally hated Esau (Mal 1:2–3; Rom 9:13) must be understood figuratively. Thus, the literal sense for the Wesleys meant the literal *theological* meaning, not merely the historical-grammatical sense, or as Luther often said, the "natural" sense.

However, in another corporeal example, one can see the liability of assuming the "literal sense" is clear, for he was more prone than might be supposed to move quickly to the spiritual sense. In his commentary on the passage concerning spiritual gifts and the metaphorical reference to the "body of Christ" in 1 Corinthians 12, Wesley assumed the metaphor would be obvious to the reader, and moved to an allegorical reading, seeing the reference to the various parts of the body as specific groups of people within the church.

The Wesleys were not, however, slaves to literalism, nor did they believe that a literal interpretation apart from the work of the Holy Spirit and the obedience of the reader in applying the Word was anything more than dead faith. "Whether the Word be preached or read," wrote Charles, "No saving benefit I gain / From empty sounds or letters dead / Unprofitable all and fain / Unless by faith Thy Word I hear" (*MSSH*). John expected that interpreters would be "masters" of the spiritual *and* literal sense, and would have "learned to apply every part of the sacred writings" (*Works* [J], 10:491). Charles perceived fluidity between the literal and the spiritual, but emphasized the need to appropriate the spiritual meaning by faith in personal application. "The meaning *spiritual* and true / The learn'd expositor may give / but cannot give the virtue too / Or bid his own dead spirit live" (*SHSS*, 2:249). Their view that the literal sense was always in relation to the message of salvation and growth in holiness meant that the Spirit was always at work to continue the work of inspiration in the present. Indeed, this canonical view of scripture was one that John Wesley followed out to its logical conclusion, holding that a valid interpretation and appropriation of the spiritual sense by faith should result in the spiritual formation of the reader in holiness.

Simultaneity of scripture. Although the Wesleys did not use the term themselves, the principle of the "simultaneity of scripture" can be observed at work in their sermons and other works as a key to their hermeneutical method of interpreting scripture theologically. Wall (in Green and Turner 2000, p. 169) has explained the principle in relation to the *analogia fidei*, writing that "every sacred part of this sacred whole, OT and NT, may be rendered coherent by the same theological beliefs and moral values of Christian faith." Such an approach is native to the biblical authors' own hermeneutical method, where the intertextuality of the biblical canon is seen in allusions to and citations of earlier texts, and the development of themes based on the expositions of earlier texts for a contemporary context as seen not only in the works of the prophets of Israel, but in the New Testament sayings of Jesus, the Gospel narratives more generally, and in the Pauline corpus. Charles exemplified the principle of simultaneity in his poetry in which, as Kimbrough (1992, p. 119) has pointed out, he bridged the world of the original settings of the text with the contemporary setting in which it is presently read.

The Wesleys' approach, however, was not indiscriminate or undisciplined. Although they appear to move freely between the interpreted original context and their contemporary setting, John was keen to point out when challenged on his order of operations, that he never moved to application before "carefully considering both the original meaning, and the secondary sense, wherein (allowing for different times and circumstances) it may be applied to ordinary Christians" (*Works* [J], 8:407).

Related to "simultaneity" is the principle that the best interpreter of scripture was the Bible itself. John Wesley asserted that plainer texts were to be used whenever possible to interpret more obscure parts of the Bible: "scripture interprets scripture; one part fixing the sense of another" (*Works* [J], 10:482). He often offered new translations from the original languages using one text to shed light on words that might be translated in multiple ways. He exhorted the English clergy "to know the literal meaning of every word, verse, and chapter," and that they ought "likewise be able to deduce the proper corollaries, speculative and practical . . . to solve the difficulties which arise . . . and to make a suitable application" (*Works* [J], 10:482–483). Thus, there is a mutual interaction between the literal sense of the text and the simultaneity of scripture, which continually inform each other, confirming an interpretation, or calling for a revision of an interpretation that is either inconsistent at any point with the whole tenor of scripture, tested ultimately by the ability of the interpretation to be applied meaningfully to the contemporary context in a way that empowers and shapes one's life in the community of faith in holiness.

Significance. The distinctively Wesleyan conviction that the authorial intentions and the soteriological functions of scripture are the primary purposes of the text may reflect the Wesleys' largely pre-critical interpretative method. However, it was firmly grounded in a commitment to the inspired and inspiring nature and function of the message of the Bible. It was the subject matter of the Christological message of salvation, as inspired by the Holy Spirit and discerned by the body of Christ through the internal testimony of the Holy Spirit, that formed the foundation for the Wesleys' belief in the spiritual authority of the message of the text. This functional and soteriological view of the spiritual basis of scripture's authority provides a criterion for the spiritual and theological integrity of the Bible's message that remains valid for the rational and textual criteria of the critical and post-critical canonical interpretations of the text. It provides a foundation for the theological integrity of the text that is not reliant on the nature of the text itself, but upon the spiritual and theological authority of the saving purpose of the text itself, as informed and inspired and illuminated by the Holy Spirit. This message and its canonical witness to the Body of Christ through the internal testimony of the Holy Spirit allows the message of the text to serve its redemptive purposes based on the ancient criterion of the internal testimony functioning to witness to the reliability of the inspired text in continuing to witness to its own saving message.

Furthermore, the canonical approach implicit within Wesleyan interpretation is intrinsically relational, creating new avenues for interpretation within the contemporary setting in the context of community, and thus lending itself well to a post-modern setting. This is relevant to a critical and post-critical age that is not convinced by truth claims based on hypothetical, rationally based assumptions about the nature of the text itself to provide theological authority.

[*See also*: Authority of the Bible; Canonical Criticism; Catholic Biblical Interpretation; Evangelical Interpretation; Historical Criticism, *subentry* Hebrew Bible; Historical Criticism, *subentry* New Testament; Intertextuality; Lutheran Interpretation; Metaphor Theory and Biblical Texts; Reformed Christian Interpretation; Textual Criticism, *subentry* Hebrew Bible; Textual Criticism, *subentry* New Testament; *and* Theological Interpretation]

BIBLIOGRAPHY

Primary Sources

Wesley, Charles. *MS Scriptural Hymns*. 1783. Methodist Archives and Research Centre, John Rylands University of Manchester. Ref. Charles Wesley Notebooks, Box 3, MA 1977/576. Cited here as *MSSH*. Taken together with Wesley's *SHHS* (q.v.), form the majority of his hymnic corpus and offer the best look into his hermeneutics.

Wesley, Charles. *The Sermons of Charles Wesley: A Critical Edition, with Introduction and Notes*. Edited by Kenneth G. C. Newport. Oxford: Oxford University Press, 2001. The most complete and only critical edition of Charles's sermon corpus.

Wesley, Charles. *Short Hymns on Select Passages of the Holy Scriptures*. 2 vols. Bristol: Farley, 1762. Cited in the preceding article as SHHS. Similar to ENNT in their attempt to offer an expository commentary upon the bible. They make up more than half of Charles's poetic corpus.

Wesley, John. *The Bicentennial Edition of the Works of John Wesley*. (Begun as The Oxford Edition of the Works of John Wesley [Oxford: Oxford University Press, 1975–]). General eds. Frank Baker et al., 20 vols. to date. Nashville, Tenn.: Abingdon, 1984–. Cited in the preceding article as Works, followed by volume number and page number (e.g., Works, 15:171). Includes some works composed by Charles Wesley, especially hymns, and some sermons. The most up-to-date and the only critical edition of Wesley's Works. Because only two volumes of the Letters have been published in this edition (Vols. 25–26) to date, recourse must be made to the Telford edition of the Letters (q.v.) or to original MSS while the remaining volumes are forthcoming. Albert C. Outler's "Introduction" to the first volume of the Works outlines five main principles of interpretation observable in John Wesley's sermons (1–102).

Wesley, John. *Explanatory Notes Upon the New Testament*. 2 vols. London: Thomas Cordeux, 1813. Cited in the preceding article as ENNT. Although largely reliant upon Bengel's Gnomon (q.v.), offers much that is original, not least an estimated 12,000 alterations to the text of the Authorized Version. Although presently out-of-print, ENNT are projected as Vols. 5 and 6 of the Works.

Wesley, John. *Explanatory Notes Upon the Old Testament.* Bristol: Pine, 1765. Cited in this article as ENOT. Even more than his Notes on the New Testament, this work relied heavily upon the work of earlier commentators, although there is evidence throughout of Wesley's own exegesis.

Wesley, John. *The Works of the Rev. John Wesley.* 3d edn. Edited by Thomas Jackson, 14 vols. London: Wesleyan Conference Office, 1872. Cited in the preceding article as *Works* (J). While the Bicentennial Edition will eventually include everything once published in the Jackson edition, it remains incomplete and several key works are still only accessible via Jackson's edition.

Secondary Sources

Abraham, William J. "The Future of Scripture: In Search of a Theology of Scripture." *Wesleyan Theological Journal* 46:1 (Spring 2011): 7–24. Proposes three arenas for exploring a Wesleyan view of scripture now and in the future, by looking at: (1) The Relation of scripture to Divine Revelation; (2) Scripture as a Means of Grace in the church; and (3) Explorations in Theological Hermeneutics.

Baker, Frank. "John Wesley, Biblical Commentator." *Bulletin of the John Rylands University Library of Manchester* 71 (1989): 110–120. An examination of John Wesley's undertaking the composition of his *Explanatory Notes,* with examples of interpretive priorities, practical theological emphases, and the process of translating from the original tongues and editing the works of Bengel and others for popular consumption by his Methodist preachers and societies.

Callen, Barry L., and Richard P. Thompson. *Reading the Bible in Wesleyan Ways.* Kansas City, Mo.: Beacon Hill Press, 2004. A collection of essays on the topic of Wesleyan Biblical interpretation from a variety of angles. Many of the essays were previously published as articles in the Wesleyan Theological Journal, and thus provide a basic compendium rather than a thoroughgoing analysis.

Campbell, Ted A. "Scripture and Tradition in the Wesleyan Tradition." In *Orthodox and Wesleyan: Scriptural Understanding and Practice,* edited by S. T. Kimbrough, Jr., 157–170. Crestwood, N.Y.: St. Vladimir's Seminary Press, 2005. A comparative survey of the role of tradition in the interpretation of scripture in Wesley and in the Wesleyan tradition. Shows how modern American Methodists' recent development of a sense of connection to the Christian tradition has roots in Wesley's own view of Christian antiquity.

Casto, Robert Michael. "Exegetical Method in John Wesley's Explanatory Notes Upon the Old Testament: A Description of His Approach, Uses of Sources, and Practice." Ph. D. Thesis, Duke University, 1977. Significant primarily for its attention to Wesley's Old Testament exegesis. Offers insights into key influences on Wesley's approach to the Old Testament, and his view of the Old Testament in relation to the New Testament and as part of the biblical canon.

Green, Joel B. *I Peter. Practicing Theological Interpretation: Engaging Biblical Texts for Faith and Formation.* Grand Rapids. Mich.: Baker Academic, 2011. The most recent of a series of articles and books on a theological approach to scripture, positing the importance of bridging the chasm that has grown between biblical studies and theological studies. Provides one chapter on John Wesley and Wesleyan interpretation specifically.

Jones, S. J. *John Wesley's Conception and Use of Scripture.* Nashville, Tenn.: Abingdon, 1995. One of the most thorough examinations of John Wesley's hermeneutics to date, although some of Jones's assumptions and conclusions have been challenged by recent scholarship, particularly his *a priori* acceptance and use of the modern construct of the "Wesleyan Quadrilateral." Jones recapitulated his conclusions with only minor amendments in his articles in several handbooks/dictionaries of biblical interpreters.

Kimbrough, S. T., Jr. "Charles Wesley as Biblical Interpreter." In *Charles Wesley: Poet and Theologian,* edited by S. T. Kimbrough, Jr., 106–136. Nashville, Tenn.: Kingswood, 1992. One of the few critical engagements with Charles Wesley's biblical hermeneutics.

Leclercq, Diane. "Wesleyan-Holiness-Feminist Hermeneutics: Historical Rendering, Current Considerations." *Wesleyan Theological Journal* 36:2 (Fall 2001): 105–132. One of the few analyses of the significance of the developments of feminist hermeneutics for a Wesleyan approach to scripture, and offers avenues for further exploration.

Maddox, Randy L. "The Rule of Christian Faith, Practice and Hope: John Wesley on the Bible." *Methodist Review* 3 (2011): 1–35. One of the most significant overviews to date of John Wesley's Bible reading habits. Based on Maddox's previous work, gives attention to what we can learn of Wesley's interpretive habits based upon the evidence of the books in Wesley's library. Includes an important excursus on the issue of Wesley and inerrancy.

McCown, Wayne. "Toward a Wesleyan Hermeneutic." In *God's Word for Today; Wesleyan Theological Perspectives,* Vol. 2, edited by Wayne McCown and James Massey, 1–30. Anderson, Ind.: Warner Press, 1982. One of the earliest attempts to demonstrate the value of a canonical approach for Wesleyan biblical interpretation. Outlines key principles of John Wesley's interpretation that are particularly relevant to this canonical approach.

Shelton, R. Larry. "John Wesley's Approach to Scripture in Historical Perspective." *Wesleyan Theological Journal* 16:1 (Spring 1981): 23–50. A presentation of lines of continuity and contrast between John Wesley's hermeneutics and the interpretive methods of the early church fathers, medieval exegetes, and the reformers.

Shelton, R. Larry. "Nature, Character, and Origin of Scripture." In *Asbury Bible Commentary*, edited by Wayne McCown and Eugene Carpenter, 19–37. Grand Rapids, Mich.: Zondervan, 1992. A contemporary and expanded look at the historical background to John Wesley's approach to scripture, demonstrating similarities and differences between Wesley and the early church, the reformers, and the church in the eighteenth century.

Turner, G. A. "John Wesley as an Interpreter of Scripture." In *Inspiration and Interpretation*, edited by J. W. Walvoord, 156–178. Grand Rapids, Mich.: Eerdmans, 1957. One of the first examinations of the topic in the twentieth century. Contains many inaccuracies, and although many of Turner's generalizations regarding Wesley's aims say more about Turner's context than Wesley's, several of his ten interpretive principles have been maintained in more recent studies.

Tyson, John R. "Charles Wesley and the Language of Evangelical Experience: The Poetical Hermeneutic Revisited." *Asbury Journal* 61:1 (2006): 25–46. An updated assessment of his earlier article on the same subject of Wesley's poetic approach to biblical interpretation. One of the few analyses of Wesley's hermeneutics in general, and specifically, his poetic imagination which lent itself to the development of Methodist ecclesiology.

Wall, Robert W. "Reading the Bible from within Our Traditions: The 'Rule of Faith' in Theological Hermeneutics" and "Canonical Context and Canonical Conversations." In *Between Two Horizons: Spanning New Testament Studies and Systematic Theology*, edited by Joel B. Green and Max Turner, 88–107 and 165–182. Grand Rapids, Mich.: Eerdmans, 2000. A demonstration of the relevance of John Wesley's understanding of the "Rule of Faith" for contemporary approaches to theological interpretation.

Wall, Robert W. "Wesley as Biblical Interpreter." In *The Cambridge Companion to John Wesley*, edited by Randy L. Maddox and Jason Vickers, 113–128. Cambridge, UK: Cambridge University Press, 2010. Provides the background for understanding John Wesley's context, and a more complete exposition of a proposal that Wesley did in fact have a functional "canon within the canon," viz. 1 John.

Weeter, Mark. *John Wesley's View and Use of Scripture*. Eugene, Ore.: Wipf and Stock, 2007. Provides a book-length summary of John Wesley's interpretive principles. Revises conclusions drawn in S. J. Jones.

Raymond Larry Shelton and David R. Wilson

WOMANIST INTERPRETATION

Womanist interpretation addresses the simultaneity of multiple and overlapping oppressions such as racism, classism, and sexism while focusing on the experiences of African American women. Womanist biblical interpretation uses a similar perspective to analyze biblical texts.

Terminology. Pulitzer Prize-winning writer Alice Walker defines the term "womanist" in the front matter of her 1983 collection of essays, *In Search of Our Mothers' Gardens: Womanist Prose*. Walker did not coin the term "womanist," which meant "womanizer" in its archaic usage. Instead, Walker redefines the term in a creative, four-part description that highlights the term's roots in African American culture. Walker writes:

> 1. From womanish. (Opp. of "girlish," i.e., frivolous, irresponsible, not serious). A black feminist or feminist of color. From the black folk expression of mothers to female children, 'You acting *womanish*,' i.e., like a woman. Usually referring to outrageous, audacious, courageous or *willful* behavior. Wanting to know more and in greater depth than is considered 'good' for one. Interested in grown-up doings. Acting grown up. Being grown up. Interchangeable with another black folk expression: 'You trying to be grown.' Responsible. In charge. *Serious*. 2. *Also*: A woman who loves other women, sexually and/or nonsexually. Appreciates and prefers women's culture, women's emotional flexibility (values tears as a natural counterbalance of laughter), and women's strength. Sometimes loves individual men, sexually and/or nonsexually. Committed to survival and wholeness of entire people, male

and female. Not a separatist, except periodically, for health. Traditionally universalist, as in 'Mama, why are we brown, pink, and yellow, and our cousins are white, beige, and black?' Ans.: 'Well, you know the colored race is just like a flower garden, with every color flower represented.' Traditionally capable, as in: 'Mama, I'm walking to Canada and I'm taking you and a bunch of other slaves with me.' Reply: 'It wouldn't be the first time.' 3. Loves music. Loves dance. Loves the moon. *Loves* the Spirit. Loves love and food and roundness. Loves struggle. Loves the Folk. Loves herself. *Regardless.* 4. Womanist is to feminist as purple is to lavender. (Walker, pp. xi–xii)

Despite its complexity, Walker's multifaceted definition of more than 200 words is often shortened to highlight a single element of the definition. For example, "womanist" is often condensed into a single phrase from part one of Walker's definition: "black feminist or feminist of color" (Walker, p. xi). Another often-quoted phrase from the definition is the analogy: "womanist is to feminist as purple is to lavender" (Walker, p. xii). The emphasis on particular elements of this term contributes to confusion regarding its meaning.

Some African American women have embraced the term "womanist" and use it to describe themselves in contrast to "feminist." Others prefer to identify as Black feminists. Of course, not all African American women identify themselves as "womanist" or as "black feminist." Some prefer to use "feminist" without an adjective. Still others do not use these terms at all. Nevertheless, due to the popularity of Walker's book and of the term "womanist," there is a common misconception within broader society and within the academy that nearly all African American women and other women of color identify themselves as womanists. Yet, discussions regarding naming take place primarily among scholars and are not significant for most women outside of the academy.

Given the fluidity of Walker's definition, the lines between womanism and black feminism are blurred. Some people treat "womanist" and "black feminist" as synonymous, but others, despite Walker's definition, contend that womanism and black feminism are not interchangeable. They regard black feminism as an offshoot of feminism, which they associate with the interests and concerns of white women. In contrast, they understand womanism as a distinct entity that focuses on the experiences of African American women. For some women, the choice to use these or other terms to define themselves and/or their work allows them to situate themselves within a particular community and to include themselves within a historical trajectory.

Despite their differences, both womanists and Black feminists share a critique of feminism as focused primarily on gender issues. They may identify as womanist or as black feminist in part as a response to what they perceive as feminism's failure to address issues of race and ethnicity. Also, both highlight the importance of treating oppressions not as additive but as multiplicative. For example, African American women face racism, sexism, and classism at the same time and experience these forms of oppression in ways that compound each other (King 1988). Similarly, a woman who is gay and a member of a religious minority group may face discrimination differently than a woman who is a member in the same religious community and who identifies as heterosexual.

Although the term "intersectionality" does not appear in Walker's definition, it has gained traction as referring to the ways in which various oppressions intersect and overlap (Crenshaw 1989, 1991). Intersectional analysis interrogates race, class, gender, and other issues not as separate and distinct but as interlocking elements. Intersectional analysis has become an important element within black feminist and womanist thought. Patricia Hill Collins distinguishes intersectionality and what she terms a "matrix of domination." While intersectionality examines these simultaneous forms of oppression, the matrix of domination "refers to how these intersecting oppressions are actually organized" (Hill Collins 2000, p. 18).

Beyond Walker. While Walker is considered to be the pioneer of womanism, she is not the only figure involved in its development as other writers have developed different notions of womanism. Nigerian writer Chikwenye Okonjo Ogunyemi (1985) claims that she developed the term "womanism" independently of Walker. Now referring to the concept as "African womanism," Ogunyemi (1996) rejects both feminism and African American womanism and offers African womanism as less individualistic, more familial, and more focused on the distinctiveness of African struggles within a global community.

Clenora Hudson-Weems (1993) has developed the concept of "Africana womanism," which she distinguishes from feminism, womanism, and African womanism. Instead of using the terms "African American," "black," or "African," Hudson-Weems uses a more inclusive term "Africana," which refers to continental Africans as well as those who are part of the African diaspora. She does not use the term "womanism" as defined by Walker. Instead, she links "womanism" with the term "woman" and with the struggles of Africana women such as nineteenth century former slave and abolitionist Sojourner Truth who challenged traditional notions of womanhood. For Hudson-Weems, Africana womanism focuses on community and on the collective work of Africana men and women. The terms as developed by Ogunyemi and Hudson-Weems are not as well known outside of the academy. Walker's definition of womanism is the most well known, but it is often simplified as merely another term for "black feminist."

Unresolved Issues in Womanist Approaches. Due to the intricacies of Walker's definition, it can be understood to embrace a variety of viewpoints simultaneously, including somewhat disparate elements such as black nationalism, pluralism, and integration/assimilation (Hill Collins 1996). Since Walker's definition was not a philosophical statement or an essay on womanism but a poetic description, its fluidity allows it to be used to support different and discordant concepts. In effect, the definition is too complex and broad to be helpful in identifying the primary elements of a womanist approach.

For example, the definition supports same-gender loving relationships as well as a commitment to both men and women. In part two of Walker's definition, Walker writes, "*Also*: a woman who loves other women, sexually and/or nonsexually" [italics original] (Walker, p. xi). In the same section, she writes: "committed to survival and wholeness of entire people, male *and* female" [italics original] (Walker, p. xi). These statements are not incompatible, but some find these notions to be inconsistent due to the fear that same-gender loving relationships constitute a threat to black families made up of black straight couples.

The exclusion of homosexuality from black feminist and womanist thought in religion-related fields is partly tied to the conservative Christian influence in these fields. As discussed by theologian Monica Coleman, in her 2006 article "Must I Be a Womanist?," womanist thought within religion-related fields has stressed heteronormativity and has created a largely "Christian hegemonic discourse" (Coleman 2006, p. 89). While some scholars offer more inclusive viewpoints, womanist thought within religion-related fields remains dominated by Christian perspectives.

One key element of womanist approaches is a focus on the lived experiences of African American women. Due to this emphasis on the personal experience and the experiences of African American women, womanist work has become the domain of African American women and other women of color. For example, sociologist Patricia Hill Collins claims, "Living life as an African American woman is a necessary prerequisite for producing Black feminist thought." (Hill Collins 1989, p. 770). Thus, black feminist thought uses standpoint theory to articulate the position of black women. Psychologist Layli Phillips (Maparyan) argues, "You're a womanist if you say you're a womanist, but others can contest you or ask you what womanism means for you" (Phillips 2006, p. xxxvi). Given the scarcity of African American female biblical scholars, this emphasis on personal experience may result in its continued failure to have an impact on the field of biblical studies.

Womanist Approaches in Religion-Related Fields Outside of Biblical Scholarship. Womanist approaches are more prevalent in religion-related fields such as theology, ethics, and homiletics than in biblical studies. For example, *Deeper Shades of Purple: Womanism in Religion and Society* (2006), edited by ethicist Stacey Floyd-Thomas, includes essays from a variety of scholars, but it does not include contributions from biblical scholars. In fact, a majority of what could be called womanist biblical interpretation has taken place outside of the field of biblical studies. Womanist scholars discuss biblical texts extensively in their work and have done so for decades. For example, Jacquelyn Grant interrogates understandings of Jesus/Christ in her work *White Women's Christ and Black Women's Jesus: Feminist Christology and Womanist Response* (1989). Delores Williams's *Sisters in the Wilderness: The Challenge of Womanist God-Talk* (1993) analyzes the Abraham/Sarah/Hagar narratives (Genesis 16 and Genesis 21) in order to construct a liberative womanist theology.

Nevertheless, due to academic disciplinary boundaries, most biblical scholars would not consider the work of these scholars to be critical biblical scholarship in the traditional sense of the term. As narrowly conceived, biblical scholarship is written and presented by those whose primary training is in the discipline of academic biblical studies, who use the tools of the discipline, and who participate in the conversations taking place within the discipline. These disciplinary boundaries are not only applied to womanist work: many scholars within other fields engage biblical texts, but biblical scholars do not consider their work to be biblical scholarship in this sense. For example, theologian David Ford, ethicist Miguel de la Torre, and homiletician Teresa Fry Brown all engage biblical texts within their work, but their work is not typically considered to be academic biblical scholarship because it is not written by those who specialize in biblical studies. Similarly, womanist scholars outside of biblical studies are biblical interpreters, but their work is not considered to be biblical scholarship by those within the field. Womanist biblical interpretation by those within biblical studies is scarce and thus has had a minimal impact on biblical scholarship.

Womanist Biblical Scholarship. Within biblical studies, the term "womanist" is commonly used to describe the scholar rather than a particular interpretive approach. That is, "womanist" is assumed to refer to a female scholar of African descent rather than to a critical approach to biblical scholarship used by that scholar. Currently, no clear consensus exists regarding what constitutes a womanist approach within biblical studies, and biblical scholars have not yet developed a significant body of scholarship that utilizes womanist approaches as a distinct critical method or set of concerns in an explicit way. Rather, African American female biblical scholars have generated womanist work that varies greatly in its relationship to Walker's definition.

Key Figures. Renita Weems is the biblical scholar who is most often associated with womanist biblical interpretation. She was the first African American woman to receive a PhD in Old Testament, having graduated from Princeton Theological Seminary in 1989. Her book *Just a Sister Away: A Womanist Vision of Women's Relationships in the Bible* (1988) was the first volume in biblical studies labeled as a womanist work. In this popular trade book, Weems focuses on the relationships between nine sets of biblical women, including Hagar and Sarah (Genesis 16 and 21) and Mary and Martha (Luke 10:38–42). Designed as a resource primarily for African American Christian women, this book provides creative interpretations of the relationships between biblical women and includes questions for thought following each chapter. It was revised and reissued as *Just a Sister Away: Understanding the Timeless Connection between Women of Today and Women in the Bible* (2005).

Many of Weems's publications are similar to *Just a Sister Away* and are intended for popular audiences. For example, in *What Matters Most: Ten Lessons in Living Passionately from the Song of Solomon* (2004), Weems focuses on helping women to identify their passions and to find personal fulfillment. Also, in her memoir, *Listening for God: A Minister's Journey through Silence and Doubt* (1999), Weems shares her personal faith crisis and describes her efforts to maintain her relationship to God.

In various scholarly publications, Weems describes womanist approaches to biblical texts as involving attention to multiple categories of oppression and as incorporating the personal experiences of African American women. For example, in her article "Womanist Reflections on Biblical Hermeneutics" (1993), Weems resists both the historical-critical method as well as the gender-focused analysis of feminist criticism. She advocates for a womanist approach that addresses multiple oppressions and suggests that women of color, having been victimized by these multiple oppressions, can bring their experiences to bear within biblical scholarship. Also, in "Re-Reading for Liberation: African American Women and the Bible" (2003), Weems argues that womanist biblical hermeneutics does not begin with the Bible; instead, it comes from the perspective of African American women's experience, in particular as survivors of slavery and as survivors of various forms of oppression. For Weems, womanist biblical hermeneutics begins with the notion that "people have power, not texts" (Weems 2003, p. 26).

Despite Weems's varied discussions of womanist approaches, she has not provided more technical discussions that illustrate the usefulness of womanist approaches for critical biblical scholarship. For example, in her only book-length exegetical work *Battered Love: Marriage, Sex, and Violence in the Hebrew Prophets* (1995), Weems states that she uses her experiences as an African American woman in her approach to prophetic literature, but she does not construct or use what she names as a womanist approach. Although Weems is regarded as one of the key figures in womanist biblical interpretation, she has not used womanist approaches in detailed exegetical treatments of biblical texts in conversation with more advanced researchers involved in the critical discipline of biblical studies.

Clarice J. Martin was the first African American woman to receive a PhD in New Testament, graduating from Duke University in 1985. In "Womanist Interpretations of the New Testament: The Quest for Holistic and Inclusive Translation and Interpretation" (1990), Martin contrasts feminist approaches and womanist approaches and contends that womanist approaches are distinct in that they focus on rediscovering not only women's voices but also the voices of the marginalized.

Martin examines the household codes (Col 3:18–41; Eph 5:21—6:9; 1 Pet 2:18—3:7) in "The Haustafeln (Household Codes) in African American Biblical Interpretation: 'Free Slave' and 'Subordinate Women" (1991)." She highlights selected African American approaches to these texts and offers a womanist perspective in order to create greater gender equality between African American men and women. In "Polishing the Unclouded Mirror: A Womanist Reading of Revelation 18:13" (2005), Martin puts into conversation the critique of ancient slavery within this text with the African American experience of slavery. Her womanist approach highlights the experiences of African American and Africana women as marginalized peoples.

Both Weems and Martin are pioneers as African-American women who are trained as biblical scholars. They are frequently cited alongside feminist biblical scholars in a misleading way, as if they are illustrative of a group of womanist scholars. While Weems and Martin are certainly key figures in womanist biblical scholarship, they are not the leading practitioners among a large number of womanist biblical scholars. In fact, they are only two of the very few biblical scholars who name themselves and their work within biblical studies as womanist (Junior 2006). Moreover, for both Weems and Martin, womanist biblical interpretation is not an exegetical method with a step-by-step procedure but an approach to engaging biblical texts in a way that focuses on the perspectives and experiences of African American women.

Other Voices. There are biblical scholars other than Weems and Martin who use womanist approaches in biblical studies, but there are only a few. Furthermore, these scholars differ greatly in their use of the term "womanist" and in the ways in which they apply womanist approaches in interpreting biblical texts. Koala Jones-Warsaw's article "Toward a Womanist Hermeneutic: A Reading of Judges 19–21" (1993) is often cited as an example of womanist biblical interpretation. Jones-Warsaw sets her work in conversation with Phyllis Trible's feminist treatment of Judges 19—21 in *Texts of Terror: Literary-Feminist Readings of Biblical Narratives* (1984). In defining her approach to a womanist reading, Jones-Warsaw uses two segments of Walker's definition: "outrageous, audacious, courageous, *willful* behavior (italics in Walker's original)" and "committed to survival and wholeness of entire people, male and female" (Jones-Warsaw, p. 182). Citing theologian Jacquelyn Grant's work, Jones-Warsaw contends that the purpose of womanist biblical hermeneutics is to "discover the significance and validity of the biblical text for black women who today experience the 'tridimensional reality' of racism, sexism, and classism" (Jones-Warsaw, p. 182). For Jones-Warsaw, womanism involves selective use of Walker's definition and provides a perspective from which to reflect on the text.

Hebrew Bible scholar Wilda (Wil) Gafney identifies herself as a feminist or as a womanist depending on the context. In "A Black Feminist Approach to Biblical Studies" (2006) Gafney highlights four key elements of womanist work, including: multidimensionality, a focus on women's experience, efforts toward the goal of eradication of human oppression, and making scholarship accessible to a "wider nonspecialist worshipping community" (Gafney, p. 392). In her translation and reading of Judges 14:1–20, Gafney names Samson's wife "Yasherah," although she is unnamed in the text, and highlights her humanity and her vulnerability. For Gafney, her role as a "black feminist biblical scholar" is to retell the story of the "silenced," "unknown," and "erased" (Gafney, p. 403). Gafney's expanded notion of "womanist" does not focus primarily on African American women's experiences although it does address multiple oppressions. Like Weems, Gafney's major book-length work, *Daughters of Miriam: Women Prophets in Ancient Israel* (2008), based on her 2006 Duke University dissertation, does not utilize a womanist approach.

New Testament scholar Raquel St. Clair describes her womanist approach in one of the first published book-length treatments of a biblical text labeled as a womanist work. In *Call and Consequences: A Womanist Reading of Mark*, a revision of her 2005 Princeton Theological Seminary dissertation, St. Clair reads the Gospel of Mark through a womanist lens. She acknowledges her debt to the work of womanist theologians. Yet, her primary exegetical method is the cultural interpretation model developed by her dissertation advisor Brian K. Blount. This cultural interpretation model uses sociolinguistics in order to focus on language and the context of language. St. Clair uses this cultural interpretation model in conjunction with a womanist hermeneutics of wholeness. This womanist hermeneutics of wholeness:

1. is focused on the wholeness of African American women;
2. is grounded in the concrete reality of African American women's lives;
3. affirms that God supports African American women in their commitment to and struggle for wholeness; and
4. asserts that the significance of Jesus is his life and ministry (St. Clair, pp. 82–83).

St. Clair develops a uniquely womanist approach that focuses on African American women but includes an especially Christian perspective.

Currently, there is no consensus on how to conduct womanist biblical interpretation. The approaches of Jones-Warsaw, Gafney, and St. Clair illustrate some of the diversity in womanist biblical interpretation as each author offers a different notion of a womanist approach that departs from the definitions of womanism by Walker and others. Yet, as is the case with Weems and Martin, these are not representative examples among a large group of scholars since there are few biblical scholars within womanist biblical interpretation.

Impact of Womanist Approaches on Biblical Studies. Womanist biblical interpretation has not had a significant impact on the field of biblical studies in terms of the production of material for scholarly discourse. Among scholarly publications, St. Clair's *Call and Consequences* is the only published monograph-length work that is labeled as a womanist approach to biblical studies. Currently, there is no edited volume in biblical studies using womanist approaches or scholarly journals dedicated to womanist biblical studies.

Within biblical scholarship, there is a limited awareness of womanist thought. The term "womanist" is sometimes mentioned in publications, but it is often linked with "feminist" and appears frequently as "feminist/womanist." Yet, even when mentioned, there is relatively little engagement with womanist thought, such that the use of the term appears to be a weak attempt at inclusion of women of color without careful engagement with the complexities underlying the term as used and developed by Walker and others.

The impact of womanist biblical interpretation has also been minimal within the scholarly guild. At the annual meetings of the Society of Biblical Literature (SBL), the largest scholarly organization for biblical studies, there is little engagement with womanist approaches. The many presentation sessions at SBL are divided among various program units and provide a way for SBL members with particular interests to converse and share ideas. While individual scholars may use womanist thought in their paper presentations, there is no program unit on womanist approaches. Active since 1880, the *Journal of Biblical Literature*, the primary publication of SBL, has not published one journal article using an explicitly womanist approach.

The limited impact of womanist biblical interpretation within biblical studies may be due, in part, to the very few women of African descent who are trained biblical scholars. Data are not available on the numbers of African American women with doctoral degrees in this field, but based on observation and anecdote, there are very few. Even among the few African American female biblical scholars, not all of those women choose to use womanist approaches to their work or develop aspects of womanist thought that would clearly distinguish their approach from feminist biblical scholarship in general.

Thus, it is understandable that womanist biblical interpretation is often linked with feminist biblical interpretation. Numerous publications include terms such as "feminist/womanist" or "black feminist/womanist." Womanist biblical interpretation is related to feminist biblical interpretation and expands on feminism's typical focus on gender to include multiple categories of difference such as gender, race/ethnicity, and class. Although womanist biblical interpretation is often regarded as analogous to feminist biblical interpretation, the two differ greatly in their influence within the field of biblical studies. While womanist biblical interpretation has had minimal impact in the guild, the impact of feminist biblical interpretation has been significant.

Feminist biblical interpretation by scholars who were trained in biblical studies emerged in the 1970s. These and other scholars have trained a second and third generation of feminist biblical scholars. Within biblical scholarship, feminist analysis is not commonplace, but it has become relatively mainstream. Many monographs, edited volumes, and journal articles using feminist approaches are published every year. *The Women's Bible Commentary*, published originally in 1992, was revised and expanded in 1998. Also, a twentieth anniversary revised edition is forthcoming. At SBL, there are some sections that engage feminist approaches, including Feminist Hermeneutics of the Bible and Women in the Biblical World, which have been active in different forms since the late 1980s. In addition, other sections include and encourage presentations that use feminist approaches, which indicates how mainstream these approaches have become.

In general terms, a feminist reading of biblical texts involves focused attention on gender and power dynamics within biblical texts. The particular elements of a feminist approach to biblical texts are contested as there are no agreed-upon steps or procedures for feminist biblical criticism. Yet, unlike womanist biblical interpretation, feminist biblical interpretation has matured to the point of having debates regarding feminist approaches and eventually achieved some consensus amidst considerable diversity due to the extensive body of feminist biblical scholarship that has been produced over the last 40 years.

Furthermore, feminist approaches have been influential to the point that attention to gender is not necessarily labeled as "feminist." For example, some scholars may prefer to identify their work as "gender analysis." Also, some scholars choose to focus on women or gender construction but prefer to identify their work with the particular exegetical method or methods that they use. Unlike womanist biblical interpretation, which is assumed to be work produced by any black female scholar, no responsible scholar would assume that a female biblical scholar was necessarily a feminist or that her work involved the use of feminist approaches.

Some may caution against comparing the impact of feminism and womanism on biblical studies because womanist interpretation is still a relative newcomer to critical biblical scholarship and has not had as much time as feminism to have a substantive impact. On this point, the example of critical disability studies is revealing. Like womanist biblical interpretation, critical disability studies is a recent addition to the discipline of biblical studies, but unlike womanist biblical interpretation, disability studies does not rely on the personal experiences of those with disabilities. Thus, having a disability does not qualify one to be a disability scholar. Scholars who engage in work on disability may or may not identify as persons with disabilities. What they have in common is a critical interest in questions regarding the construction of disability and nondisability within biblical and cognate literature.

Academic disability studies grew out of the disability rights movement, but scholars who work in disability studies are not primarily concerned with advocating for the rights of those with disabilities. Instead, they are producing critical scholarship. There are an increasing number of scholarly monographs, edited volumes, and journal articles that address issues of disability in biblical scholarship. (For examples, see Junior and Schipper, forthcoming). Also, there is an SBL program unit Healthcare and Disability in the Ancient World, which began under a different title in 2004. Given its contributions to scholarly discourse, critical disability studies is emerging as in important subfield within the discipline of biblical studies. Although both are relatively new approaches in biblical studies, womanist approaches have not reached the level of inclusion within scholarly discourse that disability studies has achieved.

Future. Given the very few numbers of African American and other women of color in biblical studies, womanist biblical interpretation will have a limited impact in the field of biblical studies as long as "womanist" refers to an individual scholar instead of to her work. It will be mentioned alongside feminist biblical interpretation as an effort at inclusive language, but it will not become a serious sub-field unless it produces critical scholarship that is in conversation with the wider discipline. The experiences of African American, African, and African diasporic women are important, but as long as womanist work remains work that is to a considerable degree "of black women, by black women, and for black women," (Coleman 2006, p. 91) it will remain on the margins of biblical scholarship.

[*See also* African American Interpretation; African Biblical Interpretation; Diaspora Studies; Disability Criticism; Feminist Biblical Interpretation; Ideological Criticism; Lesbian, Gay, Bisexual, and Transgender Interpretation; Queer Criticism and Queer Theory; *and* Race, Ethnicity, and Biblical Criticism.]

BIBLIOGRAPHY

Crenshaw, Kimberle. "Demarginalizing the Intersection of Race and Sex: A Black Feminist Critique of Antidiscrimination Doctrine, Feminist Theory and Antiracist Politics." *University of Chicago Legal Forum* (1989): 139–167. Legal essay that introduces the notion of "intersectionality" and addresses the race discrimination and sex discrimination faced by Black women plaintiffs in court cases.

Crenshaw, Kimberle. "Mapping the Margins: Intersectionality, Identity Politics, and Violence against Women of Color." *Stanford Law Review* 43, no. 6 (1991): 1241–1299. Legal essay that further explores notions of intersectionality in addressing racism and sexism affecting women of color who are victims of male violence.

Floyd-Thomas, Stacey M., ed. *Deeper Shades of Purple: Womanism in Religion and Society*. New York: New York University Press, 2006. Helpful volume on womanism from scholars in a variety of disciplines that includes responses from nonwomanist perspectives.

Gafney, Wilda. "A Black Feminist Approach to Biblical Studies." *Encounter* 67, no 4. (2006): 391–403. Provides an example of a black feminist approach to biblical studies in reading Judges 14:1–20.

Grant, Jacquelyn. *White Women's Christ and Black Women's Jesus: Feminist Christology and Womanist Response.* Edited by Susan Thistlethwaite. Vol. 64, American Academy of Religion Academy Series. Atlanta: Scholars Press, 1989. Distinguishes Christological readings of feminist and womanists.

Hill Collins, Patricia. *Black Feminist Thought: Knowledge, Consciousness, and the Politics of Empowerment.* Rev. 10th anniversary ed. New York: Routledge, 2000. Classic work that discusses key features of black feminist thought.

Hill Collins, Patricia. "The Social Construction of Black Feminist Thought." *Signs: Journal of Women in Culture and Society* 14, no. 4 (1989): 745-773. Foundational article on approaching black feminist thought that stresses black standpoint theory.

Hudson Weems, Cleonora. *Africana Womanism: Reclaiming Ourselves.* Troy, Mich., 1993. Distinguishes Africana womanism from other terms.

Jones-Warsaw, Koala. "Toward a Womanist Hermeneutic: A Reading of Judges 19–21." In *A Feminist Companion to Judges*, edited by Athalya Brenner, 172–186. Sheffield, UK: Sheffield Academic Press, 1993. Offers a womanist reading of Judges 19–21.

Junior, Nyasha. "Womanist Biblical Interpretation." In *Engaging the Bible in a Gendered World: An Introduction to Feminist Biblical Interpretation in Honor of Katharine Doob Sakenfeld*, edited by Carolyn Pressler and Linda Day, 37–46. Louisville, Ky.: Westminster John Knox, 2006. Provides an overview of womanist interpretation in biblical studies.

Junior, Nyasha, and Jeremy Schipper. "Disability Studies and Biblical Scholarship." In *New Meaning for Ancient Texts.* Edited by Steven L. McKenzie and John Kaltner. Louisville, Ky.: Westminster John Knox, forthcoming. Discusses the history and use of disability studies within critical biblical scholarship.

King, Deborah. "Multiple Jeopardy, Multiple Consciousness: The Context of Black Feminist Ideology." *Signs: Journal of Women in Culture and Society* 14, no. 1 (1988): 42–72 Moves beyond "double jeopardy" of racism and sexism and explicates the notion of "multiple jeopardy" and the necessity of addressing multiple forms of oppression.

Martin, Clarice J. "The Haustafeln (Household Codes) in African American Biblical Interpretation: 'Free Slave' and 'Subordinate Women." In *Stony the Road We Trod: African American Biblical Interpretation.* Edited by Cain Hope Felder, 206–231. Minneapolis: Fortress Press, 1991. Highlights treatment of Household Codes by African American interpreters and contrasts regulations regarding slaves and those regarding women.

Martin, Clarice J. "Polishing the Unclouded Mirror: A Womanist Reading of Revelation 18:13." In *From Every People and Nation: The Book of Revelation in Intercultural Perspective.* Edited by David Rhoads, 82–109. Minneapolis: Fortress Press, 2005. Provides an example of a womanist reading of Rev 18:13.

Martin, Clarice J. "Womanist Interpretations of the New Testament: The Quest for Holistic and Inclusive Translation and Interpretation." *Journal of Feminist Studies in Religion* 6 (1990): 41–61. Discusses the distinctiveness of womanist approaches in addressing oppressive structures.

Ogunyemi, Chikwenye Okonjo. *African Wo/Man Palava: The Nigerian Novel by Women.* Chicago: University of Chicago, 1996. Analyzes the work of eight Nigerian women and discusses the notion of "palava."

Ogunyemi, Chikwenye Okonjo. "Womanism: The Dynamics of the Contemporary Black Female Novel in English." *Signs: Journal of Women in Culture and Society* 11, no. 1 (1985): 63–85. Discusses Ogunyemi's notion of "womanism."

St. Clair, Raquel A. *Call and Consequences: A Womanist Reading of Mark.* Minneapolis: Fortress, 2008. Provides one of the first full-length womanist readings of a biblical text.

Phillips, Layli, ed. *The Womanist Reader: The First Quarter Century of Womanist Thought.* New York: Routledge, 2006. This edited volume illustrates a range of womanist approaches in multiple disciplines.

Weems, Renita J. *Just a Sister Away: A Womanist Vision of Women's Relationships in the Bible.* San Diego, Calif.: LuraMedia, 1988. The earliest work labeled as a womanist work within biblical studies.

Williams, Delores. *Sisters in the Wilderness: The Challenge of Womanist God-Talk.* Maryknoll, N.Y.: Orbis Books 1995. Constructions of a womanist liberation theology through engagement with the Hagar narratives.

Walker, Alice. *In Search of Our Mothers' Gardens: Womanist Prose.* San Diego, Calif.: Harcourt Brace Jovanovich, 1983. Collection of essays that includes famous definition of the term "womanist."

Nyasha Junior

TOPICAL OUTLINE OF CONTENTS

This outline provides a general overview of the conceptual scheme of *The Oxford Encyclopedia of Biblical Interpretation*, listing the title of each entry and subentry. Entries in the Encyclopedia are organized alphabetically. Entries in this outline are arranged under the following headings. Headings are purely heuristic and not evaluative. For instance, placing an entry under "Ideological Approaches" does not mean that it was regarded by the editors as any more ideological in orientation than other entries.

THE BIBLICAL WORLD

The Ancient World

Anthropological-Sociological Methods

Anthropological Methods

Socioscientific Criticism

THE BIBLICAL TEXT

Translation

LITERARY APPROACHES

CULTURAL APPROACHES

Afrocentric Biblical Interpretation

Asian, Asian American Interpretation

Hispanic/Latino/a Biblical Interpretation

Cultural Criticism

IDEOLOGICAL APPROACHES

Ideological Criticism

Gender Criticism

Class Criticism

Race Criticism

Sexuality Criticism

Religiously Determined Interpretation

Jewish Interpretation

Christian Interpretation

Muslim Interpretation

PHILOSOPHICAL APPROACHES

POLITICAL APPROACHES

Directory of Contributors

John Ahn
St. Edward's University
Diaspora Studies

George Aichele
Professor Emeritus, Adrian College
Poststructuralist Interpretation
Semiotics

Joel S. Baden
Yale Divinity School
Tradition-Historical Criticism

Carol Bakhos
University of California, Los Angeles
Midrash

Philip L. Barlow
Utah State University
Latter-day Saints (Mormon) Interpretation

Craig Bartholomew
Redeemer University College
Theological Interpretation

Richard J. Bautch
St. Edward's University
Form Criticism: Apocrypha and Deuterocanonical Books

Timothy Beal
Case Western Reserve University
Cultural-Historical Criticism

Dianne Bergant
Catholic Theological Union
Catholic Biblical Interpretation

C. Clifton Black
Princeton Theological Seminary
Redaction Criticism: New Testament

Paul M. Blowers
Emmanuel Christian Seminary
Eastern Orthodox Interpretation
Patristic Interpretation

Roland Boer
University of Newcastle, Australia
Class Criticism
Materialist Criticism

Ian Boxall
University of Oxford, UK
Reception Criticism and Theory

Valerie Bridgeman
Lancaster Theological Seminary
Homiletics

Edwin K. Broadhead
Berea College
Formalist Interpretation

Dexter Callender Jr.
University of Miami
Mythology and Biblical Interpretation

David M. Carr
Union Theological Seminary in New York
Source Criticism

Warren Carter
Texas Christian University—Brite Divinity School
Empire Studies and Biblical Interpretation

Corrine L. Carvalho
University of St. Thomas
Canonical Criticism

Bruce Chilton
Bard College
Genre Criticism

Dan W. Clanton Jr.
Doane College
Pop Culture and the Bible

Kelley Coblentz Bautch
St. Edwards University
Textual Criticism: Apocrypha and Deuterocanonical Books

Billie Jean Collins
Emory University
Hittitology and Biblical Interpretation

Sidnie White Crawford
University of Nebraska, Lincoln
Dead Sea Scrolls

N. Clayton Croy
Trinity Lutheran Seminary
Textual Criticism: New Testament

Adrian Curtis
The University of Manchester, U.K.
Geography and Topography in Biblical Interpretation

David A. deSilva
Ashland Theological Seminary
Rhetorical Criticism

Musa W. Dube
University of Botswana
African Biblical Interpretation

Benjamin H. Dunning
Fordham University
Gnosticism and Gnostic Interpretation

Mark W. Elliott
University of St. Andrews, UK
Allegory and Allegorical Interpretation

John T. Fitzgerald
University of Notre Dame
Greco-Roman Context

David G. Garber Jr.
Mercer University
Trauma Theory

Francisco O. García-Treto
Trinity University, Emeritus
Cuban Interpretation in the Cuban Diaspora

Stephen Garfinkel
Jewish Theological Seminary
Conservatve Jewish Interpretation

Agustinus Gianto
Pontifical Biblical Institute, Rome
Ugaritology and Biblical Interpretation

Bridget Gilfillan Upton
University of London, UK
Speech-Act Theory

Mark Goodacre
Duke University
Synoptic Problem

Norman K. Gottwald
New York Theological Seminary, Emeritus
Social Sciences: Hebrew Bible

Rhiannon Graybill
Rhodes College
Literary Criticism, Literary Theory, and the Bible

Gene L. Green
Wheaton College
Relevance Theory and Biblical Interpretation

Frederick E. Greenspahn
Florida Atlantic University
Reform Jewish Interpretation

Leonard Greenspoon
Creighton University
Translation Techniques: Ancient Versions

Leticia A. Guardiola-Sáenz
Seattle University
Latina/o Interpretation

Susan E. Haddox
University of Mount Union
Masculinity Studies

Raimo Hakola
University of Helsinki
Anti-Judaism and Anti-Semitism in the New Testament and Its Interpretation

Alan J. Hauser
Appalachian State University
Reformed Christian Interpretation

Gina Hens-Piazza
Santa Clara University
New Historicism

Bonnie Howe
Dominican University of California
Cognitive Linguistics and Biblical Interpretation

Kelly R. Iverson
Baylor University
Performance Criticism

Job Y. Jindo
New York University School of Law
Metaphor Theory and Biblical Texts

Nyasha Junior
Howard University School of Divinity
Womanist Interpretation

Walter C. Kaiser Jr.
Gordon-Conwell Theological Seminary, Emeritus
Evangelical Interpretation

Jason Kalman
Hebrew Union College
University of the Free State, South Africa
Rabbinic Exegesis

Brad E. Kelle
Point Loma Nazarene University
Diachronic Interpretation

D. Andrew Kille
Revdak Consulting
Psychological Biblical Interpretation

William W. Klein
Denver Seminary
Authority of the Bible

Robert Kugler
Lewis and Clark College
Redaction Criticism: Apocrypha and Deuterocanonical Books

Karl Allen Kuhn
Lakeland College
Phenomenological Interpretation

Won W. Lee
Calvin College
Korean Interpretation

T. M. Lemos
Huron University College at the University of Western Ontario
Cultural Anthropology: Hebrew Bible

Alan Lenzi
University of the Pacific
Assyriology and Biblical Interpretation

G. Brooke Lester
Garrett-Evangelical Theological Seminary
Inner-biblical Interpretation

B. Barry Levy
McGill University
Orthodox Jewish Interpretation

Tat-siong Benny Liew
Pacific School of Religion
Asian American Biblical Interpretation

Dennis R. MacDonald
Claremont School of Theology
Mimesis Criticism

Elvira Martín-Contreras
Spanish Council for Scientific Research (CSIC)
Masora and Masoretic Interpretation

Shelly Matthews
Texas Christian University – Brite Divinity School
Feminist Biblical Interpretation

Kathy Reiko Maxwell
Palm Beach Atlantic University
Reader-Response Criticism

Edgar V. McKnight
Furman University
Form Criticism: New Testament

Néstor Oscar Míguez
Instituto Universitario ISEDET
Central and South American Interpretation

Francis J. Moloney
Australian Catholic University, Emeritus
Synchronic Interpretation

Megan Bishop Moore
Independent Scholar
Historical Criticism: Hebrew Bible

Milton C. Moreland
Rhodes College
Historical Criticism: New Testament

Candida R. Moss
University of Notre Dame
Disability Criticism

Roger S. Nam
George Fox University
Economics and the Bible

Dietmar Neufeld
University of British Columbia
Cultural Anthropology: New Testament
Social Sciences: New Testament

Gordon Nickel
University of Calgary, Alberta
Qur'anic and Islamic Interpretation of the Bible

Susan Niditch
Amherst College
Folklore and Biblical Interpretation

Christophe Nihan
Université de Lausanne
Exegesis

David Odell-Scott
Kent State University
Semiotics

Tomohiro Omiya
Nagoya Gakuin University
Japanese Interpretation

B. J. Oropeza
Azusa Pacific University
Intertextuality

Daniel Patte
Vanderbilt University
Structuralist Interpretation

Stephen J. Patterson
Willamette University
Historical Jesus, Quest for the

David Penchansky
University of St. Thomas
Deconstruction

Raymond F. Person Jr.
Ohio Northern University
Orality Studies and Oral Tradition: Hebrew Bible

Christina Petterson
Humboldt University, Berlin
Translation Techniques: Modern Versions

Carol A. Redmount
University of California, Berkeley
Egyptology and Biblical Interpretation

Vernon K. Robbins
Emory University
Socio-rhetorical Criticism

Thomas Römer
University of Lausanne
Redaction Criticism: Hebrew Bible

Christopher Rowland
University of Oxford, UK
Ideological Criticism
Reception Criticism and Theory

Philip Ruge-Jones
Texas Lutheran University
Orality Studies and Oral Tradition: New Testament

Susanne Scholz
Southern Methodist University
Feminist Biblical Interpretation

Flip Schutte
University of Pretoria, South Africa
Autobiographical and Personal Criticism

Joseph Scrivner
Samford University
African American Interpretation

Love L. Sechrest
Fuller Theological Seminary
Race, Ethnicity, and Biblical Criticism

Raymond Larry Shelton
George Fox Evangelical Seminary
Wesleyan Biblical Interpretation

Abraham Smith
Southern Methodist University
Cultural Studies

Daniel Smith-Christopher
Loyola Marymount University
Cross-Cultural Exegesis

Kenton Sparks
Eastern University
Form Criticism: Hebrew Bible

Elsie R. Stern
Reconstructionist Rabbinical College
Reconstructionist Interpretation

David Tabb Stewart
California State University at Long Beach
Lesbian, Gay, Bisexual, and Transgender Interpretation

Ken Stone
Chicago Theological Seminary
Queer Criticism and Queer Theory

R. S. Sugirtharajah
University of Birmingham
Postcolonial Biblical Interpretation

Walter Sundberg
Luther Seminary
Lutheran Interpretation

Eve Sweetser
Univrsity of California, Berkeley
Cognitive Linguistics and Biblical Interpretation

W. Randolph Tate
Evangel University
Postmodern Interpretation

Hal Taussig
Union Theological Seminary
Canon of the Bible

John Christopher Thomas
Pentecostal Theological Seminary and Bangor University
Pentecostal Interpretation

Julio Trebolle Barrera
Universidad Complutense de Madrid
Textual Criticism: Hebrew Bible

Patricia K. Tull
Louisville Presbyterian Seminary
Narrative Criticism and Narrative Hermeneutics

David L. Turner
Grand Rapids Theological Seminary
Dispensationalist Interpretation

Arthur Walker-Jones
The University of Winnipeg
Ecological Biblical Criticism

Gerald West
University of KwaZulu-Natal, South Africa
Liberation Hermeneutics

David R. Wilson
George Fox Evangelical Seminary
Wesleyan Biblical Interpretation

K. K. (Khiok-khng) Yeo
Garrett-Evangelical Theological Seminary
Chinese Interpretation

Index

Page numbers in boldface refer to the main entry on the subject. Page numbers in italics refer to figures and tables.

H

P